ANNUAL DIGEST OF PUBLIC INTERNATIONAL LAW CASES

1919–1922

This reprinted edition published by
GROTIUS PUBLICATIONS LTD.,
LLANDYSUL, WALES, U.K.

First impression published by
Messrs. Longmans, Green & Co.

Reprinted by photolitho
by Gomer Press, Llandysul, Wales, U.K.

DEPARTMENT OF INTERNATIONAL STUDIES OF THE
LONDON SCHOOL OF ECONOMICS AND POLITICAL SCIENCE
(UNIVERSITY OF LONDON)

ANNUAL DIGEST OF PUBLIC INTERNATIONAL LAW CASES

Being a Selection from the Decisions of International and National Courts and Tribunals given during the

YEARS 1919 to 1922

EDITORS

SIR JOHN FISCHER WILLIAMS, C.B.E., K.C.
OF LINCOLN'S INN, BARRISTER-AT-LAW, SOMETIME
FELLOW OF NEW COLLEGE, OXFORD, AN ASSOCIATE
OF THE INSTITUTE OF INTERNATIONAL LAW

AND

H. LAUTERPACHT, LL.D., DR. JUR., DR. SC. POL.
LECTURER IN PUBLIC INTERNATIONAL LAW IN THE
LONDON SCHOOL OF ECONOMICS AND POLITICAL SCIENCE

LONGMANS, GREEN AND CO.
LONDON · NEW YORK · TORONTO
1932

ADVISORY COMMITTEE

CONTRIBUTORS

DECISIONS OF INTERNATIONAL COURTS AND TRIBUNALS:

Dr. H. Lauterpacht

DECISIONS OF NATIONAL COURTS:

United States of America	Professor E. DeWitt Dickinson
Latin-American Countries: Argentina, Bolivia, Brazil, Chile, Costa Rica, Cuba, Mexico, Nicaragua, Panama, Peru, Venezuela	Mr. William W. Bishop, jr. and Professor E. DeWitt Dickinson
Austria	Professor Alfred Verdross
Austria, Cases on Option of Nationality	Dr. Josef L. Kunz [1]
Belgium	Professor Fernand De Visscher
British Dominions and Colonies (except the Union of South Africa)	Professor Herbert A. Smith
Czechoslovakia	Dr. Jan Šimák
Denmark	Dr. Georg Cohn
Egypt	Professor Norman Bentwich
France	Professor A. Decencière-Ferrandière
Germany	Dr. H. Lauterpacht

[1] As in the volume for 1927-1928, Dr. Kunz, of the University of Vienna, has been responsible for the contributions covering the Austrian cases bearing on Option of Nationality. The Editors regret that by an oversight his name did not appear in the list of the contributors to that volume.

Great Britain and Northern Ireland	Dr. A. D. McNair
Greece	Professor C. G. Ténékidès
Holland	Professor J. H. W. Verzijl
Hungary	Professor Francis Faluhelyi
Italy	Professor Arrigo Cavaglieri
Japan	Professor K. Mori
Latvia	Dr. B. Akzin
Norway	Dr. C. Kruse Jensen
Poland	Professor Ludwik Ehrlich
South Africa (Union of)	Professor R. W. Lee
Sweden	Dr. E. Sandström
Switzerland	Professor Dietrich Schindler

PREFACE

THE appearance of this volume of the *Digest*, in the present financial and economic conditions, would not have been possible had it not been for the very generous help of the Carnegie Endowment for International Peace (Division of International Law under the direction of Dr. James Brown Scott), of the Benchers of the Four Inns of Court, of the Warden and Fellows of All Souls College, Oxford, and of the Governors and the Director of the London School of Economics and Political Science, under whose auspices the *Digest* is published. To all of these, pious founders and benefactors of what the Editors trust will be a work of permanence and confidently believe to be a work of utility, the Editors and the Advisory Committee tender most grateful thanks.

A capital contribution of essential importance to the usefulness of the present volume has also been supplied by the co-operation of Professor Dickinson, with the approval and active backing of the Law School of the University of Michigan. Professor Dickinson (who has accepted a place on the Advisory Committee), with the assistance of Mr. William W. Bishop, junior, undertook the collection and digesting of the cases from the United States and from all countries of the American Continent other than Canada; the University of Michigan with signal generosity has borne the whole of the expense thus involved. Those who use this volume will readily understand that the Editors are guilty of no exaggeration when they say that the value of the help thus given is inestimable.

The general scheme and arrangement of the volume follow closely the volumes already published.

As announced in the Preface to the volume for 1927-1928, there has been a partial change in the personality of the editorship. The pressure of other work has compelled Dr. McNair—without whom the *Digest* would not have existed—to put his share of the editorial work into other hands, but with the continued presence of Dr. Lauterpacht every possible effort has been (and will be) made to maintain the character and reputation of the series. The Advisory Committee, where Dr. McNair has taken a place which he has found to be no sinecure, has been strengthened by the presence of eight additional members, including Lord Atkin and Lord Tomlin.

It will be noticed that this volume differs from its predecessors in including the work of four years (1919-1922), whereas the previous volumes and that now in preparation for 1923 and 1924 cover each two years only. The years 1919 to 1922 were in fact less fertile in public international law cases, apart from the law of Prize, than the years which followed. In the earlier of those years peace after the World War had not, or had hardly, been re-established, and the international tribunals created by, or with reference to, the peace treaties—such as the Mixed Arbitral Tribunals or the German-American Claims Commission—had not been instituted or had not got into the full swing of their work.

Prize cases have as a general rule not been included in the *Digest*. The decision not to deal with Prize Law was based on several considerations—the very special nature of this branch of law, the accessibility of full reports, the serious additional expense involved, and the fact that, unless the date chosen for the commencement of the *Digest* had been altered, and thus a departure made from the fundamental intention to make this a digest of post-war public international law, only prize cases decided after the cessation of hostilities in the World War would have been included, and so only a very incomplete and imperfect picture of the contemporary developments of this branch of the international law of war would have been given. But in one or two cases, such as the famous affair of *The Blonde, Prosper and Hercules* [1] in the British Privy Council, where important points of general public international law were decided, the Editors have used their liberty to make exceptions to the general rule.

Readers will notice that in some cases it has been thought well to call attention to dissentient minority judgments recorded in the original report.

Our contributors from overseas have again been unstinting of that loyal assistance which alone makes possible the work of preparing the *Digest*, and which brings little beyond itself for reward. We have to thank them in particular for notes and further references which increase the value of this publication and which it would be impossible to compile in England.

The acknowledgment contained in the Prefaces to previous volumes of the value of the work done by the publishers, Messrs. Longmans, Green and Co., and the printers, Messrs. T. and A. Constable Limited, of the University Press, Edinburgh, is equally due on this occasion.

The help of members of the Advisory Committee, particularly in the work of revision, has been given as ungrudgingly as before, and often in the midst of pressing work of a public character ; the Editors are in special duty bound to recognise a co-operation which is all the more generous as the final word of decision has been left with themselves.

Reviewers and users of the volumes which have already appeared have been helpful in suggestions, and we have endeavoured to profit by them. If we may adapt and adopt words which Professor Maitland uses on a similar occasion,[2] we can say that " if those who have occasion to use this *Digest* " will speak their minds, every volume of the *Digest* henceforth " may be better than the last." But we may perhaps be

[1] See Case No. 288 of this volume.

[2] Introduction to the Year Book Series of the Selden Society.

allowed to repeat what was said in effect in the Preface to the 1927-1928 volume, that a *Digest* is not and cannot be either a reprint in full of reports or a case book, and that when one case, as often happens, contains decisions or discussions of more than one legal topic, the classification of material makes it necessary to treat of it in more than one entry. We have endeavoured to minimise any inconvenience which may result from this necessity, but it *is* a necessity and we cannot avoid it.

It may be useful to repeat that only those notes which are followed by the indication " Ed." are the work, and imply the responsibility, of the Editors ; all other notes are supplied by contributors.

Cross-references are, as a general rule, limited to the contents of the present volume. The adherence throughout the *Digest* to the same system of classification will, it is thought, make it easy for the reader to follow the stream or streams of decision on any one subject.

JOHN FISCHER WILLIAMS.
H. LAUTERPACHT.

1st December, 1932.

The correct method of citation of cases in this volume is :

Annual Digest, 1919-1922, Case No. .

TABLE OF CONTENTS

(*See also* CLASSIFICATION)

	PAGE
PREFACE	ix
TABLE OF CASES DIGESTED (alphabetical) .	xv
TABLE OF CASES DIGESTED (according to courts and countries)	xxiii
TABLE OF CASES CITED	xxxi
CLASSIFICATION	xxxvii
LIST OF ABBREVIATIONS	liii

PART I

INTERNATIONAL LAW IN GENERAL . . 3

PART II

STATES AS INTERNATIONAL PERSONS . . 11

PART III

STATE TERRITORY 83

PART IV

JURISDICTION 105

PART V

STATE RESPONSIBILITY 169

PART VI

PAGE

The Individual in International Law . 197

PART VII

Diplomatic and Consular Intercourse and Privileges 285

PART VIII

Treaties 313

PART IX

International Organisation and Administration 357

PART X

Disputes 367

PART XI

War and Neutrality 385

Index 493

TABLE OF CASES DIGESTED

(ALPHABETICAL)

(The figures in heavier type indicate the actual digests. The ordinary type indicates the page on which the digest appears as a cross-reference.)

A. F. *v.* Government of the Federal Country (Landesregierung) of Vienna, **219,** 259

A. L. B. *v.* (Austrian) Federal Ministry for the Interior, **20**

Administrator of *Le Progrès Industriel, In re,* **321**

Admission of Aliens (Austria) Case, **231**

Adriaenssens *v. Ministère Public,* **467**

The Adriatic, **24,** 161

Agapios *v.* Sanitary and Quarantine Council of Egypt, **201, 363,** 94

Agency of Canadian Car and Foundry Co. Ltd. *v.* American Can Co., **30,** 58

Alarcón, *In re,* **275**

Alejandro, Pojasi, *In re,* **106**

Angelini *v.* The French Government, **289**

The Anichab, **483,** 164, 445, 487

The Annette ; The Dora, **43**

The Argonaut and *The Jonas H. French,* **176,** 102, 371

Armistice Agreement (Coblenz) Case, **440,** 475

Auditeur Militaire v. G. Van Dieren, **445**

Austrian Empire (Succession) Case, **67**

Austrian Officials (Succession) Case, **73**

Aziz Hanki *v.* Russell, **40,** 162

Badische Co. Ltd., etc., *In re,* **393,** 230, 426

Baltzoudis *v.* Souliotis, **41,** 316

The Beaverton ; The Daisai Maru, **138**

Behar, *In re,* **277**

Belgium, State of, *v.* E. A. G. de Badts, **129,** 23

Belgium, State of, *v.* Malfeit and Fischer, **438,** 8

Bergverksaktiebolaget Kosmai *v.* Militär-Liquidierungsamt, of Vienna, **130,** 8, 38, 58

The Bernisse ; The Elve, **486**

Beytía, *In re,* **261**

Binon *v.* German State and the Silesian Fire Insurance Co., **390,** 341

Birge-Forbes Co. *v.* Heye, **403**

Birndörfer, *In re,* **279**

The Blonde and other Ships, **410,** 186, 326, 328, 337, 423, 428

Bochart *v.* Committee of Supplies of Corneux, **462,** 463

Bockstegen's Case, **458**

Boliotti *v.* Masse, **452,** 163, 475

Bolmer *v.* Edsall, otherwise Bolmer, **163**

De Booy *v.* German *Reich,* **124**

Bouman *v.* The State of the Netherlands, **489**

Bourgoin (Official Sequestrator) *v.* Société Belge Éloi et Cie, **449**

De Brabant and Gosselin *v.* T. and A. Florent, **463**

[References are to pages.]

Brandão & Co. *v.* Francisco Canales, **108**
Brown *v.* S.S. *Indochine*, **157**
Brühler Glashütten Co. *v.* Beaurain, **401**
Budelacci and Others *v.* El Nuevo Banco Italiano, **302**

Cambier *v.* Lebrun *et Al.*, **459**
Carapellucci *v.* Palmerio, **300**
Carinthia (Removal of Judges) Case, **467**
Carter, Darie, and Coke Webb, *In re*, **94**
The Carlo Poma, **137**
Central India Mining Co. Ltd. *v.* Société Coloniale Anversoise, **420**
Chamberlain & Hookham Ltd. *v.* Solar Zahlerwerke, **344**, 3, 230
Change of Sovereignty (Taxation) Case, **91**, 79, 202
Cheuk Gar Lim, *Ex parte*, **287**
Chryssikos *v.* Demarco, Administrator of Valmus, **346**
Cillekens *v.* De Haas, **471**
Coale *et Al.* *v.* Société Coopérative Suisse des Charbons, Basle, *et Al.*, **133**
Colliery of Gosson Lagasse and Associates *v.* Commune of Jemeppe, **461**
Collins *v.* Loisel, United States Marshal, **272**
Colombia and Venezuela, **84, 371**, 4, 95, 369, 374, 379
Comina *v.* Kite, **286**
Commercial and Estates Co. of Egypt *v.* Ball, 418
Commune of Bácsborod Case, **450**
Commune of Grace-Berleur *v.* Colliery of Gosson Lagasse and Associates, **461**
Compagnie Française de Tramways et d'Éclairage Électrique de Shanghai, *In re*, **334**
Competence of the International Labour Organisation (Organisation and Development of Methods of Agricultural Production), **357**, 350, 381
Competence of the International Labour Organisation (Regulation of Conditions of Work of Persons Employed in Agriculture), **328, 329, 338, 342, 359**
Consul of the Argentine Republic *v.* Bourgues, **301**
The Coquitlam, **171, 192**, 7
Cordova *v.* Grant, **105**
Cottam & Co. *v.* Comision Reguladora del Mercado de Henequen, **25**, 161
Couhi, *In re*, **305**
Counterfeiting of Stamps (Czechoslovakia) Case, **45**, 21
Cox, *In re*, **215**
Crédit Foncier d'Algérie et de Tunisie *v.* Restrepo and Department of Antioquia, **285**
Customs House (State Succession) Case, **68**, 315
Czechoslovak Occupation (Hungary) Case, **451**

D. N. (Greece) Case, **385**
The David J. Adams, **237, 331, 335**, 22, 24, 180, 371
Deleuze, *In re*, **265**
Delivery without Extradition (Germany) Case, **262**
Designation of the Workers' Delegate for the Netherlands Case, **361**, 350
Deutsche Bank *v.* Zirini, **324**
Diaz, Everardo, *In re*, **254**
Diaz, Juan González, *In re*, **253**
The Dirigo, The Hallingdal, and other Ships, **491**, 406
Dominguez *v.* State, **271**
Dürrenberg *v.* Polish State Treasury, **339**, 337
The Düsseldorf, **101**
Düsseldorfer Allgemeine Versicherungs-A.G. *v.* L., **441**
Dym *v.* (Austrian) Federal Ministry for the Interior, **222**

Eastern Extension, Australasia and China Telegraph Co. Ltd. *v.* United States, **58**
The Empire *v.* Chang and Others, **288**, 287
Estate and Guardianship of Tet-

[References are to pages.]

subumi Yano, a Minor, In the Matter of, **239**
Expropriated Religious Properties Case (France, Great Britain and Spain *v.* Portugal), **238**
Extradition (Germany and Czechoslovakia) Case, **259,** 73, 277
Extradition of Leocadio Rodríguez, *In re*, **269**

Fasbender *v.* Attorney-General, **211,** 423
Feldmann and Feldmann *v.* Polish State Treasury, **71**
Fenton Textile Association Ltd. *v.* Krassin, **295**
Ferdinand, Ex-Tsar of Bulgaria, *In re*, **406**
Ferdinand, S., *v.* (Austrian) Federal Chancellery, **218**
Finkelstein *v.* (Austrian) Federal Ministry for the Interior, **221**
Foà *v.* Boselli, **305**
Forté *v.* Malluk, **202**
Four Packages of Cut Diamonds *v.* United States, **314**
France and Germany (In the Matter of the Cessions relating to the Navigation of the Rhine under Article 357 of the Treaty of Versailles), **336, 349, 367**
Franz, Dame, *v.* Germany, **169**
Frasca *v.* City Coal Co., **350,** 247
French and Italian Bank *v.* Warburg & Co., **392**
French Claims against Peru, **182, 192,** 4, 248
French Clearing Office *v.* German Clearing Office, **375**
French Republic *v.* Inland Navigation Co., **132**
French State *v.* Prat, **332**
Fried Krupp Aktiengesellschaft *v.* Orconera Iron Ore Co. Ltd., **396**

G. M. *v.* (Austrian) Federal Ministry for the Interior, **219**
The Gagara, **45,** 58, 107
Galatiolo *v.* Senes, **453,** 89
Gayon *v.* McCarthy, **181,** 491
German Requisitions (Necessity and Self-Preservation) Case, **427,** 483
Gilroy, *Ex parte*, **208,** 247
Gizzarelli *v.* Presbrey, **241,** 353
Gout and Another *v.* Cimitian, **199**
The Grace and Ruby, **111**
Graves, *In re*, **307**
Grogan *v.* Walker & Sons, **327,** 111
Guardianship (Termination of Treaties) Case, **389**
Gunn *v.* Gunz, **376**

Hall *v.* Bengoa, **157**
The Hamborn, **425,** 230, 424
Handelsvennootschap onder de Firma R. Kupsch and Abtas, of Amsterdam, *v.* N. V. Amsterdam-Deli Brand- en Zeeassurantie-Maatschappij, of Amsterdam, *et Al.*, **426**
The Harrier, **180,** 490
Heim and Chamant *v.* German State, **379,** 313, 339, 344
Hein, George S., *v.* Hildersheimer Bank, **216**
Hemming Case, **170**
Henke, *In re*, **158**
Herbillon *v.* Lentz, **120**
The Home Missionary Society Case, **173, 376**
De Howorth *v.* The S.S. *India*, **156**
Hughes v. Techt; Techt *v.* Hughes, **387,** 326, 405, 423
Hungarian Soviet Government (Confiscation of Property) Case, **56**
Hurlimann, *In re*, **260,** 7, 281
Hussein Lutfi Bey, Master of the *Gul Djemal*, *Ex parte* in the Matter of, **141,** 57
Hutt *v.* French State, **306**

The Ice King, **150**
Immovables (Aliens in Germany) Case, **242,** 202, 326, 390, 441
Immunities (Foreign State in Private Contracts) Case, **118,** 292
Inglese, *In re*, **273**
International Labour Organisation. *See* Competence of the International Labour Organisation.

Ismail Pasha Sidky *v.* Sidarous Bishara, **42,** 21, 162
Italian Black Sea Co. *v.* Russian Soviet Government, **26**

J. Z., *In re*, **71**
Jackson, Jorge Alejandro, *In re*, **106,** 158
Janssens, Widow of A. van Hecke, *v.* N. V. Maatschappij Rijnschip *Barbera, et Al.*, **29**
The Jessie, The Thomas F. Bayard, The Pescawha, **175, 187,** 184
Johnstone *v.* Pedlar, **231**

Kadecka, Franz and Rosa, *v.* Government of the Federal Country (Landesregierung) of Lower Austria, **213**
The Kate, **188**
Kauhlen Case, **457**
Kirgis (Husband and Wife), Kaltenbach (Widow) and Others, *In re*, **234,** 483
Kotta, *In re*, **240**
Kotzias *v.* Tyser, **442**
Kugler *v.* (Austrian) Federal Ministry for the Interior, **220**
Kulturas Balss Co-operative Society *v.* Latvian Ministry for Home Affairs, **456**
Kwock Jan Fat *v.* White, **197**

Lakhowsky *v.* Swiss Federal Government and Colonel de Reynier, **122**
Landreau Claims against Peru, **185**
Laurent *v.* Le Jeune, **481**
Legation Buildings (Execution by Hypothecation) Case, **291**
Legation Buildings (Turnover Tax) Case, **290**
The Leonora, **429**
Loewengard *v.* *Procureur* of the Republic and Bonvier (Sequestrator), **307, 390**
Lopez *v.* Howe, Immigration Commissioner, **252**
Luther *v.* Sagor, **47,** 22, 57, 107

M. & O., *In re*, **70,** 326
The Maipo, **138**
Mann, George, & Co. (Delagoa) Ltd. *v.* The S.S. *India*, **156**
Markwald *v.* Attorney-General, **203**
Marincovich, *In re*, **100,** 3
Martin *v.* Keyaerts and Leysen, **437,** 8
Martínez, *In re*, **214**
Martorel (Martorell), *In re*, **263**
Mathot *v.* Longué, **463**
Matthews, *Ex parte*, **258**
Matys *v.* Nipanicz, **75**
McCall's Estate, *In re*, **186,** 315
Melkonian *v.* Melkonian, **204**
Menasce Roussos & Co. *v.* Holland-EgyptHandelmaatschappij,**161,** 40
Menendez, *In re*, **206**
Military Pensions (Austria) Case, **66**
Ministerio Fiscal *v.* Cecil Wilson Bertie, **309**
Monte Blanco Real Estate Corporation *v.* Wolvin Line *et Al.*, **53**
Muir, Master of *The Gleneden*, *Ex parte* in the Matter of, **143**
Muñoz, *In re*, **276**
Münster (Enemy), *In re*, **408**

Naoum and Others *v.* The Government of the Colony of French West Africa, **448**
Nazare Aga, *In re*, **286**
Neiken, *In re*, **274**
Neuburger and Kleinkramer, *In re*, **278**
Neumann, *In re*, **267**
The Newchwang, **188, 373,** 375
Ng Fung Ho *et Al.* *v.* White, Commissioner of Immigration, **257**
Niezabitowski *v.* Kowalski, **386**
De Nimal *v.* De Nimal, **447**
Nobili *v.* Emperor Charles I of Austria, **136**
The Noordam (*No.* 2) and other Ships, **430,** 428
Norway and United States (Requisition of Shipbuilding Contracts Case), **189, 191, 369, 377, 414,** 7, 24, 197, 248, 341
N. V. Süddeutsche Rückversicherungs-Aktien-Gesellschaft, of

[References are to pages.]

Munich, *v.* N. V. Companhia Nacional de Café, of Santos, Brazil, *et Al.*, **229**
N. V. Zeetjalk "De Hoop," of Amsterdam, *v.* (1) N. V. Wijnne en Barends' cargadoors- en agenturkantoren, of Delfzijl (Holland); (2) N. V. Hermes' Scheepvaart-, Handelsmaatschappij en Bank, of The Hague, **487**

Oil Industry Association Ltd., Cracow, *In re*, **245**
Olpinski *v.* Polish Treasury (Railway Division), **63**
Ospina *v.* Solveyra, **308**

Pallanca *v.* Società Ossidrica Orientale, **304**
Panama Railroad Co. *v.* Bosse, **77,** 95
Parij and Others *v.* Austro-Hungarian Treasury, **316**
Paris Agreement (9 January, 1920) Case, **313**
Pauly *v.* Custodian of Enemy Property, **225**
Payment of War Tax (Czechoslovakia) Case, **11**
Pending Actions (Danzig) Case (I), **90,** 135
Pending Actions (Danzig) Case (II), 66, **89,** 135
Penney (Custodian of Enemy Property for Scotland) *v.* Clyde Shipbuilding and Engineering Co., **397**
The Penza; The Tobolsk, **53**
People *v.* Lol-Lo and Saraw, **164**
People *v.* Perfecto, **77**
People *v.* Savic, **298**
People *v.* Wong Cheng, **110**
Pereyra Iraolo *v.* Provincia de Buenos Aires, **97**
Perkons *v.* Mezdrejs, **479**
The Pesaro, **139, 140**
Pettine, *Ex parte*, **251,** 7
Polish Loan Bank Case, **116**
(Polish) State Treasury *v.* Archduke Rainer Karl and Land Credit Bank of Lwów, **318**
(Polish) State Treasury *v.* Kurzrock, **79**
(Polish) State Treasury *v.* V. Osten, **64**
Poo Shong Hing *et Al. v.* Consolidated Steel Corporation, **402**
Poon *v.* Miller, **321,** 247, 353
The Porto Alexandre, **146**
Porto Rico Railway, Light and Power Co. *v.* Amador *et Al.*, **76**
Portugal, State of, *v.* Sauvage, **154**
Post Office Official (Austria) Succession Case, **74**
Prisoners of War (Brest Litowsk) Case, **434**
Prisoners of War (Germany) Case, **433,** 428
Procurador Fiscal *v.* Moritz Hendler, **210**
Procureur de la République (Mulhouse) *v.* Schoen, **38**
Procureur Général (Court of Appeal of Brussels) *v.* Schneider and Others, **404**
Public Prosecutor *v.* Lund, **113,** 102
Publication of Treaties (Germany) Case, **322**

Quesada, Manuel Castro, *v.* El Estado, **292**

The Rannveig, **435,** 353, 491
Republic (Poland) *v.* Felsenstadt, **33,** 35
Republic (Poland) *v.* Just (*alias* Belf) and Others, **317**
Republic (Poland) *v.* Pantol, **35,**47
Republic (Poland) *v.* Weisholc, **34, 472,** 35
Republic (Poland) *v.* Oficyński, **474**
Republic (Poland) *v.* Ralski, **457**
Republic of France *v.* Pittsburgh Steel Export Co., **134**
Rex *v.* Flannery, **280**
Rex *v.* Godfrey, **270,** 109
Rhineland (German Decrees) Case, **450,** 94, 457
Rhineland Occupation (Jurisdiction) Case, **469**
Rights of Citizenship (Establish-

[References are to pages.]

ment of Czechoslovak Nationality) Case, **17**
Rights of Citizenship (Establishment of Czechoslovak State) Case, **15**
Risse, *Ex parte*, **217**, 199
The Rogdai, **51**
De Roover *v.* Belgium and France, **120**
Rossie *v.* Garvan (Alien Property Custodian), **400**
Russian Roubles (Attempted Counterfeiting) Case, **31**
Rymenans & Co. *v.* Germany, **244**, 483

Saar Territory (Usury Decree) Case, **83**, 42
Salary Due by the Former Government (Czechoslovakia) Case, **62**
Sale of Requisitioned Object (Czechoslovakia) Case, **477**
Salti et Fils *v.* (British) Procurator-General, **419**
The Santa Luzia, **112**
The Sao Vicente, **146**
Savic *v.* City of New York, **298**
Sazonow *v.* District Land (Reform) Board of Białystok, **7**, **247**
Schmid *v.* Chemische Werke Furstenwalde, **342**, 371
Schostall *v.* Johnson, **395**
Schumacher *v.* Germany and Serb-Croat-Slovene State, **345**
Secco Maia & Co. *v.* União Federal, **444**
Security for Costs (Germany) Case, **243**, 339
Security for Costs (Treaty of Versailles) Case, **351**
Serventi, *In re*, **294**, 58
The Sidra, **100**
De Simone *v.* Transportes Maritimos do Estado, **145**
Siuta *v.* Gużkowski, **480**
Société Anonyme du Charbonnage Frédéric Henri *v.* Germany, **227**, 341
Société Siebert *v.* Burm de Belie, **466**
Solveyra *v.* Ospina, **308**
Soviet Government *v.* Ericsson, **54**
State of Arkansas *v.* State of Mississippi, **96**, 84
State of Georgia *v.* State of South Carolina, **96**
State of Missouri *v.* Holland, United States Game Warden, **4**, 316
State Succession (Notarial Act) Case, **68**
The Stigstad, **429**
Stoeck *v.* Public Trustee, **224**, 199
Strathearn Steamship Co. Ltd. *v.* Dillon, **109**
Succession of Doña Carmen de Goyeneche, *In re*, **291**
Sullivan *v.* Kidd, **347**, 334, 353
The Svanfos; *The Borgila*, **485**, 163

Tanganyika Succession Case, **61**
The Tattler (I), **235**, 184
The Tattler (II), **172**, 189
Territorial Waters (Germany) Case, **98**, 84
Terui, *In re*, **320**
The Tervaete, **148**
Tesdorpf *v.* German State, **475**, 341
The Texas Company of Mexico, S.A., *In re*, **249**
Toebinte, Theuns, *In re*; United States Government *ex parte* the *Procureur du Roi*, **121**
Tonioli, *In re*, **246**
The Treasury *v.* Gundelfinger and Kaumheimer, **399**
Trilla, Pedro, *v.* Unión Industrial y Comercial, **93**
Trott *v.* State, **6**
Turkish Purchases Commission Case, **114**, 39

Ungarische Kriegsprodukten-Aktiengesellschaft, *In re*, **72**, 35, 39
Union of South Africa *v.* Herman Grote, **22**, 23, 39
United States *v.* Bowman, **159**
United States *v.* Hicks, **443**, 441
United States *v.* Kramer, **209**
United States ex rel. Wessels *v.* McDonald, Commandant of Brooklyn Navy Yard, **431**, 385

Upper Silesia (Plebiscite Commission) Case, **179**, 43
Urios, *In re*, **107**

Del Vecchio *v.* Connio, **454**
Verdyck *v.* Voncken, **465**
Vereeniging Municipality *v.* Vereeniging Estates Ltd., **60**
The Vesta and other Ships, **424**, 230, 426
Vietti *v.* The George K. Mackie Fuel Co., **319**

W. and M. *v.* The (French) State, **439**
The Wanderer, **177**, 163, 189, 350
Weber, *In re*, **448**
West Russian Steamship Co. *v.* Captain Sucksdorff, **152**, 47
Wolff *v.* The Treasury, **422**

X, *In re*, **333**, **468**

The Zamora, **429**
Zannoni *v.* Sbisà, **28**

[References are to pages.]

TABLE OF CASES DIGESTED

[Arranged according to Courts and Tribunals (international cases) and countries (municipal cases)]

I. DECISIONS OF INTERNATIONAL COURTS AND TRIBUNALS

(The figures in heavier type indicate the actual digests. The ordinary type indicates the page on which the digest appears as a cross-reference.)

Permanent Court of International Justice

Advisory Opinion No. 1, Designation of the Workers' Delegate for the Netherlands, **361**, 350

Advisory Opinion No. 2, Competence of the International Labour Organisation (Regulation of Conditions of Work of Persons Employed in Agriculture), **328**, **329**, **338**, **342**, **359**

Advisory Opinion No. 3, Competence of the International Labour Organisation (Organisation and Development of Methods of Agricultural Production), **357**, 350, 381

Permanent Court of Arbitration

Norway and United States (Requisition of Shipbuilding Contracts Case), **189**, **191**, **369**, **377**, **414**, 7, 24, 197, 248, 341

French Claims against Peru, **182**, **192**, 4, 248

Expropriated Religious Properties Case (France, Great Britain and Spain *v.* Portugal), **238**

British-American Claims Arbitral Tribunal

The Argonaut and *The Jonas H. French*, **176**, 102, 371

The Coquitlam, **171**, **192**, 7

The David J. Adams, **237**, **331**, **335**, 22, 24, 180, 371

Hemming, H. J. R., Case, **170**

The Home Missionary Society Case, **173**, **376**

The Jessie, The Thomas F. Bayard, The Pescawha, **175**, **187**, 184

The Kate, **188**

The Newchwang, **188**, **373**, 375

The Sidra, **100**

The Tattler (I), **235**, 184

The Tattler (II), **172**, 189

The Wanderer, **177**, 163, 189, 350

[References are to pages.]

Mixed Arbitral Tribunals

(Under the Peace Treaties terminating the War of 1914-1918)

Binon *v.* German State and the Silesian Fire Insurance Co., **390,** 341

Chamberlain & Hookham Ltd. *v.* Solar Zahlerwerke, **344,** 3

Franz, Dame, *v.* Germany, **169**

The French and Italian Bank *v.* Warburg & Co., **392**

French Clearing Office *v.* German Clearing Office, **375**

Gunn *v.* Gunz, **376**

Heim and Chamant *v.* The German State, **379,** 313, 339, 344

Hein, George S., *v.* Hildersheimer Bank, **216**

Rymenans & Co. *v.* Germany, **244,** 483

Schmid *v.* Chemische Werke Furstenwalde, **342,** 371

Schumacher *v.* Germany and Serb-Croat-Slovene State, **345**

Société Anonyme du Charbonnage Frédéric Henri *v.* Germany, **227,** 341

Tesdorpf *v.* German State, **475,** 341

Special Arbitral Tribunals

Germany and France (In the Matter of the Cessions relating to the Navigation of the Rhine under Article 357 of the Treaty of Versailles), Walker D. Hines Single Arbitrator, **336, 349, 367**

Colombia and Venezuela, Swiss Federal Council Arbitrator, **84, 371,** 4, 95, 369, 374, 379

United States - Peru Landreau Claims, United States Peruvian Arbitral Commission, **185**

II. DECISIONS OF NATIONAL COURTS [1]

Argentina

Budelacci and Others *v.* El Nuevo Banco Italiano, **302**

Jackson, Jorge Alejandro, *In re*, **106,** 158

Martínez, Julio R., *In re*, **214**

Menendez, *In re*, **206**

Ministerio Fiscal *v.* Cecil Wilson Bertie, **309**

Pereyra Iraolo *v.* Provincia de Buenos Aires, **97**

Procurador Fiscal *v.* Moritz Hendler, **210**

Solveyra *v.* Ospina, Ospina *v.* Solveyra, **308**

Austria

A. F. *v.* Government of the Federal Country (Landesregierung) of Vienna (Option of Nationality), **219,** 259

A. L. B. *v.* (Austrian) Federal Ministry for the Interior, **20**

Admission of Aliens (Austria) Case, **231**

Austrian Empire (Succession) Case, **67**

Carinthia (Removal of Judges) Case, **467**

Dym *v.* (Austrian) Federal Ministry for the Interior (Option of Nationality), **222**

[References are to pages.]

[1] As in some countries it is not the practice to state the names of the parties in reporting cases, we have ventured to invent titles for these cases in the interest of convenience of citation.—[Ed.]

Ferdinand, S., *v.* (Austrian) Federal Chancellery (Option of Nationality), **218**
Finkelstein *v.* (Austrian) Federal Ministry for the Interior (Option of Nationality), **221**
G. M. *v.* (Austrian) Federal Ministry for the Interior (Option of Nationality), **219**
Hungarian Soviet Government (Confiscation of Property) Case, **56**
Immunities (Foreign State in Private Contracts) Case, **118,** 292
Kadecka, Franz and Rosa, *v.* Government of the Federal Country (Landesregierung) of Lower Austria, **213**
Kugler *v.* (Austrian) Federal Ministry for the Interior (Option of Nationality), **220**
Legation Buildings (Execution by Hypothecation) Case, **291**
Military Pensions (Austria) Case, **66**
Post Office Official (Austria) Succession Case, **74**
State Succession (Notarial Act) Case, **68**

Belgium

Adriaenssens *v.* *Ministère Public,* **467**
Auditeur Militaire *v.* G. Van Dieren, **445**
Bochart v. Committee of Supplies of Corneux, **462, 463**
Bockstegen's Case, **458**
De Brabant and Gosselin *v.* T. and A. Florent, **463**
Brühler Glashütten Co. *v.* Beaurain, **401**
Cambier *v.* Lebrun *et Al.*, **459**
Colliery of Gosson Lagasse and Associates *v.* Commune of Jemeppe, **461**
Commune of Grace-Berleur *v.* Colliery of Gosson Lagasse and Associates, **461**
Herbillon *v.* Lentz, **120**
Kauhlen Case, **457**
Laurent *v.* Le Jeune, **481**
Martin *v.* Keyaerts and Leysen, **437,** 8
Mathot *v.* Longué, **463**
De Nimal *v.* De Nimal, **447**
Procureur Général (Court of Appeal of Brussels) *v.* Schneider and Others, **404**
De Roover *v.* Belgium and France, **120**
Société Siebert *v.* Burm de Belie, **466**
State of Belgium *v.* Malfeit and Fischer, **438,** 8
State of Portugal *v.* Sauvage, **154**
Toebinte ; Theuns ; United States Government *ex parte* the *Procureur du Roi* (Civil Tribunal of Antwerp), *In re,* **121**
Verdyck *v.* Voncken, **465**
West Russian Steamship Co. *v.* Sucksdorff, **152,** 47

Bolivia

Alejandro, Pojasi, *In re,* **106**

Brazil

Brandão & Co. *v.* Francisco Canales, **108**
Cox, Walter, *In re,* **215**
Deleuze, Dr. Paulo, *In re,* **265**
Diaz, Everardo, *In re,* **254**
Graves, Lewis Vivian, *In re,* **307**
Henke, Eduardo, *In re,* **158**
Secco Maia & Co. *v.* União Federal, **444**
Tonioli, *In re,* **246**

Canada

Brown *v.* S.S. *Indochine,* **157**
Neiken, *In re,* **274**
Rex *v.* Flannery, **280**

Chile

Beytía, *In re,* **261**

[References are to pages.]

Costa Rica

Quesada, Manuel Castro, *v.* El Estado, **292**

Cuba

Trilla, Pedro, *v.* Unión Industrial y Comercial, **93**

Czechoslovakia

Austrian Officials (Succession) Case, **73**
Payment of War Tax (Czechoslovakia) Case, **11**
Rights of Citizenship (Establishment of Czechoslovak Nationality) Case, **17**
Rights of Citizenship (Establishment of Czechoslovak State) Case, **15**
Salary Due by the Former Government (Czechoslovakia) Case, **62**
Sale of Requisitioned Object (Czechoslovakia) Case, **477**

Egypt

Agapios *v.* Sanitary and Quarantine Council of Egypt, **201, 363,** 94
Aziz Hanki *v.* Russell, **40,** 162
Baltzoudis *v.* Souliotis, **41,** 316
Forté *v.* Malluk, **202**
Hall *v.* Bengoa, **157**
Ismail Pasha Sidky *v.* Sidarous Bishara, **42,** 21, 162
Melkonian *v.* Melkonian, **204**
Menasce Roussos & Co. *v.* Holland-Egypt Handelmaatschappij, **161,** 40
Pallanca *v.* Società Ossidrica Orientale, **304**

England

The Anichab, **483,** 164, 445, 487
The Annette ; The Dora, **43**
Badische Co. Ltd., *In re*, **393,** 426
The Bernisse ; The Elve, **486**
The Blonde and other Ships, **410,** 186, 326, 328, 337, 423, 428
Central India Mining Co. Ltd. *v.* Société Coloniale Anversoise, **420**
The Dirigo, The Hallingdal, and other Ships, **491,** 406
The Düsseldorf, **101**
Fasbender *v.* Attorney-General, **211,** 423
Fenton Textile Association Ltd. *v.* Krassin, **295**
Ferdinand, Ex-Tsar of Bulgaria, *In re*, **406**
Fried Krupp Aktiengesellschaft *v.* Orconera Iron Ore Co. Ltd., **396**
The Gagara, **45,** 58, 107
Gout and Another *v.* Cimitian, **199**
The Hamborn, **425,** 230, 424
The Harrier, **180,** 490
Johnstone *v.* Pedlar, **231**
Kotzias *v.* Tyser, **442**
The Leonora, **429**
Luther *v.* Sagor, **47,** 22, 57, 107
Markwald *v.* Attorney-General, **203**
Münster (Enemy), *In re*, **408**
The Noordam (*No.* 2) and other Ships, **430,** 428
The Porto Alexandre, **146**
The Rannveig, **435,** 353, 491
Rex *v.* Godfrey, **270,** 109
Salti et Fils *v.* (British) Procurator-General, **419**
Schostall *v.* Johnson, **395**
The Stigstad, **429**
Stoeck *v.* Public Trustee, **224,** 199
The Svanfos ; The Borgila, **485,** 163
The Tervaete, **148**
The Vesta and other Ships, **424,** 230, 426
The Zamora, **429**

France

Bourgoin (Official Sequestrator) *v.* Société Belge Éloi et Cie, **449**
Compagnie Française de Tramways et d'Éclairage Électrique de Shanghai, *In re*, **334**
Crédit Foncier d'Algérie et de Tunisie *v.* Restrepo and Department of Antioquia, **285**
French State *v.* Prat, **332**
Hutt *v.* French State, **306**
Kirgis (Husband and Wife), Kal-

tenbach (Widow) and Others, *In re*, **234,** 483
Lakhowsky *v.* Swiss Federal Government and Colonel de Reynier, **122**
Loewengard *v. Procureur* of the Republic and Bonvier (Sequestrator), **307, 390**
Naoum and Others *v.* The Government of the Colony of French West Africa, **448**
Nazare Aga, *In re*, **286**
Procureur de la République (Mulhouse) *v.* Schoen, **38**
Urios, *In re*, **107**
W. and M. *v.* The (French) State, **439**
Weber, *In re*, **448**
X, *In re*, **333, 468**

Germany

Administrator of *Le Progrès Industriel*, *In re*, **321**
Armistice Agreement (Coblenz) Case, **440,** 475
Change of Sovereignty (Taxation) Case, **91,** 79, 202
Counterfeiting of Stamps (Czechoslovakia) Case, **45,** 21
Customs House (State Succession) Case, **68,** 315
Delivery without Extradition (Germany) Case, **262**
Düsseldorfer Allgemeine Versicherungs-A.G. *v.* L., **441**
Extradition (Germany and Czechoslovakia) Case, **259,** 73, 277
German Requisitions (Necessity and Self-Preservation) Case, **427,** 483
The Ice King, **150**
Immovables (Aliens in Germany) Case, **242,** 202, 326, 390, 441
Legation Buildings (Turnover Tax) Case, **290**
Paris Agreement (9 January, 1920) Case, **313**
Pending Actions (Danzig) Case (I), **90,** 135
Pending Actions (Danzig) Case (II), **89,** 66, 135
Polish Loan Bank Case, **116**
Prisoners of War (Brest Litowsk) Case, **434**
Prisoners of War (Germany) Case, **433,** 428
Publication of Treaties (Germany) Case, **322**
Rhineland (German Decrees) Case, **450,** 457
Rhineland Occupation (Jurisdiction) Case, **469**
Saar Territory (Usury Decree) Case, **83,** 42
Security for Costs (Germany) Case, **243,** 339
Security for Costs (Treaty of Versailles) Case, **351**
Tanganyika Succession Case, **61**
Territorial Waters (Germany) Case, **98,** 84
Turkish Purchases Commission Case, **114,** 39
Upper Silesia (Plebiscite Commission) Case, **179,** 43

Greece

D. N. (Greece) Case, **385**
Guardianship (Termination of Treaties) Case, **389**

Holland

Bergverksaktiebolaget Kosmai *v.* Militär-Liquidierungsamt, of Vienna, **130,** 8, 38, 58
De Booy *v.* German *Reich* (The Government of Holland Intervening), **124**
Bouman *v.* The State of the Netherlands, **489**
Cillekens *v.* De Haas, **471**
Deutsche Bank *v.* Zirini, **324**
Handelsvennootschap onder de Firma R. Kupsch and Abtas, of Amsterdam, *v.* N. V. Amsterdam-Deli Brand- en Zeeassurantie-Maatschappij, of Amsterdam, *et Al.*, **426**
Janssens, Widow of A. van Hecke, *v.* N. V. Maatschappij Rijnschip *Barbera*, *et Al.*, **29**
N. V. Süddeutsche Rückversicherungs - Aktien - Gesellschaft, of

Munich, *v.* Companhia Nacional de Café, of Santos, Brazil, *et Al.*, **229**
N. V. Zeetjalk "De Hoop," of Amsterdam, *v.* (1) N. V. Wijnne en Barends' Cargadoors- en Agenturkantoren, of Delfzijl (Holland); (2) N. V. Hermes' Scheepvaart-, Handelsmaatschappij en Bank, of The Hague, **487**
The State of Belgium *v.* E. A. G. de Badts, **129,** 23
Union of South Africa *v.* Herman Grote, **22,** 23, 39

Hungary

Commune of Bácsborod Case, **450**
Czechoslovak Occupation (Hungary) Case, **451**

Italy

Angelini *v.* The French Government, **289**
Behar, *In re*, **277**
Boliotti *v.* Masse, **452,** 163, 475
Carapellucci *v.* Palmerio, **300**
Comina *v.* Kite, **286**
Consul of the Argentine Republic *v.* Bourgues, **301**
Couhi, *In re*, **305**
Foà *v.* Boselli, **305**
Galatiolo *v.* Senes, **453,** 89
Hurlimann, *In re*, **260,** 7, 281
Inglese, *In re*, **273**
Italian Black Sea Company *v.* Russian Soviet Government, **26**
Neuburger and Kleinkramer, *In re*, **278**
Nobili *v.* Emperor Charles I of Austria, **136**
Serventi, *In re*, **294,** 58
Del Vecchio *v.* Connio, **454**
Zannoni *v.* Sbisà, **28**

Japan

The Empire *v.* Chang and Others, **288,** 287
The Russian Roubles (Attempted Counterfeiting) Case, **31**

Latvia

Kulturas Balss Co-operative Society *v.* Latvian Ministry for Home Affairs, **456**
Perkons *v.* Mezdrejs, **479**

Mexico

Diaz, Juan González, *In re*, **253**
Muñoz, Ernesto Diaż, *In re*, **276**
The Texas Company of Mexico, S.A., *In re*, **249**

Nicaragua

Extradition of Leocadio Rodríguez, *In re*, **269**

Norway

Public Prosecutor *v.* Lund, **113,** 102

Panama

Darie Carter and Coke Webb, *In re*, **94**

Peru

Succession of Doña Carmen de Goyeneche, *In re*, **291**

Poland

Dürrenberg *v.* Polish State Treasury, **339,** 337
Feldmann and Feldmann *v.* Polish State Treasury, **71**
Matys *v.* Nipanicz, **75**
Niezabitowski *v.* Kowalski, **386**
Oil Industry Association Ltd., Cracow, *In re*, **245**
Olpinski *v.* Polish Treasury (Railway Division), **63**
Parij and Others *v.* Austro-Hungarian Treasury, **316**
(Polish) State Treasury *v.* Archduke Rainer Karl and Land Credit Bank of Lwów, **318**
(Polish) State Treasury *v.* Kurzrock, **79**
(Polish) State Treasury *v.* V. Osten, **64**

Republic *v.* Felsenstadt, **33**
Republic *v.* Just (*alias* Belf) and Others, **317**
Republic *v.* Oficyński, **474**
Republic *v.* Pantol, **35,** 47
Republic *v.* Ralski, **457**
Republic *v.* Weisholc, **34, 472,** 35
Sazonow *v.* District Land (Reform) Board of Białystok, **7, 247**
Siuta *v.* Guźkowski, **480**

Scotland

Penney (Custodian of Enemy Property for Scotland) *v.* Clyde Shipbuilding and Engineering Co., **397**

South Africa (Union of)

Mann, George, & Co. (Delagoa) Ltd. *v.* The S.S. *India*, **156**
Paüly *v.* Custodian of Enemy Property, **225**
The Treasury *v.* Gundelfinger and Kaumheimer, **399**
Vereeniging Municipality *v.* Vereeniging Estates Ltd., **60**
Wolff *v.* The Treasury, **422**

Sweden

Soviet Government *v.* Ericsson, **54**

Switzerland

Birndörfer, *In re*, **279**
J. Z., *In re*, **71**
M. & O., *In re*, **70,** 326
Neumann, *In re*, **267**
Ungarische Kriegsprodukten-Aktiengesellschaft, *In re*, **72,** 35, 39

United States of America

The Adriatic, **24,** 161
Agency of Canadian Car and Foundry Co. Ltd. *v.* American Can Co., **30,** 58
The Beaverton ; The Daisai Maru, **138**
Birge-Forbes Co. *v.* Heye, **403**
Bolmer *v.* Edsall, otherwise Bolmer, **163**
The Carlo Poma, **137**
Cheuk Gar Lim, *Ex parte*, **287**
Chryssikos *v.* Demarco, Administrator of Valmus, **346**
Coale *et Al. v.* Société Coopérative Suisse des Charbons, Basle, *et Al.*, **133**
Collins *v.* Loisel, United States Marshal, **272**
Cordova *v.* Grant, **105**
Cottam & Co. *v.* Comision Reguladora del Mercado de Henequen, **25,** 161
Dominguez *v.* State, **271**
Eastern Extension, Australasia and China Telegraph Co. Ltd. *v.* United States, **58**
Estate and Guardianship of Tetsubumi Yano, a Minor, In the Matter of, **239**
Four Packages of Cut Diamonds *v.* United States, **314**
Frasca *v.* City Coal Co., **350,** 247
French Republic *v.* Inland Navigation Co., **132**
Gayon *v.* McCarthy, **181**
Gilroy, *Ex parte*, **208,** 247
Gizzarelli *v.* Presbrey, **241,** 353
The Grace and Ruby, **111**
Grogan *v.* Walker & Sons, **327,** 111
Hughes *v.* Techt; Techt *v.* Hughes, **387,** 326, 405, 423
Hussein Lutfi Bey, Master of *The Gul Djemal*, *Ex parte* in the Matter of, **141,** 57
Kotta, *In re*, **240**
Kwock Jan Fat *v.* White, **197**
Lopez *v.* Howe, Immigration Commissioner, **252**
The Maipo, **138**
Marincovich, *In re*, **100, 3**
Martorel, *In re*, **263**
Matthews, *Ex parte*, **258**
McCall's Estate, *In re*, **186,** 315
Monte Blanco Real Estate Corporation *v.* Wolvin Line *et Al.*, **53**
Muir, Master of *The Gleneden*, *Ex parte* in the Matter of, **143**

[References are to pages.]

Ng Fung Ho *et Al.* *v.* White, Commissioner of Immigration, **257**
Panama Railroad Co. *v.* Bosse, **77,** 95
The Penza ; The Tobolsk, **53**
People *v.* Lol-Lo and Saraw, **164**
People *v.* Perfecto, **77**
People *v.* Savic ; Savic *v.* City of New York, **298**
People *v.* Wong Cheng, **110**
The Pesaro, **139, 140**
Pettine, *Ex parte,* **251,** 7
Poo Shong Hing *et Al.* *v.* Consolidated Steel Corporation, **402**
Poon *v.* Miller, **321,** 247, 353
Porto Rico Railway, Light and Power Co. *v.* Amador *et Al.*, **76**
Republic of France *v.* Pittsburgh Steel Export Co., **134**
Risse, *Ex parte,* **217,** 199
The Rogdai, **51**
Rossie *v.* Garvan (Alien Property Custodian), **400**
The Santa Luzia, **112**
The Sao Vicente, **146**
De Simone *v.* Transportes Maritimos do Estado, **145**
State of Arkansas *v.* State of Mississippi, **96,** 84
State of Georgia *v.* State of South Carolina, **96**
State of Missouri *v.* Holland, United States Game Warden, **4,** 316
Strathearn Steamship Co. Ltd. *v.* Dillon, **109**
Sullivan *v.* Kidd, **347,** 334, 353
Terui, *In re,* **320**
Trott *v.* State, **6**
United States *v.* Bowman, **159**
United States *v.* Hicks, **443,** 441
United States *v.* Kramer, **209**
United States ex rel. Wessels *v.* McDonald, Commandant of Brooklyn Navy Yard, **431,** 385
Vietti *v.* The George K. Mackie Fuel Co., **319**

Venezuela

Alarcón, *In re,* **275**

[References are to pages.]

TABLE OF CASES CITED

(*or otherwise mentioned in this Volume*)

A. L. B. *v.* (Austrian) Federal Ministry for the Interior, 214
The Adriatic, 144
Akerman, Julio, 211
Alcántara, Francisco Azpúrua, 262
Aldenhoff, Joseph, 267
Amazones *v.* Para, 99
The Anne, 142, 146
Aranaz, Candido Resaro, 266
Arkansas *v.* Tennessee, 96
Attorney-General *v.* Weeden, 407
The Attualita, 141
Aulicino, Julio, 256
Austro-Hungarian Consul *v.* Westphal, 347

La Bacis Gold Mining Co., 251
Badell, Manuel, 262
Baltor, Henrique, 267
Band, Isaias, 206
Bank Line *v.* Capel & Co., 395
Bank of United States *v.* Planters' Bank of Georgia, 141
Barbier, Ferdinand, 266
Bastian, Frederick, 267
Bastiann, Hermann, 266
Baumblatt, Mauricio, 257
Bercaitz, Carlos Maria, 207
Bergeron, Mario, 254
Berizzi Brothers Co. *v.* Steamship *Pesaro*, 141, 144
Berrocal, 303
Bertelli, Alfredo, 256
Beuthenot, Felippe, ou Luigi Morelli, 257
Bevilaqua, Clovis, 267
The Blonde and other Ships, 235, 430
Bochart *v.* Committee of Supplies of Corneux, 463
The Bold Buccleugh, 149
Bordone, Lorenzo, 206
Bragoseo Ltd. *v.* J. Sagor & Co., 51
Briggs, Arthur, 267
Briggs *v.* Light Boats, 148
The Broadmayne, 47
Brown *v.* United States, 407
Brulkind, Salomão, 256
Burza, Humberto, 276

Cabral, Abilio, 256
Cadenhead Case, 377
Calcabrini, David, 266, 267
Calderoni *v.* Official of Civil Status of Genoa, 455
Calleja, Andrés, 254
Canal, Victor, 276
Canellas, Antonio Bernardo, 256
Capetillo, Cipriano, 303
Carmona, Antonio Mora, 267
Carvalho, Manoel, 256
De Carzon, Isabel Forest, 304
Castillo, J. Amílcar, 269
Castro *v.* De Uriarte, 349
Chamberlain's Settlement, *In re*, 212, 213, 225
Charlton *v.* Kelly, 273, 349
Commercial and Estates Co. of Egypt *v.* Ball, 418
Commercial Pacific Cable Co. *v.* Philippine National Bank, 134
Cook *v.* Sprigg, 60
Cosacof, Salomón, 207
Do Costa, Adriano Pinto, 256
Courthieu, 303
Coury, George S., 254
The Cumene, 135
Da Cunha, Manoel Luiz, e José Maria de Carvalho, 257

Daimler Co. *v.* Continental Tyre and Rubber Co., 394, 409, 424, 425
Daubigny *v.* Davallon, 402

The David J. Adams, 377
The Davis, 140
Diez, Francisco, 211
Dobarro, Manuel, 206
Ducler y Dritman, Leon, 211
Duct de Dalarnoy, 303

The Edward and Mary, 486
Ely, Margarita, 304
Ertel Bieber & Co. *v.* Rio Tinto Co., 394, 397, 400
Esposito *v.* Bowden, 394
Estate of D'Adamo, 347
Estate of Servas, 347
Esteban, José, 211
The Exchange, 144

Faria, Alfeo dos Santos, 267
The Favourite, 179, 189
Fernandez *v.* Fernandez, 303
Filíos, Juan, 257
Flores, Pedro Alejandro, 262
Fogelzinger *v.* Pinter, 482
Foster *v.* Globe Venture Syndicate, 49
The Fox, 429
Frasca *v.* City Coal Co., 320
Freyberger, *Ex parte*, 212
Frickmann, Fritz George, 266
Fugagnoli, Benedicto, 256
Furtado *v.* Rogers, 407

Gabinsky, 211
The Gagara, 44
Gagliardi, Angelo, 207
Gagnière & Co. *v.* Eastern Company of Warehouses, etc., Ltd., 50
Galatiolo *v.* Senes, 455
García, Secondino, 445
Gemo, 304
Giglio, Salvador, 206
The Gloria, 133
Godin *v.* Godin, 460
González, Vicente, 254
Graf, Alejandro Esteban, 210
Grin v. Shine, 263
De Grospiron, Enriqueta Hauret, 304
Guadarrama, David G., 254
Guerrero, Manuel, 276

The Hakan, 491
The Hamborn, 230, 424
Hardman, William, 377
Von Hellfeld *v.* Russian Government, 135
Hermida *v.* Rios, 304
Herzenberg, Igel, 206
Hylass, Enrique, 304

International Petroleum Co. *v.* Agente de Petroleo, 251
International Petroleum Co. *v.* President, etc., 251
Iowa *v.* Illinois, 96
De Iturralde, Joaquin, 309

Jácome, Carlos Luis, 276
De Jager *v.* Attorney-General for Natal, 235
Jankelevitz, Enrique, 211
The Jassy, 137
Jenkins, Guillermo O., 310
Van der Jeucht, of Appels (Belgium) *v.* (1) N. V. Rijnschip *Barbera*, of Rotterdam; (2) C. J. van Zuijdam, Captain, *In re*, 30
The Johanna Emilie, 407
The Johnson Lighterage Co., 140
Jones *v.* United States, 31
Joo *v.* Kovacs, 482
The Jupiter, Nos. 1, 2 and 3, 44, 51, 258

Kadecka, Rosa, *v.* Government of the Federal Country of Lower Austria, 21
Kastzke, Gedale, 256
Ker *v.* Illinois, 272
Killian, 309
Kingdom of Norway *v.* Federal Sugar Refining Co., 135
Kingdom of Roumania *v.* Guaranty Trust Co., 135
Kleiber, 261
Kosching, Robert Martin, 267
Kotta, *In re*, 320
Kramer *v.* Attorney-General, 213, 216
Kunglig Jarnvagsstyrelsen *v.* Dexter and Carpenter, 133, 135, 144

Land *v.* Lord North, 407

Lapping, Ernesto, 215
Leal, Waltrudes Lopes, 267
De Leão, Luiz Francisco, *v.* Gauie and Sevilla, 308
Leiro, Jesús, 304, 309
Leivas, Luciana Narciso, 304
Leone, Carlos, 207
Leonel, Gil, 215
Lessee *v.* Anthony, 99
Liebmann, *Ex parte*, 225, 226, 405, 423
Lindo *v.* Rodney, 484
Locke *v.* United States, 172
Loewenstein *v.* Custodian of Enemy Property, 226
The Lomonosoff, 50
Long *v.* Tampico, 140
Lontrato, Pedro, 256
López, Andrés, 206
The Lotus, 271
The Lucy, 429
Luksic, Vicente, 304

M. & O., *In re*, 34
Madeira, José, 256
De Magelhaes, Manoel Calvet, 266
The Maipo, 144
Marchante, João, 257
Margulies, 405
The Marie Leonhart, 413
Martin *v.* Keyaerts and Leysen, 439
Martin, Erwin, 267
Martin, Fernando, 207
Martínez, Armando, 262
Martínez, Telmo, 207
Maru Navigation Co. *v.* Societa Commerciale Italiana di Navigazione, 144
Mary, Duchess of Sutherland, *In re*, 402
Do Mascimento, Arthur, 256
Maurine, Pedro, 257
Mayer *v.* Garvan, 400
Menaly, Pablo, 266
Mendes, José, 267
Micelle, João, 257
Mighell *v.* Sultan of Johore, 47, 49
Milligan, *Ex parte*, 431
Mineiro, João Baptista, 256
Minnesota *v.* Wisconsin, 97
Missouri *v.* Kentucky, 99
Missouri *v.* Nebraska, 98
The Möwe, 402
Muir, *Ex parte*, 140, 141, 142, 145
Munro, Donald, 303

N. V. Limburgsch Landbouw-Syndicaat, of Wijk-Maastricht *v.* German *Reich*, 129
Nebraska *v.* Yocoa [*sic*, Iowa], 98
Negrón, Simon Rojas, 262
Netherlands American Steam Navigation Co. *v.* H. M. Procurator-General, 487
The Nevada, 150
The Newbattle, 135
Niebisch, Fritz, 266
Nordman *v.* Rayner, 396
North American Dredging Co. of Texas, 236
Nunciatura Apostólica de B. A. *v.* Pérez, 309

Oetjen *v.* Central Leather Co., 26, 50
Officio al Ministro de Gobierno, 254
Oklahoma *v.* Texas, 97
Olivares, Isidro, *v.* Domingo Manfredi, 98
Oltra, Ramón, 206
The Oropa, 402
Ossa, Esbry, 309

Pagano *v.* Cerri, 347
De Paiva, Sebastião, 256
Parkinson *v.* Wentworth, 402
The Parlement Belge, 46, 137, 140, 147, 148, 154, 156, 157
Patsone *v.* Pennsylvania, 241
Patterson *v.* Bark Eudora, 110
Patterson-McDonald Shipbuilding Co., *In re*, 135
Pereira, Amaro José Marques, 256
Pereira, Antonio Manoel, 256
Peres, Manoel, 256
The Pesaro, 140, 145
Pietsch, 280
Pinedo, Martin, 304
Platten, 280
Poretti, *In re*, 261
Porter *v.* Freudenberg, 402

The Porto Alexandre, 149, 152, 156
Postmaster-General *v.* Taute, 60
Postula *v.* City of Liège, 460
De Prado, Luis, 207
Princess Paley Olga *v.* Weisz, 51
Public Prosecutor *v.* B. J. and R., 466

R. *v.* Corrigan, 275
R. *v.* Godfrey, 271
R. *v.* Sandoval, 180
Raffaele, Augustin, 206
The Rannveig, 443
Real, Domingos, 257
Reg. *v.* Jacobi and Hiller, 271
Reg. *v.* Keyn, 271
Reg. *v.* Nillins, 271
Remy, Amelius *v.* Man Sign, 95
Randjeslaagte Syndicate *v.* The Government, 60
Republic of Peru *v.* Dreyfus Brothers & Co., 184
Republic (Poland) *v.* Pantol, 35, 38
Republic (Poland) *v.* Weisholc, 33
Rex *v.* Brailsford, 127
Rex *v.* Francis; *ex parte* Markwald, 204
Ricaud *v.* American Metal Co., 26, 54
Ricciardi, José, 207
Riveros, 262
Rocca *v.* Thompson, 347
Rojas, Rubén Arturo, 262
Roméro, Modesto Pugas, 256
De la Rosa, Dioscorides, 267
Rosa, Gomez Paz, 304
The Roumanian, 484
Rowe, Joseph W., 303
Rush, *In re*, 409
Rymenans *v.* Germany, 229

Saavedra, Manoel, 257
Sánchez, Ciriaco, 207
Sanchez, Cuestra Francisco, 303
Sandberg *v.* McDonald, 110
The Sansom, 486
Santander, Carlos Gomez, 262
Santos *v.* Illidge, 50
Dos Santos, Arnaldo, 267
Santovincenzo *v.* Egan and Bennett, 303
The Sao Vicente, 142, 145
The Sapphire, 31
Scalia, Giuseppe, 257
Schaffenius *v.* Goldberg, 402
Schurmann *v.* United States, 210
Schwarts, Alexandre, 257
The Scotia, 157
The Secundus, 144
Da Silva, Manoel Pereira, 256
Simon, Manoel, 256
The Siren, 141
Sittig, *In re*, 261
Soave, Angelo, 256
Société Anonyme Belge des Mines d'Aljustrel (Portugal) *v.* Anglo-Belgian Agency, 421
Société Anonyme du Charbonnage Frédéric Henri *v.* Germany, 345
Société du Chemin de fer de Damas-Hamah *v.* Compagnie du Chemin de fer de Bagdad, 228, 344
Société Vinicole de Champagne *v.* W. de Munn, 343
Society for Propagation of the Gospel *v.* Town of New Haven, 388
Solano, Luis, 276
Soleiman, Ali, 207
Soriano, Lillie, 254
South African Republic *v.* La Compagnie Franco-Belge du Chemin de Fer du Nord, 135
Sponsito, Antonio, 207
State *v.* Hall, 271
Stevenson & Sons *v.* Aktiengesellschaft für Cartonnagen Industrie, 409
The Stigstad, 430
Stock, Paul Reinhold Ehrich, 207
Stoeck *v.* Public Trustee, 226, 333, 405
Suárez, Clodomino, 266
Sucesión de Atilio Repetto, 304
The Svanfos; *The Borgila*, 486
The Sylvan Arrow, 150

Tamiahua Petroleum Co. *v.* Secretaria de Industria, etc., 251
Tamplin Steamship Co. *v.* Anglo-Mexican Petroleum Products Co., 395
The Tattler (II), 189
The Thekla, 135
Thuysbaert, Hector, 267

Transportes Maritimos do Estado, *In re*, 144
Truax *v*. Raich, 320
The Treasury *v*. Wolff, 423

Underhill *v*. Hernandez, 50
United States *v*. Ju Toy, 209
United States *v*. Look Chaw, 110
United States *v*. McCullagh, 4
United States *v*. Rauscher, 271
United States *v*. Rockefeller, 6
United States *v*. Schwimmer, 207
United States *v*. Selkirk, 6
United States *v*. Shauver, 4
United States *v*. Strang, 134
United States *v*. Thompson, 6
United States *v*. Wilder, 140
United States, Owner of the American Steamship *Western Maid*, In the Matter of, 150

Del Val, Ramon Blanco, 262
Valin, 304
Veithardt and Hall *v*. Rylands Brothers, 395
The Vesta, 426
Vietti *v*. Mackie Fuel Co., 351
Vigneau Case, 303
Vince *v*. Tompai, 482
Vineash *v*. Becker, 298
The Vryheid, 436

Walker *v*. Baird, 233
Walneff *v*. All Russian Co-operative Society, 51
The Wanderer, 189
Waugh *v*. Morris, 422
Weber, *Ex parte*, 225, 226, 405, 423
Weiss Biheller & Brooks Ltd. *v*. German State, 229
Wells *v*. Williams, 402
Weyermann, Emile, 266
White, Child, & Beney Ltd. *v*. Eagle, Star and British Dominions Insurance Co., 51
White, Child, & Beney Ltd. *v*. Simmons, 51
Williams *v*. Bruffy, 50
Wipperman Case, 174
Wolff *v*. Oxholm, 407

The Zamora, 430
Zavagnini, Angel, 206

CLASSIFICATION

PART I

INTERNATIONAL LAW IN GENERAL

I. NATURE AND BINDING FORCE.

II. EXTENT.

III. SOURCES. *See also* PART X, ARBITRATION: The Law Applied by Arbitral Tribunals.

IV. SUBJECTS OF INTERNATIONAL LAW. *See* PART VI, THE INDIVIDUAL IN INTERNATIONAL LAW: In General; *and* PART VIII, TREATIES: Operation and Enforcement of Treaties.

V. RELATION TO MUNICIPAL LAW. *See also* PART VIII, TREATIES: Operation and Enforcement of Treaties.

VI. INTERNATIONAL COMITY.

VII. MISCELLANEOUS.

PART II

STATES AS INTERNATIONAL PERSONS

A. IN GENERAL

I. BEGINNING OF STATE EXISTENCE. (For RECOGNITION, *see below*, D.)

II. SOVEREIGNTY AND INDEPENDENCE—

i. In Foreign Relations. *See also below*, Recognition of Acts of Foreign States and Governments; PART IV, JURISDICTION; *and* PART VIII, TREATIES: Interpretation of Treaties—Agencies of Interpretation.

ii. In Matters of Domestic Jurisdiction.

iii. Acts of Sovereignty and Transactions of a Private Character. *See also* PART IV, JURISDICTION: Exemptions from.

III. EQUALITY OF STATES.

IV. RECOGNITION OF ACTS OF FOREIGN STATES AND GOVERNMENTS. *See also* PART IV, JURISDICTION: Territorial; *and below*, Recognition of States, Governments and Belligerency.

V. Continuity of States. *See also* State Succession.

VI. Extinction of States.

B. COMPOSITE AND DEPENDENT STATES AND TERRITORIES

I. Unions of States—

i. Federal States and Confederations.
ii. Other Unions (including Customs Unions).

II. British Commonwealth of Nations.

III. Protected and Vassal States and Protectorates.

IV. Mandates—

i. Sovereignty over Mandated Territories. Status of the Mandated Territories.
ii. Rights and Duties of the Mandatories.
iii. Rights and Duties of the League.
iv. Equality of Opportunity.
v. Nationality in Mandated Territories.
vi. Other Matters.

V. Territories under Joint or International Government.

C. NEUTRALISATION AND DEMILITARISATION

I. Of States.

II. Of Parts of State Territory.

III. Of Parts of the High Seas. *See also* Part III, Canals.

D. RECOGNITION. *See also above,* Recognition of Acts of Foreign States and Governments ; *and* Part IV, Jurisdiction : Territorial.

i. Of States.
ii. Of Governments.
iii. Of Insurgency.
iv. Of Belligerency.
v. Conditional Recognition.

E. STATE SUCCESSION

I. Succession in Rights.

II. Succession with regard to Contractual and other Obligations, and Concessions.

III. The Public Debt. Pensions.
IV. Succession with regard to Obligations for Delinquencies (Torts).
V. Respect of Private Rights.
VI. Upon Termination of a Rebellion.
VII. International Conventions.
VIII. In Matters of Administration. Officials.
IX. Binding Force of Laws and Judgments of Courts.

F. SUCCESSION OF GOVERNMENTS

I. In General.
II. Upon Termination of a Rebellion.

G. MISCELLANEOUS

PART III

STATE TERRITORY

A. STATE TERRITORY IN GENERAL

I. Nature of Territorial Sovereignty.
II. Acquisition of Territorial Sovereignty—
- i. Accretion and Accession. Avulsion.
- ii. Occupation. The Principle of Contiguity. Effect of Discovery.
- iii. Cession. Conditional Cession. Plebiscite.
- iv. Prescription.
- v. Conquest.

III. Loss of Territorial Sovereignty.
IV. Effects of Changes of Sovereignty. *See also* Part II, State Succession.
V. Occupation of Foreign Territory in Time of Peace.
VI. International Leases and Grants in Perpetuity.
VII. Sovereignty over the Air—
- i. Air Navigation Convention of 1919 and Similar Conventions.
- ii. Wireless Telegraphy, Telephony, etc.

See also Part XI, War and Neutrality: Air Warfare.

B. PARTS OF STATE TERRITORY

I. Boundaries—
- i. Land Boundaries.
- ii. Water Boundaries.

II. Rivers—
- i. National Rivers.
- ii. Multi-national Rivers.
- iii. International Rivers.
  - (*a*) The Principle of Freedom of Navigation on International Rivers.
  - (*b*) Functions and Competence of International Commissions on International Rivers.
- iv. The Utilisation of the Flow of Non-National and International Rivers.

III. Territorial Waters—
- i. Nature of the Maritime Belt.
- ii. Breadth of the Maritime Belt.
- iii. Jurisdiction in the Maritime Belt.
- iv. Coasting Trade and Fisheries.

IV. National Waters.

V. Straits.

VI. Bays.

VII. Canals, International—
- i. In Time of Peace.
- ii. In Time of War.

VIII. Lakes and Land-Locked Seas.

IX. Islands.

X. State Servitudes.

C. MISCELLANEOUS

PART IV

JURISDICTION

A. JURISDICTION IN GENERAL. TERRITORIAL AND PERSONAL

I. Territorial—

(*a*) Over Territory in General and Persons and Property situated therein.

See also Part II, Recognition of Acts of Foreign States and Governments, *and* Recognition of Foreign States and Governments.

(*b*) Criminal Jurisdiction over Foreigners.
(*c*) Over Ports and National Waters. *See also* PART III, TERRITORIAL WATERS.
(*d*) At the Maritime Frontier. Hovering Laws. *See also* HIGH SEAS.
(*e*) Coasting Trade.
(*f*) Fisheries.
(*g*) Exemptions from and Restrictions upon Territorial Jurisdiction.
   (i) Foreign States. *See also* PART II, SOVEREIGNTY AND INDEPENDENCE: Acts of Sovereignty and Transactions of a Private Character.
   (ii) Heads of Foreign States.
   (iii) Public Ships and other Property of Foreign States.
   (iv) Foreign Armed Forces.
   (v) Diplomatic Immunities. *See* PART VII.

II. PERSONAL—
(*a*) Over Subjects in respect of Crimes Committed outside the Realm;
(*b*) Over Subjects Abroad or on the High Seas and their Property Situate Abroad.

B. EXTRATERRITORIAL JURISDICTION

I. CONSULAR JURISDICTION. RÉGIME OF CAPITULATIONS.

C. HIGH SEAS

I. CONCEPTION OF THE HIGH SEAS AND OF THE FREEDOM OF THE SEA.

II. JURISDICTION ON THE HIGH SEAS. *See also* JURISDICTION.
i. For Ensuring the Safety of Traffic. Collisions. Salvage.
ii. For Enforcement of International Conventions.
iii. Visit, Search and Arrest by Men-of-War in Time of Peace.
iv. The Law Governing the Flag. Ship's Papers.
v. Right of Pursuit.
vi. Enforcement of Hovering, Revenue and other Municipal Laws.
vii. Piracy.

See also PART III, TERRITORIAL WATERS, BAYS *and* STRAITS.

III. SUBMARINE CABLES—
i. In Time of Peace.
ii. In Time of War.

D. MISCELLANEOUS

PART V

STATE RESPONSIBILITY

A. WHERE DOES RESPONSIBILITY REST IN FEDERAL AND OTHER COMPOSITE STATES?

B. NATURE AND KINDS OF STATE RESPONSIBILITY

I. In General. When does State Responsibility Become Engaged? Absolute Responsibility and Responsibility Based on Fault.

II. For Breaches of Treaty Obligations.

III. For Revocation of, or Interference with, Concessions or Concessionary Contracts.

IV. For Debts.

V. For Breaches of Contractual Obligations.

VI. For Wrongs Unconnected with Contractual Obligations—

(*a*) Acts and Omissions of State Organs and Officials.
- i. Denial of Justice. Exhaustion of Legal Remedies.
- ii. Executive Action or Inaction.
- iii. Connected with Legislation.
- iv. Connected with Use of Adjacent Land or Water. *See also* Part III, Rivers.
- v. Plea of Non-Discrimination against Foreigners. *See* Part IV, Territorial Jurisdiction: Expropriation.

(*b*) Acts of Insurgents, Rioters and Private Individuals in General.

VII. For Acts and Omissions of Revolutionary or *de facto* Governments.

C. CLAIMS

I. In General.

II. Nationality of Claims.

III. Assignment of Claims.

IV. State Control over Private Claims.

D. PRESCRIPTION (EXTINCTIVE PRESCRIPTION)

I. Before International Tribunals.

II. Effect of Municipal Statutes of Limitation.

III. Effect of War.

E. DAMAGES (MEASURE OF DAMAGES)

I. Award of Damages in General. Grounds for Awarding Damages.

II. Indirect Damages and Damages for Loss of Profits.

III. Punitive and Exemplary Damages.

F. INTEREST

I. In General.

II. Rate of Interest. Compound Interest.

III. The *Dies a Quo*. The *Dies ad Quem*.

G. MISCELLANEOUS

PART VI

THE INDIVIDUAL IN INTERNATIONAL LAW

A. IN GENERAL

I. Position of Individuals in International Law. *See also* Part I, International Law in General: Relation to Municipal Law; *and* Part VIII, Treaties: Operation and Enforcement of Treaties.

II. Before International Tribunals.

B. NATIONALITY

I. In General. Proof of Nationality.

II. As Affected by Changes of Sovereignty.

III. As Determining the Right of Protection of Citizens Abroad.

IV. Protected Persons and *de facto* Subjects.

V. Naturalisation.

VI. Expatriation. Loss of Nationality.

VII. Denationalisation.

VIII. Double Nationality.

IX. Option.

X. Statelessness.

XI. Nationality of Corporations. *See also* Part XI, War and Neutrality : Enemy Character.

C. ALIENS

I. Admission of Aliens.

II. Position of Aliens—

- i. Subjection to Territorial Sovereignty of the Receiving State.
- ii. Protection by the National State.
- iii. Treatment by and Responsibilities of the Receiving State. *See also* Part V, State Responsibility.
- iv. Plea of Non-Discrimination. *See* Part V, State Responsibility.
- v. Respect for Property. Expropriation. *See* Part IV, Jurisdiction : Territorial.

III. Expulsion of Aliens—

- i. Right of Expulsion.
- ii. Procedure of Expulsion.
- iii. Reception of Expelled Nationals.

D. EXTRADITION

I. Extradition in General.

II. Extraditable Crimes.

III. Extradition of Nationals.

IV. Conditions of Extradition.

V. Procedure of Extradition.

VI. Political Criminals.

E. MINORITIES (PROTECTION OF MINORITIES)

I. Minority Treaties and their Interpretation.

II. Enforcement of Minority Treaties through the League of Nations and Procedure with regard to Protection of Minorities.

III. Conception of Minority.

IV. Protection of National, Racial and Linguistic Minorities.

V. Treatment of Minorities Apart from Treaty.

F. MISCELLANEOUS

PART VII

DIPLOMATIC AND CONSULAR INTERCOURSE AND PRIVILEGES

A. PERMANENT DIPLOMATIC ENVOYS

I. Appointment and Reception of Diplomatic Envoys.

II. Position and Functions of Diplomatic Envoys.

III. Privileges and Immunities of—

- i. Diplomatic Envoys and their Staff.
- ii. Subordinate Members of the Diplomatic Staff.
- iii. The Family and Retinue of Diplomatic Envoys.
- iv. The Official House of a Diplomatic Envoy.

IV. Termination of Appointment of Diplomatic Envoy.

B. SPECIAL ENVOYS: DELEGATES AT INTERNATIONAL CONFERENCES: THEIR PRIVILEGES AND IMMUNITIES

C. RIGHT OF OTHER PERSONS TO PRIVILEGES AND IMMUNITIES

I. Officials of the League of Nations.

II. Representatives Sent by and Accredited to the League.

III. Delegates of States Attending the Assembly or International Conferences Convened by the League of Nations or the International Labour Organisation.

IV. Officials of the International Labour Office.

V. Judges and Officials of the Permanent Court of International Justice and other International Tribunals.

VI. Members of International Commissions, and Officials of International Unions and Similar Bodies.

D. CONSULS

I. Appointment and Exequatur.

II. Position and Function of Consuls.

III. Privileges and Immunities of Consuls.

E. MISCELLANEOUS

PART VIII

TREATIES

I. Conception of Treaties as International Contracts.

II. Forms of International Agreement and Methods by which they are Concluded—

- i. Treaties. Conventions. Governmental Agreements. Exchanges of Notes.
- ii. Signature. Accession and Adhesion. Tacit Renewal.

III. Multilateral Treaties.

IV. Conditions of Validity of Treaties. Registration of Treaties.

V. Parties to Treaties. Right to Conclude Treaties. Composite and Dependent States and Territories.

VI. Constitutional Limitations.

VII. Reservations.

VIII. Ratification of Treaties. Entrance into Force.

IX. Operation and Enforcement of Treaties. Necessity of Legislation. *See also* Part I, International Law in General. Relation to Municipal Law; *and* Part VI, The Individual in International Law: In General.

X. Effect of Treaties on Third Parties.

XI. Termination of Treaties—

- i. By Operation of Law.
  - (*a*) In General.
  - (*b*) Extinction and Dismemberment of Contracting Party.

(*c*) Outbreak of War. *See* PART XI, WAR AND NEUTRALITY.
(*d*) The *clausula rebus sic stantibus*. Reconsideration of Treaties under Article 19 of the Covenant.
(*e*) Merger in Subsequent Treaty.
ii. By Act of Party.
(*a*) In General.
(*b*) Mutual Consent.
(*c*) Unilateral Denunciation. Result of Non-Performance by the Other Party.
iii. Effect of Termination upon Acquired Rights.

XII. INTERPRETATION OF TREATIES—
i. Agencies of Interpretation. Construction in Accordance with the Intention of the Parties.
ii. Restrictive Interpretation.
(*a*) Restrictions of Sovereignty.
(*b*) Interpretation against the Party Responsible for the Drafting.
iii. Bilingual Treaties.
iv. Consideration of Preparatory Work.
v. Various other Rules of Interpretation.

XIII. SPECIAL KINDS OF TREATIES—
(*a*) Commercial Treaties. Most-Favoured-Nation Clause.
(*b*) Peace Treaties. *See* PART XI, WAR AND NEUTRALITY.

XIV. MISCELLANEOUS.

PART IX

INTERNATIONAL ORGANISATION AND ADMINISTRATION

A. LEAGUE OF NATIONS

I. CHARACTER OF THE LEAGUE.
II. THE ASSEMBLY.
III. THE COUNCIL.
IV. INTERPRETATION OF THE COVENANT OF THE LEAGUE.
V. THE LEAGUE AND NON-MEMBER STATES.

B. INTERNATIONAL LABOUR ORGANISATION

I. ORGANISATION AND CONSTITUTION.
II. CONCLUSION AND INTERPRETATION OF LABOUR CONVENTIONS.
III. ENFORCEMENT OF LABOUR CONVENTIONS.

C. OTHER ORGANS OF INTERNATIONAL ADMINISTRATION. *See also* PART II B (Territories under Joint or International Government), *and* PART III B (Functions and Competence of International Commissions on International Rivers).

D. MISCELLANEOUS

PART X

DISPUTES

A. ARBITRATION

I. ARBITRATION IN GENERAL—
- i. Conception and Function of Arbitration.
- ii. The Law Applied by Arbitral Tribunals. Arbitration and Judicial Settlement.
- iii. The Arbitration Treaty. Appointment and Withdrawal of Arbitrators.

II. PROCEDURE—
- i. Procedure before the Tribunal (Oral and Written Arguments).
- ii. Competence. Competence to Determine Jurisdiction.
- iii. Intervention.
- iv. Counter-Claim and Set-Off.
- v. Exceptions and Demurrers.
- vi. Costs.
- vii. Injunctions and Interlocutory Orders.
- viii. Experts.

III. RULES OF EVIDENCE. BURDEN OF PROOF. As to Consideration of Preparatory Work in the Interpretation of Treaties, *see* PART VIII, TREATIES: Interpretation of Treaties.

IV. ADMISSION OF LIABILITY. WAIVER. ESTOPPEL.

V. THE AWARD—
- i. Scope and Binding Force of the Award.
- ii. *Res Judicata.*
- iii. Appeal and Revision.

B. PERMANENT COURT OF INTERNATIONAL JUSTICE

I. ORGANISATION OF THE COURT.

II. RELATION OF THE COURT TO THE LEAGUE.

III. Contentious Jurisdiction—
  i. Competence.
  ii. Procedure.
  iii. Law Applicable.
  iv. Judgment.

IV. The Advisory Opinion—
  i. Competence.
  ii. Procedure.
  iii. Law Applicable.
  iv. Opinion.

C. CONCILIATION

I. By the Council of the League.

II. Under Special Treaties.

III. Negotiation.

D. UNILATERAL MEANS OF REDRESS SHORT OF WAR

  i. Retorsion.
  ii. Reprisals.
  iii. Pacific Blockade. Blockade under the Covenant of the League.
  iv. Intervention.

E. NEGOTIATION

F. MISCELLANEOUS

PART XI

WAR AND NEUTRALITY

A. WAR IN GENERAL

I. Definition and Technical Meaning of War. Insurgency.

II. Commencement of War.

III. Region of War.

IV. Belligerent Forces.

V. Effects of Outbreak of War—
  i. In General.
  ii. On Treaties.
    (a) During the War.
    (b) After the War.

iii. On Private Contracts.
iv. On Enemy Subjects with regard to—
(*a*) Their Personal Status in the Territory of the Belligerent. *Persona standi in judicio.*
(*b*) Their Property and other Rights.
v. On Enemy Merchant Ships in Port.
vi. On Neutral Persons and Property. Embargo. The Right of Angary.
vii. Trading with the Enemy.

VI. Enemy Character—
i. Of Individuals.
ii. Of Corporations.
iii. Of Vessels.
iv. Of Goods.

VII. The Binding Force of the Laws of War.

VIII. Enforcement of the Laws of War—
i. Reprisals.
ii. Spies.
iii. Punishment of War Crimes. Defence of Superior Orders.
iv. Compensation and Reparation.

IX. Prisoners of War.

X. Non-Hostile Relations between Belligerents, especially Armistices.

XI. Termination of War.

XII. Effects of Treaties of Peace—
i. In General.
ii. Amnesty.
iii. Revival of Treaties.
iv. Miscellaneous.

XIII. Performance of Peace Treaties.

B. WARFARE ON LAND

I. Measures and Instruments of Force.

II. Appropriation, Utilisation and Destruction of Enemy Property.

III. Occupation of Enemy Territory—
i. Nature and Effects of the Occupation.
ii. Legislative, Judicial and Administrative Functions of the Occupant.
iii. Respect of Private Property. The Public Property of the Enemy State. Requisitions and Contributions.
iv. Inhabitants. Services. Deportations. Hostages.

C. WARFARE AT SEA

I. Measures and Instruments of Force.

II. Visit, Search, Capture, and Destruction—

(*a*) Of Enemy Merchantmen.
(*b*) Of Neutral Merchantmen.

III. Restrictions on the Right of Capture (Hospital Ships, etc., Postal Correspondence, Property under Neutral Flag).

IV. Prize Law—

i. Nature and Extent of Jurisdiction in Prize Courts.
ii. Procedure.
iii. Indemnities and Damages.

D. AIR WARFARE

E. NEUTRALITY IN GENERAL

I. Nature of Duties of Neutrality.

II. Neutrals and Military and Naval Operations and Preparations.

III. Neutral Asylum.

IV. Supplies, Loans and Services to Belligerents.

V. As Affected by the Covenant of the League.

F. CONTRABAND

I. Conception of Contraband. Absolute and Relative Contraband.

II. Carriage of Contraband and Doctrine of Continuous Voyage.

III. Penalty for Carriage of Contraband.

G. BLOCKADE

I. Establishment of Blockade, Conditions of Validity.

II. Breach and Penalty.

III. Blockade and the Doctrine of Continuous Voyage. For Neutralisation *see* Part II, *above*.

LIST OF ABBREVIATIONS

OF TITLES OF COLLECTIONS OF DECISIONS, LAW REPORTS, TREATISES, PERIODICALS, ETC., QUOTED IN THE TEXT

A.C.	=	British Appeal Cases in the House of Lords and Judicial Committee of the Privy Council.
A.J.	=	The American Journal of International Law.
B. and C.P.C.	=	British and Colonial Prize Cases.
Boh.	=	Collection of the Decisions of the Czechoslovak Supreme Administrative Court (Sbírka nalezú nejvyššíjo spravniho soudu). Edited by Bohuslav. This Collection contains two series: decisions in administrative matters, abbreviated "adm.", and decisions in financial matters, abbreviated "fin."
B.Y.	=	The British Year Book of International Law.
Ch.	=	Chancery Division of the English High Court of Justice.
C.L.R.	=	Columbia Law Review.
Clunet	=	Journal du droit international.
Cornell L.Q.	=	Cornell Law Quarterly.
Dalloz	=	Recueil périodique et critique de Jurisprudence, de Législation et de Doctrine (founded by Dalloz).
Dickinson, Cases	=	Dickinson, Cases and Other Readings on the Law of Nations (1929).
E. & B.	=	Ellis and Blackburn, The English Reports (1911).
E.R.S.	=	Entscheidungen des Reichsgerichts in Strafsachen.
E.R.Z.	=	Entscheidungen des Reichsgerichts in Zivilsachen.
Fauchille	=	Fauchille, Traité de droit international public, 8th ed. of Bonfils' Manuel de droit international public, 2 vols. (1921-1926).
Fed.	=	Federal Reporter (United States).
Fiore, Int. L.	=	Fiore, International Law Codified, Borchard's trans. (1918).

Gazette du Palais = La Gazette du Palais, Supplément au Journal Judiciaire Quotidien.
H.L.R. = Harvard Law Review.
Hall, Int. L. = Hall, A Treatise on International Law, 8th Ed. (1924), ed. by Pearce Higgins.
Hallek, Int. L. = Hallek, International Law, 4th Ed. (1908), ed. by Sherston Baker.
Ill. L.R. = Illinois Law Review.
K.B. = King's Bench Division of the English High Court of Justice.
Lapradelle-Politis = Lapradelle-Politis, Recueil des arbitrages internationaux, vol. i. (1905), vol. ii. (1924).
L.J. = Law Journal Reports.
L.R. = Law Reports.
L.T. = Law Times Reports.
M.L.R. = Michigan Law Review.
Martens, N.R.G. = Martens, Recueil de Traités (Nouveau Recueil Général).
Moore = Moore, History and Digest of International Arbitrations to which the United States has been a Party, 6 vols. (1898).
Moore, Digest = Moore, A Digest of International Law, 8 vols. (1906).
Nielsen = American and British Claims Arbitration (under the special agreement of August 18, 1910), Report by Nielsen (1926).
Oppenheim = Oppenheim, International Law, 4th Ed., ed. by McNair, vol. ii. (1926), vol. i. (1928).
O.S.P. = Orzecznictwo Sądów Polskich (an unofficial collection of decisions of Polish Courts).
P. = Probate, Divorce and Admiralty Division of the English High Court of Justice.
P.C.I.J. = Publications of the Permanent Court of International Justice.
Series A—Judgments.
B—Advisory Opinions.
C—Acts and Documents relating to Judgments and Advisory Opinions given by the Court.
D—Collection of Texts Governing the Jurisdiction of the Court.
E—Annual Reports.
F—General Index.
Phillimore, Int. L. = Phillimore, Commentaries upon International Law, 4 vols., 3rd ed. (1879-1888).

Q.B.	=	Queen's Bench Division of the English High Court of Justice (time of Queen Victoria).
Ralston	=	Ralston, The Law and Procedure of International Tribunals, revised ed. (1926).
Recueil	=	Recueil des décisions des tribunaux arbitraux mixtes.
R.I.	=	Revue de droit international et de législation comparée.
S.J.		Solicitors' Journal.
Sirey	=	Recueil général des lois et des arrêts (founded by Sirey).
T.L.R.	=	Times Law Reports.
U. Pa. L.R.	=	University of Pennsylvania Law Review.
U.S.	=	United States Reporter (Supreme Court).
U.S. Stat. L.	=	United States Statutes at Large.
Váž.	=	Collection of the decisions of the Czechoslovak Supreme Court of Justice (Sbírka rozhodnutí nejvyššího soudu). Edited by Vážný. The Collection contains two series: decisions in civil and commercial matters, abbreviated "civ.", and decisions in criminal matters, abbreviated "cr."
Westlake, Int. L.	=	Westlake, International Law, 2 vols., 2nd ed. (1910-1913).
Y.L.J.	=	Yale Law Journal.
Zb. O.S.N.	=	Zbiór Orzeczeń Sądu Najwyższego (Collection of the Decisions of the Polish Supreme Court).

PART I

INTERNATIONAL LAW IN GENERAL

I.—Nature and Binding Force

International Law—In General—Restrictive Interpretation of Treaties Creating Exceptions to Generally Recognised Rules of International Law.

See Case No. 120 (*The Wanderer*).

II.—Extent

International Law—General and Universal—General International Conventions Invoked by States which have not Ratified them—The Hague Convention for the Pacific Settlement of International Disputes.

See the award of the Swiss Federal Council of 24 March, 1922 (Cases Nos. 54, 262, p. 116 of the award), for an instance of frequent invocation by both parties of Article 82 of The Hague Convention for the Pacific Settlement of International Disputes (1907), which was not ratified by either party.[1]

International Law—How far Applicable to Members of Federal States.

See Case No. 65 (*In re Marincovich*).

III.—Sources

[See also Part X, ARBITRATION: *The Law Applied by Arbitral Tribunals.*]

International Law—Sources—Municipal Enactments as a Source of Treaty Interpretation—Article 296 of the Treaty of Versailles.

See Case No. 249 (*Chamberlain & Hookham Ltd.* v. *Solar Zahlerwerke*).

[1] Article 82 lays down that in default of agreement to the contrary any dispute as to the interpretation and the execution of the award shall be submitted to the decision of the tribunal which pronounced it.

International Law—Sources of—Practice of the Parties to the Dispute as Determining the Law Applicable by the Arbitrator.

See Cases Nos. 54, 262 (*Colombia and Venezuela*) for frequent references to the practice of the disputant parties as determining the decision, for instance, on the nature of the powers of boundary commissions.

International Law—Sources—Relevance of Decisions of Municipal and International Courts—Adoption of the Reasoning of such Decisions as Basis for an International Award.

See Case No. 124 (*French Claims against Peru*).

V.—Relation to Municipal Law

[See also Part VIII, TREATIES: *Operation and Enforcement of Treaties*.]

Case No. 1

International Law—Relation to Municipal Law—Treaties as Part of the Law of the Land—United States of America—Constitutional Limitations upon Treaty-Making Power—Validity of Statutes Made under Treaties—Limitation of State Rights by Treaty.

STATE OF MISSOURI *v.* HOLLAND, UNITED STATES GAME WARDEN.

United States Supreme Court. 19 *April,* 1920.

THE FACTS.—This was a suit by the State of Missouri to prevent the enforcement of the United States Migratory Bird Treaty Act of 3 July, 1918 (40 U.S. Stat. L. 755), and of the regulations made by the Secretary of Agriculture in pursuance thereof (40 U.S. Stat. L. 1812, 1863). An earlier Act of Congress protecting migratory birds and game (37 U.S. Stat. L. 847) had been held unconstitutional (*United States* v. *Shauver,* 214 Fed. 154; *United States* v. *McCullagh,* 221 Fed. 288). The United States had thereupon concluded a Treaty with Great Britain (16 August, 1916) for the protection of migratory birds (39 U.S. Stat. L. 1702), and had enacted the statute here involved to provide for the enforcement of the Treaty. On behalf of the State of Missouri, it was contended that the statute was an unconstitutional interference with the rights reserved to the States by the Tenth Amendment to the United States Constitution. The United States District Court for the Western District of Missouri sustained a motion to dismiss the suit on the ground that the statute was constitutional.

Held, two justices dissenting: That the decree must be affirmed. Treaty and statute were constitutional. If the Treaty was valid, there could be no dispute about the validity of the statute and both Treaty and statute would be paramount in relation to conflicting State legislation. The Treaty was within the national treaty-making power conferred by Article II, § 2, of the United States Constitution. Delivering the Opinion of the Court, Mr. Justice Holmes said: " The question " raised is the general one whether the treaty and statute are " void as an interference with the rights reserved to the States. " To answer this question it is not enough to refer to the Tenth " Amendment, reserving the powers not delegated to the " United States, because by Article II, § 2, the power to make " treaties is delegated expressly, and by Article VI treaties " made under the authority of the United States, along with " the Constitution and laws of the United States made in pur- " suance thereof, are declared the supreme law of the land. . . . " Acts of Congress are the supreme law of the land only when " made in pursuance of the Constitution, while treaties are " declared to be so when made under the authority of the " United States. It is open to question whether the authority " of the United States means more than the formal acts pre- " scribed to make the convention. We do not mean to imply " that there are no qualifications to the treaty-making power; " but they must be ascertained in a different way. It is " obvious that there may be matters of the sharpest exigency " for the national well-being that an act of Congress could " not deal with but that a treaty followed by such an act " could, and it is not lightly to be assumed that, in matters " requiring national action, 'a power which must belong to " 'and somewhere reside in every civilized government' is not " to be found. . . . The treaty in question does not contravene " any prohibitory words to be found in the Constitution. The " only question is whether it is forbidden by some invisible " radiation from the general terms of the Tenth Amendment. " We must consider what this country has become in deciding " what that Amendment has reserved." Mr. Justice Holmes concluded: " Here a national interest of very nearly the first

Case No. 1 ***contd.***

"magnitude is involved. It can be protected only by national "action in concert with that of another power. The subject-"matter is only transitorily within the State and has no "permanent habitat therein. But for the treaty and the "statute there soon might be no birds for any powers to deal "with. We see nothing in the Constitution that compels the "Government to sit by while a food supply is cut off and the "protectors of our forests and our crops are destroyed. It is "not sufficient to rely upon the States. The reliance is vain, "and were it otherwise, the question is whether the United "States is forbidden to act. We are of opinion that the treaty "and statute must be upheld." [Reports: 252 U.S. 416, pp. 432, 433 and 435; 258 Fed. 479; Dickinson, *Cases*, p. 1037.]

NOTE.—See also: *United States* v. *Thompson*, 258 Fed. 257; *United States* v. *Selkirk*, 258 Fed. 775; *United States* v. *Rockefeller*, 260 Fed. 346; and (for comment) see 20 C.L.R. 692; 6 Cornell L.Q. 91; 33 H.L.R. 281; 29 Y.L.J. 445.

Case No. 2

International Law—Relation to Municipal Law—Treaties—Superseding Conflicting State Law—United States of America.

TROTT *v.* STATE.

United States, Supreme Court of North Dakota.
27 February, 1919.

THE FACTS.—The plaintiffs were British subjects, legatees under the will of a North Dakota resident, who had been taxed 25 per cent. on their inheritance of the North Dakota resident's estate. The tax was levied under N.D. Comp. Laws, 1913, § 8977, providing for a higher tax on gifts to aliens not resident in the United States than to other persons. The plaintiffs sought to recover on the ground that the North Dakota statute violated the Treaty of 1900 between Great Britain and the United States. (31 U.S. Stat. L. 1939.) The Treaty provided for testamentary succession upon the payment of "such duties only as the citizens or subjects "of the country where the property lies shall be liable "to pay in like cases." An issue as to the constitutionality of the statute was raised by the State's demurrer, and from an order overruling the demurrer the State appealed.

Held: That the order must be affirmed. The Treaty is the

"supreme law of the land," superseding all conflicting State laws, and its language is clear and unambiguous. [Report: 41 N.D. 614.]

International Law—Relation to Municipal Law—Duty of Courts to Enquire into Conformity of Laws with International Law. **Case No. 3**

SAZONOW *v.* DISTRICT LAND (REFORM) BOARD OF BIAŁYSTOK.

Poland, Supreme Court, First Division. 2 *October*, 1922.

THE FACTS.—See Case No. 174.

Held: *Inter alia*, that since the Constitution stipulates in Article 81 that courts may not enquire into the validity of statutes which have been duly promulgated, the Court could not enquire whether the Land Reform Statute of 15 July, 1920, was or was not in accordance with the principles of international law. [Reports: Zb. O.S.N., 1922, No. 81; O.S.P., II, No. 2.]

NOTE.—It has been the consistent view of Polish courts that Article 81 of the Constitution precludes their enquiring into the consistency of any Polish Acts of Parliament with the Constitution or with international law. This view seems to be in harmony with the practice of courts in many other Continental countries in applying similarly worded provisions of their laws.

International Law—Relation to Municipal Law—Municipal Law as a Source of International Arbitral Decisions—Law Applied by Arbitral Tribunals.

See Case No. 261 (*Norway and United States: Requisition of Shipbuilding Contracts Case*).

Municipal Law—Relation to International Law—Decisions of Municipal Court—Whether Binding upon the Government in Proceedings before an International Court.

See Case No. 115 (*The Coquitlam*).

International Law—Relation to Municipal Law—Abrogation of Treaty Obligations by Municipal Legislation.

See Case No. 176 (*Ex parte Pettine*).

Relation of International Law to Municipal Law—Treaties and Municipal Legislation—Extradition Treaties.

See Case No. 183 (*In re Hurlimann*).

International Law—Relation to Municipal Law—International Law as Part of Dutch Law.

See Case No. 86 *Bergverksaktiebolaget Kosmai* (*appellant*) v. *Militär-Liquidierungsamt, of Vienna* (*respondent*)).

International Law—Relation to Municipal Law—Armistices—Effect upon Private Rights and Obligations.

See Cases No. 302 (*Martin* v. *Keyaerts and Leysen*) and No. 303 (*State of Belgium* v. *Malfeit and Fischer*).

PART II

STATES AS INTERNATIONAL PERSONS

A. IN GENERAL

I.—Beginning of State Existence

[For RECOGNITION, see below, *D*.]

Beginning of State Existence—Establishment of New States—Czechoslovak Territory—Establishment of Czechoslovak Territorial Sovereignty in Bohemia, Moravia and Silesia.[1] **Case No. 4**

PAYMENT OF WAR TAX (CZECHOSLOVAKIA) CASE.

Czechoslovakia, Supreme Administrative Court.
21 *January*, 1921. (*No.* 580.)

THE FACTS.—By a Decree of the former Austrian Ministry of Finance it was made possible for tax-payers to effect payment of the war tax by bonds of the Austrian war loans. This right was, in the Czechoslovak State, abrogated by a Decree of the National Committee of 2 November, 1918, No. 19. On 14 December, 1918, the plaintiff deposited with the board of assessment of Liberec (Reichenberg, Bohemia) bonds of Austrian war loans in payment of war tax due by him. The payment was not recognised by the Czechoslovak authorities, having regard to the above Decree. The plaintiff lodged an appeal with the Supreme Administrative Court, contending that the district of Liberec was declared by Austria to belong to the territory of this latter State, as forming part of the German territory of Bohemia (*Deutschböhmen*); that on 14 December, 1918, when the payment was effected, the Czechoslovak State did not in fact exercise sovereignty in the district of Liberec as the occupation of that town by the Czechoslovak military forces did not take place before 16 December; and that therefore the payment of the tax could not be considered null and void.

Held by the Supreme Administrative Court: That the appeal failed. Before the revolution of 28 October, 1918, the

[1] See *Annual Digest*, 1925-1926, Case No. 9, footnote 1.

Case No. 4 *contd.*

former Kingdom of Bohemia formed, according to the Austrian Constitution, an autonomous unit not only from the point of view of administrative law, but also from the point of view of constitutional law. It had its separate Diet, the standing committee of which was the highest autonomous authority for the whole country. The jurisdiction of central judicial and administrative authorities, established in Prague, extended over the whole territory of the former Kingdom of Bohemia. This state of affairs lasted until 28 October, 1918. The conception of a German territory of Bohemia (*Deutschböhmen*) was not known either to the Austrian Constitution or to Austrian public administration.

The National Committee assumed power, on 28 October, 1918 (Article 3 of the Law of 28 October, 1918, No. 11 [1]), over all these central authorities, and thus over the whole territory of the former Kingdom of Bohemia, including the district of Liberec. The population of the whole former Kingdom of Bohemia recognised in fact the authority of the National Committee. It was therefore not necessary for the National Committee to fix in the Law of 28 October, 1918, No. 11, which was promulgated on the same day, the boundaries of the independent Czechoslovak State as far as the former Kingdom of Bohemia was concerned.

The situation as described above remained the same on 8 November, 1918, on which day the Decree of the National Committee of 2 November, 1918, No. 19, was promulgated. Accordingly this Decree came into force for the whole territory of the former Kingdom of Bohemia.

" The plaintiff objects that by the Decree of the Austrian " State of 25 November, 1918, No. 58, the district of Liberec " was declared to form a part of the territory of this State. He " deduces therefrom that it is not possible to consider the " payment of the tax, effected on 14 December, 1918, null and " void, as at that time the Czechoslovak State did not exercise " in fact sovereignty in the district of Liberec. This contention " cannot be admitted."

The Austrian State was established by the resolution of the provisional National Assembly of 30 October, 1918, which was not promulgated in the official collection of laws before 15 November, 1918, and does not define the boundaries of the State. Originally there was no question of an independent Austrian State, but only of a part of the German Republic (see Article 2 of the Law of 12 November, 1918, No. 5). The

[1] As to the text of this Law, see p. 16, footnote.

Decree of the State Council of 8 November, 1918 (promulgated on 17 November, 1918), established a Court of Appeal for the German territory of Bohemia with its seat at Liberec, but a provision defining the territory belonging to German Bohemia is to be found only in the Decree of the State Secretary for Justice of 25 November, 1918, No. 58, promulgated on 30 November, 1918.

Accordingly the Austrian State came into existence at a time when the independent Czechoslovak State had already exercised sovereignty over the whole territory of the former Kingdom of Bohemia. The Treaties of Peace of Versailles and of St. Germain, so far as the territory of the former Kingdom of Bohemia is concerned, merely approved a state of facts which already existed on 28 October, 1918.

The Court could not accept the contention that the National Committee, or the Czechoslovak State, exercised sovereignty in the district of Liberec only after the occupation thereof by the Czechoslovak military forces on 16 December, 1918. There could be here no question of occupation. This was not enemy territory; it was an integral part of the territory of the Czechoslovak State. From the fact that a part of the population of the district of Liberec was not disposed to recognise the sovereignty of the Czechoslovak State, and that the assistance of military forces appeared necessary for the purpose of re-establishing order, it could not be inferred that this territory was not a part of the Czechoslovak State. The plaintiff's contention, if accepted, would mean that a part of State territory in which a revolutionary movement tending to disturb the existing legal order had broken out would have to be considered as foreign—even enemy—territory, and that after the suppression of the revolution the laws and decrees promulgated in the meantime would have to be promulgated in the territory in question in order to be legally in force. [Report: Boh. 443 fin.]

Note.—(1) See the previous decision of 16 March, 1920, No. 1982 (Boh. 175 fin.), and the subsequent decision of 13 April, 1921, No. 4441 (Boh. 491 fin.), both to the same effect.

For analogous decisions on the question of the establishment of Czechoslovak territorial sovereignty in the so-called "historical "countries," *i.e.* Bohemia, Moravia and Silesia, see (i) in regard to the country of Bohemia: decisions of the Supreme Administrative Court of 27 October, 1920, No. 10.170 (Boh. 568 adm.); of 30 June, 1921, No. 4956 (Boh. 565 fin.); of 30 June, 1921, No. 4957 (Boh. 566 fin.); (ii) in regard to the country of Silesia: decisions of the Supreme Court of Justice of 15 June, 1920, No. R. II 120 (Váž. 550

Case No. 4 *contd.*

civ.); of 8 March, 1921, No. Rv. II 326/20 (Váž. 968 civ.); of 25 October, 1921, No. R. II 357 (Váž. 1266 civ.); decision of the Supreme Administrative Court quoted in *Annual Digest*, 1925-1926, Case No. 81; (iii) in regard to the countries of Bohemia, Moravia and Silesia: decisions of the Supreme Administrative Court of 24 March, 1921, No. 3336 (Boh. 470 fin.); of 25 October, 1923, No. 17.898 (Boh. 1515 fin.); of 4 December, 1923, No. 18.383 (Boh. 1579 fin.).

(2) As a consequence of the opinion that the date of 28 October, 1918, is to be considered as the date of the coming into existence of the Czechoslovak State,[1] it was held by the Czechoslovak courts that on that day the Austrian and Hungarian highest courts ceased to be competent for matter arising on the territory of the Czechoslovak State and not yet settled by them on that day.[2]

---

[1] See Case No. 5.

[2] As regards the Austrian Supreme and Cassation Court of Justice, see decisions of the Supreme Court of Justice of 30 January, 1919, No. Rv. II 12 (Váž. 34 civ.); of 11 February, 1919, No. Kr. I 27 (Váž. 8 tr.); and others. [The Czechoslovak Supreme Court of Justice was established by Law No. 5 of 2 November, 1918.]

As regards the Austrian Administrative Court, see resolution of the Supreme Administrative Court of 9 December, 1918, No. 55 pres. (Boh. I/1918), and the subsequent decisions of the Court, based upon this resolution, of 19 May, 1919, No. 1884 (Boh. 108 adm.); of 7 October, 1920, No. 9212 (Boh. 543 adm.); of 30 November, 1921, No. 15.922 (Boh. 1038 adm.); and others. The resolution of 9 December, 1918, No. 55 pres. (Boh. I/1918), reads as follows: " By the coming into existence of the Czechoslovak State, the " former Austrian Administrative Court in Vienna ceased to be competent " to administer justice in appeals against decisions and measures of adminis- " trative authorities in matters arising on the territory of the Czechoslovak " Republic in so far as it was competent in these matters according to the " law obtaining hitherto. Decisions and resolutions issued by the Austrian " Administrative Court in Vienna in respect of such appeals after 28 October, " 1918, are without any binding force, and the administrative authorities of " the Czechoslovak Republic are not bound to follow them. According to " the provisions of Law No. 3 of 2 November, 1918, only the Supreme Ad- " ministrative Court in Prague is competent from 4 November, 1918 (the date " of the coming into force of Law No. 3/1918) to decide upon appeals against " decisions and measures in the above-mentioned matters. It is therefore " also for this Court to administer justice in all appeals in these matters which, " having been lodged with the former Austrian Administrative Court in " Vienna, have not been finally settled by that Court on 28 October, 1918." [The Czechoslovak Supreme Administrative Court was established by Law No. 3 of 2 November, 1918.]

With regard to the Hungarian highest tribunals, see a similar resolution of the Senate of Conflicts of Jurisdictions of 13 November, 1920, No. 29 (Boh. adm., Vol. II, Appendix II, No. IV).

The same opinion as stated above with regard to the Austrian and Hungarian highest tribunals was held by the Supreme Administrative Court also as regards the central authorities (Ministries) of the former Austria and Hungary: see decisions of 29 October, 1919, No. 5368 (Boh. 222 adm.); of 3 February, 1921, No. 1336 (Boh. 695 adm.); of 16 March, 1921, No. 3060 (Boh. 769 adm.); of 18 May, 1922, No. 4172 (Boh. 1365 adm.); of 2 June, 1923, No. 399 (Boh. 2441 adm.); and others. [The Czechoslovak central authorities (Ministries) were established by Law No. 2 of 2 November, 1918.]

Establishment of New State—Time of Coming into Existence of the Czechoslovak State—Effect of the Treaties of Peace —Recognition—Establishment of Czechoslovak Territorial Sovereignty in Slovakia. **Case No. 5**

RIGHTS OF CITIZENSHIP (ESTABLISHMENT OF CZECHOSLOVAK STATE) CASE.

Czechoslovakia, Supreme Administrative Court.
26 *April*, 1921. (*No.* 4372.)

THE FACTS.—By a resolution of 27 March, 1920, the municipality of the town of Bratislava (Slovakia) accorded to the plaintiff, a citizen of the town of Sopron (Hungary), rights of citizenship (*Heimatrecht*). This resolution was subsequently quashed by the Ministry for Slovakia, acting in agreement with the Ministry of the Interior, on the ground that the plaintiff, being a foreigner, could not acquire rights of citizenship in a Czechoslovak commune.[1] The plaintiff lodged an appeal with the Supreme Administrative Court, contending, *inter alia*, that at the time when the municipality of Bratislava had accorded to him the rights of citizenship that town was only *de facto* in the possession of the Czechoslovak State, while *de jure* it still belonged at that time—together with the remaining Hungarian territory—to the undivided Hungarian State. It was contended that it was only as the result of the Treaty of Trianon that the occupation acquired a legal status ; the Peace Treaty was constitutive and not merely declaratory.

Held by the Supreme Administrative Court : That the appeal failed. The establishment of the Czechoslovak State was a single, undivided act. The sovereignty of the Czechoslovak Republic had in fact already come into being through the revolution of 28 October, 1918, when the National Committee in fact seized the sovereignty, having concentrated in its hands all functions of sovereignty.[2] Legal sanction was then given to this situation of fact—which, from the point of

[1] According to the former Austrian and Hungarian, now Czechoslovak, laws on the rights of citizenship, only the subjects of the State can acquire rights of citizenship in a commune of the State. See also Case No. 6.

[2] The National Committee assumed the sovereignty of the Czechoslovak State by the promulgation of the Law of 28 October, 1918, which, having been

Case No. 5 ***contd.***

view of the former State, is of course illegal, like every revolution—by the will of the Czechoslovak nation as possessor of the sovereignty. This State sovereignty, which constitutes the essential substance of a nation, and not the international treaties or the Treaties of Peace, was the source from which the Czechoslovak Republic became a State. The existence of this State as such does not depend on those treaties. They take for granted the existence in fact and in law of a State as contracting party. Their object was to give to the State access to the community of nations, to regulate the mutual relations between States already existing, or—as is the case in the Peace Treaties—to settle various questions which concern relationships that are in controversy between the States but which do not for that reason become contrary to law or mere matters of fact.

Consequently, if the Czechoslovak nation has assumed on the ground of its sovereignty the effective exercise of its sovereign rights in the commune of Bratislava as a component part of its territory, in the same way as on its other territory, it is not possible to speak of a situation as existing merely in fact and requiring legal sanction by an international treaty or a treaty of peace. By this State-creating act the town of Bratislava ceased to form a part of the territory of the former Austro-Hungarian Monarchy or of the former Hungarian State, forming a part of the Czechoslovak Republic in the same way as the other territory of Slovakia.[1] All relations of public law were severed between that town and the Hungarian territory, which thereby in relation to this town became foreign. [Report: Boh. 823 adm.]

promulgated on the same day, was subsequently inserted into the Collection of Laws and Decrees under No. 11.

The Law of 28 October, 1918, No. 11, regarding the establishment of the independent Czechoslovak State, reads as follows (translation):

"The independent Czechoslovak State has come into existence. In "order to preserve the connection between the legal system hitherto "existing and the new state of affairs, in order to avoid confusion and to "secure an undisturbed transition to the new statehood, the National "Committee as bearer of the sovereignty of the State orders on behalf of "the Czechoslovak nation as follows:

"*Art.* 1. The constitutional form of the Czechoslovak State shall be "decided by the National Assembly in agreement with the Czechoslovak "National Council in Paris. The National Committee is the organ of the "unanimous will of the nation and the bearer of the State sovereignty.

"*Art.* 2. All laws and decrees of the countries and of the Empire, "hitherto existing, remain provisionally in force.

"*Art.* 4. This law comes into force on the present day.

"*Art.* 5. The National Committee is charged with the execution of "this law."

[1] See *Annual Digest*, 1925-1926, Case No. 9, footnote 1.

NOTE.—(*a*) Also discussed: (i) Treaty between the Principal Allied and Associated Powers and Czechoslovakia, signed at St. Germain on 10 September, 1919 (Minorities Treaty), Article 3; (ii) Effect of this Treaty on subjects of third States; (iii) Relation between international treaty and municipal law.

(*b*) For a subsequent decision in the same matter see *Annual Digest*, 1925-1926, Case No. 8.

(*c*) As to the question of the establishment of the Czechoslovak State, see also decision of the Supreme Administrative Court of 16 October, 1919, No. 4407 (Boh. 114 fin.), in which the Court held: "The contention is erroneous that a State comes or could come into "existence by international recognition. On the contrary, the inter- "national recognition . . . necessarily takes the existence of an inde- "pendent State for granted. For the existence of a State such recog- "nition is not necessary in the same way as such recognition itself "would not be sufficient for this purpose. This is a recognised principle "of international theory and practice. . . . International recognition "is only a condition for the access of a State into the international "community; the State becomes through it a person of international "law, but the State draws its existence from its own internal substance. "Its existence is granted at the moment on which its sovereignty has "in fact been established. . . ." See to the same effect: decision of the same Court of 16 October, 1919, No. 4746 (Boh. 115 fin.) and others. See also decisions of the Supreme Court of Justice of 30 September, 1924, No. Rv. I 839 (Váž. 4186 civ.) and of 8 April, 1927 No. R. I 120 (Váž. 6976 civ., *Annual Digest*, 1927-1928, Case No. 94); and the decision of the Supreme Administrative Court of 15 December, 1921, No. 16.748 (Boh. 1065 adm.), Case No. 6.

(*d*) See, as to the establishment of the Czechoslovak State, Kalousek, *La Formation de l'État tchécoslovaque et la Jurisprudence*, in *Bulletin de Droit tchécoslovaque*, II, p. 67, where other decisions also are quoted in which the Czechoslovak courts had to deal with various questions in connection with the coming into existence of the Czechoslovak State (pp. 86 *et seq.*).

Establishment of New State—Coming into Existence of the Czechoslovak State—Establishment of Nationality therein —Effect of the Treaties of Peace—Recognition—Establishment of Czechoslovak Territorial Sovereignty in Bohemia. **Case No. 6**

RIGHTS OF CITIZENSHIP (ESTABLISHMENT OF CZECHOSLOVAK NATIONALITY) CASE.

Czechoslovakia, Supreme Administrative Court.
15 *December*, 1921. (*No.* 16.748.)

THE FACTS.—The plaintiffs, citizens of the town of Vienna, applied for rights of citizenship (*Heimatrecht*) in the town of Liberec (Reichenberg, Bohemia), which were accorded to them on 9 April, 1919. Subsequently, however, this acquisition of the rights of citizenship was quashed by the Ministry of the Interior on the ground

Case No. 6 ***contd.***

that the plaintiffs, being foreigners, could not acquire rights of citizenship in a Czechoslovak commune.[1]

Held by the Supreme Administrative Court: That the appeal lodged against the decision of the Ministry of the Interior must be dismissed:

(*a*) According to the provisions of paragraph 2 of the Law of 3 December, 1863, No. 105 (formerly Austrian and now Czechoslovak), as to rights of citizenship, only the subjects of the State can acquire rights of citizenship (*Heimatrecht*) in a commune, but, on the other hand, every subject of the State must have this right in a commune. This connection between rights of citizenship and nationality, declared by paragraph 2 of the Law, led to the establishment under the old régime of the doctrine that in the event of the cession by Austria of a part of her territory all Austrian subjects who possessed rights of citizenship in the ceded territory lost their Austrian nationality, and inversely, when an addition was made to Austrian territory, those who had rights of citizenship in the new territory acquired Austrian nationality. By Law No. 11 of 28 October, 1918,[2] the present territory of the Czechoslovak Republic was separated from the territory of the Austro-Hungarian Monarchy. At that time all laws of the former Monarchy ceased to be in force for the territory of the Republic; the former legal system ceased to exist. In order, however, to avoid a serious gap in public and private life, it was necessary to introduce, by a special constitutional act, a new legal system. This was done by Law No. 11 of 28 October, 1918. By this Law the new State introduced its own new legal system by means of the provisional adoption of the Austrian legal system existing hitherto (Article 2 of Law No. 11/1918). As the result of this adoption, all provisions of the former laws, in so far as they refer to Austrian subjects, were altered by the above-mentioned provision of Law No. 11/1918 in the sense that these provisions now relate only to the subjects of the Czechoslovak State, or in other words—taking into consideration the above-mentioned connection between nationality and the rights of citizenship provided for by paragraph 2 of Law No. 105/1863—concern now only such subjects as at that time possessed rights of citizenship in a commune belonging now to the territory of the Czechoslovak State.

The Law of 28 October, 1918, No. 11, had, however, also the following correlative effect, namely, that those persons who

[1] See Case No. 5 above.

[2] See p. 16, footnote.

did not previously possess a right of citizenship in a commune on the territory of the Czechoslovak State became, on the day of the promulgation of that Law, foreigners with regard to that State.[1]

(*b*) The plaintiffs contend that the new States established on the territory of the former Austro-Hungarian Monarchy acquired their territory together with their subjects only as the result of the cession of that territory by Austria, so that until the ratification of the Treaty of Peace of St. Germain there existed a general Austrian nationality; that, therefore, the plaintiffs were not foreigners and could acquire rights of citizenship in the commune of Liberec. This contention starts from the fiction that the Austrian State in its former boundaries existed until the ratification of the Treaty of Peace of St. Germain. It must, however, be observed that—as regards the Czechoslovak State—the act which created the State was the earlier revolutionary Law of 28 October, 1918, No. 11, on which day the National Committee assumed in fact the power of the State by concentrating in its hands all supreme public power in all its functions over the whole territory of the Czechoslovak State and expressing by that Law the will of the Czechoslovak nation as possessor of the sovereignty of the State. By that Law, on the basis of the sovereign will of the nation, all links with the rest of Austrian and Hungarian territory were severed and a new legal system of the Czechoslovak State was established by the reception provisionally of Austrian and Hungarian law in so far as not inconsistent with the new conditions. It is true that from the point of view of the former State the establishment of the Czechoslovak State was a revolutionary act as is any similar convulsion, but the situation of the new State was recognised in the Treaty of Peace as legal. The Treaties of Peace did not found the existence of the Succession States. On the contrary, the latter participated in the conclusion of these Treaties in the quality of contracting parties as internationally recognised possessors in fact and in law of the power of a State in a certain territory. The territory of the Czechoslovak State, with, so far as Bohemia is concerned, its historical boundaries, was separated from the rest of Austria as from 28 October, 1918, on which day independence was proclaimed, and not as from the ratification of the Peace Treaties. On that day Czechoslovak nationality was

[1] It will be noted that the Court, in dealing with the question of the coming into existence of the Czechoslovak nationality, starts here from the *positive* law, and not only from *general* considerations (as in Case No. 5).

Case No. 6 *contd.* acquired by those who at that time possessed rights of citizenship in a commune in Czechoslovak territory, and from that day onwards those who had similar rights in communes outside Czechoslovak territory became foreigners. [Report: Boh. 1065 adm.]

NOTE.—See subsequent decisions (as to the question of the acquisition of Czechoslovak nationality) of 17 May, 1924, No. 8592 (Boh. 3624 adm.), and of 17 May, 1924, No. 8595 (Boh. 3625 adm.). See also the decision of 30 June, 1923, No. 11.606 (Boh. 2588 adm.), to be digested in the forthcoming volume of the *Annual Digest.*

Case No. 7 **New States—Beginning of—Dissolution of the Old Austrian Empire—Articles 70 and 78 of the Treaty of St. Germain.**

A. L. B. *v.* (AUSTRIAN) FEDERAL MINISTRY FOR THE INTERIOR.

Austria, Administrative Court (Verwaltungsgerichtshof), Vienna. 11 *February,* 1922. (*No.* 13.021 *A.*)

THE FACTS.—The plaintiff had acquired rights of citizenship in a commune of the Austrian Republic on 20 November, 1918: this acquisition had been declared void on the ground that the plaintiff, having had at that date his rights of citizenship in Galicia, was not a national of the Austrian Republic and could not, therefore, legally acquire rights of citizenship in a commune of the Austrian Republic. He appealed, and founded his appeal on the argument that he was, at the critical date, a national of the Austrian Empire which came to an end only with the date of the coming into force of the Treaty of St. Germain.

Held: That the appeal must be dismissed. "It is a "juridical error to believe that the Austro-Hungarian Monarchy "legally existed up to the date of the coming into force of the "Treaty of St. Germain; it is, juridically speaking, an error "to believe that the new States, created on parts of the "territories of the former Monarchy, had, up to that "date, no significance except as a fact. From the moment "of the dissolution of the old Monarchy, the new States "alone possessed an organisation and exercised legislative, "administrative and judicial capacity. Even the Peace "Treaty presupposes that the new States already existed "legally before it came into force, otherwise the new States "could not have been parties. The legal existence of the new "Republic of Austria began on 30 October, 1918, the moment "when she came into life by the fundamental law of the "Provisional National Assembly. From this very moment "individuals having rights of citizenship in a commune of the "Austrian Republic became her nationals. Articles 70 and 78 "of the Treaty are based on the fiction of regulating the "nationality of citizens of the old Austrian Empire by reference to the date when the Treaty took effect, but a common-"sense interpretation of these Articles cannot overlook the "fact that if they are interpreted to mean that the nationality "laws of the new States had no legal value before that date, "the new States though legally created long before the Treaty "came into force would have previously had no nationals at "all." [Report: *Sammlung der Erkenntnisse des Verwaltungsgerichtshofes*, vol. XLVI (1922), pp. 15-20.]

NOTE.—Cf. Case No. 145 (*Franz and Rosa Kadecka* v. *Government of the Federal Country of Lower Austria*). To the same effect, see decision of 30 June, 1925, Zl. A, 319/24; cf. also the decision of the Czechoslovak Administrative Court of Prague, of 15 December, 1921, No. 16.748/21: "It is a *fiction* that the old Austrian Empire existed up to "16 July, 1920. The Peace Treaties have not created the Succession "States. Czechoslovakia legally existed from 28 October, 1918, the "moment of the proclamation of the independent Czechoslovak Re-"public by the Naródni Vybór."

As to the nationality in the Succession States in the period between the dissolution of the Austro-Hungarian Monarchy (end of October, 1918) and the coming into force of the Treaty of St. Germain (16 July, 1920) and the "fiction" referred to above, see Kunz, *Die völkerrechtliche Option*, vol. II (Breslau, 1928), pp. 108-157, 179.

States—Establishment of—Czechoslovakia—Counterfeiting of Money Abroad.

See Case No. 24 (*Counterfeiting of Stamps (Czechoslovakia) Case*).

II.—Sovereignty and Independence

i.—In Foreign Relations

[See also below, *Recognition of Acts of Foreign States and Governments*; Part IV, JURISDICTION; and Part VIII, TREATIES: *Interpretation of Treaties—Agencies of Interpretation*.]

Act of State—Power to Proclaim Martial Law—Right to Question before Courts.

See Case No. 22 (*Ismail Pasha Sidky* v. *Sidarous Bishara*).

States—Organs of—Pronouncements of Judicial Authorities—How far Expressive of the Attitude of States.

See Case No. 239 (*The David J. Adams*).

Sphere of Executive in Matters of Foreign Policy—Conclusiveness of Statements by Executive—Recognition of Foreign Governments and States.

See Case No. 26 (*Luther* v. *Sagor*).

iii.—Acts of Sovereignty and Transactions of a Private Character

[See also Part IV, JURISDICTION: *Exemptions from.*]

Case No. 8 **States in their Sovereign and other Capacities—Arrest in Holland of Goods Belonging to the Union of South Africa—Exemption of Foreign States from Jurisdiction of Dutch Courts—Acts of Sovereignty and other Acts of Foreign States Distinguished—International Status of Union of South Africa (in 1921).**

UNION OF SOUTH AFRICA *v.* HERMAN GROTE.

Holland, District Court of Amsterdam, in Summary Procedure. 14 *July*, 1921.

(Dr. L. OFFERHAUS, President.)

THE FACTS.—On 9 March, 1921, the defendant, in his capacity as master of the German s.s. *Ceres*, of Bremen, acting upon authorisation of the President of the District Court of Amsterdam of the same date, had obtained a "*conservatoir derden-arrest*" (arrest or attachment by a creditor of goods the property of his debtor in the possession of a third party, in order to secure payment of his claim) on property of the plaintiff (the Union of South Africa) in the hands of Müller & Co., of Amsterdam. The arrest was based on a claim in respect of maritime assistance which the *Ceres*, on 15 January, 1921, had rendered to the Norwegian barque *Irene*, sailing with a cargo of cement belonging to the Union of South Africa. The Government of the Union opposed the arrest and claimed in summary procedure the immediate release of the property, basing this claim on the new Article 13 (*a*) (of 1917) of the Dutch Law of 15 May, 1829, containing general provisions concerning the legislation of the Kingdom, according to which "the jurisdiction of the judiciary "is limited by the exceptions recognised by the Law "of Nations" (see Case No. 84).

Held: That the arrest must be upheld. Article 13 (*a*) gives no specific list of the exceptions recognised by the Law of Nations, to which it refers. It may safely be said that with regard to *acta imperii*, either lawful or unlawful, whether acts of war or not, a State is not subject to the jurisdiction of the judiciary of another State. The intention of the new provision was clearly to sanction this principle. However, in enacting the new law, the Legislature had not given any explicit decision with regard to cases in which foreign States are acting, not in their capacity of sovereign Powers, but as ordinary persons. In cases where the juridical acts at issue have no connection whatever with the exercise of sovereign rights, the question ought to be decided in the sense that the foreign State is subject to the jurisdiction of Dutch courts.

Moreover, the Union of South Africa, although a certain degree of independence had been granted to it, is not a sovereign State, since its authority as a self-governing community within the British Empire is derived from the Mother Country, and it lacks the right, in virtue of its own sovereignty, to send diplomatic envoys, to declare war, to make peace, and to exercise other powers of a sovereign State. [Report: *Nederlandsche Jurisprudentie*, 1921, p. 849.]

See also Note under Case No. 84, and Case No. 86.

States in their Sovereign or other Capacity—Exemption from Jurisdiction—Claim Based on Private Law Title—Counter-Claim for Acts Performed in Sovereign Capacity.

See Case No. 85 (*The State of Belgium* (*plaintiff in claim, defendant in counter-claim*) v. *E. A. G. de Badts* (*defendant in claim, plaintiff in counter-claim*)).

Jurisdiction — Exemption from — Foreign States — Acts of Sovereignty and other Acts Distinguished — Union of South Africa (in 1921).

See Case No. 8 (*Union of South Africa* v. *Herman Grote*).

III.—Equality of States

Equality of States—Jurisdiction over Foreign States—Interpretation of Treaties by Municipal Courts—Conclusiveness of—In regard to Foreign States—Whether Consistent with Equality of States.

See Case No. 239 (*The David J. Adams*).

States—Equality—Exercise of Right of Eminent Domain as against another State—Angary.

See Case No. 289 (*Norway and United States: Requisition of Shipbuilding Contracts Case*), for an instance of a tribunal refusing to accept the plea of "restraint of princes," which was invoked by the United States against Norway, on the ground that "international law and justice are based upon "the principle of equality of States."

IV.—Recognition of Acts of Foreign States and Governments

[See also Part IV, JURISDICTION: *Territorial*; and below, *Recognition of States, Governments and Belligerency*.]

Case No. 9 **Recognition of Acts of Foreign States—No Adjudication on Claims Arising out of such Acts—Requisition of Vessels by British Government.**

THE ADRIATIC.

United States District Court, E.D. Pennsylvania. United States Circuit Court of Appeals, Third Circuit. 9 *October*, 1918, *and* 7 *June*, 1919.

THE FACTS.—This was a suit for breach of charter party. The British steamer *Adriatic* was chartered for a single voyage. While on the high seas *en route* to the starting-point of the voyage, the vessel was requisitioned by the British Admiralty. The charter party contained a clause providing that if the vessel was requisitioned by the Admiralty the charter should be null and void. The charterers filed libels *in rem* against the vessel and *in personam* against the owners in the United States District Court, contending that the requisition was illegal by British law since the vessel was not in British waters when requisitioned. Counsel for the

British Embassy appeared as *amici curiae* to suggest that the *Adriatic* had been duly requisitioned and that the requisition was a Governmental act which could not be enquired into by the courts of another country.

Held: That the libels must be dismissed. "The rule "followed in like cases prevails in this, that the court should "decline to adjudicate any claim of right advanced by the "libelant which grows out of the requisitioning of the re- "spondent vessel by the government to which its master and "owners owe the duty of obedience." (253 Fed. 489, 491.) On appeal to the Circuit Court of Appeals, the British Embassy presented a certificate to the same effect.

Held: That the order must be affirmed without prejudice to the right of the libelants to institute another action in any court competent to enquire into the validity of the requisition. The Court said: "On principles of international comity, we "feel bound to accept the suggestion and avowal of the British "ambassador as conclusively establishing both the fact of the "requisition and its governmental character." "In accordance "with the rule that 'the courts of one independent govern- "'ment will not sit in judgment on the validity of the acts "'of another done within its own territory,' it is not within "the province of a court of this country to attempt to deter- "mine whether the requisition of the vessel was valid or "invalid under the laws of Great Britain; it must be here "accepted as legal, or, as it is sometimes expressed, such a "question is not justiciable." (258 Fed. 902, 904.) [Reports: 253 Fed. 489; 258 Fed. 902.]

Recognition of Acts of Foreign States—Extraterritorial Effect of Judgments of Courts in respect of Property Situate Abroad—Claim of Foreign Government to Possession. **Case No. 10**

H. T. Cottam & Co. *v.* Comision Reguladora del Mercado de Henequen.

United States, Supreme Court of Louisiana. 31 *October*, 1921.

The Facts.—The defendant Mexican corporation was heavily in debt. Proceedings had been taken against it in Yucatan (Mexico), and its property had been seized under the Mexican Law of 23 May, 1920, in satisfaction of a debt due to the Mexican Government.

Case No. 10 *contd.*

At the time of the Yucatan proceedings, one of the defendant's vessels was in New Orleans. Three months later this vessel was attached in New Orleans in a creditor's suit. When released, it was again attached in Louisiana in the present suit. The Republic of Mexico intervened, claiming to be in possession of and entitled to the vessel as a result of the proceedings in Yucatan. Judgment was rendered for the plaintiff and the intervener's petition was dismissed. On appeal,

Held: That the judgment must be affirmed. The vessel was not in the possession of Mexico, and Mexico had not taken steps to reduce it to possession within a reasonable time after the Yucatan proceedings. The Mexican statute did not provide for constructive seizure. The doctrine that the courts of one country will not sit in judgment on the acts of another Government done in its territory, laid down in *Oetjen* v. *Central Leather Co.*, 246 U.S. 297, and *Ricaud* v. *American Metal Co.*, 246 U.S. 304, does not " mean that the courts of one country " must give to the acts of the government of another, done " within its own territory, whatever extraterritorial effect the " government of that other country may claim for such acts." (149 La. 1026, 1034.) A dissenting opinion took the position that there had been a valid attachment, by " fictive " seizure, in the Mexican proceedings; and that this was a practice known also in the laws of Louisiana. [Report: 149 La. 1026.]

NOTE.—It will be observed that the Judgment speaks of the " acts " of a government " in referring to a seizure effected under an order of a court in proceedings instituted by that Government.—[Ed.]

Case No. 11

Recognition of Acts of a Foreign Government—Private Property Confiscated by Russian Government and Brought into Italian Territory—Italo-Russian Agreement of December, 1921.

ITALIAN BLACK SEA COMPANY *v.* RUSSIAN SOVIET GOVERNMENT.

Italy, Court of Appeal of Milan. 26 *July*, 1922.

THE FACTS.—The Italian Black Sea Company had acquired in March, 1920, by means of its agency at Batum in Georgia, a large quantity of silk to the value of over a million and a half Italian lire. These goods were confiscated by the Soviet Commissars when they invaded and occupied Georgia, instituting the Bolshevik Government there. Having learnt later that this merchandise was in the hands of another company in Milan, where it had been deposited in the name of Abraham Feinstein, the Genoa manager of the Commissariat for Foreign Trade of the Soviet Republic, the Italian Black Sea Company asked for and obtained an authorisation for the sequestration of the merchandise, of which a sale was being negotiated. The Public Minister [1] then intervened to ask for the revocation of the sequestration and a declaration of the inadmissibility of the action started by the plaintiff company. The Court of First Instance admitted this plea, having regard to the Royal Decree of 31 January, 1922, which declared the preliminary Italo-Russian agreement of 26 December, 1921, to be in force. The company appealed against this judgment.

Held: That the appeal must be dismissed. Article 10 of the Italo-Russian agreement provided that merchandise and goods of every kind, imported and acquired in both countries, shall not be subject to sequestration or judicial action in respect of the disposal thereof, by reason of obligations undertaken or of responsibilities incurred by a past or present Government of either country before the signing of the present convention. This provision comprises all goods regardless of the origin of the possession thereof. Any different principle would bring about an enquiry into the acts of the Russian Government and the determination of its responsibilities by an Italian judicial authority; it would thus render illusory the agreement made by the Russian Government, in whose hands is all foreign trade. It would also expose nearly all the mass of its movable goods, taken from private individuals, to a claim for the recovery thereof, including actions brought by its own subjects. The fact that the Italo-Russian agreement contains a declaration to the effect that all claims of the contracting States and their subjects against the other party concerning property or rights acquired in relation to the present or previous Government of each country shall be fairly settled in a definitive future treaty, shows that such questions have been entirely deferred for an amicable settlement by diplomatic

[1] The Public Minister represents the Italian State before the Italian judicial authorities.

Case No. 11 *contd.* negotiations between the two Governments. Pending such negotiations the courts are not in a position to assume jurisdiction over these matters. [Report: *Rivista di diritto internazionale,* 1921-1922, pp. 562-566, with a note by A. Ricci Busatti.]

Case No. 12 **Recognition of Acts of States—Act of Judicial Authorities of a New Non-Recognised State—The State of Fiume and Italy.**

ZANNONI *v.* SBISÀ.

Italy, Court of Appeal of Milan. 29 *December,* 1920.

THE FACTS.—Zannoni contracted a marriage in Florence in 1901 with Anna Sbisà. Subsequently he qualified as a subject and citizen of the State of Fiume,[1] and while resident there obtained the dissolution of the marriage by the Court of Fiume by a decree of 30 December, 1919. His wife had in the meantime also become a citizen of and resident in Fiume. He then took proceedings in an Italian court, making his wife or former wife defendant, and asking for a declaration of the validity of the decree of divorce and its registration in the registers of civil status at Florence.

Held: That the validity of the decree must be admitted. It cannot be doubted that the courts of Fiume were invested with a regular jurisdictional power, seeing that, after the dismemberment of the Austro-Hungarian Monarchy resulting from the war, a new State of Fiume was formed as a political entity in fact distinct from and independent of the dissolved Monarchy. Its judicial authorities established under the Hungarian law then in force functioned as emanations of the National Council exercising sovereign authority in Fiume. [Report: *Giurisprudenza Italiana,* 1921, pp. 1, 2, 14.]

[1] Before the war Fiume formed a distinct unit of Hungary. In October, 1918, it declared its independence, which was recognised by the Treaty of Rapallo of 2 February, 1922, and which lasted until the annexation of Fiume by Italy in January, 1924. During that period the Hungarian law remained in force in Fiume. Various Italian subjects obtained at that time Fiumen citizenship, in order to obtain a divorce in accordance with the Hungarian law.

Recognition of Judgments of Foreign Courts—Sentence of German Court-Martial in Belgium—Confiscation of Vessel —Subsequent Transfer of Property via German Buyer to Dutch Purchaser—Claim by Heirs of Original Owner in Dutch Court. **Case No. 13**

JANSSENS, WIDOW OF A. VAN HECKE, *v.* N. V. MAATSCHAPPIJ RIJNSCHIP *BARBERA, ET AL.*

Holland, District Court of Dordrecht. 17 *November,* 1920.

(Dr. K. MEYER WIERSMA, President; Drs. H. HEUVELINK and B. I. ZIJLSTRA, Judges.)

THE FACTS.—By sentence of the *Feldgericht* belonging to the military jurisdiction of the German governor of Charleroi (Hainault), in the occupied territory of Belgium, of 14 April, 1917, A. van Hecke, the original owner of the vessel claimed, was condemned to death for espionage. His vessel, then called *The Franklin,* was confiscated for the benefit of the German *Reich,* which afterwards sold it to one of its subjects, who in turn sold it again to the defendant company. In the Dutch Court the heirs of the original owner claimed the vessel, now called *The Diana* (on which they had, in the meantime, after she was brought to Holland, laid a civil embargo), from the present owner, on the ground that the confiscation of the vessel had been illegal, since German military law does not recognise the penalty of confiscation for the offence of espionage, and that, even if the punishment had been inflicted legally, the German buyer would not have acquired the property of the vessel, owing to failure to register the transfer in the shipping register.

Held : For the defendants. Even if the German *Feldgericht* had pronounced its sentence contrary to German military law, that circumstance would not alter the fact that confiscation had been pronounced by sentence of a regular court and that it remained in force until it was reversed. A Dutch court is not entitled to judge whether the confiscation was pronounced rightly or wrongly. Confiscation by virtue of a judicial sentence makes the property of the confiscated article pass *ipso facto* to the person in favour of whom it was pronounced, without any further administrative measure, such as registration of the title in the shipping register. [Reports : *Weekblad van het Recht,* 31 December, 1920, No. 10656 ; *Nederlandsche Jurisprudentie,* 1921, p. 387.]

Case No. 13 *contd.*

NOTE.—In the same sense see judgment of the Court of Appeal, The Hague, First Chamber (Jhr. Dr. R. O. van Holthe tot Echten, President; Drs. P. Polvliet and M. Polak, Judges), of 12 December, 1921 (Report: *Weekblad van het Recht,* 8 September, 1922, No. 10920), *In re G. van der Jeucht, of Appels (Belgium) (appellant)* v. (1) *N. V. Rijnschip "Barbera," of Rotterdam;* (2) *C. J. van Zuijdam, Captain (respondents).* In this case the owner had been condemned to prison only, likewise with confiscation of his vessel, *The Prins Leopold,* which was subsequently sold under the names of *Glück Auf II* and *The Barbera,* respectively, via a German subject to the Dutch company. *Held* by the Court of Appeal: "That a Dutch court is not entitled "to judge the question whether the confiscation of the vessel, which "caused the loss of the property, was pronounced in conformity with "the laws at that time in force in the occupied part of Belgium, but "that it has to admit the confiscation as a matter of fact."

V.—Continuity of States

[See also STATE SUCCESSION.]

Case No. 14

Continuity of States—Russian Revolution in 1917—Recognition of Governments—Conclusiveness of Determination by Executive Department.

AGENCY OF CANADIAN CAR AND FOUNDRY CO. LTD. *v.* AMERICAN CAN CO.

United States District Court, S.D. New York. United States Circuit Court of Appeals, Second Circuit. 5 August, 1918, *and* 21 *April,* 1919.

THE FACTS.—This was a suit to recover a sum of money. The case arose out of certain contracts made in 1915-1917 to supply the Imperial Russian Government with munitions. There had been sub-contracts, assignments and subsidiary agreements among several companies. It was acknowledged that the defendant company held a large sum of money for the account of the plaintiff companies or the Russian Government. The plaintiff companies relied upon an assignment from the Russian Government executed by the President of the Russian Supply Committee in America on 18 December, 1917. The defendant company objected that the Imperial Russian Government had been overthrown and that the Supply Committee was without authority to execute the assignment. The United States had recognised the Provisional Government which succeeded the Imperial Government, and had received an ambassador who certified to the authority of the Supply Committee.

It had not recognised the Government established after the Bolshevik Revolution of November, 1917.

Held: For the plaintiff companies. The Court said: " The " attempt was made to offer lay proof as to who were, at " present, in control of the Russian government, or, in other " words, who or what the present government of Russia is. " This line of testimony was excluded upon the well-settled " principle that the question of sovereignty is a political " question, the determination of which by the political branch " or branches of our government, *i.e.* executive and/or legis- " lative departments, binds the judicial department." (253 Fed. 152, 155.) " Since the notable precedent of *The Sapphire,* " 78 U.S. (11 Wall.) 164, 20 L. Ed. 127, the principle is firmly " established in our courts that the rights and liabilities of a " state are unaffected by a change either in the form or per- " sonnel of its government, however accomplished, whether " by revolution or otherwise. No other doctrine is thinkable, " at least among nations which have any conception of inter- " national honor." (253 Fed. 152, 157.)

On appeal to the Circuit Court of Appeals,

Held: That the decree must be affirmed subject to a modification as to interest. The Ambassador's certificate was conclusive. " Who is the sovereign *de jure* or *de facto* of a country " is a question for the political departments of the government. " It is not a judicial question. The decision of the matter by " the political departments is in this country conclusive upon " the judges. *Jones* v. *United States,* 137 U.S. 202." (258 Fed. 363, 368.) " The principle of law is well established that the " rights and liabilities of a state are not affected by a change " in the form or the personnel of a government, no matter how " that change may be affected. The obligations of a state, the " debts due to and from it, are not affected by any transforma- " tion in the internal organization of its government." (258 Fed. 363, 369.) [Reports: 253 Fed. 152; 258 Fed. 363.]

Continuity of States—Effect of Overthrow of the Recognised Régime—Counterfeiting Currencies Issued under its Authority. **Case No. 15**

THE RUSSIAN ROUBLES (ATTEMPTED COUNTERFEITING) CASE.

Japan, Supreme Court. 1919.

THE FACTS.—This was an application requesting the annulment of the confirmatory decree of the Appellate Court

Case No. 15 *contd.*

(Tokyo), whereby the act of the defendant, a Russian resident in Japan, was adjudged to be a breach of Law No. 66 of 1905, which prohibits the counterfeiting or alteration of foreign monies and notes with a view to their circulation. The accused were convicted of counterfeiting so-called Kerensky notes (*i.e.* notes issued by the Kerensky Government established in 1917 in Russia). The grounds on which the appellants relied were that: (1) the foreign country intended by the Law of 1905 must necessarily have an existence as a State with at least a *de facto* Government; (2) it must be maintaining diplomatic relations with Japan; (3) its currency must be issued under the authority, or with the acquiescence, of the existing Government and be actually in use. It was alleged in regard to the first point that Russia, since the revolution of November, 1917, was deprived of these essential requisites. For, on the one hand, the Powers had declined to recognise, because of its radical and destructive measures, the régime which the Bolshevik elements claimed to have established there. On the other hand, it was impossible to consider the embryonic political association formed by Admiral Koltchak and known as "Omsk Government" as acting for the whole people. In respect of the second head, the appellants maintained that all Russian intercourse with Japan had ceased through the extinction, by the overthrow of the legitimate administration, of the recognition afforded it by Japan. Furthermore, the so-called "Kerensky notes" were not at present compulsory legal currency. It was therefore urged that the said notes did not possess the character of foreign money within the meaning of the statute, and that, accordingly, their imitation did not constitute an offence under its provisions.

Held: That the appeal must be dismissed. It is of no consequence that Russia internally has been undergoing a political change. The primary consideration is that she has not thereby ceased to exist internationally as a State. Neither the fact of revolutionary disturbances in that country nor their effect upon the Empire can be deemed in any way to preclude culpability in regard to the offence charged. In these circumstances the enactment cited against the defendants properly applies, irrespective of the fortunes of the Government which conferred monetary value upon such foreign notes. [Report: 25 *Criminal Cases* (1919), p. 1149.]

States—Continuity of—Continuity of Present-Day Poland with the Polish State before the Partition. **Case No. 16**

REPUBLIC *v.* FELSENSTADT.

Poland, Supreme Court, Second Division. 3 *January*, 1922.

THE FACTS.—The defendant was convicted in 1921, by the District Court of Warsaw, of having, in 1915-1917, during the German occupation of Warsaw, given aid to the enemy, *viz.* the German authorities, by espionage, and of having falsely accused a certain man, before the German authorities, of espionage. The conviction having been confirmed by the Court of Appeal of Warsaw, the defendant appealed against the conviction on the first count to the Supreme Court, which

Held: That the defendant's claim that Poland during the World War was not at war with Germany because Germany did not fight Poland but proclaimed her independence in 1916, and because from the partitions to 1916 there was no Poland, was contrary to history, to law, and to the political consciousness of the nation. (See *Republic* v. *Weisholc*, Case No. 17.) Twelve years after the Third Partition and eight years before the Congress of Vienna there was reorganised an independent Polish State, called the Duchy of Warsaw, which was maintained, with territorial changes, as a result of the Congress of Vienna, under the title of the Kingdom of Poland. This State was united with Russia by a real and personal union. The Kingdom of Poland, being the only remaining fraction of the Polish State, was from the beginning of the World War at war with the Central Powers. A Polish army was fighting with the armies of the Allies in France, in Eastern Poland, on Murman and in Siberia. In 1918 the French, British, Italian and American Governments had recognised Poland as an ally of the Allied and Associated Powers in their war against Germany. In the Treaty of Versailles Poland appears as one of the Allied and Associated Powers.

The defendant's claim, that from 1795 to 1918 there was from the Polish point of view a state of absence of law, and that the only laws in force were the Polish laws of the time preceding the partitions, would lead to a more severe punishment

Case No. 16 *contd.* (death). However, the crimes of which the defendant was convicted would only be punishable if they had been committed to the detriment of Poland, and not of Russia. [Report: Zb. O.S.N., 1922, No. 2.]

[Contrast, as to the existence of Poland, *In re M. and O.* (Case No. 42).—Ed.]

Case No. 17 **States—Establishment and Extinction of—Partition of Poland—Polish View of the Continuity of the Polish State.**

REPUBLIC *v.* WEISHOLC.

Poland, Supreme Court, Second Division (Full Meeting).
17 *October*, 1919.

THE FACTS.—(See Case No. 337.) The defendant having pleaded, *inter alia*, that at the time of the alleged crime there was no Polish State,

Held: That that contention must be rejected. Of most of the lands taken by Prussia in the Second and Third Partitions there was formed in 1807 the Duchy of Warsaw (later increased in size), which was in fact an independent and large Polish State. By various treaties and acts of 1815 this State, under the style of Kingdom of Poland, was "united" (not "incorporated") irrevocably (but not entirely) with Russia, whose Emperor assumed the title of King of Poland. The Kingdom of Poland was thus a separate State and was treated as such by the Russian Emperor. Even the "Organic Statute" of 1832 did not take away the separate status of the country. It followed that the separate character of the Kingdom of Poland never perished either in the consciousness of the nation or at international law, and that there thus existed before the re-establishment of the united Polish Republic, on part of its territory, a Polish State separate from, though in union with, Russia.

As Nicholas II [1] had been at war with Germany as Emperor of Russia and King of Poland, since a Polish army was fighting in France under the Polish flag, and since the occupation of Poland by Germany was a warlike one, Germany was an enemy State within the meaning of the Penal Code.

Although the Russian authorities had for a long time tried to obscure this fact, there was, under Article 5 of the Civil Code in force in that part of Poland, a separate Polish citizenship. At the very moment when the Russians had left the

[1] The last Tsar (Emperor) of Russia.—[Ed.]

Kingdom of Poland, the Russian invasion came to an end and the statehood of that Kingdom had been revived. [Report : Zb. O.S.N., 1919, No. 65.]

NOTE.—For a discussion of this case see Berezowski, in *Gazeta Administracji i Policji Państwowej*, 1924 ; Roth, *Die Entstehung des polnischen Staates*, 63.

This decision refers to the territory in which, since 1807 (Duchy of Warsaw) and 1815 (Kingdom of Poland), there had existed a separate State organisation, although more and more limited by Russia since 1832. The decision in the case of *Republic* v. *Pantol* (see Case No. 18) refers to the question of the legal status of formerly Polish territories outside the limits of the Duchy and the Kingdom. Both decisions are in agreement as to the restoration of the state of things which was temporarily impeded by the violence of the partitioning powers (*jus postliminii*).

States—Continuity of—Partition and Re-Establishment of Polish State.

See Cases Nos. 16, 17, 18 (*Republic* v. *Felsenstadt*, *Republic* v. *Weisholc*, *Republic* v. *Pantol*).

States—Continuity—Effect of Diminution of Territory.

See Case No. 45 (*In re Ungarische Kriegsprodukten-Aktiengesellschaft*).

VI.—Extinction of States

States — Extinction of — Recognition — Re-Establishment of States—Reconstitution of Poland—Continuity of Present-Day Poland with the Polish State before the Partition. **Case No. 18**

REPUBLIC *v.* PANTOL.

Poland, Supreme Court, Second Division (Full Meeting).
30 *September*, 1922.

THE FACTS.—In 1920, during the invasion of Poland by Bolshevik armies, the defendant, an inhabitant of the city of Kobryń (situated between Brześć and Pińsk), enrolled in the service of the Bolshevik militia, and was attached to its military division. In his new capacity he arrested two local citizens, charged them with espionage on behalf of Poland, and surrendered them to the Bolshevik authorities. After the Bolsheviks had been driven out, the defendant was convicted by the District Court of Pińsk of aiding the enemy in time of war, under a provision of the Russian Penal Code (still in force) which punishes both citizens and aliens

Case No. 18 ***contd.***

for aiding the enemy of the country within its territory. The defendant appealed to the Court of Appeal and, his appeal having been dismissed, to the Supreme Court. His main contention was that in 1920 Kobryń was not part of the territory of Poland, since the Polish State had ceased to exist after the Third Partition (1795), and the reconstitution of part of the Polish State (1806, 1815) had come to an end through conquest by Russia in 1831 (after the unsuccessful revolution of 1830-1831), so that in 1918 Poland had come into existence as a new State the eastern frontiers of which were only temporarily defined in December, 1919 (the so-called Curzon Line), and that the taking over of these eastern territories by Poland in 1919 was only a military occupation, not creating Polish sovereignty over those territories.

Held : That the coming into existence of a State must be distinguished from its recognition, and that the first coming into existence of a State must be distinguished from its reconstitution, *i.e.* the restoration of the normal organs of a State which had previously existed for many centuries. Recognition *de jure* or *de facto* of a State by other States, whether solemn or tacit (through the establishment of diplomatic relations), is nothing more than the outward sign of the State's entrance into the international community, but the existence of the State is not dependent upon such recognition ; recognition constitutes the actual acknowledgment of the existence of the State, and it thus presupposes the existence of the State. The reconstitution of Poland, the recovery by the Polish nation of its independence and of its statehood, took place not by virtue of the Treaty of Versailles but by virtue of historical facts arising out of the World War and of the efforts of the Polish nation.

The restitution of the existence of a State, or, more precisely, the renewal of the activities of a State which had existed previously through many centuries, but had temporarily lost the possibility of exerting its statehood, is in reality the renewal of its necessary organs : for this purpose it is sufficient to have a steady tradition and the will of the conscious part of the nation tending constantly to recover the existence of the State, as well as friendly though interested help from outside. The tradition of Polish statehood has been in existence for at least ten centuries, and the outward expressions of the will of the nation to maintain its statehood were the self-sacrifices of hundreds of thousands of Poles who died for their country, and the constantly repeated revolutionary attempts to throw off the laws and institutions imposed by the three conquering Powers. (The Court referred to Napoleon's promises to " rebuild " Poland, to his act of organising the Duchy of Warsaw, to the history of the Polish question at the Congress of Vienna of 1814-1815 and the stipulations of the Final Act of the Congress, to the acts of Alexander I before, during and after the Congress, including his promises to add to the " Congress Kingdom " the territories then included in Western Russia—all of which constituted " external recognition of the " necessity of repairing the partitions of Poland, which had " never been accepted by the Western Powers." The Court reviewed the attitude of England and France during and after the revolutions of 1830-1831 and 1863, and concluded that " no inhabitant of territories of the old Republic may rely " on the alleged confirmation by Polish Parliaments of the " First and Second Partitions," because of the exceptional conditions of duress applied to the members of such Parliaments by Russian and German soldiers, while as for the last Partition, even the form of confirmation by a Polish Parliament was dispensed with).

It is both historically and legally a mistake to claim that Poland had ceased to exist as a result of the partitions: " States cease to exist only if the people lose their consciousness of social differentiation from the invader, if there takes " place, surely though slowly, consent to the new order, when " in general there disappears the tradition and the steady will " to keep alive the old aspirations, beliefs and forms of community life." Parts of a population and parts of territory may change, but the Polish Republic continued to exist potentially, and after the removal of the restrictions imposed by the invading Powers in November, 1918, first in Galicia and in Teshen, then in the " Congress Kingdom " and in Posnania, there came about the restoration of the native organs of State power. Poland thus recovered all her territories of 1772 (the date of the First Partition), not surrendering any territory and not being bound by the treaties concluded since the partitions in the absence of the organs of the Polish State. In 1919 Poland voluntarily decided not to claim certain of the territories which had been hers in 1772; at the same time, however, she took over others and began to exercise her sovereignty in these territories, occupying them with her army

Case No. 18 *contd.* and organising in them Polish courts and Polish administration. Poland at once occupied her eastern territories as territory under her own sovereignty, and not by way of a temporary military occupation. [Reports: O.S.P., II, No. 346; Zb. O.S.N., 1922, No. 345.]

NOTE.—For a discussion of this case see Ehrlich, *Prawo narodów*, 2nd ed., pp. 301-303, and Berezowski, in *Gazeta Administracji i Policji Państwowej*, 1924.

This decision formulates the doctrine of *jus postliminii* to be applied to the re-establishment of the Polish State in 1918. The case differs from that of *Republic* v. *Weisholc* (see Case No. 17) in that the latter case concerned the territory of the "Congress Kingdom" of Poland, organised in 1815: it was clear that the provisions of the Act of the Congress of Vienna were still in force, from the international point of view, and that Weisholc, by helping the German army, was subject to the penalty imposed by the (Russian) Penal Code in force in the territory; it was only necessary to establish that the rights of Poland to loyalty on the part of inhabitants of the territory, in a war with Germany, existed in spite of the fact that Russia no longer exercised authority over that territory. In the present case it was necessary to determine whether the territory in question was under Polish or under Russian sovereignty.

See also Phillimore, *Commentaries upon International Law*, 3rd ed., vol. I, 360, 361.

States—Extinction of—Extinction of Austro-Hungarian Monarchy—Jurisdiction of Dutch Courts in respect of Property Belonging to the Former Austro-Hungarian Monarchy—Rights of Succession States.

See Case No. 86 (*Bergverksaktiebolaget Kosmai* (*appellant*) v. *Militär-Liquidierungsamt, of Vienna* (*respondent*)).

B. COMPOSITE AND DEPENDENT STATES AND TERRITORIES

I.—Unions of States

Case No. 19 **Federal State—Nationality—German and Bavarian Nationality—Acquisition of French Nationality—Treaty of Versailles.**

PROCUREUR DE LA RÉPUBLIQUE (MULHOUSE) *v.* SCHOEN.

France, Court of Cassation (*Chamber of Petitions*).
13 *June*, 1921.

THE FACTS.—The Treaty of Versailles, Annex to Part III, Section V, paragraph 1, reads: "As from November

"11, 1918, the following persons are *ipso facto* reinstated in French nationality: (1) Persons who lost French nationality by the application of the Franco-German Treaty of May 10, 1871, and who have not since that date acquired any nationality other than German." Schoen acquired Bavarian nationality by naturalisation in 1872. Nevertheless, by the instructions of the Mayor of Mulhouse, his name was included in the roll of persons reinstated as French nationals as of full right. Objection was taken by the *Ministère Public* before the *Tribunal régional de Mulhouse,* which decided that in Schoen's case the conditions required by the Treaty were fulfilled.

Held by the Court of Cassation (on appeal by the *Procureur de la République*): That Schoen was rightly reinstated as a French national. If he acquired Bavarian nationality by naturalisation in 1872 he did not thereby acquire a nationality which was other than German. [Reports: 48 *Clunet* (1921), p. 355; *Dalloz,* 1922, Part I, p. 29.]

Composite States—Real Unions—Austria-Hungary—State Succession in regard to International Conventions.

See Case No. 45 (*In re Ungarische Kriegsprodukten-Aktiengesellschaft*).

Federal State—Conduct of Foreign Relations—Functions of Member States—Position in Germany.

See Case No. 77 (*Turkish Purchases Commission Case*).

II.—British Commonwealth of Nations

British Commonwealth of Nations—Status of the Union of South Africa in 1921—Distraint in Holland of Goods Belonging to the Union of South Africa.

See Case No. 8 (*Union of South Africa* v. *Herman Grote*).

III.—Protected and Vassal States and Protectorates

Case No. 20 **Protectorates—Effect of Declaration of British Protectorate over Egypt—Abolition of Turkish Suzerainty—Effect on National Status of Ottoman Subjects in Egypt—Jurisdiction of Mixed Courts.**

AZIZ HANKI *v.* RUSSELL.

Egypt, Mixed Court of Appeal. 30 *December*, 1919.

THE FACTS.—A Receiver was appointed by the British military authorities of the property of Ottoman subjects in Egypt. He brought an action in the Mixed Courts against an Egyptian subject on behalf of a Turkish Prince whose property in Egypt was sequestrated. Objection was made by the defendant to the jurisdiction of the Mixed Courts on the ground that the action was between two native persons and should therefore be heard by the Native Courts. The Civil Tribunal of Cairo rejected the plea, holding that Ottoman subjects in Egypt could no longer be treated as native subjects since the release of Egypt from the tribute to Turkey, the elevation of the sovereign to be Sultan, and the declaration of the British Protectorate in Egypt. On appeal to the Mixed Court of Appeal the judgment was reversed and it was

Held : (1) That the Receiver had the same national character as his principal in a case with third parties.

(2) That the Proclamation declaring Egypt to be under a British Protectorate did not affect the national character of Ottoman subjects inhabiting Egypt. They remained native subjects for the purposes of jurisdiction. It was relevant in this connection that the Protecting Power expressly declared to the sovereign of the country that the revision of the Capitulatory Treaties should be postponed till after the war. The Mixed Courts therefore retain their former competence. [Reports : *Gazette des Tribunaux Mixtes,* 1920, p. 91 ; 47 *Clunet* (1920), p. 757.]

Cf. *Menasce Roussos & Company* v. *Holland-Egypt Handelmaatschappij,* Case No. 110.

Protectorates—British Protectorate over Egypt—Power of Egypt to Conclude Treaties—A Treaty Interpreting a Convention to which One of the Signatories of the Treaty was not a Party. **Case No. 21**

BALTZOUDIS *v.* SOULIOTIS.

Egypt, Mixed Court of Appeal. 22 *April,* 1920.

THE FACTS.—The question in issue was the competence of the Mixed Courts. The plaintiff was a native of the Isle of Lemnos resident in Egypt, and in accordance with the provisions of the Treaty of Athens of 1913, by which Turkey ceded the island to Greece, he opted for Greek nationality within six months of the coming into force of the Treaty. The Egyptian Government for some years refused to recognise the Greek nationality of former Ottoman subjects resident in Egypt who had so opted. After, however, the Turkish suzerainty was abolished in December, 1914, the Egyptian Government modified its views; and in 1918 made a convention with Greece concerning the application in Egypt of the Treaty of 1913, by which it recognised as Greeks natives of the new Greek provinces who, while resident in Egypt, opted for Greek nationality. The defendant demurred to the jurisdiction on the ground that both he and the plaintiff were Greeks and therefore the case was triable by the Greek Consulate. The Court of First Instance upheld the demurrer, and on appeal,

Held: (1) That Egypt had power to enter into a convention concerning the interpretation of a treaty although she was not one of the signatory Powers of that treaty.

(2) That Egypt had in 1890, while still subject to Turkish suzerainty, entered into a convention with Greece concerning nationality, and was more certainly entitled in 1918, when all the ties with the Ottoman Empire were severed, to enter into a convention for the purpose of regulating the application on her territory of the Treaty of Athens. [Report: *Gazette des Tribunaux Mixtes*, 1920, p. 168.]

Case No. 22 **British Protectorate in Egypt—Recognition by Foreign Powers —Power of British Commander-in-Chief to Declare Martial Law—Act of State—Capitulations.**

ISMAIL PASHA SIDKY *v.* SIDAROUS BISHARA.

Egypt, Mixed Summary Tribunal of Cairo. 8 *June*, 1921.

THE FACTS.—A claim was brought in the Mixed Court for rent, based upon a proclamation of the British military authorities in Egypt concerning leases. The defendant was a foreign subject, and he demurred to the claim on the ground that the proclamation, not having been approved by the representatives of the foreign Powers, could not apply to foreign subjects. He objected also that the British authorities were not entitled to issue proclamations under cover of Martial Law when the country was at peace.

Held: (*a*) That the acceptance by the Powers of the British Occupation of Egypt, and, subsequently, the provisions of the Treaty of Versailles concerning the British Protectorate over Egypt, have implicitly but incontestably given recognition to the authority and responsibility inherent in the Commander-in-Chief of the British Forces in Egypt, among them being the right to proclaim a state of siege in case of necessity.

(*b*) That the fixing of the limits of the state of siege is a matter purely for the sovereign Power, and cannot be questioned by an action in the courts by any individual.

(*c*) That while the Egyptian Government and the Protecting Power cannot abolish or attenuate the régime of the Capitulations *proprio motu*, the juridical fiction of extraterritoriality cannot be pushed so far as to contest the right of the authorities who are responsible for maintaining order and peace to proclaim the state of siege *erga omnes*. [Report: *Gazette des Tribunaux Mixtes*, 1921, p. 162.]

V.—Territories under Joint or International Government

Saar Territory—Whether Part of Germany—Political Territory and Customs Territory.

See Case No. 53 (*Saar Territory* (*Usury Decree*) *Case*).

Territories under International Government—Inter-Allied Commission in Upper Silesia—Responsibility of Prussia for the Acts of the Officials of the Commission.

See Case No. 121 (*Upper Silesia* (*Plebiscite Commission*) *Case*).

D. RECOGNITION

[See also above, *Recognition of Acts of Foreign States and Governments*; and Part IV, JURISDICTION: *Territorial.*]

i.—Of States

Recognition of States—Absence of Formal Recognition—Co-operation of British Armed Forces with those of Foreign Provisional Government—Representation of Great Britain by a Commissioner—Statement by the British Foreign Office. **Case No. 23**

THE ANNETTE; THE DORA.

England, Admiralty[1] *Court.* 26 *February*, 1919.

THE FACTS.—The plaintiffs, Esthonian subjects, with the support of the Esthonian Government, had issued writs *in rem* claiming possession of two sailing vessels lying in the port of Liverpool. Appearances under protest were entered by the Provisional Government of Northern Russia, who thereupon moved to set aside the writs, arrests and all subsequent proceedings on the ground, *inter alia*, that the ships had been sequestered and/or requisitioned by the defendant Government and were running in the service of that Government, that they were the property of that Government, and that in these circumstances they were immune from arrest.

The learned judge, having enquired of the Foreign Office " whether [the defendant] Government was one " duly recognised by His Majesty's Government and " has all the attributes of a sovereign state," was informed on behalf of the Secretary of State for Foreign Affairs that

". . . as the title assumed by that Government " indicates, it is merely provisional in nature, and has " not been formally recognised either by His Majesty's " Government or by the Allied Powers as the Govern- " ment of a sovereign independent state."

[1] The expression " Admiralty Court " is used as an abbreviation of the full title " Probate, Divorce and Admiralty Division of the High Court of Justice, In Admiralty."—[Ed.]

Case No. 23 ***contd.***

The reply went on to state that British and Allied forces were co-operating with the Provisional Government against the Russian Soviet Government, that the British Government was represented at Archangel by a Commissioner, and that it also communicated with the Provisional Government through its representative in London.

Upon this letter the defendant Government submitted that the Court ought to infer from the fact that it " has not been formally recognised " the fact that it has been " informally recognised " as a sovereign State, and that therefore the cases were indistinguishable from *The Gagara*.[1]

Held by Hill, J. : That he was not satisfied that the British Government had recognised the Provisional Government of Northern Russia " as a sovereign State," that therefore *The Gagara* was distinguishable, and that the motions of the defendant Government, so far as they were based upon the grounds above mentioned, failed. The learned judge then proceeded to hold (1) that, even if the Provisional Government were to be regarded as a sovereign State, the ships were not at the material times in the possession of that Government, and therefore the Court by arresting the vessel would be interfering with no sovereign right of the Government. It would not be compelling the Government to submit to the jurisdiction or abandon possession ; and (2) in answer to the plea that the Court ought in its discretion to decline to exercise jurisdiction (even if it had it) in disputes between foreigners relating to foreign ships, that the Court had such jurisdiction and in the circumstances of these two cases would exercise it. Accordingly he dismissed the motions, while leaving the final rights of the parties to be determined at a later stage. [Report : L.R. [1919] P. 105.]

NOTE.—(1) It will be noticed that, although the defendants styled themselves a " Government," the cases were treated throughout as cases of the recognition of a sovereign State ; that is to say, the defendants' plea was one of State immunity.

(2) As regards point (1) see the later decisions in the case of *The Jupiter* (No. 1) (*Annual Digest*, 1925-1926, Case No. 100), where the Court took the view that if the proceedings were *in rem* it could not exercise jurisdiction even if the foreign Government were not in actual possession, since a judgment *in rem* would in fact be a decision binding upon it, although it took no part in the proceedings.

---

[1] L.R. [1919] P. 95 ; Case No. 25 in this volume.

Recognition—Effects of Non-Recognition—Counterfeiting Currency of New State Not Expressly Recognised—Czechoslovakia and Germany. **Case No. 24**

COUNTERFEITING OF STAMPS (CZECHOSLOVAKIA) CASE.

Germany, Reichsgericht in Criminal Matters. 29 *June*, 1920.

THE FACTS.—The appellants were convicted for having counterfeited, in May, 1919, certain stamps of the Czechoslovak Republic. They were convicted on the ground of § 275 of the German Criminal Code, which punishes, *inter alia*, the counterfeiting of currency and stamps of a foreign State. It was contended on behalf of the appellants that § 275 was not applicable on the ground that at that time the Czechoslovak Republic was not yet legally constituted.

Held, on final appeal on a point of law: That the conviction must stand. The decisive consideration was that in May, 1919, the Czechoslovak Republic was in fact established and that its Government was effectively in power since January, 1919. The question of recognition was irrelevant. It was not possible to accept the Opinion of the Court below that as Germany was not in a position to protest effectively against the establishment of the Czechoslovak State, she thereby tacitly recognised her as an independent State. [Report: *E.R.S.*, vol. 55, p. 81.]

Recognition of States—*De facto* Independence—Recognition Provisionally and Subject to Reservations—Esthonian National Council. **Case No. 25**

THE GAGARA.

England, Court of Appeal, on Appeal from the Admiralty[1] *Court.* 14 *February*, 1919.

THE FACTS.—In January, 1919, the plaintiffs, the West Russia Steamship Company, stated in an affidavit to be a corporate body having their registered office at Petrograd, issued a writ *in rem* in the Admiralty Division of the High Court, claiming possession of "the steamship "*Gagara*, now sailing under the name of the *Kajak*." Thereupon the Esthonian Government entered an appearance under protest and moved to set aside the writ of summons, service and all subsequent proceedings on the ground that they were the owners of the

[1] See p. 43, footnote.

Case No. 25 *contd.*

Gagara, and that, as they were an independent sovereign Government, the Court had no jurisdiction.

It appeared that the *Gagara* had been confiscated and declared national property by the Bolshevik Government; subsequently, on putting into Reval, she had been seized by the Esthonian Government *jure belli* as flying the flag of an enemy Government (the red flag), and had been condemned as prize of war "not "by bringing her before a Prize Court, but by a decree "of the Government." She was thereupon renamed, and registered at Reval as being of Esthonian nationality and the property of the Esthonian Republic, and a new master was appointed. The ship was being used for public purposes at the time of the issue of the writ.

When the motion came before the Admiralty Court, the learned judge (Hill, J.) invited the assistance of the Foreign Office as to the status of the Esthonian Government. Thereupon the Law Officers appeared and stated on behalf of the Foreign Office: (1) that "our own Government [and likewise the Govern-"ments of France and Italy] has for the time being "provisionally, and with all necessary reserva-"tions as to the future, recognised the Esthonian "National Council as a *de facto* independent body, "and accordingly has received a certain gentleman as "the informal diplomatic representative of the Pro-"visional Government. The state of affairs is of "necessity provisional and transitory . . ." (2) "that, "in the present view of His Majesty's Government, "and without in any way binding itself as to the "future, the Esthonian Government is such a Govern-"ment, as could, if it thought fit, set up a Prize "Court."

Held by the Court of Appeal (Bankes, Warrington and Duke, L.JJ.), affirming the decision of Hill, J.: That the writ of summons, the warrant of arrest, and all subsequent proceedings must be set aside. In view of the statements of the Law Officers, "I cannot but feel" (said Bankes, L.J.) "that if "the Court claimed to exercise, and did exercise, jurisdiction "in respect of such a dispute as arises in this action, they "would not be acting in accordance with what was pointed "out in *The Parlement Belge* (L.R. (1880) 5 P.D. 197) as being "the principle of international comity, and that there would "be a divergence of action as between the courts of this "country and the statements that have been made by the "Government of the country as to the attitude which this "country was prepared to take. If the Court allowed the "arrest of, and exercised jurisdiction to decide the question of "the ownership of, a vessel claimed by and actually in the "possession of a foreign government the Court would be "exercising jurisdiction over that foreign government." [Report: L.R. [1919] P. 95.]

Amongst other cases the Court referred to *Mighell* v. *Sultan of Johore*, L.R. [1894] 1 Q.B. 149, and *The Broadmayne*, L.R. [1916] P. 64. The Court also discussed the revocability of the recognition of States (see p. 103).

Recognition—New States—Retroactive Effect of Recognition of Finland by Belgium.

See Case No. 103 (*West Russian Steamship Company* v. *Captain Sucksdorff*).

Recognition—Effect of—Distinguished from Coming into Existence—Establishment of the Polish State.

See Case No. 18 (*Republic* v. *Pantol*).

ii.—Of Governments

Recognition of New Government of Foreign State—The Appropriate Organ to Grant Recognition—Consequences of *de facto* Recognition—British Recognition of Russian Soviet Government—Validity of Legislation and Administrative Acts of a Recognised Government on its own Territory. **Case No. 26**

LUTHER *v.* SAGOR.

England, High Court (King's Bench Division), and Court of Appeal. 21 *December*, 1920, *and* 12 *May*, 1921.

THE FACTS.—The plaintiffs (hereinafter also referred to as "the Russian Company") were incorporated in and under the laws of the Russian Empire in 1898 and carried on business there as manufacturers of veneer or plywood. By far the largest shareholder in the Russian Company was an English company named Venesta Limited, and the Russian Company was authorised to and did in fact mark its plywood with the trade mark or trade name "Venesta" or "V.L." At the time of the action the head office of the Russian

Case No. 26 ***contd.***

Company was in Esthonia and there was some question whether it had become an Esthonian company.

The defendants carried on business in England as importers of timber.

On 20 June, 1918, a "Decree of Council of Com- "missars for the People" was issued in Russia which purported to emanate from the Government of Russia and declared to be "the property of the Russian "Socialist Federative Republic," *inter alia,*

> "(17) All the mechanical saw mills of limited or "private Companies which have a capital of at "least 1,000,000 Roubles."
>
> "(18) All woodworking establishments equipped "with machinery which belonged to private or "limited Companies."

In 1919 certain "Commissaries," apparently as agents or officials of the Council of Commissars of the People, took possession of the Russian Company's factory in Russia and of the manufactured goods lying there.

In August, 1920, the defendants by a contract with Monsieur Krassin, the representative of the Russian Commercial Delegation in London, bought 8000 cubic metres of plywood for shipment from Russia to England.

When the plywood began to arrive in England, the defendants noticed that some part of it bore the mark "Venesta" and at once brought the fact to the attention of Venesta Limited, whereupon the writ in this action was issued, claiming (1) a declaration that the shipments of plywood in question were the unincumbered property of the Russian Company, and (2) an injunction to restrain the defendants from selling or otherwise dealing with it.

The defendants contended, *inter alia,* that the plywood bought by them was not and never had been the property of the Russian Company, and that the Russian Commercial Delegation from whom they had bought it was present in London by permission of the British Government for the purpose of entering into commercial contracts with traders in this country who were authorised by the British Government to deal with them.

In reply to letters from the plaintiffs' solicitors the

British Secretary of State for Foreign Affairs stated in a letter dated 27 November, 1920, that "for a certain "limited purpose[1] His Majesty's Government has "assented to the claim that that which Monsieur Krassin "represents in this Country is a State Government "of Russia," and that "His Majesty's Government "have never officially recognized the Soviet Govern-"ment in any way."

Held by Roche, J.: (1) That the question whether the Decree above referred to must be recognised by a British court as a valid legislative act and receive effect accordingly depended upon whether the body it emanated from was the sovereign Power in Russia; (2) that "the proper source of "information as to a foreign power, its status and sovereignty, "is the Sovereign of this country through the Government: "*Mighell* v. *Sultan of Johore*, L.R. [1894] 1 Q.B. 149; *Foster* v. "*Globe Venture Syndicate*, L.R. [1900] 1 Ch. 811"; (3) that he was satisfied upon the letters of the Secretary of State that His Majesty's Government had not recognised the Soviet Government as the Government of a sovereign State; (4) that he was therefore unable to recognise the Soviet Government as the Government of Russia and consequently was unable to recognise its Decree as a valid legislative act. Consequently he could not recognise its Decree as having the effect of depriving the plaintiffs of their property. Accordingly he gave judgment for the plaintiffs, the Russian Company. [Report: L.R. [1921] 1 K.B. 456.]

FURTHER FACTS.—The defendants appealed, but before the judgment of Roche, J., came before the Court of Appeal four months later certain events occurred which completely altered the situation. On 16 March, 1921, a Trade Agreement was entered into between the British and the Soviet Governments, and by a letter addressed to the appellants' (defendants') solicitors the British Secretary of State for Foreign Affairs stated that "His Majesty's Government recognize the "Soviet Government as the *de facto* Government of "Russia," and that the Soviet Government had succeeded to the Provisional Government (which had been recognised by His Majesty's Government) on 13 December, 1917.

[1] *I.e.* for the purpose of the carrying on of certain negotiations which ultimately resulted in the Trade Agreement.

Case No. 26 *contd.* *Held* by the Court of Appeal (Bankes, Warrington and Scrutton, L.JJ.): (1) That the effect of recognition of the Soviet Government by His Majesty's Government is that a British court cannot question the validity in Russian territory of the legislative and executive acts whereby the property in the goods in question in Russia was taken from the Russian Company and transferred to the defendants; (2) that this effect is retroactive and dates back to the time when the Soviet Government first established itself (Scrutton, L.J., did not consider it necessary to decide this point); (3) that the effect was the same whether the foreign Government is recognised as a *de facto* or as a *de jure* Government; and (4) that, accordingly, while approving of the judgment of Roche, J., upon the facts which then existed, the appeal must be allowed and judgment must be given for the defendants. [Report: L.R. [1921] 3 K.B. 532.]

NOTES.—(1) Stress was laid in the Court of Appeal upon three decisions of the Supreme Court of the United States: *Williams* v. *Bruffy*, 96 U.S. 176; *Underhill* v. *Hernandez*, 168 U.S. 250; and *Oetjen* v. *Central Leather Co.*, 246 U.S. 297.

(2) The Court of Appeal declined to accept the argument that a British court should refuse to recognise the Decree of the Soviet Government on the ground that it was confiscatory and unjust and "contrary to essential principles of justice and morality." See p. 545. Bankes, L.J., took the view that a transfer of property valid by the *lex loci rei sitae* must be recognised, and cited *Santos* v. *Illidge*, [1860] 8 C.B. (N.S.) 861 (a slavery case). See also p. 548 *per* Warrington, L.J.: "It is well settled that the validity of the acts of an independent "government in relation to property within its jurisdiction cannot be "questioned in the Courts of this country."

(3) Reference should be made to *The Lomonosoff*, L.R. [1921] P. 97, in which Hill, J., on 1 December, 1920, awarded salvage to certain British and Belgian nationals for the rescue of a steamer at Murmansk in Northern Russia in February, 1920, from the hands of certain armed men described as "Bolsheviks." The learned judge said (at p. 105): "It is obvious that this Court, respecting the comity of nations, would "never treat as a meritorious service the act of persons who in defiance "of the laws of an established government recognized by and in "friendship with this country took a ship out of the lawful control "of such a government. But at Murmansk on February 21 there "was no government recognized by this country and indeed no estab-"lished government at all."

(4) Similarly in *A. Gagnière & Co.* v. *Eastern Company of Warehouses, etc., Limited* (*The Times* newspaper, April 30, 1921), an action upon a policy of insurance which excluded "loss or damage caused ... "by persons taking part in ... civil commotions," Roche, J., held that a seizure of the goods at the Custom House at Petrograd (on a date which does not appear) by persons purporting to act on behalf of the Soviet Government was not a loss caused by "persons taking "part in civil commotions; however irregular [he said] were the "proceedings of the emissaries of the Bolshevist Government, and

"however foreign to our ideas of government, he had come to the "conclusion that such proceedings were the authorised acts of the "Government which was in fact in power at the time, and were not "acts of civil commotion, but were acts of a Government, however "irregular and rude in form it might be."

(5) This decision (*Luther* v. *Sagor*) was followed by the Court of Appeal in *White, Child & Beney Limited* v. *Simmons*; *Same* v. *Eagle, Star, and British Dominions Insurance Company* (1922), 127 L.T. 571; 38 T.L.R. 616. The case arose upon two policies of insurance which insured the plaintiffs against loss or damage "directly caused by fire, "rioters, civil commotions, war, civil war, revolutions, rebellions, "military or usurped power" and excluded claims "for confiscation "or destruction by the government of the country in which the property "is situated." The Court of Appeal (reversing Roche, J., sitting in February 1922, 38 T.L.R. 367) held in May, 1922, that the seizure of the plaintiffs' property in December, 1917, by soldiers and sailors of the Red Guard and by armed Bolshevist workmen purporting to act under the authority of an executive committee of the Commissaries of the People was an act of confiscation by a body which had since been recognised by His Majesty's Government as the *de facto* Government of Russia, and accordingly that the loss was not covered by the policies. (The judgment of Roche, J., contains a detailed narrative of the events in Russia during the material portions of the years 1917 and 1918.) At the time of the hearing of this action, the judgment of the Court of Appeal in the *Sagor* case had already been given. There was no doubt as to the recognition of the Soviet Government, and the question was the date at which the Soviet Government should be considered to have commenced its existence as a Government so that acts done in its name could be held to be the acts of the Government. (See point (2) in the judgment of the Court of Appeal in the *Sagor* case, *supra*). The relevant events in this case took place in December, 1917. The Foreign Office supplied information, but, although requested by Roche, J., to do so, refused to state the date to which His Majesty's Government's recognition of the Soviet Government should be deemed to be retrospective or the area over which that Government exercised control at different dates. These points were left to be decided by the Court on the evidence before it, and it was on the appreciation of the evidence that the Court of Appeal differed from Roche, J. The Court of Appeal thus recognised the Soviet Government as having been established as early as December, 1917.

(6) See also *Bragoseo Limited* v. *J. Sagor & Co.* (1921), 8 Lloyd's List Law Reports 388; *Walneff* v. *All Russian Co-operative Society* (1921), 9 Lloyd's List Law Reports 527; *Annual Digest*, 1925-1926, Case No. 100 (*The Jupiter*, Nos. 1, 2 and 3); and *Princess Paley Olga* v. *Weisz*, L.R. [1929] 1 K.B. 718.

Recognition—Of Governments—Conclusiveness of Action of Political Department—The Provisional Government of Russia of 1917—The Soviet Government. **Case No. 27**

THE ROGDAI.

United States District Court, N.D. California. 25 *May*, 1920.

THE FACTS.—This was a suit *in rem* to recover possession

Case No. 27 ***contd.***

of a Russian naval transport. The action was instituted by the Russian Socialist Federal Soviet Republic and Ludwig C. A. K. Martens as its representative. The " Russian Government " and Boris Bakhmetieff, appearing specially, moved to discharge the attachment. Bakhmetieff was the ambassador to the United States appointed by the Provisional Government of Russia which was overthrown in the Bolshevik Revolution of 1917. The motion was accompanied by a certificate from the United States Department of State certifying that Bakhmetieff was the duly accredited ambassador of Russia to the United States, that Martens had not been received or recognised in any representative capacity, and that the Russian Soviet Government had not been recognised by the United States.

Held : That the motion must be allowed and the attachment discharged. The Court said : " Plainly, consideration of " such an issue upon the merits would of necessity draw us " into the realm of international diplomacy ; and it is equally " plain that no useful purpose could be subserved by such an " investigation. If the court assumes the right to make an " original inquiry, it logically follows that it must exercise its " own independent judgment upon the facts thus disclosed and " reach an independent conclusion. In that view it might " recognize Martens, while Washington recognizes Bakhmetieff. " To state the proposition is to discredit it." " The question " at issue is one of state ; it involves international relations, " and is primarily for the State Department. If, as contended " by libelants, it be granted that a revolution has taken place " in Russia, and that the Soviet Republic is in actual control, " the question when, if at all, such *de facto* government shall " be recognized, is a political one. It involves considerations " of national policy, which are not justiciable, and touching it " the voice of the Chief Executive is the voice, not of a branch " of the government, but of the national sovereignty, equally " binding upon all departments." (278 Fed. 294, 296.) [Report : 278 Fed. 294.]

NOTE.—See also Case No. 28 (*The Penza ; The Tobolsk*).

Recognition—Of Governments—Effects of Non-Recognition—The Right of Non-Recognised Government to Sue. **Case No. 28**

THE PENZA; THE TOBOLSK.

United States District Court, E.D. New York.
26 *September*, 1921.

THE FACTS.—A libel was filed by the Russian Socialist Federated Soviet Republic and Martens, its agent, to recover possession of two steamships. Exceptions were taken to the libel on the ground that neither libelant could maintain the suit. Despite the *de facto* control of Russia by the Soviet Government at the time of the suit, Bakhmetieff (ambassador of the former Provisional Government of 1917) was still recognised by the United States as the representative of Russia, while neither the Soviet Government nor Martens had been so recognised.

Held: That the exceptions must be sustained and the libel dismissed. The Court will take judicial notice of the action of the political departments in such a case and is bound thereby. "Which is a sovereign, *de jure* or *de facto*, of a territory is not a judicial, but a political, question for determination." (277 Fed. 91, 92.) The cases of *The Rogdai*, 278 Fed. 294 (Case No. 27), and *Agency of Canadian Car and Foundry Co. Ltd.* v. *American Can Co.*, 258 Fed. 363 (Case No. 14), were followed. Independent enquiry by the Court into the Russian situation was refused. "The Soviet Republic never having been recognized as a sovereign state by this government, it may not maintain this libel in the federal courts. Its alleged agent would have no better or greater rights than his principal." (277 Fed. 91, 94.) [Report: 277 Fed. 91.]

Recognition of Governments—Recognition of Acts of—Retroactive Effect. **Case No. 29**

MONTE BLANCO REAL ESTATE CORPORATION *v.* WOLVIN LINE *ET AL.*

United States, Supreme Court of Louisiana. 31 *May*, 1920.

THE FACTS.—In December, 1914, the plaintiff's plantation in Mexico was invaded by forces acting under the *de facto* Carranza Government, and a quantity of coffee was seized. Some of this coffee was later sold and

Case No. 29 *contd.*

brought to New Orleans on the defendant Line's vessel. The plaintiff sued the Line and the consignee, recovering judgment for the coffee. On appeal by the consignee,

Held: That the judgment must be set aside and the suit dismissed. The defendant's title was good since it was derived from the *de facto* Government of Mexico which was later recognised with retroactive effect as the *de jure* Government. The acts of such a Government in Mexico were not subject to judicial enquiry in another country. Citing *Ricaud* v. *American Metal Co.*, 246 U.S. 304. [Report: 147 La. 563.]

Case No. 30

Recognition of Governments—Effect of Non-Recognition upon the Right to Institute Legal Proceedings on Behalf of the State—Effect of *de facto* Relations.

THE SOVIET GOVERNMENT *v.* ERICSSON.

Sweden, Supreme Court. 27 October, 1921.

THE FACTS.—The Provisional Government which was formed in Russia after the fall of the Imperial Government was recognised by Sweden. Its representative was accredited in Stockholm. When the Provisional Government fell in November, 1917, no change took place in regard to its representative in Stockholm. The succeeding Soviet Government did not request recognition and was not recognised until a long time afterwards. Nevertheless in 1918 certain *de facto* relations took place between the Swedish Government and the Soviet Government. A representative of the Soviet Government was received in Stockholm, and an agreement in regard to commercial intercourse was made. In December, 1918, the Swedish Foreign Office, however, communicated to the Soviet representation in Stockholm that they were no longer to enjoy the diplomatic privileges and immunities previously enjoyed. In this way the quasi-diplomatic relations that the Swedish Foreign Office had entertained with the Soviet Government were broken off, and in consequence thereof and of the blockade maintained by the Entente Powers in 1919 all relations with the Soviet Republic ceased. In March, 1920, commercial relations were again resumed. The Swedish Government resolved to receive a trade-delegation from the All Russian Co-operative Society, the Centro-Sojus, which delegation in its capacity as representative of the Centro-Sojus was given the right to sue and to be sued before the Swedish courts; but the Soviet Government was not *de jure* recognised by the Swedish Government.

In Sweden the right of foreigners to own real estate is subject to a special permission to be granted by the Government, and in 1918 M. Vorovsky, as "Délégué Plénipotentiaire du Conseil des Commissaires du Peuple," negotiated with the Swedish Government to obtain permission to acquire, for the premises of a legation, a house which was being built.

In January, 1919, M. Vorovsky, in the said capacity, sued A. Ericsson, a Swedish subject, before the Court of Stockholm, contending as follows: During the negotiations for the said permission Ericsson bought the house and had it registered in his name, but the acquisition was made in the interest of the Soviet Government, and M. Vorovsky paid the price and the cost of completing the building. When the Swedish Government in December, 1918, broke off relations with the Soviet Republic, M. Vorovsky attempted to make Ericsson sell the house and so let him (Vorovsky) get his money back. Ericsson refused on the pretext that he wished to keep the house as security for alleged confiscated and nationalised property in Russia. M. Vorovsky therefore asked for judgment against Ericsson for the payment of the expenses incurred. M. Vorovsky declared in the Court that the Soviet Government was the plaintiff and that he sued as representative of the Soviet Government. Ericsson objected that the Soviet Government was not entitled to institute legal proceedings before a Swedish court, as the Swedish Government had not recognised that Government nor M. Vorovsky as its representative.

In a certificate produced before the Court, the Commissary of the People for Foreign Affairs and the Commissary for Trade and Industry testified on behalf of the Soviet Government that its representative in Sweden, M. Vorovsky, in virtue of his mandate, had power to appear before the Swedish courts, and especially to bring an action against Ericsson, and that the Soviet Government acquiesced in all that M. Vorovsky had done in the matter. Counsel for the

Case No. 30 *contd.*

Soviet Government produced a power of attorney signed by the same persons giving him power to appear before all Swedish courts in behalf of the Soviet Government.

Held by the Court of Stockholm: That the case could not be considered. The Court stated in its judgment that the action was brought by the Soviet Government, that this Government was not recognised by the Swedish Government, that, moreover, there was no information as to the composition of the Soviet Government, and that in these circumstances the Soviet Government could not be allowed to appear as a party before the Court.

Held by Svea Hovrätt, on appeal by the Soviet Government: That the Soviet Government could not plead as a party before a Swedish court, and that the appeal therefore could not be taken into consideration.

Held by the Supreme Court: That the decision must be upheld.[1] [Report: *Nytt Juridiskt Arkiv*, 1921, p. 474.]

Case No. 31

Recognition—Effects of—Confiscation Decrees of Hungarian Soviet Government—Recognition of—Non-Payment of Compensation.

HUNGARIAN SOVIET GOVERNMENT (CONFISCATION OF PROPERTY) CASE.

Austria, Supreme Court in Civil Matters. 31 *October*, 1922. (*Ob. I.* 1055/22.)

THE FACTS.—The Hungarian Soviet Government seized, by Decree of 17 June, 1919, the securities and deposits in Hungarian banks. It then sold part of these effects

[1] NOTE.—In a communication sent in reply to an enquiry by the Court the adviser on public international law of the Swedish Foreign Office, Professor Undén, expressed the opinion that the non-recognition of the Soviet Government did not prevent a Swedish court from allowing the Soviet Government to plead before it. The interruption of relations with that Government in December, 1918, did not, in Professor Undén's opinion, imply that the Swedish Government had changed its view that the Soviet Government was in fact governing Russia, but could be said to be an act of retaliation for violation of "the "rights of Sweden and Swedish citizens." There was no such connection between the status of the Soviet Government in international law and the present case that the capacity of the Soviet Government to bring the action was dependent upon its being recognised by the Swedish Government. It was not a question of rights acquired by a previous Russian Government nor of the validity of acts of legislation by the Soviet Government in regard to Sweden or Swedish citizens, but the question was only whether the Soviet Government could plead before a Swedish court in respect of a transaction of civil law to which the Government had itself been a party. If this question be answered in the negative, the Soviet Government would be deprived of a

to a certain L. F., a merchant in Vienna. The owners contested the validity of the purchase and brought an action asking for a declaration that they were the owners. The Commercial Court of Vienna decided that the purchase was valid, as the effects were sold by the Hungarian Soviet Government, as that Government exercised at that time power in Hungary, and as the Austrian Government recognised and entertained relations with the Hungarian Government. The fact that no compensation was paid was irrelevant. The Upper District Court of Vienna confirmed the judgment of the Court below.

Held by the Supreme Court: That the decisions of the Courts below must be affirmed. The Soviet Government in Hungary was recognised by the Austrian Government, and it had an accredited representative with that Government. It follows that the decrees of the Soviet Government in Hungary are governmental acts which the Austrian Republic must recognise. The question whether the Allied Powers recognised the Hungarian Government is irrelevant seeing that the purchase was made in Vienna. The decrees of the Hungarian Government which succeeded the Soviet Government and which declared the acts of the latter to be null and void cannot affect the acquired rights of third persons. [Report: *Entscheidungen des Obersten Gerichtshofes in Zivilrechtssachen*, vol. IV (1922), No. 110, p. 274.]

NOTE.—As to non-payment of compensation, see Fachiri in *B.Y.*, 1925, pp. 159-171; Fischer Williams, *ibid.*, 1928, pp. 1-30.—[Ed.].

Recognition of New Government of Foreign State—Retroactive Effect.

See Case No. 26 (*Luther* v. *Sagor*).

Recognition of New Government of Foreign State—*De facto* and *de jure* Recognition.

See Case No. 26 (*Luther* v. *Sagor*).

Recognition of Governments—Effects of Non-Recognition—Upon Jurisdictional Immunities.

See Case No. 96 (*Ex parte in the Matter of Hussein Lutfi Bey, Master of the Gul Djemal*).

privilege which, not expressly denied, would belong to other Russian corporations, *e.g.*, according to the above-mentioned declaration of the Swedish Government, the trade-delegation of the Centro-Sojus. 'The decisions of the Swedish Government were not sufficient ground for such an answer.

Recognition of Governments—Conclusiveness of Statements by Executive Departments—Recognition of Russian Government by United States in 1917.

See Case No. 14 (*Agency of Canadian Car and Foundry Co. Ltd.* v. *American Can Co.*).

Recognition—Effect of Non-Recognition—Diplomatic Immunities—Non-Recognition of Soviet Russia by Italy.

See Case No. 211 (*In re Serventi*).

v.—Conditional Recognition

Recognition of States—Revocability of—Recognition of Esthonia by Great Britain.

See Case No. 25 (*The Gagara*).

E. STATE SUCCESSION

I.—Succession in Rights

State Succession—Succession in Rights—Independent of Recognition of Obligations—Succession States of the Austro-Hungarian Monarchy—Jurisdiction of Dutch Courts in Respect of Property Belonging to the Former Austro-Hungarian Monarchy.

See Case No. 86 (*Bergverksaktiebolaget Kosmai* (*appellant*) v. *Militär-Liquidierungsamt, of Vienna* (*respondent*)).

II.—Succession with regard to Contractual and other Obligations, and Concessions

Case No. 32 **State Succession—Succession with regard to Contractual and other Obligations and Concessions—Concessions Granted by Spain in the Philippines.**

EASTERN EXTENSION, AUSTRALASIA AND CHINA TELEGRAPH COMPANY LIMITED *v.* UNITED STATES.

United States Supreme Court. 12 *January*, 1920.

THE FACTS.—This was a suit to recover a subsidy stipulated in a concession granted to the plaintiff company by the Government of Spain for the construction and operation of certain cables in the Philippine Islands. The concession required the company to lay and operate the cables, give precedence to official dispatches, transmit official dispatches at special rates and pay certain taxes. In return the company was to receive an annual subsidy from the Spanish Government. The concession was granted and the cables were completed and in use before the cession of the Islands to the United States. After the cession of the Islands, United States official dispatches were given precedence and the company voluntarily accepted official dispatches at special rates. The company made claim to the subsidy in annual statements to the Philippine Government. In 1905 an official of the Philippine Government received from the company a substantial sum alleged to be due to the United States under the concession. It was not shown that any action whatever had been taken on the company's annual statements. The company first sued in the United States Court of Claims for the subsidy, contending that by virtue of the principles of State succession the United States must be deemed to have assumed the obligation. This suit was dismissed for want of jurisdiction. The decision was affirmed by the United States Supreme Court, but with the suggestion that there might be grounds for recovery on a basis of implied contract. The implied contract theory was then adopted by the company in a second suit in the Court of Claims. The Court of Claims held that there was no implied contract on the part of the United States to pay the subsidy. (54 Ct. Cl. 108.) On appeal,

Held: That the judgment of the Court of Claims must be affirmed. Questions of liability by State succession or under the treaty of cession had been excluded by the previous decision. (231 U.S. 326.) The United States Secretary of War had declined to carry out the terms of the concession agreement. An official of the Insular Government could not obligate the United States. " Such a liability can be created only by " some officer of the Government lawfully invested with power " to make such contracts or to perform acts from which they " may be lawfully implied." (251 U.S. 355, 366.) [Reports: 54 Ct. Cl. 108; 251 U.S. 355.]

Case No. 33 **State Succession—Contracts—No Liability without Express Recognition.**

VEREENIGING MUNICIPALITY *v.* VEREENIGING ESTATES LIMITED.

Union of South Africa, Supreme Court (Transvaal Provincial Division). 15 *May,* 1919.

(WESSELS AND MASON, JJ.)

THE FACTS.—The defendant company claimed to have the right to erect wires for the purpose of conveying electric current across certain streets vested in, and within the jurisdiction of, the plaintiff municipality. The source of the alleged right was a contract entered into between the Government of the late South African Republic and the company's predecessors in title.

Held : That the contract, not having been specifically recognised by the British Government after annexation, was not binding upon that Government or its successor in title. " It " has already been decided by our courts . . . that, where a " person had a personal right as against the Government of " the South African Republic, he could not vindicate that " personal right in the courts of the Transvaal Colony after " annexation. He could not set up a right that he had as " against the extinct Government. He could not set that right " up in the courts of the conqueror, because the conquest is " an act of State. That act of State would regulate the relation-" ship between the conqueror and the conquered ; it is not a " matter that can be inquired into by our courts. That is the " view taken by the English Constitution, and it has been " adopted by our courts. It is true that other systems of " jurisprudence may take a different view, but that is the " view taken by our courts and we are bound thereby " (*per* Wessels, J., at p. 163). (*Postmaster-General* v. *Taute,* [1905] T.S. 582 ; *Randjeslaagte Syndicate* v. *The Government,* [1908] T.S. 404 ; *Cook* v. *Sprigg,* [1899] A.C. 572 referred to.) [Report : *The South African Law Reports,* [1919] *Transvaal Provincial Division,* p. 159 ([1919] T.P.D. 159).)

State Succession—Succession in Obligations—Private Law Liabilities of Former Government—General Principles of Law in Matters of State Succession—German East Africa —Treaty of Versailles. **Case No. 34**

TANGANYIKA SUCCESSION CASE.

Germany, Reichsgericht in Civil Matters. 10 *October*, 1922.

THE FACTS.—Before the World War the plaintiff let a property of his to the Treasury of German East Africa. Since October, 1916, he received no rent. The present action was for arrears of rent for the period from 1 October, 1916, to 1 April, 1920. It was brought against the Treasury of the Colony (*Schutzgebiet*) of East Africa and the German *Reich* as joint debtors. In Article 119 of the Treaty of Versailles Germany renounced in favour of the Principal Allied and Associated Powers all her rights and titles over her overseas possessions. The German *Reich* denied liability.

Held, on final appeal on a point of law: That Germany was liable. As the result of the Treaty of Versailles the former Colony of East Africa ceased to exist as a territory under German protection. It has been taken over, together with all its assets, by Great Britain. According to general principles of law Great Britain would have to be responsible for the private law liabilities of the former protected territory. However, the Treaty of Versailles expressly excluded the application of this principle. Germany nevertheless had been entitled to immovable and movable property and other assets and obligations of the defunct Colony of East Africa. It cannot be maintained that the assets of the former Colony have now become without an owner, that the debtors have been freed of their liability, and the creditors have lost their rights. " Such a consequence " would be inconsistent with the requirement of a State under " the rule of law; it would also be inconsistent with the protective authority of the German *Reich*." As a matter of fact, Germany had in a number of cases undertaken to take over certain obligations of former East Africa, for instance, in the matter of pensions for officials and in regard to private law obligations which—it was contended in the present case—it had voluntarily assumed for reasons of equity. The Court sees in the assumption of liability " the express recognition and " application of a general principle." " The fact that the " public authorities of the State, it is said, have voluntarily

Case No. 34 *contd.* "undertaken as a matter of equity to take over the private law "liabilities of East Africa, cannot be properly understood with- "out assuming that there were other reasons, namely, those "of a legal nature, which prompted that course." The pretension that the *Reich* must be free to determine which private law claims deserve consideration, cannot be admitted. It is for the courts to investigate such questions in case of dispute. [Report: *E.R.Z.*, vol. 105, p. 260.]

Case No. 35 **State Succession—Succession to Obligations—Payment of Money Owing by the Former Government—Natural Law and Positive Law.**

SALARY DUE BY THE FORMER GOVERNMENT (CZECHOSLOVAKIA) CASE.

Czechoslovakia, Supreme Administrative Court.
5 *December*, 1921. *No.* 11.322.

THE FACTS.—The plaintiff was made prisoner during the war, and after his return from captivity was taken over [1] into the Czechoslovak army. Subsequently he made an application to the Czechoslovak authorities demanding payment of a certain sum of money due to him, for the duration of his captivity, by the former Austro-Hungarian military administration as part of his salary as officer. His claim was not recognised, and he lodged an appeal with the Supreme Administrative Court, contending, *inter alia*, that (i) the Czechoslovak State assumed the pecuniary obligations of the former State in regard to officials whom it had taken over, and that (ii) the Czechoslovak State, having taken over parts of the former army and in particular all military establishments of the former State with all their assets, cannot according to natural law refuse payments due to military persons for their services to the former State.

Held by the Supreme Administrative Court: That the appeal failed.

(*a*) Even if there were succession of the Czechoslovak State to the rights and obligations of the former State, such succession would relate only to the taking over of the plaintiff into the Czechoslovak army. But from this taking over, which does not mean anything else than that the person thus taken over

[1] See *Annual Digest*, 1925-1926, Case No. 67, footnote 1.

enters into the service of the new State, there cannot be deduced an obligation of the succeeding State to pay him his claims against the former State, as "it is by no means self-"evident that pecuniary obligations of public law incurred in "relations of public service pass *eo ipso* to the so-called suc-"ceeding State. Neither does international law recognise a "transference of such claims." Accordingly, a claim for the fulfilment of the obligations of the former State could arise only if the Czechoslovak State had expressed, in a binding manner, the will to take over either generally or under certain conditions pecuniary obligations of public law resulting from public service in the extinguished State. The plaintiff, however, cannot refer to any such expression of the will of the State.

(*b*) So-called natural law, as a sum of postulates which philosophy addresses to positive law, is not, except where the law provides otherwise, a real source of law, and it cannot therefore supply a positive provision. Accordingly, it is not necessary to deal more fully with the question whether mere equitable considerations can give rise to subjective legal rights which alone the Court is called upon to protect. [Report: Boh. 1041 adm.[1]]

NOTE.—For a subsequent decision to the same effect see *Annual Digest*, 1925-1926, Case No. 67.

State Succession—Succession with regard to Contractual and other Obligations—Obligations of Poland in respect of a Railway Accident on Former Austrian Railway. **Case No. 36**

OLPINSKI *v.* POLISH TREASURY (RAILWAY DIVISION).

Poland, Supreme Court, Third Division. 16 *April*, 1921.

THE FACTS.—In August, 1918, *i.e.* while certain territories of the former Polish State were still under Austrian rule, the plaintiff attempted to board a crowded train. A conductor slammed the door of the carriage, injuring the plaintiff's hand. After the re-establishment of Poland, the plaintiff brought the present action against the Polish Treasury (the Polish State having taken over Austrian State Railways on its territory).

The District Court at Jaslo gave judgment for the plaintiff, on the ground that a railway enterprise is by its nature a private undertaking, so that the Polish

[1] See also *Annual Digest*, 1927-1928, Case No. 58, Note.

Case No. 36 *contd.*

Railway Treasury is responsible for the debts and obligations which form an encumbrance on the railway property. "This . . . follows also from international "law, *viz.* from the principle, recognized in inter-"national law, of legal continuity and from the prin-"ciple of taking over of obligations localised in "territories which are taken over by a new State . . . "it is impossible to talk of taking over rights without "taking over obligations, since taking over rights "implies taking over both assets and liabilities."

The Court of Appeal of Cracow dismissed the appeal brought against that judgment, pointing out that the debt in question was not a State debt, but one of a transport enterprise, and in consequence one governed by the Civil Code. On appeal to the Supreme Court,

Held, allowing the appeal: That since the action is directed not against the Austrian but against the Polish Treasury, the plaintiff must prove a title under which the debt had passed. Now Article 318 of the Treaty of St. Germain did not provide such a title, since it only stipulated for the future issue of rules concerning the transfer of railways in the ceded territories. Nor had such rules been issued up to date. On the other hand, "the rules of civil law do not find direct "application to international relations." Moreover, they would not in this case justify an action against the Polish Treasury. The plaintiff would therefore have to sue the Austrian Treasury. [Report: O.S.P., I, No. 15.]

(For a discussion of the case see Rundstein, *ibid.*)

NOTE.—At the date of the judgment the Treaty of St. Germain had not yet been ratified by Poland, nor had it been published in the Polish Journal of Laws (see *Annual Digest*, 1927-1928, Case No. 274).

Case No. 37

State Succession—Succession with regard to Contractual and other Obligations—Leases Granted by Prussian Government—Whether Binding in Poland—Article 256 of the Treaty of Versailles.

(POLISH) STATE TREASURY *v.* V. OSTEN.

Poland, Supreme Court, Fifth Division. 9 *June*, 1922.

THE FACTS.—The Prussian State had leased to the defendants certain real property. After the re-establishment of Poland and the coming into force of the Treaty of Versailles, the Polish Treasury, which had become the owner of what was formerly Prussian and German State property in the territories now taken over by Poland, considered the contract of lease concluded between the Prussian State and the defendant as cancelled, and in December, 1920, asked the defendant either to conclude with the Polish State a new contract of lease or to quit the estate on 1 July, 1921. Ten days later the defendant was notified in writing that the Polish Treasury was willing to conclude with him a new contract of lease. A new contract not having been concluded, the Treasury brought the present action to compel the defendant to give up possession of the estate. The District Court of Bydgoszcz gave judgment for the Treasury, and the Court of Appeal of Katowice dismissed the appeal brought by the defendant. On appeal to the Supreme Court,

Held, dismissing the appeal: That the Polish State Treasury had become the (full) owner of the estate in question under Article 256 of the Treaty of Versailles, which does not on that account impose upon Poland any duty to take over obligations of Germany or Prussia. Articles 254, 255, and 92, paragraph 2, of the Treaty of Versailles relate only to the taking over of the public debt of Germany. As to the (full) ownership of the property in question, a distinction must be made between the acquisition of such ownership and between its consequences under the legal system in question. Poland had become the owner of such property under the Treaty of Versailles and not under any act of civil law, and in consequence the ownership is determined in the matter of any obligations that may accompany its acquisition by the Treaty of Versailles and not by civil law. Since, as stated, the Treaty imposes on Poland no obligation to respect the contracts of lease concluded by Prussia, " the conclusion must be drawn " that the Treasury of the Polish Republic has acquired the " said property free of all charges. It is not necessary to " decide in principle, for the purposes of the present case, " whether international custom to the contrary might give a " different legal aspect to the case. For there is no general " international custom ordering a State which acquires property " under an international treaty to respect contracts of lease " concluded by the predecessor State, unless there is a special " treaty stipulation to that effect. The Polish Treasury,

Case No. 37 *contd.*

"therefore, is not bound on the sole ground of acquisition of "ownership of State real property by any contracts of lease "concluded by the Prussian Treasury." However, once the ownership had thus been acquired on the basis of an international treaty, it was henceforth governed by the civil law of the country in which the property is situated and the new owner can on the basis of the rules of civil law ask the lessees to surrender to them his newly acquired property. Accordingly, it must be determined whether, although the contract of lease concluded between the Prussian Treasury and the defendant is not binding on the Polish Treasury, the defendants are not, nevertheless, entitled to rely on the Civil Code in bar of the plaintiff's claim. [Report: O.S.P., I, No. 504.]

State Succession—In Obligations—Actions against German Treasury—Danzig Free State.

See Case No. 55 (*Pending Actions (Danzig) Case (II)*).

III.—The Public Debt. Pensions

Case No. 38

State Succession—Succession to Liabilities—Military Pensions —Austrian Republic and the Succession States.

MILITARY PENSIONS (AUSTRIA) CASE.

Austria, Constitutional Court. 7 *May*, 1919. (*No.* 126.)

THE FACTS.—The plaintiff was conscribed in November, 1915, in the Austrian army. After the downfall of the Monarchy he claimed from the Austrian Republic a pension for his family due to him according to the military laws obtaining in the former Austrian Monarchy.

Held: That the claim must be dismissed. In Article 4 of the Law of 12 November, 1918, the Austrian Republic expressly rejected any legal succession to the defunct Monarchy. It is not generally bound to recognise claims which have arisen against the former Monarchy. There is no rule of international law which lays down that the new State of Austria is liable either jointly or severally for the obligations of the former State. The distribution of assets and liabilities of the defunct State must be decided by an international agreement between the various States which have arisen in the territory of the former Monarchy. According to the existing law the Republic of

Austria can be sued in respect of claims which have arisen against the former Monarchy only in those cases in which it has expressly announced that it succeeds in the individual case as successor to the former legal relation. [Report: *Sammlung der Erkenntnisse des österreichischen Verfassungsgerichtshofes*, vol. I (1919), No. 9, p. 17.]

NOTE.—See also to the same effect the decision of the Constitutional Court of 20 October, 1919, Nos. 253 and 254; *ibid.*, Nos. 18 and 19, pp. 36, 37.

State Succession—Succession Liabilities—Austrian Empire—Austrian Republic. **Case No. 39**

AUSTRIAN EMPIRE (SUCCESSION) CASE.

Austria, Constitutional Court. 11 *March*, 1919. (*No.* 18.)

THE FACTS.—This was a claim by a teacher against the Ministry of Education for payment of certain bonuses due to him for his work as teacher of gymnastics from 1 October, 1917, to the end of September, 1918.

Held: That the action must be dismissed. The claim was one against the Austrian Empire. That State was now defunct. "In the territory of the Austrian State there have arisen "national States—new States which are not successors of the "old State and liable for its obligations. It is true that "according to the principles of international law in cases in "which a territory is ceded by one State to another or when "several States arise out of one State, the State acquiring the "territory or the new States are bound to take over an appro-"priate part of the obligations of the former State in propor-"tion to the assets which it or they have taken over and which "have been created as the result of the activity or under the "protection of the former State. However, in individual cases "both the taking over of the liability and the extent to which "it has been taken over must be determined by international "agreement—in this case between the national States in the "former Austrian territory. For this purpose there had been "set up a Liquidation Commission composed of representatives "of those States and entrusted with the function of determin-"ing the state of the assets and liabilities. Only after the "share of liability of the German Austrian Republic has been "determined will the plaintiff be entitled to bring an action." [Report: *Sammlung der Erkenntnisse des österreichischen Verfassungsgerichtshofes*, vol. I (1919), No. 2, p. 5.]

NOTE.—See also to the same effect decisions of the Constitutional

Case No. 39 contd. Court of 5 May, 1919, No. 119, *ibid.*, No. 4, p. 8; of 6 May, 1919, No. 124, *ibid.*, No. 7, p. 12; of 8 May, 1919, No. 121, *ibid.*, No. 11, p. 22; of 8 May, 1919, No. 133, *ibid.*, No. 15, p. 28; of 20 October, 1919, No. 253, *ibid.*, No. 18, p. 36. See also the decisions of the Constitutional Court of 1921, *ibid.*, No. 29, p. 64; No. 30, p. 67; No. 69, p. 149; No. 70, p. 150; No. 73, p. 185.

V.—Respect of Private Rights

Case No. 40

State Succession—Private Rights—Whether Affected by Dismemberment of States.

STATE SUCCESSION (NOTARIAL ACT) CASE.

Austria, Supreme Court in Civil Matters. 13 *May*, 1919. (*R. II* 52/19.)

THE FACTS.—The plaintiff and the defendant concluded on 2 May, 1918, in Lemberg (part of the former Austrian Empire now forming part of Poland), a contract of sale in the form of a notarial act with an execution clause. The Vienna Court entrusted with the execution ordered the execution after the downfall of the Austrian Empire. The debtor contended that the title to execution was a foreign title and that therefore execution in the Austrian Republic was not permissible. The Court below decided against the debtor.

Held by the Supreme Court: That the appeal must be dismissed. When the notarial act was made, Lemberg formed part of Austrian territory. "Relations of private law are not "affected as the result of extinction of States. Courts survive "political changes. The dismemberment of the former terri"tory of Austria cannot effect any changes in the execution "of validly acquired titles." [Report: *Entscheidungen des Obersten Gerichtshofes in Zivilrechtssachen*, vol. I (1919), No. 33, p. 115.]

VII.—International Conventions

Case No. 41

State Succession—Treaties—Tacit Renewal of Treaties—Czechoslovakia and Germany.

CUSTOMS HOUSE (STATE SUCCESSION) CASE.

Germany, Reichsgericht in Criminal Matters. 12 *May*, 1922.

THE FACTS.—In Article 8 of the Treaty of Commerce between Germany and Austria-Hungary, concluded on

6 December, 1891, and renewed on 26 January, 1905, the parties agreed that their respective customs houses on the frontier should, so far as possible, be established in one place so as to simplify the proceedings in the collection of customs. After the dismemberment of Austria in 1918 and the establishment of the Czechoslovak State, Germany and Czechoslovakia, without concluding a new commercial treaty, maintained the régime of the common customs houses in a number of places.

In the present case the accused, who was charged with an attempt at smuggling through a customs house at the frontier, relied on the contention that as no treaty of commerce had been concluded between Czechoslovakia and Germany, the regulations obtaining hitherto on the matter were no longer existent.

Held, on final appeal on a point of law: That the conviction must stand. It was true that as the result of the dissolution of Austria-Hungary one of the parties to the Treaty ceased to exist, but this did not necessarily result in abolishing the legal position created by the Treaty. The Czechoslovak State was not the legal successor of Austria-Hungary, and it was not bound by Article 8 of the Treaty. But there was nothing to prevent either Czechoslovakia or Germany from maintaining the contractual relation, at least in regard to certain points. The continuation of this relation could have been expressly agreed; but it could also have been maintained in consequence of a tacit declaration of will. This actually happened as the result of the Czechoslovak State deciding not to interfere with the activities, on its territory, of the German customs house. As both parties have thus shown that they do not wish any change in the legal position obtaining hitherto, it must be assumed that there has taken place no change either in international or municipal law. [Report: *E.R.S.*, vol. 57, p. 61.]

NOTE.—See also *Juristische Wochenschrift*, 1920, p. 403, for a decision of the District Court of Beuthen (Upper Silesia), of 12 February, 1920, granting legal aid to a Czechoslovak subject. The Court relied, *inter alia*, on the Hague Convention on Procedure in Civil Cases of 17 July, 1905, to which both Germany and Austria-Hungary were parties. The Court assumed that Czechoslovakia, so far as the territories formerly belonging to Austria were concerned, was the successor of the Austro-Hungarian Monarchy in regard to the provisions of the said Hague Convention. But see the decision of the Upper District Court of Berlin of 2 December, 1919, *ibid.*, p. 393, in which the Court, notwithstanding the terms of the Hague Convention of 1905, required security

Case No. 41 *contd.* for costs from a person domiciled in Galicia (formerly belonging to Austria, now part of Poland) on the ground that the Austrian Monarchy had ceased to exist and that at the time of the judgment the fate of Galicia was still undecided. And see the decision of the same Court of 23 May, 1919, *ibid.*, 1919, p. 936, refusing to recognise a judgment given by a court in Galicia on the ground, *inter alia*, that, although Galicia had become part of Poland, the legal position of that province was not quite clear.

Case No. 42 **State Succession—International Conventions—Dismemberment—Switzerland and Article 287 of the Treaty of Versailles.**

IN RE M. & O.

Switzerland, Obergericht (*Court of Appeal*) *of the Canton of Zürich.* 28 *September*, 1921.

THE FACTS.—The President of the Commercial Court of the Canton of Zürich ordered the firm M. & O., of Poland, who had started an action, to give security for costs on the ground that the firm was established (*domiziliert*) in a country which was not a party to the Hague Convention on Civil Procedure. The firm appealed, and relied upon Article 287 of the Treaty of Versailles, which laid down that the contracting parties should apply, as between themselves, the provisions of the Hague Convention.

Held : That the appeal failed. (*a*) Poland had not become a party to the Hague Convention by virtue of the above provision of the Treaty of Versailles. Poland was not represented at the Fourth Conference concerning private international law. According to Article 27 of the Convention she cannot by unilateral declaration become a party to the Convention, unless she has been admitted to it by a new international agreement. Such an admission cannot, however, be made by the Peace Treaty, to which Switzerland is not a party.

(*b*) The position would be different only if Poland could be regarded according to the rules of international law as the successor State of those States which were parties to the Convention and whose territories form the present Polish State. However, Poland was created by a fusion of German and Austrian territories with parts of Russia. No dismemberment of Russia took place, though parts of Russia broke off. Poland, as such, did not exist before she gained her independence. The theory of international law points to the conclusion that a new State which has been formed by separation from another State derives neither rights nor obligations from the treaties entered into by the older State. The Hague Convention of 1905 is not a treaty which, as to either obligations or rights, related to particular parts of State territory, as, for instance, might be the case in a treaty relative to river navigation. [Report: *Blätter für zürcherische Rechtsprechung*, vol. XX, p. 354.]

As to the existence of Poland, contrast *Republic* v. *Felsenstadt*, Case No. 16.—[Ed.]

State Succession — International Conventions — Dismemberment of States—Czechoslovakia as Party to International Conventions Concluded by Austria-Hungary. **Case No. 43**

In re J. Z.

Switzerland, Obergericht (*Court of Appeal*) *of the Canton of Zürich*, 16 *February*, 1921.

The Facts.—J. Z., of Althabendorf (Bohemia), began an action against I. R., of Zürich, before the District Court of Zürich. The Court fixed a date by which the plaintiff was to give security for costs. The plaintiff appealed, contending that as Czechoslovakia was formerly a part of Austria-Hungary, which was a party to the Hague Convention on Civil Procedure, the Czechoslovak State continued to be a party to that Convention.

Held: That the appeal failed. Czechoslovakia had not declared her accession to the Hague Convention on Civil Procedure. It could therefore only be argued that this State is a party to the Convention by virtue of State succession. However, according to information given by the Swiss Legal Department, the Czechoslovak Republic refuses to be regarded as the successor of former Austria and holds that she is no party to treaties entered into by Austria-Hungary. In view of this information it is impossible to accept the view that the Hague Convention on Civil Procedure is applicable to a citizen of Czechoslovakia. [Report: *Blätter für zürcherische Rechtsprechung*, vol. XXI, p. 23.]

State Succession—Treaties—Poland and the Berne Convention of 1890. **Case No. 44**

Feldmann and Feldmann *v.* Polish State Treasury.

Poland, Supreme Court, Third Division. 8 *February*, 1921.

The Facts.—In October, 1918, certain goods were sent by railway from Germany to Cracow (then under

Case No. 44 *contd.*

Austrian rule). Both Germany and Austria were parties to the Berne Convention of 14 October, 1890. The goods arrived in Cracow in December, 1918, *i.e.* nearly two months after the re-establishment of the Polish State. Some of them had been stolen outside Polish territory, as was attested by the authorities in Vienna before the remainder of the goods entered Polish territory. The transportation document was stamped at the Polish frontier station. The plaintiffs sued the Polish Treasury (which had taken over the Austrian State Railways), claiming to base its responsibility on the Berne Convention, to which Poland became a party much later. The District Court at Cracow having decided for the plaintiffs, and the Court of Appeal of Cracow for the defendant, the Supreme Court

Held on appeal: For the defendant. The Polish railway official who had stamped the transportation document could not thereby make Poland liable for thefts committed outside Poland, nor impose on Poland obligations under the Berne Convention to which she was not a party. Although Austria had been a party to the Berne Convention, that Convention did not continue in force with regard to territories formerly Austrian but now under the sovereignty of a State not a party to that Convention. [Report: O.S.P., I, No. 16.]

Case No. 45

State Succession—International Conventions—Real Unions—Hungary as Party to the International Convention on Civil Procedure Concluded by Austria-Hungary.

IN RE UNGARISCHE KRIEGSPRODUKTEN-AKTIENGESELLSCHAFT.

Switzerland, Obergericht (Court of Appeal) of the Canton of Zürich. 5 *July*, 1920.

THE FACTS.—The President of the Commercial Court in the Canton of Zürich ordered the Ungarische Kriegsprodukten-Aktiengesellschaft of Budapest to give security for costs. The company appealed on the ground that Hungary was a party to the Hague Convention on Civil Procedure.

Held: That the appeal must be allowed. Austria-Hungary signed on 23 November, 1908, the Convention on Civil Procedure revised at The Hague on 17 July, 1905, and deposited the instrument of ratification on 24 April, 1909. By virtue of the Hungarian Act of Parliament (No. XII of 1865-67) "concerning the affairs common to the countries of the Hungarian "Crown and other countries under His Majesty's rule and the "method of their administration," it was only the conduct of the foreign affairs of the countries of the Hungarian Crown and other countries or provinces of the Emperor, that was to be common. But each of the two States of the Union had international personality, and each of them was a contracting State in the international treaties concluded by the common organs. Neither Austria nor Hungary, as a result of the dissolution of the real union existing between the two States, has ceased to be a party to the Convention on Civil Procedure. Similarly, no importance can be attached to the fact that the Hungarian territory has been diminished as the result of the Peace Treaty.[1] The present Hungarian State is still the same person of international law as that which adhered to the Hague Convention on Civil Procedure. [Report: *Blätter für zürcherische Rechtsprechung*, vol. XX, p. 267.]

State Succession—The Austro-Hungarian Empire—Extradition Treaties—Germany and Czechoslovakia.

See Case No. 182 (*Extradition* (*Germany and Czechoslovakia*) *Case*).

VIII.—In Matters of Administration. Officials

State Succession—In Matters of Administration—Succession in regard to Officials—Conditions under which Officials of the Former Austrian State Could Become Officials of the Czechoslovak State. **Case No. 46**

AUSTRIAN OFFICIALS (SUCCESSION) CASE.

Czechoslovakia, Supreme Administrative Court.
27 *March*, 1922. *No.* 2803.

THE FACTS.—The plaintiff, who had been since 1909 an official of the former Austrian Ministry of Commerce, demanded from the Czechoslovak authorities payment of a certain sum of money as salary for a certain period after the coming into existence of the Czechoslovak

[1] The Court referred here to Jellinek, *Allgemeine Staatslehre* (1900), p. 252; v. Liszt, *Völkerrecht* (1st ed.), p. 123, No. iii.

Case No. 46 *contd.*

State (28 October, 1918). His demand was dismissed on the ground that he had not been taken over into the service of the Czechoslovak State.

Held, on appeal, by the Supreme Administrative Court: That the appeal must be dismissed. The appeal was based on the opinion that the plaintiff became on 28 October, 1918, *ipso facto* an official of the Czechoslovak State with the same rank as he enjoyed hitherto. This opinion was erroneous.

The Czechoslovak State did not automatically enter as legal successor into the public service relationships of the old Austrian State before the revolution. According to Law No. 15 of 25 January, 1914, concerning the appointment and the position of officials—a law adopted by the Czechoslovak State as the result of Law No. 11 [1] of 28 October, 1918—a public service relationship with regard to the Czechoslovak State could as a rule be established only by an appointment by a competent organ of the Czechoslovak State. [Report: Boh. 1255 adm.]

Case No. 47

State Succession—Duty to Take Over Officials—Austrian Republic — Whether Universal Successor of Austrian Empire.

POST OFFICE OFFICIAL (AUSTRIA) SUCCESSION CASE.

Austria, Constitutional Court. 8 *June*, 1920.
(*No. A.* 4/20.)

THE FACTS.—The plaintiff was, on 15 July, 1918, retired on pension. He maintained that he was not pensioned in accordance with the law, and asked for the payment of a higher pension corresponding to that to which he would have been entitled if he had been taken over by the Austrian Republic.

Held: That the claim must be dismissed. The plaintiff was retired by decree of the Imperial and Royal Post Office Savings Office on 15 July, 1918, that is to say, at a time when the Austrian Republic did not exist. The Republic acquiesced in the legal position created by the former Monarchy by continuing the payment of the plaintiff's pension. However, the Republic is not the universal legal successor of the former State. It continues the relation of service between acting officials of the defunct State only in regard to such officials

[1] See *Annual Digest*, 1925-1926, Case No. 9, footnote 1.

as it has taken over individually and expressly. This was not the case with the plaintiff. Accordingly, even if his retirement was not effected in accordance with the law he could not claim payment of sums to which he would have been entitled if he had been taken over by the Republic as an active official. He had no legal right to be taken over. [Report : *Sammlung der Erkenntnisse des österreichischen Verfassungsgerichtshofes*, vol. II (1920), No. 50, p. 95.]

NOTE.—See also to the same effect the decisions of the Constitutional Court of 9 June, 1920, Z.A. 9/20, *ibid.*, No. 54, p. 101, and of 26 February, 1920, Z. 18, *ibid.*, No. 43, p. 84.

See also the decision of the Administrative Court (*Verwaltungsgerichtshof*) of 12 April, 1921, No. 1751. In this case an official of the former Monarchy claimed that he had a right to be taken over by the Republic on the ground that according to the Peace Treaty of St. Germain the Austrian Republic was the universal successor of the former Monarchy. It was held that the action must be dismissed as there was no provision in the Treaty of St. Germain which could be interpreted to the effect that the Austrian Republic was to be regarded as the successor of the Austrian Monarchy. Whenever the Treaty intended to impose upon the Austrian Republic obligations of the Austrian Monarchy it said so expressly. It followed that there is no question of universal succession. [Report : *Sammlung der Erkenntnisse des Verwaltungsgerichtshofes*, vol. XLV (1921), Administrative Part, No. 12796, p. 37.]

State Succession—Binding Force of Administrative Measures —Limitation of Rights of Proprietors Made in Interest of Predecessor State. **Case No. 48**

MATYS *v.* NIPANICZ.

Poland, Supreme Court, First Division. 14 *October*, 1920.

THE FACTS.—Certain real property, taken from Catholic monasteries, had been alienated by the Russian Government under the condition (which was entered in the land registry) that it might thenceforth pass only into the hands of persons of Russian descent. The defendant having on 1 August, 1918, sold the property to the plaintiff (a Pole), the District Court of Warsaw (in charge of the land registry) ordered the execution of the sale to be suspended until the condition entered in the land registry should have been removed. The Court of Appeal of Warsaw held, on appeal, that the execution of the sale should be suspended until the question of the right of owners of Russian descent to

Case No. 48 contd.

dispose of such property shall have been determined by legislation. On appeal to the Supreme Court,

Held : That since the condition entered in the land registry had been established solely in the political interest of the Russian State, it had lost all force at the moment when Poland regained her independence. [Report: Zb. O.S.N., 1920, No. 48.]

IX.—Binding Force of Laws and Judgments of Courts

Case No. 49

State Succession—Binding Force of Laws—Distinction between Private and Political Rights.

PORTO RICO RAILWAY, LIGHT AND POWER CO. *v.* AMADOR *ET AL.*

United States District Court for Porto Rico. 27 January, 1919.

THE FACTS.—This was a suit by a duly licensed street car company of San Juan, Porto Rico, to restrain the defendants from operating jitneys as common carriers without a licence. The Spanish civil law was the private law of Porto Rico. The Jones Act (39 U.S. Stat. L. 964) had provided that all grants of licences in Porto Rico should be made by a public service commission. The defendants claimed that they were engaging in this business by common law right and needed no licence.

Held: Against the defendants. " Although private rights " and civil law were retained in Porto Rico by the will of the " American government when it succeeded to the sovereignty " formerly held by Spain, political rights of all kinds were " thenceforward to be the same in Porto Rico as on the main- " land of the United States. . . . It is only this class of rights " which is at issue in the case at bar, and as to them whatever " is law on the mainland is to be held law in Porto Rico except " as changed by statute. Whatever rights exist as to the use " of public places in Porto Rico are to be decided according " to the principles of the freer common law prevailing in the " United States." (11 P.R. Fed. 170, 175.) [Report: 11 P.R. Fed. 170.]

State Succession—Binding Force of Laws—Political Laws—When Contrary to the Fundamental Principles of Law of the Succeeding State. **Case No. 50**

PEOPLE *v.* PERFECTO.

United States, Supreme Court of the Philippine Islands. 4 *October*, 1922.

THE FACTS.—The Spanish Penal Code, Article 256, in force in the Philippines before the American occupation, punished " any person who, by . . . writing, shall " defame, abuse, or insult any Minister of the Crown or " other person in authority." The Philippine Commission had enacted a complete Libel Law which did not make this act criminal. In the United States such attacks on authorities were permitted if not seditious. Perfecto, the editor of *La Nación,* published certain comments criticising severely the Philippine Senate. He was found guilty by the municipal Court, and again by the Court of First Instance of Manila, of violating Article 256. On appeal,

Held: That the judgment must be reversed and the defendant acquitted. The majority of the Court held the Article to be still in force, except as to ministers of the crown who were now non-existent in the Philippines; and except as to calumny, etc., by writing or printing, against an authority in the performance of his duties or arising out of that performance, the relevant provisions in relation to which matters had been repealed by the Commission's Libel Law. The minority concurred, but held that the Article had entirely lost its effect, as being " contrary to the genius and fundamental principles " of the American character and system of government " (43 P.I. 887, 901); it was classed with those laws of a political character which ceased upon the transfer of sovereignty. [Report: 43 P.I. 887.]

State Succession—Binding Force of Laws—Extent of—Rules of Common Law in the Panama Canal Zone. **Case No. 51**

PANAMA RAILROAD COMPANY *v.* BOSSE.

United States Supreme Court. 3 *March*, 1919.

THE FACTS.—Bosse brought an action in the District Court of the Panama Canal Zone for injuries caused by the

Case No. 51 ***contd.***

negligence of the Railroad Company's bus chauffeur. The judgment was for the plaintiff. This judgment was affirmed by the United States Circuit Court of Appeals for the Fifth Circuit. (239 Fed. 303.) On writ of error to the Supreme Court, it was contended that the common law responsibility of master for servant did not apply in the Canal Zone. Pursuant to an Act of Congress of 1904, § 2 (33 U.S. Stat. L. 429), the President by executive order had continued in force until changed " the laws of the land, with which " the inhabitants are familiar, and which were in force " on February 26, 1904." This was construed as continuing in force the Civil Code of the Republic of Panama. In 1912, Congress ratified and confirmed the order. (37 U.S. Stat. L. 560, 561.) It was contended that the Civil Code had been continued in force, as construed in civil law countries, and consequently that the doctrine of *respondeat superior* did not apply.

Held : That the judgment must be affirmed. As early as 1910, the Supreme Court of the Canal Zone had announced that it would look to the common law in construing Colombian statutes. Delivering the Opinion of the Court, Mr. Justice Holmes said : " The President's order continuing the law then " in force was merely the embodiment of the rule that a change " of sovereignty does not put an end to existing private law, " and the ratification of that order by the Act of August 24, " 1912, no more fastened upon the Zone a specific interpreta- " tion of the former Civil Code than does a statute adopting " the common law fasten upon a territory a specific doctrine " of the English Courts." (249 U.S. 41, 44.) The population of the Canal Zone had so changed under the American régime that the old law was no longer familiar to the inhabitants. " Whatever may be thought of the unqualified principle " that a master must answer for the torts of his servant com- " mitted within the scope of his employment, probably there " are few rules of the common law so familiar to all, educated " and uneducated alike." (249 U.S. 41, 45.) It was held that the language of the Civil Code was " not necessarily incon- " sistent with the common-law rule." [Reports : 239 Fed. 303 ; 249 U.S. 41 ; Dickinson, *Cases*, 975.]

NOTE.—See 17 M.L.R. 497.

State Succession—Judgments Given by the Courts of the Predecessor. **Case No. 52**

(POLISH) STATE TREASURY *v.* KURZROCK.

Poland, Supreme Court, Third Division. 13 *September*, 1921.

THE FACTS.—In 1915 the defendant had been ordered by the District Court of Vienna (the judgment being confirmed, on appeal, by the Court of Appeal of Vienna) to pay certain sums to the Austrian State Treasury (Army Division). After the re-establishment of Poland, the Polish State Treasury, in 1921, applied to the local court at Kozowa (now in Poland), the place of the defendant's residence, for execution of the judgment. The local court granted the application. On appeal by the defendant, the District Court at Brzezany dismissed the application of the Polish Treasury, mainly on the ground that it had no title to collect debts of the Austrian Treasury. On appeal to the Supreme Court,

Held, dismissing the appeal: That execution must be refused. Judgments of the District and Appeal Courts of Vienna, while in 1915 they were judgments of national courts from the point of view of the Court of Kozowa, must now be considered as foreign judgments. The question whether the Treaty of St. Germain is binding on the courts of Poland before having been published in the Journal of Laws is immaterial. [Report: O.S.P., I, No. 496.]

NOTE.—See *Annual Digest*, 1925-1926, Case No. 72.

State Succession—Miscellaneous—In Matters of Taxation—Liability to Taxation by the Ceding State—Taxation Claims Validly Arisen Prior to the Cession.

See Case No 57 (*Change of Sovereignty* (*Taxation*) *Case*).

PART III

STATE TERRITORY

A. STATE TERRITORY IN GENERAL

I.—Nature of Territorial Sovereignty

Territory—Customs Territory and Political Territory—Saar Territory—Whether Part of Germany. **Case No. 53**

SAAR TERRITORY (USURY DECREE) CASE.

Germany, Reichsgericht in Criminal Matters. 2 *March*, 1922.

THE FACTS.—This was a prosecution on the ground of the contravention of Article 2 of the German Usury Decree, which prohibits the export of certain articles from German territory, and of Article 134 of the Customs Law, which relates to prohibited exports from German customs territory (*Zollinland*) to foreign customs territory (*Zollausland*). The goods in question had been exported to the Saar Territory. The accused appealed on the ground that the Saar was not foreign territory.

Held, on final appeal on a point of law: That the conviction must stand.

(*a*) According to § 31 (2) of the Annex to Articles 45-50 of the Treaty of Versailles the Saar Territory is incorporated into the French customs system, and must therefore be regarded as foreign customs territory.

(*b*) It was doubtless true that politically the Saar Territory belonged to Germany seeing that the Treaty of Versailles had not separated it from Germany. In Article 49 of the Treaty Germany only renounced the government of that territory in favour of the League of Nations as trustee. However, the Saar Territory cannot be regarded as German territory for the purpose of the Usury Decree. The purpose of the latter was to secure to the Federal Government control over important articles. This purpose would be frustrated if the goods were exported to a territory over which the Federal Government exercises no control and from which the goods may be exported to yet another State. [Report: *E.R.S.*, vol. 56, p. 287.]

NOTE.—See also to the same effect the decision of the Bavarian *Oberstes Landesgericht* in Criminal Matters of 16 December, 1920, *Juristische Wochenschrift*, 1921, p. 583.

Territory—State Territory Proper and Customs Territory—Territorial Waters as Customs Territory—German Law.

See Case No. 63 (*Territorial Waters (Germany) Case*).

II.—Acquisition of Territorial Sovereignty

i.—Accretion and Accession. Avulsion

Acquisition of Territorial Sovereignty—Avulsion—River Boundaries.

See Case No. 60 (*State of Arkansas* v. *State of Mississippi*).

iii.—Cession. Conditional Cession. Plebiscite

Case No. 54

State Territory—Cession—Requirement of Formal Delivery of Possession—Whether Forming Part of International Law—Formal Delivery in regard to Territories Awarded by the Arbitrator—Declarative or Constitutive Effect of the Arbitral Award—The Principle *uti possidetis juris*—Application to Cession and to Arbitral Awards—Effectiveness of the Latter—Admissibility of Partial Executions—Tacit Consent of the Parties—Absence of Protest—Legal Nature of Boundary Commissions.

COLOMBIA AND VENEZUELA.

Swiss Federal Council as Arbitrator. 24 *March*, 1922.

THE FACTS.—On 14 September, 1881, Colombia and Venezuela concluded an arbitration agreement in which they submitted for decision by the King of Spain, acting as an "*arbitre juge de droit,*" a boundary dispute which had existed between the two countries since 1830, *i.e.* since the date of the establishment of their independence. Each of the disputant parties admitted the applicability of the principle *uti possidetis juris*, that is to say, of the rule that the boundary between them must be identical with the boundaries as laid down by the Spanish authorities between the respective territorial units prior to the establishment of the independence of the Latin-American Republics.[1] However, they disagreed as to the details of the former Spanish administrative boundaries. In a subsequent supplementary

[1] As to the principle *uti possidetis* as forming part of the fundamental laws of the two countries, see below, p. 87.

agreement of 15 February, 1886, which conferred upon the Spanish Government the exercise of arbitral functions in view of the demise of King Alphonse XII, the parties entreated the arbitrator to fix the frontier which "would approximate as closely as possible to "the available documents, in case these documents "should not be sufficiently clear." The award was given on 16 March, 1891, by the Queen Regent in the name of her son Alphonse XIII, who was then a minor. The arbitrator awarded to Colombia certain territories in the possession of Venezuela. Subsequently difficulties arose between the two States as to the execution of the award. While Colombia demanded to be permitted to take possession, without further formalities, of the territories awarded to her, Venezuela insisted on delays said to be necessitated by her internal law requiring the participation of her Legislature. Difficulties also arose as to the details of the delimitation of the frontier. After abortive negotiation aiming at the settlement of the controversy by a comprehensive *quid pro quo* in a commercial treaty, a mixed commission was appointed in 1899 charged with the task of laying down the details of the frontier. This commission, operating in two sections, agreed on certain points, but disagreed on others. In 1901 its work was suspended and never resumed. Negotiations between the two countries continued until 1915, when Colombia sent her engineers and functionaries to some of the disputed territories on the ground that they formed indisputably part of Colombia either by virtue of the principal award or in consequence of an agreement reached before the Mixed Commission. Venezuela refused to admit that such partial execution of the award of the King of Spain was permissible, and proposed that the entire question of the execution of the award be submitted to an arbitral tribunal entitled to proceed by way of summary procedure as laid down in Chapter IV of the Convention for the Pacific Settlement of International Disputes of 1907. This proposal was accepted, and on 3 November, 1916, the two States concluded an arbitration agreement in which the Swiss Federal Council was asked to decide, *inter alia*, whether, as maintained by Colombia, the arbitral award of 1891 may be executed in part, or

Case No. 54 ***contd.***

whether, as maintained by Venezuela, the right to occupy the awarded territories was dependent upon the simultaneous execution of the whole sentence. (As to other questions submitted to the arbitrator see Case No. 262.)

Before the arbitrator, Colombia contended that there was no principle of international law prescribing the inadmissibility of the execution of a treaty or of an arbitral award relating to frontiers; that such a principle would lead to absurd consequences, inasmuch as it might leave an extended boundary between two States unsettled for the mere reason that they had been unable to arrive at agreement in regard to an unimportant sector of the frontier; that there were historical examples of delimitation by stages [1]; that the award of 1891 indirectly recognised the principle of divisibility by referring to various types of sectors of the disputed frontier; that that principle was recognised in the negotiations and particular agreements between Colombia and Venezuela; that she (Colombia) was entitled to occupy without formalities the territories indisputably belonging to her by virtue of the award, in particular when that award was based on the principle *uti possidetis* recognised by both States; that there was no principle of international law enjoining formal handing over of territory in case of cession; that, even if there existed such a principle, it would apply only to cessions in which territory passed to a new sovereign, but not to cases in which the award is merely declaratory, *i.e.* confirming a pre-existing right; and that the authority of the principle of *res judicata* requires that the judgment should be executed promptly and as completely as possible, even if this can be done only by stages.

On the part of Venezuela, it was contended that the award constituted an indivisible whole; that to execute the award in regard to certain sections of the frontier only would amount to satisfying certain rights under the award and leaving other rights unsatisfied; that the award had not established priority for certain rights; that although the actual delimitation may have to proceed in stages, the execution of the sentence

[1] Colombia referred here, *inter alia*, to Moore, I, p. 219, and to the Treaty of 1886, between Bolivia and Peru, Martens, *N.R.G.*, II ser., XV, p. 770.

must constitute an indivisible whole; that according to international jurists like Rivier, Ortolan, Nys, Pradier-Fodéré, Heffter and others, an arbitral award does not operate as a transfer of territory; that the award creates merely inchoate rights which must be determined by means of delimitation; that the award is not self-executing, and that in the absence of an international organ charged with the execution of arbitral awards their fulfilment is left "to the honour and "integrity of the Parties"; that the same applies to the decision of mixed boundary commissions; and that unilateral execution of the award by one party, far from constituting a legal act, is an act of hostility.

Held: That the Venezuelan contention must be rejected. The question put in the arbitration agreement of 1916—namely, whether either of the disputant parties is entitled "to take "possession of the territories which are given to it by the "Spanish award and which are clearly defined either by nature "or in consequence of the work of the delimitation commis-"sion"—must be answered in the affirmative. The authority of arbitral awards requires that they should be executed as far as possible.

1. By virtue of the principle *uti possidetis juris* of 1810, which was recognised by both parties in their respective Constitutions and in the arbitration agreements of 1881 and 1916, they must be regarded as having had since 1810 the sovereignty over, and the possession of, the territories which had previously formed part of Spanish possessions.[1]

2. Article 3 of the arbitration agreement of 1881 provided expressly that the award by the Spanish Crown shall become executory by its publication in the official journal of the Spanish Government. The award was duly published in this manner. Neither the arbitration agreement nor the award provide for a formal handing over of the territories in question.

3. It is true that international law shows numerous examples of boundary treaties containing provisions as to formalities to be observed in the handing over of territories,

[1] The arbitrator pointed out that the parties themselves recognised in certain reciprocal declarations that they had *ipso facto* sovereignty over the territories belonging to them by virtue of the frontiers as existing in 1810. Thus in a Declaration of 21 November, 1896, it was provided that in case the contemplated treaty settling the controversy should be rejected "each of "the two Republics will assume the position and the rights recognized in "the arbitral award of 1891, and will be entitled to take possession of the "territories awarded to it." (*Sentence Arbitrale*, p. 102.)

Case No. 54 ***contd.***

but there are no absolute or obligatory rules concerning any such formalities. There are on record cases of cession and transfer of territory, in which no formal delivery took place.[1] The instances, invoked by Venezuela, of formal delivery and of taking possession of territories have reference to real cessions of territories transferred by a State which renounces sovereignty to a State which acquires it. Accordingly, even if there existed—which is not the case—a rule of international law requiring formal taking of possession in cases of transfer of territory, that principle would not be applicable to boundary relations between Colombia and Venezuela. For by virtue of the principle *uti possidetis juris*, a principle accepted by the two disputant parties and sanctioned in the award, the cession has taken place in the present case: each of the two States is presumed to have possessed since 1810 sovereignty over the territories awarded to it by the arbitrator. "A State which occupied a territory the sovereignty over "which has been recognized as belonging to another State has "no right to insist on formal delivery of territory which it retains "without legal right; its holding of the territory in question "has ceased to be legitimate with the entry into force of the "sentence. The State which continues to occupy the territory "in contradiction to the terms of the award has only one duty, "that is to say, to evacuate the territory in question. The "other State has the right to proceed to occupation subject "to such duties of courtesy as may be required by the necessity "to avoid conflicts and to inform inhabitants" (at p. 104).

4. Since the arbitral award was given in 1891 the two States have by their acts acknowledged the principle of the partial execution of the award. Both Venezuela and Colombia have occupied some of the territories held to belong to them. When in 1907 Colombia ceded to Brazil part of these territories Venezuela did not protest against the cession; neither did she protest in 1900 against the Colombian occupation of the Orinoco basin. If the arbitrator were now to adopt the view that the parties ought to restore to one another territories which they occupied by virtue of the award of 1891, then that would mean to impose upon them the duty not only to refrain from occupying what has been recognised as belonging to them, but also to restore for an indefinite period their own territory to an irregular possessor. "Thirty years have

[1] The arbitrator referred here to the cession of Lombardy by Austria to France in 1860 and to its retrocession by France to Italy, to the cession of Venice to France in 1866 and to its retrocession to Italy, and to several cases of cession under the Treaties of Versailles and St. Germain.

"elapsed since the Spanish award was given; that award "cannot indefinitely remain in the nature of a juridical "abstraction" (at p. 106).

5. As to the question which territories may be occupied, there is no doubt that the right of occupation extends to the territories defined by natural frontiers. As to other frontiers, the right of occupation extends to territories in regard to which the Mixed Commission of 1900 and 1901 arrived at a unanimous decision. According to the practice adopted by the two States mixed commissions have arbitral powers; they are not merely technical experts. Accordingly, their decisions are final and not subject to revision. The artificial frontiers unanimously laid down by them are on the same footing as natural frontiers. [Report: *Sentence Arbitrale,* Neuchâtel, Imprimerie Paul Attinger, 1922, pp. 46-112.[1]]

Territory—Cession—Annexation—Status of Occupied Territory Prior to Formal Cession—Dissolution of Austro-Hungarian Monarchy—Italian Provinces.

See Case No. 319 (*Galatiolo* v. *Senes*).

IV.—Effects of Changes of Sovereignty

[See also Part II, State Succession.]

Cession—Effect of—On Pending Actions—Loss of German Sovereignty over Danzig—Competence of a German Court of Appeal—Action against the German State. **Case No. 55**

Pending Actions (Danzig) Case (II).

Germany, Reichsgericht in Civil Matters. 6 *July,* 1922.

The Facts.—This was a claim for damages against the German State arising out of contracts made in April and May, 1919, between the plaintiff and the Danzig branch of a German administrative department for the disposal of governmental property (*Reichsverwertungsamt*). A Danzig court gave in December, 1919, judgment in favour of the defendant. The plaintiff appealed on 2 February, 1920. On 10 January,

[1] The *Sentence Arbitrale,* the Cases, Counter-cases and other documents relating to this arbitration have been published in various documents in the years 1918-1923. The *Sentence Arbitrale* is printed in a separate volume published in 1922 in Neuchâtel. The editors are greatly indebted to the Department of Foreign Affairs of the Swiss Federal Council for putting at their disposal all these documents.

Case No. 55 *contd.*

1920, the Treaty of Versailles entered into force and Danzig ceased to form part of Germany. The question then arose whether the Court of Appeal in Marienwerder in Prussia, which would have otherwise been the competent Court of Appeal, was competent to decide the appeal.

Held, on final appeal on a point of law: (*a*) If the present action were one between two private persons the German Court would no longer have jurisdiction. However,

(*b*) As according to principles of international law a State is not subject to the jurisdiction of foreign courts, and as the German State is the defendant in the present case, the German Court of Appeal continued to have jurisdiction. [Report: *Fontes Juris Gentium, Decisions of the German Supreme Court*, No. 268.]

NOTE.—See, however, as to (*a*), the case below (No. 56).

Case No. 56

Change of Sovereignty—Effect on Private Rights—Pending Actions—Appeals—Danzig and German Courts—Action against German Treasury.

PENDING ACTIONS (DANZIG) CASE (I).

Germany, Reichsgericht in Civil Matters. 1 *July*, 1921.

THE FACTS.—In September, 1915, the plaintiff concluded a contract with the authorities of the Seventeenth German Army Corps in the Danzig district concerning the employment and accommodation of a number of prisoners of war. The Army authorities undertook to pay the plaintiff the sum of 15 pfennigs per day per head. From 30 August, 1916, to 1 December, 1919, the Army authorities made no payment. The plaintiff brought the present action against the German State Treasury for the payment of the arrears due under the contract. The District Court in Danzig dismissed the claim on 6 November, 1919. The plaintiff appealed on 3 December, 1919, to the Court of Appeal in Marienwerder in Prussia, which, on 21 October, 1920, declared that German courts were no longer competent to deal with the matter.

Held, on final appeal on a point of law: That the judgment of the Court of Appeal must be set aside and that German courts had jurisdiction.

(*a*) The Court of Appeal was wrong in assuming that German courts were no longer competent in actions against the German Treasury on the ground that the Treasury of the new State which succeeded Germany (or Prussia) has become the universal successor of the latter, and that therefore there is in the present case no obligation for which Germany is liable. No such universal succession has been proved.

(*b*) It was true that since 10 January, 1920—the day on which the Peace Treaty entered into force—Danzig courts were no longer competent to deal with German actions. But this did not mean that the Court of Appeal in Marienwerder was after 10 January, 1920, no longer competent to deal with appeals, brought before that date, against decisions of Danzig courts. The Danzig District Court ceased to be a German court, but the judgments rendered by it prior to 10 January, 1920, were judgments given by a German court in respect of which, at least up to 10 January, 1920, an appeal would lie before the superior court in Marienwerder in Prussia.

(*c*) There was an additional reason which militated in favour of continued jurisdiction of the Prussian Court of Appeal. The defendant in the present action was the German Treasury. According to a recognised principle of international law a State could not be cited before the courts of a foreign State in matters of private law except in cases of voluntary submission or of the exclusive jurisdiction of that foreign State (for instance, in regard to immovable property). It followed that in the present case Danzig courts had no jurisdiction after 10 January, 1920. [Report: *E.R.Z.*, vol. 102, p. 304.]

NOTE.—But see as to (*b*), Case No. 55, above.

Effect of Change of Sovereignty—Effect on Nationality—Liability to Taxation by the Ceding State—Succession in the Matter of Taxation—Article 278 of the Treaty of Versailles. **Case No. 57**

CHANGE OF SOVEREIGNTY (TAXATION) CASE.

Germany, Federal Tribunal in Financial Matters (Reichsfinanzhof). 18 May, 1921.

THE FACTS.—The appellant had resided from 1906 in the province of Posen, which was occupied by Poland after the armistice and subsequently ceded to Poland by virtue of the Treaty of Versailles. After the Polish troops occupied the province the appellant moved to Germany. It appeared that he intended to opt for

Case No. 57 ***contd.***

German nationality. In July and September, 1920, the appellant was asked to make a declaration in connection with the German Capital Levy Act. That Act was made to apply to persons who on 30 June, 1919, were of German nationality. The Peace Treaty of Versailles was signed on 28 June, 1919. It entered into force on 10 January, 1920. The appellant contended that he was a Polish national and was not, therefore, subject to the capital levy. He also invoked Article 278 of the Treaty of Versailles, which provided as follows: " Germany undertakes to recognise any new nationality " which has been or may be acquired by her nationals " under the laws of the Allied and Associated Powers " and in accordance with the decisions of the competent " authorities of these Powers pursuant to naturalisa- " tion laws or under treaty stipulations, and to regard " such persons as having, in consequence of the acquisi- " tion of such new nationality, in all respects severed " their allegiance to their country of origin." Article 91 of the Treaty provided that: " German nationals " habitually resident in territories recognized as forming " part of Poland will acquire Polish nationality *ipso* " *facto* and will lose their German nationality."

Held: That the appeal must be dismissed.

(*a*) Although the appellant lost his German nationality by virtue of Article 91 of the Treaty, the change of nationality did not take place before 10 January, 1920, on which day the Treaty entered into force. The Court could not accept the view that the signature of the Treaty imposed upon Germany the international obligation to treat the inhabitants of the ceded territories as aliens and that the ratification of the Treaty constituted a formality which could not add anything to the obligation imposed by the Treaty.

(*b*) Article 278 of the Treaty did not help the appellant. That Article referred to the " allegiance " of former German subjects. It has no reference to individual claims, but only to the origins from which such claims arise. It has no retroactive effect. It imposes upon Germany a duty only in regard to an already accomplished change of sovereignty. The change of sovereignty does not deprive the ceding State of claims, including those arising out of taxation, which arose prior to the cession. Article 59 of the Treaty provided in regard to Alsace-Lorraine that the French Government will collect for its own account the Imperial taxes, duties and dues leviable in the ceded territory and not collected at the time of the armistice of 11 November, 1918. This provision would be superfluous if the normal result of the cession would be to deprive the ceding State of taxation claims validly arisen. [Report: *Juristische Wochenschrift*, 1921, p. 1619.]

NOTE.—See also *ibid.*, p. 1620, for a similar decision of the same Court in regard to a person who claimed to have lost his German nationality as the result of the plebiscite in Schleswig.

Changes of Sovereignty—Effect of—Nationality—Residence—Treaty of Peace of Paris between the United States and Spain. **Case No. 58**

PEDRO TRILLA *v.* UNIÓN INDUSTRIAL Y COMERCIAL.

Cuba, Supreme Court. 6 *March*, 1920.

THE FACTS.—The plaintiff was a labourer who was injured, partially losing his sight, in an industrial accident. Under Article 6 of the Workmen's Compensation Law of 12 June, 1916, an alien may have his compensation payment in a lump sum if he wishes to go abroad, instead of merely the income from the sum adjudged for compensation to which a citizen is limited. In the present case the plaintiff, who was born in Havana (Cuba), claimed to be a Spanish subject and sought the full compensation at once so that he could go abroad. He was refused this by the *Audiencia de la Habana*, which only granted him the annual income from the sum awarded. He appealed.

Held: That the appeal must be rejected and the judgment affirmed. One of the chief questions was whether he was an alien or not. The appellant had not proved that he was a Spanish citizen. A person born in Havana before the ratification of the Treaty of Peace of Paris between the United States and Spain, and still a minor when its ratification took place, does not prove that he is a Spanish subject by presenting a certificate from the Spanish consul in Havana to the effect that he is listed on the Registry List of Spanish subjects. Even assuming that his parents were not also born in Cuba, proof would be necessary that they were natives of Spain, not resident in the territory whose sovereignty Spain ceded and renounced by the said Treaty, or that, although residents in Cuba, they conserved their Spanish nationality by declaration

Case No. 58 contd.

of their intention to that effect within a year after the ratification of the Treaty in the Register of Spaniards established for the purpose of Article 9 of the said Treaty. [Reports : *Jurisprudencia al Día, Civil,* 1920, p. 73 ; *Gaceta Oficial,* 18 July, 1922, p. 1484.]

NOTE.—As to residence determining nationality in a change of sovereignty, cf. the provisions of the Treaty of Versailles, Articles 36, 84, 91, 105 and 112, and cf. Part III, Section V, Annex (3).—[Ed.]

Territory—Annexation—Effect on Nationality of Persons Resident Abroad.

See Case No. 136 (*Agapios* v. *Sanitary and Quarantine Council of Egypt*).

V.—Occupation of Foreign Territory in Time of Peace

Territory—Contractual Occupation by Foreign Power—As Distinguished from War Occupation—Armistice Agreement of 11 November, 1918.

See Case No. 315 (*Rhineland* (*German Decrees*) *Case*).

VI.—International Leases and Grants in Perpetuity

Case No. 59

Territory—Grants in Perpetuity—Panama Canal—Jurisdiction within the Panama Zone.

IN RE DARIE CARTER AND COKE WEBB.

Panama, Supreme Court. 7 *September,* 1922.

THE FACTS.—Carter was one of three American soldiers who were picked up by a car in Panama. They had just crossed the bridge of the estuary of the river Ballavista, when they overpowered the occupants of the car and robbed them. The territory into which they had passed was part of a lot taken by the United States for fortifications and ceded by Panama for that purpose. The soldiers were tried by the Sixth Circuit Court of Panama, which found Carter guilty of robbery. He appealed to the Supreme Court, claiming lack of jurisdiction in the lower Panama Court.

Held : That the judgment must be reversed, for want of

jurisdiction, although the crime was proved. The place of the crime was within property taken by the United States for fortifications. Article 2 of the Treaty of 1903 between Panama and the United States provided that: "The Republic of "Panama grants to the United States in perpetuity the use, "occupation and control of a zone . . . The Republic of "Panama further grants to the United States in perpetuity "the use, occupation and control of any other lands and "waters outside the zone above described which may be "necessary and convenient for the construction, maintenance, "operation, sanitation and protection of the said Canal." Article 3 of the same Treaty provided: "The Republic of "Panama grants to the United States all the rights, power and "authority within the zone mentioned and described . . . and "within the limits of all auxiliary lands and waters . . . which "the United States would possess and exercise if it were "sovereign over the territory within which said lands and "waters are located, to the entire exclusion of the exercise by "the Republic of Panama of any such sovereign rights, power "or authority." The later treaties and laws conformed to these provisions, so that Panama courts had no jurisdiction over the crime. [Report: *Registro Judicial*, vol. 20, p. 985.]

NOTE.—See *Amelius Remy* v. *Man Sign* (31 January, 1923), *Registro Judicial*, vol. 21, p. 155, for a refusal to carry out a judgment because Panama had no authority over the Canal Zone or its inhabitants.

Territory—Grants in Perpetuity—Panama Canal Zone—State Succession—Continuance of Civil Code of Panama.

See Case No. 51 (*Panama Railroad Company* v. *Bosse*).

B. PARTS OF STATE TERRITORY

I.—Boundaries

i.—Land Boundaries

Boundaries—Legal Nature of Boundary Commissions.

See Case No. 262 (*Colombia and Venezuela Case*).

ii.—Water Boundaries

Case No. 60 **Boundaries—Water Boundaries—Change of Course of Rivers—The *Thalweg* Doctrine—Avulsion.**

STATE OF ARKANSAS *v.* STATE OF MISSISSIPPI.
United States Supreme Court. 19 *March,* 1919.

THE FACTS.—This was a boundary dispute between two States of the United States. The Act of Congress admitting Mississippi to the Union provided for a westerly boundary " up the Mississippi River." (3 U.S. Stat. L. 348.) The Act admitting Arkansas gave that State an easterly boundary " up the middle of the " main channel of the said river." (5 U.S. Stat. L. 50, 51.) An avulsion of the river later changed its course. No definite action followed an Act providing that Mississippi and Arkansas might agree upon their boundary. (35 U.S. Stat. L. 1161.) Later Arkansas invoked the original jurisdiction of the United States Supreme Court, contending that the boundary was the middle of the channel of navigation as it existed prior to the avulsion. Mississippi contended that the boundary was a line midway between the well-defined banks of the river.

Held : That the boundary claimed by Arkansas was correct and must be determined and marked accordingly by a commission. Following *Iowa* v. *Illinois* (147 U.S. 1) and *Arkansas* v. *Tennessee* (246 U.S. 158), the Court held that " where the " States of the Union are separated by boundary lines de-" scribed as ' a line drawn along the middle of the river,' or " as ' the middle of the main channel of the river,' the boundary " must be fixed at the middle of the main navigable channel, " and not along the line equidistant between the banks." (250 U.S. 39, 43.) When the *thalweg* doctrine is applied to cases of avulsion, the rule " requires the boundary line to be " fixed at the middle of the channel of navigation as it existed " just previous to the avulsion." (250 U.S. 39, 45.) [Report : 250 U.S. 39.]

Case No. 61 **Boundaries—Water Boundaries.**

STATE OF GEORGIA *v.* STATE OF SOUTH CAROLINA.
United States Supreme Court. 30 *January,* 1922.

THE FACTS.—This was an original suit to define a river

boundary between two States of the United States. It was agreed that the boundary was determined by the Beaufort Convention concluded between the two States on 28 April, 1787. This Convention designated certain rivers as the boundary, reserved the islands in the rivers to Georgia, and declared navigation of the rivers free to the citizens of both States.

Held : That " (1) Where there are no islands in the boundary rivers the location of the line between the two States is " on the water midway between the main banks of the river " when the water is at ordinary stage ; (2) Where there are " islands the line is midway between the island bank and the " South Carolina shore when the water is at ordinary stage." (257 U.S. 516, 523.) The location of the boundary was unaffected by the *thalweg* or main navigable channel doctrine in view of the provision making navigation of the rivers free to the citizens of both States. [Report : 257 U.S. 516.]

NOTE.—See *Oklahoma* v. *Texas* (11 April, 1921), 256 U.S. 70 (river boundary located along the river bank) ; *Minnesota* v. *Wisconsin* (8 March, 1920), 252 U.S. 273 (river boundary the main channel)

Parts of State Territory—Boundaries—Water Boundaries-Rivers—Change of Course of—How far Affecting the Boundary. **Case No. 62**

PEREYRA IRAOLO *v.* PROVINCIA DE BUENOS AIRES.

Argentina, Federal Supreme Court. 11 *April,* 1921.

THE FACTS.—This was a case of the riparian boundary between two subdivisions of Argentina. In the Argentine Federation the capital, Buenos Aires, forms a federal district separate and distinct from the Province of the same name. Law 1029, of 21 September, 1880, federalising the capital, gave it the same boundaries as it had before. The provincial Legislature, by a Law of 31 October, 1867, had fixed the southern boundary as the *Riachuelo* (rivulet) *de Barracas.* Nothing was said in these laws as to the future changes in the course or channel. After 1880, its winding course had been altered considerably and straightened by artificial works. Pereyra Iraolo owned land north of the 1880 course of the *riachuelo,* but south of its new artificial channel. This property had been taxed by the Province despite its owner's contention that it lay

Case No. 62 *contd.*

within the capital and without the jurisdiction of the Province. He therefore brought an action in the Federal Supreme Court against the Province to recover road taxes and other impositions which he had paid.

Held : For the plaintiff, the Court declaring that the Province had no jurisdiction to tax this property and must refund what it had already collected. " Even under the institutions " of the American Union, in which the Supreme Court deter- " mines the boundaries between the various States, the juris- " prudence of that high Court has established that the " boundary, once fixed by law in the channel of a river that " divides two States, is not altered because this river changes " its course. In *Nebraska* v. *Yocoa* [*sic, Iowa*] it was laid down " that . . . when a boundary water-course suddenly abandons " its old bed, for whatever reason, and follows another new " course, the boundary remains unchanged in the centre of the " old channel, even though the water does not run through it. " 143 U.S. 359 ; *Missouri* v. *Nebraska*, 196 U.S. 23. This " doctrine is of even stricter application with us, where it is a " constitutional attribute of Congress to fix provincial bound- " aries, and where consequently once they are fixed by law " they can only be altered by another law."[1] (*Fallos*, vol. 133, pp. 372, 378.) [Reports : *Fallos*, vol. 133, p. 372 ; *Jurisprudencia Argentina*, vol. 6, p. 259, with a long footnote giving a Spanish translation of *Missouri* v. *Nebraska*.]

III.—Territorial Waters

i.—Nature of the Maritime Belt

Case No. 63

Territorial Waters—Nature of Maritime Belt—Whether Part of State Territory—Customs Territory and State Territory —German Law.

TERRITORIAL WATERS (GERMANY) CASE.

Germany, Reichsgericht in Criminal Matters. 11 *July*, 1921.

THE FACTS.—The motor-boat of the accused with a cargo of foreign brandy was seized by a revenue boat in

[1] See also *Isidro Olivares* v. *Domingo Manfredi* (8 August, 1923), *Fallos*, vol. 138, p. 287, an ejectment case involving jurisdiction over an island in the Rio Negro separating the territory of Rio Negro from the Province of Buenos Aires, in which it was said : " It not being expressed in the law that the boun- " dary of the territory should be either of the banks of the Rio Negro, but the " river itself, it ought to be understood that the boundary line passes through

Lübeck Bay about 1000 metres from the shore. The accused were prosecuted for having entered German territorial waters with the object of bringing the brandy into Germany without the permission of the competent authorities. The District Court adopted the view that German territorial waters form part of German territory, and found the accused guilty of an offence against the Importation Decree which punishes illicit importation into the German territory.

Held, on final appeal on a point of law: That the conviction must be quashed.

(*a*) The view of the Court below that the accused were within German frontiers is open to doubt. Article 2 of the German Constitution lays down that "Federal territory consists of the territories of the German States." The question whether territorial waters form part of State territory is a disputed one. The predominant view among writers is that they do form part of State territory, but there are also authoritative expressions of opinion to the effect that the State has over them only certain rights of sovereignty (*Hoheitsrechte*). Even those writers who favour the theory that territorial waters form part of State territory admit that the jurisdiction of the State over its territorial waters is not so intensive as over other parts of its territory, and that it is limited in certain respects by considerations of freedom of navigation on the open sea. Federal laws refer as a rule to "*Hoheitsrechte*" (rights of supremacy) over the territorial waters. In general, it is doubtful whether it is possible to answer the question by reference to existing German enactments.

(*b*) According to Article 82 (2) of the Federal Constitution the customs frontier is on the whole identical with the frontier of the *Reich*, but in regard to the sea the customs frontier is constituted by the shores of the mainland and the islands belonging to the *Reich*. It follows that for customs purposes German territorial waters must be regarded as foreign customs territory even if it were to be admitted that otherwise they are within German territory. [Report: *E.R.S.*, vol. 56, p. 135.]

"the middle of the course or channel (*cauce*), and if there are several, through "the middle of the chief or deepest course or channel." The Court quoted from *Missouri* v. *Kentucky*, 11 Wall. (U.S.) 395, and from Handly's *Lessee* v. *Anthony*, 5 Wheat. (U.S.), 374.

See also the Brazilian case *Amazones* v. *Para* (Federal Supreme Court, 3 September, 1921), *Revista Forense*, vol. 38, p. 312, in which a boundary dispute was referred to a commission of experts.

Case No. 63 *contd.*

NOTE.—See also the decision of the same Court of 11 July, 1921 (*E.R.S.*, vol. 56, p. 42), where the same distinction is made in regard to the Free Port of Hamburg which is a so-called *Zollausschluss*, *i.e.* part of German territory excluded from the customs territory of the *Reich*.

Case No. 64

Territorial Waters—Law Applicable in—In Matters of Collision.

THE SIDRA.

British-American Claims Arbitral Tribunal. 29 *November*, 1921.

(FROMAGEOT, FITZPATRICK, ANDERSON.)

THE FACTS.—This was a claim, put forward by Great Britain on behalf of the owners of the *Sidra*, for damages arising out of a collision in October, 1905, between the United States Government tug boat *Potomac* and the British merchant ship *Sidra* in the approaches of Baltimore Harbour, Maryland, in the territorial waters of the United States. The Tribunal found that while the *Potomac* was responsible for the collision by not navigating with sufficient prudence, the *Sidra* contributed to the collision by having anchored in an imprudent manner.

Held: That as the collision occurred in the territorial waters of the United States, the law applicable to the collision was, according to a well-settled rule of international law, the law of the United States. According to that law " when both " ships are to blame the damage suffered by each of them " must be supported by moiety by the other." [Reports: Nielsen, p. 453; *A.J.*, XVI (1922), p. 110.]

ii.—Breadth of the Maritime Belt

Case No. 65

Territorial Waters—Maritime Belt—Three-Mile Limit Around Islands—Fisheries.

IN RE MARINCOVICH.

United States, California Court of Appeals, Second Appellate District, Division Two. 10 *July*, 1920.

THE FACTS.—This was a petition for habeas corpus. The petitioner was arrested for violation of State Penal Code, § 636, prohibiting the use of certain dip nets in fishing in State waters. He sought release on habeas corpus on the ground that the waters where he had fished around Santa Catalina Island (some distance off the coast) were not " state waters." They had been treated as such in legislation setting up the fisheries districts. The California Constitution provided for a boundary which included a marginal belt of three marine miles in the Pacific and declared that the territory should include all " islands, harbors, and bays " along and adjacent to the coast." (Article XXI.)

Held: That the writ must be denied. The jurisdiction of California extended over a three-mile zone of sea around the island as well as along the coast. " This rule of international " usage is applicable to California just as though it were an " independent, sovereign nation, save only that its right of " exclusive control over such waters is limited in so far as " control may have been granted to the United States. . . . " Included in this territorial jurisdiction is the right of control " over fisheries, whether the fish be migratory, free-swimming " fish, or fish attached to or embedded in the soil. . . . There is " just as much reason for the extension of state sovereignty " over a three-mile belt around Catalina Island as there is for " the extension of sovereignty over a three-mile zone along " and off the shore of the mainland." (48 Calif. App. 474, 477.) [Report: 48 Calif. App. 474.]

Territorial Waters—Breadth of Maritime Belt—Measurement from Mainland or from Islands—Separation from Mainland at High Water Only. **Case No. 66**

THE DÜSSELDORF.

England, the Prize Court, and, on Appeal, the Privy Council.[1]
12 *May*, 1919; 29 *July*, 1920.

In this case the Norwegian Government succeeded in establishing its claim to the release of a German merchant ship, the *Düsseldorf*, and her cargo, on the ground that their capture by a British ship of war took place in Norwegian territorial waters. The President (Lord Sterndale) refused to award damages to the Norwegian Government, because he found that the officer in command of the capturing vessel was *bona fide* attempting to respect the neutrality of Norwegian waters, and that he unfortunately made a miscalculation as to his distance. On appeal, however, the Privy Council awarded damages to

[1] As to the jurisdiction in England in matters of Prize, see p. 491, note 1.

Case No. 66 ***contd.***

the Norwegian Government representing the cost of removing the ship from British to Norwegian or other neutral waters.

The case is only mentioned here because it involved a discussion (see L.R. [1919] P. at pp. 245-247) of the question whether the maritime belt [1] ought to be measured (*a*) from the mainland or (*b*) from some small uninhabited " islands " off the coast which at low water are connected with the mainland by a dry passage, or (*c*) from a completely separated island about 300 metres in length situated less than three miles from the mainland. It was unnecessary to decide (*c*), but Lord Sterndale held as regards (*b*) that the belt should be measured on the basis that these " islands " were part of the mainland.

[Reports: L.R. [1919] P. 245; [1920] A.C. 1034; 3 B. and C.P.C. 466; *ibid.*, 664.]

Territorial Waters—Breadth of—Norwegian " King's Resolution " of 22 February, 1812.

See Case No. 76 (*Public Prosecutor* v. *Lund*).

iv.—Coasting Trade and Fisheries

Territorial Waters—Jurisdiction in—Right of Fishery.

See Case No. 119 (*The Argonaut and The Jonas H. French*).

[1] The Norwegian Government claims that the width of the belt is four miles, but in this case did not press the claim and were content that the case should be decided on the ground that the vessels were seized within the three-mile belt.

PART IV

JURISDICTION

A. JURISDICTION IN GENERAL. TERRITORIAL AND PERSONAL

I.—Territorial

(a) Over Territory in General and Persons and Property situated therein

[See also Part II, RECOGNITION OF ACTS OF FOREIGN STATES AND GOVERNMENTS, and RECOGNITION OF FOREIGN STATES AND GOVERNMENTS.]

Jurisdiction—In General—Territorial—*De facto* Jurisdiction over Disputed Territory. **Case No. 67**

CORDOVA *v.* GRANT.

United States Supreme Court. 13 *January*, 1919.

THE FACTS.—This was a suit in the United States District Court for the Western District of Texas to determine title to land situated between the new bed and the old bed of the Rio Grande river on the international boundary between Mexico and the United States. The plaintiff derived his claim to title from Texas, a political subdivision of the United States, the defendant from Mexico. The land had been on the Mexican side of the river as late as 1852. In consequence of a change in the channel of the river, it was now on the side of the United States. The international boundary was in dispute between Mexico and the United States, but the United States exercised *de facto* jurisdiction over the territory where the land was situated. The defendant asked the District Court either to dismiss the case or to stay the trial until the international boundary should be settled. His request was denied. On writ of error,

Held: That the District Court had jurisdiction, notwithstanding the fact that the international boundary was in dispute. The District Court's decision simply meant "that the "Court finds the Government in fact asserting its authority

Case No. 67 *contd.*

"over the territory and will follow its lead. It does not "matter to such a decision that the Government recognizes "that a foreign power is disputing its right and that it is "making efforts to settle the dispute. . . . Jurisdiction is "power and matter of fact. The United States has that power "and the Courts may exercise their portion of it unless pro-"hibited in some constitutional way." (248 U.S. 413, 419.) [Report: 248 U.S. 413.]

Case No. 68

Jurisdiction—In General—Territorial—*De facto* Jurisdiction over Disputed Territory.

IN RE POJASI ALEJANDRO.

Bolivia, Supreme Court. 24 *December*, 1921.

THE FACTS.—Certain land was sold for the benefit of the owner's creditors and the titles thus conferred were confirmed by the Bolivian lower Court in Tarija. The land was in the region around Yacuiba, in the Gran Chaco, which had been disputed between Bolivia and Argentina. On appeal from the lower Court's decision,

Held: That the appeal must be rejected. The land must be treated as being in Bolivian territory, where the Court had full jurisdiction to confirm the title given by the creditors' sale. Even if there were a treaty concerning the international boundary, and if the marking of the boundary in conformity with the treaty might result in changes of territory which would put this region beyond Bolivian control, still "the "changes had not been consummated, and for that reason "both countries continue to exercise their jurisdiction over "the lands, according to the *status quo* before the treaty." Accordingly, the land in question was within Bolivian jurisdiction, even if the treaty should place it in Argentina when the new boundary was marked. [Report: *Gaceta Judicial*, No. 975, p. 37.]

Case No. 69

Jurisdiction — In General — Territorial — Over Ports and National Waters—Vessel in the Service of the British Admiralty.

IN RE JORGE ALEJANDRO JACKSON.

Argentina, Federal Court of Appeal. 1919.

THE FACTS.—The defendant, apparently a member of the crew of the English vessel *Iddesleigh*, anchored in the port of Buenos Aires, committed homicide on board the vessel and then fled ashore. He was brought for trial in an Argentine court, but contended that the Court lacked jurisdiction. At the time of the crime the *Iddesleigh* was in the service of the British Admiralty but was not a war vessel. It appeared that the crew was that of an "ordinary vessel of the merchant "marine" and the men had to provide their own outfits. The Court of First Instance held that the plea of the absence of jurisdiction must not be allowed, since the crime was one over which the Argentine courts had jurisdiction as soon as the criminal came of his own accord into their control on shore. On appeal,

Held: That, following the dictamen[1] of the Court's *Procurador-Fiscal*, the judgment must be confirmed. The *Iddesleigh* was not a war vessel, and its crew were not in military service. Accordingly, the crime came within the territorial jurisdiction of the port authorities. [Report: *Gaceta del Foro* (January, 1920), vol. 24, p. 95.]

Jurisdiction—Territorial—Effect of Condemnation of Ship as Lawful Prize by Governmental Decree.

See Case No. 25 (*The Gagara*).

Jurisdiction—Territorial—Recognition in Foreign Countries of Legislative and Executive Acts Affecting Movables within the Jurisdiction.

See Case No. 26 (*Luther* v. *Sagor*).

(b) Criminal Jurisdiction over Foreigners

Crime Committed Abroad by an Alien—Crime against the Security of the State—Competence of the French Courts. **Case No. 70**

IN RE URIOS.

France, Court of Cassation (Criminal Chamber).
15 *January*, 1920.

THE FACTS.—Urios, a Spanish national and captain of a Spanish merchant ship, was accused of having, during

[1] *Dictamen* is an opinion of the Fiscal. It is a pronouncement which may be regarded as being half-way between an Attorney-General's opinion and the report of a Master in Chancery.

Case No. 70 ***contd.***

the war, in Spain and in particular at Barcelona, been guilty of an offence against the external security of the French State by maintaining a correspondence with the enemies of France. He was arrested at Mostaganem, in Algeria, in February, 1919, and condemned on 7 November, 1919, by the Permanent Council of War of the military division of Oran to imprisonment for twenty years. Urios appealed to the Court of Cassation claiming that the French courts had no jurisdiction.

Held: That the arrest, trial and sentence of Urios in France for an act committed by him abroad were valid. Article 78 of the Penal Code, which punishes with imprisonment correspondence with the enemy such as that with which the accused was charged, was perfectly general in its terms and allowed no distinction to be drawn between Frenchmen and foreigners: Article 7 of the *Code d'Instruction criminelle* expressly provides that "any alien who, whether as principal or accomplice, is "guilty outside French territory of a crime against the security "of the State is liable to prosecution and sentence under "French law if he is arrested in France or if the Government "obtains his extradition." [Reports: 47 *Clunet* (1920), p. 195; *Dalloz*, 1920, Part I, p. 33.]

NOTE.—For a reference to this case and, generally, for a discussion of the whole question, see Donnedieu de Vabres, *Les principes modernes du droit international pénal* (1928), pp. 95 *et seq.*

Case No. 71

Jurisdiction—In General—Territorial—Criminal Jurisdiction over Foreigners for Crimes Committed Abroad.

BRANDÃO & COMPANY *v.* FRANCISCO CANALES.

Brazil, Supreme Federal Tribunal. 6 *August*, 1921.

THE FACTS.—This was a *recurso extraordinario criminal* seeking the punishment of the defendant as a member of a Spanish firm for the violation of Law 1236 of 24 September, 1904. The Spanish firm had sold in Brazil certain tins of oil in imitation of the trade-mark registered by the plaintiffs. The judge of the Fourth Chamber of São Paulo dismissed the action, and this decision was affirmed by the *Tribunal de Justiça* of that State, on the ground that the Brazilian courts had no jurisdiction.

Held: That the judgment must be affirmed. "The criminal

" act of imitation of a trade-mark was done in Malaga. The " jurisdiction of our penal law does not extend beyond the " limits of the national territory, in the terms of Article 4 of " the Penal Code." [Report: *Revista do Supremo Tribunal*, vol. 38, p. 84.]

Criminal Jurisdiction over Foreigners—Locality of the Offence —Crime Committed within Jurisdiction by Person Not Physically Present therein.

See Case No. 190 (*Rex* v. *Godfrey*).

(c) Over Ports and National Waters

[See also Part III, TERRITORIAL WATERS.]

Jurisdiction—Over Ports and National Waters—Seamen on Foreign Vessels—Claims for Wages. **Case No. 72**

STRATHEARN STEAMSHIP COMPANY LIMITED *v.* DILLON.

United States Supreme Court. 29 *March*, 1920.

THE FACTS.—This was a suit by Dillon, a British sailor, to recover one-half the wages earned on a British vessel. Dillon shipped at Liverpool under Articles which made wages payable at the end of the voyage, with no advancements abroad except at the pleasure of the master. This was a valid contract for the payment of wages under the laws of Great Britain. The demand for one-half wages earned was made in a United States port in reliance upon the United States Seamen's Act, § 4, which provides as follows: " Every " seaman on a vessel of the United States shall be " entitled to receive on demand from the master of " the vessel to which he belongs one half part of the " wages which he shall have then earned, at every " port where such vessel . . . shall load or deliver " cargo before the voyage is ended, and all stipulations " in the contract to the contrary shall be void. . . . " This section shall apply to seamen on foreign vessels " while in harbors of the United States, and the courts " of the United States shall be open to such seamen " for its enforcement." (38 U.S. Stat. L. 1164.) The demand was refused. The United States District Court held that Dillon's demand was premature. The Circuit Court of Appeals for the Fifth Circuit reversed

Case No. 72 *contd.*

this decision and held that Dillon was entitled to recover. (256 Fed. 631.) On certiorari,

Held: That the judgment of the Circuit Court of Appeals must be affirmed. It was clear that Congress intended to give the benefit of the Act to seamen on foreign vessels. The jurisdiction of the United States over foreign merchant vessels in its ports was such as to give Congress authority to make provisions of this character. *Patterson* v. *Bark Eudora*, 190 U.S. 169, followed. *Sandberg* v. *McDonald*, 248 U.S. 185, arising under § 11 of the Seamen's Act, distinguished. [Reports: 256 Fed. 631; 252 U.S. 348.]

Case No. 73

Jurisdiction—Territorial—Over Ports and National Waters—Foreign Merchant Vessels—Smoking of Opium Distinguished from Possession of Opium.

PEOPLE *v.* WONG CHENG.

United States, Supreme Court of the Philippine Islands.
19 *October*, 1922.

THE FACTS.—This was a prosecution for the offence of smoking opium. The information charged that the offence was committed on an English merchant vessel anchored two miles and a half from shore in Manila Harbour. The defendant demurred on the ground that the Court lacked jurisdiction of the offence. The demurrer was sustained by the Court of First Instance of Manila. The Attorney-General appealed.

Held: That the demurrer must be overruled. The Court said that there are two views of the law governing crimes committed on merchant vessels in territorial waters. According to the French view, only the flag State has jurisdiction unless the crime affects the peace and security of the port. According to the English view, which is followed by the United States, such crimes can be tried in the courts of the territorial jurisdiction. In *United States* v. *Look Chaw*, 18 P.I. 573, this Court had taken the position that mere possession of a forbidden substance on a foreign merchant vessel in territorial waters does not constitute a crime triable locally. " But " to smoke opium within our territorial limits, even though " aboard a foreign merchant ship, is certainly a breach of the " public order here established, because it causes such drug " to produce its pernicious effects within our territory. It "seriously contravenes the purpose that our Legislature has "in mind in enacting the aforesaid repressive statute." (46 P.I. 729, 733.) [Report: 46 P.I. 729.]

Jurisdiction—Over Ports and National Waters—Transportation of Whisky through United States National Waters—Eighteenth Amendment to the Constitution.

See Case No. 236 (*Grogan* v. *Walker & Sons*).

(d) At the Maritime Frontier. Hovering Laws

[See also HIGH SEAS.]

Jurisdiction on the High Seas—Enforcement of Hovering, Revenue and other Municipal Laws—The Maritime Frontier. **Case No. 74**

THE GRACE AND RUBY.

United States District Court, D. Massachusetts.
18 *September*, 1922.

THE FACTS.—This was a libel to forfeit a British schooner for violations of U.S. Rev. Stat., §§ 2872, 2874 (forbidding deliveries in night-time within the United States of "merchandise brought in any vessel from any "foreign port" and authorising forfeitures for unlawful delivery), and for violations of the National Prohibition Act (41 U.S. Stat. L. 305). The schooner cleared from the Bahama Islands for St. John, N.B., with a cargo of liquor. Part of the cargo belonged to one Sullivan, of Salem, Mass., who was on board. The vessel proceeded directly to a point about six miles off Gloucester, Mass., and set Sullivan on shore. Two days later Sullivan came out in a motor-boat to bring provisions and take off liquor. At that time the schooner was about ten miles from land. The motor-boat was loaded with liquor, three members of the schooner's crew went aboard, a dinghy belonging to the schooner was taken in tow, presumably for use in landing the liquor or to enable the members of the crew to return to their ship, and the motor-boat started for shore under cover of darkness. The motor-boat was apprehended and seized. Two days later the *Grace and Ruby* was arrested about four miles from land. Exceptions to the libel raised the question of jurisdiction.

Case No. 74 *contd.*

Held: That the exceptions must be overruled. There was an unlawful unlading at night within the territorial limits of the United States in violation of U.S. Rev. Stat., §§ 2872, 2874. "The act of unlading, although beginning beyond the three-"mile limit, continued until the liquor was landed, and the "schooner was actively assisting in it by means of her small "boat and three of her crew, who were on the motor-boat for "that purpose." (283 Fed. 475, 476.) "The line between "territorial waters and the high seas is not like the boundary "between us and a foreign power. There must be, it seems "to me, a certain width of debatable waters adjacent to our "coasts. How far our authority shall be extended into them "for the seizure of foreign vessels which have broken our laws "is a matter for the political departments of the government "rather than for the courts to determine. . . . The *Grace and* "*Ruby* had committed an offense against our law, if my view "as to the unlading is right, and was lying just outside the "three-mile limit for purposes relating to her unlawful act. "In directing that she be seized there and brought into the "country to answer for her offense, I am not prepared to say "that the Treasury Department exceeded its power." (283 Fed. 475, 478, 479.) [Report: 283 Fed. 475.]

Case No. 75

Jurisdiction—Territorial—At the Maritime Frontier.

THE SANTA LUZIA.

United States District Court, S.D. Florida. 7 October, 1921.

THE FACTS.—The Chinese Exclusion Act imposed penalties on "the master of any vessel who shall knowingly "bring within the United States on such vessel, and "land, or attempt to land, or permit to be landed any "Chinese laborer." (23 U.S. Stat. L. 115.) A later section of the Act provided for the forfeiture of the offending vessel. The *Santa Luzia* was libelled by the United States for forfeiture under this statute on the ground that it had brought certain Chinese labourers from Cuba to a point about ten miles off the Florida coast and had permitted them to leave the vessel with the intent that they be landed. On exceptions to the libel,

Held: That the exceptions must be sustained and the libel dismissed. The wording of the statute made the offence consist in bringing Chinese labourers within the United States. The libel only alleged that they were brought within ten miles of the coast. It was conceded that a marine league from the coast was the limit of territorial jurisdiction. Consequently the vessel could not be forfeited. [Report: 287 Fed. 152.]

Jurisdiction—In the Maritime Frontier—Extent of Territorial Waters—Criminal Jurisdiction in respect of Unlawful Sale of Spirits. **Case No. 76**

PUBLIC PROSECUTOR *v.* LUND.

Norway, Supreme Court. 22 *March*, 1922.

THE FACTS.—By a judgment pronounced by the District Court of Fredrikstad on 20 December, 1921, a Danish subject, Jens Hansen Lund, was convicted of an infraction of an Act of 30 September, 1921, extending the application of the Customs regulations in Norwegian waters to within a boundary of ten miles from the outermost isle or rock which is not permanently submerged by the sea. The Court found it to be proved that he had, on 12 October, 1921, sold spirits to various persons from a vessel called *Kattegat* whilst lying at the mouth of the Oslo Fjord within the ten-mile limit. It appeared that the sale had taken place within a limit of about three and a half miles from shore. The accused pleaded that according to Section 12 (4) of the Norwegian Criminal Law an act such as the one of which he was accused, when committed by an alien abroad, was not justiciable under Norwegian law. The term "abroad" in this connection must mean outside the territorial limit of three miles. Section 1 of the Act of 30 September, 1921, extending the Customs control to ten miles, could not, he contended, be interpreted as making any alteration in the provision of Section 12 (4) of the Criminal Law. The District Court rejected this contention and asserted that the Act of 1921 had been intended to apply also to aliens on foreign vessels. The accused appealed to the Supreme Court.

Held: That the appeal must be dismissed. The point to be decided was whether Section 1 of the Act of 30 September, 1921, as referred to above, could be applied in the present case. There was nothing in its wording to suggest that the provision was applicable to Norwegians and Norwegian vessels only.

Case No. 76 *contd.* Consequently it must apply also to aliens on foreign vessels. [Report : *Norsk Rettstidende* (*Norwegian Judicial Journal—Law Reports*), 1922, pp. 499-503.]

NOTE.—The Supreme Court rejected as erroneous the view of the Court below that the general limit of Norwegian territorial waters was three miles. According to the " King's Resolution " of 22 February, 1812, the limit of territorial waters was fixed at one sea-mile from shore, which corresponded approximately to four ordinary (nautical) miles. This rule still held good. The Supreme Court also referred to the suggestion made in the Court below that Norway during the war had confined herself to enforcing the three-mile limit, for instance as regards neutrality. The Supreme Court pointed out that there was nothing to prove that contention, and that in any case such a voluntary limitation could not be interpreted as implying a definite giving up of the one sea-mile territorial limit as fixed by the above-mentioned resolution.

(g) Exemptions from and Restrictions upon Territorial Jurisdiction

(i) FOREIGN STATES

[See also Part II, SOVEREIGNTY AND INDEPENDENCE : *Acts of Sovereignty and Transactions of a Private Character.*]

Case No. 77 **Exemption from Jurisdiction—Submission to Jurisdiction and Submission to Execution—Implied Submission—General and Limited Submission—The Turkish Military Purchases Commission in Berlin—The Political Status of Turkey in the Post-War Period.**

TURKISH PURCHASES COMMISSION CASE.

Germany, Prussian Tribunal for Conflicts of Jurisdiction.
29 *May*, 1920.

THE FACTS.—This was an action against the Turkish military treasury, represented by a Purchases Commission of the Imperial Turkish Ministry of War, for payment of a sum representing the value plus interest of iron goods sold by the plaintiff to the Purchases Commission. The plaintiff asked for the attachment of the property of the Turkish Treasury, and in particular of the banking account opened by it for the purpose of buying goods through the Purchases Commission. In the contract of sale the parties recognised the jurisdiction of German courts for any disputes arising out of the contract. The District Court of

Berlin issued the order of attachment. The Turkish Treasury appealed. However, before the appeal was heard, the Prussian State Ministry[1] raised, in an action before the Tribunal for Conflicts of Jurisdiction, the question of competence. It contended that as the action concerned a foreign sovereign State which was not liable to the jurisdiction of German courts the political departments of the State were the proper authority to deal with the matter.

Held: That the objection of the Prussian State Ministry must be sustained so far as the general attachment is concerned, but that it must be overruled in regard to the attachment of the banking account of the Purchases Commission.

(*a*) The recognition in the contract of the jurisdiction of German courts did not in general carry with it subjection *ipso facto* to measures of enforcement including attachment. Accordingly, German courts had no jurisdiction to decree the attachment of the entire property of the Turkish State in Germany.

(*b*) However, in individual cases a foreign State or its representative may be deemed by its conduct to have submitted to the specific jurisdiction of German courts even in the matter of enforcement. This took place in the present case. It appeared from the evidence that in view of the misgivings of German firms in the matter of the fulfilment of its obligations by the Commission, the latter arranged for a larger sum of money to be deposited in a special banking account in its name from which the claims of the German firms could be satisfied. This appeared to have been the condition, well known to the Turkish Commission, under which the German firms were prepared to supply it with munitions and other war material. The only purpose of the banking account thus opened was to satisfy the claims of German private firms. This being so, the Commission must be held as having impliedly agreed to measures of execution by German courts in regard to the banking account opened by it.

In acting thus the Commission must be deemed to have acted within the scope of its competence. Even if it were not so, the superior Turkish authorities must have envisaged the necessity of such submission to jurisdiction which in any case must be deemed to have been subsequently ratified by them. [Report: *Juristische Wochenschrift*, 1921, p. 773.]

[1] See below, Note (*c*).

Case No. 77 *contd.*

NOTE.—(*a*) See, to the same effect, the decision of the same Tribunal of 13 November, 1920, in *Juristische Wochenschrift*, 1921, p. 1478.

(*b*) The Tribunal rejected the view of the Berlin District Court that as Turkey was in consequence of the outcome of the war largely subject to the control of foreign Powers, she could no longer be regarded as a fully sovereign foreign State which alone is entitled to jurisdictional immunities. The Tribunal pointed out that such foreign control, temporary in its nature, did not deprive Turkey of her status as an independent State.

(*c*) It was contended on the part of the plaintiffs that as the objection to the jurisdiction was raised by reference to international law and to the foreign relations of Germany, the Prussian State Ministry was not competent to bring the matter before the Tribunal seeing that the conduct of foreign affairs was in the hands of the Federal (*Reich*) Ministry for Foreign Affairs. The Tribunal rejected this view. It pointed out that although only the Federal Ministry for Foreign Affairs was (subject to exceptions laid down in Article 78 (2) of the Constitution of 1919) competent to conduct negotiations with foreign Powers, the authorities of the individual States had still to fulfil a number of functions in this field. In particular, they were competent to deal with and prevent situations which might give rise to complaints of and negotiations with foreign Powers. This was so in particular in view of the fact that by virtue of the German Constitution the *Reich* was not always competent to adopt measures within the territories of the individual States calculated to deal with situations of international importance. This function devolved upon the States. Before the Weimar Constitution of 11 August, 1919, there was a single government for Prussia and the *Reich*. The Weimar Constitution restored the dual government which obtained before the Federal Constitution of 16 April, 1871. However, in view of the tendency, clearly expressed in the Weimar Constitution, to make the conduct of foreign affairs a matter of the *Reich* rather than of the individual States, no separate ministry for foreign affairs was created in Prussia. These functions were taken over by the State Ministry as such. See on this subject, Anschütz, *Die Verfassung des deutschen Reichs vom 11 August*, 1919 (1921), p. 142, and Strupp in *Juristische Wochenschrift*, 1921, p. 1478.

Case No. 78

Exemption from Jurisdiction—Foreign State—Indirectly Impleading a Foreign State—Action against the Debtor of the Foreign State—Action in Germany against the Polish State Bank.

POLISH LOAN BANK CASE.

Germany, Prussian Tribunal for Conflicts of Jurisdiction.
12 *March*, 1921.

THE FACTS.—During the German occupation of the Polish part of Russia the plaintiffs established there an extensive book-selling and newspaper business. After the evacuation of this part of Poland by German troops the Polish provisional Government established at

Warsaw appropriated and sold all the assets belonging to the plaintiffs' business. The plaintiffs held the Polish Government responsible for the damage thus caused to their property, which they estimated at 10 million Marks. For part of this sum they brought an action against an institution styled the Polish Loan Bank (Polska Krajowa Kasa Pożyczkowa) and closely associated with the Polish State. The Bank was originally set up by the German occupation authorities. It was entrusted with the issue of paper money in the form of treasury notes signed by the German Governor-General. The Polish State then took over the Bank and conferred upon it a special status. On the whole, its position—including the privilege of issuing treasury notes—remained the same as during the German occupation. According to its constitution, it remained a separate juristic person distinct from that of the Polish State. The plaintiffs contended, however, that at the same time the Bank was permanently in a position in which it owed money to the Polish State; it was the central bank of the various State authorities and received large advances from which it effected payments at the order of the Government. As the Bank was thus in a position of a debtor in relation to the Polish State it could, it was contended, be sued for the liabilities of the Polish State. Being a separate juristic person it could not, it was said, rely on jurisdictional immunities to which the Polish State was entitled. The plaintiffs relied particularly on Article 1166 of the *Code Civil*—obtaining at that time in Poland—according to which the debtor's debtor can be sued by the creditor. In February, 1919, the plaintiff obtained an order attaching the deposits of the defendant Bank with the Deutsche Bank in Berlin.

The Prussian State Ministry,[1] in an action before the Tribunal for Conflicts of Jurisdiction, raised the question of jurisdiction, maintaining that German courts were not competent to entertain the action against a foreign State, and asking that the attachment order be set aside.

Held: That the German courts were not competent to entertain the action and that the order of attachment must

[1] See above, p. 116, Note (*c*).

Case No. 78 *contd.* be set aside. It was true that the action was brought against the Bank and that that institution was a juristic person distinct from that of the Polish State. But the cause of action was grounded in the alleged responsibility of the Polish State as such. The claim was not based on any fact arising from or legally connected with the activities of the Bank. The claim was in fact directed exclusively against the Polish State. According to international law a foreign State, both in its public capacity and in transactions of a private law nature, is not subject to the jurisdiction of the courts of another country except in cases of voluntary submission and in matters involving immovable property. This rule applied also to Poland, whose independence Germany recognised in Article 87 of the Treaty of Versailles. It did not matter that the Treaty was ratified on 11 January, 1920, *i.e.* after the order of attachment was issued. The decisive date is that of the present judgment. [Report: *Juristische Wochenschrift*, 1921, p. 1481.]

NOTE.—The other aspects of this case, dealt with in detail in the judgment, do not raise questions of general interest and are not digested. For interesting notes on this case see Rukser and Strupp, *ibid.*, pp. 1481-1483. See also *ibid.* p. 1485, for a similar decision of the same Tribunal of 4 December, 1920.

Case No. 79 **Jurisdiction—Exemption from—Foreign States—Contracts in Private Law Matters—Exterritoriality of Legation Buildings—Fiction of Exterritoriality—Object of Diplomatic Immunities.**

IMMUNITIES (FOREIGN STATE IN PRIVATE CONTRACTS) CASE.

Austria, Supreme Court in Civil Matters. 5 *January*, 1920. (*R. II* 282/19.)

THE FACTS.—A foreign ambassador concluded in Austria a contract concerning the execution of various works in the Embassy building. No payments were subsequently made in connection with the contract, and the plaintiff thereupon brought in the local court at Vienna a civil action against the State represented by the ambassador. The Court of First Instance dismissed the action on the ground that it had no jurisdiction seeing that a foreign State cannot be sued before the courts of another State even on account of private law claims except in cases of voluntary submission or actions involving immovable property. The Court of

Appeal held that Austrian courts had jurisdiction. It pointed out that the State which in the territory of another State concludes a private law contract of this nature cannot complain that its sovereignty has been violated if it is asked to comply with its obligations in that State. Whoever chooses to participate in business intercourse within a State must put up with the jurisdiction of courts in that State. Without such jurisdiction business intercourse would remain without legal protection. Further, the Court pointed out that the alleged exterritoriality of the Embassy building was a mere fiction. The Embassy building must be regarded as property situated in Austria.

Held by the Supreme Court: That the judgment of the Court of Appeal must be upheld. Austrian courts had jurisdiction. The view that the sovereignty of a State involves for that State absolute freedom from responsibility before the courts of a foreign State is not accurate. It is true that in cases in which the sovereignty of the foreign State is involved Austrian courts have no jurisdiction. However, if the foreign State appears in Austria as a subject of private rights and concludes contracts which have to be fulfilled in Austria, then it " enters the legal system of the Austrian State." It can no longer remain independent of it. In such cases the foreign State is subject to the jurisdiction of the courts of the State in which the contract has been made. The purpose of exterritoriality is merely to prevent such jurisdiction as may hinder the ambassador in the fulfilment of his mission. This is not the case in the present action. [Report: *Entscheidungen des Obersten Gerichtshofes in Zivilrechtssachen*, vol. II (1920), No. 1, p. 3.]

NOTE.—See, however, the decisions, in the period under review, of the Supreme Court of Justice of Czechoslovakia, which held repeatedly that the fiscus of a foreign State cannot be sued before the Czechoslovak courts, except in cases of voluntary submission (decisions of 23 December, 1919, No. R. I 364 [Váž. 343 civ.]; of 31 August, 1920, No. R. I 337 [Váž. 639 civ.]; of 12 October, 1920, No. R. II 211 [Váž. 705 civ.]), or in cases concerning immovable property situated in Czechoslovakia (decision of 19 October, 1920, No. R. I 863 [Váž. 712 civ.]).

See also decision of the same Court of 26 April, 1928, No. R. I 305 (Váž. 8000 civ.), in *Annual Digest*, 1927-1928, Case No. 111.

Case No. 80

Jurisdiction—Exemption from—Foreign State—French Restitution Commission in Belgium.

HERBILLON *v.* LENTZ.

Belgium, Civil Tribunal of Huy. 10 *February*, 1920.

THE FACTS.—The French Restitution Commission having seized a cow belonging to the plaintiff, the latter brought an action for compensation for the loss against the person who had sold her the animal, basing her claim on the fact that it was a chattel of German origin forming part of the war booty of the Allied and Associated armies. The defendant contended that since the said Commission was not under the duty to establish its right to the seizure in each particular case, seizure by it was nothing more than an interference in fact with possession, and not the adverse claim of right which Article 1626 of the *Code Civil* requires as a condition for a claim for a breach of warranty of title.

Held : For the plaintiff. The requisition carried out by the French Restitution Commission, an official organisation operating in Belgium with the consent of the Belgian Government, cannot be regarded as merely an interference in fact with the possession. Commissions of this kind " share in the " sovereignty of the Government which instituted them and " determined their powers. In consequence, whatever mistakes " of fact the commissions may commit, it is not for the courts " to give redress." As the seizures made by these commissions are presumed to be based on law, they fall within the conception of the adverse claim of right referred to in Article 1626 of the *Code Civil.* [Report : *Pasicrisie belge,* 1920, III, pp. 145 *et seq.*]

Case No. 81

Jurisdiction—Exemption from—Foreign State—Requisition on Behalf of Naval Base of a Foreign Allied State.

DE ROOVER *v.* THE STATES OF BELGIUM AND FRANCE.

Belgium, Civil Tribunal of Antwerp. 2 *February*, 1920.

THE FACTS.—On 15 March, 1919, the Municipality of Antwerp, acting under the order of the Belgian military authorities, requisitioned part of a hotel belonging to the plaintiff, in order to establish there the French naval base. The plaintiff maintained (1) that the requisition was irregular, seeing that the Belgian Law of 14 August, 1887, provided only for requisitions for the billeting of troops and the establishing of a foreign transport base on the lines of a commercial enterprise; (2) that the French military authorities prevented him from making use of the parts of the property which were not actually requisitioned. On this latter point he asked for an order against the French naval base to give him the full enjoyment of those parts of the building.

Held: That the Tribunal has no jurisdiction to entertain the claim. Military requisitions are in effect acts by public authority; they depend solely on the will of the State exercised in the public interest; it is immaterial that the property requisitioned has been appropriated for the use of the French naval base, seeing that this latter constituted an organisation indispensable for the requirements, the maintenance and the provisioning of the French troops both in Belgium and in the occupied part of Germany. The forces of the Allied and Associated Powers are an indivisible unit, under one command, so that requisitions made for any of these forces are to be regarded as national requisitions.

As to the writ against the French State, represented by the commander of the naval base, it was held that the latter had no authority to represent the French State. If he had such authority, the Tribunal would not be competent to deal with this part of the charge, seeing that the sovereignty of States, their mutual independence and their absolute autonomy do not permit that a State be submitted against its will to the control and jurisdiction of the judicial authority of another State. [Report: *Pasicrisie belge*, 1920, III, pp. 93 *et seq.*]

Jurisdiction—Exemption from—Foreign State—Military Service—Public Order. **Case No. 82**

In re Toebinte; Theuns; United States Government *ex parte* the *Procureur du Roi* (Civil Tribunal of Antwerp).

Belgium, Court of Appeal of Brussels. 24 June, 1920.

The Facts.—An action for damages had been brought against the United States Government as the result of a collision at Antwerp between Toebinte's car driven by Theuns and a lorry driven by Gibson, a soldier from the American naval base. The Civil Tribunal of Antwerp having declared itself competent to deal with this matter (20 January, 1920), the

Case No. 82 *contd.*

Procureur du Roi in his official capacity appealed against the judgment.

Held : The Court quashed the judgment appealed against. It declares itself incompetent to entertain the claim on the grounds that Gibson was a soldier in the United States army and that at the time of the collision he was carrying out his duty in driving a car belonging to that army. " The judge in " the court of first instance . . . could not, without contra- " vening public order, assume the right to censure the acts of " a foreign Government in its capacity of a public authority." [Report : *Pasicrisie belge*, 1920, II, pp. 122 *et seq.*]

Case No. 83

Suit against Foreign State—Exemption from Jurisdiction—Distinction between Acts in a Public and other Capacity—Hague Convention of 17 July, 1905, on Civil Procedure—Suits against Non-Diplomatic Representatives of States.

LAKHOWSKY *v.* SWISS FEDERAL GOVERNMENT AND COLONEL DE REYNIER.

France, Tribunal de Commerce of the Seine (*Eighth Chamber*). 26 *December*, 1919.
Court of Appeal of Paris (*First Chamber*). 16 *March*, 1921.

THE FACTS.—A " Swiss Office of Foreign Transports " was established to assure the service of supplies to Switzerland during the war. Lahkowsky claimed that he had concluded agreements with this Office on 8 October, 1918, for obtaining charters of 25,000 tons of shipping for the carriage of cocoa from Java to Cette at the rate of 1275 francs per ton. He declared that the alleged agreements had not been carried out, and sued the Office of Transports by its Paris representative, Colonel de Reynier, and the Swiss Federal Government, on whose behalf the Office of Transports had acted, asking for rescission and damages. The Swiss Federal Council pleaded to the jurisdiction. It relied on the principle of the immunity of foreign States. It also objected to the jurisdiction of the French courts " *ratione loci* " on the ground of the Franco-Swiss Convention of 15 June, 1869.[1]

[1] Article 1 of the Convention of 1869 provides as follows : " Dans les " contestations en matière mobilière et personnelle, civile ou de commerce " qui s'élèveront, soit entre Français et Suisses, soit entre Suisses et Français, " le demandeur sera tenu de poursuivre son action devant les juges naturels du " défendeur."

Held by the *Tribunal de Commerce*: That the Court had no jurisdiction "*ratione loci*" in consequence of the provisions of the Franco-Swiss Convention of 15 June, 1869.

It rejected, however, the plea that the Court was incompetent "*ratione personae.*" Although sovereign States, such as the Swiss Federal State, are absolutely independent of other States in virtue of the essential principles of international law, it must be remarked that this immunity from jurisdiction exists only for acts in a sovereign capacity or administrative acts—acts of public authority. The Federal Government has renounced the right to claim immunity from jurisdiction by procuring the contract to be signed not in its own name but in that of the Swiss Office of Foreign Transports whose representative at Paris was not the Swiss diplomatic representative. [Report: *Gazette du Palais*, 1920, vol. II, p. 282.]

FURTHER FACTS.—Lakhowsky appealed. The Swiss authorities refused to serve on the Federal Government the notice of appeal on the ground that Article 4 of the Hague Convention of 1905 on Civil Procedure gave the State to which the request was addressed the right to refuse the service of a writ on its territory in cases when in its opinion the service would be prejudicial to its sovereignty or security. Accordingly, the Swiss Government, which maintained the objection to the jurisdiction put before the Court of First Instance, asserted that it was not properly cited and that the proceedings were therefore null and void.

Held by the Court of Appeal: That the Court was not competent, but not for the same reasons as those of the Court below.

(*a*) The principle of immunity from jurisdiction, based on the mutual independence of States, is universally recognised, and nothing in the attitude of the Swiss Government and its relations with Lakhowsky implies the abandonment of this principle. While the distinction drawn by the *Tribunal de Commerce* between a political and a business act may be accepted, still the alleged agreements were not made with a commercial object but corresponded to political considerations, in both the international and the domestic fields, wholly remote from any idea of profit or speculation. Moreover, the establishment of the Swiss Office of Foreign Transports is connected with the Order of 3 August, 1914, concerning the measures necessary to ensure the safety of the country and the maintenance of its neutrality.

Case No. 83 *contd.* (*b*) The immunity from jurisdiction enjoyed by the foreign State attaches also to the acts of its official representative. Accordingly, French courts had no jurisdiction to entertain an action against Colonel Reynier.

(*c*) As Colonel Reynier was not domiciled in France, assumption of jurisdiction would be contrary to the Convention of 1869. [Report: *Clunet*, vol. XLV (1921), p. 179.]

NOTE.—As to the Hague Convention the Court held that, whatever the attitude adopted by the foreign State where process is to be served, the Convention is not to be enforced by making the proceedings a nullity. A State cannot be allowed the power of paralysing at its own discretion suits brought in a foreign country against its nationals.

Case No. 84 **Jurisdiction—Foreign States—Exemption from—Conformity of Municipal Law with International Law—Acts of War by Germany in Belgium in regard to Neutral Property—Claim for Compensation against German *Reich* in Dutch Court—Judgment for the Plaintiff in Default of Appearance by the *Reich*—Claim by Dutch Government to have the Judgment Revoked—Lack of Jurisdiction of the Court—Disturbance of Friendly Relations by Municipal Decision—Insufficiency of Dutch Legislation Remedied by Enactment of New Supplementary Law.**

DE BOOY *v.* GERMAN *Reich* (The Government of Holland Intervening).

Holland, District Court of Rotterdam, First Chamber. 19 *April*, 1920.

(Dr. A. RIETEMA, President; Drs. W. LUNSINGH TONCKENS and H. W. M. VAN HELTEN, Judges.)

THE FACTS.—During the Great War, in October, 1914, the German military authorities in Belgium, acting in exercise of their belligerent rights, destroyed in Mechlin a 320-ton vessel, with a cargo of coal, belonging to B. A. de Booy, a Dutch merchant of Rotterdam. According to Article 126 of the Dutch Code of Civil Procedure, which entitles Dutch subjects to institute legal proceedings in the court of their own domicile against any defendant "who has no recognised residence in the Kingdom," the owner of the property destroyed sued the German *Reich* for damages in the District Court of Rotterdam. When the case came under discussion, the German *Reich* allowed judgment against itself to go by default, and was ordered by the Court, on 25 September, 1916, to pay to the plaintiff

Belg. frs. 24,600, plus interest at the rate of 5 per cent. from 7 July, 1916, the date of the " commencement of " the proceedings." [Reports: *Weekblad van het Recht*, No. 10022; *Nederlandsche Jurisprudentie*, 1917, p. 13.]

The successful plaintiff then intimated his intention to proceed to execution of the judgment by seizing certain property of the *Reich* in Holland. The Dutch Government was of opinion that this judgment against a foreign State for acts performed in the exercise of its sovereign belligerent powers was contrary to the Law of Nations. As, however, the Dutch Government did not possess sufficient authority under Dutch constitutional law to interfere with decisions of the judiciary, it took proceedings of a summary nature before the President of the same District Court that had given judgment against the *Reich* (the President being this time Dr. J. H. van Meurs), in order to have the execution of the judgment stayed pending decision on a formal claim to have it definitively annulled. The President, on 13 January, 1917, found for the Government and ordered a stay of execution. [Reports: *Weekblad van het Recht*, No. 10038; *Nederlandsche Jurisprudentie*, 1917, p. 133.] De Booy appealed against the judgment of the President of the District Court to the Appellate Court of The Hague, which, in its turn, refused to allow the appeal, apparently on the ground that it was contrary to international law to sue a foreign State in a Dutch court (judgment of 23 March, 1917). [Reports: *Weekblad van het Recht*, No. 10170; *Nederlandsche Jurisprudentie*, 1917, p. 38.]

In the meantime [1] the Dutch Government, aware of its lack of sufficient constitutional and legal powers to prevent the execution of judgments contrary to international law, had introduced on 12 January, 1917, a bill designed to fill this gap in Dutch legislation. The bill was passed by Parliament and published in the *Staatsblad* (Official Journal) No. 303 of 1917 (Law of 26 April, 1917, inserting in the Law of 15 May, 1829, *Staatsblad* No. 28, " containing general provisions con- " cerning the legislation of the Kingdom," a new Article 13 (*a*), reading as follows: " The jurisdiction

[1] Gradually the case grew to a " *cause célèbre* " as the result of discussion in legal periodicals and of questions in Parliament.

Case No. 84 *contd.*

"of the judiciary and the possibility of the execution "of judicial decisions and of acts of public authorities "are limited by the exceptions recognised by the Law "of Nations"). Thereupon, by Royal Decree of 29 May, 1917, *Staatsblad* No. 446, a corresponding provision was inserted in *Règlement* No. IV of 1838, concerning the service of officers of the Court, obliging them to refuse to act on a writ, in the event of a notice given to them by, or on the authority of, the Minister of Justice, to the effect that action on the writ would be contrary to the international obligations of the State.

Independently of the law thus passed, the Dutch Government determined to have recourse to ordinary remedies of civil procedure, with the view to having the original judgment against the German *Reich* formally annulled by means of "third-party opposition" (*derdenverzet*) according to Articles 376 ff.[1] of the Code of Civil Procedure. Thus the case came up once more in the District Court of Rotterdam (First Chamber), in consequence of a summons issued by the Government against the two parties to the original suit, B. A. de Booy and the German *Reich* (the latter for purely formal reasons only). This time the Court was composed of other judges than in 1916, only one of the judges of 1916 sitting on the Chamber. Before the Court the Dutch Government contended that, according to the Law of Nations, a sovereign State may not be subjected against its will to the jurisdiction of a foreign court, and that in any case a judgment against such a State

[1] Articles 376 ff. of the Code of Civil Procedure provide as follows:

(376) "Third parties are entitled to ask for the revision of a judgment "which injures their rights, if neither they themselves in person or their "legal representatives, nor the persons they represent, have been summoned in the suit, or have been a party to it by intervention."

(377) "The Court which gave the decision decides upon the request "for revision. The matter is brought before the Court by a summons "served upon all parties to the original proceedings, and the general "provisions as to procedure apply."

(379) "The Court which is seized of a request of third parties for "the revision of a judgment may, if there are grounds for so doing, stay "the execution of the judgment until it has decided the application for "revision."

(380) "If the decision is in favour of revision, the judgment shall be "amended to the extent only to which it has injuriously affected the rights "of third parties, unless it is impossible to draw a distinction between the "several parts of the judgment and it is therefore necessary to quash "it *in toto*."

is not susceptible of execution against the property of that State situate in Holland. Therefore the Dutch Government asked the Court to annul its decision of 1916 by virtue of Articles 376 ff. of the Code of Civil Procedure, under which third parties are entitled to ask for the revision of a judgment, given without notice to them and calculated to injure their rights.

Held, adopting the contention of the Dutch Government: "That a sovereign State may not be subjected against its will "to the jurisdiction of another State; that, consequently, "States are bound to abstain from any act which presupposes "the existence of such jurisdiction; that the existence of such "an obligation implies the right not to be impeded in its "fulfilment; that, if the judicial authorities of the State render "decisions which conflict with such an obligation, they injure "the rights of their own State." On these grounds the Court annulled its own judgment of 1916. [Reports: *Weekblad van het Recht*, 19 November, 1920, No. 10638; *Nederlandsche Jurisprudentie*, 1921, p. 853.]

Held, on appeal, by the Appellate Court (22 December, 1922: Dr. S. Gratama, Wzn., President; Drs. Jhr. J. L. W. C. von Weiler and J. van Gelein Vitringa, Judges): That Article 376 of the Dutch Code of Civil Procedure entitles third parties whose rights are injured by the judgment of a civil court rendered between other litigants to ask for the revision of that judgment in the court which rendered it; that, although the main object of this Article is to safeguard interests of third parties which are protected by the civil law, there is nothing in the law which limits this particular form of procedure to the case of a judicial decision involving private interests only; that there is no reason, therefore, to deny this legal protection to one whose interest is protected by other law—*e.g.* international law; that the Court below was justified in holding that its original judgment injured an interest of its State protected by the Law of Nations; that the judgment therefore violated not only the international rights of the German *Reich*, but also the right of the State of The Netherlands not to have its friendly relations with a foreign State endangered by decisions of its judiciary, contrary to international law [1]; that the lower Court

[1] On this point of the character in municipal law of acts calculated to disturb friendly relations, reference may be made to the English case of *Rex* v. *Brailsford*, L.R. [1905] 2 K.B. 730. See also Fischer Williams, *Chapters on Current International Law and The League of Nations* (Longmans, London, 1929), p. 246, n.

Case No. 84 ***contd.*** had rightly set aside its original judgment of 1916; and that, consequently, the appeal must be dismissed. [Reports: *Weekblad van het Recht*, 9 July, 1923, No. 11050; *Nederlandsche Jurisprudentie*, 1923, p. 609.]

Held, on further appeal, by the Supreme Court (21 March, 1924: Dr. J. A. A. Bosch, President; Drs. A. Fentener van Vlissingen, H. Hesse, Jhr. Rh. Feith, and J. Kosters, Judges): That the appeal must be allowed. It was true that the original judgment was contrary to international law and ought not to have been given. However, that judgment could not be annulled by way of a civil action, the legal procedure of "opposition by third parties" not being intended to cover claims such as those entered by the State of The Netherlands. Accordingly, the original decision of 1916 must be maintained and put into force.

The claim of the Dutch Government depended on the rule of unwritten customary law according to which, apart from voluntary recognition of jurisdiction, a civil court has no jurisdiction in regard to claims brought against a foreign State on account of acts committed by it in its capacity under public law. According to the Law of Nations, the State of The Netherlands is bound to fulfil the obligations arising from this rule and, therefore, to have it enforced by means of its organs (in the present case, by means of its judiciary). However, this obligation of the State of The Netherlands to foreign States is not accompanied by a right under civil law against private persons to have the rule of international law respected. The Law of Nations is silent on that issue and Dutch law does not recognise any such right. Strict enforcement of the rules of international law is undoubtedly of paramount interest to the State, but in order to justify the procedure of "opposition by "third parties" under the Code of Civil Procedure, the interest in question ought to have been sanctioned by the law and raised to the rank of a subjective right. [Reports: *Weekblad van het Recht*, 1 December, 1924, No. 11269; *Nederlandsche Jurisprudentie*, 1924, p. 535.]

NOTE.—(*a*) Since, however, in the meantime (1917), Dutch legislation had been completed by a new Article 13 (*a*) of the Law of 1829 containing general provisions concerning the legislation of the Kingdom (see THE FACTS, above), the final solution of the controversy under civil law had no practical effect, the Article in question authorising the Government to prevent the execution of a sentence deemed by it to be contrary to international law.

(*b*) The fact that the Supreme Court limits itself to mentioning acts of a foreign State in its capacity under public law does not mean that its judgment recognises jurisdiction with regard to acts done in some other capacity. See the note at the foot of the judgment in *Weekblad van het Recht*, No. 11269. Cf. also for this civil lawsuit Dr. L. van Praag in *Revue de droit international privé*, 1923, p. 436, and Dr. J. Kosters, *Les fondements du droit des gens*, in *Bibliotheca Visseriana*, vol. IV, pp. 270 ff.

(*c*) This series of cases has been the object of prolonged discussions in Dutch legal literature. Cf., *inter alia*, *Weekblad van het Recht*, Nos. 10023 and 10024 (parliamentary interpellation in writing by Dr. J. H. W. Q. ter Spill and answer of the Minister of Justice); 10028 and 10045 (Dr. W. Heineken); 10029 (the Editors); 10030 (Dr. W. van Rossem); 10036 (Dr. Nolst Trenité); 10036, 10045 and 10049 (Dr. L. van Praag); 10038 and 10058 (bill of 12 January, 1917, with parliamentary documents); 10041 (leading article by the Editors); 10042 (Dr. Denekamp); 10047 (Dr. J. A. Levy). Parliamentary documents and debates in: *Handelingen van de Tweede Kamer der Staten-Generaal*, 1916/1917, pp. 1805-1821, and *Bijlagen*, No. 346, 1-7; *Handelingen van de Eerste Kamer der Staten-Generaal*, 1916/1917, pp. 384 ff., 458, 459, 477-480, 489-496; Dr. J. Kosters, *op. cit.*, vol. IV, pp. 270-272.

(*d*) Only two months after the original decision of the District Court of Rotterdam, the District Court of Maastricht had given a contrary decision, dated 23 November, 1916 [Reports: *Nederlandsche Jurisprudentie*, 1917, p. 12; 48 *Clunet* (1921), p. 632], according to which a State is not, with certain exceptions recognised by the Law of Nations itself, under positive international law subject to the jurisdiction of a foreign court, unless it submits voluntarily: *N. V. Limburgsch Landbouw-Syndicaat, of Wijk-Maastricht (plaintiff)* v. *German Reich (defendant, in default)*. In this suit the Court refused to order the *Reich* to compensate the losses which the plaintiff had suffered in consequence of the seizure by the *Reich*, *jure imperii*, in the Belgian invaded territory, of certain quantities of beetroots belonging to him.

Jurisdiction—Immunity of States from Suit—Claims and Counter-Claims—States in their Sovereign and other Capacities—Belgium as Defendant in Counter-Claim—Counter-Claim in respect of Acts Performed in Sovereign Capacity. **Case No. 85**

THE STATE OF BELGIUM (plaintiff in claim, defendant in counter-claim) *v.* E. A. G. DE BADTS (defendant in claim, plaintiff in counter-claim).

Holland, District Court of Rotterdam. 24 *November*, 1922.

(Dr. H. W. B. THOMAS, President; Drs. S. G. CANES and B. I. ZIJLSTRA, Judges.)

THE FACTS.—A shipowner and shipbroker of Rotterdam was sued by the Belgian Government for an account of the sale of a certain cargo of wheat which one of his ships had transported for the Belgian State, in October or November, 1914. In opposing this claim,

Case No. 85 *contd.*

the defendant brought a counter-claim against the Belgian Government for hire of vessels requisitioned by that Government during the war. The Belgian Government having invoked the Court's lack of jurisdiction with regard to this counter-claim,

Held: That the Court had no jurisdiction to take cognisance of the counter-claim against the Belgian State. A State which is entitled to claim immunity from foreign jurisdiction does not lose this right by the fact that it submits to that jurisdiction in another suit. The correctness of this statement is not impaired by the circumstance that the two actions are, for the sake of convenience, joined in the same proceedings, since the counter-claim does not lose, in consequence thereof, its independent character. This is so particularly in cases in which the plaintiff Government bases its claim on a private law title, but in counter-claim is sued for acts performed in its sovereign capacity. [Reports: *Weekblad van het Recht*, 22 January, 1923, No. 10978; *Nederlandsche Jurisprudentie*, 1923, p. 618.]

Case No. 86

Jurisdiction—Exemption from—Foreign States—Attachment in Holland of Money Belonging to Former Austro-Hungarian Monarchy or its Successor States—Exemption of Foreign States from Jurisdiction of Dutch Courts—States in Liquidation—State Succession—Lack of Jurisdiction.

Bergverksaktiebolaget Kosmai (appellant) *v.* Militär-Liquidierungsamt, of Vienna (respondent).

Holland, Court of Appeal of Amsterdam, First Chamber. 29 *April*, 1921.

(Dr. B. Simons, President; Drs. G. Kirberger and W. A. van Woudenberg Hamstra, Judges.)

The Facts.—On 23 September, 1920, the President of the District Court of Amsterdam, in summary procedure, ordered the raising of a "*conservatoir derden-arrest*" (arrest or attachment by a creditor of goods the property of his debtor in the possession of a third party, as security for his claim) which a Swedish company had procured on a sum of fl. 1,800,000, in possession of the Amsterdamsche Bank and belonging to the *Militär-Liquidierungsamt* of Austria-Hungary in its capacity of agent for that Monarchy. The Swedish company appealed to the Court of Appeal against the raising of this attachment, asserting the inapplicability to the case under consideration of the new Article 13 (*a*) (1917) of the Dutch Law of 15 May, 1829, " containing general " provisions concerning the legislation of the King- " dom " (cf. Case No. 84), since that provision has not in view foreign States who no longer exist and who find themselves in a state of liquidation.

The Court, in conformity with an advisory opinion *ex officio* of the Attorney-General, Dr. S. J. M. van Geuns,

Held, dismissing the appeal : " That, although the Austro- " Hungarian Monarchy has ceased to exist, it did not appear " that the assets of that Monarchy were actually without an " owner ; that the former Dual Monarchy consisted of the " States of Austria and Hungary and that, therefore, the " assets of that Monarchy were in reality the property of those " two States *pro indiviso* ; that those States had continued to " exist, while new States had been constituted out of what " were formerly parts of their territory ; that, from the nature " of things, the former possessions of the Austro-Hungarian " Monarchy had become the property of the old States Austria " and Hungary and the new States, even though the latter " would perhaps not recognise all obligations of the old " Monarchy ; that the above is confirmed by Article 4 of the " Austrian Law of 12 November, 1918, 'Concerning the Con- " 'stitution and Government of German-Austria,' according " to which the 'K. und K.' [1] and the 'K.K.' [2] Ministries were " dissolved ; and as the national States outside Austria, which " had come into existence on the territory of the former " Austro-Hungarian Monarchy, maintained their claims to " the property which those Ministries administered, the " Government of the Republic of Austria continued to manage " provisionally as 'trustee of all interested nations' the " common property lying within the Austrian territory ; " that, consequently, there is every reason to admit that " the appellant party intends to attach in Holland goods " belonging to other sovereign States, or in any case goods to " which other sovereign States lay claim ; that the Law of " Nations recognises that the jurisdiction of a State does not " extend to such sums of money as are the property of foreign " sovereign States, or to which others have a claim, unless those

[1] K. und K., *i.e. Kaiser- und Königlich* (Emperor and King), indicating ministries common to Austria and Hungary, like the ministry of war.—[Ed.]

[2] K.K., *i.e. Kaiser-Königlich* (of the King-Emperor), indicating the separate Austrian ministries.—[Ed.]

Case No. 86 contd. "States submit voluntarily to that jurisdiction." [Report: *Weekblad van het Recht*, 8 August, 1921, No. 10750.]

See also Case No. 8, and Note under Case No. 84.

NOTE.—After the raising, in consequence of the above judgment, of the attachment, the Swedish company tried to obtain a judicial decision in Holland against the *Militär-Liquidierungsamt* of Vienna, recognising its right to pecuniary compensation for the damages which the military administration of the former Austro-Hungarian Monarchy had caused to the company's possessions in Serbia during the Great War. *Held* (by the District Court of Amsterdam, Second Chamber (Dr. W. J. Huysinga, President; Drs. J. Slingenberg and A. J. van Royen, Judges), on 9 June, 1922): That the Court had no jurisdiction. The defendant was an official organ of the sovereign State of Austria, charged with the administration of property of one or more of the States formed from the dissolution of the former Dual Monarchy. It is generally recognised in international law that sovereign States are not, in matters relating to the public administration of their country, subject to the jurisdiction of the courts of another State. The defendant had declared itself unwilling to submit to such jurisdiction. Accordingly, in application of Article 13 (*a*) of the Dutch law containing general provisions concerning the legislation of the Kingdom, the Court had no jurisdiction. [Reports: *Weekblad van het Recht*, 27 September, 1922, No. 10928; *Nederlandsche Jurisprudentie*, 1923, p. 292.]

Case No. 87

Exemptions from Jurisdiction—Foreign States—Counter-Claim

FRENCH REPUBLIC *v.* INLAND NAVIGATION CO.

United States District Court, E.D. Missouri.

21 *February*, 1920.

THE FACTS.—The French Republic sued the defendant company to recover $330,000 paid on a contract. The defendant company claimed that it had been damaged by an alleged breach of the contract on the plaintiff's part and counter-claimed for $600,000. The plaintiff admitted that any damages to the defendant arising out of breaches of the contract might be used as a defence or set-off, but denied that the mere act of bringing suit subjected it to a counter-claim amounting to an affirmative action. The plaintiff moved to strike out such parts of the defendant's answer as attempted to set up a counter-claim for affirmative relief.

Held: That the motion to strike out must be allowed. In bringing suit the foreign State did not waive its immunity with respect to the counter-claim. Such a counter-claim was distinguished from matters of procedure to which the plaintiff must admit. The difficulty of enforcing an affirmative judgment on the counter-claim was pointed out. United States State decisions to the effect that a private individual sued by a State of the United States may not counter-claim for affirmative relief against the State were cited. Reliance was also placed upon the case of *Kingdom of Roumania* v. *Guaranty Trust Co.*, 250 Fed. 341. The Court said: "Keeping in mind "the nature and effect of an action by way of counterclaim, "I think the authorities, the analogous cases, and the reason "of the thing, all sustain the conclusion, which I reach, that "such a proceeding is not permissible. While there is scarcely "a dissenting view upon the point that, as against a sovereign "electing to sue an individual or a public or private corpora-"tion in its own courts, or in the courts of a friendly foreign "jurisdiction, such defendant may, as a defense to the demand "of the sovereign, set off a part, or the whole, of plaintiff's "demand by pleading a demand which might otherwise form "the subject-matter of a counterclaim . . . and that such a "foreign sovereign is amenable, just as is any other plaintiff, "to mere matters of practice and procedure, yet no affirmative "judgment can be sustained as upon a counterclaim against "the sovereign, whereby the sovereign shall be compelled or "adjudged to pay money or any other thing of value." (263 Fed. 410, 413.) [Reports: 263 Fed. 410; Dickinson, *Cases*, p. 630.]

NOTE.—See *The Gloria*, 286 Fed. 188, 266 U.S. 328, *Annual Digest*, 1923-1924; *Kunglig Jarnvagsstyrelsen* v. *Dexter and Carpenter*, 32 F. (2nd) 195 (certiorari denied: 280 U.S. 579), 43 F. (2nd) 705 (certiorari denied: 282 U.S. 896); *A.J.*, XXV (1919), p. 335; 29 M.L.R. 894.

Exemptions from Jurisdiction—Foreign States—Corporation Controlled by Foreign State. Case No. 88

COALE *ET AL.* *v.* SOCIÉTÉ COOPÉRATIVE SUISSE DES CHARBONS, BASLE, *ET AL.*

United States District Court, S.D. New York. 20 *May*, 1921.

THE FACTS.—This was an action for breach of contract. In 1917, the Swiss Federal Council delegated to the Department of Commerce the power to control the importation and distribution of coal. In March, 1919, this Department caused the Société Coopérative Suisse des Charbons to be organised to purchase abroad and import coal. The members of the company were Swiss nationals who had imported coal in large quantities. The company's charter and rules were not to be valid

Case No. 88 *contd.*

until approved by the Swiss Government. Seven of the seventeen directors of the company were to be appointed by the Government. The Government was to receive the net earnings in excess of 6 per cent. The Société contracted to buy coal from the plaintiffs. The contract was signed by the Swiss Minister to the United States on behalf of the Société and the Swiss Federation. The plaintiffs brought this action on the contract for failure to take and pay for coal. The Société claimed immunity.

Held : That the Société was not immune. The Court said : " If the Swiss government chose to do its business by means " of the Société, the latter, as a corporate entity, was liable " for its corporate obligations. . . . If the Société had con- " tracted as agent for the Swiss government, the case might " have been different ; but in this instance the Swiss minister " signed the contract for the corporation. The interest of the " government in any balance after those contributing the " capital received 6 per cent. interest is like the case of a bank " where the government owns all the stock. The decisions " hold that the corporation is liable under such circumstances." (21 F. (2nd) 180, 181.) The Court cited *Commercial Pacific Cable Co.* v. *Philippine National Bank*, 263 Fed. 218, 269 Fed. 1022 ; and *United States* v. *Strang*, 254 U.S. 491. The Court added that, " The joinder of the Swiss government will not " defeat the cause of action. . . . The action may proceed " against the party served. . . . Any profits which might " become due to the government after payment of 6 per cent. " to those furnishing capital would resemble dividends ; " property of the corporation taken on execution would not " be property of the Swiss Federation." (21 F. (2nd) 180, 181.) [Reports : 21 F. (2nd) 180 ; Dickinson, *Cases*, p. 559.]

Case No. 89

Exemptions from Jurisdiction—Foreign States—Waiver—Counter-Claim.

REPUBLIC OF FRANCE *v.* PITTSBURGH STEEL EXPORT COMPANY.

United States, New York, City Court of the City of New York, Special Term. July, 1920.

THE FACTS.—The Republic of France sued for the purchase price of wire sold to the defendant corporation. The defendant counter-claimed for failure to deliver certain quantities of nails. The plaintiff demurred to the counter-claim on the ground that the Court lacked jurisdiction.

Held: That the demurrer to the counter-claim must be sustained. "The Republic of France, a friendly foreign "sovereign power, may not be sued in our courts without its "consent, and by bringing this suit it has not waived this "immunity to the extent that the defendant may ask for "affirmative relief against it. *Kingdom of Roumania* v. "*Guaranty Trust Co.*, 250 Fed. Repr. 341. While, in the circum-"stances of this case, the defendant might set up a counter-"claim which arose out of the same transaction declared on "in the complaint, and then only to the extent necessary to "defeat it, an affirmative judgment against the plaintiff may "not be rendered without its consent. The counter-claim "alleges a distinct and collateral transaction in no way con-"nected with the cause of action pleaded in the complaint." (112 Misc. (N.Y.) 688, 689.) [Report: 112 Misc. (N.Y.) 688.]

NOTE.—See to the same effect: *South African Republic* v. *La Compagnie Franco-Belge du Chemin de Fer du Nord*, [1898] 1 Ch. 190; *In re Patterson-McDonald Shipbuilding Company*, 293 Fed. 192, *Annual Digest*, 1923-1924. Affirmative judgments on counter-claims have been allowed in *Kingdom of Norway* v. *Federal Sugar Refining Company*, 286 Fed. 188, *Annual Digest*, 1923-1924; *Kunglig Jarnvagsstyrelsen* v. *Dexter and Carpenter*, 300 Fed. 891, 32 F. (2nd) 195, although no execution was allowed against State property, 43 F. (2nd) 705, 29 M.L.R. 894; and *von Hellfeld* v. *Russian Government*, 5 *A.J.*, 490 (Germany). See also *The Newbattle*, 10 P.D. 33; *The Thekla*, 266 U.S. 328; van Praag, *Juridiction et droit international public*, s. 105; and *The Cumene*, *Annual Digest*, 1925-1926, Case No. 126.

Exemption from Jurisdiction—Foreign States—Germany before Danzig Courts after 10 January, 1920.

See Case No. 56 (*Pending Actions* (*Danzig*) *Case* (*I*)).

Exemption from Jurisdiction—Foreign States—Germany—Jurisdiction of Danzig Courts.

See Case No. 55 (*Pending Actions* (*Danzig*) *Case* (*II*)).

(ii) Heads of Foreign States

Case No. 90 **Jurisdiction—Exemption from—Heads of States—Obligations of Private Law.**

Nobili *v.* Emperor Charles I of Austria.

Italy, Court of Cassation of Rome. 11 *March,* 1921.

The Facts.—Nobili had started legal proceedings of a private nature against the Archduke Charles Francis Joseph. The latter, having become Emperor of Austria during the course of the hearing, claimed that he henceforth enjoyed, by virtue of Austrian laws and the principles of international law, immunity from jurisdiction, and that therefore neither the commencement nor the continuance of any judicial proceedings against him were admissible.

Held: That such a contention cannot be allowed. The appeal by the Emperor's representative against the judgment of the Court of Appeal of Ancona, pronounced against him in default of appearance, must be dismissed. It is not permissible to invoke a prerogative of immunity from jurisdiction in favour of a foreign sovereign in Italy, where even the national sovereign is subject to ordinary law for his obligations of a proprietary nature. The present proceedings do not relate to acts done by the Emperor of Austria as head of his own State. The engagements in question have their origin in contracts and acts of a private nature which arose in Italy. The provisions of Article 105 of the Italian Code of Civil Procedure therefore make the Italian judicial authorities competent in relation to a foreigner who has no residence in the kingdom but who is not merely casually present there. Nor is it sound to oppose to such a conclusion the consideration that Austrian laws recognise, in favour of the Emperor, full exemption from the jurisdiction of the courts. Such a consideration cannot be invoked in foreign States. Nor is it proper to make an appeal, as the appellant does, to the principle of international law of reciprocity, which cannot be prayed in aid by a foreigner so as to be accorded a privilege which the local law does not grant to any of its own citizens and which is contrary to the fundamental principle of modern constitutions based on the juridical equality of the State before the law, even though the State be actuated with regard to foreigners by the very singular generosity of Article 3 of the Italian Civil

Code.[1] [Report: *Giurisprudenza Italiana*, vol. I (1922), pp. 1, 472.]

(iii) PUBLIC SHIPS AND OTHER PROPERTY OF FOREIGN STATES

Exemptions from Jurisdiction—Public Ships—Ships Employed in Trade. **Case No. 91**

THE CARLO POMA.

United States Circuit Court of Appeals, Second Circuit. 14 *May*, 1919.

THE FACTS.—A shipper libelled the Italian merchant vessel *Carlo Poma* in the United States District Court for the Southern District of New York. The Italian ambassador suggested to the Court that this was a Government-owned vessel and therefore immune. This suggestion was accompanied by a certificate from the United States Secretary of State to the effect that the suggestion was signed by the Italian ambassador but without his taking responsibility for the contents. Proctors appeared specially for the Kingdom of Italy and secured on motion an order staying the execution of process. On appeal,

Held: That the order must be affirmed. The United States, like Great Britain, allows immunity to the property of foreign sovereigns, whatever the purpose for which it is used. The British cases of *The Parlement Belge*, 5 P.D. 197, and *The Jassy*, [1906] P. 270, were cited. The Court said: "The law of the United States is the same, except that the "immunity of property of a sovereign, whether the United "States or a foreign sovereign, depends, not merely upon the "ownership, but also upon the actual possession by the "sovereign of the property at the time process is served." (259 Fed. 369, 370.) [Report: 259 Fed. 369.]

NOTE.—This decree was vacated by the United States Supreme Court, 255 U.S. 219, on the ground that a jurisdictional question required a direct appeal to the Supreme Court. The decision of the District Court stood.

---

[1] Article 3 provides as follows: "A foreigner shall be admitted to the "enjoyment of all civil rights allowed to citizens . . ."

Case No. 92

Exemptions from Jurisdiction—Public Ships—Ships Employed in Trade.

THE MAIPO.

United States District Court, S.D. New York.
21 February, 1919.

THE FACTS.—The *Maipo* was a merchant vessel owned and operated by the Chilean Government. The Commercial Shipping Co. brought a suit against it in the United States District Court. Upon motion to discharge the vessel on the ground that it belonged to the Government of Chile,

Held: That the motion to discharge must be granted. Judge Hough said: " I do not think the enormous extension " of sovereign privilege demanded by vessels in all kinds of " business of late months and years indicates any change or " advance in the law at all. The law remains the same. " What has changed is the view which the governments of the " world assume towards public duties or public enterprises. " Why was a war vessel exempt from seizure? Not because " it was a war vessel, but because it was a part of the exercise " or manifestation of sovereign power. . . . If the Republic of " Chile considers it a government function to go into the " carrying trade, as would appear to be the case here, that is " the business of the Republic of Chile; and if we do not " approve of it, if we do not like it, if we do not wish any " longer to accord that respect to the property so engaged, " which has hitherto been accorded to government property, " then we must say so through diplomatic channels, and not " through the judiciary." (259 Fed. 367, 368.) [Report: 259 Fed. 367.]

Case No. 93

Exemptions from Jurisdiction—Public Ships—Chartered Ships —Ownership or Possession as Test of Immunity.

THE BEAVERTON. THE DAISAI MARU.

United States District Court, S.D. New York. 28 July, 1919.

THE FACTS.—There was a collision between the *Beaverton* and the *Daisai Maru*, and the latter vessel was libelled in the United States District Court. The *Daisai Maru* was under charter at the time to the French Republic, although neither owned by the Republic nor in its possession.

Held : That the decree must be against the *Daisai Maru.* The Circuit Court of Appeals for the Second Circuit had concluded in the *Carlo Poma*[1] case, 259 Fed. 369, that " the test " of immunity was the possession of the foreign sovereign, not " its ownership." " *A fortiori,*" said Judge Learned Hand, " the relation of charterer will not give immunity." (273 Fed. 539, 540.) [Report : 273 Fed. 539.]

Exemptions from Jurisdiction—Public Ships—Method of Claiming Immunity. **Case No. 94**

THE PESARO.

United States Supreme Court. 28 *February,* 1921.

THE FACTS.—This was a suit *in rem* in the United States District Court for the Southern District of New York against the Italian steamship *Pesaro* to recover for damage to cargo, the libel alleging that the *Pesaro* was a " general ship engaged in the common carriage of " merchandise by water, for hire." The arrest was vacated on a direct suggestion by the Italian ambassador that the ship was owned by the Italian Government and in its possession at the time of arrest. The libelants objected that this was an improper means of claiming immunity, but they were not allowed to controvert the suggestion. A direct appeal was taken to the United States Supreme Court.

Held : That the decree must be reversed. With respect to the ambassador's suggestion, the Court said: " Apart from " that suggestion, there was nothing pointing to an absence of " jurisdiction. On the contrary, what was said in the libel " pointed plainly to its presence. The suggestion was made " directly to the court and not through any official channel " of the United States. True, it was accompanied by a certifi-" cate of the Secretary of State stating that the Ambassador " was the duly accredited diplomatic representative of Italy, " but while that established his diplomatic status it gave no " sanction to the suggestion. The terms and form of the " suggestion show that the Ambassador did not intend thereby " to put himself or the Italian Government in the attitude of " a suitor, but only to present a respectful suggestion and " invite the court to give effect to it. He called it a ' suggestion ' " and we think it was nothing more. In these circumstances,

[1] Case No. 91.

Case No. 94 *contd.* "the libelants' objection that, to be entertained, the suggestion should come through official channels of the United States was well taken. *Ex parte Muir*, 254 U.S. 522." (255 U.S. 216, 218.) [Report: 255 U.S. 216.]

Case No. 95

Exemptions from Jurisdiction—Public Ships—Ships Employed in Trade.

THE PESARO.[1]

United States District Court, S.D. New York.
1 *October*, 1921; 13 *December*, 1921.

THE FACTS.—This was a suit against the Italian steamship *Pesaro* to recover for damage to cargo. The vessel was owned by the Italian Government, was in its possession, and was being operated by it in a commercial service carrying goods and passengers for hire. It was not exempt from process in the Italian courts. It appeared that United States Government-owned vessels similarly employed were likewise subject to process in the Italian courts. Upon a suggestion of immunity by the Italian ambassador, the District Court vacated the arrest. The United States Supreme Court reversed this decision, on appeal, on the ground that the suggestion must come through official channels of the United States. (*The Pesaro*, 255 U.S. 216.) Objections were then made to the jurisdiction in the District Court on the agreed facts.

Held by Judge Mack: That the objections must be overruled. Government-owned merchant vessels are not entitled to State immunity in admiralty suits. The English cases following *The Parlement Belge*, 5 P.D. 197, proceeded on the principle that "a ship cannot be libelled *in rem* where the "owner cannot under the common law be impleaded *in* "*personam*." "This doctrine," said Judge Mack, "would "appear to be peculiar to English admiralty and is not "accepted as a part of the maritime law in this and other "countries." (277 Fed. 473, 480.) Reference was made to *dicta* in *United States* v. *Wilder*, Fed. Cas., No. 16694, and to decisions in *The Davis*, 10 Wall. 15; *The Johnson Lighterage Co.*, 231 Fed. 365; *Long* v. *Tampico*, 16 Fed. 491; *The*

[1] As stated in the Note below, the decision of the District Court was subsequently reversed by the Supreme Court. However, the Editors deem it expedient to include a detailed digest of Judge Mack's decision.—[Ed.]

Attualita, 238 Fed. 909; and *The Siren*, 7 Wall. 152, as indicating some departure from the rule of absolute sovereign immunity. The language of *Bank of United States* v. *Planters' Bank of Georgia*, 9 Wh. (U.S.) 904, followed in suits involving the States of the United States, was quoted with approval: "It is, we think, a sound principle that when a government "becomes a partner in any trading company, it divests itself, "so far as concerns the transactions of that company, of its "sovereign character, and takes that of a private citizen." (277 Fed. 473, 476.) Although little weight was given to the fact that Italy did not grant immunity to Government-owned merchant vessels of the United States, it was said that "the "fact that the steamship *Pesaro* itself is subject to the ordinary "processes of the Italian court would seem to be vital and "decisive. There is no reason of international comity or "courtesy which requires that Italian property not deemed "*extra commercium* in Italy should be treated as *res publica* "and *extra commercium* in the United States." (277 Fed. 473, 483.) To the argument that subjecting the vessel to process might cause international complications, it was replied: "It would seem that foreign relations are much less likely to "be disturbed if the rights and obligations of foreign states "growing out of their ordinary civil transactions were dealt "with by the established rules of law, than if they were made "a matter of diplomatic concern." (277 Fed. 473, 485.) [Reports: 277 Fed. 473; see also 255 U.S. 216; 13 F. (2nd) 468; 271 U.S. 562.]

NOTES.—(1) The order in the principal case was later vacated with the consent of the parties. The case was again argued before the same Court, this time before Judge Augustus N. Hand, and the libel was dismissed for want of jurisdiction (13 F. (2nd) 468). This decision was affirmed by the United States Supreme Court in *Berizzi Brothers Co.* v. *The Steamship Pesaro*, 271 U.S. 562, *Annual Digest*, 1925-1926, Case No. 135. See also Case No. 97, *Ex parte Muir*, and Note.

(2) See 20 M.L.R. 771; 70 U. Pa. L.R. 322.

Exemptions from Jurisdiction—Public Ships—Effect of Non-Recognition of Government—United States and Turkey—Method of Claiming Immunity. **Case No. 96**

EX PARTE IN THE MATTER OF HUSSEIN LUTFI BEY, MASTER OF THE *GUL DJEMAL*.

United States Supreme Court. 6 *June*, 1921.

THE FACTS.—This was a suit *in rem* against the steamer *Gul Djemal* to recover for wharfage, fuel, supplies, etc.

Case No. 96 ***contd.***

The vessel's master, Hussein Lutfi Bey, appeared specially to ask the vessel's release on the ground that it was owned, manned and operated by the Turkish Government. The United States and Turkey had not yet resumed diplomatic relations broken off during the World War. The United States Department of State declined to ask the Attorney-General to present a suggestion of immunity. Upon the Court declining to order the vessel's release, the master sought writs of prohibition and mandamus from the United States Supreme Court.

Held : That the writs must be refused. The case was a proper one for the exercise of discretion. "The questions "involved are, first, whether the ship of a foreign government "which it uses and operates as a merchant vessel is, when "within the waters of the United States, immune from process "in suits such as have been described ; and, secondly, whether "such immunity properly can be claimed in respect of the "ship of a government which has severed and not resumed "diplomatic relations with the United States. Both questions "are important and also new. Their proper solution is not "plain but debatable. . . . A writ of prohibition goes as a "matter of right only where the absence of jurisdiction is plain. "Where the jurisdiction is debatable, the granting or refusal "of the writ is discretionary. *Ex parte Muir,* 254 U.S. 522." (256 U.S. 616, 618.) [Report : 256 U.S. 616.]

FURTHER FACTS.—Subsequently the District Court decreed for libelants on the ground that the *Gul Djemal* was not entitled to immunity. (296 Fed. 567.) On appeal to the United States Supreme Court,

Held on 18 February, 1924 : That the judgment of the District Court must be affirmed. Replying upon *Ex parte Muir,* 254 U.S. 522, the Court said : "Such immunity will not "be granted upon the mere claim of the master, especially "when the United States has no diplomatic relations with the "sovereign owner. Such claim can be made only by one duly "authorized to vindicate the owner's sovereignty." While the master was a naval officer, he was performing no naval or military duty and could not be held to have the necessary authority from the Turkish Government, especially since it had been held in *The Anne,* 3 Wh. 435, and *The Sao Vicente,* 260 U.S. 151, that a consul lacks authority to present a claim of sovereign immunity. [Report : 264 U.S. 90, 94.]

Exemptions from Jurisdiction—Public Ships—Method of Claiming Immunity. **Case No. 97**

EX PARTE IN THE MATTER OF MUIR, MASTER OF *THE GLENEDEN*.

United States Supreme Court. 17 *January*, 1921.

THE FACTS.—This was a suit in the United States District Court for the Eastern District of New York to recover damages in a case of collision between an Italian vessel and the *Gleneden*, a privately owned steamship requisitioned by the British Government for transport use. Counsel for the British Embassy appeared as *amici curiae* and filed a suggestion that process be quashed and jurisdiction over the *Gleneden* declined on the ground that it was a Government vessel, in Government service, carrying wheat during the war. An affidavit of the vessel's master accompanied this suggestion. The libelant objected that the suggestion was not presented through official channels and disputed the facts alleged. The Court decided that the *Gleneden* was not a public ship entitled to immunity, and ordered it to be released only upon giving bond. The Circuit Court of Appeals for the Second Circuit had meanwhile refused to issue writs of prohibition and mandamus on the ground that it lacked jurisdiction at this stage of the proceedings. (255 Fed. 24.) Counsel then petitioned the United States Supreme Court for writs of prohibition and mandamus to prevent the District Court from proceeding with the suit or interfering with the *Gleneden*, to direct it to vacate the order made when the suggestion on behalf of the Embassy was overruled, and to enter an order of release without security.

Held : That the writs must be refused. Where the jurisdiction of the Court below was not clearly unlawful, but at most debatable, it was within the Court's discretion to refuse the writs. The Court did not decide the question of immunity. "The principal question sought to be presented—whether the "*Gleneden* is such a public vessel of the British Government "as to be exempt from arrest in a civil suit *in rem* in admiralty "in a court of the United States—is one of obvious delicacy "and importance. No decision by this court up to this time "can be said to answer it. The nearest approach is in the

Case No. 97 ***contd.*** "case of *The Exchange*, 7 Cranch, 116, where an armed ship "of war, owned, manned and controlled by a foreign government at peace with the United States, was held to be so "exempt. To apply the principle or doctrine of that decision "to the *Gleneden* would be taking a long step, and the present "posture of this litigation is such that we find no occasion to "consider whether there is proper warrant for taking it." (254 U.S. 522, 531.) The Court held that *prima facie* the District Court had jurisdiction over the vessel and that the burden of proving lack of jurisdiction lay upon those who denied it. With respect to the method of raising the objection of State immunity, the Court said: "As of right the British "Government was entitled to appear in the suit, to propound "its claim to the vessel and to raise the jurisdictional question. ". . . Or with its sanction, its accredited and recognized "representative might have appeared and have taken the "same steps in its interest. . . . And, if there was objection "to appearing as a suitor in a foreign court, it was open to "that government to make the asserted public status and "immunity of the vessel the subject of diplomatic representa-"tions to the end that, if that claim was recognized by the "Executive Department of this government, it might be set "forth and supported in an appropriate suggestion to the "court by the Attorney General, or some law officer acting "under his direction. . . . The reasons underlying that "practice are as applicable and cogent now as in the beginning, "and are sufficiently indicated by observing that it makes for "better international relations, conforms to diplomatic usage "on other matters, accords to the Executive Department the "respect rightly due to it, and tends to promote harmony of "action and uniformity of decision. . . . Of course, the sug-"gestion as made could not be given the consideration and "weight claimed for it." (254 U.S. 522, 532-533.) [Report: 254 U.S. 522.]

NOTE.—(1) In *Berizzi Brothers Co.* v. *Steamship Pesaro* (7 June, 1926), 271 U.S. 562, *Annual Digest*, 1925-1926, Case No. 135, the Supreme Court finally decided that State-owned vessels employed in trade are entitled to immunity.

(2) For other cases—in addition to those reported in this volume—involving procedural questions concerning the claim of immunity, see *The Secundus*, 15 F. (2nd) 711; *In re Transportes Maritimos do Estado*, 264 U.S. 105; *Maru Navigation Co.* v. *Societa Commerciale Italiana di Navigazione*, 271 Fed. 97, 280 Fed. 334, 259 U.S. 584; *Kunglig Jarnvagsstyrelsen* v. *Dexter and Carpenter*, 300 Fed. 891, 32 F. (2nd) 195, 280 U.S. 579; *The Adriatic*, 253 Fed. 489, 258 Fed. 902; *The Maipo*, 252 Fed. 627, 259 Fed. 367.

Exemptions from Jurisdiction—Setting up an Answer—Whether Amounting to Waiver of Immunity—Withdrawal of Waiver—Public Ships. **Case No. 98**

DE SIMONE *v.* TRANSPORTES MARITIMOS DO ESTADO.

United States, New York Supreme Court, Appellate Division, First Department. 13 *January and* 3 *March,* 1922.

THE FACTS.—The plaintiff sued the defendants in the New York Supreme Court for certain goods sold. The defendants answered that admiralty actions for the same causes were already pending against them and their vessels in the United States District Court for the Southern District of New York. Furthermore, the defendants claimed to be a department of the Portuguese Government and consequently entitled to immunity from suit. This was verified by the Portuguese Vice-Consul-General. The Court sustained a demurrer by the plaintiff to these defences. On appeal,

Held: That the demurrer to the defence of sovereign immunity must be overruled. The defendant could set up in answer matter other than the claim of sovereign immunity, without being held to have waived that immunity. The sovereign could at any time withdraw its consent to be sued and its waiver of immunity. A general appearance was at the most only equivalent to personal service within the jurisdiction, which would not be enough to subject a foreign sovereign to jurisdiction. The claim to sovereign immunity must be considered, however it may have been presented.[1] After the United States Circuit Court of Appeals for the Second Circuit had held the defence of sovereign immunity insufficient in the admiralty actions noted elsewhere,[2] a motion was made for re-argument of the appeal.

Held: That the motion must be denied. The same reasons were given as in the former Opinion.[3] The Court also pointed out that the Federal Court's decision was primarily grounded on cases dealing with the immunity of States of the United States, which this Court felt to be quite different from State immunity in international law. [Reports: 199 App. Div. (N.Y.) 602; 200 *ibid.* 82.]

[1] But see *Ex parte Muir*, 254 U.S. 522, Case No. 97 and Note.

[2] *The Sao Vicente*, 281 Fed. 111, affirmed 260 U.S. 151. See also 264 U.S. 105.

[3] The Court also distinguished the course here followed by the defendant from that followed in *The Pesaro*, 255 U.S. 216, where a suggestion by the Italian ambassador was held insufficient to present the claim to immunity.

Case No. 99

Exemptions from Jurisdiction—Public Ships—Method of Claiming Immunity—Competence of Consul.

THE SAO VICENTE.

United States Supreme Court. 13 *November*, 1922.

THE FACTS.—These were suits to recover for supplies and labour furnished vessels belonging to the *Transportes Maritimos do Estado* of Portugal. It was contended that the owner was a department of the Government of Portugal and as such not subject to the jurisdiction of the United States courts. The United States District Court for the Southern District of New York denied immunity. Appeals to the Circuit Court of Appeals for the Second Circuit were dismissed. (281 Fed. 111, 115.) Writs of certiorari were issued from the Supreme Court on petition of the Consul-General of Portugal.

Held : That the writs were improvidently awarded and should be dismissed. Relying chiefly upon *The Anne,* 3 Wh. 435, the Court said : " The Consul-General was not a party to " any of the proceedings below, and is not competent, merely " by virtue of his office, to appear here for his Government " and claim immunity from process in the manner attempted." (260 U.S. 151, 154.) [Reports : 281 Fed. 111, 115 ; 260 U.S. 151.]

Case No. 100

Jurisdiction—Exemptions from—Foreign Government's Ships Engaged in Trade—Claim for Salvage.

THE PORTO ALEXANDRE.

England, Court of Appeal, on Appeal from the Admiralty Court.[1] 10 *November*, 1919.

THE FACTS.—In August, 1916, the Portuguese Government requisitioned a German merchant ship, and in January, 1917, the Portuguese Prize Court adjudged her to be a lawful prize of war. Apparently, she did not become the actual property of the Portuguese Government and was merely detained pending the conclusion of peace.

In September, 1919, this ship, which had been renamed the *Porto Alexandre,* while carrying from Lisbon to Liverpool a cargo shipped by and consigned to the Portuguese Import and Export Company, ran aground in the Mersey. Salvage services were rendered by three

[1] See p. 43, footnote.

Liverpool tugs, and a writ *in rem* was issued by their owners, masters and crew against "the owners of the "Portuguese steamship *Porto Alexandre*, her cargo and "freight."

Appearance was entered under protest on behalf of the owners of the ship and freight, and a motion was made on their behalf to set aside the writ, the warrant for arrest and all subsequent proceedings on the ground that the ship and the freight "were and are the public "national property of and/or requisitioned by and in "the possession and public use and service of the "Portuguese Government."

The motion was supported by (i) a communication by the Portuguese Chargé d'Affaires to the British Secretary of State for Foreign Affairs to the effect that the ship was "a state-owned vessel belonging to the "Government of the Portuguese Republic," (ii) an affidavit by the Portuguese vice-consul in Liverpool to the effect that the ship had been requisitioned by the Portuguese Government for the service of the State and was employed under the orders of the Government, and (iii) a further written statement by the Portuguese consul (? vice-consul) at Liverpool in reference to the particular voyage in question that the freight on the cargo had been paid before shipment and belonged solely and entirely to the Portuguese Government.

The plaintiffs sought to distinguish such cases as *The Parlement Belge* (1880), 5 P.D. 197, on the ground that the immunity of foreign public ships did not extend to the case of a foreign State-owned merchant ship engaged on an ordinary mercantile voyage and earning freight for a foreign Government. (The proceedings against the cargo which was privately owned were not in question.)

Held by the Court of Appeal (Bankes, Warrington and Scrutton, L.JJ.), affirming the judgment of Hill, J.: That, so far as concerned the *Porto Alexandre* and her freight, the writ, warrant for arrest and all subsequent proceedings must be set aside. The ship was the property of a foreign State and was destined to public use. It was therefore impossible to distinguish the case from *The Parlement Belge* (*supra*). The fact that State property is employed in trading does not destroy its immunity any more than a foreign sovereign or ambassador

Case No. 100 ***contd.*** forfeits his personal immunity by engaging in trade. The deductions made by Brett, L.J., in *The Parlement Belge* (*supra*), from the judgment in the American case *Briggs* v. *Light Boats* (1865), 93 Mass. 157, were adopted by Warrington, L.J. [Report: L.R. [1920] P. 30.]

NOTE.—On the matter of remedying the practical difficulties arising out of the jurisdictional immunities of State-owned ships engaged in commerce, Scrutton, L.J., said: "The remedy is not in these Courts. " *The Parlement Belge* excludes remedies in these Courts. But there " are practical commercial remedies. If ships of the state find them- " selves left on the mud because no one will salve them when the " state refuses any legal remedy for salvage, their owners will be apt " to change their views. If the owners of cargoes on national ships " find that the ship runs away and leaves them to bear all the expenses of " salvage, as has been done in this case, there may be found a difficulty " in getting cargoes for national ships. These are matters to be dealt " with by negotiations between Governments, and not by Governments " exercising their power to interfere with the property of other states " contrary to the principles of international courtesy which govern " the relations between independent and sovereign states." (At p. 39.)

Case No. 101

Jurisdiction—Exemptions—Public Ships—Maritime Lien—Position after Sale to Private Persons.

THE TERVAETE.

England, Court of Appeal, on Appeal from the Admiralty Court.[1] 12 *July*, 1922.

THE FACTS.—In 1920 a collision occurred in a Spanish port between the British vessel *Lynntown* and the Belgian vessel *Tervaete*, which was at that time the property of the Belgian Government and was carrying coal for the purposes of that Government. After the collision the Belgian Government sold the *Tervaete* to a Belgian company, and in 1922 the owners of the *Lynntown* served upon the *Tervaete*, while she was in a British port, a writ of summons in an action *in rem* to recover damages for collision. In consideration of an undertaking by the solicitors acting for the owners of the *Tervaete* to put in bail she was not arrested. Appearance was entered on behalf of the *Tervaete* under protest, and a motion was made to set aside the writ and discharge the undertaking to put in bail, on the ground that a maritime lien in respect of the collision did not attach to the *Tervaete* being a State-owned vessel and therefore could not revive against her when she passed into private ownership (citing *The Parlement*

[1] P. 43, footnote.

Belge (1880), 5 P.D. 197, *The Porto Alexandre,* [1920] P. 30, Case No. 100 in this volume, and similar cases).

A maritime lien " travelled with the thing, into " whosesoever possession it may come " (*The Bold Buccleugh* (1852), 7 Moo. P.C. at p. 284).

The learned President (Sir Henry Duke) said (at p. 202) the question was: " Is the immunity from " foreign jurisdictions of sovereign states and their " agents and their property due to a principle that " their acts can involve no legal consequences and " their property is subject to no legal obligations, or is " such immunity due only to absence of jurisdiction in " the Court ? " Applying this test he held that a maritime lien attached to the *Tervaete* at the time of the collision ; " the immunity from legal process of the " public ship of a foreign state, while it is in the hands " of the state, does not arise from a rule that the " vessel is, to use the language of the civilians, *extra* " *commercium* . . ." ; that " this immunity does not " involve the conclusion that such a ship is incapable " of becoming subject to obligations to which individual owners may subject ships " ; and that " a " foreign state by its authorized agents may impose a " lien or charge upon one of its public ships," which can be enforced as soon as this can be done without the assertion of any jurisdiction over the foreign State or its property. Accordingly he declined to set aside the writ and discharge the undertaking to put in bail. (L.R. [1922] P. at pp. 206-208.) On appeal,

Held by the Court of Appeal (Bankes, Scrutton and Atkin, L.JJ.), reversing the decision of the learned President: That a maritime lien must have its root in the personal liability of the vessel: that though a foreign sovereign may be liable for a breach of contract or a tort, a maritime lien is a process or remedy which is part of the right of action against the owner, and consequently if there is no right of action against the owner because he possesses immunity there can be no lien against his property. Consequently no maritime lien attached to the *Tervaete* at the time of the collision, the writ must be set aside, and the undertaking to put in bail discharged.

Per Scrutton, L.J.: " In the present case no lien attached " against the Belgian Government, nor could their ship have " been arrested *in rem*. But if they could only sell the ship

Case No. 101 *contd.*

" subject to the lien, their property would be affected by the " lien, in that they would receive less than the value of the " ship free from encumbrances or liens. The result would be " that our law would assert a right over the property of a " foreign sovereign not arising from any voluntary action on " his part which adversely affected his property." (At p. 272.) [Report: L.R. [1922] P. 157 and 259.]

See *Annual Digest*, 1925-1926, Case No. 134, *The Nevada*, and *The Sylvan Arrow* (No. 2), L.R. [1923] P. 220 (to be digested in *Annual Digest*, 1923-1924.

The decision of the Court of Appeal in this case proceeds entirely on the basis that a maritime lien is in its nature a first step in proceedings against the shipowner or his vessel, and therefore no lien on property belonging to a person against whom no proceedings can be taken can arise. The case in the Supreme Court of the United States, *In the Matter of the United States, owner of the American Steamship " Western " Maid,"* 257 U.S. 419 [1922], may also be consulted. It was held in this case that no liability for damages for collision to a citizen of the United States could attach to a vessel in the possession of the United States.—[Ed.]

Case No. 102

Jurisdiction—Exemptions from—Government-Owned Vessels Engaged in Trade—Express or Implied Waiver of Immunity.

THE ICE KING.

Germany, Reichsgericht in Civil Matters. 10 *December*, 1921.

THE FACTS.—On 24 August, 1919, there took place a collision between the *Jonas Sell* belonging to the plaintiff and the *Ice King*, a steamer belonging to the United States of America. The plaintiff maintained that the damage done to the *Jonas Sell* was due to bad navigation on the part of the *Ice King*, and claimed damages from the United States. The defendant pleaded to the jurisdiction on the ground that being a sovereign State it was not amenable to the jurisdiction of German courts. The Court of First Instance rejected the plea to the jurisdiction. The Court of Appeal, following a decision of the *Reichsgericht* of 12 December, 1905 (*E.R.Z.*, vol. 62, p. 165), reversed the judgment and dismissed the claim.

Held, on final appeal on a point of law: That German courts had no jurisdiction.

(*a*) *Jurisdiction in General.* The view that a State which makes itself responsible for a commercial undertaking in a foreign country subjects itself, in actions arising therefrom, to the jurisdiction of the courts of that foreign country has not received general or predominant recognition in the practice of courts. It was true that there has recently been a tendency, in particular in the literature of international law, to do away with immunity of State property engaged in private business.[1] However, this tendency has not become so general as to alter an invariably recognised principle of international law which the Court by virtue of Article 4 of the Constitution [2] was bound to apply. Accordingly, it must be held that a foreign State is in principle immune from the jurisdiction of the courts of foreign States even in purely private law actions. It remains to examine whether in the present case there are reasons justifying an exception from this general rule.

(*b*) *Alleged Exceptions*: (1) *Ships as Immovable Property.* It has been maintained that, as in regard to immovable property a foreign State is in any case liable to the jurisdiction, the courts ought, for analogous reasons, to have jurisdiction in regard to foreign Government-owned ships which happen to be in Germany. This argument cannot be admitted. Immovable property forms an integral part of State territory; it can be subject only to the rule of that State, and that State alone can give effect to a judgment in respect of such real property. This is the reason why immunity from jurisdiction cannot be enjoyed in respect of immovable property. But this reason does not apply to ships seeing that claims against them are independent, for their realisation, of the ship's stay in the country whose jurisdiction is being invoked.

(2) *Express or Implied Waiver of Immunity.* The fact that the United States—like other States, for instance, Soviet Russia—have acquired a large commercial fleet for the purpose of taking part on a large scale in international commercial intercourse, cannot be regarded as an implied waiver of immunity. A State frequently has direct commercial interests in transport in foreign countries in regard to railways and land navigation, but this does not deprive it of privileges of immunity. Waiver of immunity cannot be assumed unless there is an express declaration of will to this effect. There has been no such consent on the part of the United States. In Section 7

[1] The Court referred here, *inter alia*, to the so-called Hague Rules adopted in 1921 by the International Law Association (33rd Report, vol. II, p. 251).

[2] That Article provides: "The universally recognised rules of International Law are valid as binding constituent parts of German Federal Law."

Case No. 102 *contd.*

of the Act of 9 March, 1920, "authorising suits against the "United States in admiralty" the authorities of the United States are expressly instructed to claim jurisdictional immunity abroad in respect of ships owned by the United States. It was true that Section 9 of that Act provided that "such "vessels while employed solely as merchant vessels shall be "subject to all laws, regulations, and liabilities governing "merchant vessels," but that section cannot, having regard to the Act as a whole, be read as implying a waiver of immunity. It has reference only to substantive private law and not to procedural questions of immunity. [Report : *E.R.Z.*, vol. 103, p. 275.]

NOTE.—The Court also dealt with the argument that the granting of immunity to foreign Government-owned merchant vessels must hamper trade in an inequitable manner. The Court pointed out that such immunity is also connected with certain disadvantages arising out of the usual restrictions in regard to entry and stay to which foreign Government-owned vessels are liable. Also, the Court said, the elasticity of commercial intercourse may be counted upon to discover without special difficulties proper counter-measures calculated to meet the disadvantages arising out of the immunity of such vessels. See the somewhat drastic remedies suggested for some cases by Scrutton, L.J., in the *Porto Alexandre*, [1920] P. 30, at p. 39. For a discussion of the *Ice King* case see Garner in *B.Y.*, 1925, pp. 133, 134, 142, and Feine in Strupp, *Wörterbuch*, vol. I, p. 543.

Case No. 103

Jurisdiction—Exemption from—Foreign States—Capture or Requisition of a Vessel in virtue of the Right of Angary by a Foreign State—Provisional Arrest at Suit of the Owner —Lack of Jurisdiction of Municipal Courts—Failure to Claim Immunity from Jurisdiction—Recognition of New States—Retroactive Effect of.

WEST RUSSIAN STEAMSHIP COMPANY *v.* CAPTAIN SUCKSDORFF.

Belgium, Commercial Tribunal of Antwerp. 9 *February*, 1920.

THE FACTS.—In November, 1918, the Senate of Finland decided that vessels seized at Helsingfors, amongst which was the steamer *Joulan* owned by the West Russian Steamship Company, should be used for the transport of food supplies from foreign countries for the account of the Finnish Government, and that they should be placed under Finnish command and manned by a Finnish crew. On putting in to the port of Antwerp in January, 1920, the *Joulan*, flying the Finnish flag and under the command of the Finnish Captain Sucksdorff, was arrested at the instance of the

West Russian Steamship Company. At the same time (17 January) the company asked the Court to order the removal of Captain Sucksdorff from the ship and claimed possession as owners.

The State of Finland, which had been made party to the action, contended that it had acquired legitimate ownership of the steamer: alternatively, if the capture could not be held to be definitive, owing to the absence of a judgment of a prize court, it contended that it exercised a right of angary in respect of the steamer, having appropriated it for a public service.

The West Russian Steamship Company contested the acquisition of ownership by the Finnish State on two grounds: (1) that the capture had not been confirmed by a prize court; (2) that it had taken place at a time when the State of Finland was still without international existence. As for the right of angary, it could only have effect within the frontiers of Finland; and moreover, as the *Joulan* had made a voyage for account of a private individual and proposed to sail in ballast, she could not be considered to have been appropriated for a public service.

Held: That, on account of the respect due to Finnish sovereignty, the action brought by the West Russian Steamship Company did not lie. The Tribunal said: "On the 10th June, "1919, the Belgian Government officially recognised the "Finnish Republic [1]; . . . a sovereign State is not subject "to the jurisdiction of foreign courts; the very idea of a State "having jurisdiction in regard to a foreign State is incompatible "with the notion of the sovereignty of States and their mutual "independence." It was not possible to base an argument, as the West Russian Steamship Company sought to do, on the principle that the sovereignty of a State is limited to its territory, and that a State has authority outside its territory only in so far as this is recognised by rules of international law. The vessel having been captured in Finnish territory, the question is whether a Belgian court is competent to deprive the State of Finland of the possession of the ship.

For the same reasons the Finnish State cannot be put to

[1] The vessel was captured before the recognition by the Belgian Government of the State of Finland. See, in favour of the retroactive effect of recognition of States, Fauchille, *Traité*, I, i, p. 307. According to Fedozzi, *Corso di diritto internazionale*, I (Padova, 1931), pp. 102 *et seq.*, the international personality of States is independent of recognition.

Case No. 103 *contd.* proof of the fact that the vessel was really appropriated for a public service. To do this would be tantamount to subjecting the Finnish State to the jurisdiction of the Court. Moreover, a public vessel used for private or commercial purposes does not thereby lose the advantages of its public status.[1]

Finally, it cannot be alleged that by making a claim to have the arrest set aside and for payment of damages the State of Finland has submitted itself to the jurisdiction of Belgium. In fact, the very argument put forward by that Government is that the judge who ordered the arrest was not competent to do so by reason of the fact that the State of Finland was in possession of the vessel. Any other view "would result in putting the foreign State in the dilemma "either of allowing itself to be dispossessed of the vessel, and "of suffering without compensation the loss caused by the "distraint, or of submitting under compulsion to foreign "jurisdiction." Moreover, a waiver is not to be presumed. "The Finnish State has never declared itself willing to renounce "its sovereign rights and to submit to a tribunal the question "whether its possession of the *Joulan* could or could not be "the subject of a legal proceeding." [2]

Warrant for arrest of the *Joulan* was set aside.

[Reports: *Belgique Judiciaire*, 1920, cols. 211 *et seq.*; *Pasicrisie belge*, 1922, III, pp. 3 *et seq.*]

Case No. 104 **Jurisdiction—Exemption from—Foreign State—Public Vessel —Invalidity of Arrest—Incompetence of Local Courts— Setting aside the Warrant of Arrest.**

STATE OF PORTUGAL *v.* SAUVAGE.

Belgium, Court of Appeal of Brussels. 27 *June*, 1921.

THE FACTS.—The defendant, on the ground that he was a creditor of the *Transportos Maritimos da Estado*, had procured the arrest of two steamers, the *Lima* and the *Pangim*, belonging to this undertaking. The Portu-

[1] In this sense see Westlake, *International Law*, 1910, I, p. 265, following the judgment of the Court of Appeal of 27 February, 1880 (*The Parlement Belge*, L.R. [1880] 5 P.D. 197; Moore, *Digest*, I, p. 591); but see for a contrary view, van Praag, *Juridiction et droit international public*, 1915, No. 158; Fauchille, *Traité*, I, 2, pp. 891 *et seq.*

[2] See Ch. de Visscher in *R.I.*, 3rd ser., vol. III (1922), pp. 315 ff., who expresses the view that it is impossible to renounce immunity from jurisdiction in matters affecting the exercise of the public authority of the State. However, see Fischer Williams, *Chapters on Current International Law and the League of Nations* (1929), p. 298, n. 2, and the authorities there quoted. See also Oppenheim (4th Ed., ed. by McNair), § 451 (*a*).

guese State lodged an appeal against the order of the President of the Commercial Tribunal of Antwerp authorising the arrest. It demanded that the warrant of arrest be set aside, mainly on the ground that international usage, in its opinion, upheld the freedom from seizure of goods belonging to States or appropriated by them for a public service. These two vessels, of German origin, were requisitioned by the Portuguese State in 1916 to facilitate the revictualling of the country, and had been assigned in turn to two State services. The present service, organised by decree of 30 April, 1919, was known as the "Direction of Maritime Transport."

Held: That the Belgian courts have no jurisdiction to order an arrest of this kind; the order must be quashed and the ships released. The decree of 30 April, 1919, creating the service in which the two steamers were engaged, leaves no doubt that it acquired the characteristics of a public utility and the quality of a State service. It is true that the service is declared to be autonomous and that it is laid down that the expenses incurred in pursuance of the decree are to be borne by the receipts from working, but it is not permissible to deduce from these arrangements that the service constitutes a body corporate distinct from the State, nor that its budget is not to be included in the State budget. This interpretation is confirmed by the title of the undertaking, "*Transportos* . . . "*da Estado*." As to the ownership of the vessels, Germany had expressly renounced its rights in favour of the former owners (Treaty of Versailles, paragraph 1 of Annex III, Part VIII), and it was not disputed that the appellant had acted continuously as owner.

The goods seized are goods belonging to the State of Portugal. It is Portugal which has really been affected by the arrest, and the goods were appropriated by Portugal to the public service. But "Belgian law does not permit the issue "of a writ of execution against the Belgian State. . . . According "to the principle of international law which recognises "the equality of States, this immunity must be accorded "equally to other States . . . at least when they do not allow "in their countries their national property to be taken in "execution. . . . This limitation of sovereignty is based on "international courtesy and on the mutual duty not to disturb "the conditions of their existence." The arrest has in effect deprived the Portuguese State of the free disposition of its

Case No. 104 *contd.* property, and, although taken as an interlocutory proceeding, it constitutes "the first step on the way to execution." [Report: 49 *Clunet* (1922), pp. 739 *et seq.*]

NOTE.—In the case reported above, as in that analysed in Case No. 103, the decision appeared to be based on the character of the owner of the vessels seized rather than on the public character of the vessels. It does not seem, therefore, that either of these two judgments can be invoked in support of the one or the other theory in regard to the conception of "public vessel." See especially on this question, van Praag, *Juridiction et droit international public*, 1915, p. 385, n. 1002.

Case No. 105

Jurisdiction—Exemption of Foreign State-Owned Vessels used for Public Purposes.

(1) DE HOWORTH *v.* THE S.S. *INDIA*.
(2) MANN, GEORGE & CO. (DELAGOA) LTD. *v.* THE S.S. *INDIA*.
Union of South Africa, Supreme Court (Cape Provincial Division). 5 *April*, 1921.
(Motions heard together by consent of parties.)
(GARDINER, J.)

THE FACTS.—Application was made to the Court to attach the ship, in the first case *ad fundandam jurisdictionem*, in the second case in an admiralty action *in rem*, in which the Court had jurisdiction under the Colonial Courts of Admiralty Act, 1890 (53 & 54 Vict. c. 27), Section 2 (2).

The ship was the property of the Portuguese Government, and was under the control of the *Transportes Maritimos da Estado*, a board of naval officers appointed by the Portuguese Government. She carried mails and sometimes troops to the Portuguese colonies, also passengers and cargo, and her earnings were the property of the Portuguese Government. Apparently she flew the Portuguese mercantile flag.

Held: That the vessel was not liable to attachment. "The conclusion I have come to is that ships, the property of a foreign State and used for public purposes, are not subject to attachment under an order of the local court. . . . In my opinion any use of a vessel for the purpose of obtaining revenue for the State is a public purpose, just as its use for the protection of the State is public" (*per* Gardiner, J., at p. 464).

Authorities cited, *inter alia*: *The Parlement Belge*, L.R. 5 P.D. 197; *The Porto Alexandre*, [1920] P. 30; Moore, *Digest*, vol. II, §§ 257, 258. [Report: *The South African Law Reports* [1921], *Cape Provincial Division*, p. 451 ([1921] C.P.D., 451).]

Immunity of State Ships—Vessel Engaged in Trade. **Case No. 106**

BROWN *v.* S.S. *INDOCHINE.*

Canada, Exchequer Court, Quebec, Admiralty Division. 19 *October*, 1922.

THE FACTS.—The S.S. *Indochine* was the property of the Government of Indo-China, a French possession. Her officers and crew were in the employment of that Government and the ship was on a voyage in its interest. She was arrested on a claim made by the owners of the Danish ship *Sammatia* as the result of a collision on 11 August, 1922.

Held: That recognising the established rule that foreign sovereigns and their property are exempt from the jurisdiction of municipal courts, the action must be dismissed. The fact that the ship was engaged in trade made no difference to this decision. [Report: *Canada Law Reports*, 21 *Exchequer*, 406.]

NOTE.—This case is an application of the principle established by such cases as *The Parlement Belge* (1880), L.R. 5, P.D. 197, and *The Scotia*, [1903] A.C. 501.

Jurisdiction—Foreign State—Government Vessel Engaged in Commerce. **Case No. 107**

HALL *v.* BENGOA.

Egypt, Mixed Court of Appeal. 24 *November*, 1920.

THE FACTS.—A British vessel belonging to the Controller of Shipping collided in Egyptian waters with a foreign ship. An action for damages was brought against the Captain, who demurred to the jurisdiction on the ground that the Court could not entertain a suit against a foreign State and produced a certificate of the Registrar-General of the Office of Shipping that the vessel was the property of His Britannic Majesty represented by the Shipping Controller. The Court rejected the demurrer.

Held (following previous decisions): That the rule by which a foreign State cannot be sued in the courts of another State applies only where the action which gives rise to the suit is done in the exercise of the powers of the State in its public capacity, and not where a civil wrong has been done by an

Case No. 107 *contd.* employee of the foreign State in the management of its private interests and without any connection with its political action.

The incompetence of the courts with regard to a foreign State is only relative, since a foreign State may bring an action in the courts against persons subject to the jurisdiction, and must bring in those courts an action relating to any immovables which it owns within the jurisdiction. [Reports: *Bulletin de Législation et Jurisprudence Égyptiennes*, 1920-1921, p. 25; *Clunet*, 1921, p. 270.]

Jurisdiction—Exemption from—Public Vessels—Vessel in the Service of the British Admiralty—Crimes Committed on Board of.

See Case No. 69 (*In re Jorge Alejandro Jackson*).

II.—Personal

(a) Over Subjects in respect of Crimes Committed outside the Realm

Case No. 108 **Jurisdiction—Personal—Over Subjects Abroad—On Ships in Foreign Port—Jurisdiction of the State of the Port.**

In re Eduardo Henke.

Brazil, Supreme Federal Tribunal. 16 *August*, 1920

The Facts.—The accused was a Brazilian member of the crew of the Brazilian merchant vessel *Guandú*. He killed another member of the crew, also a Brazilian, on 20 April, while the vessel lay at anchor in the French port of Marseilles. The French authorities commenced proceedings against him, but upon request from the Brazilian consul he was turned over to the Brazilian authorities. He was detained on the boat for some time and not brought back to Brazil for trial until 20 July. Criminal proceedings were then commenced, but on 22 July he secured release on habeas corpus on the ground that too long a period had elapsed while he was in custody without proceedings being started against him. On appeal by the State,

Held: That habeas corpus must be refused and instructions given that the Brazilian courts should proceed with the trial. Article 4 of the Brazilian Penal Code does not include in the definition of Brazilian territory Brazilian merchant vessels when in foreign ports. " But that Article ought to be "interpreted in accordance with public international law, "which makes the following distinction: If crimes com- "mitted on board a merchant vessel in a foreign port do not "have external consequences, nor affect the police of terri- "torial waters, nor the public order of the territory, the com- "petent criminal jurisdiction is that of the nation to which "the ship belongs: If the crimes committed on board might "disturb the public security or tranquillity, or have a begin- "ning on land, or are of such a nature that the captain of the "ship is shown impotent to repress them, or can have any sort "of external consequences, the competent criminal jurisdic- "tion for these cases will be the territorial jurisdiction." The crime here concerned was perpetrated on board, and did not in the least threaten the tranquillity of the port. France therefore surrendered the criminal.

Article 14 of Law 2416, 28 June, 1911, places in the hands of national justice the prosecution and judgment of crimes perpetrated abroad by a Brazilian against Brazilians where the penalty is two years' imprisonment at least, adding, in section 3, that the Federal justice is *always* competent to take cognisance of crimes committed on foreign territory. Thus the crime fell within the jurisdiction of the Brazilian courts, and habeas corpus could not be granted on account of the necessary delay in bringing the prisoner to Brazil, since the crime was not committed on Brazilian territory. [Report: *Diario Official* for 4 September, 1921, p. 17078.]

NOTE.—See *Revista do Supremo Tribunal*, vol. 52, p. 164, holding that, under Article 1 of Law 221, 1894, and *Decreto* 848, Article 15, § 1, 1890, local justice in Brazil is competent in case of crimes committed on board Brazilian merchant vessels so long as they are not political crimes.

Jurisdiction—Personal—Over Subjects Abroad or on the High Seas—United States Criminal Code—Crimes against Private Individuals and Crimes against the Government. **Case No. 109**

UNITED STATES *v.* BOWMAN.

United States Supreme Court. 13 *November*, 1922.

THE FACTS.—This was a criminal prosecution of United States nationals commenced in the United States District Court for the Southern District of New York for conspiracy to defraud a corporation in which the United States was a stockholder. The prosecution was instituted under the United States Criminal Code, § 35, as amended on 23 October, 1918 (40 U.S. Stat.

Case No. 109 ***contd.***

L. 1015), which provided, *inter alia*, for the punishment of any one who should " enter into any agree-" ment, combination, or conspiracy to defraud the " Government of the United States, or any depart-" ment or officer thereof, or any corporation in which " the United States of America is a stockholder, by " obtaining or aiding to obtain the payment or allow-" ance of any false or fraudulent claim." It was charged that the offence had been committed on the high seas, in the port and harbour of Rio de Janeiro, and in the city of Rio de Janeiro. For the defendants it was contended that paragraph 35 was applicable only to offences committed within the territory of the United States. The District Court held that it was without jurisdiction. (267 Fed. 588.) On writ of error,

Held : That the judgment must be reversed. Delivering the Opinion of the Court, Chief Justice Taft said : " We have " in this case a question of statutory construction. The neces-" sary *locus*, when not specially defined, depends upon the " purpose of Congress as evinced by the description and nature " of the crime and upon the territorial limitations upon the " power and jurisdiction of a government to punish crime " under the law of nations." (260 U.S. 94, 97.) Crimes against private individuals must of course be committed within the territory, unless the legislature has expressly asserted a more comprehensive jurisdiction. " But the same rule of " interpretation should not be applied to criminal statutes " which are, as a class, not logically dependent on their locality " for the Government's jurisdiction, but are enacted because " of the right of the Government to defend itself against " obstruction, or fraud wherever perpetrated, especially if " committed by its own citizens, officers or agents. Some such " offences can only be committed within the territorial juris-" diction of the Government because of the local acts required " to constitute them. Others are such that to limit their *locus* " to the strictly territorial jurisdiction would be greatly to " curtail the scope and usefulness of the statute and leave open " a large immunity for frauds as easily committed by citizens " on the high seas and in foreign countries as at home. In " such cases, Congress has not thought it necessary to make " specific provision in the law that the *locus* shall include " the high seas and foreign countries, but allows it to be " inferred from the nature of the offense." (260 U.S. 94, 98.)

Other examples of such statutes were cited from United States Criminal Code, Chapter 4, "Offenses against the Operations "of the Government," in which § 35 is included. (35 U.S. Stat. L. 1088, 1093.) With respect to § 35, the Court concluded: "We can not suppose that when Congress enacted "the statute or amended it, it did not have in mind that a "wide field for such frauds upon the Government was in private "and public vessels of the United States on the high seas and "in foreign parts and beyond the land jurisdiction of the "United States, and therefore intend to include them in the "section." (260 U.S. 94, 102.) The defendants were citizens of the United States, and "clearly it is no offense to the dignity "or right of sovereignty of Brazil to hold them for this crime "against the government to which they owe allegiance." (*Ibid.*) [Report: 260 U.S. 94.]

(b) Over Subjects Abroad or on the High Seas and their Property Situate Abroad

Jurisdiction—Over Property Situate Abroad—Judgments of Court.

See Case No. 10 (*H. T. Cottam & Co.* v. *Comision Reguladora del Mercado de Henequen*).

Jurisdiction—Over Property Situate Abroad—Right to Requisition Ships in Foreign Waters.

See Case No. 9 (*The Adriatic*).

B. EXTRATERRITORIAL JURISDICTION

I.—Consular Jurisdiction. Régime of Capitulations

Jurisdiction of Mixed Courts—Incompetence with regard to Subjects of State which Fails to Adhere to the Prorogation of the Courts—Effect of British Protectorate and Treaty of Versailles on Capitulations in Egypt. **Case No. 110**

MENASCE ROUSSOS & COMPANY *v.* HOLLAND-EGYPT HANDELMAATSCHAPPIJ.

Egypt, Mixed Commercial Tribunal of Cairo. 1 *March*, 1921.

THE FACTS.—Holland failed to adhere to the prorogation of the Mixed Courts of Egypt in 1920; and the Decree

Case No. 110 *contd.*

of October, 1920, which renewed the power of the Courts provides that the prorogation should not affect Dutch subjects. In accordance with the Statute of Judicial Organisation, any Power which did not adhere to the extension of the jurisdiction of the Mixed Courts was in the position which existed before the Judicial Reform of 1875 (which initiated that system). An action was brought in the Mixed Court, a few days before the publication of the Decree, against a Dutch company for cancellation of a contract. The defendants pleaded that the Court was not competent and that the action should be brought before the Dutch Consular Court. It was argued that the effect of the declaration of the Protectorate was to put an end to the Capitulatory régime in Egypt because the Capitulations were based on treaties between the Powers and Turkey, which was no longer suzerain.

Held : (*a*) That the provisions of the Egyptian Decree concerning the prorogation of the Mixed Courts clearly intended to place Dutch subjects outside the jurisdiction of those Courts : and their case is altogether different from that of other foreign subjects who have been deemed within that jurisdiction though belonging to States which have not adhered to the Judicial Reform.

(*b*) That the proclamation of the British Protectorate over Egypt and the recognition of that Protectorate by the Powers which signed the Treaty of Versailles have not affected the Capitulatory régime. Consequently, an action against a Dutch subject must be brought before the Dutch Consulate in accordance with the rule, *Actor sequitur forum rei*, which obtained by custom prior to the institution of the Mixed Courts. [Report : *Gazette des Tribunaux Mixtes*, 1921, p. 176.]

Capitulations—Jurisdiction of Mixed Courts in Egypt—Declaration of British Protectorate over Egypt—Effect on National Status of Ottoman Subjects in Egypt.

See Case No. 20 (*Aziz Hanki* v. *Russell*).

Capitulations—Whether Affecting the Right to Proclaim Martial Law—British Protectorate over Egypt.

See Case No. 22 (*Ismail Pasha Sidky* v. *Sidarous Bishara*).

Capitulations—Capitulatory Régime in Territory under Enemy Occupation—Turkish Territory Occupied by Italy.

See Case No. 318 (*Boliotti* v. *Masse*).

C. HIGH SEAS

II.—Jurisdiction on the High Seas

[See also JURISDICTION.]

i.—For Ensuring the Safety of Traffic. Collisions. Salvage

Civil Salvage—Rescue and Recapture of Neutral Ships.

See Case No. 345 (*The Svanfos; The Borgila*).

iii.—Visit, Search and Arrest by Men-of-War in Time of Peace

Open Sea—Jurisdiction in—Restrictive Interpretation of Agreements Providing for the Right of Visit and Search.

See Case No. 120 (*The Wanderer*).

iv.—The Law Governing the Flag. Ship's Papers

High Seas—Jurisdiction on the High Seas—Law of the Flag—Validity of a Marriage Contracted on Board a Vessel. **Case No. 111**

BOLMER *v.* EDSALL, OTHERWISE BOLMER.

United States, New Jersey Court of Chancery. 28 *March*, 1919.

THE FACTS.—This was a suit for annulment of a marriage performed by a ship's surgeon, claimed to be a minister, on the S.S. *Algonquin* while it was proceeding between two ports of the Dominican Republic. It was not shown what flag the vessel flew, nor whether the marriage was performed on the high seas or in territorial waters. The special master reported adversely to the suit, considering the grounds of annulment insufficient. There was a question as to the validity of the marriage. On exceptions by the plaintiff to the master's report,

Case No. 111 *contd.* *Held:* That the exceptions to the report must be sustained and the petitioner given leave to present further testimony. The Court said that the validity of a marriage was governed by the *lex loci contractus*. A vessel on the high seas was subject to the jurisdiction of the flag State. If the *Algonquin* were an American vessel, the validity of the marriage would be determined by the law of the State where the vessel was registered and owned. [Report: 90 N.J. Eq. 299.]

NOTE.—The petitioner later proved the vessel to have been owned and registered in the United States, and received a *decree nisi*, 90 N.J. Eq. 313.

v.—Right of Pursuit

Open Sea—Hot Pursuit.

For possible analogy in case of maritime prize see Case No. 344 (*The Anichab*).

vii.—Piracy

Case No. 112 **High Seas—Piracy—Robbery and Rape—Piracy Committed in Territorial Waters of a Foreign State.**

PEOPLE *v.* LOL-LO AND SARAW.

United States, Supreme Court of the Philippine Islands. 27 February, 1922.

THE FACTS.—This was a prosecution for piracy. Certain Moros from the Philippines boarded a small Dutch boat in the vicinity of the Dutch East Indies, attacked the men on board, violated the women, and took the cargo. They left the men on board the vessel, after scuttling it so that it would sink, and carried off with them two women whom they repeatedly raped. The men escaped drowning and reached land after many privations, while the women escaped when the Moros put into a port of the Dutch East Indies. After the Moros returned to the Philippines, two of them were arrested and charged with piracy in the Court of First Instance of Sulu. A demurrer based on an alleged lack of jurisdiction and on failure of the facts to constitute an offence under the present laws was overruled. They were convicted and sentenced to life imprisonment. The Penal Code of Spain, in force in the Philippines, provided for punishment of piracy against

Spaniards or subjects of countries at peace with Spain. On appeal by the prisoners to the Supreme Court of the Philippines,

Held: That the appeal must be disallowed, but that sentence must be modified so as to inflict the death penalty on Lol-lo, who had been guilty of rape. The Court held that it had jurisdiction. Delivering the Opinion of the Court, Justice Malcolm said: " All of the elements of the crime of piracy are " present. Piracy is robbery or forcible depredation on the " high seas, without lawful authority and done *animo furandi*, " and in the spirit and intention of universal hostility. . . . " Pirates are in law *hostes humani generis*. Piracy is a crime " not against any particular state but against all mankind. It " may be punished in the competent tribunal of any country " where the offender may be found or into which he may be " carried. The jurisdiction of piracy unlike all other crimes has " no territorial limits. As it is against all so may it be punished " by all. Nor does it matter that the crime was committed " within the jurisdictional 3-mile limit of a foreign state." (43 P.I. 19, 22.) When the United States took over the Philippine Islands, the provisions on piracy in the old penal code remained in force, but with the substitution of " United " States " for " Spain." These provisions were not inconsistent with the corresponding provisions against piracy in the United States statutes, and the death penalty could be imposed in aggravated circumstances such as those presented by the present case. [Report: 43 P.I. 19.]

PART V

STATE RESPONSIBILITY

B. NATURE AND KINDS OF STATE RESPONSIBILITY

I.—In General. When does State Responsibility Become Engaged ? Absolute Responsibility and Responsibility Based on Fault

State Responsibility—In General—Plea of *Force Majeure*—Admissibility of—Article 231 of the Treaty of Versailles. **Case No. 113**

DAME FRANZ *v.* GERMANY.

Franco-German Mixed Arbitral Tribunal. 11 *February*, 1922.

(SJOEBORG, FORTIN.[1])

THE FACTS.—This was a claim against Germany, under Article 297 (*e*) of the Treaty of Versailles, for compensation for loss suffered by the plaintiff, whose luggage, forwarded on 31 July, 1914, from Germany to France, was during the war detained and sold by order of the German Railway Company. It was contended by Germany that the contract of registration of the luggage ought to be governed by German law; that according to German railway regulations the company is entitled in certain cases to dispose of the luggage by sale; and that in the present case the railway administration was compelled by *force majeure, i.e.* in consequence of the state of war, to sell the luggage.

Held : That Germany was liable. German municipal law was only applicable in so far as it was not inconsistent with the Treaty of Versailles. In Article 231 of that Treaty Germany accepted responsibility for causing the loss and damage to which the Allied and Associated Powers had been subjected as a consequence of the war. It follows that Germany cannot, as against nationals of the Allied and Associated Powers, avail herself of the plea of *force majeure* arising out of the war. It is an uncontested principle that one cannot plead as an excuse the existence of a fact for which one is responsible. [Report : *Recueil*, vol. I (1922), p. 781.]

[1] The German judge seems to have refused to sign the decision.

V.—For Breaches of Contractual Obligations

Case No. 114

Responsibility of States—Acts of Officials outside the Scope of their Competence—Subsequent Tacit Ratification.

H. J. R. HEMMING CASE.

British-American Claims Arbitral Tribunal.
18 *December,* 1920.

(FROMAGEOT, FITZPATRICK, ANDERSON.)

THE FACTS.—This was a claim put forward on behalf of H. J. R. Hemming, an English lawyer, who in 1894 and 1895 was engaged by the consul of the United States at Bombay in the prosecution of certain persons accused of counterfeiting United States gold coin in India. The United States did not deny that Hemming was engaged by the consul and that he rendered legal services. It contended, however, that the consul was not authorised to employ private counsel in the matter of a prosecution which might well have been conducted by the authorities of the Crown. It appeared from the correspondence laid before the Tribunal that the Government of the United States was aware at the time of the employment of Hemming, and that it did not object to his continued employment during the progress of the case.

Held : That the conduct of the Government of the United States must be regarded as an implicit ratification of the contract entered into by the consul. In view of this it was immaterial whether the consul entered rightly or wrongly into the contract. [Reports : Nielsen, p. 622 ; *A.J.*, XV (1921), p. 292.]

NOTE.—In awarding the amount, the Tribunal took into account the expense undergone by the claimant in the attempt to obtain satisfaction and the delay in payment.

VI.—For Wrongs Unconnected with Contractual Obligations

(a) Acts and Omissions of State Organs and Officials

(ii) Executive Action or Inaction

Responsibility of States—Executive Action—Responsibility for Errors of Judgment of Officials—Probable Causes of Seizure—Errors of Judgment as to Facts and as to the Law—Decisions of Municipal Court—Whether Binding upon a Government. **Case No. 115**

The Coquitlam.

British-American Claims Arbitral Tribunal.
18 *December*, 1920.

(Fromageot, Fitzpatrick, Anderson.)

The Facts.—This was a claim by Great Britain for compensation on the ground of the alleged unlawful seizure of the steamer *Coquitlam* by a United States cutter in the Behring Sea. The *Coquitlam* was a British registered ship chartered for the purpose of conveying supplies to a number of schooners and receiving in return their catch of seals. In June, 1892, the *Coquitlam* was seized by a United States revenue cutter and handed over to the Collector of Taxes. In July, 1892, she was charged with a number of offences against the United States revenue laws by receiving or unloading merchandise and cargo in the waters and within four leagues of the coast of the United States, by having no manifest in writing of the cargo brought into a United States harbour and the like. Her cargo and appurtenances were condemned by a decree of a District Court of Alaska, but on appeal a United States Circuit Court of Appeals reversed the decree of forfeiture and dismissed the libel of information against the *Coquitlam*. The Court of Appeal held that there had taken place no infringement of the statutes of the United States. Before the Tribunal the United States denied liability on account of wrongful seizure. It contended that the construction put by the Court of Appeal on the language of the statutes was a very technical construction, that the construction under which the customs authorities acted was supported by previous

Case No. 115 *contd.*

decisions of the United States courts, that the authorities acted in the *bona fide* belief that there had taken place an infringement of the statutes, and that there was probable cause for this belief.

Held: That the United States were liable.

(*a*) The good faith and fair conduct of the authorities of the United States were not open to question, but even though this fact may be taken as an adequate explanation given by the authorities to their Government " . . . it can not operate " to prevent their action being an error in judgment for which " the Government of the United States is liable to a foreign " Government."

(*b*) The fact that the interpretation of the United States customs statutes had given rise to some doubt does not constitute a probable cause of seizure. Probable cause of seizure, as defined by Chief Justice Marshall, " imports a seizure made " under circumstances which warrant suspicion."[1] Such probable cause implied the existence of certain facts which *prima facie* created a liability to seizure. This means that the doubt must relate to the existence of the fact, and not to its legality. In the present case the doubt was not as to the facts, but as to the meaning of the United States statutes.

(*c*) As it had been finally decided by a court of the United States that the customs authorities put a wrong construction upon the United States revenue statutes, the United States must be deemed responsible. " This decision of the Judicial " Authorities of the United States is binding upon the " Government." [Reports: Nielsen, p. 447; *A.J.*, XV (1921), p. 301.]

Case No. 116

State Responsibility—Executive Action—Erroneous Refusal of Licence—Seizure of Vessels Operating without a Licence Erroneously Refused—Question of Liability.

THE TATTLER (II).

British-American Claims Arbitral Tribunal.
18 *December*, 1920.

(FROMAGEOT, FITZPATRICK, ANDERSON.)

THE FACTS.—The *Tattler* was an American vessel which in December, 1905, was seized and detained by Canadian officials on the ground that in October of that year she shipped, without having the required

[1] *Locke* v. *United States*, 1813, 5 Cranch, 339, at p. 348.

licence, a number of men as members of the crew. It appeared from the evidence that the master of the vessel applied in October, 1905, for the licence, but the Canadian authorities, being under a mistaken impression as to the status of the vessel, refused the licence. In November of that year the owners of the vessel were informed that the refusal was due to a mistake and that they were ready to issue the licence on receipt of the proper fee. The owners thereupon mailed the amount required to the Canadian authorities at North Sydney. When, in December, the *Tattler* entered North Sydney for shelter she was seized and detained on the charge of having in October shipped men without a licence. She was detained for a period of three days.

Held : That the *Tattler* was entitled to an indemnity. " It " is difficult to admit that a foreign ship may be seized for not " having a certain document when the document has been " refused to it by the very authorities who required that it " should be obtained." An error of judgment of the Canadian officials ought not to result in prejudice to the ship affected by the error. [Reports : Nielsen, p. 490 ; *A.J.*, XV (1921), p. 297.]

State Responsibility—Executive Inaction—Responsibility for Damage Done to Property of Aliens in the Course of Riots. **Case No. 117**

THE HOME MISSIONARY SOCIETY CASE.

British-American Claims Arbitral Tribunal. 18 *December*, 1920.

(FROMAGEOT, FITZPATRICK, ANDERSON.)

THE FACTS.—This was a claim presented by the Government of the United States on behalf of an American religious body known as the " Home Frontier and " Foreign Missionary Society of the United Brethren " in Christ." The claim was for compensation for damage sustained by the Society and some of its members during a rebellion of natives in 1898 in the British Protectorate of Sierra Leone. The rebellion followed upon the collection of a new tax imposed on the district. In the course of the rebellion, which was promptly suppressed, the property of several missions was destroyed and a number of missionaries were murdered. The United States contended that the

Case No. 117 ***contd.***

British authorities in the Protectorate had notice that the collection of the tax would meet with forcible resistance; that at the time of the rising only inadequate forces were stationed in the vicinity of the missions although there were adequate forces in the Protectorate as a whole; and that the British Government was responsible for the losses suffered by the Society because of its neglect or failure to give proper protection.

Held: That the claim must be dismissed. "It is a well-"established principle of international law that no government "can be held responsible for the act of rebellious bodies of "men committed in violation of its authority, where it is itself "guilty of no breach of good faith, or of no negligence in sup-"pressing insurrection."[1] There was no evidence to support the contention that the British Government had failed in its duty to afford adequate protection for life and property. The tax in question—even if it were admitted that it was the actual cause of the rebellion—was a fiscal measure in accordance with general usage in colonial administration and the usual practice in African countries. The British Government was entitled, in the legitimate exercise of its sovereignty, to impose the tax as part of its policy and its administrative system. "Of these "requirements it alone could judge." It had no reason to believe that the imposition of the tax would lead to a widespread and murderous revolt. It is impossible to apply, in respect of the system of police and protection of life and property in force in backward regions of Africa, the standards of social order and respect of authority obtaining in countries with a higher civilisation. In the present case no lack of promptitude or courage was alleged against the British forces in the Protectorate. The Home Missionary Society must have been aware of the risks involved in its work in a savage region, and the contempt for difficulty and peril was the reason why missionary zeal was successful in fields which mere commercial enterprise could not profitably enter. [Reports: Nielsen, p. 423; *A.J.*, XV (1921), p. 294.]

NOTE.—(1) As to the recommendation of an *ex gratia* payment see Case No. 266.

(2) The Tribunal referred with approval to the *Wipperman* case, Ralston (1st ed.), No. 491, p. 231.

---

[1] The Tribunal referred here to Moore, pp. 2991-2992; Moore, *Digest*, vol. VI, p. 956, vol. VII, p. 957.

Responsibility for Acts of Officials—*Bona fide* Action contrary to International Law—Whether Involving State Responsibility—Unlawful Interference with Foreign Vessels.

Case No. 118

THE JESSIE, THE THOMAS F. BAYARD, THE PESCAWHA.

British-American Claims Arbitral Tribunal.
2 December, 1921.

(FROMAGEOT, FITZPATRICK, ANDERSON.)

THE FACTS.—This was a claim put forward on behalf of the owners of the above British vessels on account of the interference, in June, 1909, with their sealing operations in the North Pacific Ocean by the United States revenue vessel. It was contended on behalf of the United States that the officer commanding the revenue cutter acted *bona fide* in the belief that his action, consisting in sealing the firearms and ammunition found on board the British vessels, was covered by the joint regulation adopted by the United States and Great Britain for the protection of the fur seals in the Behring Sea. The United States admitted that there existed in 1909 no agreement permitting such action.

Held : That the United States were responsible. It was a fundamental principle of international maritime law that, in the absence of a special convention or except in time of war, interference with a foreign vessel pursuing a lawful activity on the high seas is illegal, and constitutes a violation of the sovereignty of the State whose flag the vessel flies. The fact that the authorities of the United States acted *bona fide* might be invoked as an explanation of their action to their own Government, but if their conduct constituted an error of judgment, "any government is responsible to other governments for "errors in judgment of its officials purporting to act within "the scope of their duties and vested with power to enforce "their demands."

As to damages see Case No. 127. [Reports : Nielsen, p. 479 ; *A.J.*, XVI (1922), p. 114.]

Case No. 119

Responsibility of States—Executive and Judicial Action—Wrongful Seizure and Confiscation of Boats and Seines—Declared Intention of Executive Organs to Effect an Illegal Seizure—Jurisdiction within Territorial Waters—Rights of Fishery—Conclusiveness of Findings of the Municipal Court.

THE ARGONAUT AND *THE JONAS H. FRENCH.*

British-American Claims Arbitral Tribunal. 2 *December,* 1921.

(FROMAGEOT, FITZPATRICK, ANDERSON.)

THE FACTS.—This was a claim by the United States Government on account of the alleged wrongful seizure and confiscation by the Canadian authorities of boats and seines of two American vessels, the *Argonaut* and the *Jonas H. French,* and the threatened seizure of the vessels themselves. The boats and seines of the vessels were seized and subsequently confiscated by a decision of a Canadian court on the ground that they were illegally engaged in fishing within three miles of the Canadian coast. It appeared that the owners of the vessels were under the impression that they were fishing outside the three-mile limit. After the seizure of the boats and seines the owners abandoned the trip. On returning they heard that it was the intention of the Canadian authorities to seize the vessels themselves even if found outside the territorial waters of Canada. The claim of the United States seems to have been based on the following grounds: (*a*) that the seizure took place outside the three-mile limit; (*b*) that there was in any case no intention of fishing inside the three miles; (*c*) that the owners suffered loss as the result of the threatened seizure of the vessels outside the territorial waters.

Held: That the claim must be dismissed.

As to (*a*). The Tribunal found that the seizure of the boats and seines had in fact taken place within the Canadian territorial waters.

As to (*b*). It is a universally recognised principle of international law that a State has jurisdiction over sea-fishing within its territorial waters, and is entitled to apply thereto its municipal law, and to impose in respect thereof such prohibitions as it may think fit. As the boats and seines were, at the time of the seizure, inside Canadian territorial waters, they were, according to international law, subject to the municipal law and the jurisdiction of Canada. The question whether the owners of the vessels acted in good faith and whether the Canadian courts properly applied and interpreted Canadian statutes was a question of municipal law and not of international law to be decided by the Tribunal.

As to (*c*). The mere intention of Canadian authorities, even if such intention existed, to seize the vessels themselves could not constitute a basis for indemnity unless it was manifested by some wrongful act. No evidence was offered to show that an order of seizure was given or that any other measure of execution was taken against the vessels.[1] [Reports: Nielsen, p. 509; *A.J.*, XVI (1922), p. 106.]

State Responsibility—Executive Action—Responsibility in Cases of a Government Exercising Delegated Authority on behalf of Another Government—*Bona fides* of Executive Action and the Question of Responsibility—Restrictive Interpretation of Agreements Constituting an Exception from General Principles of International Law. **Case No. 120**

THE WANDERER.

British-American Claims Arbitral Tribunal.
9 *December*, 1921.

(FROMAGEOT, FITZPATRICK, ANDERSON.)

THE FACTS.—This was a claim by Great Britain for damages arising out of the seizure and detention of the British sealing schooner *Wanderer*. A British Act of Parliament passed on 23 April, 1894, with the view to giving effect to the award in the Behring Sea Arbitration of 15 August, 1893, provided in Section 3, paragraph 3, as follows: "An Order in Council under "this Act may provide that such officers of the United "States of America as are specified in the order may, "in respect of offences under this Act, exercise the "like powers under this Act as may be exercised by a "commissioned officer of Her Majesty in relation to a "British ship." Article 6 of the *Regulations*, annexed

[1] For another aspect of the question of liability, in international law, for administrative measures which have not as yet resulted in actual damage, see *Annual Digest*, 1925-1926, Case No. 148. And see the attitude of the United States in the matter of the British request for arbitration in regard to the act of Congress concerning the Panama Canal Tolls: Lauterpacht, *Law and the Judicial Function in the International Community* (1932), chapter VII.

Case No. 120 *contd.*

to the Behring Sea Award and declared, like other Articles of the *Regulations*, to form part of the above Act of Parliament, provided that the use of nets, firearms and explosives shall be forbidden in the fur-seal fishing. On 10 June, 1894, the *Wanderer*, a British schooner, was seized and detained by the United States authorities following upon a search which resulted in the discovery on board the schooner of an unsealed gun and ammunition. Before the Tribunal the United States denied liability on the ground: (*a*) that her authorities acted in the *bona fide* belief that an infraction of the *Regulations* of the Behring Sea Award had been committed; (*b*) that the United States officers were acting on behalf of the British Government and that, therefore, the liability to pay damages would rest with the British Government even if it were assumed that the seizure was made without probable cause.

Held: That the United States were responsible.

(*a*) According to a fundamental principle of international maritime law no nation can exercise a right of visitation and search over foreign vessels pursuing a lawful avocation on the high seas, except in time of war or by special agreement.[1] In the present case it was, therefore, for the United States to show that its naval authorities acted under special agreement. "Any such agreement, being an exception to the general principle, must be construed *stricto jure*."

As the Behring Sea *Regulations* prohibited only the use of firearms and munitions, the mere possession of them could not be regarded as being in contravention of the *Regulations*. Accordingly, even if it were admitted that the United States authorities acted on behalf of the British Government under the Behring Sea Act, it was clear that "such a delegation of power only gave them authority to act within the limits of that Act, and as the seizure was made for a reason not provided for by that Act, it is impossible to say that in this case they were exercising that delegated authority."

The *bona fides* of the United States naval officers could, in the circumstances of the case,[2] be admitted; the United States Government was, nevertheless, liable for the error of

[1] It will be noted, however, that in the present case it was not the right of visit and search which was at issue, but of seizure and detention.

[2] The United States *Regulations* in question prohibited also the possession of firearms.

judgment committed by its agents. [Reports: Nielsen, p. 459; *A.J.*, XVI (1922), p. 305.]

NOTE.—See also, to the same effect, *The Favourite*, Nielsen, p. 515; *A.J.*, XVI (1922), p. 301.

Responsibility of States—Responsibility for the Acts of Foreign Authorities—Responsibility of Prussia for the Acts of the Inter-Allied Plebiscite Commission in Upper Silesia. **Case No. 121**

UPPER SILESIA (PLEBISCITE COMMISSION) CASE.

Germany, Upper District Court (Oberlandesgericht) of Breslau. October, 1922.

THE FACTS.—On 11 April, 1921, the District Officer of Oppelm (Upper Silesia), an official appointed by the Inter-Allied Plebiscite Commission in Upper Silesia, requisitioned a motor-car belonging to the plaintiff. In August, 1921, the Inter-Allied Commission restored the car to the owner and paid him 24,500 Marks as compensation for the use of the car. The owner contended that 40,000 Marks was the sum which he was entitled to receive, and brought an action for the balance against the Prussian State.

According to § 3 of the Annex to § 88 of the Treaty of Versailles the Inter-Allied Commission was entrusted with all the powers exercised by the German or Prussian Government, except those of legislation and taxation.

Held: That the action must be dismissed. It was true that in view of the circumstances of the case the requisition was unlawful. However, the Prussian law on the responsibility of State officials had no application to wrongful acts of the officials of the Inter-Allied Commission. Although the Treaty of Versailles provided that the Inter-Allied Commission shall exercise the powers hitherto exercised by the *Reich* or Prussia, it did not have the effect of substituting, as a matter of constitutional law, the officials of the Inter-Allied Commission for those of the *Reich* or of Prussia. The fact that the Treaty of Versailles was published as part of German law is irrelevant. The effect of such publication was merely to bring about a duty, under municipal law, on the part of individuals and officials to observe the international obligations undertaken by Germany. In particular, it had the effect of obliging individuals and State officials in Upper Silesia to

Case No. 121 *contd.* recognise the authority of the Plebiscite Commission. But it cannot be interpreted as meaning that the Prussian law on the responsibility of the State for the acts of its organs applies also to the acts of the officials of the Inter-Allied Commission. [Report : *Juristische Wochenschrift*, 1923, p. 191.]

Responsibility of States—Judicial Action—Judicial Interpretation of Treaties by Municipal Courts—How far Subject to Review by International Courts—Denial of Justice.

See Case No. 239 (*The David J. Adams*).

v.—PLEA OF NON-DISCRIMINATION AGAINST FOREIGNERS

[See Part IV, TERRITORIAL JURISDICTION : *Expropriation*, and Part VI, C II.]

(b) Acts of Insurgents, Rioters and Private Individuals in General

Case No. 122

Responsibility of States—Duty to Prevent Dispatch of Hostile Expedition Intended to Promote Revolution in Friendly State—Seizure of Ship—British Foreign Enlistment Act, 1870.

THE HARRIER.

England, Admiralty Court.[1] 29 *July*, 1921.

THE FACTS.—In this case (which was undefended) the Court was informed by the Attorney-General that a warrant for the seizure, search and detention of the steamship *Harrier* has been issued by the Secretary of State for Foreign Affairs under the Foreign Enlistment Act, as the result of information received to the effect that two Venezuelan generals were organising in Europe a revolution in Venezuela for the overthrow of President Gomez and were conspiring with a certain person in London with a view to acquiring the *Harrier*, formerly a British gunboat, for the purpose of arming and equipping her to take part in the revolution. The warrant had been executed at Swansea. His Majesty's Procurator-General now asked for a decree of forfeiture of the vessel under the Foreign Enlistment Act, 1870.

Held by Hill, J. : That the *Harrier* must be forfeited to His Majesty. [Report : 8 Lloyd's List Law Reports 488.[2]]

[1] See p. 43, footnote.

[2] See, for a similar case, *R.* v. *Sandoval*, 3 T.L.R. 411.—[Ed.]

Responsibility of States—Duty to Prevent Revolutionary Preparations of a Military Character against a Friendly Government—Enlistments. **Case No. 123**

GAYON *v.* McCARTHY.

United States Supreme Court. 1 *March*, 1920.

THE FACTS.—This was an indictment for conspiracy to enlist a United States citizen in military forces in revolt against the Government of Mexico. Gayon and another Mexican, Naranjo, were active partisans of the revolt. An American citizen, Averitt, recently resigned from the United States Naval Academy, called at Gayon's office in New York and received letters of introduction to Naranjo in Texas and to one of the leaders of the revolt in Mexico. Gayon declined to commission Averitt or to advance expenses, on the ground that this would violate United States neutrality laws, but he intimated that both commission and expenses would be forthcoming in Mexico. Averitt called on Naranjo in Texas, received further instructions, and was arrested while attempting to cross into Mexico. Gayon was arrested in New York. The United States Criminal Code, § 10, as amended, provides that " whoever, within the territory or jurisdiction of the United States, enlists or enters himself, " or hires or retains another person to enlist or enter " himself, or to go beyond the limits or jurisdiction of " the United States with intent to be enlisted or " entered in the service of any foreign prince, State, " colony, district, or people as a soldier or as a marine " or seaman on board of any vessel of war, letter of " marque, or privateer, shall be fined not more than " $1000 and imprisoned not more than three years." (40 U.S. Stat. L. 39.) The same Code, § 37, provides that " if two or more persons conspire either to commit any offense against the United States, or to " defraud the United States in any manner or for any " purpose, and one or more of such parties do any act " to effect the object of the conspiracy, each of the " parties to such conspiracy shall be fined not more " than ten thousand dollars, or imprisoned not more " than two years, or both." (35 U.S. Stat. L. 1088, 1096.) Gayon was denied habeas corpus and a warrant

Case No. 123 *contd.*

was issued for his removal to Texas for trial. On appeal,

Held: That the judgment must be affirmed. Engaging another to go to Mexico to join revolutionary forces, under promise of a commission and probable reimbursement for expenses, is a "retaining" within the meaning of § 10 of the Criminal Code. Delivering the Opinion of the Court, Mr. Justice Clarke said: "While the narration of what took "place between Gayon and Averitt does not show a hiring of "the latter in the ordinary sense of the word, yet, when taken "with the conduct of Averitt in going immediately to Texas, "and in attempting to cross into Mexico, plainly, it tends to "show that Gayon retained Averitt in the sense of engaging "him to go to Mexico, that he was induced to enter into that "engagement by the promise that he would be given a com-"mission in the forces of Diaz when he arrived there and that "he would probably be reimbursed for his expenses." (252 U.S. 171, 177.) [Report: 252 U.S. 171.[1]]

VII.—For Acts and Omissions of Revolutionary or *de facto* Governments

Case No. 124

State Responsibility—Responsibility for the Acts of a *de facto* Government—Legislation Annulling Acts of *de facto* Governments—How far Applicable to Aliens—Decisions of Municipal and International Courts.

French Claims against Peru.

Permanent Court of Arbitration. 11 *October*, 1921.

(Ostertag, Sarrut, Elguere.)

The Facts.—By a contract concluded in August, 1869, the State of Peru sold to Dreyfus Brothers & Company (a firm whose members were French subjects) two million tons of guano. The company was also by another contract granted rights in the nature of a monopoly for the sale of guano in return for a loan. A number of disputes arose subsequently in the matter of these contracts between the company and the Peruvian Government. In April, 1879, a war broke out between Peru and Chile. As the result of the

[1] On the question of revolutionary activities against foreign States see Lauterpacht in *A.J.*, XXII (1928), pp. 105-130, and, with special reference to the practice of the United States, Curtis in *A.J.*, VIII (1914), pp. 1-37, 224-252.

events of the war a revolution broke out in December, 1879, in Peru. Nicolas de Piérola seized the power and was proclaimed head of the Republic. In April, 1880, he was entrusted by the Dreyfus Company with the decision of all questions in dispute between themselves and the Peruvian Government. In November, 1880, he gave a decision, approved by the Peruvian Court of Accounts, which fixed the balance of the credit of the Dreyfus Company at the sum of about 17 million Peruvian soles, being equivalent to £3,214,388. In October, 1886, an Act was passed in Peru declaring null all the internal acts of government performed by Nicolas de Piérola, and the Peruvian Government then refused to effect any payments to the company. The French Government intervened on behalf of Dreyfus Brothers. In December, 1912, a Peruvian law was passed authorising the Government to conclude an arbitration agreement for submission of the case to the Permanent Court of Arbitration at The Hague, provided that in no case should the Government of Peru be bound to make a payment exceeding 25,000,000 francs for the claims in question. On 2 February, 1914, a protocol was signed between France and Peru submitting for arbitration, *inter alia*, the claim of Dreyfus Brothers. Before the Tribunal Peru relied both on the mere *de facto* character of the Piérola Government and on the Law of 1886 declaring null the internal acts of this Government.

Held: That Peru was liable for the sum as approved in 1880 by the Peruvian Court of Accounts. It was bound by the acts of the Piérola Government so far as foreigners were concerned. Nicolas de Piérola was proclaimed supreme chief of the Republic with the apparent consent of large sections of the population, including that of the National Assembly. He in fact exercised legislative, executive and, in part, judicial powers. His Government was recognised by many States, including France, England, Germany and Belgium. "The High Court of "Justice of England (decree of February 23, 1888), the Court "of Appeals of Brussels (decree of July 10, 1888), the Franco-"Chilean Arbitral Court (award called Award of Lausanne of "July 5, 1901), being decrees and an award of which the "arbitral court adopts the reasons, have deemed that this "government represented and bound the nation."

Case No. 124 ***contd.***

The Law of 1886 could not "be applied to foreigners who "treated in good faith." [Reports: *The Hague Court Reports* (Second Series, edited by J. B. Scott), p. 33; *A.J.*, XVI (1922), p. 480.]

NOTE.—The English case referred to by the Tribunal is the case of *Republic of Peru* v. *Dreyfus Brothers & Co.*, L.R. (1888) 38 Ch. D. 348.

The decision of the Belgian Court of Appeals is reported in *La Belgique Judiciaire*, XLVI (1888), p. 1218.

The decision of the Franco-Chilean Arbitral Tribunal of 5 July, 1901, is printed in a separate volume entitled *Tribunal Arbitral Franco-Chilien* (1901). The relevant passage from this award (p. 288) runs: "According to a principle of the law of nations, at first denied theoretically "in the dynastic interest by the diplomacy of European monarchies, "applied, however, in fact in a series of cases to-day universally "admitted, the capacity of a government to represent the State in "its international relations depends in no degree whatever upon the "legitimacy of its origin; so that foreign states no longer refuse to "recognize governments *de facto*, and the usurper who exercises power "in fact, with an express or tacit consent of the nation, acts and "concludes validly in the name of the state treaties which the legiti-"mate government, upon its restoration, is bound to respect." (As translated in Scott, *op. cit.*, pp. viii, ix.)

C. CLAIMS

I.—In General

Claims—In General—Nature of—Whether Claim Presented by a Government is Identical with the Private Claim which it Espouses.

See Case No. 163 (*The Tattler (I)*).

Claims—In General—Effect of Presentation by Government—Evidence as to *bona fides* of the Claim.

See Case No. 118 (*The Jessie, The Thomas F. Bayard, The Pescawha*).

Claims—Liability in General—Liability not Affected by Exaggeration or Fraudulent Character of the Claim for Damages.

See Case No. 127 (*The Jessie, The Thomas F. Bayard, The Pescawha*)

II.—Nationality of Claims

Claims—Nationality of—Claims Accruing before the Naturalisation of the Claimant—Point not Open on the Terms of the Protocol. **Case No. 125**

LANDREAU CLAIMS AGAINST PERU.

United States-Peruvian Arbitral Commission.[1]
26 *October*, 1922.

(VISCOUNT FINLAY, President; BARTON SMITH, CARLOS H. PREVOST.)

THE FACTS.—This was a claim by the United States on behalf of the heirs and assignees of a naturalised American citizen, John Célestin Landreau, arising out of a Peruvian Decree of 1865 providing for the payment of rewards to his brother, John Théophile Landreau, and of contracts made between the Peruvian Government and the two brothers. It was contended before the Commission that as the claim accrued to John Célestin Landreau while he was still a French subject, his subsequent naturalisation as a citizen of the United States did not justify the United States in taking up the claim.

Held: That that contention must be rejected. " The fact " that any claim had accrued before naturalization might " form one element to be considered by the United States " before deciding to take up the case, but it is quite impossible " to say that it would on such ground be *ultra vires* of the " United States to take it up. This tribunal cannot enter " into the question whether it was proper for the United States " Government to take up the case. All that the tribunal has " to do is to decide the dispute in the terms of the protocol." [Report: *A.J.*, XVII (1923), p. 157, at p. 172.]

[1] Constituted by a special agreement signed on 21 May, 1921, relating to this case only.

Case No. 126 **Claims—Nationality of Claims—Claims under the Alsop Award—Treaties and Not-Ratified Protocols.**

In re McCall's Estate.

United States, Pennsylvania, Orphans' Court for Philadelphia County. 1 *April*, 1919.

The Facts.—Edward McCall, an American citizen, was a partner in the Chilean firm of Alsop & Co. As a result of its dealings in South America and of the Chilean seizure of Arica in the War of the Pacific, Alsop & Co. had large claims against Chile. The United States took the matter up with Chile. While the claim of the United States was disallowed on the ground that Alsop & Co. were a Chilean partnership, the King of England, as " *amiable compositeur* " under a protocol, made an award in favour of the United States on behalf of its citizens who were interested in the company. The award was paid in 1911. McCall had died domiciled in Pennsylvania in 1874. The United States Department of State referred claims to the sum awarded to the courts. The auditing judge on McCall's claim ordered distribution to the next-of-kin of McCall, who were American nationals living at the time of distribution. Certain Peruvians, claiming to be McCall's next-of-kin under Peruvian law, took exception to the order.

Held : That the exceptions must be dismissed. Under an international settlement between Chile and the United States, the United States represents only the interests of its nationals. It would be an act of bad faith for the United States to receive this sum from Chile and pay it to Peruvians. It is true that protocols do not have the force of municipal law unless ratified like treaties, but they pledge the good faith of the country. Unless the Senate expressly refuses to ratify a protocol if and when submitted for ratification, " courts of equity may and " will be bound by all representations and proceedings under " a protocol where equity and justice require it." (28 Pa. Dist. Ct. 433, 448.) [Report : 28 Pa. Dist. Ct. 433.]

Claims—Nationality of—Enemy Character—Effect of Divesting of Enemy Nationality by Claimants in Prize Proceedings.

See Case No. 288 (*The Blonde and other Ships*).

E. DAMAGES (MEASURE OF DAMAGES)

II.—Indirect Damages and Damages for Loss of Profits

Damages—Consequential and Indirect—Alleged Exaggerated and Fraudulent Claims—Claims for Damages and Question of Liability—Presentation by a Government as Evidence of the *bona fides* of the Claim.

Case No. 127

THE JESSIE, THE THOMAS F. BAYARD, THE PESCAWHA.

British-American Claims Arbitral Tribunal. 2 *December*, 1921.

(FROMAGEOT, FITZPATRICK, ANDERSON.)

THE FACTS.—(See Case No. 118.) It was contended by the United States that the claims for damages should be rejected as there was no evidence as to the alleged damage except the declarations of the claimant party, and that the claims in question were of an exaggerated and fraudulent nature.

Held : (*a*) That the points as to the alleged insufficiency of proof and as to the alleged exaggeration and fraudulent character of the claims had a bearing only on the determination of damages and indemnity. They did not affect the question of liability.

(*b*) The exaggeration of the claims, even if proved to be correct, did not justify the charge that they were fraudulent. The mere fact that they were presented by the British Government was, so far as the Tribunal was concerned, sufficient evidence of their *bona fides*.

(*c*) That the United States were liable to compensate the claimants : (i) for the special expense incurred in engaging crews specially trained for the enterprise in question ; (ii) " for " the trouble occasioned by the illegal interference." [Reports: Nielsen, p. 482 ; *A.J.*, XVI (1922), p. 114.]

NOTE.—The part of the decision dealing with the question of damages is somewhat obscure. It appears from the decision that the claim was for damages caused not only by the frustration of a fur-seal-catching expedition, but also of an otter-hunting enterprise. This dual aspect of the claim does not appear in the statement of the facts by the Tribunal.

In assessing the amount of damages the Tribunal regarded as relevant the fact that the amount claimed was based merely on statements made by the interested parties or on statistics affording no

Case No. 127 contd.

evidence as to the "sea otters caught by other British schooners, "similarly equipped and manned, hunting during the same period and "in the same localities as the three schooners in question intended "to hunt."

Case No. 128

Damages—Indirect Damages—Legal Expenses as an Element of Damages—Loss of Profits.

THE NEWCHWANG.

British-American Claims Arbitral Tribunal. 9 *December,* 1921.

(FROMAGEOT, FITZPATRICK, ANDERSON.)

THE FACTS.—(See Case No. 263.) The claim in this case was not only for damage suffered by the *Newchwang* as the result of the collision with the United States navy collier, the *Saturn,* and the cost of her repair, but also for the legal expenses incurred by the company owning the *Newchwang* in connection with the action originally brought by the United States before the British Supreme Court for China and Korea.

Held : That this item of the claim must be rejected. It was true that these expenses were damages indirectly consequent upon the collision ; but it was "a well known principle "of the law of damages that *causa proxima non remota* "*inspicitur.*"

As to the claim for loss of profits, the Tribunal held that as no sufficient evidence was adduced to prove the loss occasioned by the deprivation of use, the damage must be computed according to the ordinary rule of demurrage at 4d. per ton gross tonnage. [Reports: Nielsen, p. 414 ; *A.J.*, XVI (1922), p. 323.]

Case No. 129

Damages—Loss of Profits—Calculation of—Damages in Cases of Illegal Detention.

THE KATE.

British-American Claims Arbitral Tribunal. 9 *December,* 1921.

(FROMAGEOT, FITZPATRICK, ANDERSON.)

In this case the Tribunal awarded damages for loss of profits by estimating the probable catch of a vessel on the basis of the actual catch on another vessel in the corresponding period. This method was adopted by the Tribunal (the details of the calculation are given) at the instance of the claimants, who asked for its application in regard to compensation for loss of catch for the period during which the *Kate* was illegally prevented from sealing. [Reports: Nielsen, p. 472; *A.J.*, XVI (1922), p. 328.]

NOTE.—And see *The Wanderer* (Case No. 120), where the Tribunal adopted a similar although less definite basis for calculating the amount of damages for loss of profits. The Tribunal admitted that the evidence offered as a basis for the estimate was indefinite and inconclusive, but it was of the opinion that in view of the fact of illegal detention it was justified in adopting " a liberal estimate of the profits " which the vessel would have made if she had not been unlawfully detained. [Nielsen, p. 470.] See also *The Favourite*, *ibid.*, p. 515; *A.J.*, XVI (1922), p. 301.

In *The Tattler* (*II*) (see Case No. 116) the Tribunal regarded as relevant the fact that no evidence was produced as to the certainty of the prospective catch. " Nobody can say whether the vessel would " have made such a catch, or whether it would have encountered some " mishap of the sea." [*Ibid.*, p. 494; *A.J.*, XV (1921), p. 297.]

Damages—Measure of—In Case of Angary—Requisition of Norwegian Shipbuilding Contracts by the United States. **Case No. 130**

NORWAY AND UNITED STATES (REQUISITION OF SHIPBUILDING CONTRACTS CASE).

Permanent Court of Abritration. 13 *October*, 1922.

(VALLOTON, ANDERSON,[1] VOGT.)

THE FACTS.—(See Case No. 289.) After having decided that in view of the circumstances in which the claimants were deprived of their property they were entitled to compensation, the Tribunal considered what factors ought to serve as the basis for assessing compensation. Both parties agreed that just compensation as it is understood in the United States should be liberally awarded, and that it should be based on the net value of the property taken.

Held: That not only " the fair actual value of the property " taken " but also its value at the time and place it was taken and all the surrounding circumstances must be considered. The value of the shipbuilding contracts must be assessed *ex aequo et bono*. Consideration must be paid to the fact that

[1] See Case No. 267 as to the participation of Mr. Anderson in the rendering of the award.

Case No. 130 ***contd.***

owing to the exceptional circumstances created by the scarcity of ships in 1917 many of the shipbuilding transactions were of a speculative character. As a rule abnormal circumstances and speculative prices cannot form the legal basis of the award. On the other hand, decisive importance could not be attached to " artificial reduction of hire, chartering or purchase price of " ships, as fixed under compulsion, requisition or other govern- " mental action during the war."

The Tribunal was not bound by those municipal enactments of the United States which limited the right of the claimants to receive immediate and full compensation (see Case No. 289). Just compensation in the present case included either full compensation as from 6 October, 1917—the day of the requisition—for the taking away of Norwegian property, or, alternatively, compensation for use of that property during the war, plus, as from 1 July, 1919, damages for unlawful retention of title and use of the ships after all emergency ceased.[1] [Reports : *A.J.*, XVII (1923), pp. 362-399.]

[1] In assessing the amount of compensation the Tribunal took into account the following circumstances : " the date of each contract or sub-contract "between shipbuilder and shipowner ; the technical characteristics and " qualities of each contract (type and dead weight tonnage of the ship ; its " speed, etc. ; the reputation, experience, technical and financial situation " of the shipyard) ; the legal value of the contract, namely the liens, rights " and interests of each original contract, etc. ; the original contract (or sub- " contract) price ; the progress (and brokerage) payments made by each of " the parties on the original contract price ; the date of delivery promised in " the contract ; the date of delivery which was expected at or about the date " of the general requisition order and about the date of the effective requisition " of each contract as far as these can be ascertained ; the various elements " pertaining to the value and degree of completion of the tangible objects of " completion, as, for instance, the percentage of materials ordered, and the " percentage of materials on hand ; the date at which the keel was laid, before " or after the general requisition ; and the date when the ship was launched ; " the contracts, settlements, etc., made by the United States and by Nor- " wegian or other shipowners, or by third parties, whether governments or " private persons, whether with shipowners or shipbuilders, for the con- " struction or purchase or hire of ships ; the statistics, reports and opinions " of experts produced by the parties ; the award of the United States Claims " Committee on the present claims ; the reports of the Ocean Advisory Com- " mittee on just compensation for certain American ships lost in the service " of the government ; etc."

F. INTEREST

I.—In General

Interest—In Case of Exercise of Right of Angary—Compound Interest.

Case No. 131

NORWAY AND UNITED STATES (REQUISITION OF SHIPBUILDING CONTRACTS CASE).

Permanent Court of Arbitration. 13 *October*, 1922.

(VALLOTON, ANDERSON,[1] VOGT.)

THE FACTS.—See Cases Nos. 130, 289.

Held[2]*:* That, as this was a case of expropriation, interest ought to be awarded. The Tribunal took into consideration the fact that the United States had the use and profits of the claimants' property for five years; that the compensation awarded to them by the United States Requisition Claim Committee had not been paid; and that the United States had the benefit of the progress payments made by the Norwegian owners to the shipbuilders.

As to the claim for compound interest, there was no precedent of its being granted in other arbitration cases. No sufficient reason was adduced why it should be granted in the present case. The Tribunal decided to allow to each claimant a lump sum in respect of interest, and held that some claimants are, in view of special circumstances, entitled to a higher rate of interest than the others. [Reports: *A.J.*, XVII (1923), pp. 362-399.]

NOTE.—It will be noted that the award refers only to interest for the period up to the date of the award. In regard to interest after the date of the award the arbitration agreement laid down that "any "amount granted by the award rendered shall bear interest at the "rate of six per centum per annum from the date of the rendition of "the decision until the date of payment."

[1] See Case No. 267 as to the participation of Mr. Anderson in the rendering of the award.

[2] Citing Nichols, *The Law of Eminent Domain* (New York, 1917), p. 216; and Lewis, *A Treatise on the Law of Eminent Domain* (Chicago, 1909), Section 742.

II.—Rate of Interest. Compound Interest

Case No. 132

Interest—Compound Interest.

FRENCH CLAIMS AGAINST PERU.

Permanent Court of Arbitration. 11 *October*, 1921.

(OSTERTAG, SARRUT, ELGUERE.)

THE FACTS.—(See Case No. 124.) The French Government asked for compound interest on the sums claimed.

Held: That the claim for compound interest must be rejected. The right to compound interest can result only " from a stipulation or from circumstances of fact making clear " the consent of the debtor to assume such an onerous obliga- " tion." No such consent of the Peruvian Government has been alleged in the present case. [Reports: *The Hague Court Reports* (Second Series, edited by J. B. Scott), p. 33; *A.J.*, XVI (1922), p. 480.]

III.—The *Dies a Quo*. The *Dies ad Quem*.

Case No. 133

Interest—Award of—No Award of Interest from the Time a Government Expresses Readiness to Comply with Request for Compensation.

THE COQUITLAM.

British-American Claims Arbitral Tribunal. 18 *December*, 1920.

(FROMAGEOT, FITZPATRICK, ANDERSON.)

THE FACTS.—(See Case No. 115.) Subsequently to the judicial proceedings in the case of the *Coquitlam*, the Secretary of State of the United States, in a letter addressed on 21 December, 1904, to the British ambassador, declared that his Government was prepared to admit liability and to recommend payment of a reasonable indemnity. The British Government was asked to submit proofs showing the nature and the extent of the damage caused by the seizure in order to enable the Department of State of the United States to consider the amount of the liability and to make a definite recommendation. There was no evidence to show that the British Government complied with this request.

Held : That interest must be allowed for the period from 16 May, 1897 (this being six months after the date on which a United States Court of Appeal reversed the decision of a lower court ordering the seizure) to 21 December, 1904 (the date of the communication to the British Government of the willingness of the United States to admit liability). [Reports : Nielsen, p. 447 ; *A.J.*, XV (1921), p. 301.]

NOTE.—The decisions of the Tribunal on the matter of interest must be read in the light of Article IV of the Terms of Submission annexed to the Special Arbitration Agreement of 18 August, 1910, between Great Britain and the United States (Nielsen, p. 3). That Article provided as follows : " The Arbitral Tribunal, if it considers equitable, may include in its award in respect of any claim interest at a rate not exceeding 4 per cent. per annum for the whole or any part of the period between the date when the claim was first brought to the notice of the other party and that of the confirmation of the schedule in which it is included." The Schedule of Claims annexed to the Special Agreement provided for the settlement of four categories of claims : (*a*) Claims based on alleged denial in whole or in part of real property rights ; (*b*) Claims based on the acts of the authorities of either Government in regard to the vessels of the nationals of the other Government, or for the alleged wrongful collection or receipt of customs duties or other charges by the authorities of either Government ; (*c*) Claims based on damages to the property of either Government or its nationals, or on personal wrongs of such nationals, alleged to be due to the operations of the military or naval forces of the other Government or to the acts or negligence of the civil authorities of the other Government ; (*d*) Claims based on contracts between the authorities of either Government and the nationals of the other Government. The Schedule of Claims was ratified by an exchange of notes on 26 April, 1912.

PART VI

THE INDIVIDUAL IN INTERNATIONAL LAW

A. IN GENERAL

I.—Position of Individuals in International Law

[See also Part I, INTERNATIONAL LAW IN GENERAL: *Relation to Municipal Law*; and Part VIII, TREATIES: *Operation and Enforcement of Treaties*.]

II.—Before International Tribunals

Individuals—Position of—Before International Tribunals.

See Case No. 289 (*Norway and United States: Requisition of Shipbuilding Contracts Case*) for the statement that "it is "common ground between the parties to this arbitration that "the fifteen claims against the United States are presented "by the Government of the Kingdom of Norway," which Government, and not the individual claimants, "is the sole "claimant before this Tribunal."

B. NATIONALITY

I.—In General. Proof of Nationality

Nationality—Admission to—Abuse of Administrative Discretion—"Fundamental Rights of Men." Case No. 134

KWOCK JAN FAT *v.* WHITE.

United States Supreme Court. 7 *June*, 1920.

THE FACTS.—This was a petition for habeas corpus alleging unlawful detention under the Chinese Exclusion Laws. In 1915, intending to leave the United States on a temporary visit to China, the petitioner secured a "preinvestigation of his claimed status as an American "citizen by birth"[1] and was found to be an American citizen. However, while he was away, another inves-

[1] This means an administrative investigation by immigration official provided by statute in order that the petitioner may have his status established in advance of leaving the United States so that he can leave the United States with confidence as to his right of re-admission notwithstanding provisions of the immigration laws.

Case No. 134 ***contd.***

tigation was initiated upon anonymous information and the finding was reversed. On his return, Kwock Jan Fat was excluded by the immigration authorities. The case was reopened by the Commissioner of Immigration, who, on investigation, adhered to his decision denying admission. Some of the evidence before the Commissioner was obtained from witnesses whose identity could not be disclosed; and the examining inspector had failed to record an important part of the testimony of three white witnesses in petitioner's favour. The only reason given for the Commissioner's decision was that "the claimed American citizenship "is not established to my satisfaction." The Commissioner's decision was approved by the Secretary of Labor. The District Court denied the writ, and on appeal to the Circuit Court of Appeals for the Ninth Circuit the judgment was affirmed. (255 Fed. 323.) On certiorari,

Held: That the judgment denying the writ must be reversed. The decision of the Secretary of Labor is conclusive unless the proceedings are "manifestly unfair," "such as to "prevent a fair investigation," or show "manifest abuse of "discretion." The Court concluded that there had been a denial of "fair hearing." Delivering the Opinion of the Court, Mr. Justice Clarke said: "The acts of Congress give great "power to the Secretary of Labor over Chinese immigrants "and persons of Chinese descent. It is a power to be administered, not arbitrarily and secretly, but fairly and openly, "under the restraints of the tradition and principles of free "government applicable where the fundamental rights of men "are involved, regardless of their origin or race. It is the "province of the courts, in proceedings for review, within the "limits amply defined in the cases cited, to prevent abuse of "this extraordinary power, and this is possible only when a "full record is preserved of the essentials on which the executive "officers proceed to judgment. For failure to preserve such a "record for the information, not less of the Commissioner of "Immigration and of the Secretary of Labor than of the "courts, the judgment in this case must be reversed. It is "better that many Chinese immigrants should be improperly "admitted than that one natural born citizen of the United "States should be permanently excluded from his country." (253 U.S. 454, 464.) [Reports: 255 Fed. 323; 253 U.S. 454.]

Proof of Nationality—Nature of Proof—Enemy Character.

See Case No. 149 (*Ex parte Risse*).

Nationality—In General—Determination of—Within the Exclusive Competence of the Home State.

See Case No. 156 (*Stoeck* v. *Public Trustee*).

II.—As Affected by Changes of Sovereignty

Nationality—Effect of Change of Sovereignty—Meaning of "Resident" and "Ordinarily Resident" Occurring in British Orders in Council—Analogy of Domicile Rejected. **Case No. 135**

GOUT AND ANOTHER *v.* CIMITIAN.

British Empire, Privy Council, on Appeal from His Britannic Majesty's Supreme Court for Egypt (*Cairo*). 17 *November*, 1921.

THE FACTS.—On 5 November, 1914, by the Cyprus Annexation Order in Council Cyprus was annexed to and became part of His Britannic Majesty's Dominions. On the same day and under the same Order in Council the British High Commissioner for Cyprus issued a Proclamation which provided as follows: (1) "Ottoman subjects born in Cyprus and now resident in "Cyprus are British subjects. (2) Ottoman subjects "not born in Cyprus are allowed one year from the "date of this Proclamation within which to leave "Cyprus. Ottoman subjects mentioned in this Pro-"clamation who do not leave Cyprus within the said "period of one year will, on expiration of the said year, "be British subjects."

On 3 March, 1915, this Proclamation was revoked by a further Proclamation which provided that: "Under and by virtue of the said Order in Council "the following provisions have effect: (1) All Otto-"man subjects resident in Cyprus on November 5, "1914, have become British subjects. (2) Any Otto-"man subject resident in Cyprus on November 5, "1914, desiring to retain Ottoman nationality may by "notice under his hand elect to do so within one month "of the coming in operation of this proclamation, and "any such person electing so to do must leave Cyprus "within two months after the date of his election and

Case No. 135 *contd.*

" take up his residence elsewhere, failing which he " would be treated as a British subject."

On 27 November, 1917, the Cyprus Annexation Amendment Order in Council was made, whereby for the purpose of removing doubts arising under the Order in Council of 5 November, 1914, and the Proclamation of 3 March, 1915, made thereunder, it was provided that: " The following persons shall be " deemed to have become British subjects under and " by virtue of the Cyprus Annexation Order in Council, " 1914, and the Proclamation of the High Commissioner " of March 3, 1915. (1) (*a*) Any Ottoman subject " who was ordinarily resident and actually present in " Cyprus on November 5, 1914."

The plaintiff was born at Kaiserie in the Ottoman Dominions in 1878 of Ottoman parentage, and from 1893 to 1913 resided and carried on business in Cairo. In December, 1913, he went to Cyprus for the sake of his health, was joined by his family after three or four months, and resided there for twenty-three months, renting a house by the month. Thus he was present in Cyprus at the dates of the Order in Council and Proclamation of 5 November, 1914, and of the Proclamation of 3 March, 1915. In October, 1915, without giving the notice referred to in paragraph (2) of the Proclamation of 3 March, 1915, he returned to Cairo, having received a passport from the High Commission of Cyprus in which he was described as a British subject. On 2 October, 1915, he was registered as a British subject in Cairo by the defendant Gout, who was at all material times His Majesty's vice-consul at Cairo, and this registration was thrice renewed. In January, 1919, the plaintiff's further application for renewal of his registration was refused by the defendant Gout. The plaintiff sued for a declaration that he (together with his wife and children) was entitled to a renewal of his registration as a British subject in Cairo. The second defendant was His Majesty's consul at Cairo at the time of the commencement of the action.

The defendants' objection may be summarised by saying that they contended that the plaintiff was neither " resident " nor " ordinarily resident " in Cyprus but was a mere sojourner there, and that permanent residence akin to domicile was intended. The acting judge of His Britannic Majesty's Court for Egypt at Cairo held that the plaintiff was " resident " in Cyprus on 5 November, 1914, within the meaning of the Proclamation of 3 March, 1915, and therefore became a British subject under the first Order in Council and the two Proclamations referred to, but that he was not " ordinarily resident " there within the meaning of the Order in Council of 27 November 1917. On appeal by the defendants and a cross-appeal by the plaintiff against the finding that he was not " ordinarily resident " in Cyprus,

Held by the Privy Council (Judicial Committee) (Lords Sumner, Parmoor, Wrenbury, and Carson, and Sir Arthur Channell): That the plaintiff was " ordinarily resident and " actually present " in Cyprus on 5 November, 1914, and had consequently made out his claim to be a British subject. " The motive which caused him to leave Cairo and take up " his residence in Cyprus is immaterial to the question which " [their Lordships] are called upon to decide." [Report: L.R. [1922] 1 A.C. 105.]

See also on the meaning of " residence " *Annual Digest*, 1925-1926, Case No. 337, and *ibid.*, 1927-1928, p. 445, footnote, and Case No. 372.

Nationality—Consequences of Annexation—National Character of Cypriotes Resident Abroad. **Case No. 136**

AGAPIOS *v.* SANITARY AND QUARANTINE COUNCIL OF EGYPT.

Egypt, Mixed Court of Appeal. 21 *January*, 1920.

THE FACTS.—A person born in Cyprus but for many years resident in Egypt brought an action for damages against the Sanitary and Quarantine Council of Egypt before the Mixed Court of Alexandria. He claimed to be a British subject on the strength of the annexation of Cyprus to Great Britain. This Court declared itself incompetent on the ground that: (1) the claimant must be deemed to be a native or Ottoman subject; and (2) the defendant was a native corporation, and therefore the case was within the competence of the Native Courts. On appeal by the claimant to the Mixed Court of Appeal on the question of jurisdiction,

Held (as to the nationality of the plaintiff): That the Order in Council of 1914 which declared Cyprus annexed to Great

Case No. 136 *contd.* Britain did not render all persons born in Cyprus *ipso facto* British subjects. Ottomans born in the island but residing elsewhere from 1914 to 1919 did not acquire British nationality but remained Ottomans. [Report: *Gazette des Tribunaux Mixtes d'Egypte*, 1920, p. 49.]

[See same case, No. 259, where it appears that the decision appealed from was reversed on the ground that the defendant corporation was not of Egyptian national character.—Ed.]

Nationality—As Affected by Changes of Sovereignty—Cession —Persons Born or Domiciled in the Ceded Territory but Resident Abroad.

See Case No. 169 (*Immovables (Aliens in Germany) Case*).

Nationality—Effects of Changes of Sovereignty—Article 278 of the Treaty of Versailles.

See Case No. 57 (*Change of Sovereignty (Taxation) Case*).

IV.—Protected Persons and *de facto* Subjects

Case No. 137

Protected Persons—Renunciation of Protection during War—Whether Admissible without the Consent of the Protecting State—Jurisdiction of Mixed Tribunals.

FORTÉ *v.* MALLUK.

Egypt, Mixed Court of Appeal. 12 *December*, 1922.

THE FACTS.—An action was brought in the Mixed Courts by an Egyptian plaintiff against the defendant, who was alleged to be an Austro-Hungarian protected person though born in Egypt. The defendant objected to the jurisdiction of the Mixed Court on the ground that he renounced the Austro-Hungarian protection during the war, and therefore acquired the character of a local Egyptian subject. The Court of First Instance rejected the plea. But, on appeal by the defendant,

Held: That the renunciation by a local Egyptian subject of Austro-Hungarian protection during the war was admissible without the consent of the Austro-Hungarian Government, since all relations between Egypt and Austria-Hungary were broken off; and the renunciation implied the return of the local subject to his original character. [Report: *Gazette des Tribunaux Mixtes*, 1923, p. 171.]

V.—Naturalisation

Naturalisation—When Taking Place in British Self-Governing Dominion—Local Operation—Person Naturalised in Australia in 1908 not a British Subject in England. **Case No. 138**

MARKWALD *v.* ATTORNEY-GENERAL.

England, Court of Appeal, on Appeal from the Chancery Division of the High Court of Justice. 14 *January,* 1920.

THE FACTS.—This was an action for a declaration that the plaintiff " is no alien in England but a liege subject " of His Majesty the King, and entitled to the pro- " tection of His Majesty the King in all parts of His " Majesty's Kingdom and Dominions."

The plaintiff was born in Berlin in 1859; left Germany in 1878; went to Australia in 1881; never took up residence in Germany again; was naturalised in Australia in 1908, and in the same year came to England, where he had resided ever since. It was assumed by the Court, though it was unnecessary to decide it, that the plaintiff had ceased to be of German or Prussian nationality.

The scheme of the (Imperial) Naturalisation Act, 1870,[1] was, in the words of Warrington, L.J. (at p. 367), " by means of naturalization to grant to an alien " certain rights, powers, and privileges, but local in " each case; local in the United Kingdom if granted " under that Act; local in one of the colonies if that " colony should legislate on the subject and natural- " ization should be granted in pursuance of that " legislation."

The Commonwealth of Australia passed in 1903 an Australian Naturalisation Act, by section 8 of which a naturalised person " shall in the Commonwealth be " entitled to all political and other rights, powers and " privileges and be subject to all obligations to which " a natural-born British subject is entitled or subject " in the Commonwealth."

It was under this Act that the plaintiff was naturalised and had taken the oath of allegiance. (There appears to have been some doubt whether or not he

[1] The scheme of the British Nationality and Status of Aliens Act, 1914, which has replaced the Act of 1870, is different.

Case No. 138 *contd.*

had taken the oath, but it was assumed by the Court of Appeal that he had done so.)

Astbury, J., declined to make the declaration asked for by the plaintiff.

Held by the Court of Appeal (Lord Sterndale, M.R., Warrington and Younger, L.JJ.), affirming the decision of Astbury, J.: That neither as the result of the certificate of naturalisation nor of the oath of allegiance nor of the two combined had the plaintiff ceased to be an alien in England. It was clear that under the legislation above referred to the plaintiff's naturalisation was limited in scope. Moreover, it was conditional upon taking the oath of allegiance, and the effect of taking that oath was coextensive with the scope of operation of the rights and liabilities which thereupon attached to the person taking the oath. [Report: L.R. [1920] 1 Ch. 348.]

NOTE.—This case was in effect an appeal from the judgments of the Divisional Court (Darling, Bray and A. T. Lawrence, JJ.) in *Rex* v. *Francis*; *ex parte Markwald*, L.R. [1918] 1 K.B. 617, in which the conviction of the plaintiff on a charge of failing to furnish the particulars required by the Aliens Restriction (Consolidated) Order, 1916, was affirmed.

By the Australian Nationality Act, 1920-1925, the Commonwealth of Australia adopted Part II of the British Nationality and Status of Aliens Act, 1914, as amended in 1918 and 1922, and a person naturalised in Australia after that adoption is also a British subject in Great Britain and Northern Ireland.

Case No. 139

Naturalisation—Condition of Invalidity in the Event of Return to Country of Origin—Non-Communication of Condition to Foreign Powers—Egyptian Independence—Burden of Proof.

MELKONIAN *v.* MELKONIAN.

Egypt, Mixed Court of Appeal. 7 June, 1922.

THE FACTS.—The question at issue on a preliminary point was the nationality of the defendant. The defendant was born in Asiatic Turkey an Ottoman subject but had been inscribed as a Greek national in the Island of Syra. Subsequently, in 1911, he applied to the Turkish Government for authorisation to be naturalised as an Austrian subject. The certificate granting the authorisation bore a note that if the person naturalised returned to Ottoman territory he would be treated as an Ottoman subject. The defendant did not pursue the application for Austrian naturalisation, and at a later date applied to the Egyptian Government to recognise him as Greek. The Egyptian Government by letter in November, 1914, granted this recognition, but later, in 1921, declared that they considered him as a "local subject" because his naturalisation as a Greek was not effective in Egypt as that country remained part of Ottoman territory till 1914. The Greek Government claimed that he was a Greek national. There was no proof that the Declaration of the Turkish Government with regard to not recognising naturalisation when the person returned to Turkey was communicated to the Powers, as required by the Turkish Memorandum on the Nationality Law of 1869. The Egyptian and Greek Governments were unable to agree as to the defendant's nationality, and the point had to be decided by the tribunal whose jurisdiction depended upon it.

Held : That the nationality of the defendant must be taken to be Greek. (*a*) The Turkish Imperial *Iradè* of 28 April, 1893, according to which an authorisation to be naturalised was to be granted only on condition that the person concerned should not return to Ottoman territory, could not be recognised by the Court as it had not been published or communicated to the Powers.

(*b*) The non-ratification of the Treaty of Sèvres did not prevent the Court from recognising the independence of Egypt in relation to Turkey which was the practical result of the British Proclamation of December, 1914, and established by the statute which the Sovereign gave to Egypt. "Egypt had "in fact always asserted a relative independence even though "it was part of the Ottoman dominions down to 1914; and a "person who claimed to be a subject of Egypt could not contest "the validity of the act of his Sovereign."

(*c*) On the production of documents establishing Greek naturalisation and originating from the Greek diplomatic agent, the naturalisation should be held to be in order unless the contrary were established by the party alleging that the naturalisation was obtained by fraud and in contravention of the law of the foreign country. [Reports : *Gazette des Tribunaux Mixtes*, 1923, p. 74; 50 *Clunet* (1923), p. 1008.]

NOTE.—"Local subject" is the name given in the Egyptian legislation

Case No. 139 *contd.* to Ottomans resident in Egypt who are entitled to vote in elections and come within the jurisdiction of the Egyptian " Native " courts. There was no law of Egyptian nationality till 1926.

Case No. 140

Naturalisation—Requirement of Good Morals in Addition to Statutory Requirements.

IN RE MENENDEZ.

Argentina, Federal Court of Appeal of the Capital.
29 *November*, 1919.

THE FACTS.—Menendez had been refused naturalisation by Judge Escobar in the lower Federal Court. He had complied with the residence requirement of the Argentine naturalisation laws, but had not proved his good character. He appealed.

Held: That the judgment must be affirmed. " Although " it is true that the law of citizenship and naturalization only " requires, outside the cases to which paragraph 2 of Article 2 " refers, a residence of two years continuously in the country " and the will [to become naturalized] manifested before the " Federal district judges, it is none the less true, considering " the nature of the matter, that even though the said law has " not expressly stipulated the information *de vita et moribus*, " it has not been possible to grant the benefit of citizenship " except to those foreigners whose incorporation represents " positive good to the country and in no way appears unsuitable " or undesirable." [Report: *Jurisprudencia Argentina*, vol. 3, p. 1001.]

NOTE.—See the case of *Andrés López* (*Cámara Federal*, 11 March, 1921), *Gaceta del Foro*, vol. 31 (March, 1921), p. 94, in which naturalisation was denied to a foreigner who had been found guilty of a crime meriting corporal punishment by Argentine law.

See also the cases of *Isaias Band* (*Juzgado Federal*, 24 June, 1919, Judge Escobar), *ibid.*, vol. 21 (June, 1919), p. 355; *Ramón Oltra* (*Juzgado Federal*, 7 December, 1921, Judge Escobar), *ibid.*, vol. 36 (January, 1922), p. 36; *Manuel Dobarro* (*Juzgado Federal*, 16 December, 1921), *ibid.*, vol. 36 (January, 1922), p. 163; and *Lorenzo Bordone* (*Juzgado Federal*, 28 March, 1922, Judge Escobar), *ibid.*, vol. 37 (April, 1922), p. 281, all refusing naturalisation to persons who " did " not enjoy an effective reputation for good habits " (*buenas costumbres*).

Similar cases, in which naturalisation is refused to those convicted of crimes, are *Augustin Raffaele* (*Juzgado Federal*, 24 June, 1919, Judge Escobar), *ibid.*, vol. 21 (June, 1919), p. 33; *Igel Herzenberg* (*Cámara Federal*, 1 September, 1921), *ibid.*, vol. 34 (September, 1921), p. 79; *Angel Zavagnini* (*Cámara Federal de la Capital*, 7 June, 1922), *Jurisprudencia Argentina*, vol. 8, p. 572; and *Salvador Giglio* (*Cámara*

Federal, 5 July, 1922), *Gaceta del Foro*, vol. 39 (August, 1922), p. 376. In the case of *José Ricciardi* (*Cámara Federal*, 15 February, 1922), *ibid.*, vol. 36 (February, 1922), p. 344, naturalisation was refused to one who had undergone bankruptcy. In the cases of *Carlos Leone* (*Cámara Federal*, 3 July, 1922), *ibid.*, vol. 39 (July, 1922), p. 103, and *Fernando Martin* (*Cámara Federal de la Capital*, 3 October, 1924), *Jurisprudencia Argentina*, vol. 14, p. 396, it was held that naturalisation must not be granted to those proceeded against for crimes who had received temporary stay of proceedings.

But see the case of *Telmo Martínez* (*Cámara Federal*, 15 February, 1922), *Gaceta del Foro*, vol. 37 (March, 1922), p. 60, which allowed naturalisation to one who had been made the subject of criminal investigation (*indagado*), reversing the refusal by Judge Escobar below. And see the decision of the *Cámara Federal de la Plata*, of 1 April, 1925, in the case of *Antonio Sponsito* (*Jurisprudencia Argentina*, vol. 15, p. 510), holding by a divided Court, contrary to the decision of the lower Court in the same case, that naturalisation must be allowed, even though the police *informe* showed that the applicant had been convicted of crimes in the country. " Such a ground [for denying " naturalisation] is contrary to the express letter of the said law, which " in Article 2, paragraph 1, attributes the character of citizen by " naturalisation to the foreigners over 18 years of age, who reside " continuously in the Republic for two years, and manifest before the " federal district judges their desire to become such. . . . The scope " of the law cannot be dismissed by limiting and restrictive interpreta- " tion ; only the national Congress, enacting a new law of naturalization " of foreigners, could make rules to carry out Article 20 of the Constitu- " tion and explain its concept. Meanwhile, the judges are not permitted " to restrict the right of those who, with two years' residence, elect " citizenship."

See the case of *Ciriaco Sánchez* (*Juzgado Federal de la Plata*, 4 June, 1924), *Gaceta del Foro*, vol. 51, p. 156, refusing citizenship to a foreigner who would not take an oath of fidelity to the Constitution and laws of the country because he was not ready to defend the country in case of war.[1] The Court (Judge Matienzo) held this to be an essential requirement of citizenship. And see the case of *Salomón Cosacof*, *Revista Judicial* of Salvador, vol. 26 (1921), p. 96, in which Judge Escobar refused naturalisation to a Russian who had lived fifteen years in a Jewish colony in the Argentine but could not write Spanish, and who petitioned for citizenship in the Slavonic alphabet. He was held to be a person who had " remained refractory to the influence of the " Argentine surroundings and atmosphere."

See also the case of *Luis de Prado* (*Juzgado Federal*, 20 May, 1919), *Gaceta del Foro*, vol. 20 (May, 1919), p. 147, refusing Argentine citizenship to one under eighteen. See further on naturalisation the cases of *Angelo Gagliardi*, *Jurisprudencia Argentina*, vol. 3, p. 1000 ; *Ali Soleiman*, *Gaceta del Foro*, vol. 28 (February, 1924), p. 299 ; *Paul Reinhold Ehrich Stock*, *ibid.*, vol. 50 (May, 1924), p. 108 ; and *Carlos Maria Bercaitz*, *ibid.*, vol. 49 (April, 1924), p. 344.

---

[1] For the law of the United States on this point see *United States* v. *Schwimmer* in the Supreme Court of the United States (1929), 49 Sup. Ct. 448 ; also reported in *A.J.*, XXIII (1917), p. 652.—[Ed.]

Case No. 141 **Naturalisation—Implied Renunciation of—Treaty of 1868 between Germany and the United States—Internment of Aliens during War—Review by Courts.**

EX PARTE GILROY.

United States District Court, S.D. New York. 31 *March,* 1919.

THE FACTS.—This was a petition for habeas corpus. Alexander was held in custody on a presidential warrant as an enemy alien under U.S. Rev. Stat. § 4067. It was contended that Alexander was an American citizen. His father was born in Germany, came to the United States, was naturalised in the United States when barely of age, and eight years later returned to Germany; he then secured a divorce in the United States as an American citizen on temporary visit abroad, and subsequently married in Germany in 1890. Alexander was born in Germany in 1893. His father lived in Germany until his death in 1914, but secured a copy of his naturalisation certificate in 1901 and an American passport in 1908, stating that he resided in New York (perhaps meaning that he was domiciled there). Alexander had accompanied his father on two short trips to the United States. U.S. Rev. Stat. § 1993 provides that persons born abroad of fathers who were United States citizens at the time of their birth shall be citizens of the United States. The Treaty of 1868 between Germany and the United States (15 U.S. Stat. L. 616) provided that if a German naturalised in the United States should renew his residence in Germany without intent to return to the United States he should be held to have renounced his naturalisation, and that "the intent not to return "may be held to exist when the person naturalized "in the one country resides more than two years in "the other country." When the war broke out in 1914, Alexander served as a voluntary member of the Automobile Club on the Eastern front, driving for the Red Cross and the German army without pay and without army uniform. He refused offers of a commission in the German army and finally secured a passport as an American citizen from the American ambassador in Berlin, coming to the United States late in 1915. After the United States entered the war, Alexander registered under the Selective Service Act, asked deferred classification for physical incapacity and stated in full his service in the German motor corps, but did not claim exemption as a German. Gilroy, his legal adviser, suggested to the draft board that he should be exempted or deferred in view of the policy of exempting enemy aliens. He was placed in class A-1, included in the United States army, and served at Camp Wadsworth until honourably discharged in December, 1918. After his discharge he was taken into custody as an enemy alien. The questions were, *inter alia*, (1) whether the executive acts in interning aliens were reviewable, and (2) whether it was shown on the facts that he was not a citizen of Germany.

Held: That the writ must be granted and the relator discharged from custody. (1) Since there was no provision for hearing, it was held that the courts could review the executive action. Action under this internment statute was differentiated from that upheld in *United States* v. *Ju Toy*, 198 U.S. 253. (2) The evidence showed that Alexander was an American citizen by birth, unless his father had lost his American citizenship by more than two years' residence in Germany. However, American practice under the Treaty had treated the two years' residence as inconclusive with respect to intention to return, and at most as merely *prima facie* proof of abandonment of naturalisation. In his service in the automobile force Alexander had done nothing to forfeit his American citizenship. [Report: 257 Fed. 110.]

Naturalisation—Cancellation for Disloyalty.

Case No. 142

UNITED STATES *v.* KRAMER.

United States Circuit Court of Appeals, Fifth Circuit.
23 *December*, 1919.

THE FACTS.—This was a proceeding to cancel a naturalisation certificate. Kramer, a German, was naturalised in Texas in 1912. He manifested open sympathy for Germany during the war with that country in 1917, made statements derogatory to the United States, and tried to help the German cause by supplying information. The United States brought this suit on the ground that naturalisation had been fraudulently

Case No. 142 contd.

and unlawfully obtained. The District Court dismissed the bill. On appeal,

Held: That the judgment must be reversed. The statements and actions clearly showed disloyalty to the United States and continuing loyalty to Germany. The statutes made a certain length of residence out of the United States *prima facie* evidence of a lack of real intent to become a permanent citizen. "If mere removal is sufficient evidence of "fraud," said the Court, "why not subsequent acts of dis-"loyalty, or statements indicating his want of allegiance?" (262 Fed. 395, 397.) [Report: 262 Fed. 395.]

NOTE.—See *Schurmann* v. *United States* (May 3, 1920), 264 Fed. 917, cancelling naturalisation of one born in Germany and naturalised as an American citizen because during the war he made statements favouring the cause of Germany as opposed to the United States. The Court said: "One who spoke in that way . . . must have taken the oath "of full faith and allegiance with a reserved determination, to be kept "down, but nurtured, until a momentous time might come. In years, "however, the time did come, and the criterion of original fraud must "be the later conduct, which, in its relation to the earlier attitude, "will furnish safe ground for judgment." (264 Fed. 917, 920.)

Case No. 143

Naturalisation—Cancellation—Reasons of.

PROCURADOR FISCAL *v.* MORITZ HENDLER.

Argentina, Federal Court of Appeal. 3 *October,* 1921.

THE FACTS.—Hendler was granted naturalisation in Argentina in 1908. He was shown to have been engaged in immoral business enterprises and to have been a disturber of the public peace. In 1919 a civil action was brought against him to cancel his naturalisation papers. The lower Court cancelled them, and he appealed.

Held, by a vote of 3 to 2: That the judgment must be affirmed. Law 7029 enacts that an alien whose entry into the country is prohibited, as well as those referred to by Law 4144, cannot become naturalised; and, if granted naturalisation despite this, the naturalisation may be annulled. Law 4144 referred, *inter alia,* to all aliens whose conduct compromised the national security or disturbed the public order, or those whose antecedents merited their inclusion among those expressly enumerated.[1] (Judge Escobar held with the majority,

[1] See the case of *Alejandro Esteban Graf* (*Cámara Federal,* 3 June, 1921), *Gaceta del Foro,* vol. 32 (June, 1921), p. 246, annulling citizenship because the naturalised citizen had failed to perform his military service obligations. Cf.

but thought this a penal proceeding and not a civil action.[1]) [Report : *Gaceta del Foro*, vol. 35 (December, 1921), p. 295.]

VI.—Expatriation. Loss of Nationality

Nationality—British Nationality Law—Loss of Nationality—Effect of Marriage during War of British Woman to Enemy Subject. **Case No. 144**

FASBENDER *v.* ATTORNEY-GENERAL.

England, High Court of Justice, Chancery Division.
24 November, 1921.

THE FACTS.—The plaintiff, a natural-born British subject, married on 3 November, 1919, a German subject. The Treaty of Peace of Versailles did not come into force until 10 January, 1920, so that at the time of the marriage Great Britain and Germany were still in a state of war.

The effect of certain Treaty of Peace Orders made in pursuance of the Treaty of Peace Act, 1919, was to place a charge upon the property in Great Britain of German subjects. The plaintiff was the owner of certain shares in an English limited company at the

the cases of *José Esteban* (*Cámara Federal*, 29 August, 1924), *Gaceta del Foro*, vol. 54 (January, 1925), p. 92 (refusing to revoke naturalisation after the one-year prescriptive period had run) ; and *Francisco Diez* (*Cámara Federal*, 26 August, 1921), *Gaceta del Foro*, vol. 34, p. 47 (to a similar effect).

See also the case of *Julio Akerman* (31 July, 1922), *Fallos*, vol. 136, p. 438, in which the Supreme Court based its decision on a procedural point, but in which the *Cámara Federal* (30 June, 1921), *Gaceta del Foro*, vol. 33 (July, 1921), p. 45, allowed cancellation, saying that although the national Constitution wanted to attract aliens and make their incorporation into the nation easy, in order to populate the country, it only wanted to attract and incorporate useful elements. "The nation, in conferring political rights upon aliens as a gift, " for supreme reasons of political organisation and public good, . . . does not " grant irrevocable rights, nor would it be able to grant them, because no one " can acquire irrevocable rights against laws of public order ; and just as the " beneficiary can renounce the tie at any moment by naturalisation in another " country, the nation can deprive it of its effect whenever the same supreme " reasons of public order and welfare so require." Although naturalisation was granted before Law 7029, the infractions were later in time, so that this was not an *ex post facto* application of the law.

[1] On the nature of this proceeding see the case of *Gabinsky* (1 August, 1923), *Fallos*, vol. 138, p. 281. On other points of procedure connected with cancellation of naturalisation see the cases of *Leon Ducler y Dritman* (21 July, 1922), *ibid.*, vol. 136, p. 389 ; and *Enrique Jankelevitz* (*Cámara Federal*, 26 August, 1919), *Gaceta del Foro*, vol. 22, p. 60.

As to the cancellation of naturalisation in British law see Section 7 of the British Nationality and Status of Aliens Act, 1914 (as amended in 1918). See McNair, *Legal Effects of War* (1920), pp. 6-8, and W. E. Davies, *Law Relating to Aliens* (1931), pp. 302-307.

Case No. 144 *contd.*

time of her marriage and on 10 January, 1920, when the charge took effect. She claimed a declaration that she was then and at all material times a British subject and that her property was not subject to the above-mentioned charge.

Section 10 of the British Nationality and Status of Aliens Act, 1914, contains the following passage: "The "wife of a British subject shall be deemed to be a "British subject, and the wife of an alien shall be "deemed to be an alien. . . ." [1]

The plaintiff did not dispute that by German nationality law she had acquired German nationality upon her marriage, but contended (*a*) that during time of war the marriage of a British woman to an alien enemy did not operate so as to divest her of her British nationality, and (*b*) that the charge above-mentioned did not take effect upon the property of one who like her had both German nationality and another nationality.

Held by Russell, J.: (*a*) That section 10 of the Act operated in time of war as well as in time of peace, so that the plaintiff upon her marriage lost her British and acquired German nationality. The reasoning underlying *R.* v. *Lynch*, L.R. [1903] 1 K.B. 444 (voluntary naturalisation in an enemy State), and *Ex parte Freyberger*, L.R. [1917] 2 K.B. 129 (declaration of alienage during war), did not apply to a marriage: "alienage "is not the sole object of the marriage, or even its primary "object; nor can it be reasonably said to fall within its "objects at all." (*b*) The second point therefore did not arise. Had it arisen, the learned judge would have followed *In re Chamberlain's Settlement*, L.R. [1921] 2 Ch. 535.[2] Accordingly,

[1] Which appears to mean that she is deemed to be the particular kind of alien that her husband is.

[2] This decision demands a short note. The question was whether the charge created by the Treaty of Peace and the Orders made in pursuance of the Treaty of Peace Act, 1919, took effect upon the property (in the hands of trustees in England) of one Houston Stewart Chamberlain, a natural-born British subject, who obtained German nationality by means of a certificate of naturalisation on 5 August, 1916, that is, during the war. It was held by P. O. Lawrence, J., that, whatever the effect of his naturalisation might be upon his British nationality according to the law of this country (and his act amounted to a crime), he certainly became and remained a "German national" according to German municipal law. He was therefore a "German national" within the meaning of the Treaty and Orders, and it did not matter whether he had also another nationality. Accordingly, his property in Great Britain became subject to the charge on 10 January, 1920, when the Treaty came into force.

the plaintiff's property was subject to the charge. [Report: L.R. [1922] 1 Ch. 232.]

NOTE.—The decision of Russell, J., was affirmed by the Court of Appeal (Lord Sterndale, M.R., Warrington and Younger, L.JJ.) on substantially the same grounds. There was some discussion as to the plaintiff's domicile at the time of her marriage. [Report: L.R. [1922] 2 Ch. 850.]

At the same time the Court of Appeal heard an appeal from the decision of Astbury, J., in *Kramer* v. *Attorney-General*, and affirmed his decision to the effect that the expression "German national" in the Treaty of Peace and Orders above-mentioned includes all persons who answer to that description according to German law, whether they also have any other nationality or not—*per* Lord Sterndale, M.R., and Warrington, L.J.; Younger, L.J., dissenting. [Report: L.R. [1922] 2 Ch. 850.] The decision of the Court of Appeal was affirmed by the House of Lords. [Report: [1923] A.C. 528.]

The effect of the decision in *Kramer's* case is to affirm the decision of P. O. Lawrence, J., in *In re Chamberlain's Settlement* (*supra*).

Loss of Austrian Nationality Previously Acquired under Austrian Law—Treaty of St. Germain, Article 70. **Case No. 145**

FRANZ AND ROSA KADECKA *v.* GOVERNMENT OF THE FEDERAL COUNTRY (LANDESREGIERUNG) OF LOWER AUSTRIA.

Austria, Administrative Court (*Verwaltungsgerichtshof*), *Vienna.* 11 *November*, 1921. (*No.* 12.946 *A.*)

THE FACTS.—The plaintiffs had acquired Austrian nationality by virtue of a declaration, made according to the Austrian law on nationality of 5 December, 1918. A deportation order was issued against them by the *Landesregierung* of Lower Austria after the coming into force of the Treaty of St. Germain, the plaintiffs having become, by virtue of the Treaty, aliens, namely Czechoslovak nationals. They appealed.

Held: That the appeal must be dismissed. It is true that the plaintiffs had acquired Austrian nationality, according to the Austrian Law of 5 December, 1918, which provided that Austrian nationality may be acquired by virtue of a simple declaration, without acquisition of rights of citizenship in a commune of the Austrian Republic. But they had not acquired such rights of citizenship in a commune of the Austrian Republic prior to 16 July, 1920, the date of the coming into force of the Treaty of St. Germain. Their Austrian nationality was therefore automatically lost on that date, as the Treaty (Article 70) provides that every national of the old Austrian

Case No. 145 *contd.* Empire automatically acquires, to the exclusion of Austrian nationality, the nationality of the State exercising sovereignty over the territory where he possesses rights of citizenship. The plaintiffs had therefore acquired the Czechoslovak nationality. This effect of the Peace Treaty was confirmed by the Treaty of Brünn of 7 June, 1920, concluded between Austria and Czechoslovakia. [Report : *Sammlung der Erkenntnisse des Verwaltungsgerichtshofes*, vol. XLV (1921), pp. 105-108.]

NOTE.—Cf. Case No. 7, *A. L. B.* v. (*Austrian*) *Federal Ministry for the Interior*. To the same effect see the decisions of 4 November, 1922, No. 9070, of 14 October, 1924, No. 13.641, vol. XLVIII (1924), pp. 351-353; of 25 October, 1924, No. 13.652 A, vol. XLVIII (1924), pp. 370, 371; the Austrian Constitutional Court (*Verfassungsgerichtshof*) had already given a decision in this sense on 12 October, 1920, Z.B. 15/20: " In consequence of Article 70, St. Germain, Austrian nation-" ality, acquired by virtue of a declaration, according to the Austrian " law of 5 December, 1918, is annulled." On the other hand, options for a Succession State other than the Austrian Republic made according to the above-mentioned Austrian law became void with the coming into force of the Treaty of St. Germain, if the person in question had rights of citizenship in Austria: Austrian Administrative Court, decision of 25 October, 1924, No. 13.653 A, vol. XLVIII (1924), pp. 371-374.

Case No. 146

Nationality—Expatriation—Argentine Law—Loss of Nationality and Loss of Political Rights—Naturalisation.

IN RE JULIO R. MARTÍNEZ.

Argentina, Federal District Court. 7 *April*, 1919.

(SÁUL ESCOBAR, Judge.)

THE FACTS.—Martínez was an Argentine by birth. He obtained naturalisation papers in Uruguay in 1915. He now came before the Court seeking to become restored to his status as an Argentine.

Held : That the petition must be refused, since it was not within the jurisdiction of the Court to act in such a situation. Law 346 declared that those naturalised in foreign countries could not exercise political rights in Argentina, and that only Congress could restore their rights to those who had lost the exercise of citizenship. The Court could not restore to him his political rights. According to Argentine law, he had never lost his character of an Argentine national, although he was deprived of political rights by naturalisation abroad. " It is " not possible to restore the petitioner to his status as an " Argentine, since he has continued to be one." This decision was largely based on Zeballos and Alcorta, whom the Court quoted: "In the Republic, the vassalage [of citizenship] is "perpetual. Argentine nationality is never lost, even though "political rights can be lost."[1] [Report: *Gaceta del Foro* (April, 1919), vol. 19, p. 243.[2]]

VIII.—Double Nationality

Nationality—Double Nationality—Military Service—British Subject Born in Brazil of British Parents Born in Brazil —Registration in British Consulate—Effect of. **Case No. 147**

In re Walter Cox.

Brazil, Supreme Military Tribunal. 29 *December*, 1920.

The Facts.—Cox was born in Brazil of British parents who had also been born in Brazil. He had registered as a British citizen, in accordance with the British law, in the British Consulate at Pernambuco. He was ordered by the Brazilian authorities to enrol for military service. The *Junta de Revisão e Sorteio do Estado de Pernambuco* refused him relief against this order, holding him a Brazilian citizen.

Held: That the decision must be affirmed. By Article 69 of the Brazilian Constitution, among those who are Brazilian citizens are included "all those who are born in Brazil, even "though of a foreign father, if he is not living there in the "service of his nation." The enrolment of Cox at the British Consulate had no juridicial effect. The quality of Brazilian citizen can only be lost according to the strict terms of the Constitution. [Report: *Revista Forense*, vol. 35, p. 393.]

Note.—See also the case of *Gil Leonel* (14 April, 1920), *Revista do Supremo Tribunal*, vol. 42, p. 5. See the treaty on this subject between Brazil and Great Britain of 29 July, 1922, reported in the *American Bar Association Journal*, vol. IX, p. 245.

---

[1] Amancio Alcorta, *Curso de Derecho Internacional Privado* (1887), vol. I, p. 406. See on this point the case of *Ernesto Lapping, Jurisprudencia Argentina*, vol. 6, p. 398, for a decision of the *Cámara Federal de la Capital* (23 May, 1921), holding that a *naturalised* citizen who later becomes naturalised in another country completely loses his Argentine nationality.

[2] German nationality law before 1914 admitted the possibility for a German national to retain his German nationality in spite of naturalisation abroad. By Article 278 of the Treaty of Versailles, Germany undertook to regard any of her nationals who had acquired or sought thereafter to acquire the nationality of any of the other parties to the Treaty as having "in all respects "severed their allegiance to their country of origin."—[Ed.]

Case No. 148

Double Nationality—Effect on Claims—German Subject Naturalised in Great Britain—Article 296 of the Treaty of Versailles—Certificate of Naturalisation—Limitation of the Right to Diplomatic Protection.

GEORGE S. HEIN *v.* HILDERSHEIMER BANK.

Anglo-German Mixed Arbitral Tribunal.
26 *April and* 10 *May*, 1922.

(BOREL, VAUGHAN WILLIAMS, ZACHARIAS.)

THE FACTS.—Article 296 of the Treaty of Versailles provided, *inter alia*, machinery for recovery of pre-war debts through Clearing Offices. Hein, who was born in Germany but was naturalised in Great Britain in 1901 and resident there on the date of the entrance into force of the Treaty, sought to recover under Article 296 a sum of money standing to his account with the Hildersheimer Bank. The German Clearing Office denied liability on the ground that as the plaintiff had not according to German law lost German nationality,[1] he could not as a British subject avail himself of the procedure laid down in Article 296. It was also contended that the creditor could not rely, as against the German Government, on his naturalisation certificate, as it contained a reservation to the effect that within the limit of his country of origin the holder of the certificate would not be deemed a British subject.

Held: That it was immaterial whether the claimant had or had not lost his German nationality. He had become a British national, and as he was residing in Great Britain at the time of the entrance into force of the Treaty he had acquired the right to claim under Article 296 through the British Clearing Office. [Report: *Recueil*, II (1923), p. 70.]

[1] As to the position under the British Treaty of Peace Order of a person who possesses both British and German nationality, see *Kramer* v. *Attorney-General*, L.R. [1923] A.C. 528.—[Ed.]

Enemy Character—Double Nationality—Nature of the Burden of Proof. **Case No. 149**

EX PARTE RISSE.

United States District Court, S.D. New York, 17 *February*, 1919.

THE FACTS.—This was a petition for habeas corpus. Stallforth was held in custody during the war in reliance on U.S. Rev. Stat. § 4067, dealing with enemy aliens. He was born in Mexico in 1882 of a German father. His father went to Mexico in 1861 and set up in business there. In 1893, Stallforth went to Germany with his father and stepmother. His father died *en route* in Chicago. His stepmother took up her domicile in Germany. He was educated there, married a German woman in England, and returned to Germany to stay until 1907, when he went to Mexico to take over his father's business. From 1907 to 1910 he travelled back and forth between Mexico and Europe. Since 1913 he had lived in the United States and had established his business there. The Constitution and laws of Mexico provide that persons born of Mexican parents, naturalised foreigners, and foreigners acquiring property in Mexico or having Mexican children, provided they do not declare their intention to retain their nationality, are Mexicans. Provision is made for the declaration, and its omission is held equivalent to declaring for Mexican citizenship. There was no evidence of any declaration by Stallforth's father. The Mexican law provides further that children born in Mexico of an alien father shall be regarded as Mexican unless within a year after becoming of age they make a declaration to the civil authorities of the place where they reside that they follow the parent's citizenship. The Law of 1 June, 1870, of the North German Confederation provided that children of a North German acquired their father's citizenship, even though born abroad; but provided for the loss of citizenship by ten years' residence abroad, unless registered, etc. There was no evidence of registration by Stallforth's parents. There was evidence that in 1905, 1916 and 1917 Stallforth had referred to himself as "a German "citizen, born in Mexico."

Held: That the writ must be dismissed. The Court said:

Case No. 149 *contd.* " The burden is . . . on relator to show illegal restraint, and, " on habeas corpus, he must satisfy the court that he is not a " native, citizen, denizen, or subject of the hostile nation or " government. In this case, the question is not whether " Stallforth is a subject of the republic of Mexico ; but whether " he is not a native, citizen, or subject of Germany." (257 Fed. 102, 104.) Without passing directly upon the question whether Stallforth was a Mexican citizen, or whether his father had retained German citizenship despite the ten-year provision, it was concluded that " whatever may be relator's status, he " has not satisfied the court that he is not a German citizen " or subject." (257 Fed. 102, 109.) [Report : 257 Fed. 102.]

IX.—Option

Case No. 150 **Nationality—Option—Whether Constitutive or Declaratory—Date of Acquisition of Nationality Subsequent to Option.**

S. Ferdinand *v.* (Austrian) Federal Chancellery.
Austria, Administrative Court (*Verwaltungsgerichtshof*), *Vienna.* 23 *December*, 1924. (*No.* 13.713 *A.*)

The Facts.—The plaintiff had opted for Austria in accordance with Article 80 of the Treaty of St. Germain. His option was recognised. However, the Federal Chancellery decided that he had acquired Austrian nationality at the date of its decision and not at the date of his declaration. He appealed.

Held : For the appellant. That the decision of the Federal Chancellery must be annulled as being unfounded in law. It is true that the Austrian Ordinance concerning options, of 20 August, 1920, St. G. Bl. No. 397, provides that the acquisition of Austrian nationality by way of option shall date from the date of the decision by the competent authority. However, this rule is in contradiction with the terms of the Treaty, seeing that Articles 78 and 80 provide that a person who makes his declaration of option has *exercised* his right to opt. The acquisition of Austrian nationality by way of option dates therefore from the moment of the declaration. The decision by the competent authority stating that the conditions of the exercise of the right to opt had been fulfilled is only *declaratory* in character. [Report : *Sammlung der Erkenntnisse des Verwaltungsgerichtshofes*, vol. XLVIII (1924), pp. 458-461.]

Note.—To the same effect see the decisions of 13 November, 1924, No. 13.673 A (vol. XLVIII (1924), p. 408), and the decision of the

Austrian Constitutional Court (*Verfassungsgerichtshof*), of 28 April, 1921, Z.B. 2/21. Whereas according to the system in force before 1914, the validity of options was dependent on the fulfilment of *all* conditions (declaration, emigration, etc.), and whereas, therefore, the final decision rendered by the competent authority was *constitutive* in character, the Peace Treaties adopted a new system, according to which the right to opt is *exercised* by the declaration. The right to opt has thus become a *unilateral* and *constitutive* act of the optant, the decision and the certificate handed over by the competent authority has only a declaratory meaning. The above-quoted decision gives effect to the new system adopted by the Treaty of St. Germain. Cf. on this problem: Kunz, *Die völkerrechtliche Option*, vol. I (1925), pp. 157 *et seq.*, 188-190; vol. II (1928), pp. 17, 204, 309.

Nationality—Option by Persons over Eighteen Years of Age. **Case No. 151**

G. M. *v.* (AUSTRIAN) FEDERAL MINISTRY FOR THE INTERIOR.

Austria, Administrative Court (*Verwaltungsgerichtshof*), *Vienna.* 20 *March*, 1922. (*No.* 13.047 *A.*)

THE FACTS.—The plaintiff had opted for Austria for himself and for his son, who was over eighteen years of age. The option was not recognised. He appealed.

Held: That the decision of the Federal Ministry for the Interior must be annulled, as unfounded in law, in so far as it concerns the son. As the son was over eighteen years of age, the Federal Ministry was bound to examine separately whether the conditions on which the validity of the option depends were or were not fulfilled in the case of the son. [Report: *Sammlung der Erkenntnisse des Verwaltungsgerichtshofes*, vol. XLVI (1922), pp. 25, 26.]

NOTE.—The Peace Treaties adopted the system of *collective* option. Article 78 of the Treaty of St. Germain provides that option by parents will cover their children under eighteen years of age. Cf. decisions of the same Court of 1 January, 1922, No. 151, of 22 May, 1922, No. 13.097 A, vol. XLVI (1922), p. 52.

Nationality—Option—Expulsion Subsequent to Option—Treaty of St. Germain, Articles 63 and 80. **Case No. 152**

A. F. *v.* GOVERNMENT OF THE FEDERAL COUNTRY (LANDESREGIERUNG) OF VIENNA.

Austria, Administrative Court (*Verwaltungsgerichtshof*), *Vienna.* 12 *January*, 1921. (*No.* 12.727 *A.*)

THE FACTS.—The Government of the Federal Country of Vienna had issued a deportation order against the

Case No. 152 *contd.*

plaintiff. His objection on the ground that he had opted for Austria in accordance with Article 80 of the Treaty of St. Germain was overruled. He appealed to the Court.

Held: That the deportation order must be annulled on the ground of defective procedure. It is true that according to Austrian law deportation is within the discretion of the competent administrative authorities and that the legal situation in this respect has not been changed by Article 63 of the Treaty of St. Germain, which provides only guarantees for full and complete protection of life and liberty for all inhabitants of Austria, but not for an absolute right of residence in Austria. However, as the Austrian law allows expulsion only against foreigners, the administrative authority was bound to examine and clear up the legal question of the option by the plaintiff. For if the plaintiff had acquired Austrian nationality by way of option, expulsion was no longer admissible. [Report: *Sammlung der Erkenntnisse des Verwaltungsgerichtshofes*, vol. XLV (1921), p. 5.]

NOTE.—Cf. also the decision of the same Court of 11 November, 1921, No. 8528. The mere fact that a person has presented a demand to exercise the option, which demand had been returned to the competent authority in order to be completed and had not been presented again, cannot be opposed to a deportation order, the person in question being a foreigner: Austrian Supreme Court (*Oberster Gerichtshof*), decisions of 11 November, 1921, Os. 376/21, and of 14 February, 1922, Os. 56/22. To the same effect: Austrian Constitutional Court (*Verfassungsgerichtshof*), decisions of 13 October, 1921, Z.B. 20/21, and of 22 June, 1921, Z.B. 28/22.

Expulsion is admissible against nationals of the Succession States who have become foreigners by virtue of the Treaty of St. Germain: Austrian Administrative Court, decision of 22 December, 1922, No. 10.469, vol. XLVI, No. 13.198, pp. 129, 130.

However, expulsion is not admissible against a person who acquired Austrian nationality, not by way of option, but " *ipso facto* and without " the requirement of any formality," in virtue of a disposition to this effect of the Treaty of St. Germain: Austrian Supreme Court, decision of 29 April, 1921, Os. 83/21.

Case No. 153

Nationality—Option—Woman's Right to Opt Individually—Treaty of St. Germain, Article 78.

KUGLER *v.* (AUSTRIAN) FEDERAL MINISTRY FOR THE INTERIOR.

Austria, Administrative Court (*Verwaltungsgerichtshof*), *Vienna.* 29 *September*, 1921. (*No.* 12.891 *A.*)

THE FACTS.—The husband of the plaintiff, who had his

rights of citizenship (*Heimatrecht* [1]) in Czechoslovakia, had not been heard of since the end of the war in 1918. The plaintiff opted for Austria in accordance with Article 80 of the Treaty of St. Germain. Her application for option was refused by the Federal Ministry for the Interior on the ground that the change of nationality of a married woman cannot be effected except through her husband so long as the wife has not been legally divorced. She appealed.

Held, dismissing the appeal: That the decision of the Federal Ministry for the Interior was correct in law. [Report: *Sammlung der Erkenntnisse des Verwaltungsgerichtshofes*, vol. XLV (1921), pp. 80, 81.]

NOTE.—To the same effect see the decisions of 20 March, 1922, No. 13.047 A, vol. XLVI, pp. 25, 26, and of 29 April, 1924, No. 13.529 A, vol. XLVIII, pp. 176, 177. These decisions seem to be in conformity with Article 78 of the Treaty of St. Germain providing that "option by "a husband will cover his wife." The Peace Treaties adopted the system of *collective*, and not of *individual* option. Cf. Kunz, *Die völkerrechtliche Option*, vol. I (1925), pp. 111-116, 182; vol. II (1928), p. 201. It has been held that even the consent of the husband, expressly given, to the option of the wife, is not sufficient if the husband himself has not exercised his right to opt: Austrian Administrative Court, decision of 29 April, 1924, No. 13.529 A, vol. XLVIII (1924), pp. 176, 177. On the other hand, women over 18 years of age who are not married have the right to independent option: Austrian Administrative Court, decision of 14 May, 1921, No. 12.810, vol. XLV (1921), p. 50. The same applies to legally divorced women: Austrian Administrative Court, decision of 6 October, 1925, No. 13.980 A, vol. XLIX (1925), pp. 453, 454.

Nationality—Option—Article 80 of the Treaty of St. Germain —Burden of Proof on the Optant. **Case No. 154**

FINKELSTEIN *v.* (AUSTRIAN) FEDERAL MINISTRY FOR THE INTERIOR.

Austria, Administrative Court (*Verwaltungsgerichtshof*), *Vienna.* 9 *June*, 1921. (*No.* 12.830 *A.*)

THE FACTS.—The plaintiff, who had his rights of citizenship (*Heimatrecht*) at Stanislau, Poland, had opted for Austria in accordance with Article 80 of the Treaty of St. Germain. His option was refused by the Federal Ministry for the Interior on the ground that he had not given evidence of his belonging to the German race.

[1] In addition to nationality proper, Austrian law recognises a so-called right of citizenship (*Heimatrecht*) in a territorial district, usually referred to as a commune (*Gemeinde*).—[Ed.]

Case No. 154 ***contd.***

His appeal was based on the argument that the *onus probandi* is not on the optant, but on the competent authority.

Held, dismissing the appeal: That the burden of proof is always on the person exercising the right to opt. The appeal must therefore be dismissed. [Report: *Sammlung der Erkenntnisse des Verwaltungsgerichtshofes*, vol. XLV (1921), pp. 59-61.]

NOTE.—Persons fulfilling certain conditions are entitled to opt, and the contracting parties undertook, in Article 81 of the Treaty of St. Germain, "to put no hindrance in the way of the exercise of the right "which the persons concerned have under the present Treaty." However, the above decision shows that they must produce evidence of their fulfilling the conditions laid down by the Treaty, and that it is for the competent authorities to decide whether the proof is sufficient or not. See, to the same effect, the decisions of 5 May, 1921, No. 5.730, and of 2 January, 1922, No. 12.993 A, vol. XLVI (1922), p. 3.

Case No. 155

Nationality—Option—Article 80 of the Treaty of St. Germain —Meaning of "Race."

DYM *v.* (AUSTRIAN) FEDERAL MINISTRY FOR THE INTERIOR.

Austria, Administrative Court (*Verwaltungsgerichtshof*), *Vienna*. 9 *June*, 1921. (*No.* 12.828 *A*.)

THE FACTS.—Article 80 of the Treaty of St. Germain provides:

"Persons possessing rights of citizenship in territory forming part of the former Austro-Hungarian "Monarchy and differing in race and language from "the majority of the population of such territory, shall "within six months from the coming into force of the "present Treaty severally be entitled to opt for "Austria, Italy, Poland, Roumania, the Serb-Croat-"Slovene State, or the Czecho-Slovak State, if the "majority of the population of the State selected is of "the same race and language as the person exercising "the right to opt. The provisions of Article 78 as to "the exercise of the right of option shall apply to the "right of option given by this Article." Under this Article the plaintiff had purported to opt for Austria. The Federal Ministry for the Interior declined to recognise the option on the ground that the plaintiff had not given evidence of his being of the same race as the (German) majority of the population of Austria. He appealed.

Held : That the appeal must be dismissed. The burden of proof is on the person exercising the right to opt. It is not sufficient to prove belonging to the majority of the Austrian population as regards *language*. Evidence must also be given of belonging to the German majority of Austria as regards *race*. It is clear that the Treaty does not mean the same thing by the two different terms " language and race." The Treaty demands the fulfilment of two different conditions. *Both* must be proved. The language spoken by an individual is no proof that he belongs to a certain race. The language of an individual may be chosen *freely*. But the race is " an inherent quality, " born with the individual, characterised by physiological and " psychological facts, of a permanent character, a status inde- " pendent of the will of the individual in question and which " cannot be thrown off or changed arbitrarily. Certificates " proving that a person has visited German schools give " evidence as to language, but not as to race." As the plaintiff had not fulfilled the obligation, incumbent on him, to prove his belonging to the German race by providing evidence through " conclusive characteristics " (*fassbare Merkmale*), his option cannot be recognised. [Report : *Sammlung der Erkenntnisse des Verwaltungsgerichtshofes*, vol. XLV (1921), pp. 55-57.]

NOTE.—This is the leading decision in this matter. It has formed a precedent for a long series of decisions to the same effect, rendered in 1921 and in the following years : decisions of 9 June, 1921, No. 12.830, vol. XLV (1921), pp. 59-61 ; of 1 December, 1921, No. 12.965 A, vol. XLV (1921), pp. 116, 117 ; of 12 December, 1921, No. 9863 ; of 27 December, 1921, No. 12.988 A, vol. XLV (1921), pp. 133-135 ; " Race " is not to be confounded with religion " : decision of 19 December, 1921, No. 12.982 A, vol. XLV (1921), pp. 128, 129 ; of 24 April, 1922, No. 13.069 A, vol. XLVI (1922), p. 36 ; of 9 January, 1922, No. 12.997 A, vol. XLVI (1922), p. 4 ; of 13 February, 1922, No. 1419 ; of 20 March, 1922, No. 2701 ; of 27 March, 1922, Nos. 2896, 2897, 2898 ; of 16 May, 1922, No. 4546 ; of 8 July, 1922, Nos. 5285, 5286 ; of 3 April, 1922, Nos. 2953, 3167 ; of 14 April, 1922, No. 3084 ; of 2 November, 1922, No. 8973 ; of 8 June, 1923, No. 13.300 A, vol. XLVII (1923), pp. 123-125 ; of 29 December, 1925, No. 14.072 A, vol. XLIX (1925), pp. 586-588. Neither has the necessity of giving evidence, by the production of conclusive characteristics, that an optant belongs to the German majority of Austria, also as regards race, been removed by Article 9 of the Austro-Czechoslovak Treaty of Brünn of 7 June, 1920, which provides that the interpretation of the terms " race and language " in Article 80 of the Treaty of St. Germain should be made in a liberal sense, and that *in the first instance* the language should be taken into consideration. See decisions of 31 October, 1921, No. 12.937 A, vol. XLV (1921), p. 97, and of 20 December, 1921, No. 10.095.

Cf. on this question, Kunz, *Die völkerrechtliche Option*, vol. II (1928), pp. 199-201, 210, 219, 226-229, 307.

X.—Statelessness

Case No. 156 **Statelessness—Status Recognised by English Municipal Law —Determination of Nationality—German Law as the Test of a "German National."**

STOECK *v.* PUBLIC TRUSTEE.

England, High Court of Justice, Chancery Division.
28 *April*, 1921.

THE FACTS.—The plaintiff was born in Rhenish Prussia in 1872, went to reside in Belgium in 1895, and obtained his discharge from Prussian nationality in 1896. He never subsequently applied for, or obtained, the nationality of any German State. In 1896 he came to England and made it his permanent home. He did not become naturalised in England, was deported to Holland in 1916, and since then had resided in Germany.

The effect of the Treaty of Peace Orders, 1919, and of sections III to VII of Part X of the Treaty of Peace of Versailles was to place a charge, with a view to its retention and liquidation, upon all the property "within His Majesty's Dominions or Protectorates "belonging to German nationals at the date when the "Treaty comes into force," namely, 10 January, 1920.

The plaintiff sued the Public Trustee and the Attorney-General for a declaration that he was not on that date a German national within the meaning of the Treaty of Peace Order, 1919, and the Treaty of Peace. He contended, *inter alia*, that he had been completely divested of his Prussian nationality and German nationality in 1896, had never acquired any other nationality and was therefore a stateless person. Evidence was given by two German lawyers to the effect that German law recognised him as stateless and that he possessed no shred or remnant of Prussian or German nationality.

The defendants contended, *inter alia*, that he still retained a remnant of his former nationality, that the condition of statelessness was not recognised by law, international or municipal, and that the words "German national" in the Treaty of Peace and the

Order giving effect to it included a person who was a German national by English law.

Held, by Russell, J.: (1) Accepting the evidence of the German lawyers, that the plaintiff had lost his German nationality for all purposes; (2) that English law recognises the condition of statelessness; and (3) that the plaintiff was not a "German national" at the material time. He further held (4) that the question "whether a person is a national of a "country must be determined by the municipal law of that "country. . . . There is not and cannot be such an individual "as a German national according to English law." [Report: L.R. [1921] 2 Ch. 67.]

NOTES.—(1) The learned judge distinguished *Ex parte Weber*, L.R. [1916] 1 K.B. 280 n.; [1916] 1 A.C. 421, and *Ex parte Liebmann*, L.R. [1916] 1 K.B. 268, on the question of the completeness of the loss of German nationality.

(2) As to point (4) above, the judgment of Russell, J., was followed in the case of *In re Chamberlain's Settlement, Chamberlain* v. *Chamberlain*, L.R. [1921] 2 Ch. 533.

Nationality—Loss of German Nationality—Statelessness. **Case No. 157**

PAULY (appellant) *v.* CUSTODIAN OF ENEMY PROPERTY (respondent).

Union of South Africa, Supreme Court (Appellate Division). 26 *January*, 1922.

(INNES, C.J.; MAASDORP, J.A.; JUTA, J.A.)

THE FACTS.—The appellant Pauly claimed certain properties held by the Custodian of Enemy Property. Pauly was a German subject by origin, who left Germany in 1884, had never returned except for a holiday visit in 1910, and had never registered his name at any German consulate. In 1920 he received a grant of naturalisation in The Netherlands. The properties in question had come into the hands of the Custodian at an unascertained date before the last-named event.

Held: (1) It is a general rule of law that questions of nationality must be determined by the municipal law of the country concerned.

(2) (On proof that (*a*) statelessness is recognised by German

Case No. 157 *contd.* municipal law; (*b*) by a Prussian statute of 1870, the operation of which was in 1871 extended to the whole German Empire, Germans who remained abroad for an uninterrupted period of ten years without registering their names at a German consulate thereby lost their German nationality and became stateless) The applicant was not a German national at the date of the Treaty of Versailles or at the date when his assets came into the hands of the Custodian or at any intermediate date. In these circumstances the Custodian was not entitled to retain the assets in question.

In the course of his judgment, Innes, C.J., commented upon *Ex parte Weber*, [1916] 1 A.C. 421; *Ex parte Liebmann*, [1916] 1 K.B. 268; and *Stoeck* v. *Public Trustee*, [1921] 2 Ch. 67, "which upon the facts was a case exactly on all fours with "the present dispute. . . . Any State is entitled to provide "that its nationals, who have lost their original status, may "be naturalised more easily than foreigners. And the fact "that it confers upon its former nationals special facilities for "regaining citizenship specially declared to have been lost does "not seem to me a sufficient reason for holding that it was "never lost at all." [In *Ex parte Weber, ubi sup.*; *Ex parte Liebmann, ubi sup.*, it was held that German nationals who had resided abroad for ten years had not lost their original nationality "for all purposes." [Report: *The South African Law Reports*, [1922] *Appellate Division*, p. 161 ([1922] A.D. 161).]

NOTE.—In the case of *Loewenstein* v. *Custodian of Enemy Property* in the Transvaal Provincial Division of the Supreme Court of South Africa (*South African Law Reports*, [1921] *Transvaal Provincial Division*, p. 606 [1921 T.P.D. 606]) it was held by Gregorowski, J., that where a person, born in Germany, had resided in the South African Republic, but without acquiring nationality, from 1881 to 1896, when he returned to Germany and since remained there, he had not completely divested himself of his German nationality; that assuming a condition of statelessness to be possible (a question left undecided), he had not become a stateless person in consequence of his prolonged absence from Germany; and that since he was not shown to have become a national of the South African Republic he could not in any circumstances have become a British subject by annexation. It was held (on the facts) that he had not retained his Transvaal domicile.

Statelessness—Loss of German Nationality—Article 297 of the Treaty of Versailles.

See Case No. 285 (*Procureur Général* v. *Schneider and Others*).

XI.—Nationality of Corporations

[See also Part XI, WAR AND NEUTRALITY: *Enemy Character*.]

Nationality—Of Corporations—*Siège Social*—Nationality of Majority of Members—Article 297 of the Treaty of Versailles—French and English Texts of Article 297 (*e*). **Case No. 158**

SOCIÉTÉ ANONYME DU CHARBONNAGE FRÉDÉRIC HENRI *v.* GERMANY.

Franco-German Mixed Arbitral Tribunal. 30 *September*, 1921.
(ASSER, BONDI, GANDOLPHE.)

THE FACTS.—This was a claim against the German Government under Article 297 (*e*) of the Treaty of Versailles. The claimants, a company constituted under German law and having its principal place of business in Germany but composed mostly of French shareholders, asked for a decision ordering the German Government to assure the re-registration of the company as it existed on 1 August, 1914, and for the registration of its property taken away in connection with the exceptional war measures adopted by Germany. It was contended on behalf of Germany that the Tribunal had no jurisdiction on the ground that the claimants being a German company could not be considered a national (*ressortissant*) of an Allied or Associated Power. The claimants contended that they were in reality a French company seeing that the majority of the shareholders were French.

Held: That the Tribunal has jurisdiction. The claimants must be deemed to be a French company:

(*a*) Corporations do not, properly speaking, possess a nationality. For nationality confers rights and imposes duties which apply only to physical persons. Corporations are created by a contract between physical persons. They owe their existence as moral persons to a legal fiction. The rules which govern the relations of these moral persons are rules of private law of the State where they are registered and where they have their *siège social*. However, apart from the corporation there exist its members, who determine the character and the nature of the undertaking. These members possess a nationality.

(*b*) In answering the question whether in applying Article 297 (*e*) of the Treaty of Versailles the Tribunal ought to con-

Case No. 158 ***contd.***

sider as decisive the *siège social* or the nationality of the majority of the shareholders, it ought to regard as relevant the manner in which the exceptional war measures dealt with in Article 297 (*e*) were applied to corporations during the war. It appeared, as a matter of fact, that they were applied having regard rather to the composition of the company than to its *siège social*. Thus the German Ordinance of 31 July, 1918, laid down, in regard to the liquidation of British (and other) businesses, that those undertakings should be liquidated of which the greater part of the capital belonged to British nationals.

(*c*) The interpretation adopted by the Tribunal found support in other parts of Article 297, for instance, in paragraphs (*a*) and (*b*), which treated on the same footing nationals of the Allied and Associated Powers and the companies and associations in which they are interested. The same applied to paragraph (*e*) of that Article. The obscurity of the French text of this paragraph could be removed by inserting a comma between the words " *intéressés* " and " *sur le territoire français*," an amendment which seems justified when we consider that in the English text there is a comma between the words " interested " and " in German territory." [1] [Report : *Recueil*, vol. I (1922), p. 423.]

NOTE.—As to (*a*) and (*b*), see also to the same effect the decision of another section of the Franco-German Mixed Arbitral Tribunal (Botella, Serruys, Scholz) of 31 August, 1921, in the case *Société du Chemin de fer de Damas-Hamah* v. *Compagnie du Chemin de fer de Bagdad* (*Recueil*, vol. I (1922), p. 401). This decision develops in some detail the view that the relevant provisions of the Treaty of Versailles are, in regard to corporations, based on the theory of " control " as distinguished from that of " *siège social*." According to the Tribunal the theory of control implies that it is not necessary that the *absolute majority* of the shareholders should be of enemy nationality. It is sufficient if the enemy group has a decisive influence.

---

[1] The French text of the first sentence of Article 297 (*e*) runs as follows : " Les ressortissants des Puissances alliées ou associées auront droit à une " indemnité pour les dommages ou préjudices causés à leurs biens, droits ou " intérêts, y compris les sociétés ou associations dans lesquelles ils étaient " intéressés sur le territoire allemand, tel qu'il existait au 1er août 1914, par " l'application, tant des mesures exceptionnelles de guerre que des mesures " de disposition qui font l'objet des paragraphes 1 et 3 de l'Annexe ci-jointe."

The English text of the first sentence of Article 297 (*e*) runs as follows : " The nationals of Allied and Associated Powers shall be entitled to com- " pensation in respect of damage or injury inflicted upon their property, " rights or interests, including any company or association in which they are " interested, in German territory as it existed on August 1, 1914, by the " application either of the exceptional war measures or measures of transfer " mentioned in paragraphs 1 and 3 of the Annex hereto."

It will be observed that the Anglo-German Mixed Arbitral Tribunal, in the case, digested below (Case No. 249), of *Chamberlain & Hookham Ltd.* v. *Solar Zahlerwerke*, rejected the theory of control in favour of that of the *siège social* in regard to a claim under Article 296 of the Treaty relating to pre-war debts and the clearing procedure.

As to (*c*), see also, to the same effect, the decision of the Anglo-German Mixed Arbitral Tribunal in the case *Weiss Biheller & Brooks Ltd.* v. *German State* decided on 22 and 24 February, 1922 (Borel, Vaughan Williams, Zacharias), and reported in *Recueil*, vol. I (1922), p. 850. In that case the Tribunal refused to attach importance to the absence of the comma in the French text of Article 297 (*e*). It regarded it as " unreasonable to rely upon an interpretation of the French text of " Article 297 (*e*) which is in apparent conflict with the clear English text " of that article as opposed to an interpretation which is completely " in accord with the English text and also in accord with all the other " provisions in the Treaty, in which the same words appear, viz. Article " 297 (*a*) and the Annex to Articles 297 and 298, paragraphs 4, 6, and " 12." See also the case *Rymenans* v. *Germany*, decided on 11 February, 1922, by the Germano-Belgian Mixed Arbitral Tribunal (*Recueil*, vol. I (1922), p. 878), in which the Tribunal in interpreting Annex 1 to Article 297 of the Treaty pointed out that " il faut être prudent dans les arguments tirés de la présence ou de l'absence d'une virgule " (at p. 881). This had reference to the interpretation of the passage " in pursuance " of war legislation with regard to enemy property, rights or interests."

Nationality of Corporations—Enemy or Neutral Character of a Corporation—Brazilian Company Founded and Conducted by Germans—Shipment from Brazil to Sweden, with Ultimate Destination to Germany—Insurance of Cargo against Molestation—Formal Criterion of Place of Registered Office, or Substantial Criterion of Nationality of Founders and Managers. **Case No. 159**

N. V. SÜDDEUTSCHE RÜCKVERSICHERUNGS-AKTIEN-GESELLSCHAFT, of Munich (appellant) *v.* N. V. COMPANHIA NACIONAL DE CAFÉ, of Santos, Brazil, *ET AL.* (respondents).[1]

Holland, Court of Appeal of Amsterdam, First Chamber.
18 *March*, 1921.

(Dr. W. BOOT, President; Drs. G. KIRBERGER and W. A. VAN WOUDENBERG HAMSTRA, Judges.)

THE FACTS.—In January, 1916, the appellant company had insured against molestation 1000 bales of coffee, which the respondent shipped from Santos (Brazil) to Malmö (Sweden) *per* s.s. *Foerde*, for an appraised value of fl. 46,000. According to the insurance policy the insurance covered only neutral property. The cargo

[1] " N. V." is the usual abbreviation of the words " *naamlooze vennootschap*," which term is equivalent to the French " *société anonyme*."

Case No. 159 *contd.*

was seized as prize by the British authorities, brought into a British port and confiscated in 1917. The owners of the coffee, having abandoned the same to the insurance company as a total loss, brought an action against that company for the amount insured. The District Court of Amsterdam considered that the fact that the ultimate destination of the cargo was Germany was established, *inter alia*, by the evidence given in the British Prize proceedings, and put on the claimants the onus of proof of the neutral character of the shipping company at the time of the insurance, the shipment and the seizure of the coffee.

Held on appeal: For the appellant. The Companhia Nacional de Café proved to have been founded by a German subject, Trinks, who was at the same time the true owner of the overwhelming majority of the shares, and to be managed by another German subject, Jagoir, the rest of the persons concerned being figureheads only. This being so, the company was not justified in asserting that it is sufficient to prove that it was founded under Brazilian law and has its head office in Brazil. The " neutral property " clause in the insurance policy clearly means property which is neutral in the eyes of the belligerent States. It is self-evident that the Prize Court of a belligerent Power, in determining the nationality of a company, not only enquires after the place of its headquarters, but at the same time investigates who are the natural persons behind the corporate entity. If it were otherwise, the interests of those Powers could only too easily be prejudiced by their enemies under a false cover of neutral nationality. The British Prize Courts, too, recognise that principle, as appears, *inter alia*, from the decision concerning the *Hamborn* [1] of 12 December, 1917, according to which the Prize Courts " will " penetrate through and beyond forms and technicalities to " the facts and realities." [Report: *Weekblad van het Recht*, 27 July, 1921, No. 10745.]

Nationality of Corporations—Test of Control—*Siège Social.*

See Cases Nos. 249, 276, 293 and 294 (*Chamberlain etc.* v. *Solar etc.*, *In re Badische Company Limited*, *The Vesta* and *The Hamborn*).

[1] L.R. [1918] P. 19.

C. ALIENS

I.—Admission of Aliens

Aliens—Admission of—Equality with Subjects of the State—Articles 62 and 63 of the Treaty of St. Germain. **Case No. 160**

ADMISSION OF ALIENS (AUSTRIA) CASE.

Austria, Constitutional Court. 22 *June,* 1922. (*B.* 28/22.)

THE FACTS.—The appellant, who had lost Austrian nationality, was expelled from the Austrian Republic. He appealed on the ground that according to Articles 62 and 63 of the Peace Treaty of St. Germain aliens were placed on a footing of equality with Austrian subjects.

Held: That the appeal must be dismissed. The Articles in question placed aliens on an equal footing with Austrian subjects only in regard to protection of life and property, but not in regard to the right of residence. [Report: *Sammlung der Erkenntnisse des österrischen Verfassungsgerichtshofes,* vol. II (1922), No. 120, p. 57.]

II.—Position of Aliens

i.—Subjection to Territorial Sovereignty of the Receiving State

Aliens—Subjection to Territorial Sovereignty of Receiving State—Aliens in British Territory—Local and Temporary Allegiance—Forfeiture of Protection of Crown—Plea of "Act of State." **Case No. 161**

JOHNSTONE *v.* PEDLAR.

Great Britain and Ireland (*United Kingdom of*), *House of Lords, on Appeal from the Court of Appeal in Ireland.* 24 *June,* 1921.

THE FACTS.—The plaintiff, who was born in Ireland, had become an American citizen by naturalisation. Returning to Ireland in 1916 he took part in the Easter 1916 rebellion in Dublin. He was deported to England, and on being released in 1917 he returned to Ireland and was again deported. He again returned to Ireland and in 1918 he was arrested there and convicted on a

Case No. 161 *contd.*

charge of illegal drilling. When arrested he had with him cash amounting to £124 and a cheque for £4. 15s. 6d. The cash and the cheque were seized and detained by the police. Shortly after his release from prison he instituted proceedings against the Chief Commissioner of the Dublin Metropolitan Police to recover the cash and the cheque. The statement of defence contained the following paragraph:

"4. The Plaintiff is an alien and the said monies "and cheque were taken by an Officer of the Crown "by the direction of the Crown as an Act of State "for the Defence of the Realm and for the prevention "of crime, which is the detention and conversion "complained of."

The Chief Secretary for Ireland gave a certificate (which was put in at the trial) in which he stated that he did "in my capacity as a minister of the Crown and "officer of State and official superior of the [defendant] " . . . hereby formally ratify, adopt and confirm the "said seizure of the said cash and cheque and the "detention of the same by the [defendant] on the "grounds aforesaid."

The defendant also contended that the said monies and cheque were the property of an illegal association and were in the plaintiff's possession for the illegal purpose of the said association, but the defendant failed to obtain from the jury a finding to this effect, so that the substantial defence of the action was the plea of "act of State" coupled with the allegation of alienage.

The judge of first instance (Pim, J.) directed the jury to enter a verdict for the defendant. The Divisional Court (Dodd, Gordon and Moore, JJ.) dismissed the plaintiff's motion to set aside the verdict and judgment in favour of the defendant. The Court of Appeal (Ronan and O'Connor, L.JJ.; *dissentiente* O'Connor, M.R.) allowed the plaintiff's appeal on the ground that the defence of "act of State" could not be pleaded against the subject of a State at peace with His Majesty. The defendant's counsel informed the House of Lords "that he had advisedly taken up the "position that an allegation of alienage was a good "defence to an action in respect of an act of State in "Ireland." On appeal,

Held by the House of Lords (Viscount Finlay, Viscount Cave, Lords Atkinson, Sumner and Phillimore), dismissing the appeal: That paragraph 4 of the defence is bad in law and the plaintiff is entitled to judgment. In the case of a wrong done by or on behalf of the Crown, an officer of the Crown may be sued in respect of the wrongful act by the person wronged. "This rule of law has, however, been held subject to qualification in the case of acts committed abroad against a foreigner. If an action be brought in the British Courts in such a case it is open to the defendant to plead that the act was done by the orders of the British Government, or that after it had been committed it was adopted by the British Government. In any such case the act is regarded as an act of State of which a municipal Court cannot take cognizance. The foreigner who has sustained injury must seek redress against the British Government through his own Government by diplomatic or other means," *per* Viscount Finlay, at p. 271. The rule applies if the person wronged is a British subject (*Walker* v. *Baird*, L.R. [1892] A.C. 491), and for this purpose, as for most others, an alien once admitted to and resident in British territory is in the same position as a British subject. Accordingly, "the defence of act of State cannot be made good as to acts in the King's Dominions on a bare averment that the plaintiff is an alien" (*per* Viscount Finlay, at p. 275).

Per Lord Phillimore: "An alien ami is never ex lex, he is never subject to the arbitrary dispositions of the King. His rights may be limited, but whatever rights he has he can enforce by law just as an ordinary subject can. That is, I believe, both international law and the law of this country. . . . The alien ami, once he is resident within the realm, is given the same rights for the protection of his person and property as a natural born or naturalised subject" (at p. 296).

On the argument that the plaintiff had by his conduct forfeited the rights of an alien ami, Lord Atkinson said (at p. 284): "The protection to a resident alien is given by the Crown. The Crown alone can withdraw it. The [plaintiff] is still the subject of a State at amity with Great Britain. He does not come within the definition of alien enemy, and the Crown has given no indication whatever that it has withdrawn his implied licence to reside within this realm." His conduct does not *ipso facto* terminate the protection of the Crown.

[Report: L.R. [1921] 2 A.C. 262. The judgments of the Irish Courts are reported in [1920] 2 Irish Reports 450.]

Case No. 161 contd.

NOTE.—(1) Their Lordships speak of the alien ami "resident" within the realm, but it is submitted that for the purpose "residence" amounts to no more than "presence within the realm" with the express or tacit permission of the Crown.

(2) The question whether the defence of "act of State" is available against an alien resident abroad when the injury takes place within the realm would appear to be still open: see *Commercial and Estates Co. of Egypt* v. *Ball*, [1925] 1 K.B. at pp. 290, 297.

Case No. 162

Aliens—Position of—Subjection to Territorial Sovereignty—Aliens of German Nationality on French Occupied Territory—Crime of Communication with the Enemy—Arrest in Lorraine during the Provisional Régime Established by the Armistice—Assimilation to the National Territory—Competence of the French Courts.

IN RE KIRGIS (HUSBAND AND WIFE), KALTENBACH (WIDOW) AND OTHERS.

France, Fourth Council of War of Paris. 18 *June*, 1919.

THE FACTS.—The accused were German nationals. They were at Laon, in France, when the Great War broke out, and conformed to the regulations of the French police concerning enemy subjects. They were charged with having committed acts amounting in French law to communication with the enemy (*intelligence avec l'ennemi*) when the district of Laon was occupied by the German army. One of the Kirgis was arrested at St. Avold, the other at Bitche (Lorraine), while Lorraine was under French occupation in accordance with the régime established by the Armistice Agreement of 11 November, 1918. The accused disputed the jurisdiction of the Council of War on the ground that they were German nationals, that the alleged offence was committed on the territory occupied by the enemy, and (in one case) that their arrest did not take place on French territory. They contended that according to Article 43 of the Hague Regulations on the Laws and Customs of War on Land the occupation by the enemy suspended the sovereignty of the national authorities, and that therefore Article 3 of the *Code Civil*[1] was inapplicable at least in regard to enemy nationals. They also contended that in view of the character of modern warfare a new principle of international law

[1] Article 3 provides as follows: "Les lois de police et de sûreté obligent "tous ceux qui habitent le territoire . . ."

was created which assimilated subjects of enemy States to enemy combatants and rendered possible the application to them of the provisions of Article 31 of the Hague Convention Concerning the Laws and Customs of War.[1]

Held: That the Council of War had jurisdiction. The crimes with which the accused were charged were committed in France. According to Articles 63, 64 and 269 of the *Code de Justice Militaire* all persons, including civilians and aliens, are subject to the jurisdiction of the Council of War in regard to crimes laid down in that Code and committed within the theatre of war.[2] The Kirgis were arrested in Lorraine, and thus on French territory in accordance with the principle that " France is wherever the French flag flies. . . ."

As to the Hague Convention, it could not be maintained that France is bound in relation to Germany to apply the terms of a convention which Germany has herself violated since the outbreak of hostilities. In any case the Council of War had jurisdiction also by virtue of Article 31 of that Convention.[3] (Reports: 46 *Clunet* (1919), p. 737; *Gazette du Palais*, 1920, I, p. 78.]

ii.—Protection by the National State

Aliens—Treatment of—Protection by the Home State—Renunciation by the Alien of Legal Remedies—How far Binding upon the Home State. **Case No. 163**

THE TATTLER (I).

British-American Claims Arbitral Tribunal.

18 *December*, 1920.

(FROMAGEOT, FITZPATRICK, ANDERSON.)

THE FACTS.—This was a claim on behalf of the owners of the American schooner *Tattler* which on 10 April,

[1] Article 31 provides as follows: " A spy who, after rejoining the army to "which he belongs, is subsequently captured by the enemy, is treated as a "prisoner of war, and incurs no responsibility for his previous acts of espionage."

[2] See Sirey, 1918-1919, Part II, p. 47, for a decision of 20 December, 1915, to the effect that French courts have no jurisdiction over an alien for a crime committed in 1914 in German territory occupied by France and subsequently annexed by her.

[3] As to the application of the Hague Conventions, see the case of *The Blonde, etc.*, Case No. 288 (L.R. [1921] P. 155, and, on appeal, [1922] 1 A.C. 313). As to "territorial" liability for treason, see the case of *De Jager* v. *Attorney-General for Natal* (L.R. [1907] A.C. 326).—[Ed.]

Case No. 163 ***contd.***

1905, was seized and detained by Canadian authorities for a period of six days on a charge of having contravened certain provisions of the Treaty of 1818 between Great Britain and the United States [1] and the relevant Canadian statute. The vessel was then released on payment of a fine of five hundred dollars and on an undertaking given by the owners and guaranteeing the British Government against all claims, before any court or tribunal, on account of the detention and the seizure. The owners paid the fine under protest, but no protest or reservations appear to have been made against the guarantee. It was contended by the United States that the renunciation and the guarantee against any claim for damages on account of the seizure and the detention were not binding upon the Government of the United States which presented the claim.

Held : That that contention must be rejected. The only right which the Government of the United States was supporting in the present case was that of its national. Consequently, the United States could not rely on legal grounds other than those which would have been open to its national. [Reports : Nielsen, p. 490 ; *A.J.*, XV (1921), p. 297.]

NOTE.—The present case raises, it is believed, a question similar to that involved in the so-called Calvo Clause. See *North American Dredging Company of Texas* case (*Annual Digest*, 1925-1926, Case No. 218). It will be noted that the decision in the case here digested is based on a principle different from that usually underlying decisions in cases involving the Calvo Clause. The question whether the claim put forward by a Government is identical with the private claim which it espouses is both of practical and theoretical interest. In the present case the contention of the United States was that a wrong against one of its nationals was a wrong against the United States, *i.e.* that it was not identical, and that any modification of responsibility, as the result of a declaration of the individuals concerned, was not binding upon the United States.

[1] See p. 331.

iii.—Treatment by and Responsibilities of the Receiving State

[See also Part V, STATE RESPONSIBILITY.]

Aliens—Treatment of—Exercise of Privileges not Granted by International Law—Sudden Withdrawal of—Absence of Notice—Question of Liability—American Fishery Rights in Canadian Waters—Treaty of 1818. **Case No. 164**

THE DAVID J. ADAMS.

British-American Claims Arbitral Tribunal. 9 *December*, 1921.

(FROMAGEOT, FITZPATRICK, ANDERSON.)

THE FACTS.—(See Cases Nos. 239 and 243.) It appeared that for various reasons the British Government refrained for a considerable period of time from enforcing some of the provisions of the British Act of 1819 (see Case No. 239) which, in pursuance of the Treaty of 1818, prohibited to foreign fishermen entrance into Canadian ports for purposes other than those specified in the Treaty. In 1885, following upon the denunciation of some previous arrangements governing the matter, a *modus vivendi* was agreed upon by the British and American Governments to terminate on 1 January, 1886. That *modus vivendi* provided that the purchasing of bait (which was not included in the fishery rights allowed by the Treaty of 1818) should continue until January, 1886, and that no impediments should be placed during that period in the way of the local traffic incidental to fishing. In March, 1886, before the beginning of the fishing campaign of 1886, the Canadian Government gave a public warning announcing its intention not to permit in the future to foreign fishermen the exercise of activities not permitted by the Treaty of 1818. The warning reproduced the text of the Treaty of 1818 and of a Canadian Act of 1868 concerning fishing of foreign vessels. It did not reproduce the Act of 1819. It was contended by the United States that the seizure of the *David J. Adams* for purchasing bait within the Canadian waters was a violation of international law because "as a "matter of international law, where for a long con-"tinued period a Government has, either contrary to "its laws or without having any laws in force covering

Case No. 164 *contd.*

"the case, permitted to aliens a certain course of "action, it can not, under the principles of international "law, suddenly change that course and make it affect "those aliens already engaged in forbidden transac-"tions as the result of that course and deprive aliens "of their property so acquired, without rendering "themselves liable to an international reclamation."

Held: That the American contention must be rejected.

(*a*) It appeared from the evidence presented to the Tribunal that it was admitted by the United States, at least once, that the American fishermen were enjoying access to the Canadian ports for purchasing bait "only by sufferance," and could at any time be deprived of it "by the enforcement of existing "laws or the re-enactment of former oppressive statutes."

(*b*) It appeared from the evidence that this was not a case "of a sudden and unexpected change of a government's con-"duct towards a foreigner suddenly surprised by that change." Thus the Tribunal attached, *inter alia*, importance to the fact that the master admitted that he knew the Canadian law; that he informed the authorities that he entered the harbour to see his relatives; that he gave false information as to possession of bait; and that he took away the ship's papers. [Reports: Nielsen, p. 526; *A.J.*, XVI (1922), p. 315.]

NOTE.—It will be noted that the Tribunal dealt on its merits with the contention that withdrawal, without due notice, of privileges granted in excess of what is due by international law gives rise to international liability. International cases bearing on this subject are few, and it has therefore been deemed necessary to digest the present case in some detail. See, as bearing on a similar question, the arbitration between Great Britain and Argentina of 1870 concerning the closure of the port of Buenos Aires to traffic coming from Monte Video (Moore, pp. 4916-4925, and Lapradelle-Politis, vol. II, pp. 637-667). Some of the pronouncements of international commissions on the limitation of the right of expulsion of aliens touch also on the matter. See Lauterpacht, *Law and the Judicial Function in the International Community* (1932), Chapter XIV.

Case No. 165

Aliens—Treatment of—Confiscation of Property of Aliens—Duty of Compensation—Portuguese Religious Properties.

THE EXPROPRIATED RELIGIOUS PROPERTIES CASE.
(FRANCE, GREAT BRITAIN AND SPAIN *v.* PORTUGAL.)

The Permanent Court of Arbitration. 2 and 4 September, 1920.
(ROOT, DE SAVORNIN LOHMAN, LARDY.)

THE FACTS.—After the revolution of October, 1910, which established the Republic in Portugal, the Provisional

Government enacted a law which confiscated certain religious properties. The British, French and Spanish Governments took up the case of their nationals affected by this measure. In July, 1913, an agreement was concluded submitting the claims of these Governments to arbitration.

Held: (*a*) That, with the exception of two cases,[1] the Portuguese Government shall retain as proprietor the property seized; (*b*) that compensation shall be paid to the persons affected. In formulating its decision [2] the Tribunal took into consideration " the circumstances under which the claimants " possessed the property claimed in Portugal, as well as the " burdens resulting therefrom, and especially the fact that they " had introduced capital into that country "; the fact that " it was not the intention of the Government of the Portuguese " Republic to seek in the seizure of the said property a source " of pecuniary gain, any more than it had been the intention " of the claimants to violate the respect due to the laws and " institutions of Portugal "; and that the award had " to " satisfy the respective legitimate expectations of the parties." [Reports: *The Hague Court Reports* (Second Series, edited by J. B. Scott), p. 3; *A.J.*, XV (1921), p. 99.]

NOTE.—For comments on this case see Scott in *A.J.*, XV (1921), p. 73, and Fachiri in *B.Y.*, 1925, pp. 167-169.

Aliens—Position of Aliens—Treatment by the Receiving State —Aliens as Guardians—Japanese Subject in California. **Case No. 166**

IN THE MATTER OF THE ESTATE AND GUARDIANSHIP OF TETSUBUMI YANO, A MINOR.

United States, Supreme Court of California. 1 *May*, 1922.

THE FACTS.—Yano, a Japanese resident in California, paid for certain land and had it conveyed directly to his baby daughter who had been born an American citizen. This was after the Law of 1913 forbidding aliens disqualified for citizenship from holding land (Statutes, 1913, p. 206), but before a later statute which also forbade aliens to act as guardians of minors

[1] A chapel was to be placed at the disposal of the Papal Nuncio at Lisbon, and an educational institution for young girls was to be continued for the same purpose.

[2] The substance of the award was agreed upon by the parties in a settlement out of court, and thus it is not wholly clear how far the Tribunal in formulating the decision was expressing its own views on the legal points involved.—[Ed.]

Case No. 166 *contd.*

whose property they could not hold. (Statutes, 1921, p. lxxxvii.[1]) He was denied letters of guardianship of the person and estate of his daughter. Upon appeal,

Held : That the order must be reversed. The father of a minor under fourteen is entitled as a matter of right to the guardianship of the minor, including guardianship of the estate, unless he is shown to be incompetent under California law. Alienage does not constitute such incompetence. The daughter was a citizen, was entitled to take title to the land, and received a good title.[2] It was contended in a dissenting opinion that this was a mere evasion of the alien land law and that the minor had no right to have her parent appointed as guardian if he were legally incompetent to discharge the office. [Report : 188 Calif. 645.]

Case No. 167

Aliens—Position of Aliens—Treatment by the Receiving State —Discrimination against—When Admissible.

IN RE KOTTA.

United States, Supreme Court of California. 12 *September*, 1921.

THE FACTS.—This was a petition for habeas corpus. The petitioner, a Mexican citizen, was held in custody for failure to pay a Californian poll tax levied on aliens. He contended that, since no such tax was laid upon citizens, the tax law was unconstitutional as a violation of the equal protection clause of the Fourteenth Amendment to the Constitution of the United States. The tax law was solely a revenue measure.

Held : That the petitioner must be discharged from custody. The Fourteenth Amendment extends the right of equal protection to aliens and citizens alike. The classification of aliens apart from citizens bore no such reasonable relation to the object of the tax law as to justify the discrimination. " The " constitutional guaranty, in so far as an alien is concerned, " has no application to laws of a state relating to such matters " as the regulation or distribution of the public domain, or of " the common property or resources of the people of the state,

[1] Commonly cited, through typographical error, as p. lxxxiii. See *ibid.*, p. 2272.

[2] Although this was not necessary to the decision of the case, the Court said that the later statute prohibiting such aliens from acting as guardians did not violate the Treaty with Japan (37 U.S. Stat. L. 1504), but did violate the " equal protection clause " of the Fourteenth Amendment to the Constitution of the United States.

" or, it is suggested, laws relating to the devolution of the real " property therein. . . . But that it does guarantee the alien " 'equal laws' in the matter of the imposition of such burdens " on him and his property as taxes seems clear." (187 Cal. 27, 32.) [Report: 187 Cal. 27.]

Aliens—Position of Aliens—Treatment by the Receiving State —Commercial Treaties—Equality of Treatment—Not Applicable to Regulations concerning Security for Persons and Property. **Case No. 168**

GIZZARELLI *v.* PRESBREY.

United States, Supreme Court of Rhode Island. 6 *June*, 1922.

THE FACTS.—Gizzarelli, an Italian, sought mandamus to compel the granting of a licence to him to operate a motor-bus in Providence. The city ordinance requiring such licence forbade its issuance to one who was not a citizen. The Treaty of 1913 between Italy and the United States provided that citizens of each country should enjoy in the other the same rights and privileges as nationals. Gizzarelli claimed that the ordinance was invalid as violating this Treaty and as a denial of " equal protection " under the Fourteenth Amendment to the Constitution of the United States.

Held: That the writ must be denied. The right to use the public highways as a common carrier was not a privilege covered by the Treaty. The Court quoted from *Patsone* v. *Pennsylvania*, 232 U.S. 138, as follows: " the equality of rights " that the treaty assures is equality only in respect of protec- " tion and security for persons and property." (44 R.I. 333, 334.) Various cases upholding police power regulations discriminating against aliens were cited, the Court saying: " We " think it fairly may be said that as aliens as a class are natur- " ally less interested in the state, the safety of its citizens and " the public welfare, than citizens of the state, to allow them " to operate motor buses would on the whole tend to increase " the danger to passengers and to the public using the highways. " It is clear that we can not say that the evil to be apprehended " and the proposed remedy are so dissociated as to warrant " the court in holding the ordinance to be invalid. . . . The " test of such legislation is not whether there is discrimination " against aliens, but rather is there any proper basis for such " discrimination " (44 R.I. 333, 335.) [Report: 44 R.I. 333.]

Case No. 169 **Aliens—Treatment of—Acquisition of Immovable Property—Requirement of Reciprocity—Armistice Agreement of November, 1918—Cession of Territory—Effect on Nationality—Residence Outside the Ceded Territory—Article 291 (2) of the Treaty of Versailles.**

IMMOVABLES (ALIENS IN GERMANY) CASE.

Germany, Reichsgericht in Civil Matters. 20 *October*, 1922.

THE FACTS.—By a notarial contract concluded on 2 October, 1918, the plaintiff sold to the defendant, a Russian subject resident in Hessen (Germany) but born in a part of Russia now forming part of Poland, a piece of land situated in Germany. The contract was concluded under the condition that it should not be executed should the fact of the Russian nationality of the defendant prove to be an obstacle to the continued validity of the contract. On 3 May, 1919, the plaintiff finally parted with the property through a so-called *Auflassung* and the defendant's title was registered in the land registry. In August, 1920, the plaintiff brought an action asking for a declaration that the contract was null and void on the ground that the defendant failed to obtain the consent of the State authorities which, according to Article 88 of the Introductory Law to the Civil Code and also to the law of Hessen where the property was situated, is necessary for the validity of acquisition of land by aliens. According to the above-mentioned German laws, in cases in which Germany does not enjoy reciprocity of treatment, the consent of the Ministry of Justice is required for the valid acquisition of real property by aliens.

In 1894 a commercial treaty was concluded between Germany and Russia which provided for reciprocity of treatment in the matter of acquisition of real property. This Treaty was again put into force by the Peace Treaty of Brest Litowsk concluded on 3 March, 1918, between Germany and Russia. In the Armistice Agreement of November, 1918, Germany waived all rights belonging to her by virtue of the Treaty of Brest Litowsk. Article 292 of the Treaty of Versailles provided for the abrogation of all treaties between Germany and Russia. In Article 291 of the Treaty of Versailles Germany undertook to grant to the subjects of the Allied and Associated Powers, should they make a request to this effect, all the rights and privileges enjoyed before 1 August, 1914, as the result of treaties, by the subjects of Austria, Hungary, Bulgaria and Turkey.

Held, on final appeal on a point of law: That the contract was invalid as the State had not given the required authorisation.

(*a*) The commercial treaty with Russia of 1894 which provided for reciprocity had been abrogated by the war. The reciprocity secured by the Treaty of Brest Litowsk was no longer existent in May, 1919, in view of the provisions of the Armistice Agreement of November, 1918, which must be regarded as forming part of German law. Accordingly, as a Russian subject, the defendant required the State authorisation provided in the law.

(*b*) Assuming that the defendant resident in Germany had become a Polish subject as the result of the part of Russia where he was born having become Polish territory—a question which the Court, unlike the Court of Appeal,[1] found it unnecessary to decide—there was no evidence that Poland availed herself of the provision of Article 291 (2) of the Treaty of Versailles. Accordingly, as a Polish subject, the defendant could not dispense with the required authorisation. [Report: *E.R.Z.*, vol. 105, p. 169.]

Aliens—Treatment of—Free Access to Court—Whether Implying Exemption from Security for Costs—Article 277 of the Treaty of Versailles—Interpretation of. **Case No. 170**

Security for Costs (Germany) Case.

Germany, Reichsgericht in Civil Matters. 18 *March*, 1922.

The Facts.—The plaintiff, a Polish subject, appealed against the decisions of the courts below requiring him to deposit security for costs in an action brought by him against a German subject. Article 277 of the Treaty of Versailles laid down that the subjects of the Allied and Associated Powers shall have free access to German courts.

Held, on final appeal on a point of law: That the appeal must be rejected. The obligation to give security for costs has

[1] The Court of Appeal held that the defendant did not acquire Polish nationality as he was not resident in that part of Russia which became Polish territory.

Case No. 170 *contd.* no direct connection with the question of free access to German courts. Free access means that the alien shall at any time be entitled to invoke the protection of German courts. Such protection is not impaired by the fact that the alien—as was the case in many States prior to the Hague Convention of 17 July, 1905, on Civil Procedure—is bound to deposit security for costs in case he loses his action. The requirement of such security cannot be regarded as a limitation of the right to bring actions in German courts.

The precise terms of Article 277 referring to " free access to " courts " do not admit of an extensive interpretation. Whenever the Allied and Associated Powers who were responsible for drafting the Treaty intended, in the conditions of peace imposed upon Germany, to secure special privileges for their subjects, they used detailed language for the purpose of specifying the German obligations. [Report : *E.R.Z.*, vol. 104, p. 189.]

Case No. 171

Aliens—Treatment of—Requisitions—Plea of Non-Discrimination—Requisitions in Time of War—Enemy Aliens—Articles 297 (*e*) and 298 (*b*) of the Treaty of Versailles.

RYMENANS & CO. *v.* GERMANY.

Germano-Belgian Mixed Arbitral Tribunal. 11 *February*, 1922.

(MORIAUD, HOENE, ROLIN.)

THE FACTS.—This was a claim against Germany, under Article 297 (*e*) of the Treaty of Versailles, for compensation on account of the requisition by Germany during the war of certain property belonging to the claimant.[1] It was contended by Germany that the exceptional war measures envisaged in that Article referred only to so-called differential measures, *i.e.* measures taken exclusively against enemy property and not applicable equally to German nationals. In support of this contention she relied, *inter alia*,[2] on

[1] Article 297 (*e*) provides as follows : " The nationals of Allied and " Associated Powers shall be entitled to compensation in respect of damage or " injury inflicted upon their property, rights or interests, including any " company or association in which they are interested, in German territory " as it existed on August 1, 1914, by the application either of the exceptional " war measures or measures of transfer mentioned in paragraphs 1 and 3 " of the Annex hereto."

[2] The Tribunal dealt at length with other reasons adduced by Germany. These parts of the decision do not raise any questions of general principle, and are, therefore, not digested here, but the above decision is of interest in regard to the much discussed question of the meaning of " exceptional war " measures."

Article 298 (*b*), which laid down for Germany the obligation " not to subject the property, rights or interests " of the nationals of the Allied or Associated Powers " to any measures in derogation of property rights " which are not applied equally to the property, rights " and interests of German nationals, and to pay " adequate compensation in the event of the application of these measures."

Held : That Germany was liable. Article 298 (*b*) applied to the time of peace. The assimilation, in time of peace, of the alien to the national is easily explained by the fact that in peace time the alien takes part in the economic and social life of the country where he is established and where he holds property. This does not apply to the time of war, in particular in regard to an alien enemy, who cannot be expected to take part, directly or indirectly, in the struggle against his country. This view seems also to have inspired Articles 44, 49 and 52 of the Fourth Hague Convention. [Report : *Recueil*, vol. I (1922), p. 878 at p. 885.]

Aliens—Position of—Companies Formed by Aliens—Nationality of—Whether Immune from Restrictions Imposed upon Aliens Individually. **Case No. 172**

IN RE OIL INDUSTRY ASSOCIATION LIMITED, CRACOW.

(Appeal by the Procurator-General of the Republic of Poland.)

Poland, Supreme Court, Third Division (*Full Meeting*). 12 *November*, 1921.

THE FACTS.—Under a statute of 1920 (passed during the period of inflation in order to prevent large estates from passing into alien hands for sums which were comparatively trifling), aliens can acquire real property in Poland only on obtaining the consent of the Council of Ministers. Two aliens formed a limited liability company for the purpose, *inter alia*, of acquiring (and selling) real estate. The law requires the registration of limited liability companies with the competent court. The District Court of Cracow (Commercial Division) rejected the request for registration, since such registration would make the company a Polish one and would thus enable the two partners to accomplish what individually they would be prevented by the law from doing. The Court of Appeal of Cracow allowed the

Case No. 172 *contd.*

appeal lodged against that decision, and held that the seat of the company is the sole criterion, under the law, of its national or foreign character ; that the nationality of the corporators is of no consequence in this connection, such companies being rather a form of association of capital ; that limitations of the right of aliens to purchase real estate do not apply to national companies ; and that questions of extending prohibitions and restrictions aimed at aliens to alien capital lie in the field of legislative policy and transcend the field of the jurisdiction of courts. On appeal to the Supreme Court, the latter

Held, reversing the decision of the Court of Appeal : That since neither partner had the capacity to acquire real estate, they did not have such capacity jointly and they cannot confer it upon themselves by forming a company of which they are the sole shareholders. [Report : O.S.P., I, No. 589.]

(For a discussion of the case see Professor S. Wróblewski, *ibid.*, Nos. 509-511, n. 2. Followed in later decisions, see *ibid.*, No. 509, n. 1.)

Case No. 173

Position of Aliens—Discrimination in the Receiving State—Brazilian Constitution—Habeas Corpus.

In re Tonioli.

Brazil, Supreme Federal Tribunal. 31 *May*, 1922.

The Facts.—The State of São Paulo, by Article 5, § 2, No. 3 of Law 1750 (8 December, 1920), and regulations carrying it into effect, enacted that in all private establishments of learning the Chair of Portuguese must be filled by one born either in Portugal or Brazil, and that of Geography and History of Brazil by a Brazilian-born. This was not obeyed by the *Externato Italo Brasileiro*, where the plaintiff was Professor and Director. The plaintiff had lived in Brazil for twenty-seven years, and, although foreign-born, had become a voter and magistrate. Thereupon an order was issued forbidding instruction in the school with the plaintiff as Director. The plaintiff applied for habeas corpus, alleging that undue restriction was put on his personal liberty inasmuch as he was not allowed to enter the school and exercise his profession. He claimed that this law violated §§ 2 and 24 of Article 72 of the

Brazilian Constitution. The *Tribunal de Justiça do Estado de São Paulo* rejected this petition, since the petitioner was neither arrested nor threatened with restraint. On appeal,

Held : That the appeal must be allowed and habeas corpus granted, so that the petitioner could carry on his profession of instructing in these subjects. "Habeas corpus is not exclusively a guaranty against imprisonment or threat of imprisonment. . . . The distinction between naturalized Brazilian and Portuguese born, or between Brazilian and foreigner, established by the Paulist law 1750 of 1920 as to private individual instruction in certain subjects . . . is contrary to the rules of §§ 2 and 24 of Article 72 of the Constitution of the Republic." [Report : *Revista do Supremo Tribunal*, vol. 42, p. 38.]

Aliens—Internment of—During War—Review by Courts.

See Case No. 141 (*Ex parte Gilroy*).

Aliens—Treatment of—Discrimination Against—Interpretation of Treaties of Commerce.

See Case No. 254 (*Frasca* v. *City Coal Co.*).

Aliens—Position of—Discrimination Against—Engaging in Trade—Regulation of State Property.

See Case No. 232 (*Poon* v. *Miller*).

iv.—Plea of Non-Discrimination

[See Part V, State Responsibility.]

Aliens—Position—Respect for Property—Confiscation—Plea of Non-Discrimination. **Case No. 174**

Sazonow *v.* District Land (Reform) Board of Białystok.

Poland, Supreme Court, First Division. 2 October, 1922.

The Facts.—The Constitution of Poland provides in Article 95, paragraph 2, that "aliens enjoy, on condition of reciprocity, equality of rights with citizens of the Polish State and are subject to duties equal to

Case No. 174 *contd.*

"those of the latter, unless Polish citizenship is expressly required by statute." Article 99 (last sentence) of the Constitution provides that "statutes "will determine the right of the State compulsorily to "buy up land and to regulate dealings in land . . ." and also that "it is only by statute that it can be "determined how far rights of citizens and of their "legally recognized associations to use freely land, "waters, minerals and other natural resources, may be "limited for public reasons." Under statutes concerning land reform, the defendant Board directed that the plaintiff's land should be bought up (in confirmation of the decision of the local land [reform] commission), because it had been found that the estate in question had for a long time been badly administered. The plaintiff brought the present action, alleging, *inter alia*, that the Constitution permits of limitations of free user of land only with regard to citizens, and that, under the statute in question, which allows compensation only with regard to one-half the value of the land bought up under the scheme for land reform, there really takes place confiscation of half the value, confiscation of an alien's property being contrary to international law.

Held: *Inter alia*, that the Constitution grants to aliens, on condition of reciprocity, equality of rights with citizens, but not preferential treatment, and that the same applies to the Land Reform Law of 1920. [Reports: Zb. O.S.N., 1922, No. 81; O.S.P., II, No. 2.]

See the same case, No. 3.

Aliens—Treatment of—Plea of Non-Discrimination—Internal Decrees Annulling Acts of *de facto* Government—How far Binding upon Aliens.

See Case No. 124 (*French Claims against Peru*).

Aliens—Respect of Property of—Non-Discrimination—Right of Angary—Requisition of Norwegian Shipbuilding Contracts by the United States.

See Case No. 289 (*Norway and United States: Requisition of Shipbuilding Contracts Case*).

v.—Respect for Property. Expropriation

[See Part IV, JURISDICTION : *Territorial*.]

Aliens—Respect for Property of—Corporation Controlled by Aliens—Nationalisation of Petroleum in Mexico. **Case No. 175**

IN RE THE TEXAS COMPANY OF MEXICO, S.A.

Mexico, Supreme Court. 30 *August*, 1921.

THE FACTS.—Article 27 of the Mexican Constitution of 1917, which became effective on 1 May of that year, provided that petroleum should be nationalised and that rights to exploit it should be granted only in certain ways.[1] Article 14 of the same Constitution provided that no law should be given retroactive effect.[2]

On 28 April, 1917, three days before the Constitution became effective, the owners of lot 36 of Zazamixtle granted oil leases to one Ravise for a higher

[1] The pertinent provisions of the Constitution of 1917, Article 27, are: "The ownership of lands and waters comprised within the limits of the "national territory is vested originally in the nation, which has had and has "the right to transmit title thereof to private persons, thereby constituting "private property. . . .

"4. In the nation is vested direct ownership of all minerals or substances "which in veins, layers, masses, or beds constitute deposits whose nature is "different from the components of the land, such as minerals from which "metals and metaloids used for industrial purposes are extracted; beds of "precious stones, rock salt, and salt lakes formed directly by marine waters; "products derived from the decomposition of rocks, when their exploitation "requires underground work; phosphates which may be used for fertilisers; "solid mineral fuels; petroleum and all hydrocarbons, solid, liquid, or "gaseous.

"5. In the nation is likewise vested the ownership of the waters of territorial seas. . . .

"6. In the cases to which the two foregoing paragraphs refer, the ownership of the nation is inalienable and may not be lost by prescription; the "Federal Government shall be able to grant concessions to private parties "or to civil or commercial corporations organised under the laws of Mexico, "only on condition that regular works are established for the development of "such resources, and on the further condition that they carry out the provisions which the laws require.

"Legal capacity to acquire ownership of lands and waters of the nation "shall be governed by the following provisions: (1) Only Mexicans by birth "or naturalisation and Mexican companies have the right to acquire ownership in lands, waters, and their appurtenances or to obtain concessions to "develop mines, waters, or mineral fuels in the Republic of Mexico. The "nation may grant (*podrá conceder*) the same right to foreigners, provided they "agree before the Department of Foreign Affairs to be considered Mexican "in respect to such property, and accordingly not to invoke the protection "of their Governments in respect to the same, under penalty, in case of "breach, of forfeiture to the nation of property so acquired."

[2] Article 14 provides as follows: "To no law shall retroactive effect be "given, to the prejudice of any person."

Case No. 175 ***contd.***

price than leases for agricultural use would have commanded. In September, 1917, Ravise assigned these leases to the Texas Company of Mexico, a Mexican corporation controlled by a corporation organised in the United States. In reliance upon a Presidential Decree of 8 August, 1918, giving retroactive effect to the provisions of Article 27, one Cortina "denounced" claims to lot 36 and secured from the Secretary of Industry, despite the protest of the Texas Company of Mexico, the right to exploit these petroleum lands. The Texas Company of Mexico sought relief of *amparo* [1] against the President and the Secretary of Industry on the ground that Article 14 and other provisions of the Constitution were violated. In behalf of the President and the Secretary of Industry it was contended that Article 27 must be understood as an exception to Article 14. The District Judge decided against the plaintiff, holding that the Presidential Decree and acts under it did not exceed the provisions of Article 27 which itself ended all private rights to petroleum. On appeal to the Supreme Court,

Held: That the judgment must be reversed. Laws enacted by the ordinary legislature cannot be given retroactive effect, to the prejudice of any person, in view of Article 14 of the Constitution. Laws enacted by the constituent legislature on the other hand should be applied retroactively, notwithstanding Article 14.

Paragraph 4 of Article 27 of the Constitution was not retroactive, either in letter or spirit. "Not by its letter, "because it does not contain the express order in a retroactive "sense, nor is this necessary from its wording. Nor by its "spirit, because such a non-retroactive interpretation is in "accordance with the other Articles of the same Constitution, "which recognise in general the old principles on which rest "the rights of man, and grant them full guarantees; and "because, holding it as not retroactive, it is also in harmony "with the principles expressed in the paragraphs which "immediately precede it . . . and with the provisions relative "to petroleum, which follow it, as integral parts of the same "Article 27 of the Constitution." Rights legitimately acquired

[1] *Amparo* is an extraordinary constitutional writ for relief against infringement of individual guarantees or encroachment upon the federal system. See Benito Flores, *Writ of Amparo*, in *American Bar Association Journal*, vol. VII, p. 388.

before 1 May, 1917, were respected. [Report: *Semanario Judicial*, vol. 9, 5ª *Epoca*, p. 432.]

NOTE.—Although this case does not treat the question as one involving international law or the rights of aliens or foreign corporations, it has been digested as being the principal adjudication upon the meaning of Article 27 as it affected petroleum concessions and petroleum-bearing lands owned by foreigners in Mexico. There was considerable diplomatic correspondence on this question, particularly between Mexico and the United States. On the international law question see Bullington, *Problems of International Law in the Mexican Constitution of* 1917, in *A.J.*, vol. XXI (1927).

There has been some doubt as to just how much the Court held in this case. For an account of the decision and its effects see Schuster, *The Texas Company's Amparo Case*, in *American Bar Association Journal*, vol. VII, p. 583.

See to the same effect *International Petroleum Co.* v. *President, etc.* (8 May, 1922), *Semanario Judicial*, vol. 10, 5ª *Epoca*, p. 886. See also the cases *International Petroleum Co.* v. *Agente de Petroleo* (10 May, 1922), and *Tamiahua Petroleum Co.* v. *Secretaria de Industria, etc.* (12 May, 1922, two cases), reported without opinion in *ibid.*, vol. 10, p. 1146.

See also the case of *La Bacis Gold Mining Co.*, *ibid.*, vol. 13, p. 428, and footnote.

See for later decrees, diplomatic correspondence and other material on the Mexican oil controversy, Gaither, *The Mexican Constitution of* 1917, in *American Law Review*, vol. LV, p. 481, and the same, *Interpretation of Confiscatory Phases of the Mexican Constitution.*, *ibid*, vol. LVI, p. 39. See cases noted in the footnote to *La Bacis Gold Mining Co.* case, *supra*; and also, *inter alia*, A. Campillo, *Derecho Constitucional Mexicano*, vol. I, pp. 651-691; José Colomo, *La Industria del Petroleo en Mexico* (1927); Diaz Dufoo, *La Cuestión del Petroleo* (1921), especially chap. XIV; Gonzales Roa, *Las Cuestiones Fundamentales de Actualidad en Mexico* (1927), especially pp. 11-48; Salvador Mendoza, *La Controversia del Petroleo*; Genaro Fernandez MacGregor, *La Propriedad Raiz de los Extranjeros en Mexico*, in *Revista Mexicana de Derecho Internacional*, vol. I, p. 28, and the same, *La Fr. 1, Art.* 27 *de la Constitución ¿Viola los Tratados?*, in *ibid.*, vol. I, p. 316; and Francisco G. de Cosio, *El Art.* 27 *de la Constitución . . . en relación con los Tratados*, in *ibid.*, vol. I, p. 561.

III.—Expulsion of Aliens

i.—Right of Expulsion

Aliens—Expulsion—Anarchists—Expulsion Laws Contrary to Treaties—Abrogation of Treaties by Subsequent Legislation. **Case No. 176**

EX PARTE PETTINE.

United States District Court D. Massachusetts. 3 *June*, 1919.

THE FACTS.—This was a petition for habeas corpus.

Case No. 176 *contd.*

Certain Italian aliens in the United States were ordered to be deported as philosophical anarchists under 39 U.S. Stat. L. 874 and 40 *ibid.* 1012. These statutes provided for deportation of aliens who advocated anarchy, and more specifically singled out for deportation those advocating the overthrow of governments, those disbelieving in all government, those proposing assassinations of state heads, etc.

Held: That the petition must be denied. Congress has constitutional power to order the deportation of those aliens whose teachings are considered dangerous to American government and to include philosophical anarchists among those to be deported. In reply to the contention that American citizens were entitled to liberty of speech and that, by a treaty between Italy and the United States, Italians in the United States were entitled to similar privileges, the Court pointed out that the Act of Congress was later in time. A later statute supersedes an earlier inconsistent treaty in so far as its effect as domestic law is concerned. It was said that the enactment was "based upon the idea that the government possesses the "right to determine who shall be members of its community—"a right which may be exercised by all nations." (259 Fed. 733, 736.) [Report: 259 Fed. 733.]

Case No. 177

Aliens—Expulsion—Philosophical Anarchists.

LOPEZ *v.* HOWE, IMMIGRATION COMMISSIONER.

United States Circuit Court of Appeals, Second Circuit. 14 *May*, 1919.

THE FACTS.—This was a petition for habeas corpus. Lopez was a Spanish national who had lived fifteen years in the United States. He was described as a prominent philosophical anarchist working along educational and propagandist lines for conditions of society without organised government. He did not favour the use of force in any way for these ends. He was ordered to be deported under the Immigration Act of 5 February, 1917. (39 U.S. Stat. L. 874.) Section 3 of that Act provided for the exclusion of anarchists without limiting the class to those advocating forcible action. Section 19 provided for deportation within five years of entry of any alien who was within a class prohibited by law; and it provided for deportation at any time of "Any alien who . . . shall be found "... advocating or teaching anarchy, or the overthrow "by force or violence of the government of the United "States or of all forms of law or the assassination of "public officials." The deportation of Lopez was approved by the Secretary of Labor. The writ was refused by the United States District Court. On appeal,

Held: That the appeal must be dismissed. Congress had the right to exclude or expel aliens at any time. The Immigration Act is to be construed as authorising the deportation of all who advocate anarchy, whether by peaceable education or by violent overthrow of the existing government. "While "the student of social science may discriminate between "philosophical anarchists and other kinds of anarchists, the "act of Congress now under consideration does not." (259 Fed. 401, 405.) [Report: 259 Fed. 401.]

Aliens—Expulsion—Mexican Law in the Matter of. **Case No. 178**

IN RE JUAN GONZÁLEZ DIAZ.

Mexico, Supreme Court. 19 *August*, 1919.

THE FACTS.—Diaz and two relatives were Spanish citizens living in Mexico. They were imprisoned and ordered to be expelled from the country at the direction of the President of Mexico. Relief of *amparo*[1] and *suspención* was asked in their behalf on the ground that their constitutional guarantees had been violated. The District Judge refused them relief, whereupon they appealed, contending that they were "of well-"known rank and property, of quiet habits, hard-"working business men, with houses established in "Vera Cruz, Spanish, and of real property which "yielded enough for them to live on, while they had "never interfered in the political affairs of the country." Article 33 of the Mexican Constitution provided, with reference to aliens, that: "The Executive of the Union "shall have exclusive power to cause all foreigners "whose remaining he deems undesirable at once and

[1] As to *amparo*, see p. 250, footnote.

Case No. 178 *contd.*

"without need of prior legal proceedings to leave the "national territory."

Held: That the judgment must be affirmed. The terms of Article 33 gave the Executive the power to deport aliens without interference by the courts. "Given the power granted to "the President of the Republic by law, the only thing which "would remain for review would be whether the person to "whom it [the power of expulsion] is applied are foreigners or "not. Here that status is proved, by the admission of the "complainant." [Report: *Semanario Judicial,* vol. 5, 5ª *Epoca,* p. 337.]

NOTE.—See the case of *Andrés Calleja* (1 February, 1919), *Semanario Judicial,* vol. 4, 5ª *Epoca,* p. 323, to the same effect.

See also the cases of *Lillie Soriano* (25 August, 1921), *Semanario Judicial,* vol. 9, 5ª *Epoca,* p. 409, and (17 January, 1924), *ibid.,* vol. 14, p. 286; *George S. Coury* (10 November, 1922), *ibid.,* vol. 11, p. 1024; *Mario Bergeron* (2 July, 1924), *ibid.,* vol. 15, p. 25; *Vicente González* (7 October, 1924), *ibid.,* vol. 15, p. 890; and *David G. Guadarrama* (9 December, 1924), *ibid.,* vol. 15, p. 1268. And see A. Campillo, *Derecho Constitucional Mexicano,* vol. I, p. 797.

See also the Chilean case of *Barrios* (31 December, 1918), *Revista de Derecho, Jurisprudencia, y Ciencias Sociales,* vol. 16, p. 576.

And see the Peruvian case of *Oficio al Ministro de Gobierno* (20 June, 1920), *Anales Judiciales,* 1920, p. 243, in which the Supreme Court approved the Executive's power to watch over the interests of the country, but held illegal a law providing for substitution of police functionaries for the judiciary in matters of expulsion of aliens.

Case No. 179

Aliens—Expulsion—Brazilian Law—Expulsion as a Measure of Self-Defence.

IN RE EVERARDO DIAZ.

Brazil, Supreme Federal Tribunal. 8 *November,* 1919.

THE FACTS.—Diaz was a Spanish anarchist, well known as a communist and anarchist and as a counsellor of the use of violence. He had helped with a bombing in the Argentine in 1909, and had served six years in prison as a result. He had issued various revolutionary statements and writings, including attempts to induce the soldiers of Brazil to strike. In consequence, he was ordered to be expelled. He applied for habeas corpus, claiming that he had six children born in Brazil, that he was an elector, and that he had been naturalised by virtue of the fact that he was in the country in 1889 when the Republic was declared and had not chosen to retain his nationality of origin. Consequently he claimed that he could not be expelled.

Held : That habeas corpus must be denied. Diaz had failed to prove himself a Brazilian. There was not sufficient evidence that he had been in Brazil in 1889 and had not declared for his former nationality. The declaration of a single witness was insufficient. Although he had Brazilian children and lived in Brazil, he had not married a Brazilian, nor did the evidence show that he owned realty in Brazil. His qualification as an elector did not prove his nationality, since such registration as an elector would prove Brazilian nationality only if given before 1908. It was true that Diaz had been resident in the country for more than two continuous years (Article 3, *decreto* 1641 of 1907), but this Article, which enacts that a foreigner resident in the Republic for more than two continuous years cannot be expelled, was revoked by Decree 2741 of 1918. The expulsion of a foreigner, despite guarantees of the Brazilian Constitution, was justified : " It is an accepted " principle in Public International Law that the State has the " power, as an attribute of sovereignty, to expel from its terri- " tory or to prohibit from entering it foreigners harmful to the " social security or public order. It is a right of conservation, " of defence, inherent in the organisation of the State ; it does " not depend on the law that recognises it ; it is enough that " the law does not prohibit its exercise." Neither Article 72 of the Constitution nor any other constitutional provisions secure to the alien the right to enter into Brazil, to reside there, or to remain there when a duly proven serious reason which concerns the defence of the State, its social tranquillity, or the public order, demanded that he should be prevented from landing or that he should withdraw from the national territory. Except when there is a law to the contrary, the time of residence, however long, did not prevent the application of this right of expulsion. The civil equality between resident aliens and nationals was not complete. However, since the foreigner had the right of resort to the judicial power by habeas corpus, there existed a remedy against the possible abuse of the right of expulsion. According to Article 1 of the Decree of 1907, the first of the causes of expulsion was that a foreigner, for whatever reason, placed the public security or tranquillity in danger. The State had no obligation to be burdened with the difficult work, at times ineffective, of constant vigilance over the actions of foreigners putting their theory into practice. It need not

Case No. 179 ***contd.*** await overt action on the part of such aliens. [Report: *Revista do Supremo Tribunal*, vol. 26, p. 19.]

NOTE.—There was a strong dissent based on the ground that the Constitution had been violated.

See the case of *Angelo Soave* (5 May, 1920), *ibid.*, vol. 26, p. 296, and *ibid.*, vol. 24, p. 55.

For a different state of affairs, created by Law 4247 of 6 January, 1921, see the case of *Modesto Pugas Roméro* (27 May, 1921), *Revista do Supremo Tribunal*, vol. 31, p. 40, and *Revista de Direito*, vol. 67, p. 324: "At present Article 2 of law 4247 . . . orders that there cannot be "expelled from national territory any alien who resides in the country "for more than five years uninterruptedly. Now, it is certain that an "examination of the papers shows clearly that the applicant is Spanish, "is an anarchist, is a dangerous element, and for this alone was expelled "by the order of 21 February. But it is also certain that . . . he has "resided in the country for over ten years and for that reason that his "expulsion is clearly contrary to law."

Upholding expulsion of a foreigner, see the cases of *Antonio Manoel Pereira* (28 July, 1924), *Revista do Supremo Tribunal*, vol. 67, p. 440 ("element harmful to public order and national security"); *Manoel Peres* (24 September, 1923), *ibid.*, vol. 63, p. 23 ("dangerous to public "order"); *Benedicto Fugagnoli* (29 November, 1919), *ibid.*, vol. 23, p. 220, and *José Madeira* (30 May, 1921), *ibid.*, vol. 35, p. 32 (anarchists); *Sebastião de Paiva* (5 July, 1920), *ibid.*, vol. 24, p. 212 (bolshevist); *Amaro José Marques Pereira* (1 October, 1920), *Revista Forense*, vol. 37, p. 385, and *Julio Aulicino* (24 September, 1919), *Revista do Supremo Tribunal*, vol. 21, p. 464 (various crimes). On necessary proof of crime before allowing expulsion, see the cases of *Arthur do Mascimento* (29 November, 1922), *ibid.*, vol. 51, p. 60; *Gedale Kastzke* (31 January, 1924), *ibid.*, vol. 83, p. 15; *Manoel Pereira da Silva* (9 June, 1924), *ibid.*, vol. 83, p. 25; and *Salomão Brulkind* (1 and 8 December, 1923), *ibid.*, vol. 83, p. 7.

That only an alien can be expelled, see the cases of *Antonio Bernardo Canellas* (20 April, 1920), *Revista de Direito*, vol. 61, p. 84; and *Adriano Pinto do Costa* (3 December, 1919), *Revista Forense*, vol. 34, p. 501, holding the criminal to be a Portuguese. That one tacitly naturalised by living in Brazil, having Brazilian children, and acquiring Brazilian realty cannot be expelled, since he is in the same legal position as a citizen, see the case of *Manoel Carvalho* (14 June, 1920), *Revista do Supremo Tribunal*, vol. 25, p. 149. Allowing expulsion, however, of one who had proved himself an elector, see the principal case and that of *Adriano Pinto do Costa* (8 November, 1919), *Revista Forense*, vol. 35, p. 89.

That a foreigner cannot be expelled if he has been resident for more than five years, see the cases of *Modesto Pugas Roméro*, above, and *Manoel Simon* (3 December, 1921), *Revista do Supremo Tribunal*, vol. 40, p. 49, and *ibid.*, vol. 39, p. 25; *João Baptista Mineiro* (16 May, 1921), *ibid.*, vol. 31, p. 38; *Pedro Lontrato* (23 October, 1922), *ibid.*, vol. 65, p. 7; and see also the case of *Abilio Cabral*, *ibid.*, vol. 24, p. 211. Holding that an order of the President is not sufficient for expulsion of a resident alien, see the case of *Alfredo Bertelli* (21 June, 1919), *Revista de Direito*, vol. 62, p. 105.

That those ordered to be expelled or deported must not be kept in prison indefinitely or for more than thirty days, see the cases of *João Marchante* (25 October, 1920), *Revista Forense*, vol. 37, p. 387; *Alexandre Schultz or Schwart* (10 July, 1922), *Revista do Supremo Tribunal*, vol. 51, p. 48, and *ibid.*, vol. 52, p. 51; *Giuseppe Scalia* (16 July, 1923), *ibid.*, vol. 62, p. 33; *Juan Filíos* (1 August, 1923), *ibid.*, vol. 62, p. 40; *Pedro Maurini* (3 September, 1923), *ibid.*, vol. 75, p. 13.

For a case in which the criminal had been ordered to be expelled, then seized to be surrendered in extradition, and when the requesting country failed to go through with the extradition the police again ordered expulsion, see the case of *Felippe Beuthenot ou Luigi Morelli* (12 and 31 May, 1924), *ibid.*, vol. 64, pp. 167 and 485.

Decisions dealing with the return of an alien once expelled, and with the prescription of the offence of returning, include the cases of *Mauricio Baumblatt* (21 July, 18 August, 15 September, 1924), *ibid.*, vol. 67, p. 331, *ibid.*, vol. 69, p. 403, and *ibid.*, vol. 89, p. 20; *Manoel Luiz da Cunha e José Maria de Carvalho* (26 August, 1922, and 3 December, 1923), *ibid.*, vol. 50, p. 65, and *ibid.*, vol. 62, p. 89; and *Domingos Real* (10 May, 1924), *ibid.*, vol. 65, p. 32.

Other cases where expulsion was allowed include those of *Manoel Saavedra* (4 October, 1920), *ibid.*, vol. 26, p. 34; *João Micelle* (17 April, 1922), *Diario Official* for 13 July, 1922; and *Alexandre Schwarts* (12 June, 1922), *Diario Official* for 20 August, 1922.

On this general topic see Francisco de Paula Lacerda de Almeida, *O Decreto n.* 1641 *sobre expulsão de estrangeiros*; and Bevilaqua's *Direito Publico Internacional*, vol. II, pp. 65-71.

ii.—Procedure of Expulsion

Aliens—Expulsion of Aliens—In Cases of Claim to Citizenship—Procedure.

Case No. 180

NG FUNG HO *ET AL. v.* WHITE, COMMISSIONER OF IMMIGRATION.

United States Supreme Court. 29 *May*, 1922.

THE FACTS.—These were petitions for habeas corpus by Chinese held for deportation under warrants issued by the Secretary of Labor pursuant to the United States Immigration Act of 1917, § 19 (39 U.S. Stat. L. 874, 889). The petitioners had entered the United States before the Immigration Act became effective, but within five years of the commencement of the deportation proceedings, and they contended that they could be deported only under the Chinese Exclusion Acts which required judicial proceedings. Two of the petitioners claimed that they were foreign-born children of native-born citizens and that they had been examined upon arrival at San Francisco, and had been ordered to be admitted as citizens. The District Court

Case No. 180 *contd.*

remanded petitioners to the custody of the immigration authorities. The judgment was affirmed by the Circuit Court of Appeals for the Ninth Circuit, except as to one appellant who was ordered to be released. (266 Fed. 765.) On certiorari,

Held: That the judgment must be affirmed as to petitioners not claiming citizenship; but that, as to those claiming citizenship, writs of habeas corpus should issue remanding them to the District Court to have their citizenship determined. Chinese who entered the United States before the Immigration Act of 1917 could be deported nevertheless, on the ground of remaining unlawfully in the United States. Remaining unlawfully in the United States was a deportable offence separate and distinct from unlawful entry. Those who claimed to be citizens and had shown sufficient evidence of citizenship to obtain an order admitting them as such were entitled to judicial trial. "Jurisdiction in the executive to order deportation "exists only if the person arrested is an alien. The claim of "citizenship is thus a denial of an essential jurisdictional fact. ". . . If the jurisdiction of the Department of Labor may not "be tested in the courts by means of the writ of habeas corpus "when the prisoner claims citizenship and makes a showing "that his claim is not frivolous, then, obviously, deportation of "a resident may follow upon a purely executive order, whatever "his race or place of birth." (259 U.S. 276, 284.) This would contravene the provisions of the Fifth Amendment to the Constitution of the United States guaranteeing due process of law. [Report: 259 U.S. 276.]

Case No. 181

Aliens—Expulsion—Procedure in Case of Non-Recognition of Alien's Government.

EX PARTE MATTHEWS.

United States District Court, W.D. Washington.
3 *October*, 1921.

THE FACTS.—This was a petition for habeas corpus. The petitioner was found to be a native of Kamenetz, in the province of Podole, Ukrainia, and was ordered to be deported to Ukrainia.[1] The United States had no diplomatic relations with Ukrainia. Meanwhile the petitioner had been held in confinement.

[1] As to the status of the Ukrainian Soviet Socialist Republic, see *The Jupiter, Annual Digest*, 1925-1926, Case No. 100 (The Facts).

Held: That the writ must be granted. An alien held in confinement on a deportation warrant which the Government is unable to execute because of uncertainty as to the country of his nativity or the absence of a recognised Government there is entitled to discharge on habeas corpus. [Report: 277 Fed. 857.]

Aliens—Expulsion—Expulsion Subsequent to Option of Nationality.

See Case No. 152 (*A. F.* v. *Government of the Federal Country (Landesregierung) of Vienna*).

D. EXTRADITION

I.—Extradition in General

Extradition—In General—International Law of Extradition Independent of Extradition Treaties—Principle that a Person must only be tried for the Offence for which he is Extradited—Extradition Treaties and State Succession as between Austria-Hungary and Czechoslovakia. **Case No. 182**

EXTRADITION (GERMANY AND CZECHOSLOVAKIA) CASE.

Germany, Reichsgericht in Criminal Matters. 4 *April,* 1921.

THE FACTS.—The accused was extradited from Czechoslovakia on the charge of larceny coupled with the charge of being a habitual thief. There was at that time no extradition treaty between Czechoslovakia and Germany, and the extradition took place by virtue of an *ad hoc* agreement. The accused was subsequently convicted in Germany not only of the crime for which he had been extradited, but also of the unlawful export of horses. The public prosecutor himself then appealed against the conviction on the ground that as the accused was extradited for larceny only, the conviction ought to have been confined to this crime.

Held, on final appeal on a point of law: That the appeal must be allowed.

The pre-war extradition treaty between Germany and Austria was not applicable to Czechoslovakia although her territory was largely composed of former Austrian territory. For the States which have arisen on the territories of the

Case No. 182 *contd.* Austrian Empire cannot be regarded as succeeding automatically to the rights and duties of that Empire. In the absence of an extradition treaty between the two countries, questions of extradition were governed by relevant rules of international law which recognise, *inter alia*, the so-called principle of speciality according to which the requesting State may prosecute the extradited person only for those offences in respect of which extradition was granted. This principle applies also to extradition treaties or to special *ad hoc* extradition agreements except when they contain provisions to the contrary. [Report: *E.R.S.*, vol. 55, p. 284.]

Case No. 183

Extradition—In General—Treaty Provisions and Municipal Legislation in the Matter of.

In re Hurlimann.

Italy, Criminal Court of Cassation (Second Division).
7 October, 1921.

The Facts.—Hurlimann, a Swiss subject, charged with frauds committed at Lugano to the total amount of 98,000 francs, fled to Milan. The Swiss Government asked for his extradition, on the basis of a warrant of the Public Prosecutor of Lugano dated 21 July, 1921. The *sezione d'accusa* of the Court of Appeal of Milan, by a judgment of 15 September, 1921, rejected Hurlimann's application for release and decided that it could consent to his extradition to the Swiss Government. Hurlimann appealed against this judgment to the Court of Cassation. He based his appeal on the alleged breach of Article 641 of the Italian Code of Criminal Procedure, inasmuch as the *sezione d'accusa* granted extradition without first making an investigation ordained by such Article to see whether or not there existed sufficient evidence of guilt on the part of the accused in order to ascribe the crime to him.[1]

Held by the Court of Cassation: That the appeal must be dismissed and the judgment confirmed. Article 635 of the Code of Criminal Procedure provides, so far as it relates to extradition, that conventions and international usages are to be observed, and that it is only in the absence of these that the

[1] Article 641 (*c*) is to the effect that the Court must see if the particulars of the charge offer sufficient indication of guilt as regards the accused.—[Ed.]

provisions of Articles 640-650 of the Code of Criminal Procedure (which relate to extradition) apply. "Since the convention "between Switzerland and Italy (which cannot be altered "without openly breaking it, not even by a statute made by "us afterwards, but only by a new treaty made between the "contracting parties) prescribes in Article 9 thereof that "extradition must be granted on the basis of the mere pro- "duction of a warrant, it precludes any enquiries as to the "sufficiency of the *prima facie* case as to the crime with which "the accused is charged." There was no breach of Article 641 of the Code of Criminal Procedure seeing that that Article is inapplicable in face of the provisions of Article 9 of the Italo-Swiss Extradition Treaty. [Reports: *Giurisprudenza Italiana*, 1921, p. 454; *Procedura Penale*, 1921, p. 462.]

NOTE.—See to the same effect the case of *Kleiber*, decided by the Italian Criminal Court of Cassation (First Division) on 31 July, 1920 (*Procedura Penale*, 1921, p. 50). See also to the same effect *In re Poretti*, decided by the Italian Criminal Court of Cassation (First Division) on 10 April, 1922. The case was decided on the basis of the special convention of 22 July, 1868, between Italy and Switzerland according to which the mere presentation of the warrant of arrest is sufficient for the grant of extradition. [Report: *Foro Italiano*, 1922, Part II[a], pp. 224, 225.] See also *In re Sittig*, decided by the Court of Cassation on 20 June, 1914 (*Repertorio del Foro Italiano*, 1915).

There are, however, other conventions (for example, Article 9 of the Treaty of Extradition between Italy and England of 25 March, 1873) according to which the extradition of an accused person cannot be granted unless there be some evidence against him that would justify his arrest in the territory of either of the two contracting States. See *Foro Italiano*, 1922, Part II[a], pp. 69, 70.

Extradition—Extradition in Absence of Extradition Treaty. **Case No. 184**

IN RE BEYTÍA.

Chile, Supreme Court. 16 April, 1920.

THE FACTS.—Beytía, a Chilean, had altered certain legal documents with fraudulent intent. Investigations were made and an order of arrest issued against him. He did not appear, and it was learned that he had fled to Bolivia. The papers were then sent up to the Supreme Court for its decision as to whether the extradition should be requested from Bolivia.

Held: That extradition should not be requested. The Supreme Court passes on the question whether Chile should request extradition. There was no treaty with Bolivia, and the request "would have to be based upon the principles of

Case No. 184 *contd.* "international law, or reciprocity," which in this case could not be offered. This crime was not one for which Chilean penal legislation authorised the Government to surrender criminals, except under treaty. [Report: *Revista de Derecho, Jurisprudencia, y Ciencias Sociales*, vol. 18, p. 391.]

NOTE.—On the practice of the courts before requesting extradition, see the cases of *Carlos Gomez Santander* (21 March, 1919), 1[er] *Sem., Gaceta de los Tribunales*, p. 139; *Ramon Blanco del Val* (2 April, 1921), 1921, 1[er] *Sem., ibid.*, p. 562; and *Pedro Alejandro Flores* (28 August, 1923), 1923, 2° *Sem., ibid.*, p. 341. See also the case of *Riveros* (20 October, 1920), *Revista de Derecho, Jurisprudencia, y Ciencias Sociales*, vol. 19, p. 409. In the last case request for extradition was disapproved on the ground that there was insufficient proof as to just what offence the accused had committed and that he could only be tried for the crime for which he was extradited.

On the same practice in Venezuela see the Venezuelan cases of *Francisco Azpúrua Alcántara* (12 December, 1922, and 8 February, 1923), *Memoria*, 1923, p. 197; *ibid.*, 1924, p. 121; *Armando Martínez* (9 March, 1920), *ibid.*, 1921, p. 122; *Manuel Badell* (24 June, 1920), *ibid.*, 1921, p. 134; *Rubén Arturo Rojas* (13 July, 1920), *ibid.*, 1921, p. 136; and *Simon Rojas Negrón* (23 April, 1923), *ibid.*, 1924, p. 133.

Case No. 185

Extradition—In General—Handing over of Accused without Extradition Proccedings.

DELIVERY WITHOUT EXTRADITION (GERMANY) CASE.

Germany, Reichsgericht in Criminal Matters. 24 *March*, 1922.

THE FACTS.—This was a prosecution for fraud and forging documents. The accused fled into Dutch territory, from where, without any extradition proceedings, he was brought by a Dutch policeman over the frontier and handed over to German authorities. The accused contended that as there had been no extradition proceedings, as provided in the Extradition Treaty between Germany and Holland of 31 December, 1896, the prosecution could not be proceeded with.

Held, on final appeal on a point of law: That the absence of extradition proceedings was irrelevant. The extradition treaty with Holland does not contain any provision which confers upon an accused person who has been handed over without any extradition proceedings the right to invoke the absence of extradition proceedings as a reason preventing prosecution. The fact that the accused succeeded in crossing the frontier does not therefore confer upon him the right to claim impunity. [Report: *Juristische Wochenschrift*, 1922, p. 1588.]

II.—Extraditable Crimes

Extradition—Extraditable Crimes—Procedure of Extradition —Construction of Extradition Treaties—Amendment of Request. **Case No. 186**

IN RE MARTOREL (MARTORELL).

United States District Court for Porto Rico.

29 *July and* 10 *August*, 1920.

THE FACTS.—This was a petition for habeas corpus by Martorel, a Cuban, held for extradition on request of the Cuban Consul-General under an Extradition Treaty (33 U.S. Stat. L. 2265) and by warrant of the United States Commissioner. The extradition was asked for on the ground that Martorel had committed the crime of " falsification of public documents." Among the extradition crimes included in the Treaty were forgery, or falsification of official acts or documents of government or public authority ; while under another heading were included perjury and subornation of perjury. The Treaty provided that extradition should be in conformity with the laws of the rendering State. The United States statute provided for extradition hearings before a judge or commissioner. (U.S. Comp. Stat. [1918] § 10110 ; see 9 U.S. Stat. L. 302.) If the judge or commissioner considered the evidence sufficient to sustain the charge, he should give a certificate to that effect, send a copy of the testimony to the Secretary of State, and issue a warrant for commitment to jail of the person charged. Some of the evidence introduced against Martorel was hearsay of a kind allowed in Spanish-Cuban procedure but not at common law, but there was other evidence before the Commissioner. The evidence submitted tended to prove that Martorel had secured a person to give false evidence so as to acquire certain property.

Held : That the prisoner must be kept in custody, pending final order, so that Cuba might issue a new request. The Commissioner could properly hold his hearing before certifying the testimony to the Secretary of State, and the prisoner could be remanded in custody pending such certification. (*Grin* v. *Shine*, 187 U.S. 181.) On habeas corpus, the hearing before the Commissioner could only be reviewed to determine whether

Case No. 186 ***contd.*** the crime alleged is within the Treaty and whether the evidence would justify commitment for trial. There was evidence enough before the Commissioner to justify the remand. Although the Spanish terms might be so broad that the offence which the proof tended to show would come under the words translated " falsification of public documents," it would seem that the offence was rather that of subornation of perjury. Therefore the Cuban officials should have a chance to request his extradition for that offence.

> FURTHER FACTS.—On a later hearing it was contended that the proceedings in Cuba were for "*falsedad en* "*documentos oficiales*," which was not the same as " falsification of public documents " and was not a treaty crime. There was in addition some evidence presented that Martorel had caused certain persons to make false or forged statements in a deed.

Held: That the petitioner must be remanded in custody for extradition. The "*falsedad*" referred to was covered by the spirit of the English phrase. Although Martorel could not be tried for an entirely different offence from that for which his extradition was asked, nothing prevented the Cuban courts from changing their theory of action in the penal proceedings there to agree with the crime for which Martorel was extradited. " In the construction of extradition treaties, technicalities in " criminal proceedings are applicable only to a limited extent, " since an exact correspondence between the laws of the two " countries cannot be expected." (12 P.R. Fed. 77, 79.) In the civil law, a deed was in some respects a quasi-judicial proceeding. The Court was not bound to look too technically into whether the act was a common law forgery, where " the " wickedness of the act, the fraudulent intent with which it " was committed, and the final success by which the fraud " was perpetrated, are undoubted." (12 P.R. Fed. 77, 81.) Furthermore, by Porto Rican law all persons engaged in any way in the commission of a crime are principals; while in Cuba it had been held that one procuring another to sign a deed falsely was himself guilty of falsification of a public document. Accordingly, the procuring of this deed was here an additional reason for extradition. [Report: 12 P.R. Fed. 50, 77.]

Extradition—Extraditable Crimes—Extradition of Nationals—Conditions of Extradition—Procedure—Political Criminals—Trading with the Enemy as a Political Crime. **Case No. 187**

In re Dr. Paulo Deleuze.

Brazil, Supreme Federal Tribunal. 29 *April*, 1922.

The Facts.—France asked Brazil to extradite Deleuze for the crimes of *escroquerie* (cheating) and trading with the enemy of which he had been convicted by a French court although he was in Brazil at the time. Deleuze, through his attorney Ruy Barbosa, sought preventive habeas corpus against extradition, alleging, *inter alia :* (*a*) the acts for which he had been convicted did not constitute crimes ; (*b*) trading with the enemy was not a crime by Brazilian law, and in any case was a political crime for which extradition could not be granted, while *escroquerie* was connected with the political crime ; (*c*) he had been convicted without service of notice of the proceedings and in default ; (*d*) French courts lacked jurisdiction, since the acts were done in Brazil and Switzerland ; (*e*) the crime, if any, had, by the time of the action, been affected by a statute of limitation ; (*f*) he was a resident foreigner who could not be extradited, since France refused reciprocal surrender of nationals.

Held : That the petition for habeas corpus must be refused, since none of the grounds enumerated were available to the petitioner.[1]

(*a*) The acts charged were made criminal by French law. Habeas corpus is granted when the acts, even if committed by defendants, would not be a crime ; but not where it is necessary to decide whether in the alleged facts the elements of the crime are found fully expressed.

(*b*) Deleuze was convicted of two different crimes. Although trading with the enemy was political from its nature, yet the *escroquerie* was a common crime. The judgment did not speak of any connection between the two crimes. Furthermore, " our " law only refuses to concede extradition when the crime was " political, and not when there was connected with it a viola- " tion of the ordinary law."

(*c*) (*d*) (*e*) It was not possible to go behind the terms of

[1] As a preliminary question, the majority of the Tribunal considered that habeas corpus was a proper remedy.

Case No. 187 ***contd.*** the French judgment on the questions of notice, territorial jurisdiction, or prescription, since the French judgment specifically covered these matters.[1] The State requested has only to judge the external questions of the extradition petition, for instance, the identity of the person sought, the formal defects of the documents presented, etc. As has been said, "the justice of the country of asylum does not judge the "alleged criminal, but only the extradition." "If, in the "adjudication on the extradition petition, we cannot question "the facts given as proved by French justice, *a fortiori* we "cannot do so in this most summary action of habeas corpus."

(*f*) Law 2146, Article 1, § 2, provided : "Lack of reciprocity "shall not impede extradition in the case of one naturalised "after the commission of the crime charged by the petition "of the country where the offence was committed." Brazil had made some concessions towards surrender of nationals ; and, even where they were not handed over, there was usually an "exception for naturalised citizens, when the crime had "been committed before the naturalisation, for all publicists "and authorised jurisconsults teach that naturalisation does "not have retroactive effect." This exception ought to be applied to resident foreigners where the residence has been effected subsequent to the acts charged in the petition. Thus want of reciprocity did not prevent the surrender. [Reports : *Revista do Supremo Tribunal*, vol. 44, p. 35 ; *ibid.*, vol. 39, p. 277 ; and *Revista Forense*, vol. 39, p. 172, with dissent in *ibid.*, vol. 40, p. 159.]

NOTE.—Cases granting extradition, where all legal or treaty requirements were satisfied, include those of *Ferdinand Barbier* (4 June, 1921), *Revista do Supremo Tribunal*, vol. 38, p. 137 (and see *ibid.*, vol. 69, p. 3) ; *David Calcabrini* (30 November, 1921), *Diario Official* for 1 April, 1924, p. 8702 ; *Manoel Calvet de Magelhaes* (28 January, 1922), *Revista do Supremo Tribunal*, vol. 52, p. 19 ; *Hermann Bastiann* (31 January, 1923), *ibid.*, vol. 52, p. 163 ; and *Erwin Martin Mertin* (17 September, 1924), *ibid.*, vol. 77, p. 145 (and see also *ibid.*, vol. 71, p. 377).

On requisite papers, see the cases of *Fritz Niebisch* (19 May, 1920), *ibid.*, vol. 26, p. 358 ; *Clodomino Suárez* (6 May, 1922), *ibid.*, vol. 77, p. 144 ; *Pablo Menaly* (25 October, 1922), *ibid.*, vol. 57, p. 1 ; and *Candido Resaro Aranaz* (12 July, 1924), *ibid.*, vol. 77, p. 144.

On procedural questions, see the cases of *Fritz Georg Frickmann* (17 July, 1922), *ibid.*, vol. 47, p. 58 (and *ibid.*, vol. 51, p. 57) ; and *Emile Weyermann* (June, 1922), *ibid.*, vol. 52, p. 43, *ibid.*, vol. 44, p. 161, *ibid.*, vol. 51, p. 46, *ibid.*, vol. 41, pp. 189 and 226.

---

[1] The French judgment spoke of Deleuze as "*en fuite*," "*sans domicile* "*connu*," and "*non comparant, bien que régulièrement cité*," and said that the crimes were committed "*sur le territoire français et à l'étranger*" and "*depuis* "*un temps non prescrit.*"

See, to the effect that nationals will not be surrendered under treaty with Uruguay, the case of *Waltrudes Lopes Leal* (26 September, 1921), *Diario Official* for 13 July, 1922, p. 13598. Insisting on a promise not to inflict the death penalty on one extradited, see the case of *Hector Thuysbaert* (7 April, 1923), *Revista do Supremo Tribunal*, vol. 52, p. 164. See the case of *Joseph Aldenhoff* (12 July, 1922), *ibid.*, vol. 44, p. 163, to the effect that while Brazilian law did not punish the counterfeiting of foreign money, yet this involved defrauding and therefore was an extraditable crime.

That extradition should be requested through diplomatic channels and passed upon by the Federal Supreme Court rather than in other ways or by inferior courts, see the cases of *Henrique Baltor* (11 April, 1921), *ibid.*, vol. 29, p. 27, and *Revista de Direito*, vol. 68, p. 138; and *Arnaldo dos Santos* (10 December, 1919), *Revista do Supremo Tribunal*, vol. 36, p. 15.

Approving *prisão preventiva* or *provisoria*, see the cases of *David Calcabrini* (23 November, 1921), *ibid.*, vol. 51, p. 7; *Antonio Mora Carmona* (9 April, 1923), *ibid.*, vol. 55, p. 34; *Frederick Bastian* (24 January, 1923), *ibid.*, vol. 55, p. 30; and *Erwin Martin* (18 August, 1924), *ibid.*, vol. 75, p. 37. But that this must not continue longer than 60 or 70 days, respectively, without petition being presented, see the cases of *Dioscorides de la Rosa* (7 August, 1922), *ibid.*, vol. 55, p. 7; and *Robert Martin Kosching* (6 August, 1923), *ibid.*, vol. 62, p. 40. Allowing habeas corpus where extradition had been granted but had not been effected within twenty days by the requesting country, see the case of *Alfeo dos Santos Faria* (7 June, 1920), *ibid.*, vol. 28, p. 13.

On extradition in Brazil in general, see Puente in M.L.R., vol. 28, p. 665; and the cases of *Arthur Briggs, Extradicão* (1909); *Clovis Bevilaqua, Direito Publico Internacional*, vol. II, pp. 123 ff.; and *José Mendes, ibid.*, vol. II, pp. 402 ff.

III.—Extradition of Nationals

Extradition—Extradition of Nationals—Resumption of Criminal Prosecution against German Citizen in the Canton where the Offence was Committed (Canton of Thurgau) after the Request to Take up Proceedings was Refused by the German Authorities. **Case No. 188**

In re Neumann.

Switzerland, Federal Court. 18 *June*, 1921.

The Facts.—Fritz Neumann, a German citizen, formerly resident in the Canton of Thurgau (Switzerland), was indicted for blackmail by the Criminal Prosecutor of that Canton. As he had in the meantime transferred his residence to Germany (Baden), the Governing Council of Thurgau through the Swiss Department of Justice asked the German authorities to take over the criminal proceedings. The request was refused on the

Case No. 188 ***contd.***

ground of the German Amnesty Decree of 7 December, 1918, in favour of persons who participated in the war. The Criminal Prosecutor of Thurgau then decided to resume proceedings against the accused, who was sentenced *in contumaciam* by the *Kriminalkammer* of Thurgau to hard labour, banishment from the country for life, and restitution of the money extorted. Counsel for Neumann appealed to the Federal Court on the ground of the violation of the German-Swiss Extradition Treaty.[1] The violation of the Treaty consisted, in his opinion, in the fact that the accused was prosecuted in the Canton of Thurgau notwithstanding the amnesty granted in his home State. As, according to Article 2 of that Treaty,[2] it was not admissible to extradite the accused, the Canton of Thurgau was, it was urged, bound to hand over the question of punishment to the home State and to put up with the manner in which that home State disposed of the prosecution.

Held: That the appeal must be dismissed. The provision of Article 2, paragraph 1, of the German-Swiss Extradition Treaty exempting the nationals of the contracting parties from extradition is an exception from the reciprocal engagement to extradite persons who are prosecuted or have been sentenced for an extraditable offence in one State whilst resident in the territory of the other. The effect of this provision is merely to confer upon the prosecuted or convicted person a claim against his own State not to be extradited. It does not confer upon the home State a right to prosecute; neither does it impose an obligation on the requesting State (which is generally the State where the offence was committed) not to prosecute. In addition, it follows from paragraph 2 of Article 2 of the German-Swiss Extradition Treaty, where in the case of non-extradition a mutual duty of legal assistance is stipulated, that in such cases the home State, which may deny extradition, is not bound to proceed with the prosecution and conviction. The extradition treaty cannot be regarded as

[1] According to Article 113, No. 3, of the Swiss Federal Constitution, the Federal Court is competent, *inter alia*, to deal with complaints of private individuals against violations of treaties.

[2] Article 2, paragraphs 1 and 2, provide as follows: "However, there shall "be no extradition of a German to the Swiss Government and no extradition "of a Swiss to the German Government. If according to the laws of the "home State of the accused he is liable to prosecution, then the other State "shall transmit to the home State all information and documents necessary "for the elucidation of the facts."

violated by the resumption of the prosecution in the Canton of Thurgau. Even if prosecution and conviction had been admissible by German law, the right of Thurgau to prosecute would still remain unaffected. The latter's right would only have been affected by a completed prosecution in Germany, as the result of the operation of the maxim *ne bis in idem*. [Report: *Entscheidungen des schweizerischen Bundesgerichtes*, 47, I, p. 332.]

Extradition—Extradition of Nationals—Treaty Right to Refuse Extradition—Not Excluding the Faculty of Extradition. **Case No. 189**

IN RE EXTRADITION OF LEOCADIO RODRÍGUEZ.

Nicaragua, Supreme Court. 14 *May and* 20 *June*, 1919.

THE FACTS.—Criminal proceedings in Honduras, for theft committed there, were instituted against Rodríguez. He was arrested in Nicaragua and his extradition to Honduras was requested. He objected to extradition on the ground, *inter alia*, that he was a Nicaraguan citizen. On the first hearing, the Supreme Court held that extradition must be granted. The Court held that the proof offered as to his Nicaraguan nationality and his presence in Nicaragua at the time of the crime was insufficient. Rodríguez petitioned again for relief, this time presenting a birth certificate.

Held: That extradition must be allowed. " Although it " is true that Article 4 of the Convention of Extradition, signed " at Washington on 20 December, 1907, established that the " high contracting parties are not obliged to surrender their " nationals, it is also true that it does not establish a strict " obligation to deny extradition, but a mere faculty or right " to be able to do so when judged suitable, for reasons of " general welfare; which leads this Supreme Court to consent " to the extradition, since it thinks that, when the criminal is " judged by the authorities of the jurisdiction where the crime " was committed, the interested parties will contribute to the " cause the necessary elements for the best elucidation of the " truth of the facts, so avoiding impunity for crimes." [Report: *Boletin Judicial de la Gaceta*, 1919, pp. 2333 and 2387.]

NOTE.—See also the case of *J. Amilcar Castillo* (5 April, 1921), *Boletin Judicial de la Gaceta*, p. 3255, likewise allowing surrender of a national.

IV.—Conditions of Extradition

Case No. 190 **Extradition—Crime Committed in a Country by Person Not Physically Present therein—British Extradition Act, 1870.**

REX *v.* GODFREY.

England, High Court of Justice, King's Bench Division. 22 October, 1922.

THE FACTS.—This was an application for a writ of habeas corpus in order to test the legality of the proposed extradition of the applicant to Switzerland on the charge of obtaining goods by false pretences.

By Article 1 of the Extradition Treaty between Great Britain and Switzerland of 26 November, 1880, each party undertook to deliver up to the other criminals of certain kinds " who . . . shall be found " within the territory of that other," but excluding by Article 2 Swiss nationals.

By Section 26 of the Extradition Act, 1870, " the " term ' fugitive criminal ' means any person accused " or convicted of an extradition crime committed " within the jurisdiction of any foreign state who is " in or is suspected of being in some part of [His] " Majesty's dominions ; and the term ' fugitive criminal " ' of a foreign state ' means a fugitive criminal accused " or convicted of an extradition crime committed " within the jurisdiction of that state."

It was alleged that the applicant had obtained goods in Switzerland by false pretences made in Switzerland by his partners upon his procuration or instigation so that he was an accessory before the fact to the offence and therefore, the offence being a misdemeanour, was liable as a principal and ought to be extradited to Switzerland, although he had not been there when the alleged crime was committed or since.

The main contention on behalf of the applicant was that a person could not be a " fugitive criminal " unless he had fled from the country in which he was alleged to have committed the crime. It was also claimed that certain words used in Article 2 of the Swiss treaty (relating to the non-extradition of Swiss nationals) lent support to this view.

Held by the King's Bench Division (Lord Hewart, C.J.,

Avory and Sankey, JJ.) : That the application must be dismissed and the extradition must take place. Neither the Swiss treaty nor the Extradition Act, 1870, required the physical presence of the criminal in the country in which he is alleged to have committed the crime. It is not necessary to the idea of " fugitiveness " that there should be refuge from a foreign country ; refuge from the penal consequences of a criminal act is also comprised within it. The English case of *Reg.* v. *Nillins* (1884), 53 L.J. (M.C.) 157, and the American case of *State* v. *Hall*, 44 Amer. St. Rep. 501, were followed. [Report: L.R. [1923] 1 K.B. 24.]

NOTE.—The main reason why this case is digested is that it illustrates the rule that a crime may be committed within the jurisdiction of a State by one who is not physically present therein, as is shown by the decision of the majority of the Permanent Court of International Justice in *The Lotus* (*Annual Digest*, 1927-1928, Case No. 98), where *R.* v. *Godfrey* is cited. See also *Reg.* v. *Keyn* (1877), L.R. 2 Ex. D. 63 (not an extradition case), and *Reg.* v. *Jacobi and Hiller* (1881), 46 L.T. 595 (note).

Extradition—Arrest by Expeditionary Force in Hot Pursuit of Bandits Analogous to Extradition—Application of Principle of Speciality—Forcible Kidnapping. **Case No. 191**

DOMINGUEZ *v.* STATE.

United States, Texas Court of Criminal Appeals. 24 *June*, 1921.

THE FACTS.—In pursuance of orders given by the War Department authority, a detachment of United States troops crossed the border into Mexico in hot pursuit of certain bandits. Dominguez, a Mexican citizen, was captured and brought back by the expedition. He was subsequently released by the expedition, since it appeared that he was not one of the bandits whom they were pursuing. He was then arrested by Texas authorities and placed on trial for murder. He was convicted, and appealed on the ground of lack of jurisdiction.

Held : That the judgment must be reversed. The entry of troops into Mexico was presumably in accordance with arrangements approved by the Mexican Government. The right of the United States to hold Dominguez was no greater than if he had been extradited. A defendant extradited for one crime could not be tried for another crime unless he had been given a chance to leave the country. (*United States* v. *Rauscher*, 119 U.S. 407.) Where a defendant was not extradited, but was forcibly kidnapped or abducted from a foreign country, he

Case No. 191 *contd.* might be tried if he were brought into the State and there arrested. (*Ker* v. *Illinois*, 119 U.S. 436.) The question was which principle governed the present case. The Court held that this action by the expedition, under the authority of the United States, and presumably pursuant to agreement with Mexico, was not an unlawful kidnapping. "If the apprehension "of appellant was due solely to an honest mistake of fact as "to his identity, the act was not criminal kidnapping or "abduction." (90 Tex. Crim. 92, 98.) Therefore the arrest must be treated as an arrest for extradition, and the principle prohibiting trial for other crimes applied. "The same moral "obligation that would restrain the United States Government "from transgressing the implied limitations upon it under its "treaty with Mexico, would necessarily prevail with reference "to the agreement resting upon the 'comity of nations,' and "if the legal obligation is the same, the appellant cannot be "held for the offense which we are now considering without "the opportunity to return to his country in order that it may "there determine whether he shall be surrendered for trial "under the treaty of extradition." (90 Tex. Crim. 92, 98.) [Reports: 90 Tex. Crim. 92; Dickinson, *Cases*, 755.]

NOTE.—See 20 M.L.R. 536.

Case No. 192 **Conditions of Extradition—Differing Designation of Potential Crimes—Principle that a Person must only be Tried for the Offence for which he is Extradited—Statutes and Extradition Treaties.**

COLLINS *v.* LOISEL, UNITED STATES MARSHAL.

United States Supreme Court. 29 *May*, 1922.

THE FACTS.—This was a petition for habeas corpus. Collins was held in Louisiana for extradition to India to be tried for obtaining property by false pretences. Two questions were involved in the present appeal: (1) Obtaining property by false pretences was included among the extraditable crimes enumerated in the Treaty of 13 December, 1900, between Great Britain and the United States. (32 U.S. Stat. L. 1864.) The Indian Penal Code, like that of Louisiana, made it a crime. However, while the Indian Code referred to it as "cheating," common law "cheating" was not among the crimes enumerated in the Treaty. (2) The evidence introduced at the hearing tended to show that Collins had obtained a pearl button by false pretences.

The law of Louisiana permitted a person charged with crime to produce evidence on his own behalf before the committing magistrate. However, Collins was only allowed to testify to matters which might explain ambiguities or doubts in the *prima facie* case. His petition for habeas corpus was denied by the District Court. On appeal,

Held : That the judgment must be affirmed. (1) " The law " does not require that the name by which the crime is described " in the two countries shall be the same ; nor that the scope of " the liability shall be coextensive, or, in other respects, the " same in the two countries. It is enough if the particular act " charged is criminal in both jurisdictions." (259 U.S. 309, 312.) (2) As pointed out in *Charlton* v. *Kelly*, 229 U.S. 447, 461, there was a distinction between evidence in defence, which may not be given in extradition hearings, and evidence rebutting probable cause for extradition, which must be admitted. Although the procedural law of Louisiana must be followed in an extradition hearing in that State, " no procedural rule of a State could " give to the prisoner a right to introduce evidence made " irrelevant by a treaty." (259 U.S. 309, 317.) [Reports: 259 U.S. 309 ; Dickinson, *Cases*, 733.]

Extradition — Conditions of — Principle that a Person must only be Tried for the Offence for which he is Extradited —Meaning of. **Case No. 193**

IN RE INGLESE.

Italy, Criminal Court of Cassation (First Division).
10 *January*, 1919.

THE FACTS.—A certain Inglese, employed by the State Railways and attached to the Milan Central Station, during the night of the 15th to the 16th April, 1916, abstracted from the management an amount of over three hundred thousand lire contained in bags sent from different railway stations. He then made for Domodossola and succeeded in crossing the frontier. He was quickly identified and arrested by the Swiss authorities and, following a request for extradition, was handed over to the Italian authorities. The extradition was asked and granted for the crime of theft. The Milan Court, by sentence of 4 December, 1917, declared Inglese to be guilty of the crime of peculation and condemned him to a punishment of

Case No. 193 *contd.*

about seven years' imprisonment. The sentence was confirmed by the Court of Appeal of Milan. Inglese now applied for the annulment of the sentence, mainly on the grounds of breach of Article 648 of the Code of Criminal Procedure and of the clauses of the Italo-Swiss Extradition Treaty, which provided that an individual cannot be subjected to punishment for a crime different from that for which extradition is conceded.

Held by the Court of Cassation: That the appeal must be dismissed. Inglese was sentenced for the act committed by him, for and on account of which his extradition was requested from Switzerland. The objection that Inglese was sentenced for a crime (peculation) different from that for which his extradition was requested (theft) is not sound. It is the specific fact constituting the crime that is decisive, and not merely its legal definition. The State granting extradition has only a political interest that the extradited person be not subjected to proceedings in respect of some act different from that for which the extradition was granted. The legal definition of such act may differ in Italian legislation and in that of the foreign State. In fact, Articles 5 and 9 of the Extradition Treaty between Italy and Switzerland speak of alleged acts, and not of crimes, and hardly therefore of the legal definition of those acts. Article 10 of the Treaty includes amongst the acts for which extradition is allowed, misappropriation of money committed by officials and public functionaries. Accordingly, the Court of Appeal was right in holding that, when the extradition of an accused person for a definite criminal act has been consented to by a foreign State, it would be absurd to hold that the national jurisdiction cannot give that act its precise legal definition and apply to the guilty person the appropriate punishment. [Reports: *Giurisprudenza Italiana*, vol. II (1919), p. 199; *Giustizia Penale*, 1919, p. 760; *Monitore dei Tribunali*, 1919, p. 672.]

Case No. 194

Extradition—Identity of Offence Charged with that for which Extradition is Granted.

IN RE NEIKEN.

Canada, District Court of Alberta, Edmonton. 3 *February*, 1922.

THE FACTS.—An application was made for the extradition to Denmark of Neiken, who was charged with :—

(1) Defrauding a person of a gold watch;
and (2) Larceny of an automobile.

Held : (1) That the evidence of the first charge was altogether too vague to justify extradition.

(2) That the evidence seemed to suggest that the second offence was rather fraud by a bailee than actual larceny, and in the Extradition Treaty with Denmark of 1873 these two offences come under different headings. It had been decided that a person cannot be tried for an offence other than that for which he is extradited, and conversely it would seem that a person cannot be extradited for an offence different from that with which he is to be charged. Moreover, fraud by a bailee is not larceny by common law and only became theft by statute, and it would be necessary therefore to prove that it also constitutes larceny by statute in Denmark.

The application was refused.

[Report : (1922) 1 *Western Weekly Reports*, 515.]

NOTE.—The statutory crime of " theft," as defined in the Canadian Criminal Code, includes both the English common law crime of " larceny " and certain other offences of a fraudulent nature.

Compare the recent English case of *R.* v. *Corrigan* (1931), 100 L.J.K.B. 55, 22 Crim. App. R. 106.

Extradition—Conditions of Extradition.

Case No. 195

IN RE ALARCÓN.

Venezuela, Court of Federal Affairs and of Cassation. 10 *October*, 1922.

THE FACTS.—Colombia requested the extradition of Alarcón from Venezuela for the crime of homicide. The necessary papers were appended to the request. Venezuelan penal laws forbade the extradition of a fugitive for any crime which carried a penalty of death or life imprisonment in the requesting country. The Colombian Penal Code of 1889-1890, still in force, made premeditated homicide, in certain cases, the crime of *asesinato* and punished the crime with death. But a Colombian law of 1910 [1] enacted that " the legislature " will not be able to impose the death penalty in any " case," and provided that crimes previously punishable with death should thereafter have a penalty of twenty years' imprisonment. The question of extradition was referred to the Court.

Held : That extradition must be granted. The requisites

[1] *Acto Legislativo de* 1910, No. 3.

Case No. 195 *contd.* of the *Acuerdo del Congreso Boliviano* were fulfilled. The later Colombian legislation prevented the death penalty from being applied. [Report: *Memoria*, 1923, p. 163.]

NOTE.—(1) On the question of death penalty, see Puente, *Principles of International Extradition in Latin America*, in M.L.R., XXVIII, pp. 665, 702, 703; and Reeves, *Extradition Treaties and the Death Penalty*, in *A.J.*, XVIII, p. 298.

(2) For cases granting extradition see the *Humberto Burza* (30 January, 1920), *Memoria*, 1921, p. 107; *Carlos Luis Jácome* (2 August, 1922), *ibid.*, 1923, p. 156; *Luis Solano* (20 April, 1923), *ibid.*, 1924, p. 131; and *Manuel Guerrero* (27 June, 1923), *ibid.*, p. 135. To the effect that papers presented were insufficient, see the case of *Victor Canal V.* (23 July, 1923), *ibid.*, 1924, p. 136.

Case No. 196

Extradition—Conditions of Extradition—Change of Government in State Demanding Extradition.

IN RE ERNESTO DIAZ MUÑOZ.

Mexico, Supreme Court. 8 *July*, 1921.

THE FACTS.—Muñoz was a Spanish subject who came to Mexico from Cuba. At the request of the Cuban Legation he was arrested in Mexico for extradition to Cuba on charges of *robo* (theft) committed in Cuba. A District Judge of the capital held that extradition would be improper on the papers presented, and the President of Mexico thereupon refused the request. A fresh request for extradition was then made, accompanied by new papers, and Muñoz was again taken into custody. These papers were held to be sufficient and extradition was ordered. Subsequently Muñoz appealed to the Supreme Court, contending, *inter alia*, that he could not be extradited because, owing to a change in the Cuban Government, the Legation could not properly request his extradition.

Held: That the judgment must be affirmed. It is within the sole competence of the Executive to grant the request for extradition of the complainant, presented by the Cuban Legation, as coming from the representative of a foreign Government accredited to this country, if the legal requisites are judicially considered satisfied. "It does not fall to the judicial power of "the Federation to pass on or decide concerning the existence "or non-existence of a foreign legation, nor the attributes "which it can exercise." [Report: *Semanario Judicial*, vol. 9, 5ª *Epoca*, p. 112.]

Extradition—Conditions of—Principle that a Person must only be Tried for the Offence for which he has been Extradited —Conventional and Customary International Law Rules of Extradition.

See Case No. 182 (*Extradition* (*Germany and Czechoslovakia*) *Case*).

V.—Procedure of Extradition

Extradition—What is a Demand for—Procedure—Request to Italian Authorities by the Inter-Allied Police at Constantinople through the Italian Ambassador. **Case No. 197**

In re Behar.

Italy, Criminal Court of Cassation (*First Division*).
21 *January*, 1921.

The Facts.—The Italian ambassador at Constantinople had telegraphed to the under-prefect of Brindisi to arrest Behar, an individual of uncertain nationality born in Italy, who had just landed from the steamship *Baron Beck*. Behar was sought for by the inter-allied police as an alleged accomplice in a murder committed at Constantinople. The ambassador added that a detachment of Italian carbineers formed part of such police, and that after Behar had been handed over to them he would be held in custody in the Italian consular prisons in Constantinople and would not be tried without the previous authorisation of the Italian Government, to whom it would fall to make the decision regarding the competent Court. Behar was in fact arrested on his landing at Brindisi. He appealed against this action to the *sezione d'accusa* (chamber for prosecutions) of the Court, which, however, gave judgment to the effect that it was not its place to consider the request for the release of the accused. Behar appealed against this verdict to the Court of Cassation (Article 642 of the Code of Criminal Procedure dealing with the formalities of extradition).

Held by the Court of Cassation: That the appeal must be dismissed and the verdict of the *sezione d'accusa* confirmed. The Court said: " The present case was not one of extradition " within the meaning of the law. Such a question would occur

Case No. 197 *contd.* "if the request had been made by a foreign Government with "the object of proceeding criminally in respect of certain "crimes in the territory of the Government making the request. "In this case the request did not come from the Ottoman "Government but from the Italian Ambassador; the person "arrested is to be taken to the Italian consular prisons so that "the Italian Government may decide on the court competent "to judge the responsibility for the matter. It must be con- "cluded, therefore, that all the essential elements of an extradi- "tion proceeding are lacking here. The case must be regarded "as a police measure on the part of an Italian political author- "ity not subject to the control of the criminal magistrate." [Reports: *Rivista Penale*, vol. 93 (1921), p. 474; *Procedura Penale*, 1921, p. 120.]

Case No. 198 **Extradition—Simultaneous Request by Two Foreign Governments—Competence to Determine the Order of Extradition.**

In re Neuburger and Kleinkramer.

Italy, Criminal Court of Cassation (First Division).
21 December, 1921.

The Facts.—Neuburger and Kleinkramer, neither of whom were of Italian nationality, were arrested in Turin on charges of forgery and fraud committed in Turin. During the preliminary criminal proceedings the Government of Bulgaria and the Government of Roumania asked the Italian Government for the extradition of the two accused for crimes of forgery and fraud committed by them at Sofia and Bucharest respectively. A month before, an identical request for extradition had been presented by the Government of Germany for the crime of embezzlement. The *sezione d'accusa* of the Court of Appeal of Turin, by a judgment of 11 August, 1921, gave a favourable opinion on this request. Afterwards, by another judgment of 13 October, 1921, the same *sezione d'accusa* declared that, provided the proceedings in respect of the crimes committed at Turin be first terminated, the extradition of the two accused asked for by the Governments of Bulgaria and Roumania could also be consented to.

The accused appealed against the last-mentioned judgment, on the ground that new grants of extradition were not possible seeing that extradition had already been granted to Germany by the completed judgment. It was not permissible to speak of eventual preferences between different requests for extradition, not presented contemporaneously. Germany, which has in its favour a sentence preceding the second one by more than a month, has an undoubted acquired right.

Held : That the appeal must be rejected. The Turin *sezione d'accusa* was not competent to decide difficulties which might arise from the fact that, after the extradition of an accused person has been consented to at the request of a given foreign Government, consent was also given to further extraditions of the same person to other Governments. The *sezione d'accusa* must in matters of extradition do no more in any given case than see that the conditions laid down in Article 641 of the Code of Criminal Procedure are adhered to. It is for the Italian Government to decide in each case whether or not extradition should be granted, and to determine the formalities of the grant, and to settle any resulting difficulties in deciding to which of several foreign Governments who have successively asked for the extradition of the same accused person he should be handed over.[1] [Reports: *Scuola Positiva,* vol. II (1922), pp. 289-291, with a note by Professor Cavaglieri; *Rivista Penale,* vol. XCVII, p. 240; *Giustizia Penale,* 1922, p. 598.]

Extradition—Delivery of Objects Connected with the Extraditable Offence. Case No. 199

IN RE BIRNDÖRFER.

Switzerland, Federal Court. 12 *February,* 1921.

THE FACTS.—The German authorities asked for the extradition of the Hotel Manager Birndörfer, who was accused of having bribed police officials in order to frustrate a search in the hotel premises for goods acquired by illicit secret traffic.

Held : That extradition on account of bribery (Article 1 (22) of the Extradition Treaty with Germany) must be granted, but that delivery of the money and other objects found on the

[1] It is understood that before any extradition could take effect the accused would have to serve any sentence of imprisonment pronounced by the Italian Court for the offence committed in Italy.—[Ed.]

Case No. 199 ***contd.*** prisoner must be refused.[1] The first sentence of Article 9 [2] of the German-Swiss Extradition Treaty seemed *prima facie* to support the argument that the extradition is to include all objects found in the possession of the accused irrespective of their connection with the offence for which extradition is sought. This had been the practice of the Federal Council in cases which it had dealt with directly in the absence of opposition. However, the Federal Court adopted in the cases of *Platten* and *Pietsch* (*B.G.E.*, 31, I, p. 694; 34, I, p. 368) a restrictive interpretation, and allowed the delivery of objects only if they had some connection, immediate or remote, with the offence for which extradition was sought. This attitude was not only compatible with the text of the Treaty, but was also in harmony with the nature of extradition and the development of the law of extradition as laid down in the Swiss Extradition Act of 1892 and in the latest extradition treaties. There was no practical objection to a decision on these lines. [Report: *Entscheidungen des schweizerischen Bundesgerichtes*, 47, I, p. 121.]

Case No. 200 **Extradition—Waiver of Extradition by Offender—Trial Limited to Offence for which Extradition could have been Granted.**

REX *v.* FLANNERY.

Canada, Supreme Court of Alberta, Appellate Division.
7 July, 1923.

THE FACTS.—The accused had committed a serious assault on a woman in Canada, and had fled to the United States. He was arrested on a charge of attempted murder, waived extradition, and returned to Canada. An alternative count was added to the indictment charging him " with intent to do grievous bodily harm," a non-extraditable offence. The trial judge struck out

[1] The case came before the Federal Court in the following way: The German request for extradition was directed to the Federal Council, which had the accused interrogated. In the course of the interrogation the accused was asked—in accordance with Article 21, paragraph 2, of the Federal Law of 22 January, 1892, concerning extradition abroad—to declare whether he consented to his immediate extradition or whether, and if so why, he objected to being extradited. As he resisted extradition the Federal Council was bound, according to Article 23, paragraph 1, of the above-mentioned Law, to transmit the documents to the Federal Court, which had, according to Article 24, to decide whether the extradition ought to be granted or not.

[2] The first sentence of Article 9 is as follows: " The objects, instruments " and tools which have been stolen or which are in the possession of the con- " victed or accused and which he used for the purpose of committing the " crime or misdemeanour shall, together with other means of proof, be handed " over at the same time as the arrested person is being extradited."

the second count. Flannery was convicted on the first count. He appealed.

Held : That there had been no evidence to prove intent to kill, and the conviction was set aside. The Court in the exercise of its discretion under Section 108 of the Criminal Code refused to grant an order for a new trial, on the grounds that if Flannery had been extradited and charged with an offence other than that on which he had been extradited, and one which was not in itself extraditable, then there would have been a breach of faith towards the extraditing country ; if, therefore, in this case, the accused, having waived extradition, was convicted of a non-extraditable offence, there would be a breach of faith towards him. [Report : (1923) 3 *Dominion Law Reports*, 689 ; *Alberta Law Reports*, 613.]

NOTE.—The theory upon which this decision rests would appear to be that an accused person who voluntarily returns to his country of origin can claim to have made a contract with his own Government extending to him as an individual the benefits of the extradition treaty. Both on grounds of international and of constitutional law this theory is open to obvious objections. Any favour shown towards the accused person in such cases should rest upon executive discretion and not upon legal grounds.

Extradition—Procedure—Establishment of *prima facie* Case.

See Case No. 183 (*In re Hurlimann*).

PART VII

DIPLOMATIC AND CONSULAR INTERCOURSE AND PRIVILEGES

A. PERMANENT DIPLOMATIC ENVOYS

III.—Privileges and Immunities of

i.—Diplomatic Envoys and their Staff

Diplomatic Agents—Claim to Exemption from Jurisdiction—Position when not Acting for the Foreign Sovereign. **Case No. 201**

CRÉDIT FONCIER D'ALGÉRIE ET DE TUNISIE *v.* RESTREPO AND DEPARTMENT OF ANTIOQUIA.

France, Civil Tribunal of the Seine (*First Chamber*). 11 *December*, 1922.

THE FACTS.—The Government of Antioquia, one of the constituent members of the Republic of Colombia, had issued a loan in France, and a certain number of these bonds had been given as security to the *Crédit Foncier d'Algérie et de Tunisie.* Difficulties arose with regard to the currency in which interest and redemption payments were to be made, and thereupon the *Crédit Foncier d'Algérie* sued the Government of Antioquia in the person of M. Restrepo, Secretary of Legation and Chargé d'Affaires of Colombia. The latter invoked his diplomatic immunity.

Held: For the plaintiffs. Restrepo, as Chargé d'Affaires of the Republic of Colombia at Paris, could not take advantage of his immunity from jurisdiction as a diplomatic agent in the case before the Court. He was sued neither in his own name nor as the representative of the Republic of Colombia, but " as " the mandatory of a department of Colombia which, as it is " not a sovereign State, can legally be sued before the French " courts in accordance with Article 14 of the Civil Code." [Reports: 50 *Clunet* (1923), p. 857; *Gazette du Palais*, 1923, I, p. 439, in both places with the conclusions of M. le substitut Lyon-Caen.]

Case No. 202 **Diplomatic Immunities—Exemption from Civil Jurisdiction —Relations of Private Law not Connected with the Mission.**

COMINA *v.* KITE.

Italy, Court of Cassation of Rome (Combined Division). 31 *January,* 1922.

THE FACTS.—This was an appeal from the judgment of the Court of Appeal which held that the Italian courts are not competent to decide as to obligations assumed by a foreign diplomatic agent in his capacity as a private person.

Held by the Court of Cassation: That the judgment of the Court of Appeal must be reversed. "The absolute immunity "put forward from historical times is now ended and is one "of the political doctrines that have been superseded; it is "contrary to justice and to legal logic. The acts that a diplo- "matic agent does outside his public functions have no relation "to the exercise of sovereignty; they do not constitute a "manifestation of the activity of the Government represented "by the agent; they are not extraterritorial acts of the "Government itself; hence it is not necessary for them to "be protected by the principle of immunity. They are there- "fore subject to the laws of the country. . . . The nature "and completeness of the mission confided to the representa- "tives of foreign governments, their dignity, their prestige, "do not undergo any diminution when a citizen pleads the "*lex loci* against them to regulate private relations which "are not relevant to the mission as such. It is not admissible "that a minister or other foreign diplomatic agent should "contract debts and not satisfy them, make contracts and "not fulfil them, and invoke our laws only for his advantage "and deny their application to his detriment." [Reports: *Foro Italiano,* vol. I (1922), pp. 343-351, with a critical note by Professor Cavaglieri; *Rivista di diritto internazionale,* 1924, pp. 173-175, with a critical note by Professor Anzilotti.]

See *Annual Digest,* 1927-1928, Case No. 246.

Case No. 203 **Diplomatic Agents—Immunity from Jurisdiction—Obligations Incurred before Commencement of Mission.**

IN RE NAZARE AGA.

France, Procureur Général (Appeal in interests of the law), Court of Cassation (Civil Chamber). 3 *August,* 1921.

THE FACTS.—Youssef Khan Nazare Aga, counsellor of

the Persian Legation in Paris, signed a promissory note for 11,000 francs which had not been paid. At the time of signature (March, 1913) he was not yet in a diplomatic capacity. The *Tribunal de Commerce* of the Seine and the Paris Court of Appeal refused to accept the plea of diplomatic immunity because he could not show that he was acting in any diplomatic capacity in March, 1913, and in any case he could not prove that his Government authorised him to rely on diplomatic immunity.

Held : That the decision of the Paris Court must be quashed. Diplomatic immunity which is founded on the necessity for the mutual independence of States extends to every effective member of the Legation. It can only be set aside by a clear and regular acceptance by these persons of the jurisdiction of the courts before which they are proceeded against. It is irrelevant whether the defendant contracted his obligation before or after he began his official duties. It is sufficient that he possesses his official character at the time when proceedings against him are initiated. He has no need of an authorisation from his Government when he invokes a privilege essential to protect him from disturbance in the fulfilment of his mission. [Reports : 48 *Clunet* (1921), p. 922 ; *Dalloz*, 1925, Part I, p. 87.]

NOTE.—See Case No. 205 (*The Empire* v. *Chang and Others*) in regard to proceedings after the diplomatic character had been lost.

iii.—The Family and Retinue of Diplomatic Envoys

Permanent Diplomatic Envoys—Privileges and Immunities—The Family. **Case No. 204**

EX PARTE CHEUK GAR LIM.

United States District Court, N.D. California.
18 *December*, 1922.

THE FACTS.—This was a petition for habeas corpus by the minor son of an accredited Chinese official who had been admitted to the United States. Though accompanying his father, the petitioner had been denied admission on the ground that he was suffering from a contagious disease. The same section of the Immigration Law which excluded aliens suffering from contagious diseases provided that " nothing in

Case No. 204 *contd.*

" this Act shall be construed to apply to accredited " officials of foreign Governments, nor to their suites, " families, or guests." (39 U.S. Stat. L. 878.) On demurrer,

Held : That the demurrer must be overruled and the petitioner discharged. The act expressly exempted members of families of accredited officials. The Court said : " I see no " reason for holding that the act does not mean what it says." [Report : 285 Fed. 396.]

Case No. 205 **Privileges and Immunities of Diplomatic Envoys—Retinue of Envoys—Liability after Termination of Diplomatic Employment.**

THE EMPIRE *v.* CHANG AND OTHERS.

Japan, Supreme Court. 1921.

THE FACTS.—The accused were charged with breach of the Decree concerning explosives at the time when they were employed as attendants at the Chinese Legation. Their employment with the Legation terminated before the prosecution. They were convicted by the District Court of Tokyo. They appealed on the ground that their immunity continued after the termination of their employment as members of the retinue of the Chinese Minister. Their appeal was dismissed. On further appeal,

Held : That the conviction must stand. The exercise of a nation's sovereignty is, as the necessary consequence of its statehood, co-extensive with its entire territory. It is true that the admission of diplomatic privilege tends more or less to restrict the nation's jurisdiction. But this concession does not imply the total exemption therefrom of the persons granted such immunities to the extent of permitting them to enjoy unqualified liberty of action. As a corollary, an offence committed by such persons is not purged of its *prima facie* quality as an illegal act. Whilst they may not be tried in the territorial courts during the term of their office or employment, this may naturally be effected when they become divested of it except in cases where such a procedure is no longer admissible owing to prescription. [Report : 27 *Criminal Cases* (1921), p. 187.]

iv.—The Official House of a Diplomatic Envoy

Diplomatic Privileges—Jurisdictional Immunity of Legation Buildings—Extent of Immunity. Case No. 206

ANGELINI *v.* THE FRENCH GOVERNMENT.

Italy, Arbitral Commission at Rome for Leases of Business Premises.[1] 29 *June,* 1921.

THE FACTS.—Angelini summoned before this Commission, by an application dated 6 April, 1921, the Government of the French Republic, in the person of M. Barrère, the French ambassador, for the purpose of obtaining the renewal of the claimant's lease of certain premises situate in Via Giulia and ordinarily used as coach-houses and stables. The French Government replied that such places must be considered as French territory, and that consequently the provisions of the ordinary law did not apply to them. On the merits of the case it was contended that the French Embassy needed the premises let to the claimant for use as offices of the French Consulate.

Held : That the so-called extraterritoriality of the palace, the seat of the French Embassy, cannot be understood to mean that diplomatic privilege extends in such a way as to make the seat of the diplomatic representative foreign territory. The privilege is justified on the grounds of the necessity of guaranteeing the absolute independence of the diplomatic function. Immunity from jurisdiction is, according to diplomatic custom, limited to the building where the diplomatic representative has his seat, and does not extend to any other immovable property owned by the diplomatic representative of a foreign State. The present action *ad rem* started by Angelini might, therefore, only be met with a valid defence of the privilege of jurisdictional immunity in case the objection to the renewal of the lease, made by the ambassador, had its foundation in his right to the free exercise of his diplomatic function. This is a question of fact. It must therefore be ascertained whether the property where Angelini carries on his coaching business is or is not part of the Farnese Palace, the

[1] These were State Tribunals presided over by a magistrate. They were set up during the war for the purpose of dealing, largely on the basis of equity, with disputes as to rents for dwelling-houses and business premises.

Case No. 206 *contd.* seat of the French ambassador. This is alleged by the representative of the ambassador and denied by Angelini. If this plea be made out, there should be an irrebuttable presumption of the validity of the defence of jurisdictional immunity. The Commission accordingly ordered proceedings for an investigation of this aspect of the question. [Report : *Giurisprudenza Italiana,* 1922, p. 339.]

Case No. 207 **Legation Buildings—Position of—Fiction of Extraterritoriality.**

LEGATION BUILDINGS (TURNOVER TAX) CASE.

Germany, Federal Tribunal for Financial Matters (Reichsfinanzhof). 7 *March,* 1922.

THE FACTS.—The appellant bought in May, 1920, at an auction in the building of the former Russian Legation in Berlin, a number of carpets belonging to the Legation. He was asked by the tax authorities to pay a "turn-"over tax" (*Umsatzsteuer*) at a rate fixed for the sale of goods brought from abroad. The tax authority contended that, in view of the extraterritoriality of the Legation building, goods bought therein must be regarded as bought abroad. The Court of the lower instance upheld this contention of the tax authorities. On appeal,

Held : For the appellant. The territory of the *Reich* consists, according to Article 2 of the German Constitution, of all the territories of the German States. Accordingly, a Legation building in a German State forms part of the territory of the *Reich.* International and constitutional law prohibit the exercise of German jurisdiction in the building of a Legation, which is, therefore, regarded for certain purposes as being foreign territory. This fiction of extraterritoriality has no relevance to the turnover tax, whose purpose is to protect the home producer from the effects of the influx of foreign goods. If the view of the Court below were adopted, then goods bought by the personnel of the Legation would not be liable to turnover tax at all, seeing that according to the Turnover Tax Law goods sent abroad are exempt from the turnover tax. [Report : *Juristische Wochenschrift,* 1923, p. 194.]

Diplomatic Immunities—Legation Buildings—Immunity of—Registration of Charging Orders. **Case No. 208**

LEGATION BUILDING (EXECUTION BY HYPOTHECATION) CASE.

Austria, Supreme Court in Civil Matters. 15 *March*, 1921. (*Ob. III.* 134/21.)

THE FACTS.—The District Court of Vienna ordered entry of a charge in the land registry in regard to an Embassy building belonging to a foreign State. It was held on appeal that the order, being in the nature of an execution, could not be permitted.

Held by the Supreme Court: That the execution could not be permitted. "Embassy buildings of a foreign State are not an "object for execution." [Report: *Entscheidungen des Obersten Gerichtshofes in Zivilrechtssachen*, vol. III (1921), No. 32, p. 69.]

Diplomatic Privileges—Permanent Diplomatic Envoys—Fiction of Extraterritoriality—Domicile. **Case No. 209**

IN RE SUCCESSION OF DOÑA CARMEN DE GOYENECHE.

Peru, Supreme Court. 13 *May*, 1921.

THE FACTS.—The Peruvian laws fixed a higher tax on property passing by inheritance to Peruvians not domiciled in Peru than to those domiciled in the Republic. The property of Doña Carmen de Goyeneche went to Don Juan Mariano de Goyeneche and his sister Doña Maria Josefa de Goyeneche. He was, and had been for years, the Peruvian minister to the Holy See; his sister lived with him in Rome. They claimed to remain domiciled in Peru, however, by virtue of the extraterritoriality of a diplomatic minister and his household. The lower Court held that Don Juan was only obliged to pay the tax of a person domiciled in Peru, but that his sister must pay the higher rate. The Superior Tribunal held that both should pay the lower rate. On appeal,

Held: That the judgment must be reversed and both directed to pay at the rate fixed for persons domiciled abroad. Neither of them could be considered as domiciled in Peru. The fiction of extraterritoriality cannot establish the purely

Case No. 209 *contd.* civil fact of domicile, since the immunities which international law accords the diplomatic representative, to assure his independence, do not modify the rules of private law to which he is subject in his own country. If, in virtue of these immunities, his residence is admitted to form part of the national territory, this does not have the result of attributing to him a domicile which he had already renounced, as in this case. It was well known that when Don Juan Mariano de Goyeneche was appointed Minister of the Republic to the Holy See he then had no domicile in Peru, because he had for many years established his voluntary domicile abroad. [Report: *Anales Judiciales*, 1921, p. 26.]

Diplomatic Immunities—Exterritoriality—Legation Buildings—Jurisdictional Immunities of Ambassadors when Acting for their State in Matters of Private Contract—Purpose of Jurisdictional Immunities.

See Case No. 79 (*Immunities* (*Foreign State in Private Contracts*) *Case*).

IV.—Termination of Appointment of Diplomatic Envoy

Case No. 210 **Diplomatic Envoys—Overthrow of Government by which they have been Appointed—Termination of Mission by *de facto* Governments.**

MANUEL CASTRO QUESADA *v.* EL ESTADO.

Costa Rica, Court of Cassation. 17 *August*, 1922.

THE FACTS.—This case involved the diplomatic representation of a Government which had been overthrown. Castro Quesada was appointed Costa Rican minister to the United States on 29 June, 1915, took office, and drew his pay until January, 1917, when Tinoco, the revolutionary leader, seized the presidency and suspended the minister's salary. Quesada continued to occupy the Legation and carry out the duties of his office until April, 1918. Tinoco accepted the minister's resignation on 1 February, 1917, though it had not been asked for or handed in. After Tinoco was ousted, the Costa Rican Congress declared that all acts of the usurping régime from 27 January, 1917, to 2 September,

1919, were of no legal effect. Quesada brought an action for payment of his salary for the period from January, 1917, to April, 1918, claiming that he had been recognised by the United States as the minister and that the Government was at least obligated to him by quasi-contract, since the acceptance of his resignation had been among the acts which the Congress later declared invalid. The claim was contested on the ground that he had ceased to be the diplomatic representative. The lower Court found against him, saying: "The recognition or non-recognition by a foreign "Government of a minister accredited to it is an "essential factor in his ability to carry out the mission "which causes his appointment; but its effects cannot "extend to affecting the validity of an act which is one "of the manifestations of the sovereignty of the State. "If the Constitutional Government of Costa Rica dis- "appeared in a *coup d'état* of 27 January, 1917, by "virtue of what legal fiction could the plaintiff continue "to represent a Government which had already dis- "appeared? . . . If the Constitutional Government of "Costa Rica disappeared on 27 January, 1917, all "representation of it must necessarily have dis- "appeared." On appeal, the *Sala Primera de Apelaciones* reversed the decision of the lower Court and allowed the claim, chiefly on quasi-contractual grounds and relying upon the Congressional declaration of nullity of Tinoco's acts. The Government appealed to the Court of Cassation.

Held: That the decision of the Court of Appeal must be reversed and the judgment of the Court of First Instance affirmed. There was no valid quasi-contractual claim. The reasoning of the Court of First Instance was approved to the effect that, "by the fall, on account of revolution, of the "Government which accredited a diplomat, he ceases to function "as such, even though, by general custom, the minister con- "tinues to enjoy the prerogatives of his high office." [Report: *Sentencias de la Corte de Casacion*, 2° *Sem.*, 1922, p. 202.]

B. SPECIAL ENVOYS: DELEGATES AT INTERNATIONAL CONFERENCES: THEIR PRIVILEGES AND IMMUNITIES

Case No. 211 **Diplomatic Privileges—Members of Commercial Mission—Soviet Russia—Effect of Non-Recognition by Italy.**

In re Serventi.

Italy, Court of Appeal of Rome. 20 *May*, 1921.

The Facts.—On the evening of 23 March, 1921, Serventi assaulted and threatened M. Vaslav Worovsky, head of the Russian commercial mission accredited to the Italian Government, using abusive expressions and then striking him a blow on the arm. Serventi was then prosecuted under Article 130 of the Criminal Code, which extends to crimes committed against the representatives of foreign States accredited to the Italian Government the punishments provided for crimes committed against public officials in the course of their duties. On the question whether the Russian commercial delegation and its head had the character of a representative of a foreign State, the statement of the Minister for Foreign Affairs, which was put in evidence, was to the effect that the Russian delegation had an official character, but it did not expressly declare whether M. Worovsky had been granted the status of a diplomatic agent.

Held: That Article 130 of the Criminal Code did not apply to the present case. The acts imputed to Serventi, as regards the injuries caused to M. Worovsky, should be considered on the same footing as injuries done to private individuals.

A State acquries an international personality only when it is recognised by other States, and it is from such recognition that is derived the exercise of its fundamental rights, such as, for example, that of being represented by its own diplomatic agents accredited to other States. The Socialist Soviet Republic in Russia had not yet been recognised, *de jure*, by the Italian State, which had not yet opened up diplomatic relations with it. Worovsky cannot therefore be considered as representing a foreign State, since the State which he would represent has not yet an international legal personality and, in consequence, has not yet been accorded the right to have a legation.[1] It follows, therefore, that the character of the delegation presided over by Worovsky excludes him from the status of representative of a foreign State. Article 130 of the Criminal Code speaks of representatives of foreign States accredited to His Majesty's Government. It is necessary that the representative be accredited by means of the solemn presentation of his credentials to the head of the State. This has not in fact been done by the head of the Russian delegation. That delegation has come to Italy solely for economic and commercial reasons, in pursuance of an activity which is purely technical and indeed extraneous to the representation of a foreign State and to its own juridical existence as an international person. [Reports: *Monitore dei Tribunali*, 1922, p. 31; *Scuola Positiva*, 1921, with a note by Professor Marinoni.]

NOTE.—The Court also observed that the absence from the Russian delegation of any diplomatic character could also be inferred from the fact that while there is universally accorded to diplomatic agents the privilege of exemption of their baggage from any customs examination, the baggage of Worovsky and of the other members of the Russian commercial delegation had been subjected to a customs examination at the Rome Railway Station.

Diplomatic Immunity — Special Representatives — Effect of Special Agreement between Governments Defining Status and Immunities—Representatives of a Foreign Government Recognised *de facto* only—Representatives Not Received by the Sovereign. **Case No. 212**

FENTON TEXTILE ASSOCIATION LIMITED *v.* KRASSIN.

England, Court of Appeal, on Appeal from the King's Bench Division of the High Court of Justice. 16 December, 1921.

THE FACTS.—On 16 March, 1921, the British Government entered into a " Trade Agreement " [2] with the Russian Soviet Government, from Article V of which the following is an extract:

" Either party may appoint one or more official " agents to a number to be mutually agreed upon, to " reside and exercise their functions in the territories " of the other, who shall personally enjoy all the rights " and immunities set forth in the preceding Article " and also immunity from arrest and search provided

[1] It will be noticed that the Court treats the non-recognition of the Soviet Government as equivalent to the non-recognition of the Russian State.—[Ed.]

[2] Parliamentary Paper, Cmd. 1207.

Case No. 212 ***contd.***

"that either party may refuse to admit any individual "as an official agent who is *persona non grata* to itself "or may require the other party to withdraw him "should it find it necessary to do so on grounds of "public interest or security. Such agents shall have "access to the authorities of the country in which they "reside for the purpose of facilitating the carrying out "of this Agreement and of protecting the interests of "their nationals. . . .

"Russian official agents in the United Kingdom "shall enjoy the same privileges in respect of exemp-"tion from taxation, central or local, as are accorded "to the official representatives of other foreign Govern-"ments. British official agents in Russia shall enjoy "equivalent privileges, which, moreover, shall in no "case be less than those accorded to the official agents "of any other country.

"The official agents shall be the competent author-"ities to visa the passports of persons seeking admission "in pursuance of the preceding Article into the terri-"tories of the parties."

Thereupon the defendant Krassin took up his position in London as the official agent of the Russian Soviet Government under that Agreement. To an action brought against him (and also against the Russian Socialistic Federative Soviet Republic and the All-Russian Co-operative Society Limited) for the balance of the price of goods sold and delivered a conditional appearance was entered by him, and later he made an application to set aside the service upon him of the writ on the ground that he was the authorised representative of a foreign State and entitled as such to immunity from process.

The application having been refused by Branson, J., the defendant now appealed to the Court of Appeal, and it was argued on his behalf that he was discharging functions wider than those involved in connection with the Agreement, that the Agreement necessarily implied that the persons to whom it gave immunity from process and taxation were persons entitled to diplomatic privileges, and that he was a public minister within the meaning of the Diplomatic Privileges Act, 1708, and the diplomatic representative of a foreign Sovereign Power, and as such immune from process. It was not suggested that he was protected from civil process by the express provisions of the Agreement.

A letter from the Foreign Office to the defendant's solicitors was read in which it was stated that M. Krassin's position and privileges were defined in Articles 4, 5 and 6 of the Trade Agreement, and that the Foreign Office list of persons entitled to diplomatic privileges only contained the names of the diplomatic representatives of countries which had received *de jure* recognition as Sovereign Independent States and, the Soviet Government having only been recognised *de facto*, his name did not appear therein.

In answer to an enquiry addressed by the Court of Appeal to the Foreign Office, a reply was received from the Secretary of State for Foreign Affairs which may be summarised as follows: M. Krassin has not been received by His Majesty, and "no representative of "the Soviet Government would be received by His "Majesty's Government because the Soviet Govern-"ment has not been recognised *de jure* as a State (*sic*). "Since the signature of the Trade Agreement M. "Krassin has been received at the Foreign Office as "the official agent of the Soviet Government under the "provisions of Article 5 of the Agreement for purposes "covered by the Agreement." Apart from that, advantage had been taken of his presence in London by officials of the Foreign Office to discuss other matters with him, such as the repatriation of Russian refugees and the famine in Russia.

Held by the Court of Appeal (Bankes, Scrutton and Atkin, L.JJ.): That M. Krassin was not entitled to the immunity claimed by him and the service of the writ was therefore effective, for he had not been "recognized by any "competent authority in this country in any capacity other "than that of official agent" under the Agreement; *per* Bankes, L.J., at p. 261, "that status is clearly insufficient to "carry with it the immunity accorded to accredited and "recognized representatives of foreign States"; *per* Scrutton, L.J., and *per* Atkin, L.J., at p. 262, that the privileges to be granted to the official trade agents were defined in the Trade Agreement itself and immunity from civil process was not included. [Report: 38 T.L.R. 259.]

NOTE.—Scrutton, L.J., pointed out (p. 261) that the statute of

Case No. 212 *contd.*

1708 was not exhaustive. The common law gave further protection in respect of diplomatic immunity. The diplomatic staff of an embassy and a chargé d'affaires were entitled to immunity at common law although they were neither "received by His Majesty" nor were "domestic servants" in the words of the statute of 1708.

The opinion of Lord Ellenborough in *Vineash* v. *Becker*, 3 M. & S., at p. 298, that this statute "was declaratory . . . of the extent to "which the law is to be carried" was no longer accurate. "The "question of the exact limits of diplomatic privilege is so important "as to justify me in declining to lay down any general principle unless "the facts of the case require it. It is sufficient to say that so long as "our Government negotiates with a person as representing a recognised "foreign State about matters of concern as between nation and nation, "without further definition of his position, I am inclined to think that "such representative may be entitled to immunity though not ac-"credited to or received by the King. If the question in the present "case had been the position of M. Krassin when he was as representing "the Russian Soviet Government negotiating the Trade Agreement "I should have been inclined to think . . . that M. Krassin should "be exempted from the process of the Court. But . . ." and the L.J. went on to explain that M. Krassin's present position was different from that defined in the Trade Agreement.

Atkin, L.J., stated (p. 262) that, even if the official agents appointed under the Trade Agreement would have been entitled to full diplomatic immunity in the absence of an agreement between the two Governments to the contrary, nevertheless if there was such an agreement limiting the immunities of the agent "such restricted immunity can alone be "recognized by the municipal Courts."[1]

D. CONSULS

I.—Appointment and Exequatur

Case No. 213

Consuls—Appointment and Exequatur—Termination of Mission—By Withdrawal of Exequatur or Removal by Sending Government—Privileges and Immunities.

PEOPLE *v.* SAVITCH (otherwise known as Savic).
SAVIC *v.* CITY OF NEW YORK.

United States, New York Court of General Sessions for the County of New York; New York Supreme Court, New York Special Term; New York Supreme Court, Appellate Division, First Department. September, 1921; *February,* 1922; 3 *November,* 1922.

THE FACTS.—Savic had been Consul-General in New York of the Kingdom of the Serbs, Croats and Slovenes.

[1] It appears from the report that the following factors are not conclusive against the recognition of diplomatic immunity: (*a*) that the representative has not been personally received by the sovereign; (*b*) that he is the representative of a foreign Government recognised *de facto* only.—[Ed.]

His exequatur was revoked by the President of the United States on 23 June, 1921. He was indicted on 21 July, 1921, for a crime alleged to have been committed while he was serving as Consul-General. United States Federal courts have exclusive jurisdiction in suits against consuls. (36 U.S. Stat. L. 1160.) Savic moved to dismiss the indictment.

Held by the Court of General Sessions: That the motion to dismiss must be denied. When the indictments were filed Savic was no longer a consul. He had therefore become subject to the State courts for unofficial acts done while consul. (116 Misc. (N.Y.) 531.)

Savic furnished bail and then sued in the Supreme Court, New York Special Term, to recover the bail on the ground that he was still consul, since he had not been removed by his own Government, and consequently was immune from arrest for crime and requirement of bail in the State courts.

Held by the Supreme Court, New York Special Term: That the complaint must be dismissed. The revocation of his exequatur terminated his status as consul. The President's action in revoking the exequatur was conclusive for the courts. "Consular status does not exist in the absence of the president's "recognition of the person accredited by the foreign state." (118 Misc. (N.Y.) 156, 158.) On appeal to the Supreme Court, Appellate Division, First Department,

Held: That the judgment must be affirmed. In so far as the question was a political one, it was determined by a communication from the United States Secretary of State to the effect that Savic was not considered a consular officer, within the meaning of the statute, after the revocation of his exequatur. In so far as the question was a judicial one, the decision below was correct. Consuls do not enjoy immunity from civil or criminal process by international law. [Reports: 116 Misc. (N.Y.) 531; 118 Misc. (N.Y.) 156; 203 App. D. (N.Y.) 81.]

NOTE.—See 35 H.L.R. 752. See also 28 M.L.R. 591; and Surridge, *Jurisdiction over Suits against Foreign Consuls in the United States*, 80 U. Pa. L.R. 972.

II.—Position and Function of Consuls

Case No. 214

Functions of Consuls—Right to Collect Evidence—Hague Convention on Civil Procedure.

CARAPELLUCCI *v.* PALMERIO.

Italy, Court of Appeal of Aquila. 2 *May*, 1919.

THE FACTS.—In the course of the proceedings of the present case it was necessary to hear certain witnesses resident at São Paulo in Brazil. The President of the Court of Appeal deputed the collecting of such evidence to the Italian consul at São Paulo, and as the length of time fixed for this was not sufficient, he extended it for another six months. The appellants contended that the President could not entrust the Italian consul with such functions, seeing that the latter was not competent to collect evidence and that therefore the proofs received through him would be null and of no value.

Held: That the plea of the appellants must be allowed. The President's ordinance, which appointed the Italian consul at São Paulo to receive the depositions of the witnesses, cannot be considered as legally valid because the Italian consul lacked the jurisdiction and the power to exercise such legal functions as those which had been entrusted to him. Article 65 of the Consular Law says that in countries where, by reason of treaties and usages, consuls exercise jurisdiction over their compatriots, such a practice must be kept within the limits of those treaties and usages. The application of this provision presupposes, therefore, that one is dealing with a country where the consul has the right to exercise jurisdiction, that is, with a country where the régime of capitulations is in operation. In such a case the consuls are effectively judges, and in that capacity have full and entire competence to execute requests for evidence on commission. This law is not, however, applicable in other countries where the consul has no power of jurisdiction, and therefore it is scarcely possible to apply the provisions of the Consular Law (Articles 74, 84, 85, 95) with regard to the examination of witnesses, which provisions relate to the powers reserved to a consul as judge. Nor is it in point to cite the provisions of the Hague Convention of 1905 on Civil Procedure which authorise consular functions of this nature, because these relate to Italy and the various States of Europe which are signatories of the Convention. It is not possible, therefore, to extend them to other countries which did not join in such Convention. The Italian judicial authority should consequently have referred exclusively to the judicial authority of the country where the proofs of evidence were to be taken. [Report: *Monitore dei Tribunale*, 1919, p. 508.]

NOTE.—The Court of Appeal of Milan has twice rendered judgment to the same effect as the Court of Appeal of Aquila (judgments of 16 October, 1893, and of 27 October, 1896). Possibly this view is in contradiction to Article 171 of the Italian Consular Law, which says that the courts of the consul's State can address requests for evidence to consuls independently of the special provisions of the Hague Convention (Article 15).

Consuls—Functions of—Whether Representatives of their State. **Case No. 215**

CONSUL OF THE ARGENTINE REPUBLIC *v.* BOURGUES.

Italy, Court of Appeal of Genoa. 9 June, 1921.

THE FACTS.—This was an action relating to the devolution of the estate of an Argentine citizen who died in Italy without leaving any testamentary or other successors entitled under the general law. The Argentine consul intervened in the proceedings for the purpose of claiming that the estate should devolve on the Argentine State. A preliminary objection was taken on the ground that the Argentine consul intervening in the proceedings had not made out his claim to represent the Argentine Republic in the action. On the objection being overruled, an appeal was taken.

Held: For the appellant. The consul has shown neither an express authorisation to become a party to the suit before the Italian courts, granted by the governmental authority competent to confer it upon him, nor has he made out his claim to the right to represent his own State on the ground either of an implied provision of an Argentine law or of a treaty between the two States. It is a principle prevailing by international custom and approved by the authority of textbooks that consuls are not charged with the legal representation of the interests of their States. They are not, in a strict sense, the representatives of the State itself. Their function is to watch the commercial interests of their countries, and to render assistance to business men and other of their compatriots who happen to be in the territory of the State to which they have been sent. Consuls may intervene by virtue of their office and without special authority only when it is a question of asking for precautionary measures to safeguard the pecuniary interests of

Case No. 215 *contd.* nationals who are minors or who are absent. There was no substance in the view advanced that there was a constant tradition to the effect that the consul is the representative of the economic interests of his own State abroad. It is one thing to speak of a specific kind of representation exercised by their direct intervention in an administrative capacity in relation to the local authorities, and another thing to claim a general recognition in international relations of the power of the consuls to institute suits and to intervene in civil actions in the name of their own States. [Report: *Foro Italiano*, vol. I (1922), p. 82.]

Case No. 216

Consuls—Administration of Estates—Scope of.

ANGEL BUDELACCI AND OTHERS *v.* EL NUEVO BANCO ITALIANO.

Argentina, Federal Supreme Court. 9 December, 1919.

THE FACTS.—This was a case of consular administration of a deceased alien's estate. Budelacci, an Italian, died in Santa Fé. The Italian vice-consul secured a decree from the *Juez de Paz* there, by which the deceased's property was inventoried and turned over to him as depositary. This included a savings account in the defendant bank which the bank paid to the vice-consul. The representatives of certain minor heirs then sued the bank for their part of the account. The bank defended on the ground that it had paid the person legally entitled. The *Juez de la Primera Nominación en lo Civil*, of Santa Fé, held for the plaintiffs in this action, though for a lesser amount than was claimed. The basis of the decision was that neither by the general law on consular intervention in administration of estates, nor under the most-favoured-nation clause of the Treaty with Italy, had the Italian vice-consul any right to the account. (The defendant invoked the most-favoured-nation clause of the Treaty with Italy, relying on an earlier Treaty with Germany giving consuls such rights, in so far as it was consistent with the laws of the country.) The *Superior Tribunal de Justicia* affirmed this part of the judgment. Since a question of treaty interpretation was involved, an extraordinary appeal was taken to the Argentine Supreme Court.

Held : That the judgment must be affirmed. Italian consuls accredited in this country have not greater powers in that respect than those which the laws of the nation grant to foreign consuls. The Consular Convention of 1885 with Italy provided, in Article 13, that " the intervention of the consuls " of both nations will be ruled by the laws and regulations that " may be in force in the country where the succession is opened." Law 163, in force since 1865, regulated consular intervention. According to that law, the intervention of the consul is reduced to the taking of measures merely conservatory of the property of the foreigner, such as joining with the local authorities in sealing the movables and papers of the deceased. Given the limited character and object of this intervention, which does not exclude or impair the jurisdiction of the ordinary judges over the successions of aliens dying in the Republic, it is not possible to maintain that consuls have the power to take possession of the property, collect the credits, and receive the funds belonging to the deceased's estate ; and even less, that they can perform these acts without the knowledge of the judge of the case. The Treaty of 1825 with Great Britain, and the Treaty of 1857 with Germany, did not through the most-favoured-nation clause help the Italian consul. It was not shown that the Italian Government had granted, or was willing to grant, these rights to Argentine consuls in Italy.[1] [Report : *Fallos*, vol. 130, p. 328.]

NOTE.—On this general subject see the *Berrocal* case (*Cámara Civil Segunda de la Capital*, 2 July, 1924), *Gaceta del Foro*, vol. 51 (August, 1924), p. 425. Holding that the consular administration may intervene, see the cases of *Cuestra Francisco Sanchez* (*Juzgado Civil*, 20 September, 1920), *ibid.*, vol. 28 (September, 1920), p. 155 ; *Vigneau* (*Cámara Civil Primera de la Capital*, 7 June, 1922), *Jurisprudencia Argentina*, vol. 8, p. 582 ; and *Cipriano Capetillo* (*Cámara Civil Primera*, 17 June, 1919), *Gaceta del Foro*, vol. 21, p. 181. Cf. the Mexican case of *Joseph W. Rowe* (Mexican Supreme Court, 14 May, 1919), *Semanario Judicial*, vol. 4, 5ª *Epoca*, p. 1092.

On the capacity of the consular administration to litigate, see *Fernandez* v. *Fernandez* (*Cámara Civil Segunda*, 27 August, 1924), *Jurisprudencia Argentina*, vol. 13, p. 818 ; and the case of *Donald Munro* (*Juzgado Civil*, 9 September, 1924), *Gaceta del Foro*, vol. 52, p. 113.

On termination of consular administration by recognition of heirs or declaration of vacancy, see the cases of *Courthieu* (*Cámara Civil Segunda*, 8 March, 1922), *Jurisprudencia Argentina*, vol. 8, p. 165 ; *Duct de Dalarnoy* (*Cámara Civil Primera*, 22 March, 1922), *Gaceta del Foro*,

[1] For a decision of the Supreme Court of the United States on a similar point see *Santovincenzo* v. *Egan and Bennett* (1931), reported in *A.J.*, vol. XXVI (1932), p. 395.—[Ed.]

Case No. 216 *contd.*

vol. 37, p. 182; *Margarita Ely* (*Cámara Civil Primera*, 5 July, 1921), *ibid.*, vol. 33, p. 219.

On costs and expenses, see the cases of *Enriqueta Hauret de Grospiron* (7 December, 1922), *Fallos*, vol. 135, p. 320; and *Luciana Narciso Leivas* (*Cámara Civil Primera*, 14 August, 1919), *Gaceta del Foro*, vol. 22, p. 43. Cf. the case of *Sucesión de Atilio Repetto* (Panama Supreme Court, 4 January, 1924), *Registro Judicial*, vol. 22, p. 38.

On other points see the cases of *Enrique Hylass* (*Cámara Civil Primera*, 23 May, 1922), *Jurisprudencia Argentina*, vol. 8, p. 443; *Hermida* v. *Rios* (*Cámara Civil Segunda*, 27 February, 1919), *ibid.*, vol. 3, p. 90; *Valin* (*Cámara Civil Primera*, 26 April, 1923), *ibid.*, vol. 10, p. 262; *Jesús Leiro* (*Cámara Civil Primera*, 22 September, 1920), *Gaceta del Foro*, vol. 28, p. 199; *Gomez Paz Rosa* (*Cámara Civil Segunda*, 20 July, 1921), *ibid.*, vol. 33 (July, 1921), p. 198; *Vicente Luksic* (*Cámara Civil Segunda*, 10 December, 1923), *Jurisprudencia Argentina*, vol. 11, p. 1275; *Gemo* (*Cámara Civil Primera*, 12 February, 1924), *ibid.*, vol. 12, p. 218; *Isabel Forest de Carzon* (Supreme Court, 3 November, 1924), *Gaceta del Foro*, vol. 53, p. 192. See also the Chilean case of *Martin Pinedo* (*Corte de Apelaciones de Iquique*, 23 May, 1919), *Gaceta de los Tribunales*, 1er *Sem.*, 1919, p. 493.

Case No. 217

Consuls—Position of—Fiction of Extraterritoriality.

PALLANCA *v.* SOCIETÀ OSSIDRICA ORIENTALE.

Egypt, Italian Consular Court of Cairo. 4 March, 1921.

THE FACTS.—On 12 February, 1902, articles of a limited partnership having for its object the purchase of oxygen and hydrogen gas and the sale thereof in Egypt were signed in the British Consulate at Milan before the British consul. The contracting parties were three Italians and a Swiss. The partnership purported to fix its seat at Cairo, and an administrative office in Milan. Litigation arose in Egypt between the partnership and one Pallanca, who sued for the cost of certain work done by him at Cairo for the partnership. The jurisdiction of the Italian Consular Court depended on what was the national law applicable to the contract of partnership.

Held: That as the articles of partnership were agreed at Milan, in Italy, between contracting parties of different nationalities, by virtue of Article 9 of the preliminary provisions of the Italian Civil Code the law to be applied to the contract is Italian law, the *lex loci contractus*, there being no question of a different intention of the parties. The contract, although signed in the presence of the British consul, does not cease to be subject to Italian law. "It "cannot be admitted that the document has been signed "outside the country, because the sovereignty of the State "does not allow of any derogation in any part of its territory. "Indeed the concession of extraterritoriality within the "confines of the territory of the State is absurd, both in logic "and in law. Diplomatic and consular authorities do not "alter the nationality of the place where they reside. They "enjoy purely and simply a personal right, recognised by the "State in which they exercise their functions and conferring "upon the place where they have their seat immunity within "certain limits." [Report: *Giurisprudenza Italiana*, 1922, p. 339.]

III.—Privileges and Immunities of Consuls

Consuls—Position of—Extraterritoriality of Consular Premises. **Case No. 218**

In re Couhi.

Italy, Criminal Court of Cassation (*Third Division*).
11 *February*, 1921.

The Facts.—An Italian, one Couhi, was found guilty of making and uttering a forgery by having obtained, under a false name, the grant of a passport from an Italian consulate, signing the document with the false name and then presenting it to the authorities in Italy and abroad. It was contended for the prosecution that for the purposes of the sentence the crime should be treated as having been committed in Italian territory.

Held: That a crime committed in a foreign country at an Italian embassy, legation or consulate, by an Italian who does not belong to the diplomatic or consular service, must be held to be committed abroad. Hence Article 5 of the Italian Criminal Code, according to which a crime committed out of the kingdom carries with it a smaller punishment, is applicable. [Report: 49 *Clunet* (1922), p. 192.]

Consular Privileges—Immunity of Archives—Meaning of. **Case No. 219**

Foà *v.* Boselli.

Italy, Court of Appeal of Turin (*Third Division*).
21 *October*, 1921.

The Facts.—Foà, a firm having a credit against Boselli, an employee of the French Consulate at Turin, served the French consul, at the consular offices, with process

Case No. 219 *contd.*

in the nature of a garnishee order *nisi* (*atto di pignoramento*) for the amounts due from the consul to Boselli. The firm then had recourse to the Court to make the order absolute and to order the French consul to pay to it the sums due from him to Boselli.

Held : That the garnishee order must be declared null and the application of the firm of Foà dismissed. The garnishee order, served in the consular office and on the consul as such, amounted to an act of execution which should not be carried out. On the basis of the Consular Convention in force between Italy and France, consular archives are inviolable, and by archives must be understood all the rooms used in connection with them at the office of the Consulate, the very place where the order in question was served. [Report : *Giurisprudenza Torinese,* 1921, col. 1283, with a note by Magistrate Rivera.]

Case No. 220

Consuls—Offences Committed by Consuls—Personal Immunity—Waiver of Privilege by the Consul's Government.

HUTT *v.* FRENCH STATE.

France, Court of Cassation (*Criminal Chamber*).
25 *September,* 1919.

THE FACTS.—Hutt, a former American consular officer, was prosecuted for embezzlement as a result of a complaint lodged by the United States consul at Bordeaux. The Ambassador of the United States in France waived so far as Hutt was concerned the personal immunities recognised by the Franco-American Consular Convention of 23 February, 1853. A decision was given against Hutt by the *Chambre des mises en accusation* (Prosecuting Department) of the Court of Appeal of Bordeaux. On appeal to the Court of Cassation by Hutt, who still continued to claim personal immunity,

Held : That the appeal must be dismissed. The privileges extended to consuls, vice-consuls, and consular agents by the Convention between France and the United States of America were conferred on those agents not in their own personal interests, but to safeguard the independence of the State which has accredited them. Accordingly, the Government of the State in question could waive the immunity which a convention conferred upon its agent. [Reports : 47 *Clunet* (1920), p. 186 ; Sirey, 1921, Part I, p. 140 ; *Dalloz,* 1921, Part I, p. 5.]

Consuls—Distinguished from Diplomatic Agent—Sequestration in Wartime—Maintenance of Sequestration of Personal or Professional Property of a Consul of Enemy Nationality. **Case No. 221**

LOEWENGARD *v.* *PROCUREUR* OF THE REPUBLIC AND BONVIER (SEQUESTRATOR).

France, Court of Appeal of Lyons (First Chamber).
13 *October*, 1921.

THE FACTS.—Loewengard, a German national, had been German consul since 1907 at Lyons, where he was engaged in business and owned considerable real property. He left France definitely on 2 August, 1914. His property was then sequestrated. In 1921, when his property was about to be liquidated, he brought an action against the *Procureur* of the Republic and the Sequestrator asking for a declaration that " as he was " a consul, his personal property could not be liquid- " ated," and consequently for an order discharging the sequestration. The *Tribunal Civil* declined jurisdiction on the ground that French legislation with regard to sequestration gave the *Chambre du Conseil* and the *Juge du Référé* exclusive jurisdiction, but at the same time rejected the claim of Loewengard to special treatment *quâ* consul. On appeal,

Held : That the appeal must be dismissed. Loewengard had never been an official " *de carrière*." He was only a consul engaged in business (*consul commerçant*). Foreign consuls, even consuls " *de carrière*," who carry on no business in France outside their official functions, have neither the title, nor the rank, nor the privileges of diplomatic agents. " While certain pre- " rogatives or even privileges are accorded to them as a matter " of courtesy and purely *ex gratia* with a view to facilitating the " performance of their mission in peace time, it is clear that any " such prerogatives or privileges, which have no legal founda- " tion, disappear on the outbreak of war." [Report : 49 *Clunet* (1922), p. 391.]

Consuls—Immunities—Crimes not Connected with the Consular Office. **Case No. 222**

IN RE LEWIS VIVIAN GRAVES.

Brazil, Fourth Criminal Court of Rio de Janeiro. 17 *May*, 1920.

THE FACTS.—Graves was a British vice-consul in Brazil.

Case No. 222 *contd.*

He was about to be tried for a crime committed there which had no connection with his consular duties. Upon his claim to consular immunity,

Held : That he was subject to the ordinary criminal jurisdiction for private offences. Article 4 of the Penal Code makes its provisions applicable to all persons on Brazilian territory, regardless of nationality, except where the Constitution, or international law, creates exceptions. " Consuls are not among " those excepted, and consequently do not enjoy ' personal " ' immunity ' in criminal matters, except in crimes related to " their functions." [Report : *Revista Forense*, vol. 34, p. 105.]

NOTE.—Amongst other authors the Court quoted with approval João Barbalho, *Constitucion Federal Commentado*, p. 237 : " Consuls are " mere commercial agents, do not have diplomatic status, do not enjoy " extraterritoriality, and are subject to the justice and police of the " country where they perform their duties. There is no reason, then, to " give them a special forum, which diplomats have."

See on this point Bevilaqua, *Direito Publico Internacional*, vol. I, pp. 493 ff. See also the case of *Luiz Francisco de Leão* v. *Gauie and Sevilla* (Supreme Federal Tribunal, 17 May, 1924), *Revista de Direito*, vol. 77, p. 478, where plaintiffs in a maritime action sought to appeal from the release of the ship upon bond given by the Peruvian consul. Their appeal was dismissed, and the Court said : " In such a case, in " accordance with public international law, the consul is not subject to " the local tribunals ; the injury to individual rights can only be re- " dressed by diplomatic means."

Case No. 223

Consuls—Privileges and Immunities—Consular Premises.

GUILLERMO SOLVEYRA *v.* GUILLERMO OSPINA, CONSUL-GENERAL OF COLOMBIA. GUILLERMO OSPINA *v.* GUILLERMO SOLVEYRA.

Argentina, Federal Supreme Court. 9 *and* 28 *August*, 1922.

THE FACTS. — There were cross-actions between the Colombian Consul-General (Ospina) and an Argentine citizen (Solveyra) from whom the consul rented the building used as his house and consular offices. Solveyra brought a suit for ejectment in the Supreme Court, claiming that the case was within its original jurisdiction because it concerned a foreign consul. (Argentine Constitution, Article 101.) Ospina then sued Solveyra in the same Court for damages for breach of contract.

Held : That the Supreme Court lacked original jurisdiction, since these were cases concerning the private business of a foreign consul rather than cases involving the privileges or exemptions of the consul in his public character. [Report: *Fallos*, vol. 137, pp. 23, 73.]

NOTE.—See the case of *Esbry Ossa* (Supreme Court, 13 June, 1921), *Fallos*, vol. 134, p. 228, to the same effect, in a criminal proceeding. See also the case of *Joaquin de Iturralde* (5 September, 1932), *ibid.*, vol. 138, p. 381, in which it was held that the ordinary courts of the capital have criminal jurisdiction in a case of calumny and libel against the Spanish consul for newspaper statements made by him in his official capacity. And see the case of *Jesús Leiro, su suc.* (*Cámara Civil Primera*, 30 September, 1919), *Gaceta del Foro*, vol. 22 (October, 1919), p. 342, where it was held that a foreign consul is not exempted from the tax requirement of using stamped paper for his legal acts.

But see as to *diplomatic* immunities proper the case of *Killian* (Supreme Court, 2 July, 1924), *Fallos*, vol. 141, p. 131 (more detailed report in *Jurisprudencia Argentina*, vol. 13, p. 281), upholding the original jurisdiction of the Supreme Court in a criminal case against the British minister's chauffeur for negligent injury caused by the minister's car in which the minister was riding at the time. See also *Nunciatura Apostólica de B.A.* v. *Pérez* (Supreme Court, 27 March, 1925), *Jurisprudencia Argentina*, vol. 15, p. 198, in which an ejectment case brought by the Papal Nuncio against the tenant of property bequeathed by the Pope was held to be within the original jurisdiction of the Supreme Court.

Consuls—Privileges and Immunities—Consular Premises. **Case No. 224**

MINISTERIO FISCAL *v.* CECIL WILSON BERTIE.

Argentina, Federal Supreme Court. 6 *September*, 1920.

THE FACTS.—The chancellor in charge of the Uruguayan Consulate filed an information against the defendant, an electric company employee, for *violación de territorio*. The defendant had entered the vestibule of the Consulate building under pretext of examining the meter. The La Plata Federal Court held that the foreign consul, as informant, was not a party to the litigation, that, consequently, it had jurisdiction, and that the case did not fall within the original jurisdiction of the Supreme Court. The *Cámara Federal* held that the informant must have meant *violación de domicilio* (amounting to trespass), since the facts constituted only this offence; therefore it reversed the decisions and held the crime to be entirely outside the Federal Court's jurisdiction and solely a matter for the local courts. On appeal to the Supreme Court,

Held: That the appeal must be dismissed. "The privilege "of extraterritoriality, and others of a diplomatic character, do

Case No. 224 *contd.* " not extend to consuls nor their agents." The opinion of the *procurador general* holding that neither " territory " nor diplomatic privilege was violated by the defendant, and that the case was not one that concerned diplomats or consuls, was approved. There was no ground for federal jurisdiction. [Report : *Fallos*, vol. 132, p. 212.]

NOTE.—See also the Mexican case of *Guillermo O. Jenkins* (Supreme Court, 12 August, 1920), *Semanario Judicial*, vol. 7, 5ª *Epoca*, p. 654, holding that the Federal courts, rather than local courts, had jurisdiction of crimes committed by one who was American consul at the time of the alleged offences, although he was a private person at the time of the trial.

Consuls—Position of—Determination by Political Department —Privileges and Immunities.

See Case No. 213 (*People* v. *Savic : Savic* v. *City of New York.*)

PART VIII

TREATIES

I.—Conception of Treaties as International Contracts

Treaties—Construction of—Analogy to Statutes—Application to Questions of Preparatory Work.

See Case No. 268 (*Heim and Chamant* v. *The German State*).

II.—Forms of International Agreement and Methods by which they are Concluded

i.—Treaties. Conventions. Governmental Agreements. Exchanges of Notes

Treaties—Forms of—Formal Treaties *stricto sensu*—Inter-Governmental Agreements Concluded without the Consent of Legislative Organs—The Polish-German Paris Agreement of 9 January, 1920. **Case No. 225**

PARIS AGREEMENT (9 JANUARY, 1920) CASE.

Germany, Reichsgericht in Civil Matters. 22 *June*, 1922.

THE FACTS.—At the end of December, 1919, the plaintiff bought from the defendant, the State of Prussia, a quantity of timber. He paid 30 per cent. of the price, *i.e.* 8550 German marks. The forests from which the timber was produced passed in January, 1920, to Poland, and the plaintiff, in order to maintain the contract, had to pay to the Polish Treasury the full price of 28,500 marks.[1] He then brought an action against the Prussian State asking for the repayment of the 8550 German marks. The action was brought, *inter alia*, on the ground of unjustified enrichment. Prussia contended that there was no unjustified enrichment on the ground, *inter alia*, that by virtue of the Paris Agreement of 9 January, 1920, between Germany and Poland, by which Prussia also was bound, Germany was bound to regard the payment made by the plaintiff as

[1] He paid them in Polish marks, which, according to Polish law, were equivalent to German marks. In fact, the value of the Polish mark was at that time 30 per cent. less than that of a German mark—a fact which the Court took into consideration.

Case No. 225 *contd.*

a payment made to Poland and to credit it to the latter. The Agreement, which was concluded in order to put into effect some of the provisions of the Peace Treaty, was never published in the Journal of the Laws of the *Reich*. The plaintiff contested both the validity of the Agreement and its ability to affect private rights.

Held, on final appeal on a point of law: That the claim must be dismissed. There was no reason to doubt the validity of the Agreement. It was concluded by the representatives of the German and Polish Governments. It contained no provision for ratification, and no ratification was necessary. It is true that according to Article 45 of the German Federal Constitution the conclusion of treaties with foreign States lies within the competence of the President of the *Reich*. But that does not mean that every treaty must be personally concluded or formally approved by the President. As pointed out by Laband (*Staatsrecht des deutschen Reichs*, 5th ed., vol. II, p. 152), there exists, in addition to the solemn form of treaties, an informal type of agreements. In regard to the first, the State representatives are merely authorised to agree on a draft of a treaty which is finally concluded only by the competent constitutional authorities. In regard to the second, the representatives of the State are authorised to conclude a final agreement which comes into being by the signature of a common document or the exchange of separate documents. It is in this informal way that the Agreement of 9 January was concluded. There is no reason to doubt its validity.

It may be admitted that an internationally valid treaty does not *per se* affect private rights. However, the question does not arise in the present case. Germany—and, through her, Prussia—have undertaken to credit Poland with the amount received from the plaintiff. This being so, there is no question of unjustified enrichment on which the plaintiff bases his action. [Report: *E.R.Z.*, vol. 105, p. 156.]

Case No. 226

Forms of International Agreement—Conventions Concluded not in Accordance with Municipal Provisions Concerning the Treaty-Making Power—Whether Constituting Treaties—United States and Universal Postal Convention.

FOUR PACKAGES OF CUT DIAMONDS *v.* UNITED STATES.

United States Circuit Court of Appeals, Second Circuit.

15 *January*, 1919.

THE FACTS.—This was a libel by the United States to

forfeit four packages of diamonds. Forfeiture was decreed. (247 Fed. 354; 255 Fed. 314.) On rehearing, however, it was agreed that one package, which had been marked "loose diamonds, dutiable," and imported from Cuba by registered mail, was not subject to forfeiture because of false or fraudulent invoice. If forfeited at all, it could only be on the ground that it had been imported "contrary to law" under U.S. Rev. Stat. 3082. The only provision forbidding the importation was a rule of the Universal Postal Convention, to which both Cuba and the United States were parties, prohibiting the insertion of dutiable articles in ordinary or registered correspondence. (35 U.S. Stat. L. 1639.) On the part of the United States, the Universal Postal Convention had been concluded by the Postmaster-General, "by and with the "advice and consent of the President," pursuant to authority given by U.S. Rev. Stat. 398.

Held: That the package must not be forfeited. Referring to the Universal Postal Convention, the Court said: "Such "conventions are not treaties, because not made by and with "the advice and consent of the Senate, and they are not laws, "because not enacted by Congress." (256 Fed. 305, 306.) [Report: 256 Fed. 305.]

Treaties—Operation of—Protocols not Submitted to Ratification.

See Case No. 126 (*In re McCall's Estate*).

Treaties—Forms of—Protocols not Submitted to Ratification.

See Case No. 126 (*In re McCall's Estate*).

ii.—Signature. Accession and Adhesion. Tacit Renewal

Treaties—Tacit Renewal—Germany and Czechoslovakia—State Succession.

See Case No. 41 (*Customs House (State Succession) Case*).

V.—Parties to Treaties. Right to Conclude Treaties. Composite and Dependent States and Territories

Treaties—Parties to—Treaty Interpreting a Convention to which One of the Signatories of the Treaty was not a Party.

See Case No. 21 (*Baltzoudis* v. *Souliotis*).

VI.—Constitutional Limitations

Treaties—Constitutional Limitations—United States of America—Limitation of State Rights by Treaty.

See Case No. 1 (*State of Missouri* v. *Holland, United States Game Warden*).

VIII.—Ratification of Treaties. Entrance into Force

Case No. 227 **Treaties—Ratification and Entrance into Force—Reliance on Non-Ratified Treaties—Treaty of St. Germain, Articles 177 and 179.**

PARIJ AND OTHERS *v.* AUSTRO-HUNGARIAN TREASURY.

Poland, Supreme Court (*Full Meeting*). 31 *January*, 1920.

THE FACTS.—The plaintiffs were interned by Austrian authorities during the World War. Under an Austrian statute of 1918 they were entitled to claim against the Treasury damages for certain illegal acts of Austrian civil and military authorities, the competent court being in their case the (then Austrian) Court of Appeal of Lwów. After the re-establishment of Poland they brought the present action before the Court of Appeal of Lwów, which refused to entertain the action on the ground that the Austro-Hungarian Monarchy having ceased to exist, the States formed out of it had never declared themselves ready to form a body which would be the representative of the former Austro-Hungarian State Treasury.

On appeal to the Supreme Court (of which the competent Divisional Court demanded a full meeting),

Held : That the claim cannot be entertained. The Austrian statute in question presupposed the continued existence of the

Austrian State and Treasury, and thus had ceased to operate. The plaintiffs, being now Polish and no longer Austrian citizens, could not in Polish territory sue an Austrian State, not existing on that territory, before a non-existent Austrian court. This view found confirmation in the Peace Treaty of St. Germain, " which, although so far not ratified, may be quoted in support " of the views of the Court of Appeal as pointing as clearly as " could be to the true nature of the claim and to the proper " way of enforcing it " : here the Court quoted Articles 177-179 of the Treaty of St. Germain, establishing the responsibility of Austria and her allies for causing all the loss and damage to which the Allied and Associated Governments and their nationals had been subjected as a result of the war imposed upon them by the aggression of Austria-Hungary and her allies, including damage caused by cruelty, violence or maltreatment (Annex I), and designating the Reparation Commission as the proper authority to investigate the claims in question. [Report : Zb. O.S.N. Og., 1918-1921, C. No. 3.]

Treaties—Ratification and Entrance into Force—Non-Ratified Treaties—Legal Basis of Conditions Abroad Although Not Ratified in the State of the Tribunal. **Case No. 228**

REPUBLIC *v.* JUST (*alias* BELF) AND OTHERS.

Poland, Supreme Court, Third Division. 27 September, 1922.

THE FACTS.—The defendants were convicted by a jury, before the District Court of Lwów, of having, early in 1921, counterfeited " public credit papers accepted " as (or passing for) money " (definition contained in the Austrian Penal Code of 1853 still in force in that part of Poland), *viz.* bank notes of the late Austro-Hungarian Bank of Issue (the Austro-Hungarian Bank) of the face value of 1000 Kronen. In their appeal to the Supreme Court the defendants contended, *inter alia*, that such bank notes were not, in 1921, public credit paper accepted as money in Poland.

The notes were formerly legal currency in Austria.

Under Article 206 of the Treaty of St. Germain, each so-called Succession State was to stamp notes of the late Austro-Hungarian Bank within two months of the coming into force of the Treaty ; within twelve months of the same date each was to withdraw such notes from circulation, replacing them by its own

Case No. 228 *contd.*

currency, and within another two months they were to place the withdrawn notes in the hands of the Reparations Commission. The notes of the Bank were stamped in various Succession States in 1919 and 1920; after April, 1920, they ceased to be legal currency in Poland. In certain States, however, notably in Roumania and Italy, the withdrawal of unstamped notes was still in progress during 1921. The Treaty of St. Germain had not been ratified in Poland in 1921 or 1922.

Held, affirming the conviction: That although the Treaty of St. Germain was not yet ratified by Poland, the Court "must take it into account as forming the legal basis of conditions existing abroad"; that the notes were thus "accepted for money," being "*de facto* in circulation in Poland, mainly because of their circulation" in certain foreign States. [Report: O.S.P., vol. II, No. 294.]

Case No. 229

Treaties—Ratification—Entrance into Force—Operation and Enforcement.

(POLISH) STATE TREASURY *v.* ARCHDUKE RAINER KARL AND LAND CREDIT BANK OF LWÓW.

Poland, Supreme Court, Third Division. 10 *May*, 1921.

THE FACTS.—The defendant, a former Austrian Archduke, owned the estate of Izdebnik in the district of the Court of Appeal of Cracow. After the re-establishment of Poland, the estate was placed by the Polish Government in the hands of a public administrator. The defendant Archduke then sold the estate to the defendant Bank. The Polish Treasury brought the present action to have the sale declared void: (1) because, contrary to the law, the consent of the Land Reform Office had not been obtained; and (2) because under Article 208 of the Treaty of St. Germain (at that time not yet ratified by or published in the Official Journal of Poland) the estate in question, being the property of a member of the former royal family of Austria-Hungary, was to become the property of the Polish State.

The District Court of Wadowice dismissed the action, *inter alia*, because the Treaty of St. Germain was not yet ratified. The Court of Appeal of Cracow reversed this decision, holding that Article 208 relates, *inter alia*, to the private property of (members of) the former royal family. The fact that the Treaty of St. Germain was not yet ratified could not suffice to bar the claim. The Treaty, even before ratification, was in any case a State act. The owner could not of his own will frustrate the stipulations of the Treaty.

On appeal to the Supreme Court,

Held, reversing the decision of the Court of Appeal: For the defendants. The introduction of compulsory administration may have had for its purpose either the safeguarding of the interests of the Polish State or the safeguarding of those of the absent owner, and that by itself does not deprive the owner of the right of disposing of his property. The Treaty of St. Germain, not having been ratified, has no binding force. [Reports: O.S.P., vol. I, No. 328; P.P.A. (1921), p. 45.]

NOTE.—For a discussion of this case see *O.S.P.*, vol. I, p. 315, n.; and *G.S.W.* (1921), p. 235.

IX.—Operation and Enforcement of Treaties. Necessity of Legislation

[See also Part I, INTERNATIONAL LAW IN GENERAL: *Relation to Municipal Law*; and Part VI, THE INDIVIDUAL IN INTERNATIONAL LAW: *In General*.]

Treaties—Operation of—Overriding Conflicting Statutory Provisions. **Case No. 230**

VIETTI *v.* THE GEORGE K. MACKIE FUEL CO.

United States, Supreme Court of Kansas. 7 May, 1921.

THE FACTS.—This was a proceeding in Kansas to recover workmen's compensation for Italian dependents residing in Kansas. The Kansas Workmen's Compensation Law (Law 1917, ch. 226, § 3) limited the amount of compensation to $750 if the workman did not leave dependents who were "citizens of and residing in" the United States or Canada. The Treaty between Italy and the United States (38 U.S. Stat. L. 1669) provided that aliens and nationals should receive like treatment under laws establishing civil responsibility

Case No. 230 *contd.*

for injuries or for death caused by negligence or fault.[1] The lower Court interpreted the Kansas Act to mean that either citizenship *or* residence was enough to allow compensation in excess of $750 and made an award of over $3000. On appeal,

Held: That the judgment must be affirmed. The construction of the statute by the lower Court was erroneous; but the effect of the Treaty, overriding any conflicting statutory provisions, was to prevent any restriction of the right to compensation on account of nationality. The Court also thought, in view of *Truax* v. *Raich*, 239 U.S. 33, that the statute violated the Fourteenth Amendment to the Constitution of the United States.[2] [Report: 109 Kans. 179.]

Case No. 231

Treaties—Operation and Enforcement—Overriding Conflicting State Legislation.

In re Terui.

United States, Supreme Court of California. 12 *September*, 1921.

The Facts.—This was a petition for habeas corpus. The petitioner, a Japanese subject resident in California, was held in custody for failure to pay a poll tax levied on aliens. There was no such tax levied on citizens, nor were aliens exempted from other taxation on account of alienage. The Treaty of 1911 between Japan and the United States provided for the liberty of the citizens of each State to enjoy the same rights and privileges in the other State as natives; and further that "they "shall not be compelled, under any pretext whatever, "to pay any charges or taxes other or higher than those "that are or may be paid by native citizens or sub-"jects." (37 U.S. Stat. L. 1504.) It was contended that the alien poll tax law was invalid as a violation of the Fourteenth Amendment to the Constitution of the United States and of the Treaty with Japan.

Held: That the prisoner must be discharged. The Treaty overruled contrary State legislation and specifically prevented such a tax levied solely upon aliens. [Report: 187 Calif. 20.]

[1] See the text quoted in *Frasca* v. *City Coal Co.*, 97 Conn. 212, Case No. 254.
[2] See *In re Kotta* (Case No. 167).

Treaties—Operation and Enforcement—Overriding Conflicting State Law—Interpretation—Alien's Privilege of Engaging in Trade. **Case No. 232**

POON *v.* MILLER.

United States, Texas Court of Civil Appeals, San Antonio.
2 *November*, 1921.

THE FACTS.—The plaintiff, a Chinese subject residing in Texas, bought fish-market space from the defendant and secured from him a contract that the defendant would not engage in the fish business in the city. The defendant failed to keep his agreement. The plaintiff sued for damages and an injunction. The Treaty between China and the United States provided for most-favoured-nation treatment. (22 U.S. Stat. L. 827.) The plaintiff claimed to be entitled, under the Treaty, to the privilege of engaging in trade and doing anything necessary or incident thereto on the same terms as citizens. The lower Court found for the defendant on the ground that a Texas statute (Vernon's Sayles' Statutes, Art. 3987) prohibited engaging in the wholesale fish-dealing business without a licence, which should not be granted to aliens. On appeal,

Held: That the judgment must be reversed. The Treaty was superior to the conflicting State law. Although Texas had entered the Union in a way different from the other States, it had no greater rights. The law in question was distinguished from laws forbidding aliens to fish, since the latter were a regulation of State property in wild fish and game. After fish came to the wholesaler, the State no longer had a property right in them sufficient to justify such a discrimination against aliens. [Report: 234 S.W. Rep. 573.]

Treaties—Operation of—How far Affecting Relations between one Party and its own Subjects—§ 1 of Annex to Articles 297 and 298 of the Treaty of Versailles—German Measures of Compulsory Administration in Belgium and German Nationals. **Case No. 233**

IN RE ADMINISTRATOR OF *LE PROGRÈS INDUSTRIEL.*

Germany, Reichsgericht in Civil Matters. 19 *November*, 1920.

THE FACTS.—During the war the German occupation authorities in Belgium appointed the plaintiff as ad-

Case No. 233 *contd.*

ministrator and receiver of the factories belonging to the company *Le Progrès Industriel*. In November, 1918, before the German troops left Belgium, the factory supplied the defendant, a German subject, with certain machines in respect of which the present action was brought. In § 1 of the Annex to Articles 297 and 298 of the Treaty of Versailles all war measures adopted by the German occupation authorities in Belgium, including those of compulsory administration, were declared null and void. The defendant contended that in view of the above provision of the Treaty the plaintiff was no longer entitled to bring the action.

Held, on final appeal on a point of law: That the Administration was entitled to bring the action. The nullity of administrative measures, as laid down in the Annex to Articles 297 and 298, must be regarded as bearing only upon the relations between enemy States and their subjects on the one side, and Germany and her subjects on the other. The Peace Treaty regulates only such relations. It does not affect internal German relations, for instance, those arising out of German war measures in relations between Germans according to German law. For, and as against, Germans the legal transactions of the compulsory administrator remain valid; and his office continues in so far as this is necessary for the liquidation of the administration. [Report: *E.R.Z.*, vol. 101, p. 3.]

NOTE.—The Court pointed out that there is a special reason why in this case the above interpretation of the legal position must be adopted. The nullity of the administrative measures, as laid down in the Annex, entails the obligation on Germany to make reparation to the owners in accordance with Articles 231 *et seq.* of the Treaty. Germany, in the fulfilment of her duty of compensation, must duly clear up the relations arising out of the compulsory administration and collect the outstanding debts.

Case No. 234

Treaties—Operation and Enforcement of—German Constitution—Effect of Publication in the Journal of Laws—Function of Publication—Deposit of Ratifications.

PUBLICATION OF TREATIES (GERMANY) CASE.

Germany, Reichsgericht in Criminal Matters. 25 *September*, 1920.

THE FACTS.—The Journal of the Laws of the *Reich* (*Reichsgesetzblatt*) published on 13 January, 1920, an announcement by the German Minister for Foreign Affairs of 11 January, 1920, to the effect that the

Treaty of Versailles had been ratified by the signatory States, and that the first protocol on the deposit of ratifications was signed on 10 January, 1920. According to the German Constitution, German laws become effective within fourteen days of their publication in the Journal of Laws. The Court below held that as in view of this provision of the Constitution the Treaty of Versailles became effective, as between the *Reich* and German subjects, on 27 January, 1920, the offence of the accused committed during the period from 14-19 January was not punishable under the provisions of the Treaty.

Held, on final appeal on a point of law: That the Opinion of the Court below cannot be accepted. The announcement of the Minister of 11 January, 1920, did not have reference to any decision of the German Parliament. It contained no legal provision. It merely stated the fact that the Treaty had been ratified and that the ratifications had been exchanged. Article 71 of the new Constitution is identical with Article 2, paragraph 3, of the old Constitution. The latter had been consistently interpreted by the *Reichsgericht* to the effect that treaties acquire through publication the force of law; it was not necessary that they should be accompanied by a clause ordering that they should be obeyed. In the present case no such clause was necessary, for the additional reason that there had already been passed on 16 July, 1919, a law ordering the publication of the Treaty. Article 440, paragraph 7, of the Treaty of Versailles laid down that the Treaty shall enter into force with the fulfilment of a certain condition, namely, with the signature of the protocol of deposit of ratifications. The announcement of 13 January, 1920, merely states that that protocol was signed, *i.e.* that the Treaty entered into force. The announcement had the same function as the announcements of the ratifications of other treaties in the Journal of Laws. The Conventions concluded at the Second Hague Conference were announced in this way. These announcements were not in the nature of commands ordering that these treaties should be obeyed. They defined the time and scope of their operation. [Report: *Fontes Juris Gentium,* Series A, Section II, vol. I, No. 205.]

NOTE.—The facts and contentions which gave rise to this decision do not appear clearly from the available report, but the observations of the Court on the points indicated in the heading are of sufficient general interest to warrant inclusion.—[Ed.]

Treaties—Operation of—Effect of Publication.

See Case No. 121 (*Upper Silesia (Plebiscite Commission) Case*).

X.—Effect of Treaties on Third Parties

Case No. 235 **Treaties—Effect upon Third Parties—Recognition by Courts of States not Parties—Effect upon Individuals—Jurisdiction of Dutch Court with regard to Contractual Relation between German Company and Greek Subject Domiciled in Holland—Claim for Money Received by London Branch of German Bank during the War on Account of Greek Customer—Applicability of Article 304 (*b*), paragraph 2, of Treaty of Versailles.**

DEUTSCHE BANK *v.* ZIRINI.

Holland, District Court of The Hague. 7 February, 1922.

(Dr. A. H. DU MOSCH, President; Drs. W. J. BERGER and W. LUNSINGH TONCKENS, Judges.)

THE FACTS.—In this suit the Deutsche Bank, of Berlin, sought to have a judgment, which the same Court had rendered, on 8 March, 1921, in favour of the plaintiff, a Greek subject, resident at The Hague, annulled. By that judgment (which was a judgment by default) the Court had ordered the Deutsche Bank to pay to the plaintiff the sum of £275. 12s. 11d., plus interest at the rate of 6 per cent. from the date of the writ, this sum being the proceeds of a bill of exchange which the plaintiff Zirini, then living at Dresden (Germany), had lodged with the Bank, in 1914, for collection in London, by its branch office there. The bill had been duly honoured by the acceptor, on 8 August, 1914, but the proceeds of the same had not been paid out to the plaintiff, owing to the fact that the British Government had placed an embargo, shortly after the outbreak of the war, on all assets of the London branch of the Deutsche Bank and continued, after the conclusion of peace, to refuse payment of the proceeds in question, all efforts of the Bank with the Custodian of Enemy Property to get the remittance carried through having been in vain. The Deutsche Bank was not prepared to answer for an interference by the British Government with the property of a Greek subject, but only to remit to the owner of the sum all money which it might itself obtain either from the British or from the German Government, and to assign to him its own claims against the British Government. The plaintiff was not prepared to wait till the end of the liquidation of the branch office in London pursuant to Article 297(*b*) of the Treaty of Versailles, nor to rely on the engagement of the German Government under Article 297 (*i*) of that Treaty, and, therefore, sued the Deutsche Bank in the court of his Dutch residence, according to Article 126 of the Dutch Code of Civil Procedure. In seeking the annulment of the original judgment, the Deutsche Bank urged the Court to decide that it had no jurisdiction, in view of the fact that the claim was comprised in Article 304 (*b*), paragraph 2, of the Treaty of Versailles, to which both the plaintiff's and the defendant's countries were parties, and that, consequently, the matter was within the exclusive jurisdiction of the Mixed Arbitral Tribunal.

Held: That the Court had jurisdiction. Article 304 of the Treaty of Versailles contains an express exception to the jurisdiction of the Mixed Arbitral Tribunals in respect of questions which, under the laws of the Allied, Associated or Neutral Powers, are within the jurisdiction of the national courts of those Powers. In the case under consideration the Dutch Court has jurisdiction under the Code of Civil Procedure (Article 126), which authorises the judiciary of the Kingdom to hear and decide all claims brought before it by plaintiffs resident in Holland against respondents who have no recognised residence in that country, whatsoever the nationality of the parties to the suit might be. Accordingly, the Treaty of Versailles, although obligatory between Germany and Greece, did not preclude the Greek plaintiff from suing the Deutsche Bank in a Dutch court. Apart from the question of the applicability of Article 297 of the Treaty of Versailles to pecuniary debts such as that under discussion, Article 296 of that Treaty is not applicable to the case, since the latter refers only to debts due by a national of one of the contracting Powers, resident within its territory, to a national of an opposing Power, resident within its territory. In the present case the appeal of the Deutsche Bank on the ground of *force majeure* was not justified since, in spite of the retention of the proceeds of the bill of exchange by the British Government, the Bank was

Case No. 235 *contd.* quite able to pay the sum to the plaintiff out of its cash in Germany. [Report: *Weekblad van het Recht*, 6 April, 1923, No. 11010.]

NOTE.—The Court of Appeal of The Hague, on 30 November, 1922 (Dr. F. N. L. Aberson, President; Drs. K. W. Brevet and L. A. M. Sassen, Judges), confirmed the judgment of the Court of First Instance and approved of the reasons underlying the Court's decision. [Report: *Weekblad van het Recht*, 19 October, 1923, No. 11094.] The Supreme Court (in a judgment of 10 January, 1924), while confining itself to the interpretation of Dutch law, confirmed the decision of the Appellate Court. [Reports: *Weekblad van het Recht*, 24 March, 1924, No. 11161; *Nederlandsche Jurisprudentie*, 1924, p. 281.]

Treaties—Effect on Third Parties—Effect of Armistice Agreement of November, 1918, on the Treaty of Brest Litowsk.

See Case No. 169 (*Immovables* (*Aliens in Germany*) *Case*).

Treaties—Effect upon Third Parties—Provisions of the Treaty of Versailles as to the Continuance of Certain International Conventions—Article 287 of the Treaty—Effect upon Switzerland.

See Case No. 42 (*In re M. & O.*).

XI.—Termination of Treaties

i.—By Operation of Law

(*a*) In General

Treaties—Termination —Termination of Some Provisions and Maintenance of Others.

See Case No. 271 (*Hughes* v. *Techt*; *Techt* v. *Hughes*).

Termination of Treaties—Relevance of Rules of Municipal Law as to Discharge of Contracts.

See Case No. 288 (*The Blonde and other Ships*) (Note 1).

(*c*) Outbreak of War

See Part XI, War and Neutrality: A, V, ii.

ii.—By Act of Party

(*a*) In General

Termination of Treaties—By Act of Party—Implied Repeal by Statute—Eighteenth Amendment to the Constitution of the United States. **Case No. 236**

Grogan *v.* Walker & Sons.

United States Supreme Court. 15 *May*, 1922.

The Facts.—These were suits to forbid interference with the transportation and transhipment of whisky. In the first case the United States District Court for the Eastern District of Michigan enjoined the Collector of Internal Revenue, at the suit of a Canadian corporation, from interfering with the shipping of whisky from Canada by way of Detroit in bond through the United States to Mexico and Central or South America. (275 Fed. 373.) In the second case the United States District Court for the Southern District of New York refused an injunction sought by a British corporation to prevent interference with the transhipment of whisky from one British ship to another in New York harbour. (280 Fed. 870.) The plaintiffs relied upon a Treaty between Great Britain and the United States of 8 May, 1871 (17 U.S. Stat. L. 863), authorising transit of merchandise through the United States without payment of duty, and U.S. Rev. Stat. § 3005, as amended, providing for a similar exemption. The Eighteenth Amendment to the Constitution of the United States prohibited " the manufacture, sale, or " transportation of intoxicating liquors within, the " importation thereof into, or the exportation thereof " from, the United States and all territory subject to " the jurisdiction thereof for beverage purposes." The National Prohibition Act of 28 October, 1919, provided for the enforcement of the Eighteenth Amendment. (41 U.S. Stat. L. 305.)

Held, three justices dissenting: That the decree granting an injunction must be reversed and the decree denying an injunction affirmed. While it is true that the repeal of statutes, and *a fortiori* of treaties, by implication is not to be favoured, the letter of the later law was too strong in this case. Delivering the Opinion of the Court, Mr. Justice Holmes said: " The

Case No. 236 *contd.*

"Eighteenth Amendment meant a great revolution in the policy "of this country, and presumably and obviously meant to upset "a good many things on as well as off the statute book. . . . It "is obvious that those whose wishes and opinions were em- "bodied in the Amendment meant to stop the whole business." (259 U.S. 80, 89.)

The dissenting justices contended that the importation, transportation or exportation involved in these cases was not of the kind intended to be prohibited by the Amendment and the Prohibition Act, and that the Treaty should not be considered as abrogated or repealed by the later legislation. [Report: 259 U.S. 80.]

NOTE.—See 21 M.L.R. 911.

Termination of Treaties—By Act of Party—Unilateral Denunciation—Results of Non-performance by Other Party —Waiver of Right to Repudiate.

See Case No. 288 (*The Blonde and other Ships*).

Treaties—Abrogation of—Unilateral—By Subsequent Legislation.

See Case No. 176 (*Ex parte Pettine*).

XII.—Interpretation of Treaties

i.—Agencies of Interpretation. Construction in Accordance with the Intention of the Parties

Case No. 237

PERMANENT COURT OF INTERNATIONAL JUSTICE. ADVISORY OPINION No. 2.

Treaties—Interpretation—Conduct of the Parties Subsequent to the Conclusion of the Treaty—Action Taken under the Treaty.

COMPETENCE OF THE INTERNATIONAL LABOUR ORGANISATION.

(Regulation of Conditions of Work of Persons Employed in Agriculture.)

12 *August*, 1922.[1]

THE FACTS.—(See Case No. 257.) After having arrived at the conclusion that there was no ambiguity in the provisions of the Treaty of Versailles in regard to the competence of the

[1] The Court was composed as follows: Loder, President; Weiss, Vice-President; Lord Finlay, Nyholm, Moore, de Bustamante, Altamira, Oda, Anzilotti, Judges; Negulesco, Deputy-Judge. Judge Weiss and Deputy-Judge Negulesco dissented.

International Labour Organisation to deal with the international regulation of conditions of work of persons employed in agriculture, the Court considered the question whether, if there were any ambiguity, it might consider, for the purpose of construing the text, the action taken under the Treaty.

Held: That such action "might suffice to turn the "scale in favour of the inclusion of agriculture, if there "were any ambiguity." Although the Treaty was signed in June, 1919, and although in the intervening period the subject of agriculture was discussed and dealt with in various forms, it was not until October, 1921, that the question was raised whether the International Labour Organisation was competent to deal with the regulation of agricultural work. The second session of the International Labour Conference in 1920 was devoted entirely to seamen, and the same Conference adopted a recommendation concerning the regulation of work in the fishing industry. It was never suggested that either navigation or fisheries were outside the competence of the International Labour Organisation. But the arguments for the exclusion of agriculture can with equal force be used for the exclusion of the other above-mentioned industries. [Report: P.C.I.J., Series B, Nos. 2 and 3, pp. 40, 41.]

Treaties—Interpretation—General Purpose of the Treaty—Context as a Whole—Overriding Literal Interpretation—Exceptional Departures from the General Purpose of the Treaty—Effect on Interpretation of the Treaty as a Whole.

Case No. 238

PERMANENT COURT OF INTERNATIONAL JUSTICE.

ADVISORY OPINION No. 2.

COMPETENCE OF THE INTERNATIONAL LABOUR ORGANISATION.

(Regulation of Conditions of Work of Persons Employed in Agriculture.)

12 *August*, 1922.

THE FACTS.—(See Case No. 257.) The argument of the Governments opposing the competence of the International Labour Organisation to regu-

Case No. 238 *contd.*

late the conditions of work of persons employed in agriculture rested almost entirely on the contention that the words "*industrie*" and "*industrielle*" occurring in the French text of some of the relevant clauses ordinarily refer to manufactures, and that Part XIII of the Treaty must therefore be confined to these limits. While not admitting fully the linguistic part of this argument,[1] the Court

Held : That although in general the above terms are used in a special and restrictive sense, the decisive question is in what sense these clauses should be interpreted when reading the Treaty as a whole. "At the "present day the adjective is, especially in French, "most commonly used in relation to the arts or manu- "factures, and would ordinarily be so understood, "unless the context indicated that it was to be inter- "preted otherwise. But the context is the final test, "and in the present instance the Court must consider "the position in which these words are found and the "sense in which they are employed in Part XIII of "the Treaty of Versailles."

As the Court found—by reference to the general purpose of the Treaty (see Case No. 257)—that the International Labour Organisation was competent to deal with conditions of work of persons employed in agriculture, the natural inference would be to interpret provisions of the Treaty alleged to be doubtful by reference to the findings on the major question. Thus when Article 412 of the Treaty provided a panel "of "persons of industrial experience," the French text reading "*personnes compétentes en matières industrielles,*" the phrase "*matières industrielles*" when taken in conjunction with other parts of the Treaty ought to be interpreted as including the industry of agriculture. "But, even if it were not so read, the consequences

[1] The Court referred to the French dictionary by Littré and the Oxford Dictionary as showing that the words "*industrie*" and "industry," although as a rule used in the restricted meaning, referred also generally to "toutes "les opérations qui concourent à la production des richesses" or to "habitual "employment in some useful work."

"would be that there would seem to be merely a "defect in the constitution of the machinery in this "particular instance, and not that the powers given "to the international organisation with regard to con- "ditions of labour were to be similarly limited." [Report: P.C.I.J., Series B, Nos. 2 and 3, pp. 35-37.]

Interpretation of Treaties—In General—Interpretation by Municipal Courts—How far Binding upon Foreign Governments—Pronouncements of Judicial Authorities in Matters of Treaties—How far Internationally Effective—How far Expressive of the Official Interpretation of the State Concerned—Interpretation of Municipal Exactments by Municipal Courts—Whether Liable to Review by International Tribunals—Denial of Justice. **Case No. 239**

THE DAVID J. ADAMS.

British-American Claims Arbitral Tribunal. 9 *December*, 1921.

(FROMAGEOT, FITZPATRICK, ANDERSON.)

THE FACTS.—This was a claim put forward by the United States on account of the seizure and subsequent condemnation of the schooner *David J. Adams.*

By the Treaty of London of 20 October, 1818, the United States renounced the liberty of fishing in Canadian waters in the following terms: "The United "States hereby renounce forever, any liberty, hereto- "fore enjoyed or claimed by the inhabitants thereof, "to take, dry or cure fish on, or within three marine "miles of, any of the coasts, bays, creeks, or harbours "of His Britannic Majesty's Dominions in America not "included within the above-mentioned limits; Pro- "vided, however, that the American fishermen shall be "admitted to enter such bays or harbours for the "purpose of shelter and of repairing damages therein, "of purchasing wood, and of obtaining water, and "for no other purpose whatever." (*United States Memorial*, p. 375.) The *David J. Adams* was seized and condemned for entering Canadian waters for purposes other than those specified above, in particular for the purpose of purchasing bait contrary to the provisions of the Treaty of 1818 and of various British and Canadian enactments. It seems to have been contended by Great Britain that the Tribunal could not disregard the finding of the Canadian court on the question

Case No. 239 ***contd.***

whether the owners of the *David J. Adams* have by their action contravened the terms of the Treaty of 1818.

Held: That the mere fact that a British court, however authoritative, interpreted a treaty in a certain manner, cannot be accepted by the Tribunal as a conclusive interpretation binding upon the United States. "The duty of this international Tribunal is to determine, from the international point of view, how the provisions of the treaty are to be interpreted and applied to the facts, and consequently whether the loss resulting from the forfeiture of the vessel gives rise to an indemnity." The subjection of one State to an interpretation of a treaty asserted by the other or its authorised organs, including its judicial authorities (see below), would in fact place one State under the jurisdiction of the other; it would thus be opposed to the "fundamental principle of the juridical equality of States." Such a unilateral interpretation of an essentially bilateral contract could not be binding upon another State by the mere fact that it was given by a judicial, legislative or other authority of the State.

Great Britain and Canada, acting by their properly constituted judicial authorities, were entitled to interpret and to apply legislation enacted for the purpose of giving effect to the Treaty, but such judicial action was internationally effective only in so far as—like the Act which it applied—it was consistent with the Treaty.

The decision of the Canadian judicial authorities must be taken as an authorised expression of the position assumed on this question by Great Britain, and "so far as such decision implies an interpretation of said treaty, it must be taken as the authorized expression of the Canadian interpretation."

On the other hand, the Tribunal was not called upon to pronounce whether the Canadian authorities had justly and properly applied the municipal enactments in question. Denial of justice was not alleged in the present case. [Reports: Nielsen, p. 526; *A.J.*, XVI (1922), p. 315.]

Case No. 240

Interpretation of Governmental Agreements—Franco-American Agreement on Military Jurisdiction in France.

French State *v.* Prat.

France, Court of Cassation (Criminal Chamber).

13 *August*, 1920.

The Facts.—Prat, a Captain in the American Army, was charged and arrested for having fraudulently appropriated goods at Montoir and St. Nazaire to the prejudice of the French State. The competent American authorities intimated that as Prat was not accused of theft to the prejudice of the American State and had been demobilised at the date of his arrest, the American military courts had no jurisdiction over him. The French and American Governments were thus agreed that the French courts had jurisdiction. The *Tribunal correctionnel* and the Court of Rennes (by a decision of 29 June, 1920) nevertheless declared that they were not competent because the agreement concluded between France and the United States of America in 1918 and prolonged on 5 September, 1919, seemed in such cases to give jurisdiction to the American military courts.

Held, by the Court of Cassation: That the French courts had jurisdiction. The agreement between the two Governments was a diplomatic convention and, being an intergovernmental act, could only be interpreted by the Governments themselves. The Governments in question had already recognised that the Franco-American Agreement of 1918 was inapplicable in the present case. In these circumstances the finding of the Court of Rennes was contrary to Article 3 of the *Code Civil* which says that "the laws for the security of persons "and property (*les lois de police et de sécurité*) are binding upon "all those who live on French territory." [Reports: 48 *Clunet* (1921), p. 970; *Dalloz*, 1921, Part I, p. 58.]

NOTE.—As to refusal of a municipal court to criticise a treaty, see the remarks of Lord Russell (then Russell, J.) in *Stoeck* v. *Public Trustee*, L.R. [1921] 2 Ch. 67, at p. 71.

Interpretation of Treaties—Competence of Courts in the Matter of Interpretation—Interpretation for Purposes of Municipal Law by Government concerned—Franco-Spanish Convention of 7 January, 1862—Tax on War-Profits. **Case No. 241**

IN RE X.

France, Council of State. 11 *June*, 1920.

THE FACTS.—The claimant was assessed for the payment of the special tax on war-profits. His contention that he was not liable was based on the terms of Article 4 of the Franco-Spanish Convention of 7 January, 1862, which provided that: "French nationals in Spain and

Case No. 241 *contd.*

"Spanish nationals in France shall be exempt from all "taxation for war purposes, payments in advance, "borrowings, war loans and all other extraordinary "impositions of whatever nature levied in either "country under exceptional circumstances, except in "so far as such impositions may be levied on landed "property." The *Commission Supérieure des Bénéfices de Guerre* decided that the claimant was liable.

Held: That the claim must be dismissed. The *Commission Supérieure* had only adopted the interpretation given by the Government. "In the absence of any special agreement "between the Governments concerned, in France the French "Government alone is competent to interpret the meaning "and scope of the provision for exemption from taxation "contained in the article in question." [Report: Sirey, 1922, Part III, p. 36.]

See Case No. 252 (*Sullivan* v. *Kidd*).

Case No. 242

Interpretation of Treaties for Purposes of Municipal Law by Government Concerned—French Settlement at Shanghai—Concession of Public Services.

In re Compagnie Française de Tramways et d'Éclairage Électrique de Shanghai.

France, Council of State. 27 January, 1922.

The Facts.—A dispute arose between the company and the Municipal Council of the French Settlement at Shanghai as to authorising the company to raise the water and electricity rates on account of the abnormal rise in the price of coal and other necessary materials used in the company's business. The company contended that the French Settlement at Shanghai was a French administrative unit, and that therefore the dispute could be settled by an administrative court in accordance with the principles governing the relations between French administrative authorities and their concessionaries.

Held: That the claim must be dismissed. In principle there was no objection to the creation by the French Government on a foreign territory, with the consent of the Government concerned, of an organisation intended to provide for certain collective French interests, especially by making regular public utility contracts in French legal form which, as such, would be subject to the administrative jurisdiction. But the character of the contracts in question in this case depended upon the meaning to be given to the treaties concluded between France and China on 27 November, 1844, at Whampoa, and 27 June, 1858, at Tien-tsin, and also the subsequent agreements made between French consuls and the local Chinese authorities. "The interpretation of these "different diplomatic conventions from this point of view can "only be made by the French Government, and according to "the interpretation given by the Ministry of Foreign Affairs "the contracts between the appellant company and the "Municipal Council of Shanghai do not, in the special con-"ditions in which they were made, constitute concession con-"tracts for public utilities." [Reports: *Gazette du Palais*, 1922, I, p. 283; *Recueil des Arrêts du Conseil d'État*, 1922, p. 87.]

Treaties—Interpretation—Literal Interpretation—Intention of Negotiators—Relevance of Subsequent Action of One of the Contracting Parties. **Case No. 243**

THE DAVID J. ADAMS.

British-American Claims Arbitral Tribunal. 9 December, 1921.

(FROMAGEOT, FITZPATRICK, ANDERSON.)

THE FACTS.—(See also Case No. 239.) It was contended by Great Britain that the provision of the Treaty of 1818 according to which American fishermen shall be permitted to enter Canadian bays and harbours for shelter, repairing damages, purchasing wood and obtaining water, "and for no other purpose whatever," meant that American fishermen were not entitled to enter these bays and harbours to purchase bait. According to the United States, the renunciation on their part, in the Treaty of 1818, of their former right to fish in Canadian waters, had as a counterpart the obligation of Canada to admit American fishermen for shelter, repairs, wood and water, and for no other purpose. But, it was contended, although Canada was entitled to prohibit the admittance of American fishermen for other purposes than the four mentioned above, so long as the entrance for the purpose of purchasing bait was not prohibited by Canadian legislation it must be considered as the exercise of a legal right of access. The United States pointed out that "the literal mean-

Case No. 243 *contd.*

" ing of an isolated clause is often shown not to be the " meaning really understood or intended." The United States adduced in support of their contention the negotiations preceding the signature of the Treaty.

Held : (*a*) That a provision laying down that fishermen shall be admitted for certain enumerated purposes and " for no other " purpose whatever " is perfectly clear. It meant that for the specified purposes the fishermen had the right of entrance and that for any other purpose they had no such right. It is difficult to contend that by such plain words the right of entrance for the purpose of purchasing bait has not been denied.

(*b*) No evidence has been presented to the effect that the intention of the negotiators was to contradict the literal meaning of the Treaty.

(*c*) Immediately after the conclusion of the Treaty, a British Act of Parliament was passed in 1819 (59 Geo. III, c. 36, § III) which expressly provided that the entrance into Canadian bays and harbours for other purposes shall not be lawful. The relevant section was as follows : " Be it enacted " that it shall be lawful for any fishermen of the said United " States to enter into such bays or harbours of His Britannic " Majesty's Dominions in America as are last mentioned for " the purpose of shelter, and repairing damages therein, and " of purchasing wood, and of obtaining water, and for no other " purposes whatever." If the entrance for other purposes was not lawful, it is difficult to say that such entrance is not prohibited. [Reports: Nielsen, p. 526; *A.J.*, XVI (1922), p. 315.]

Case No. 244

Treaties—Interpretation—Effectiveness of Treaty Provisions —Interpretation by Reference to other Provisions of the same Treaty.

GERMANY AND FRANCE.

(In the Matter of the Cessions relating to the Navigation of the Rhine under Article 357 of the Treaty of Versailles.)

8 *January*, 1921.

(WALKER D. HINES, Arbitrator.)

THE FACTS.—As stated in Case No. 260. (See also Case No. 253.) It was contended by France that by virtue of Article 357 of the Treaty she was entitled to the cession of shares in certain German navigation companies in addition to the cession of tugs and vessels. One of the reasons adduced by France was that these companies, in addition to operating tugs and vessels, performed other functions, like loading and unloading of freight, storing freight in warehouses, etc.; that these functions are proper and necessary incidents to navigation; that it was the purpose of the Treaty to provide for the legitimate needs of France by means of organisations already established and adequately equipped; and that France ought not to be left in a position where she would have to depend upon the goodwill of German agencies for the performance of these auxiliary services.

Held: That the French contention must be accepted. (*a*) It was just and reasonable that Germany should cede to France shares in a German Rhine navigation company conducting sufficiently extended business.[1] As no practical purpose will be accomplished by the cession of a mere minority interest, it was necessary and proper to require, in order to carry out the purpose of Article 357, the cession of enough shares to give France control of the company.

(*b*) The French contention was also supported by reference to Article 339 of the Treaty of Versailles which, in addition to providing for the cession of tugs and vessels on certain rivers to Allied and Associated Powers, laid down that Germany "shall in the same way cede material of all kinds necessary to "the Allied and Associated Powers concerned for the utilisation "of those river systems." That latter clause was not found in Article 357. However, there was no reason why the Treaty should give France, in connection with the restoration of her rights on the Rhine, less than Article 339 gives to the other Allied and Associated Powers in regard to newly-acquired rights on other river systems. [Report: *A.J.*, XVII (1923), pp. 786-805.]

Treaties—Interpretation—Construction in Accordance with the Intention of the Parties—Spirit of the Treaty—Technical and Legal Expressions.

See Case No. 246 (*Dürrenberg* v. *Polish State Treasury*).

Interpretation of Treaties—Relevance of Rules of Municipal Law as to Interpretation of Contracts.

See Case No. 288 (*The Blonde and other Ships*) (Note 1).

[1] The company in question was the Rheinschiffahrts Aktien Gesellschaft, with an annual business of about 2,000,000 tons.

ii.—Restrictive Interpretation

(a) Restrictions of Sovereignty

Case No. 245

PERMANENT COURT OF INTERNATIONAL JUSTICE.

ADVISORY OPINION No. 2.

Treaties—Interpretation—Restrictive Interpretation—Infringement of Sovereignty.

Competence of the International Labour Organisation.

(Regulation of Conditions of Work of Persons Employed in Agriculture.)

12 *August*, 1922.

The Facts.—(See Case No. 257.) It was urged on behalf of the Governments, which contended that the Treaty of Versailles did not confer upon the International Labour Organisation the right to deal with the regulation of conditions of work of persons employed in agriculture, that as the establishment of the International Labour Organisation involved a relinquishment of rights derived from national sovereignty, the competence of the Organisation should not be extended by interpretation.

Held : That although there may be some force in the above argument, " the question in each case must " resolve itself into what the terms of the Treaty " actually mean." It was from this point of view that the Court proposed to examine the question.[1] [Report : P.C.I.J., Series B, Nos. 2 and 3, p. 23.]

[1] This was the first of the long series of cases decided by Judgments and Advisory Opinions in which the parties pleaded the principle of restrictive interpretation on the ground of infringement of sovereignty. See Judgment No. 1, Series A, No. 1, p. 25 ; Advisory Opinion No. 10, Series B, No. 10, p. 21 ; Advisory Opinion No. 11, Series B, No. 11, pp. 37-39 ; Advisory Opinion No. 12, Series B, No. 12, p. 25 ; Advisory Opinion No. 13, Series B, No. 13, p. 22 ; Advisory Opinion No. 14, Series B, No. 14, p. 35 ; Judgment No. 16, Series A, No. 23, p. 26. In the present case one of the Counsel (Professor de Lapradelle) admitted that the measure of the infringement of State sovereignty as the result of the adoption of Part XIII of the Treaty of Versailles is not considerable, but he urged that in view of the fact that some restriction was placed on national sovereignty the text must be construed strictly and in a narrow sense. He said : " It is a fundamental principle that " States, justly jealous of their sovereign prerogatives, do not abandon them " willingly and that all limitations of their sovereignty must be formally " embodied in the text. One of the great principles of civil law is that, in

(*b*) Interpretation against the Party Responsible for the Drafting

Treaties—Interpretation—Provisions Drafted by the Party which Imposed the Obligation.

See Case No. 170 (*Security for Costs* (*Germany*) *Case*).

Treaties—Interpretation—Provisions Inserted in the Interest of One Party.

See Case No. 268 (*Heim and Chamant* v. *The German State*).

iii.—Bilingual Treaties

Treaties—Interpretation—Bilingual Treaties—Relation to Municipal Law—Official Translation into a Third Language—Article 256 of Treaty of Versailles—Spirit of the Treaty. **Case No. 246**

Dürrenberg *v.* Polish State Treasury.

Poland, Supreme Court, Fifth Division. 29 *September*, 1922.

The Facts.—The plaintiff had been, until 1908, a member of the dynasty of "*Reuss Jüngere Linie*," a German princely house. Under the family law of the dynasty, which was part of the law of the State and was recognised by the legislation of the *Reich*, the plaintiff had given up his family name, assuming the name and style of Count Dürrenberg, thus giving up all the privileges derived from being a member of the dynasty.

Article 256 of the Treaty of Versailles made Poland acquire all property and possessions situated in Polish territory which until the war had been under German sovereignty and belonged to the German Empire or the German States, such property and possessions including, *inter alia*, "the private property of the former "German Emperor and other Royal personages" (*et des autres personnes royales*).

In 1920 a statute was passed in Poland which pro-

" cases of doubt, liberty cannot be presumed to have been restricted ; *a fortiori*, when important legal personalities such as States are concerned, it " is a principle that, in cases of doubt, their special attributes, which include " not merely liberty but sovereignty, cannot be considered as having been in " any way restricted. In such matters, the questions involved are so important that the text is bound to be precise." (Series C, No. 1, p. 174.) See also Series C, No. 12, p. 63, for a similar argument by Professor Borel.

Case No. 246 ***contd.***

vided that in all cases where, *inter alia,* " the former " German Emperor or other members of German ruling " houses " are entered in the land registry as owners of real estate in the formerly Prussian parts of Poland, the Polish courts, on the basis of Article 256 of the Treaty of Versailles, must substitute the entry of the Polish Treasury for that of such persons. This was done in 1921 in regard to the plaintiff's estate, whereupon the plaintiff brought the present action to have his name restored as that of the owner, since he was not a " royal personage." The District Court of Ostrow and (on appeal) the Court of Appeal of Poznan, gave judgment for the plaintiff. On appeal by the Treasury to the Supreme Court, the latter, dismissing the appeal,

Held: That neither the official Polish translation of the Treaty of Versailles, published in the Polish Official Journal of Laws alongside the French and English texts (both of which are authentic), nor the expression in the statute of 1920 " other " members of German ruling houses," are binding upon the Court, " since the Polish text of the Versailles Peace Treaty " does not possess decisive importance in view of the provision " contained (in that Treaty) after Article 440, that the French " and English texts are authentic, while the statute of 14 July, " 1920, does not imply that it was intended to give a statutory " binding interpretation of the expression ' *des autres personnes* " ' *royales,*' since this would have to be expressly stated in the " statute, and that, therefore, it is only possible to rely on the " authentic text(s) of the Treaty."

Since the Treaty itself does not define more precisely the meaning of the expression *autres personnes royales*, and since it cannot be defined by comparison with other Articles, *e.g.* Article 56 which relates to France—because the Treaty deals differently with the rights of France and with those of Poland, and could have been intended to define differently for each country the group of persons whose property will be taken over by the State—and since the expression is not one generally accepted either in international or in constitutional law, it is necessary to determine the meaning of the expression on the basis of the spirit of the Treaty. The expression in question was intended to refer to constitutional conditions which had prevailed in Germany before the Revolution of November, 1918. Consequently, it is necessary to determine in each individual case, on the basis of the constitutional law of the particular

German State in question, whether the person concerned had been a "royal personage." Accordingly, since under the constitutional law of *Reuss Jüngere Linie* the plaintiff could not have been considered a member of the dynasty of that State since 1908, it was not necessary for the Court to define further the meaning of the expression in Article 256, nor the meaning of "private property." [Report: O.S.P., II, No. 332.]

Treaties—Bilingual—Authoritative Text—Hague Convention of 1907 for the Pacific Settlement of International Disputes.

See Case No. 261 (*Norway and United States: Requisition of Shipbuilding Contracts Case*), in regard to the interpretation of the term "principles of law and equity" for the statement that "it is common ground that the United States, as well as "Norway, are bound by the French text" of the above Convention.

Treaties—Interpretation—Bilingual Treaties—Drafting in English—Literal Translation into French—Anglo-American Doctrine of the Effect of War on Contracts—Adaptation of English Text to Continental Conditions.

See Case No. 274 (*Binon* v. *German State and the Silesian Fire Insurance Co.*).

Treaties — Interpretation — Bilingual Treaties — Recourse to Both Texts.

See the case *Tesdorpf* v. *German State* decided by the Anglo-German Mixed Arbitral Tribunal; *Recueil*, III (1924), p. 22, at p. 28.

Treaties—Interpretation—Bilingual Treaties—Interpretation of French Text by Reference to the English Text—Article 297 (*e*) of the Treaty of Versailles.

See Case No. 158 (*Société anonyme du Charbonnage Frédéric Henri* v. *Germany*) (*c*).

iv.—Consideration of Preparatory Work

Case No. 247
PERMANENT COURT OF INTERNATIONAL JUSTICE.
ADVISORY OPINION No. 2.

Treaties—Interpretation—Preparatory Work.

COMPETENCE OF THE INTERNATIONAL LABOUR ORGANISATION.

(Regulation of Conditions of Work of Persons Employed in Agriculture.)

12 *August*, 1922.

THE FACTS.—See Case No. 257.

The question of admissibility of preparatory work for the interpretation of the relevant provisions of the Treaty of Versailles having been raised, the Court did not think it necessary to discuss the various contentions on the matter as it had already " on the construction of the text itself reached the conclusion " that agricultural labour is within the competence of " the International Labour Organisation." There was " certainly nothing in the preparatory work to disturb " this conclusion." [Report : P.C.I.J., Series B, Nos. 2 and 3, p. 41.]

NOTE.—It will be noted that the Court did in fact consider the preparatory work from the point of view of its compatibility with the conclusion reached in another way. The Court having answered this question in the affirmative, it could decline to pronounce on the question of admissibility, which, in these circumstances, did not arise.

Case No. 248

Treaties—Interpretation of—Preparatory Work—Article 299 (*b*) of the Treaty of Versailles—Execution of Contracts " in " the General Interest "—Competence of Mixed Arbitral Tribunals.

SCHMID *v.* CHEMISCHE WERKE FURSTENWALDE.

Franco-German Mixed Arbitral Tribunal.

30 *July*, 1921.

(SJOEBORG, FORTIN, VON RICHTHOFEN.)

THE FACTS.—Article 299 (*b*) of the Treaty of Versailles provided as follows: " Any contract of which the " execution shall be required in the general interest, " within six months from the date of the coming into " force of the present Treaty, by the Allied or Associated

" Governments of which one of the parties is a national, " shall be excepted from the dissolution under this " Article." In the present case the plaintiff asked the Tribunal to declare, under Article 299 (*b*), that a contract between him and the defendant in 1913 ought to be maintained in the public interest. The defendant contended that the Tribunal had no jurisdiction seeing that the determination whether a contract ought to be maintained in the public interest was a matter left by the Treaty to the Allied and Associated Powers.

Held: That the Tribunal had no jurisdiction.

(*a*) The text of Article 299 (*b*) seems to indicate that the Allied and Associated Powers wished to reserve for themselves the determination of the question whether a contract ought to be maintained in the general interest. If they had not had this intention they would have expressly stated that there was no right to demand the execution of the contract unless it had been ascertained that the maintenance of the contract was in the public interest. There is a special reason why, had they wished to confer this function upon the Mixed Arbitral Tribunal, they would have said so expressly. This reason is that the decision as to what is required in the general interest is not a matter which is as a rule in the hands of judicial authorities. It is rather a matter for governmental authorities.

(*b*) The notes exchanged at the Peace Conference between the German Delegation and the Allied and Associated Powers showed that there was tacit agreement to the effect that this question shall be excluded from the competence of the Mixed Arbitral Tribunal. In fact, the German Note pointed out that according to the Article in question the decision as to what is dictated by general interest would be left to the discretion of the Allied and Associated Powers, and that this was inadmissible. The Allied and Associated Powers answered in reply that the continuation of the contract would only be insisted upon when required in the general interest, and that they themselves, and not private individuals, could decide on the matter. No mention was made in any of these Notes of the Mixed Arbitral Tribunals. [Report: *Recueil*, vol. I (1922), p. 345.]

NOTE.—It will be observed that the correspondence exchanged between the German Delegation and the Allied and Associated Powers immediately before signing the Treaty of Versailles had a more authoritative character than that of " preparatory work " (*travaux préparatoires*) of the ordinary kind. See Case No. 268. See also *Société Vinicole de Champagne* v. *W. de Mumm*, decided on 4 March, 1921, by

Case No. 248 contd. the Franco-German Mixed Arbitral Tribunal (*Recueil*, vol. I (1922), p. 22 at pp. 25, 26), where the Tribunal has recourse to the preparatory work of the Treaty of Versailles and the Notes exchanged between the German Delegation and the Allied and Associated Powers for the purpose of determining the scope of the jurisdiction of the Mixed Arbitral Tribunals under Article 304 of the Treaty.—[Ed.]

Treaties—Preparatory Work—Consideration of—When Emanating only from the Contracting Party—The Analogy of Treaties and Statutes in the Matter of Preparatory Work —Preparatory Work as New Facts Relevant to Revision of Arbitral Awards.

See Case No. 268 (*Heim and Chamant* v. *The German State*).

v.—Various other Rules of Interpretation

Case No. 249

Treaties—Interpretation—Interpretation by Reference to the Action of the Parties under the Treaty—Article 296 of the Treaty of Versailles—Nationality of Corporations—*Siège Social.*

CHAMBERLAIN & HOOKHAM LTD. *v.* SOLAR ZAHLERWERKE.

Anglo-German Mixed Arbitral Tribunal. 16 *December*, 1921, *and* 6 *February*, 1922.

(BOREL, VAUGHAN WILLIAMS, ZACHARIAS.)

THE FACTS.—The plaintiffs, who brought the action under Article 296 of the Treaty of Versailles, were a company registered under English law. The defendants were a company with limited liability incorporated and registered at Hamburg in Germany. The claim was for the balance, on 4 August, 1914, to the credit of the plaintiff company for goods sold and delivered. The German Clearing Office contested the claim on the ground that the creditors held the whole capital of the debtor company; that the creditors and the debtors were in fact the same person; that the Hamburg company was therefore not of German nationality; that it was in fact subjected during the war to compulsory administration in Germany; and that therefore Article 296 of the Treaty was not applicable. The German Clearing Office also quoted a decision of the Franco-German Mixed Arbitral Tribunal in the case of *Société du Chemin de fer de Damas-Hamah* v. *Compagnie du Chemin de fer de Bagdad* (*Recueil*, vol. I (1922), p. 401), in which the Tribunal adopted as the criterion of the nationality of the company in question not its *siège social* but the nationality of the physical persons by whom it was in fact controlled.

Held: That the Tribunal had jurisdiction. While it must be admitted that the criterion of the *siège social* has been much shaken during the World War, " the Tribunal are bound " to examine whether this new conception has been really " contemplated by the High Contracting Parties in the Peace " Treaty generally, and more especially with regard to the " working of the clearing of debts according to Article 296." The relevant measures taken by Great Britain and Germany in the domain of municipal law show that they have interpreted and understood Article 296 as including in the category of nationals of a State those companies which have been incorporated under the laws of the State in question. This was expressly " declared in the Treaty of Peace Order 1919, para- " graph 2, which runs as follows: 'The expression nationals " 'in relation to any State includes the subjects or citizens " 'of that State and any company or corporation therein " 'according to the law of that State.' " The German law (of 31 August, 1919) to give effect to the Peace Treaty contained analogous provisions. [Report: *Recueil*, vol. I (1922), p. 723.]

NOTE.—See Note to Case No. 227 (*Société anonyme du Charbonnage Frédéric Henri* v. *Germany*) for a suggestion of a further reason for the apparently divergent decision in that case in the matter of the nationality of corporations.

Treaties—Interpretation of—Interpretation by Reference to the Terms of a Treaty Concluded Subsequently—Article 297 (*h*) (2) of the Treaty of Versailles—Articles 248 (*d*) (3) and 271 (2) of the Treaty of St. Germain—Articles 231 (*d*) and 254 of the Treaty of Trianon. **Case No. 250**

SCHUMACHER *v.* GERMANY AND SERB-CROAT-SLOVENE STATE.

Germano-Yugoslav Mixed Arbitral Tribunal. 1 *October*, 1922.

(LOGOZ, HEINZE, ARANGÉLOVITCH.)

THE FACTS.—This was a claim arising out of certain requisitions and liquidation of the plaintiff's property. The claim was brought under Article 297 (*h*) of the Treaty of Versailles, of which the second paragraph provided as follows: " In the case of liquidations effected in new " States, which are signatories of the present Treaty as " Allied and Associated Powers, or in States which are

Case No. 250 *contd.*

"not entitled to share in the reparation payments to "be made by Germany, the proceeds of liquidations "effected by such States shall, subject to the rights "of the Reparation Commission under the present "Treaty, particularly under Articles 235 and 260, be "paid direct to the owner." It was contended on the part of Yugoslavia that she was not a "new State," and that therefore the provisions of Article 297 (*h*) (2) could not be applied.

Held: That Yugoslavia was not a "new State" within the meaning of the Treaty and that the action, in so far as Yugoslavia was concerned, failed. The Treaty of Versailles did not indicate what was the meaning of the term "new State." However, there are articles in treaties concluded subsequently to the conclusion of the Treaty of Versailles, in which the Yugoslav State is excluded from the category of new States. Thus Article 248 (*d*) (3) of the Treaty of St. Germain speaks "of the new States of Poland and the Czechoslovak State." Article 271 (2) of the same Treaty contains the phrase "subject "to the special provisions laid down in Article 248 (*d*) for the "case of the new States." If the States signatory to the Treaty of St. Germain had regarded as new States not only Poland and Czechoslovakia but also Yugoslavia, which is a party to that Treaty, they would have said in Article 271 (2) "for Poland and Czechoslovakia" or "for certain new States" instead of "for the case of new States." The Treaty of Trianon contained identical provisions: Articles 231 (*d*) and 254. This was one of the reasons why Yugoslavia could not be regarded as a new State within the meaning of the Treaty. [Report: *Recueil,* vol. II (1923), p. 602 at p. 608.]

Case No. 251

Treaties—Interpretation—Clause "so far as the Laws of each Country Permit."

CHRYSSIKOS *v.* DEMARCO, ADMINISTRATOR OF VALMUS.

United States, Maryland Court of Appeals. 24 *June,* 1919.

THE FACTS.—Valmus, a Greek citizen, died intestate in Maryland without relatives of legal age there but with relatives in Greece. Administration was granted Demarco, following the Maryland laws allowing administration to be granted at the discretion of the Orphans' Court when there were no relatives of certain classes. Chryssikos later petitioned, as representative of the Greek Consul-General, to have the letters of administration of Demarco set aside and administration granted to himself under the Consular Convention of 1903 between Greece and the United States. (33 U.S. Stat. L. 2122.) The Convention provided that consular officers should have the same rights in all matters relating to administration of estates as were granted the consuls of the most-favoured nation. It was contended that this gave the Greek consul the same rights as those stipulated in the Convention of 1911 between Sweden and the United States, which provided that the consul or his representative "shall, so far as the "laws of each country permit," take charge of property pending appointment of an administrator of such estate. (37 U.S. Stat. L. 1479.) Chryssikos' petition was dismissed. On appeal,

Held: That the decree must be affirmed. The clause "so "far as the laws of each country permit" qualified the right of appointment as administrator as well as the right to take charge of property pending administration. Therefore the Treaty did not override the Maryland statutes but yielded to them. Although there were cases holding that similar treaty clauses gave consuls a right of administration, the Court here followed *Rocca* v. *Thompson*, 223 U.S. 317, decided under an earlier treaty; and *Austro-Hungarian Consul* v. *Westphal*, 120 Minn. 122; *Estate of D'Adamo*, 212 N.Y. 214; *Estate of Servas*, 169 Cal. 240; and *Pagano* v. *Cerri*, 93 Ohio St. 345. The right of administration given the consul under the Treaty was not exclusive and paramount to the exercise of State authority. [Report: 134 Md. 533.]

Treaties—Interpretation—Securing Equality in Exchange of Privileges—Most-Favoured-Nation Clause—Relevance of Construction by Executive Department. **Case No. 252**

SULLIVAN *v.* KIDD.

United States Supreme Court. 3 *January*, 1921.

THE FACTS.—A British subject residing in Canada claimed as devisee a share in the proceeds of Kansas land. Reliance was placed upon the Treaty of 2 March, 1899, between Great Britain and the United States, governing the inheritance of real property within the territories of each of the contracting parties by citizens or subjects

Case No. 252 ***contd.***

of the other, and providing for the sale of such property and withdrawal of the proceeds. (31 U.S. Stat. L. 1939.) Article IV provided that " the stipulations of the " present Convention shall not be applicable to any of " the Colonies or foreign possessions of Her Britannic " Majesty unless notice to that effect shall have been " given, on behalf of any such Colony or foreign posses- " sion, by Her Britannic Majesty's Representative at " Washington to the United States' Secretary of State " within one year from the date of the exchange of the " ratifications of the present Convention." Article VI provided further that " Her Britannic Majesty or " the United States shall also have the right separately " to terminate the present Convention at any time, on " giving twelve months' notice to that effect in regard " to any British Colony, foreign possession, or depend- " ency, as specified in Article IV, which may have " acceded thereto." Citizens or subjects of each of the contracting parties were assured most-favoured-nation treatment " in all that concerns the right of disposing " of every kind of property." As to the Dominion of Canada no notice of adhesion had been given. The British Government had interpreted the Treaty as giving to British subjects wherever resident the right to inherit property in the United States. According to this interpretation, notice of adhesion as to Canada was necessary only to give effect to the Treaty as to Canadian lands. The United States Government, on the other hand, had interpreted the Treaty as requiring notice as to Canada in order to bring within its operation either property in Canada or British subjects residing therein. The lower Court held the Treaty applicable. On appeal,

Held : That the judgment must be reversed. " For lack of " notice of the adhesion of Canada to the terms of the treaty, " the law of Kansas was not superseded in favor of British " subjects resident in Canada, and it determined the right of " aliens to inherit lands in that State." (254 U.S. 433, 443.) This interpretation was consistent with " the general purpose " and object of such conventions to secure equality in exchange " of privileges and reciprocity in rights granted and secured." (254 U.S. 433, 440.) The provision of Article VI with respect to termination supported this interpretation. Nor was the specific provision of Article IV overcome by the most-favoured-nation clause. "That clause has been held in the practice of "this country to be one not extending rights acquired by "treaties containing it because of reciprocal benefits expressly "conferred in conventions with other nations in exchange for "rights or privileges given to this Government." (254 U.S. 433, 441.) Of the persuasive effect of an executive interpretation of the Treaty, it was said: "While the question of the construction of treaties is judicial in its nature, and courts when "called upon to act should be careful to see that international "engagements are faithfully kept and observed, the construction placed upon the treaty before us and consistently adhered "to by the Executive Department of the Government, charged "with the supervision of our foreign relations, should be given "much weight. Charlton *v.* Kelly, 229 U.S. 447, 468. See also "Castro *v.* De Uriarte, 16 Fed. Rep. 93, 98 (opinion by Judge "Addison Brown)." (254 U.S. 433, 442.) [Report: 254 U.S. 433.] See Case No. 241 (*In re X.*).

Treaties—Interpretation—Alternative or Cumulative Obligations. **Case No. 253**

GERMANY AND FRANCE.

(In the Matter of the Cessions relating to the Navigation of the Rhine under Article 357 of the Treaty of Versailles.)

8 *January*, 1921.

(WALKER D. HINES, Arbitrator.)

THE FACTS.—(See Case No. 260.) Article 357 of the Treaty of Versailles provided, *inter alia*, that Germany shall cede to France certain tugs and vessels, or shares in German Rhine navigation companies. Before the Tribunal France asked for the cession of shares in some of the companies in addition to the cession of tugs and vessels. Germany contended that Article 357 required the cession of either boats or shares, and that she was entitled to choose which she will cede.

Held: That Germany was not entitled to determine the character of the property to be ceded under Article 357. That Article obviously contemplated that all questions as to the amount and specifications of the cessions to be made in relation to the legitimate needs of the parties shall be determined by the arbitrator. This was also the reason why the arbitrator

Case No. 253 *contd.*

was authorised to require the cession of shares as well as the cession of tugs and vessels if he found that the object of the Article could best be promoted by the cession of shares of one or more companies simultaneously with the cession of tugs and vessels. (See also Case No. 244.) [Report: *A.J.*, XVII (1923), pp. 786-805.]

Treaties—Interpretation of—Treaties Creating Exceptions to Generally Recognised Rules of International Law.

See Case No. 120 (*The Wanderer*).

Treaties—Interpretation—Rules of—*Ejusdem Generis*—"And Other Measures."

See Case No. 256 (*Competence of the International Labour Organisation: Organisation and Development of Methods of Agricultural Production*).

Treaties—Interpretation—Rejection of Interpretation Producing Inequitable Results—Article 389 (3) of the Treaty of Versailles—International Labour Conference—Nomination of Labour Representatives.

See Case No. 258 (*Designation of the Workers' Delegate for the Netherlands*).

XIII.—Special Kinds of Treaties

(a) Commercial Treaties. Most-Favoured-Nation Clause

Case No. 254

Treaties of Commerce—Interpretation—Treatment of Aliens—Discriminations against.

FRASCA *v.* CITY COAL CO.

United States, Supreme Court of Errors of Connecticut.
21 *February*, 1922.

THE FACTS.—This was a proceeding in Connecticut to recover workmen's compensation for an Italian dependent residing in Italy. Connecticut General Statutes, § 5350, provided that workmen's compensation to alien dependents not resident in the United States or Canada should only be one-half the compensation otherwise payable. The Treaty of 1871 between Italy and the United States (17 U.S. Stat.

L. 845), as amended in 1913 (38 U.S. Stat. L. 1669), provided that the citizens of each party " shall receive " in . . . the other the most constant security and " protection for their persons and property and for " their rights, including that form of protection granted " by any State or national law which establishes a civil " responsibility for injuries or for death caused by " negligence or fault and gives to relatives or heirs of " the injured party a right of action, which right shall " not be restricted on account of the nationality of " said relatives or heirs; and shall enjoy in this " respect the same rights and privileges as are or shall " be granted to nationals, provided that they submit " themselves to the conditions imposed on the latter." From an award of half compensation the claimant appealed.

Held: That the award must be affirmed. The Treaty applied primarily to Italians in the United States, rather than to Italians in Italy. The discrimination was not based on nationality alone, but on nationality and non-residence. The Compensation Act made a distinction between classes of dependents, not between alien workmen and citizens. The result would have been the same if the employee had been a citizen. The case of *Vietti* v. *Mackie Fuel Co.*, 109 Kans. 179,[1] was distinguished on the ground that the statute in that case discriminated against resident alien dependents. [Report: 97 Conn. 212.]

Most-Favoured-Nation Clause—Treaty Provisions of Analogous Character—Article 276 of the Treaty of Versailles—Conditional Interpretation. **Case No. 255**

SECURITY FOR COSTS (TREATY OF VERSAILLES) CASE.

Germany, Upper District Court (Oberlandesgericht) of Frankfort-on-the-Main. 11 *December,* 1922.

THE FACTS.—This was an appeal by a French plaintiff against an order to deposit security for costs in an action brought by him against a German subject. Section 110 of the German Code of Civil Procedure lays down that aliens appearing as plaintiffs before German courts must at the defendant's request deposit a security for costs. This provision does not apply to

[1] Case No. 230.

Case No. 255 *contd.*

aliens whose own State does not demand security for costs from Germans appearing as plaintiffs. A convention concluded at The Hague on 14 November, 1896, between a number of States, including Germany and France, exempted the subjects of the contracting parties from the duty to deposit security for costs. This convention was not included in the number of those which, according to Article 287 of the Treaty of Versailles, were to be regarded as revived between the Allied Powers and Germany. In Article 291 (1) of that Treaty Germany undertook "to secure to the Allied "and Associated Powers, and to the officials and "nationals of the said Powers, the enjoyment of all "the rights and advantages of any kind which she "may have granted to Austria, Hungary, Bulgaria or "Turkey, or to the officials and nationals of these "States by treaties, conventions or arrangements "concluded before August 1, 1914, so long as those "treaties, conventions or arrangements remain in "force." The second paragraph of that Article provided that: "The Allied and Associated Powers "reserve the right to accept or not the enjoyment of "these rights and advantages." There existed between Germany and Bulgaria a treaty providing for the exemption, on the basis of reciprocity, from the duty to deposit security for costs. In a Note, communicated to Germany in April, 1921, the French Government informed the German Government that it wished to avail itself of the relevant provisions of the Treaty between Germany and Bulgaria. The plaintiff did not prove that in France German subjects were exempt from depositing security for costs in actions brought against French subjects.

Held: That the appeal must be dismissed. Article 291 of the Treaty of Versailles did not oblige Germany to grant to French subjects wider privileges than those granted to the subjects of the former Central Power. The Treaty with Bulgaria was based on reciprocity. As France did not grant such reciprocal treatment, her subjects were not entitled to an exemption from the duty to deposit security for costs. [Report: *Juristische Wochenschrift*, 1923, p. 191.]

Treaties of Commerce—Interpretation of—Treatment of Aliens —Equality of Treatment.

See Case No. 168 (*Gizzarelli* v. *Presbrey*).

Commercial Treaties—Interpretation of—Right to Engage in Trade—Limitations of.

See Case No. 232 (*Poon* v. *Miller*).

Most-Favoured-Nation Clause—Interpretation—Relevance of Construction by Executive Department.

See Case No. 252 (*Sullivan* v. *Kidd*).

XIV.—Miscellaneous

Interpretation—Miscellaneous—Treaty Permitting Trade between Neutral Country and Enemy Country—Restriction to Trade Consistent with Neutrality and Exclusive of Trade in Contraband.

See Case No. 301 (*The Rannveig*).

PART IX

INTERNATIONAL ORGANISATION AND ADMINISTRATION

B. INTERNATIONAL LABOUR ORGANISATION

I.—Organisation and Constitution

International Labour Organisation—Competence of—Examination of Proposals for the Organisation and Development of Methods of Agricultural Production—When Incidental to Regulation of Conditions of Work.

Case No. 256

PERMANENT COURT OF INTERNATIONAL JUSTICE.

ADVISORY OPINION No. 3.

COMPETENCE OF THE INTERNATIONAL LABOUR ORGANISATION.

(Organisation and Development of Methods of Agricultural Production.)

12 *August*, 1922.[1]

THE FACTS.—On 18 July, 1922, the Council of the League of Nations requested the Court to give an Advisory Opinion on the question whether examination of proposals for the organisation and development of methods of agricultural production falls within the competence of the International Labour Organisation. (It does not appear that an affirmative answer to this question was urged by any interested party. In a statement made before the Court, the Director of the International Labour Organisation declared that that Organisation never considered any intervention of the nature indicated in the question submitted to the Court, and submitted that the organisation and development of agricultural production are not within the competence of the International Labour Organisation. However, the French Government urged that notwithstanding this disclaimer the matter should be the subject

[1] The composition of the Court was the same as in the case of the Second Advisory Opinion. (See p. 359.)

Case No. 256 ***contd.***

of an authoritative Opinion on the part of the Court.)

Held: That the question, properly construed,[1] must be answered in the negative. The object of the International Labour Organisation, as stated in the Preamble to Part XIII of the Treaty of Versailles, is to improve the lot of wage-earners by the amelioration of conditions of work, prevention of unemployment, protection against sickness, protection of children, young persons and women, freedom of association and "other "measures." The expression "other measures" "must "mean measures to improve the conditions of labour "and to do away with injustice, hardship and priva-"tion." The consideration and development of the means of production from the economic point of view are not committed to the Organisation and are alien to its sphere of activity as laid down in the Treaty.

On the other hand, the Organisation could not be precluded from considering matters expressly entrusted to it by the Treaty on the ground that this may incidentally involve the consideration of methods or means of production, or of the effect which the proposed measures would have on production. Thus, for instance, "if it should appear that a particular measure "would involve a material diminution of production, "this might be a matter proper to be considered by "the Organisation before deciding on its adoption, "although it might be desirable in other respects. So, "for instance, protection against sickness, disease and "injury arising out of employment may involve the "consideration of methods and processes of produc-"tion, such as the use of white phosphorus, and of "white lead, both of which have been dealt with as "subjects within the scope of international regulation "as affecting the conditions of labour." [Report: P.C.I.J., Series B, Nos. 2 and 3, pp. 53-59.]

[1] The Court considered the question to be "whether the consideration of "the excess of jurisdiction in itself, and apart from the specific points in respect "of which powers are conferred upon the International Labour Organisation "by the Treaty, falls within the competence of that Organisation."

International Labour Organisation—Competence of—Regulation of Conditions of Work of Persons Employed in Agriculture—Part XIII of the Treaty of Versailles—General Purpose of the Treaty.

Case No. 257
PERMANENT COURT OF INTERNATIONAL JUSTICE.
ADVISORY OPINION No. 2.

COMPETENCE OF THE INTERNATIONAL LABOUR ORGANISATION.

(Regulation of Conditions of Work of Persons Employed in Agriculture.)

12 *August*, 1922.[1]

THE FACTS.—In March, 1920, the Governing Body of the International Labour Office included in the agenda of the third session of the International Labour Organisation a number of questions relating to the regulation of conditions of work in agriculture. A number of Governments objected to these questions being included in the agenda of the Conference on the ground that Part XIII of the Treaty was not intended to regulate the conditions of work of persons employed in agriculture. The third conference of the International Labour Organisation held in October, 1921, adopted by a majority vote a resolution affirming its competence to deal with matters concerning agricultural labour. It also adopted a number of draft conventions and recommendations relating to the protection of agricultural workers. The French Government then brought the matter before the Council of the League of Nations proposing that the Permanent Court of International Justice be requested to give an Advisory Opinion on the question, *inter alia*, whether the International Labour Organisation is competent to deal with questions of agricultural labour. On 18 May, 1921, the Council

[1] The Court was composed as follows: Loder, President; Weiss, Lord Finlay, Nyholm, Moore, de Bustamante, Altamira, Oda, Anzilotti, Judges; Negulesco, Deputy-Judge. Judge Weiss and Deputy-Judge Negulesco dissented.

Case No. 257 ***contd.***

decided to put this question before the Court for an Advisory Opinion.

Held: That the competence of the International Labour Organisation does extend to international regulation of conditions of labour of persons employed in agriculture.

The Court refused to attach decisive importance to the fact that most of the relevant provisions of the Treaty referred to "industry," which term a number of Governments regarded as excluding agriculture. " . . . it is obvious that the Treaty must be read as a " whole, and that its meaning is not to be determined " merely upon particular phrases which, if detached " from the context, may be interpreted in more than " one sense."

Part XIII of the Treaty stated expressly that the intention of the Contracting Parties was to establish a permanent labour organisation. Agriculture, which is the most ancient and the greatest of all industries, employing over half of the world's wage-earners, could not be considered as left outside the scope of the International Labour Organisation for the mere reason that it was not expressly mentioned by name. There were in the Treaty many indications of the comprehensive character of Part XIII as relating to labour in general, and not to one of its particular aspects. This was in particular true of the Preamble to Part XIII which defined in general terms the competence of the International Labour Organisation in language that "could hardly be more comprehensive." [1] Equally the general principles enunciated in Article 427 of the Treaty on the protection of work was as applicable to agriculture as to any other form of labour. Accordingly, although the adjective "*industriel*" is generally

[1] The Court referred here in particular to those passages of the Preamble to Part XIII which declared that " conditions of labour (*conditions de travail*) " exist involving such injustice, hardship and privation to large numbers of " persons as to produce unrest so great that the peace and harmony of the " world are imperilled," and which stressed the importance of international regulation of conditions of work on the ground that " the failure of any nation " to adopt humane conditions of labour is an obstacle in the way of other " nations which desire to improve the conditions in their own countries."

used in a special and restrictive sense, the question put to the Court must be answered by reference to the Treaty read as a whole. [Report: P.C.I.J., Series B, Nos. 2 and 3, pp. 23-35.[1]]

NOTE.—See also for the other aspects of the same case, from the point of view of interpretation of treaties, Cases Nos. 237, 238.

Case No. 258

PERMANENT COURT OF INTERNATIONAL JUSTICE.

ADVISORY OPINION No. 1.

International Labour Organisation—Constitution of—Nomination of Delegates—Designation of Non-Government Delegates—Article 389 (3) of the Treaty of Versailles—Interpretation of Treaties—Rejection of Interpretation Producing Inequitable Results.

DESIGNATION OF THE WORKERS' DELEGATE FOR THE NETHERLANDS.

31 *July*, 1922.[2]

THE FACTS.—The delegation of each State to the General Conference of the International Labour Organisation is composed of four persons, of whom two are the delegates of the Government and the other two represent the employers and the workers respectively. The third paragraph of Article 389 of the Treaty of Versailles provides as follows: "The Members undertake "to nominate non-Government Delegates and "advisers chosen in agreement with the industrial organisations, if such organisations exist, "which are most representative of employers "or workpeople, as the case may be, in their "respective countries."

In 1921 there existed in Holland the following five important organisations of labour: (1) The Netherlands Confederation of Trades Unions, numbering, in April, 1921, 218,596 members; (2) The Confederation of Catholic Trades Unions, numbering, in April, 1921, 155,642 members; (3) The Confederation of

[1] See on this case Chateau, *De la compétence de l'Organisation internationale du Travail en matière de travail agricole* (1924); Mahaim in *R.I.*, 3rd ser., vol. III (1922), pp. 503-524.

[2] The Court was composed as follows: Loder, President; Weiss, Lord Finlay, Nyholm, Moore, de Bustamante, Altamira, Oda, Anzilotti, Judges; Beichmann, Negulesco, Deputy-Judges.

Case No. 258 ***contd.***

Christian Trades Unions, numbering, in April, 1921, 75,618 members; (4) The Netherlands General Confederation of Trades Unions, numbering, in April, 1921, 51,195 members; (5) The National Labour Secretariat, numbering, on 1 January, 1921, 36,038 members. When the question of the selection of the workers' representative for the third session of the International Labour Conference arose, these organisations could not agree on a common nominee to be suggested to the Netherlands Government. Eventually, the second, third and fourth organisations agreed on a nominee who was eventually appointed by the Netherlands Government. The Netherlands Confederation of Trades Unions considered that it was entitled to propose the workers' delegate and objected to the nomination made by the Netherlands Government. The International Labour Conference admitted the delegate appointed by the Government, but adopted a resolution urging that the Council of the League of Nations should request the Permanent Court of International Justice to give an Advisory Opinion as to the interpretation of Article 389. On 12 May, 1922, the Council requested the Court to give an Advisory Opinion on the following question: "Was the Workers' Delegate for the Netherlands at the Third Session of the International Labour Conference nominated in accordance with the provisions of paragraph 3 of Article 389 of the Treaty of Versailles?"

Held: That the question must be answered in the affirmative. The Treaty contains no definition of the expression "most representative" as applying to organisations from which the person nominated must be chosen. "The most representative organisations for this purpose are, of course, those organisations which best represent the employers and the workers respectively.

" What these organisations are, is a question to be " decided in the particular case, having regard to the " circumstances in each particular country at the time " when the choice falls to be made " (at p. 19). Numbers are an important and, other things being equal, a decisive test. But they are not the only test. It is for the Government, acting in good faith, to decide in each case what organisations are most representative.

There was no reason for assuming that the Government was bound by the views of the one organisation most important among those representative of the workers. If that were so, a situation might arise in which a substantial minority of the workers would have the decisive influence upon the nomination of the delegate. " Such a result is enough to condemn the " interpretation which would make it possible, and " unequivocal terms would be required to compel its " adoption " (at p. 23).

Paragraph 3 of Article 389 could not be interpreted as meaning that an agreement of *the* most representative organisations on the question of nomination was essential. Such a construction " would make it possible " for one single organisation, in opposition to the " wishes of the great majority of workers, to prevent " the reaching of an agreement. A construction which " would have this result must be rejected " (at p. 25). [Report: P.C.I.J., Series B, No. 1, *passim.*]

C. OTHER ORGANS OF INTERNATIONAL ADMINISTRATION

[See also Part II B (*Territories under Joint or International Government*), and Part III B (*Functions and Competence of International Commissions on International Rivers*).]

International Administration — International Character of Sanitary and Quarantine Council of Egypt—International Health Convention of Venice, 1892. **Case No. 259**

AGAPIOS *v.* SANITARY AND QUARANTINE COUNCIL OF EGYPT.

Egypt, Mixed Court of Appeal. 21 *January*, 1920.

THE FACTS.—See Case No. 136.

Case No. 259 ***contd.***

Held: (*a*) That the Sanitary and Quarantine Council of Egypt, which was constituted by an Egyptian Decree of 1881 modified by a Decree of 1893, and which is charged with the execution of the measures prescribed in the International Convention of Venice of 1892, is not to be regarded as a purely Egyptian Administration, and therefore as having Egyptian national character. The Council, which is concerned not only with the sanitary but also with the pecuniary interests of foreign subjects, is subject to the jurisdiction of the Mixed Courts of Egypt in all pecuniary claims, even by native subjects.

(*b*) The Decree of 1893 which defined the functions of the Council is not to be regarded as an act simply of the Egyptian sovereign. It was designed to give effect to the Convention of 1892 drawn up at the meeting of the contracting Powers which was held for the purpose of introducing modifications in the sanitary system applied to shipping in Egypt. The Council is, therefore, an emanation of the International Convention.

(*c*) The international character of the Council is further indicated by its composition, as it comprises delegates of fourteen Powers and only four Egyptian officials, and also by the right of foreign Powers to correspond directly with the Council. [Report: *Gazette des Tribunaux Mixtes d'Egypte*, 1920, p. 49.]

PART X

DISPUTES

A. ARBITRATION

I.—Arbitration in General

i.—Conception and Function of Arbitration

Arbitration—Arbitration as Adjudication upon Interests—Decision as to " Legitimate Needs of the Parties." **Case No. 260**

GERMANY AND FRANCE.

(In the Matter of the Cessions relating to the Navigation of the Rhine under Article 357 of the Treaty of Versailles.)

8 *January*, 1921.

(WALKER D. HINES, Arbitrator.)

Article 357 of the Treaty of Versailles provided as follows :

" Within a maximum period of three months from the " date on which notification shall be given Germany shall " cede to France tugs and vessels, from among those re- " maining registered in German Rhine ports after the " deduction of those surrendered by way of restitution " or reparation, or shares in German Rhine navigation " companies.

" When vessels and tugs are ceded, such vessels and " tugs, together with their fittings and gear, shall be in " good state of repair, shall be in condition to carry on " commercial traffic on the Rhine, and shall be selected " from among those most recently built.

" The same procedure shall be followed in the matter of " the cession by Germany to France of :

" (1) the installations, berthing and anchorage accom- " modation, platforms, docks, warehouses, plant, etc., " which German subjects or German companies owned on " August 1, 1914, in the port of Rotterdam, and

" (2) the shares or interest which Germany or German " nationals possessed in such installations at the same date.

" The amount and specifications of such cessions shall " be determined within one year of the present treaty by " an arbitrator or arbitrators appointed by the United

Case No. 260 *contd.*

"States of America, due regard being had to the legitimate "needs of the parties concerned.

"The cessions provided for in the present article shall "entail a credit of which the total amount, settled in a "lump sum by the arbitrator or arbitrators mentioned "above, shall not in any case exceed the value of the "capital expended in the initial establishment of the ceded "material and installations, and shall be set off against the "total sums due from Germany; in consequence, the "indemnification of the proprietors shall be a matter for "Germany to deal with."

In deciding upon the amount and specification of these cessions having regard to the "legitimate needs of the parties "concerned," the arbitrator had seldom occasion to apply rules of international law proper (but see Cases Nos. 244 and 253), but the case is noted here as an instance of judicial determination of interests, the decision as to the legitimate needs of the parties having been left to the arbitrator. It may be convenient to refer to some specific questions showing the manner in which the arbitrator exercised his function.[1]

In regard to the traffic to be considered in estimating the legitimate needs of the two countries, Germany and France agreed to adopt the traffic on the Rhine for the year 1913 as the basis of the estimate. Germany contended that the arbitrator ought to exclude the 1913 traffic in coal moving down the Rhine from the Ruhr to the sea destined for French ports, and that the 1913 traffic in ore coming by sea from the French colonies should be excluded from the Rhine traffic having a relation to the legitimate needs of France, on the ground that France did not participate in this traffic before the war and that therefore it is not a legitimate need of hers. *Held*, that this contention must be rejected. As at that time France had no base on the Rhine it was not to be expected that she would participate in this traffic.

France contended that to the 1913 Rhine traffic there must be added reparation coal from the Ruhr to French sea ports. *Held*, that this contention must be rejected for the reason, *inter alia*, that Germany was in fact, by virtue of the provisions of the Treaty, herself responsible for the transport of the reparation coal, and also because Article 357 ought to be construed rather as providing for normal commercial activity than as

[1] It is believed that in view of the frequent distinction between decisions on the basis of existing law and adjudication upon interests this case may merit attention.

having reference to reparation necessarily temporary in character.

As to the amount of shipping required to perform France's part of the traffic in respect of the traffic which is of joint interest to the two countries,[1] that is, which moves from one of them to the other, the arbitrator decided that each country has a right to possess a portion of the existing German Rhine fleet, and that "it is a legitimate need of each of the two "countries to have one-half of the boats needed to transport "such traffic."

As to the cession of tugs and vessels or shares in German Rhine navigation companies, see Cases Nos. 244, 253. [Report: *A.J.*, XVII (1923), pp. 786-805.]

NOTE.—See also *ibid.*, XVIII (1924), pp. 186-197, for the award of 14 June, 1921, by the same arbitrator in the matter of the cessions by Germany to Czechoslovakia under Article 339 of the Treaty of Versailles of certain property pertaining to certain river systems specified in Article 331 of the Treaty. The Treaty provided that the amount and specifications of these cessions shall be determined by an arbitrator appointed by the United States.

Arbitration—Nature of—Legal Character of Boundary Commissions.

See Case No. 262 (*Colombia and Venezuela*).

ii.—The Law Applied by Arbitral Tribunals. Arbitration and Judicial Settlement

International Arbitration—Law Applied by Arbitral Tribunals —Application of the Municipal Law of the Parties—Meaning of the Terms "Law and Equity." **Case No. 261**

NORWAY AND UNITED STATES (REQUISITION OF SHIPBUILDING CONTRACTS CASE).

Permanent Court of Arbitration. 13 *October*, 1922.

(VALLOTON, ANDERSON,[2] VOGT.)

THE FACTS.—(See Case No. 289.) The special arbitration agreement between the United States and Norway of 30 June, 1921, providing for submission to arbitration of claims of Norwegian shipowners whose shipbuilding

[1] The arbitrator accepted it as evident that no country could claim boats to enable it to participate in the internal traffic of the other country.

[2] See Case No. 267 as to the participation of Mr. Anderson in the rendering of the award.

Case No. 261 *contd.*

contracts were requisitioned by the United States, laid down that the Tribunal " shall examine and decide the " aforesaid claims in accordance with the principles of " law and equity." It was maintained by the United States that the Tribunal was bound to apply the municipal law of the United States in regard to matters within the jurisdiction of the United States which came for decision by the Tribunal. Norway contended that in the absence of an agreement to the contrary, the Tribunal, far from being bound to apply the municipal law of any country, was bound to apply international law.

Held: (*a*) That the Tribunal had no power to modify contracts of private law or their consequences, except when the public law of one of the parties affecting these contracts was contrary to international public policy (*ordre public international*), in which case an international tribunal is not bound by the municipal law of the parties.

As to the terms " principles of law and equity " the parties were bound by the French text of the Convention for the Pacific Settlement of International Disputes of 18 October, 1907. Article 73 of that Convention provided as follows:

> " Le Tribunal est autorisé à déterminer sa compétence " en interprétant le compromis ainsi que les autres actes " et documents qui peuvent être invoqués dans la matière " et en appliquant les principes du droit."

The term was also referred to in Article 37 of that Convention, which laid down as follows:

> " L'arbitrage international a pour objet le règlement de " litiges entre les Etats par des juges de leur choix et sur " la base du respect au droit."

According to the generally accepted view,[1] this meant that the Tribunal was bound in the first instance to apply rules of positive international law. The phrase " law and equity " used in the special agreement of 1921 could not be interpreted in the technical sense attributed to it in the Anglo-Saxon jurisprudence. " The majority of international lawyers seem to " agree that these words are to be understood to mean general " principles of justice as distinguished from any particular " system of jurisprudence or the municipal law of any state."

[1] The Tribunal referred here to Lammasch, *Die Rechtskraft internationaler Schiedssprüche*, p. 37, and Scott, *The Hague Court Reports* (1916), p. xxi.

The Tribunal is not at liberty to ignore the municipal law of the parties to the dispute, unless that law " is contrary to " the principle of the equality of the parties, or to the principles " of justice which are common to all civilized nations." The Tribunal is entitled to examine the statutes of the United States from the point of view of their conformity with these principles as well as with conventional and customary international law binding upon the United States. [Reports : *A.J.*, XVII (1923), pp. 362-399 ; *British and Foreign State Papers.*]

II.—Procedure

ii.—Competence. Competence to Determine Jurisdiction

International Tribunals—Competence of—Right to Review Judicial Decisions of Municipal Courts—Denial of Justice.

See Case No. 239 (*The David J. Adams*).

International Arbitration—Right to Review Judicial Decisions of Municipal Courts.

See Case No. 119 (*The Argonaut and The Jonas H. French*).

Arbitration—Competence—Decision as to Whether Contracts Ought to be Maintained in the General Interest.

See Case No. 248 (*Schmid* v. *Chemische Werke Furstenwalde*).

viii.—Experts

Arbitration—Boundary Commissions—Technical Experts—Character of—Whether Endowed with Arbitral Powers. **Case No. 262**

COLOMBIA AND VENEZUELA.

(SWISS FEDERAL COUNCIL AS ARBITRATOR.)

24 *March*, 1922.

THE FACTS.—(See also Case No. 54.[1]) Article 3 of the Arbitration Agreement of 3 November, 1916, between Colombia and Venezuela provided as follows : " The " High Contracting Parties agree to entrust the " arbitrator with the task of laying down and de-

[1] On the question of occupation as provided in Article 1, see Case No. 54.

Case No. 262 ***contd.***

"limiting the frontier, which task he will perform "through experts immediately after the award has "been given. The experts shall be of the same nation- "ality as the arbitrator. They shall fulfil their task "within the period indicated by the arbitrator, and "they shall take into account, before or in the course "of the delimitation, the cases, plans, and other "documents submitted to them by the parties." Subsequently the question arose as to the powers of the said commission of experts. Colombia maintained that the correct interpretation of the Arbitration Agreement was that the arbitrator (the Swiss Federal Council) had no power to decide as to the details of the delimitation, that task having been reserved for the experts only and exclusively. Venezuela was of the opinion that by virtue of the special agreement the final decision as to laying down the frontier rested with the Swiss Federal Council; that the experts were merely agents entrusted with the execution of the award; and that the Federal Council was entitled to give instructions to the experts and to reserve its decision until after having received their report.[1]

Held: That the correct interpretation of Article 3 of the Arbitration Agreement was that the task of deciding questions of boundary and their delimitations did not fall upon the Swiss Federal Council; that this was the task to be fulfilled by experts nominated by the Federal Council; and that the experts were to possess arbitral powers exercised as the result of delegation from the Federal Council. It was clear from the evidence that a long series of precedents in the relations between Colombia and Venezuela attributed to members of technical boundary commissions the character of arbitral tribunals. (See also Case No. 54 (5).) [Report: *Sentence Arbitrale*, pp. 87-91, 113-116.]

[1] Attention ought perhaps to be drawn to the practical consequences of the divergency of views as outlined above. While the result of the adoption of the Colombian contention would be a definite settlement of the boundary controversies, the Venezuelan view might have had the result of postponing the final settlement until the receipt by the arbitrator of the report of the experts or otherwise. It will be noted that in *Venezuelan Reply*, p. 270, the view was expressed that as a rule of international practice the findings of the experts are subject to approval on the part of the respective Governments.

IV.—Admission of Liability. Waiver. Estoppel

Arbitration—Evidence—*Res Judicata*—Decisions of Municipal Courts—*Res Judicata* in relation to International Tribunals—Admission of Liability. **Case No. 263**

THE NEWCHWANG.

British-American Claims Arbitral Tribunal. 9 *December*, 1921.

(FROMAGEOT, FITZPATRICK, ANDERSON.)

THE FACTS.—In May, 1902, there occurred a collision near the mouth of the Yangtse river between the *Newchwang*, a steamship owned by a British company, and the *Saturn*, a navy collier owned and operated by the Government of the United States. In July, 1902, the Government of the United States instituted, before the British Supreme Court for China and Korea at Shanghai, proceedings in admiralty against the *Newchwang* to obtain damages for the injuries to the *Saturn*. In January, 1903, the Court dismissed the petition of the United States on the ground that the *Saturn* was at fault. The United States appealed, but then withdrew the appeal. Subsequently a bill was introduced in the Congress of the United States with a view to conceding compensation to the owners of the *Newchwang*, but no definite action was taken. In the course of the proceedings before the Committee on Claims of the House of Representatives, the Chairman of that Committee expressed in a letter a view favourable to the passage of the bill granting compensation to the owners. The present claim was put forward by Great Britain on behalf of the owners. Great Britain contended that the question of the responsibility of the *Saturn* was *res judicata* as the result of the judgment of the Supreme Court for China and Korea seeing that the parties were the same, that the judgment of that Court was on the merits and that the United States withdrew the appeal. For these reasons, it was contended, the United States were estopped from denying that the *Saturn* was at fault. Also, it was maintained that the Tribunal ought to take into consideration the admission of liability contained in the letter of the Chairman of the Committee of the House of Representatives.

Case No. 263 ***contd.***

Held: (*a*) That the contention as to *res judicata* must be rejected. It was a well-established rule of law that the principle of *res judicata* applied only when both the issue and the parties were the same. The question before the Supreme Court of China and Korea was the liability of the *Newchwang*, whereas the present Tribunal had to determine whether the *Saturn* was at fault.[1]

(*b*) Although the decision of the British Supreme Court of China and Korea could not be regarded as having the force of *res judicata* in regard to the liability of the *Saturn*, it could be taken into consideration as showing what were the conclusions reached by a competent municipal tribunal.[2]

(*c*) As to the contention that, as the result of the letter of the Chairman of the Committee on Claims, the United States were estopped from denying liability, the Tribunal held that as that letter was merely a personal or private recommendation of the Chairman of the Committee, and had never been officially published, it could not be regarded as an admission of liability on the part of the United States. [Reports: Nielsen, p. 414; *A.J.*, XVI (1922), p. 323.]

NOTE.—The Terms of Submission forming part of the Arbitration Agreement provided, *inter alia*: " II. The Arbitral Tribunal shall take " into account as one of the equities of a claim to such extent as it shall " consider just in allowing or disallowing a claim any admission of " liability by the Government against whom a claim is put forward.

" III. The Arbitral Tribunal shall take into account as one of the " equities of a claim to such extent as it shall consider just in allowing " or disallowing a claim, in whole or in part, any failure on the part of " the claimants to obtain satisfaction through legal remedies which are " open to him or placed at his disposal, but no claim shall be disallowed " or rejected by application of the general principle of international " law that the legal remedies must be exhausted as a condition pre- " cedent to the validity of the claim."

The finding of the Tribunal must be read in the light of these provisions.

Acquiescence—Absence of Protest—Relevance of.

See Case No. 54 (*Colombia and Venezuela*).

[1] It must be noted that the British Supreme Court for China and Korea refused, on the ground of lack of jurisdiction, to entertain the counter-claim of the owners of the *Newchwang* against the *Saturn*.

[2] At the same time the Tribunal pointed out that that evidence was not conclusive of the question at issue on the ground: (*a*) that before the municipal court in question the burden of proof was on the *Saturn*, whereas before the present Tribunal it was on the *Newchwang*; (*b*) that evidence was put before the Tribunal which was not before the Court.

Arbitration—Evidence—Estoppel—As the Result of *Res Judicata*—As the Result of Admission of Liability.

See Case No. 263 (*The Newchwang*).

V.—The Award

i.—Scope and Binding Force of the Award

Arbitration — Declaratory Judgments — Abstract Questions of Principle. **Case No. 264**

French Clearing Office *v.* German Clearing Office.

Franco-German Mixed Arbitral Tribunal. 8 July, 1922.

(Sjoeberg, Fortin, Herwegen.)

The Facts.—This was an application by the French Clearing Office for a declaration that the German Clearing Office was not entitled to make the recognition of debts claimed by a representative of the claimant dependent upon the production of a power of attorney. The application, which was opposed by the German Office, had no reference to any specific case.

Held: That the application must be rejected.

(*a*) In the present case the plaintiff, without submitting to the Tribunal a concrete case, asks for a decision on a question of principle which has arisen between the two offices. There is, as stated in a decision of the Tribunal in a previous case,[1] no provision of the Treaty or of the Rules governing the procedure of the Tribunal prohibiting it from deciding on abstract questions.

(*b*) However, although the Tribunal is entitled to give such decisions, it is not bound to give them. It must exercise its discretion in each particular case. In particular, it ought to refuse to give an abstract decision whenever the principle which it is asked to lay down is such as to be liable to considerable modifications by reason of special circumstances. The present application raises a principle of this nature. [Report: *Recueil*, vol. II (1923), p. 282.]

[1] *French Clearing Office* v. *German Clearing Office*, decision of 15 December, 1921: *Recueil*, vol. I (1922), p. 593.

Case No. 265

Arbitration—Award—*Stare Decisis*—The Practice of the Mixed Arbitral Tribunals.

GUNN *v.* GUNZ.

Anglo-German Mixed Arbitral Tribunal. 25 *July*, 1922.

(BOREL, VAUGHAN WILLIAMS, ZACHARIAS.)

THE FACTS.—The German Clearing Office contended that the dissolution of contracts provided for in the first paragraph of Article 296 of the Treaty of Versailles did not extend to contracts of loan, and asked the Tribunal to reconsider the reasons for which they decided another decision in the opposite sense. The agent of the British Government objected on the ground that it was not admissible to impugn a decision already given and to reopen a question which had been finally solved by this decision.

Held: That this contention must be rejected. "The "Tribunal are of opinion that considering the nature of their "task and their position as a final Arbitral Court created by the "Peace Treaty, a decision given by them in a case cannot be "deemed as unreservedly binding for future cases. They must "reserve to themselves the right of reconsidering in a new case "a legal question dealt with by them in a former decision. "Likewise, any of the parties may not only bring before the "Tribunal a new case which they consider as not identical with "a former case already decided, but also request the Tribunal "with regard to the new case to reconsider a legal question on "which a former decision has been grounded. The Tribunal "trust that this will not be done without serious reasons." [Report: *Recueil*, vol. II (1923), p. 202.]

Case No. 266

Arbitration—Award—Dismissal of Claims—Recommendation of Payment as an Act of Grace—"Equity."

THE HOME MISSIONARY SOCIETY CASE.

British-American Claims Arbitral Tribunal. 18 *December*, 1920.

(FROMAGEOT, FITZPATRICK, ANDERSON.)

For THE FACTS and the Decision see Case No. 117.

In this case the Tribunal, while dismissing the claim on behalf of the Home Missionary Society for damage done to its property during a rebellion in the British Protectorate of Sierra Leone, added that it would be an act of grace which the Tribunal could not refrain from recommending warmly to the generosity of the British Government, if that Government, in consideration of the services which the Society had rendered and was still rendering to the development of the Protectorate and of its population, could avail itself of any fund from which to repair, so far as possible, the losses sustained by the Society in the course of the revolt. See also for a similar recommendation, in deference to the unfortunate circumstances of the claimants, the case of the *David J. Adams* (Case No. 164; Nielsen, p. 536).[1] And see *ibid.*, p. 495, for a similar recommendation in the case of *William Hardman* decided on 18 June, 1913, and p. 506, in the *Cadenhead* case decided on 1 May, 1914.

It will be noted that the Tribunal was by Article 7 of the Arbitration Agreement instructed to decide the cases submitted to it in accordance with "treaty rights and with "the principles of international law and equity." The fact that the Tribunal in a number of cases found it necessary, while dismissing the claim, to recommend payments as an act of grace suggests that it did not consider that "equity" entitled it to depart from rules of international law applicable to the disputes.

Arbitration—Award—Excess of Jurisdiction—Neutral Arbitration—Dissenting Opinions under the Hague Convention of 1907—Signature of the Award—Execution of the Award—Reservation as to the Force of the Award as a Precedent. **Case No. 267**

NORWAY AND UNITED STATES (REQUISITION OF SHIPBUILDING CONTRACTS CASE).

Permanent Court of Arbitration. 13 *October*, 1922.

(VALLOTON, ANDERSON, VOGT.)

See Cases Nos. 261, 289.

On the day on which the award was given the American

[1] In this case the Tribunal, while disallowing the claim, expressed the desire that the defendant Government might consider favourably the allowance as an act of grace of compensation to the descendants of the claimant. In recommending this course the Tribunal took into consideration the fact that although the criminal acts in question had been effectively prohibited for a long time, the particular penalty was enacted posterior to the seizure of the vessel; that the owner of the vessel was not in fact responsible for the illicit conduct of the master of the ship; that he was a poor man whose livelihood was destroyed as the result of the condemnation of the vessel; and that a possibly successful appeal against the judgment of the lower court had to be abandoned owing to lack of pecuniary means on the part of the owner of the vessel.

Case No. 267 *contd.*

arbitrator addressed a letter to the Secretary-General of the Permanent Court of Arbitration, informing him that he refused to be present when the award was announced, on the ground that the two other members of the Tribunal disregarded the terms of submission and exceeded the authority conferred upon them by the special agreement. (See *A.J.*, XVIII (1923), p. 399.)

It appears from a note (printed *ibid.*, p. 399) communicated by the American arbitrator that the Tribunal interpreted the relevant provisions of the Hague Convention of 1907 for the Pacific Settlement of International Disputes (Articles 78-90) to the effect that it did not contain an authorisation for filing a dissenting opinion or for a note of dissent. The American arbitrator—after communicating with the Government of the United States—finally acquiesced in that interpretation of the Hague Convention as precluding a dissenting opinion on the law and the facts, but he "refused to appear to acquiesce in "the action of the Tribunal by his presence and silence when "the award was announced."

On 26 February, 1923, the Government of the United States, while forwarding to the Government of Norway the amount of $12,239,852.47 awarded to the claimants, addressed to it a communication stating that although the Government of the United States felt it incumbent upon it to comply with the award, it would not accept certain apparent bases of the award as being declaratory of international law or as binding the Government of the United States. The latter protested both against certain aspects of the substantive law applied by the Tribunal and alleged non-compliance with the rules of procedure laid down in the Hague Convention. In regard to the first, the United States maintained that, contrary to the view adopted by the arbitrators, "due process of law applied uniformly, and "without discrimination to nationals and aliens alike and "offering to all just terms of reparation or reimbursement "suffices to meet the requirements of international law; and "thus the requisitioning state is free to determine the extent "and duration of its own emergency." In regard to the second, it was alleged that the Tribunal disregarded the terms of Article 79 of the Hague Convention by not giving a detailed exposition of reasons which determined the amounts awarded and the variations in the amount of interest. (Scott, *The Hague Court Reports* (2nd series), p. 81; *A.J.*, XVII (1923), pp. 287-289.[1])

[1] For some comments on the protest of the United States, see Scott in *A.J.*, XVII (1923), pp. 289, 290.

Arbitration—Award—Effectiveness of—Admissibility of Partial Execution.

See Cases Nos. 54, 262 (*Colombia and Venezuela*).

Arbitration—Award—How far Based on Available Sources of Evidence.

See Case No. 54 (*Colombia and Venezuela*) (FACTS) and *Sentence Arbitrale*, p. 12, for a reference to an arbitration agreement according to which in the absence of clear documentary evidence the award is " to approximate so far as " possible to the existing documents."

iii.—Appeal and Revision

Arbitration—Revision of Award—New Facts—Questions of Fact and of Law—Discovery of " Preparatory Work." **Case No. 268**

HEIM AND CHAMANT *v.* THE GERMAN STATE.

French-German Mixed Arbitral Tribunal.
7 August and 22 September, 1922.
(MERCIER, GANDOLPHE.)

THE FACTS.—Paragraph 80 of the Rules of Procedure of the French-German Mixed Arbitral Tribunal provided that a party may ask for the revision of an award given by the Tribunal in consequence of " the discovery of a " new fact such as would have exercised a decisive " influence on the award and which, before the termina- " tion of the proceedings, was unknown to the Tribunal " and to the party asking for revision." In the course of 1921 the Tribunal gave a number of decisions in the case of *Heim and Chamant* v. *The German State*. Subsequently Germany asked for revision of these decisions on the ground of discovery of new facts. The new facts were said to consist of the minutes, previously inaccessible, of the so-called Alsace-Lorraine Conference, a meeting of statesmen and jurists which took place before the Paris Peace Conference. It was maintained that the proceedings of this meeting influenced considerably the Alsace-Lorraine Committee at the Peace Conference, and that the Committee's projects as to regulation of the question of Alsace-Lorraine nationality had almost, in their entirety, become part

Case No. 268 *contd.*

of the Treaty of Versailles; that the minutes in question could therefore fittingly be regarded as part of the preparatory work of the Treaty of Versailles; that they showed conclusively that Alsace-Lorrainers were to be regarded as of German nationality during the war; that they rejected the idea of the retroactive effect of the reintegration of Alsace-Lorrainers into French nationality—a thesis rejected by Germany but adopted by the Tribunal as one of the principal reasons for its decision.

Held: That the request for a revision must be rejected. (*a*) The Tribunal in introducing "revision" into its procedure intended to adopt for international arbitration an institution which serves a definite function in municipal law. In view of the risks involved in the effort to ascertain the facts amidst unusual and troubled circumstances, the Tribunal thought it necessary to provide for safeguards against errors. It was not the intention of the Tribunal to create indirectly an appeal procedure not provided for in the Treaty of Versailles, which considered the decisions of the Tribunal as final (Article 304 *g*). Accordingly, the request for revision was limited solely to discovery of new *facts*.

(*b*) The conception of "facts" is in itself an elastic and relative one. It ought to be interpreted restrictively so as not to injure the course of international justice, in which as a rule there exists only one instance and no possibility of appeal. Neither can this conception be made too comprehensive in disregard of the requirements of certainty and stability. The conception of "facts" cannot be rigidly opposed to that of law. It embraces all means of proof relating to questions of law and, by way of exception, the law itself in all cases in which the principle *jura novit curia* does not apply and in which the proof of the law applicable rests upon the party invoking it. The Tribunal could not therefore reject the request of Germany *a limine*.

(*c*) However, as Germany in invoking the minutes of the Alsace-Lorraine Conference has assimilated them to the preparatory work or the motives of a law within the State, the Tribunal observes that the assimilation of a treaty to a legislative enactment is not accurate. A treaty is a contractual act. Undoubtedly a treaty, like an enactment, has the force of law, but it does not follow that the same rules of interpretation apply to treaties and statutes. In any case, even in municipal law the discovery of new facts in the shape of preparatory work cannot have the effect of putting the procedure of revision in motion.

(*d*) There are particular reasons which in international law tend to diminish the weight of preparatory work. While within the State the source of preparatory work is on the whole uniform, in the international sphere it proceeds from divergent and opposing conceptions and interests. It is also frequently secret and inaccessible to the judge in its entirety. Special procedure is required in this respect in the matter of treaties, for while in municipal law the State may remedy the effects of an incautious resort to preparatory work, there is no such possibility in the international sphere.

(*e*) While, as a rule, in regard to a multilateral treaty it would not be possible to attach decisive importance to preparatory work confined to one of the contracting parties, an exception could be made in the case of treaty provisions concerning only one contracting party. This was the case in the matter of Alsace-Lorraine, in respect of which the Allied and Associated Powers left to France in the first instance the elaboration of the relevant treaty provisions. However, such preparatory work if it is to be authoritative must emanate from the competent authorities of the State in question and not, as in the present case, from purely private sources. [Report: *Recueil*, III (1924), p. 50.]

B. PERMANENT COURT OF INTERNATIONAL JUSTICE

IV.—The Advisory Opinion

i.—Competence

Permanent Court of International Justice—Advisory Opinions —Non-Contentious Questions.

See Case No. 256 (*Competence of the International Labour Organisation: Organisation and Development of Methods of Agricultural Production:* The Facts) for an example of a request for an Advisory Opinion on a matter which was not actually contentious and on which " an authoritative opinion " on the part of the Court " was desired.

PART XI

WAR AND NEUTRALITY

A. WAR IN GENERAL

I.—Definition and Technical Meaning of War. Insurgency

War—Definition—Technical Meaning of Belligerency—Armed Resistance to Troops Invading National Territory. **Case No. 269**

D. N. (GREECE) CASE.

Greece, Court of Appeal of Athens. 1922. (*No.* 833.)

THE FACTS.—D. N., an officer in the Greek army, was killed while offering armed resistance, with the troops under his command, by order of his superiors, to the French troops which had landed at the Piræus with a view to taking possession of Greek military material.

The Greek State, in a proceeding instituted for recovery of a pension, denied that there was any question of a state of war at the time of the officer's death, and refused to grant the pension.

Held: That the fact that a country offers armed resistance to troops invading its territory constitutes a case of legitimate self-defence and creates a state of hostilities as laid down in Article 6 of Law No. 680, providing for the granting of a pension to the relations of officers and soldiers killed in such circumstances. For this purpose a declaration of war or a state of war is not essential. [Report: Themis, vol. 33, p. 249.]

III.—Region of War

Theatre of War—New York as Theatre of War during the World War.

See Case No. 298 (*United States ex rel. Wessels* v. *McDonald, Commandant of Brooklyn Navy Yard*).

IV.—Belligerent Forces

Case No. 270 **Belligerent Forces—*De facto* Belligerents—The Forces of the West-Ukrainian Republic in 1918.**

NIEZABITOWSKI *v.* KOWALSKI.

Poland, Supreme Court, Third Division. 28 *July*, 1921.

THE FACTS.—In 1919, while the Ukrainian army [1] was holding the district of Rudki, some Ukrainian soldiers took a cow from the plaintiff without payment or receipt. Subsequently the animal was alienated by the Ukrainian authorities to the defendant. On the re-establishment of order, the plaintiff brought the present action to recover the cow from the defendant. The local court at Rudki decided that the Hague Rules of Land Warfare did not apply to the Ukrainian army, which was one of insurgents, and that, consequently, that army had no right to requisition private property and thus divest the plaintiff of his title. The Court added that this made it unnecessary to point out that the alleged requisition did not take place in the manner stipulated by Article 52 of the Hague Rules. On appeal, the District Court of Sambor held that the appeal must be dismissed since the alleged requisitions were merely illegal acts, and that even had the defendant believed those acts to be legal, they were objectively illegal and thus could not deprive the plaintiff of his title. On appeal to the Supreme Court,

Held: That the appeal must be dismissed, the grounds adduced by the courts below being unassailable. [Report: O.S.P., I, No. 231.]

For a discussion of the case see Rundstein, *ibid.*, 212-214, n. 1.

---

[1] The Ukrainian armed forces belonged to an organisation which called itself the West-Ukrainian Republic and which, after the collapse of the Austrian Empire, established itself at the end of October, 1918, in the Eastern part of Galicia now forming part of Poland. See *Annual Digest*, 1927-1928, Case No. 362.—[Ed.]

V.—Effects of Outbreak of War

ii.—On Treaties

(*a*) During the War

War—Effect on Treaties—When Maintained notwithstanding State of War—Treaty of 1848 between Austria and the United States — Alien Enemies and Alien Friends — Classification of. **Case No. 271**

Hughes *v.* Techt ; Techt *v.* Hughes.

United States, New York Supreme Court, and New York Court of Appeals. March, 1919, *and* 8 *June,* 1920.

The Facts.—Hannigan, an American citizen, died intestate in New York on 27 December, 1917, owning land in New York. He left two daughters, Mrs. Hughes and Mrs. Techt. The latter had married an Austro-Hungarian in 1911 and so had become an Austro-Hungarian national, although living in the United States. On 7 December, 1917, war had been declared between Austria-Hungary and the United States. Mrs. Hughes brought an action to bar the claims of her sister, Mrs. Techt, to Hannigan's property on the ground that Mrs. Techt was an enemy alien. The New York statutes allowed *alien friends* to hold real property. Mrs. Techt had not been interned as an enemy, nor had she come under any of the special disabilities placed on alien enemies by the Trading with the Enemy Act and other regulations. The Treaty of 1848 between Austria and the United States (9 U.S. Stat. L. 944), in force at the outbreak of the war, provided that nationals of each country could take land by descent within the other country, sell it within two years, and remove the proceeds. It was held in the Court of First Instance that Mrs. Techt's claim was not barred. In view of the modern rules making actual residence the test of enemy character for matters of trading with the enemy, Mrs. Techt, a resident of the United States, was an alien friend within the meaning of the New York Real Property Law, § 10. Furthermore, the Treaty provision, which would of course supersede contrary State legislation, had not been annulled by

Case No. 271 ***contd.***

the outbreak of war. Mrs. Techt thereafter secured a judgment for partition of the property, which was affirmed by the Appellate Division of the Supreme Court, and the question was then certified to the Court of Appeals whether she had an estate of inheritance in the property.

Held: That the judgment must be affirmed and the question answered in the affirmative. Judge Cardozo's Opinion went at length into the treatment given resident nationals of enemy States in time of war. He concluded: " The truth is " that they are enemies, who, within the limits placed by the " sovereign upon a revocable license, enjoy the privileges of " friends. Their identification with friends is never com- " plete." (229 N.Y. 222, 229.) Despite the privileges given them, they remained enemy aliens, rather than alien friends, for the purpose of the New York Real Property laws. The Trading with the Enemy Act only defined and classified aliens as enemies and friends for the purpose of preventing intercourse across the line of war. Commercial domicile was not to be confused with questions of alienage.

However, the Treaty provision remained valid and effective notwithstanding the outbreak of war. " The effect of war upon " the existing treaties of belligerents is one of the unsettled " problems of the law. The older writers sometimes said that " treaties ended *ipso facto* when war came (3 Phillimore Int. L. " 794). The writers of our own time reject these sweeping " statements (2 Oppenheim Int. L. sec. 99; Hall Int. L. 398, " 401; Fiore Int. L. [Borchard's Transl.] sec. 845). Inter- " national law to-day does not preserve treaties or annul them " regardless of the effects produced. It deals with such " problems pragmatically, preserving or annulling as the neces- " sities of war exact. It establishes standards, but it does not " fetter itself with rules. . . . Treaties of alliance fall. Treaties " of boundary or cession, 'dispositive' or 'transitory' con- " ventions, survive (Hall Int. L. pp. 398, 401; Westlake Int. " L. II, 34; Oppenheim, *supra*). So, of course, do treaties " which regulate the conduct of hostilities (Hall, *supra*; " 5 Moore Dig. Int. L. 372; *Society for Propagation of the* " *Gospel* v. *Town of New Haven*, 8 Wheat. 464, 494). Intention " in such circumstances is clear. These instances do not " represent distinct and final principles. They are illustrations " of the same principle. They are applications of a standard. " When I ask what that principle or standard is, and endeavour "to extract it from the long chapters in the books, I get this, "and nothing more, that provisions compatible with a state of "hostilities, unless expressly terminated, will be enforced, and "those incompatible rejected." (229 N.Y. 222, 240, 241.) "The mere fact that other portions of the treaty are suspended "or even abrogated is not conclusive. The treaty does not fall "in its entirety unless it has the character of an indivisible "act." (229 N.Y. 222, 243.) To the argument that treaties of commerce and navigation are suspended or abrogated by war, Judge Cardozo replied: "But stipulations do not touch "commerce because they happen to be embodied in a treaty "which is styled one to regulate or encourage commerce. . . . "There is a line of division, fundamental in importance, which "separates stipulations touching commerce *between* nations "from those touching the tenure of land *within* the territories "of nations." (229 N.Y. 222, 246.) Judge Cardozo concluded: "I find nothing incompatible with the policy of the "government, with the safety of the nation, or with the "maintenance of the war in the enforcement of this treaty so "as to sustain the plaintiff's title." (229 N.Y. 222, 244.) [Reports: 106 N.Y. Misc. 524; 229 N.Y. 222; 254 U.S. 643; Dickinson, *Cases*, 1116.]

NOTES.—See 5 *Cornell L.Q.* 209; 15 *Ill. L. Rev.* 459; and 30 *Y.L.J.* 176.

War—Effect on Treaties—Termination—No Effect on Vested Rights. **Case No. 272**

GUARDIANSHIP (TERMINATION OF TREATIES) CASE.

Greece, Court of Appeal of Salonica. 1919. (*No.* 57.)

THE FACTS.—This was an action for eviction. Certain of the plaintiffs who were infants were represented by a guardian appointed before the entry of Greece into the Great War by a Moslem religious authority (Mufti), pursuant to Article 11 of the Treaty of 14 November, 1913, between Greece and Turkey, which Treaty was duly ratified by an Act of the Greek Parliament. It was objected that the effect of the entry of Greece into the Great War in opposition to Turkey was to terminate the Treaty of 1913 and thus render the appointment of the guardian invalid.

Held: That this contention could not be accepted. The guardian was appointed according to the Treaty and the

Case No. 272 *contd.* relevant provisions of Greek law several months before the entry of Greece into the Great War. The guardian was not deprived of his office by this event. [Report: Themis, vol. 31, p. 39.]

(*b*) AFTER THE WAR

Case No. 273

War—New Treaty—Effect on Treaties—Treaty of Frankfort of 10 May, 1871—Most-Favoured-Nation Clause.

LOEWENGARD *v.* *PROCUREUR* OF THE REPUBLIC AND BONVIER (SEQUESTRATOR).

France, Court of Appeal of Lyons (First Chamber).
13 *October*, 1921.

THE FACTS.—(See Case No. 221.) Loewengard declared that in accordance with the terms of certain diplomatic agreements the consuls of a number of States enjoyed diplomatic immunities in France subject to the condition of reciprocity; he cited in his favour the most-favoured-nation clause included in the Treaty of Frankfort. On appeal,

Held: That the appeal must be dismissed. The Treaty of Frankfort ceased to exist as from the date of the declaration of war, and the Treaty of Versailles has taken its place. The French Government had made no declaration on the subject of the immunities of German consuls reviving the rights enjoyed before the war. [Report: 49 *Clunet* (1923), p. 391.]

War—Effect on Treaties—Commercial Treaties—Germany and Russia.

See Case No. 169 (*Immovables (Aliens in Germany) Case*).

iii.—On Private Contracts

Case No. 274

War—Effect on Contracts—Anglo-American Doctrine—Compared with the Continental Practice—Interpretation of Treaties Drafted on the Basis of Anglo-American Doctrine—Article 296 (2) of the Treaty of Versailles.

BINON *v.* GERMAN STATE AND THE SILESIAN FIRE INSURANCE CO.

Germano-Belgian Mixed Arbitral Tribunal. 1 *June*, 1922.
(MORIAUD, HOENE, ROLIN.)

THE FACTS.—This was an action brought by a Belgian national against the German State, a German Company in whose employment he had been before, and at the outbreak of, the war, and a German Fire Insurance

Company. The only point in the action which is material for the purposes of this digest was the claim against the Fire Insurance Company for the value of the plaintiff's furniture in Germany which had been insured with that company and destroyed by fire. On this head the preliminary point was—whether the contract with the Insurance Company had given rise to a debt to which Article 296 (2) of the Treaty of Versailles applied, as being a debt "of which the total "or partial execution was suspended on account of the "declaration of war." If the Article applied, it was contended that the plaintiff should have taken steps to have his debt settled through the Clearing Office and not sought to enforce it by a direct proceeding.

Held: That the concluding words of the provision of Article 296 (2) relating to "Debts which became payable during "the war to nationals of one Contracting Power residing "within its territory and arose out of transactions or con-"tracts with the nationals of an Opposing Power, resident "within its territory, *of which the total or partial execution* "*was suspended on account of the declaration of war*" must as a matter of construction be read as follows: "*of which the* "*total or partial execution was suspended on account of the* "*declaration of war, or, subsequently, as the result of the pro-*"*hibition of commercial intercourse with the enemy.*" This construction must be adopted for the following reasons: On the Continent of Europe the declaration of war did not have the result of suspending, as a matter of law, the execution of contracts between subjects of belligerents. The suspension, if any, was one of fact. It was not the automatic consequence of the declaration of war, as is the case in England by virtue of the Anglo-American doctrine according to which the execution of contracts between enemies is suspended as the result of the declaration of war in all cases in which the contract is not totally abrogated. The explanation of the existing text of Article 296 (2) is that it was drafted by Englishmen and that the French translator did not think of the difficulties which a literal translation of this passage was likely to cause when applied to Continental nations. The correct interpretation of this paragraph must therefore attempt to find a formula which when applied to relations on the Continent corresponds to what was intended in the English text by reference to the consequences of the declaration of war. As the equivalent of the

Case No. 274 contd.

declaration of war in England there must be regarded on the Continent the Decrees prohibiting commercial intercourse with the enemy such as the French Decree of 27 September, 1914, and the Belgian Decree of 10 December, 1916. The latter Decree made it impossible for the plaintiff to continue the payment of the insurance premiums to the German insurance company. It thus had the result of making impossible, in part, the execution of the contract. Accordingly, the contract in question falls within the provision of Article 296 (2) of the Treaty and the plaintiff must apply to the Belgian Clearing Office in respect of his claim against the Fire Insurance Company. [Report: *Recueil*, vol. II (1923), p. 217.]

Case No. 275

War—Effect on Contracts—Pre-War Contracts—Meaning of—Contract Concluded by Means of a Letter Sent before and Received after the Declaration of War—Article 296 of the Treaty of Versailles.

THE FRENCH AND ITALIAN BANK *v.* WARBURG & CO.

Franco-German Mixed Arbitral Tribunal. 3 *June*, 1922.

(SJOEBORG, HERWEGEN, FORTIN.)

THE FACTS.—This was a claim under Article 296 of the Treaty of Versailles.[1] The branch of the plaintiff bank in São Paolo (Brazil) was instructed by the head office in Paris, by letter dispatched on 24 July, 1914, to collect the proceeds of a bill of exchange for the account of the defendants. The bill was accordingly collected on 7 January, 1915. The defendants claimed from the plaintiffs the amount of the bill, and this claim was admitted by the German and French Clearing Offices. The plaintiffs appealed, on the ground that the claim was not covered by Article 296, as it arose out of a contract concluded after the outbreak of the war.

Held: That the claim was based on a contract concluded by means of a letter which was sent before the declaration of war but which reached its address after the declaration of war;

[1] Article 296 provides as follows: "(1) There shall be settled through "the intervention of clearing offices to be established by each of the High "Contracting Parties within three months of the notification referred to in "paragraph (*e*) hereafter the following classes of pecuniary obligations:

"(2) Debts which became payable during the war to nationals of one "Contracting Power residing within its territory and arose out of trans-"actions or contracts with the nationals of an Opposing Power, resident "within its territory, of which the total or partial execution was suspended "on account of the declaration of war."

such a contract must be regarded as concluded after the outbreak of the war. It followed that the present claim was not a pre-war debt within the meaning of Article 296 to be settled through the Clearing Offices. [Report: *Recueil*, vol. II (1923), p. 249.]

NOTE.—It will be observed that the Tribunal treated the letter from the head office of the Bank in Paris to its branch in Brazil as the instrument by which the contract between the plaintiffs and defendants was concluded.—[Ed.]

War—Effects of Outbreak—Contract with Enemy Not Wholly Performed on the Outbreak of War—Performance Involving Intercourse with the Enemy—Clause Suspending Deliveries during War—National Character of Limited Company—Frustration of Contract—Doctrine of *rebus sic stantibus*. **Case No. 276**

IN RE BADISCHE COMPANY LIMITED.
IN RE BAYER COMPANY LIMITED.
(And certain other companies registered in England.)

England, High Court of Justice, Chancery Division.
28 *July*, 1921.

THE FACTS (in the Bayer Company's case, which may be regarded as typical).[1] The Bayer Company (hereinafter referred to as the B. company) was registered as a company with limited liability in England in 1895. Both then and at the outbreak of war all the shares but a very few were held by persons resident in Germany or by the Farbenfabriken Company which manufactured dye-stuffs in Germany (hereinafter referred to as "the German company"). On the outbreak of war the German company held 9912 of the 10,000 shares of £10 each in the B. company. Two directors resident in England held respectively 4 and 20 shares, and the holders of the remainder were apparently all resident in Germany.

The B. company was in substance the English selling agency of the German company. In form the German company sold dye-stuffs to the B. company, who in turn sold them as independent principals to English customers. The German company was "vitally "interested not only in the contract between itself "and the [B.] company but also in the contract be-

[1] A full statement of the facts would be both lengthy and complicated, but it is believed that the brief statement given in the text does not omit anything material to the purposes of this volume.

Case No. 276 ***contd.***

" tween the [B.] company and the English customer. " . . . At every moment of time down to the out- " break of war the control of the limited company, its " business, its affairs and its acts, were in the hands, " and at the mercy, of the German directors, the " German shareholders and, ultimately in the last " resort, the " German company (*per* Russell, J., at p. 342). The prices at which the B. company sold the dye-stuffs would, if necessary, be settled by the German company.

A controller of the B. company had been appointed under the Trading with the Enemy Amendment Act, 1916, for the purpose of winding up its business. The controller now applied to the Court for directions on the question whether he should admit as debts due from the B. company certain claims by purchasers in respect of pre-war contracts made by the B. company for the sale of dye-stuffs, the claims being mainly for damages for non-performance of these contracts.

The question of the effect of the outbreak of war upon these contracts was thus raised. The main contentions will appear from the following summary of the judgment.

Held by Russell, J. : (1) That, upon applying the " control " test enunciated by the House of Lords in *Daimler Co.* v. *Continental Tyre and Rubber Co.*, L.R. [1916] 2 A.C. 307 (and more particularly in the speech of Lord Parker at p. 336), the B. company upon the outbreak of war " *eo instanti* assumed " enemy character," so that the uncompleted contracts in question then became " contracts with an enemy " and were therefore dissolved.

(2) Nor, upon the authority of *Ertel Bieber & Co.* v. *Rio Tinto Co.*, L.R. [1918] A.C. 260, were the contracts preserved from dissolution by the presence of clauses providing for a suspension of deliveries pending the duration of certain events including war, as such clauses were void as being contrary to public policy.

(3) Further, that even if they had not been contracts with enemies, they were dissolved upon the outbreak of war because they were contracts for the supply of goods to be obtained from Germany, and their further performance involved intercourse with the enemy and therefore became illegal [1] (*Veithardt*

[1] See *Esposito* v. *Bowden* (1857), 7 E. & B. 763, for a simple illustration of this rule.

and Hall v. *Rylands Brothers* (1917), 116 L.T. 706; 86 L.J. (Ch.) 604). Nor were they saved by the suspensory clauses (see (2) above).

(4) Further, that the contracts were dissolved by the operation of the doctrine of frustration (*Bank Line* v. *Capel & Co.*, L.R. [1919] A.C. 435, and *Tamplin Steamship Co.* v. *Anglo-Mexican Petroleum Products Co.*, L.R. [1916] 2 A.C. 397); for "the parties contracted on the footing that peace "would continue to exist between the country of the con-"tracting parties and the country of the source of supply, and "that the source of supply would remain open" (at p. 380). [Report: L.R. [1921] 2 Ch. 331.]

War—Effects of Outbreak—Pre-War Contracts with Enemy Subjects. **Case No. 277**

SCHOSTALL *v.* JOHNSON.

England, High Court of Justice, King's Bench Division.
20 *November*, 1919.

THE FACTS.—In 1912 the plaintiff, an Austrian subject, entered into a contract with the defendants, London sugar brokers, whereby for three years he was to be employed in association with the defendants and to be remunerated by way of a commission and a share of the profits arising from business introduced or initiated by him, subject to a minimum annual sum guaranteed by the defendants.

In August, 1914, war broke out between Great Britain and Austria. The plaintiff was not interned and was granted a travelling permit which enabled him to attend at the defendants' place of business.

On 30 September, 1914, one of the defendants wrote to the plaintiff as follows: "Please note that under "present circumstances your agreement with me dated "the 21st August, 1912, is null and void." The plaintiff continued to be ready and willing to perform his contract, though in fact after the outbreak of the war there was little or no business for him to do. The plaintiff claimed damages for breach of contract.

Held by Avory, J.: That the defendants' repudiation of the contract was wrongful, and the plaintiff was entitled to recover the sums becoming due to him under the agreement up till the date of its expiry on 1 September, 1915. The fact

Case No. 277 *contd.* that the plaintiff was the subject of an enemy State did not terminate the contract, nor did the circumstances show a frustration of the contract. The learned judge followed *Nordman* v. *Rayner* (1916), 33 T.L.R. 87, an even stronger case, for there the plaintiff was interned. [Report: 36 T.L.R. 75.]

Case No. 278 **War—Effects of Outbreak—Executory Contract for Supply of Goods to Enemy Country—Effect of Clause Suspending Deliveries during War.**

FRIED KRUPP AKTIENGESELLSCHAFT *v.* ORCONERA IRON ORE COMPANY LIMITED.

England, House of Lords (on Appeal from the Court of Appeal and the Chancery Division of the High Court of Justice). 31 *January,* 1919.

THE FACTS.—In 1873 the Orconera Iron Ore Company (hereinafter referred to as "the English company"), being a company formed to work certain mines and railways in Spain, entered into a contract with the predecessor of the Fried Krupp Aktiengesellschaft (hereinafter called "the German company") for the supply of a large annual quantity of Spanish iron ore during a period of ninety-nine years.

Clause 15 of this contract provided that "If by "reason of war or civil disturbance the [English] "company shall be obstructed or hindered in the raising, getting or leading away or transport of ore . . . "so that the company shall be unable in any year to "deliver to Fried Krupp his full and proper quantity "of ore according to the arrangement then in force ". . . Fried Krupp shall be entitled to receive and "the company shall deliver to him . . . during the five "years next succeeding the cessation of such war or "civil disturbance the amount of ore by which the "quantity of ore fell short of the full and proper "quantity. . . ."

Clause 18 provided that the agreement and everything therein contained, except clauses 18 and 23 (which provided for the settlement of disputes by arbitration) and all provisions necessary for the settlement of accounts between the parties, should "cease "to have any force during any period of time in which "an unavoidable cause shall exist preventing the

" company from delivering or Fried Krupp from " receiving ore but shall revive and be in full force " on the cessation or removal of such cause."

In 1903 the German company, which carried on the business of steel and munition manufacturers at Essen in Germany, succeeded to the rights of its predecessor and continued to receive iron ore under the agreement until the outbreak of war between Great Britain and Germany in August, 1914.

The short question was whether the effect of the outbreak of war upon the contract (which admittedly " could not be carried out without such a degree of " contact and trading with the enemy as would be " plainly illegal ") was to dissolve it or merely to suspend its operation. The sum due upon the outbreak of war by the German company to the English company had already been paid by the British Custodian of Enemy Property out of monies in his hands belonging to the German company.

Held by the House of Lords (Lords Birkenhead, Buckmaster, Finlay, Dunedin, Atkinson and Shaw), affirming the decision of Younger, J., and of the Court of Appeal, and following *Ertel Bieber & Co.* v. *Rio Tinto Co.*, L.R. [1918] A.C. 260: That the contract was dissolved by the outbreak of war and not merely suspended. [Reports: 120 L.T. 386; 88 L.J.Ch. 304.]

NOTE.—The main ground of the *Ertel Bieber* decision on the effect of a suspensory clause is stated in the Judgment of Lord Dunedin at p. 275.

War—Effects of Outbreak on Private Contracts—Abrogation of Executory Contract—Preservation of Rights Already Accrued. **Case No. 279**

PENNEY (Custodian of Enemy Property for Scotland) *v.* CLYDE SHIPBUILDING AND ENGINEERING COMPANY.

Scotland, Court of Session, and, on Appeal therefrom, the House of Lords. 10 *December*, 1918; 20 *February*, 1919; 15 *March*, 1920.

THE FACTS.—By a contract made in July, 1913, the Clyde Shipbuilding and Engineering Company (hereinafter referred to as " the Scottish company ") agreed to build a steamer for the Royal Hungarian Sea Navigation Company " Adria," of Budapest (hereinafter referred to as " the Hungarian company ").

Case No. 279 ***contd.***

On 12 August, 1914, when war broke out between Great Britain and Austria-Hungary, the steamer was not yet finished ; work was stopped ; four instalments of the purchase money had already been paid by the Hungarian company to the Scottish company, amounting (less a small contra account) to some £79,000. On 18 February, 1915, the steamer was requisitioned by the British Admiralty, who paid the Scottish company £86,000 therefor.

On 10 August, 1917, the Board of Trade made an Order under the Trading with the Enemy Acts vesting the said sum of £79,000 in the pursuer, the Custodian of Enemy Property for Scotland, who on 19 April, 1918, raised the present action against the Scottish company to recover that sum. The Scottish company, however, claimed the right to retain that sum on the ground that (in the words of Lord Ormidale—[1919] S.C. at p. 371—" on the outbreak of war the contract was abrogated or " cancelled, with the result that it became illegal and " therefore impossible for them to complete the vessel " for delivery, and that, on the other hand, any claim " that the Adria Co. might have had for repayment of " the instalments had ceased to exist."

Held by the Lord Ordinary (Lord Ormidale) and the First Division of the Court of Session (Lords Strathclyde (Lord President), Mackenzie and Cullen) : That the pursuer was entitled to recover the sum of £79,000. The effect of the outbreak of war upon this executory contract between a Scottish company and an alien enemy in enemy territory was to dissolve it as from the date of the outbreak of war. " But rights which, " prior to that date, had accrued were not destroyed, although " during the continuance of a state of war they were not " enforceable. . . . What rights, under the contract before us, " had accrued in favour of the alien enemy when war was " declared ? " ([1919] S.C. at p. 375.) The property in the steamer had already passed to the Hungarian company so that the steamer became on the outbreak of war the movable property of an alien enemy, of which the pursuer as Custodian was entitled to take possession. Instead of that, however, she was requisitioned by the Admiralty, who paid the Scottish company therefor. " Had the vessel not been so requisitioned " and sold, she would have remained in the hands of the " builders as custodiers for the [Hungarian] company, whose

" property the builders had expressly agreed she was. But, " instead of the unfinished ship, the builders held in their " hands her value . . . the sum sued for in this action. In " other words that sum of money represented, and was a " surrogatum for, the unfinished ship " (per the Lord President, [1919] S.C. at p. 376). Therefore the pursuer was entitled to a decree for payment of it.

Lord Mackenzie ([1919] S.C. at p. 378) said: " Although the " contract could not be executed it still subsisted for the " purpose of winding-up. An alien enemy cannot sue for or " receive during the war any property belonging to him in this " country, but his property as such is not confiscated. It is " for the purpose of winding-up that the aid of the Custodian " is invoked."

On appeal by the Scottish company, the House of Lords, in terms of an agreement arrived at between the parties upon the Lord Chancellor's suggestion, affirmed the judgment of the First Division, subject to a modification arising from the allowance of a counter-claim of which it is unnecessary to give particulars. Interest on the sum of £79,000 was awarded to the Custodian, not from the date of the outbreak of war, but from that of the interlocutor of the First Division. [Reports: [1919] *Session Cases*, 363; [1920] *Session Cases*, 68.]

War—Effects of Outbreak—Partnership Dissolved by Residence of One of the Partners in Enemy Territory—Vesting of Enemy Partner's Rights in Custodian of Enemy Property. **Case No. 280**

THE TREASURY *v.* GUNDELFINGER AND KAUMHEIMER.

Union of South Africa, *Supreme Court* (*Transvaal Provincial Division*). 15 *August*, 1919.

(MASON, CURLEWIS AND GREGOROWSKI, JJ.)

THE FACTS.—This was an action brought by the Custodian of Enemy Property under Union of South Africa Act No. 39 of 1916 claiming in respect of a sum of money alleged to be due to one Benno Gundelfinger, with whom the two defendants were in partnership. This person was an enemy subject. At the outbreak of war he was resident in England. On 31 December, 1916, he was repatriated to Germany, and thenceforth resided in Germany. The remaining partners continued in possession of the partnership assets and carried on business on their own account.

Held: That the partnership was dissolved not from the

Case No. 280 *contd.*

date of the outbreak of war, but from the date at which one of the partners became resident in enemy territory. The Custodian of Enemy Property, in whom the enemy partner's rights and interests had been vested, was entitled to claim an account as at that date, and payment of the enemy partner's share on that basis.

Mason, J. (at p. 331): "It is settled law that the mere fact "of a partner being an enemy subject does not cause dissolu- "tion of a partnership with persons who are British subjects; "he must be resident in an enemy country." [Report: *The South African Law Reports* [1919], *Transvaal Provincial Division*, p. 329 ([1919] T.P.D. 329).]

Case No. 281

War—Effects of Outbreak on Private Contracts—Partnerships.

ROSSIE *v.* GARVAN (Alien Property Custodian).

United States District Court, D. Connecticut. 3 *June*, 1921.

THE FACTS.—This was a suit against the Alien Property Custodian to recover partnership property. The partnership had been formed before the war between Germans and citizens of the United States. After the outbreak of war between Germany and the United States, the United States assets of the partnership were taken by the Alien Property Custodian. The United States partners claimed that the partnership was ended by the declaration of war, and that upon its dissolution they were entitled to their share of the assets.

Held: That decrees must be for the complainants. Although such a partnership could not be dissolved by war under the German law, but only by proceedings in a German court, it was said that, "By the settled law and policy of this "country all executory contracts with enemies of the United "States, including partnerships, are abrogated by the declara- "tion of war between this country and such enemy." (274 Fed. 447, 450.) *Mayer* v. *Garvan*, 270 Fed. 229, and *Ertel Bieber & Co.* v. *Rio Tinto Co.*, [1918] A.C. 260, were relied upon as supporting the application of the United States rather than the German law. Since the partnership was dissolved by the outbreak of war it could not be an enemy partnership, and consequently the Alien Property Custodian could not hold its assets under the Trading with the Enemy Act. (40 U.S. Stat. L. 411.) [Report: 274 Fed. 447.]

NOTE.—See also *Mayer* v. *Garvan* (17 January 1922), 278 Fed. 27.

iv.—On Enemy Subjects with regard to

(*a*) Their Personal Status in the Territory of the Belligerent. *Persona standi in judicio.*

Effects of War—Personal Status of Enemy Subjects in the Territory of the Belligerent—*Persona standi in judicio* —Armistice—Right of Appeal. **Case No. 282**

Brühler Glashütten Company *v.* Beaurain.

Belgium, Court of Appeal of Brussels. 19 *May*, 1919.

The Facts.—The Brühler Glassworks, a German company established in Brühl (Prussia), lodged an appeal from the judgment of the Commercial Tribunal of Brussels given during the German occupation (12 May, 1917). This appeal came up for hearing after the armistice but before the ratification of the Treaty of Versailles. As, moreover, the appeal came from a company of enemy character, it raised the question of the right of enemy subjects to appear in a Belgian court (Belgian Decree of 10-16 December, 1916, concerning the suspension of economic relations with the enemy).

Held: That the appellant, having been the subject of an adverse decision in a Belgian court, has the right to appeal. The Court ignored any argument based on the armistice, which is " not a partial or temporary peace, but simply a suspension of " military operations." [1] Referring then to the variations in former practice in regard to the *persona standi in judicio* of enemy subjects, the Court declared that the Decree of 10-16 December, 1916, on the subject of the interruption of economic relations with the enemy, had been issued in accordance with and in execution of the resolutions of the Economic Conference of Allied Governments at Paris (14-17 June, 1916). One of these resolutions provided that " the laws and regulations prohibiting " commerce with the enemy shall be co-ordinated." In its report to the King on the above-mentioned Decree the Belgian Government expressly declared itself to be guided by these resolutions. For the interpretation of this Decree the judge must therefore bear in mind the entirety of laws and regulations prohibiting trade with the enemy. " In case of obscurity or " doubt he can, and even must, take into account the course of

[1] See however Fauchille, vol. II, p. 81. If the armistice does not necessarily put an end to the prohibition of trade with the enemy, " it tends at any rate " to mitigate it."

Case No. 282 *contd.*

" the decisions which from time immemorial or recently have " been given by the courts of the Allied Powers. . . ." Now " at all times the English judge has been able to give a hearing " to an enemy subject who has obtained from the King express " or implied licence to remain in the country; the authorities " record many cases where enemy subjects have been allowed " to appear in Court (Oppenheim, *International Law* (1912), " vol. II, p. 133)." In France also, the principle of denial of access to the Court has undergone during the last four years modifications dictated either by special circumstances or by considerations of humanity. Some recent English decisions have rightly laid down that when sued before an English judge, an enemy subject and an enemy company have the right to resort to all the means of defence allowed by the law; that, in particular, they cannot be refused the right to appeal when judgment has been given against them. [Report: *Pasicrisie belge*, 1919, vol. II, p. 86.]

NOTE.—See Nys, *Persona standi in judicio*, in *Belgique Judiciaire*, 1919, cols. 801 *et seq*.

As to the British practice during the World War see *Porter* v. *Freudenberg*, [1915] 1 K.B. 857; *In re Mary, Duchess of Sutherland*, [1915] 31 T.L.R. 394 and [1921] 65 S.J. 513; *The Möwe*, [1915] P. 1 at p. 15. See Oppenheim (4th Ed., ed. by McNair), § 100 a, and McNair, *Legal Effects of War* (1920), pp. 26-58.—[Ed.]

Case No. 283

Effects of Outbreak of War on Enemy Subjects—*Persona standi in judicio*—In Extraterritorial Court.

POO SHONG HING *ET AL.* v. CONSOLIDATED STEEL CORPORATION.

United States Court for China. 19 *November*, 1920.

THE FACTS.—This was a suit brought in the United States Court for China, by a firm consisting of two Chinese nationals and a German residing in China, before the termination of the war between China and the United States on the one side and Germany on the other. The defendant demurred on the ground that the German plaintiff could not sue in a United States court.

Held: That the demurrer must be overruled. To the general rule forbidding an alien enemy to sue in time of war there was an exception in favour of alien enemies allowed to remain after the outbreak of war. *Wells* v. *Williams*, 1 Ld. Raym. 282; *Daubigny* v. *Davallon*, 2 Anstr. 462; *Porter* v. *Freudenberg*, [1915] 1 K.B. 857; *Schaffenius* v. *Goldberg*, [1916] 1 K.B. 284; *Parkinson* v. *Wentworth*, 11 Mass. 26; *The Oropa*,

255 Fed. 132; and other cases. " Thus it has come about in " both countries [Great Britain and the United States] that the " test of the right to sue in such cases is not nationality but the " place of carrying on business." (2 Extraterritorial Cases 39, 43.) Had the German plaintiff resided in the United States, there could be little doubt of his right to sue. His right to sue in the United States Court for China must depend upon his status in China. Although China had ordered the repatriation of enemy subjects, various classes had been allowed to remain. It was to be presumed from the German plaintiff's continued residence in China that he was within the classes allowed to remain unless the defendant could make an affirmative showing to the contrary. [Report: 2 Extraterritorial Cases (Lobingier) 39.]

Effects of Outbreak of War on Enemy Subjects—*Persona standi in judicio*—Judgment for an Alien Enemy. **Case No. 284**

BIRGE-FORBES COMPANY *v.* HEYE.

United States Supreme Court. 12 January, 1920.

THE FACTS.—Heye, a Bremen cotton-broker, sold cotton for the Texas firm of Birge-Forbes Co. In consequence of the fact that the cotton did not correspond to description, Heye had to pay the buyers more than 300,000 marks, this sum being determined by arbitration in accordance with the contracts and the Bremen Cotton Exchange rules. Heye paid part of the sum, sued Birge-Forbes Co. in the United States District Court to recover the amount paid, and secured a directed verdict in his favour. (212 Fed. 112.) Certiorari was denied by the Supreme Court. (234 U.S. 759.) Heye later paid the rest of the arbitration award and sued to recover the sum not included in his former judgment. A judgment for Heye in the District Court was taken to the Circuit Court of Appeals for the Fifth Circuit. At this stage war was declared between the United States and Germany. A motion was made to dismiss or suspend the suit, but the Court affirmed the judgment and ordered that it be paid to the clerk of the lower Court and by him turned over to the Alien Property Custodian. (248 Fed. 636.) On certiorari,

Held: That the judgment must be affirmed. Delivering the Opinion of the Court, Mr. Justice Holmes said: " There is

Case No. 284 *contd.* "nothing 'mysteriously noxious' . . . in a judgment for an "alien enemy. Objection to it in these days goes only so far "as it would give aid and comfort to the other side. . . . Such "aid and comfort were prevented by the provision that the "sum recovered should be paid over to the Alien Property "Custodian, and the judgment in this respect was correct." (251 U.S. 317, 323.) [Reports: 248 Fed. 636; 251 U.S. 317.]

Case No. 285 **Enemy Character of Individuals—Statelessness—Freedom from Sequestration of their Property—Article 297 of the Treaty of Versailles.**

Procureur Général (Court of Appeal of Brussels) *v.* Schneider and Others.

Belgium, Court of Cassation. 20 January, 1921.

The Facts.—The Decree-Law of 10 November, 1918, provides for the sequestration of the movable and immovable property of subjects of enemy countries. In the present case the defendant had renounced his German nationality; since 1884 he had had his permit (*lettres de congé*) under German law and had remained without nationality. The Court of Appeal of Brussels had decided on 12 April, 1919, that there was in this case no reason to place the property under sequestration. The *Procureur Général* appealed against this decision on the ground that the enemy origin should be sufficient for the application of the terms of the Decree-Law.

Held: That the appeal must be dismissed. The sequestration enacted by the Decree-Law against subjects of enemy countries, "a very harsh measure which the Treaty of Ver-"sailles describes as 'an exceptional war measure,'" was not capable of any extension. As for the conception of a person without nationality (*heimatlos*), even if since the Law of 8 June, 1909, Belgian nationality could only be lost by the acquisition of another nationality, the same was not necessarily the case in a foreign country. Each State had absolute authority in regard to the political composition of its subjects. The idea of a complete loss of nationality still obtained in almost every country, and even in Belgium legal provision had been made in more than one connection for the position of a person without nationality. Thus the Belgian law subjected to conscription for military service aliens who did not prove that they possessed a definite nationality. As the law thus assimilated them to Belgian citizens it would be inconceivable that it should assimilate them to subjects of enemy nations in order to deprive of their patrimony those who may have served under the Belgian flag. The argument for the Government would, further, have the result—that a person without nationality, in contrast to a person who remains a German subject, would in defiance of justice be liable to expropriation without compensation, Germany being bound, under the terms of Article 297 (1) of the Treaty of Versailles, to indemnify only its own nationals. The loss of nationality must not be "fictitious," and the person of foreign origin should not have had recourse to it as a mere expedient for favouring the designs of the enemy. The judges who decide on the merits of the case had full authority to determine whether the person in question has shown that he is no longer, in reality, a subject of one of the States which were at war with Belgium; if his denationalisation was not genuine, they should declare it ineffectual and maintain the sequestration. [Reports: *Pasicrisie belge*, 1921, vol. I, pp. 32 *et seq.*; 48 *Clunet* (1922), p. 1030.]

NOTE.—On the question of sequestration the Belgian courts have generally followed this decision; see, for instance, decisions of the Court of Appeal of Liège of 30 April, 1919, and of 5 July, 1919 (*Pasicrisie belge*, 1919, II, p. 69, and 1920, II, p. 29; 47 *Clunet* (1920), p. 739), and of 21 May, 1920, 47 *Clunet* (1920), p. 741. See also the judgment of the Court of Cassation of 21 April, 1921 (*Pasicrisie belge*, 1921, I, p. 330) which, although the Decree-Law of 10 November, 1918, does not expressly give any one who is not a Belgian subject or a subject of an allied or neutral country the right to oppose a sequestration order, extends this right to aliens of indeterminate nationality (*Margulies* case). See also in this sense the decision of the Court of Appeal of Brussels of 26 April, 1920 (47 *Clunet* (1920), p. 722). In contradistinction to this decision an award of the same Court of 6 May, 1919 (*Pasicrisie belge*, 1919, II, p. 67) had denied this right to stateless persons.

It is to be noted that the two judgments of the Court of Cassation (20 January (digested above) and 21 April, 1921 (above mentioned) impose upon the plaintiff, although he is a denationalised enemy, the burden of proving that his denationalisation is not fictitious and that he is no longer "in reality" a subject of an enemy nation).[1]

Outbreak of War—Effect on Enemy Subjects.

See Case No. 271 (*Hughes* v. *Techt*; *Techt* v. *Hughes*).

[1] For the attitude of the English Courts during and after the war to the question of the loss of German nationality, see the cases of *Ex parte Liebmann*, L.R. [1916] 1 K.B. 268; *Ex parte Weber*, L.R. [1916] 1 A.C. 421; and *Stoeck* v. *Public Trustee*, L.R. [1921] 2 Ch. 76.—[Ed.]

Effect of Outbreak of War on Enemy Subjects—*Persona standi in judicio*—Prize Court.

See Case No. 349 (*The Dirigo, The Hallingdal, and other Ships*).

(*b*) THEIR PROPERTY AND OTHER RIGHTS

Case No. 286

Effects of Outbreak of War—Property in Great Britain Belonging to an Enemy—Private Property of an Enemy Monarch—Effect of British Trading with the Enemy Acts upon Common Law Right of Forfeiture.

IN RE FERDINAND, EX-TSAR OF BULGARIA.

England, Court of Appeal, on Appeal from the Chancery Division of the High Court of Justice. 30 *July*, 1920.

THE FACTS.—At the outbreak of war between Great Britain and Bulgaria in October, 1915, Ferdinand, then Tsar of Bulgaria, owned, not as Tsar but in his private capacity, certain securities in England, namely, certain bearer bonds (which were not before the Court on this occasion) and certain securities registered, as to some in his own name, and as to others in the names of trustees. The indicia of title were deposited with Coutts & Co., of London, his bankers.

On 29 September, 1918, an armistice was declared between Great Britain and Bulgaria, but the state of war still continued at the date of the hearing of this appeal. On 3 October, 1918, the Tsar Ferdinand abdicated the Bulgarian throne.

On 10 July, 1919, upon a commission issued by the Crown to enquire into the ownership of the property above mentioned, an inquisition was held and the jury found that the securities were at the outbreak of war in the beneficial ownership of the ex-Tsar Ferdinand and were forfeited to the Crown. On 19 November, 1919, an order was made by the Board of Trade under Section 4 of the Trading with the Enemy Act, 1916, vesting the securities in the Custodian of Enemy Property in case of its being held that no forfeiture to the Crown had taken place.

In due course, upon the petition of the Crown, orders were made by Eve, J., and P. O. Lawrence, J., declaring that the securities had by virtue of the outbreak of war become forfeited to and vested in the

Crown and making the necessary consequential orders. The ex-Tsar Ferdinand appealed.

The main points taken on his behalf were that, excluding maritime property, the mere outbreak of war never operated *ipso facto* a forfeiture of an alien enemy's movable property found within the United Kingdom; that an enemy monarch was in no worse position as regards his private movable property than an enemy subject; and that if ever the Crown had the power to forfeit such property it had been lost (*a*) by abandonment, or if not, then (*b*) by assenting to the Trading with the Enemy Acts passed during the Great War, which by constituting a Custodian of Enemy Property had established a system of dealing with enemy private property inconsistent with its forfeiture.

Held, by the Court of Appeal (Lord Sterndale, M.R., Warrington and Younger, L.JJ.): (1) That the right of the Crown "to seize private enemy property" found in the United Kingdom on the outbreak of war still existed, and (2) "that "nothing had occurred up to the beginning of the war with "Bulgaria to deprive the Crown of that right unless that were "the effect of the Trading with the Enemy Acts" (*per* Lord Sterndale, M.R., at pp. 124-128, referring to the following, amongst other, cases: *Attorney-General* v. *Weeden* (1699), Parker 267; *Land* v. *Lord North* (1785), 4 Doug. 266; *Furtado* v. *Rogers* (1802), 3 Bos. and P. 191; *Brown* v. *United States* (1814), 8 Cranch 110; *Wolff* v. *Oxholm* (1817), 6 M. & S. 92; *The Johanna Emilie* (1854), Spink's Prize Cases, 14).

(3) That, however, the Crown by assenting to the Trading with the Enemy Acts must be taken to have abandoned this common law right. "A power to vest property in a custodian "to be dealt with at the end of the war as His Majesty should "by Order in Council direct is inconsistent with an intention "of preserving a power to insist on an absolute forfeiture at "common law" (at p. 131).

(4) That, accordingly, the appeal must be allowed and the forfeiture must be set aside.

The Court also discussed a number of recent judicial *dicta* to the effect that enemy private property found within the realm on the outbreak of war was immune from confiscation. [Report: L.R. [1921] 1 Ch. 107.]

NOTE.—(1) It must not be assumed from the fact that the forfeiture was set aside that the ex-Tsar recovered his property, for it fell under

Case No. 286 contd.

the operation of the order vesting it (conditionally) in the Custodian of Enemy Property. Presumably it was thereupon impounded under the provisions of the Treaty of Peace with Bulgaria.

(2) A great deal of the argument on behalf of the ex-Tsar will be found in two articles by his junior counsel, Mr. Farrer, in the *Law Quarterly Review*, vol. 37, pp. 217-241 and 337-362.

(3) The Court considered that the fact that the property in question was that of an enemy sovereign was irrelevant. The case was decided on the same footing as if the property had been that of any Bulgarian national. (See p. 124, *per* Lord Sterndale.)

Case No. 287

Effects of Outbreak of War—Private Property of Enemy Subjects Found in Opposing Belligerent's Territory—Position of apart from Treaty Provisions.

In re Münster (Enemy).

England, High Court of Justice, Chancery Division.
19 *December*, 1920.

The Facts.—Alexander, Prince Münster of Derneberg, an enemy subject, was at the outbreak of war between Great Britain and Germany the owner of a large estate in the county of Sussex and of shares and securities in British companies. All this property was, by two Orders made under Section 4 of the Trading with the Enemy Act, 1914, vested in the Public Trustee as Custodian of Enemy Property. The total income resulting from the property amounted to between £4000 and £5000 per annum.

The Special Commissioners of Income Tax claimed to assess the Custodian to super-tax in respect of this income, and he disputed the legality of the assessment. Accordingly he issued a summons under the above-mentioned Act in which he asked for the directions of the Court, and the Commissioners of Inland Revenue were made parties to it. The Custodian disputed the assessment on the grounds (*a*) that Prince Münster retained no interest in the property but only a *spes restitutionis*, Section 5 of the above-mentioned Act having completely destroyed his interest, and (*b*) that the Custodian was not the agent or receiver of Prince Münster but dealt with the property without reference to him.

Held by Russell, J., upon an analysis of the provisions of the Trading with the Enemy Act, 1914 (which it is not considered necessary to reproduce in this digest): (1) That,

" pending its disposition by Order in Council after the deter-
" mination of the war, the property is removed from the control and from the beneficial ownership of the enemy. At the termination of the war fresh considerations will arise; and whether the enemy will recover, and to what extent he will recover, the beneficial ownership will depend upon the arrangements made at the conclusion of peace. . . ."

The learned judge then proceeded to deal with the objection raised by the Commissioners of Inland Revenue to such a construction of the Act, namely, that it involved confiscation and "that confiscation of the property of enemy subjects is not the law of this country." . . . "In *Hugh Stevenson & Sons* v. *Aktiengesellschaft für Cartonnagen Industrie* [1] Lord Finlay, L.C., says, 'It is not the law of this country that the property of enemy subjects is confiscated. Until the restoration of peace the enemy can, of course, make no claim to have it delivered up to him, but when peace is restored he is considered as entitled to his property with any fruits which it may have borne in the meantime.' Lord Haldane in the same case remarks: 'The law of this country does not in general confiscate the property of an enemy. He cannot claim to receive it during war, but his right to his property is not extinguished; it is merely suspended.' The passages no doubt accurately state the law of this country apart from the provisions of any statute or of the treaty of peace.[2] Lord Parker in *Daimler Co.* v. *Continental Tyre and Rubber Co.*[3] makes this clear when he says: 'Subject to any legislation to the contrary or anything to the contrary contained in the treaty of peace when peace comes, enemy property in this country will be restored to its owners after the war just as property in enemy countries belonging to His Majesty's subjects will or ought to be restored to them after the war.' In my judgment the Act of 1914 does not depart from these principles or involve confiscation. Under its provisions the enemy is deprived of beneficial ownership during the war, and the custodian after the termination of the war is bound to deal with it in such manner as His Majesty (keeping no doubt in view the arrangements made at the conclusion of peace) may by Order in Council direct. . . .

[1] L.R. [1918] A.C. 239, 244, 247. See, however, *In re Ferdinand*, [1921] 1 Ch. 107, Case No. 286.

[2] See also Younger, L.J., in *In re Rush*, L.R. [1923] 1 Ch. 69, 70.

[3] L.R. [1916] 2 A.C. 307, 347.

Case No. 287 *contd.*

" In the result I come to the conclusion that the profits and " gains in question have only been received by the custodian " in respect of Prince Münster, that they do not in the hands " of the custodian belong to the Prince, and, accordingly, that " the custodian has not received those profits and gains, and " does not hold them in any sense as an agent or receiver or " trustee for Prince Münster.

" In answer to the summons I declare that the custodian " is not liable to make a return to super-tax, nor is he liable to " be assessed to super-tax, as agent or receiver for Prince " Münster in respect of the four years in question."

(2) Nevertheless, in view of the fact that Prince Münster could never properly ask to receive back the property except subject to a deduction representing the amount of super-tax which but for the war he would have been liable to pay, the learned judge, in the exercise of the wide discretion vested in him by Section 5, Sub-Section 1, of the Act of 1914, and upon the analogy of the provision of an enemy's debts, directed the Custodian to pay to the Commissioners out of the money in his hands the amount of super-tax " which Prince Münster, but " for the war, would have been liable to pay." [Report: L.R. [1920] 1 Ch. 268.]

v.—On Enemy Merchant Ships in Port

Case No. 288

Effect of Outbreak of War—Enemy Merchant Ships in Port—Enemy Ships in British Port upon Outbreak of War—Sixth Hague Convention—Order for Detention—Application by Procurator-General for Condemnation after Conclusion of Peace—Mutuality of the Convention—Repudiation of the Convention—Waiver of Right to Repudiate Convention—Reprisals—Effect of Change of Nationality of Enemy Shipowners—Status of the Free City of Danzig.

THE BLONDE AND OTHER SHIPS.

England, Privy Council, on Appeal from the Prize Court.
10 *February*, 1922.

THE FACTS.—Upon the outbreak of war between Great Britain and Germany three enemy merchant ships, the *Blonde*, the *Prosper*, and the *Hercules*, were seized in British ports and were proceeded against in Prize. In due course orders were made for their detention in the form of what came to be known as " the *Chile* order," [1] and later they were requisitioned for the use of His

[1] L.R. [1914] P. 212.

Majesty. The *Blonde* and the *Hercules* were lost while under requisition, the former by grounding, the latter through being struck by an enemy torpedo, while the *Prosper* remained in the hands of the British Crown at the conclusion of peace. The ships were registered at Danzig, and the release of the *Prosper* and the value of the other two were claimed by a shipping company registered and carrying on business at Danzig and claiming to be nationals of the Free City of Danzig established by the Versailles Treaty of Peace of 1919.

The Sixth Hague Convention of 1907 contains the following provisions:

Art. 1: "When a merchant ship belonging to "one of the belligerent Powers is at the commence- "ment of hostilities in an enemy port, it is desirable "that it should be allowed to depart freely, either "immediately, or after a reasonable number of days "of grace. . . ."

Art. 2: "A merchant ship which, owing to "circumstances beyond its control, may have been "unable to leave, may not be confiscated. The "belligerent may merely detain it, on condition of "restoring it after the war, without payment of "compensation, or he may requisition it on condition "of paying compensation."

Art. 6: "The provisions of the present Conven- "tion do not apply except between Contracting "Powers, and then only if all the belligerents are "parties to the Convention."

Both Great Britain and Germany were parties to this Convention so far as concerned the three Articles quoted above. Of the Powers belligerent in some theatre or other and against one combination of opponents or another during the World War, Serbia and Montenegro never ratified the Sixth Hague Convention. The United States of America were not parties to it at all. At the dates of the detention orders made in respect of these ships "Germany had not "declared war on Serbia, nor had Serbia become "formally the ally of Great Britain, and, so far as "their Lordships are aware, actual hostile action by "Germany against Serbia and actual military support "to Serbia by Great Britain both belong to later "stages of the war."

Case No. 288 ***contd.***

Through the good offices of the United States of America. negotiations (the nature of which will appear later) took place between Great Britain and Germany upon the outbreak of war regarding the treatment of detained merchant ships.

By Article 297 (*b*) of the Treaty of Peace of Versailles " the Allied and Associated Powers reserve the " right to retain and liquidate all property, rights and " interests belonging at the date of the coming into " force of the present Treaty to German nationals, or " companies controlled by them, within their terri- " tories, colonies, possessions and protectorates . . ."

After the conclusion of peace the question of the ultimate fate of the *Prosper* and the values of the *Blonde* and the *Hercules* arose.

In the Prize Court the shipowners based their claim to the release of the vessels on the following grounds:

(i) that after the outbreak of war the British and German Governments had reached an agreement on the basis of the Sixth Hague Convention (it was not contended that the Convention itself applied) to the effect that at the end of the war detained merchant ships should reciprocally be restored or that, if requisitioned and not restored, compensation should be paid;

(ii) that, assuming the conclusion of such an agreement, it was not for the Prize Court to say that the agreement had come to an end owing to breaches by Germany of international law or treaty obligations, for the Prize Court has no power to take reprisals;

(iii) that, even if such an argument were valid against German nationals, it did not avail against claimants who had become nationals of the Free City of Danzig by virtue of the Treaty of Peace;

and (iv) that Article 297 of the Treaty, which permitted the Allied and Associated Powers to retain and liquidate the property of German nationals, did not apply to the property of those who had become by virtue of the Treaty nationals of the Free City of Danzig.

The learned President (Sir Henry Duke) held (i) that no such agreement as was alleged had been reached by the two Governments; (ii) that therefore " the common " law of prize (that is the law of prize which depends on " immemorial or universal usage) " applied; and (iii) that, upon the construction of the Treaty of Peace, the claimants were in the same position as if they had remained German nationals. There was no provision requiring that property of which they had become lawfully divested during the war when they were German citizens should be restored to them. Accordingly, following his decision in *The Marie Leonhart*, L.R. [1914] P. 212 (though the circumstances of the two cases and the grounds of his two decisions are not identical), he condemned the three vessels.

On appeal, it was also contended on behalf of the claimants that, while Article 1 of the Sixth Hague Convention was not obligatory and merely stated a *desideratum*, Article 2 was independent of Article 1 and was binding upon the parties.

Held by the Judicial Committee of the Privy Council (Present: Lords Sumner and Parmoor and Sir Arthur Channell): (i) That the negotiations between the two opposing Governments after the outbreak of war were not directed to an agreement which would displace the Sixth Hague Convention but resulted in a mutual conviction that the two Governments intended to observe the provisions of Article 2 of the Convention;

(ii) that the prohibition upon confiscation contained in Article 2 was obligatory and did not "depend on a prior "election to do what art. 1 desiderates but does not require" (at p. 329);

(iii) that, whatever grounds Germany might have afforded to Great Britain, by her disregard of international law and treaty obligations in her conduct of the war or otherwise, to repudiate the Convention, this was not done and the British Government continued, down to the conclusion of peace, to regard the Convention as binding;

(iv) that the British Government by acting upon the Convention during the war had waived any right it might have had to plead that the Convention was not binding by reason of the fact that Serbia, Montenegro and the United States of America, all belligerents, were not parties, as to which right their Lordships expressed no final opinion;

(v) that the fact that the claimants had upon the conclusion of peace become under the Treaty of Peace the subjects of a newly constituted State could not frustrate proceedings which were regular from the beginning.

Accordingly, their Lordships allowed the appeal and set

Case No. 288 *contd.* aside the decrees of condemnation. They directed that the *Prosper* in specie and the appraised values of the *Blonde* and the *Hercules* should be released "to the custodian of enemy property to be delivered up to the claimants, if after the lapse of six months no proceedings have been begun [*scilicet,* under Article 297 of the Treaty of Peace] for delivery up to the Crown, but otherwise to abide the final determination of such proceedings." [Reports: L.R. [1921] P. 155; 3 B. and C.P.C. 875; L.R. [1922] 1 A.C. 313; 3 B. and C.P.C. 1031.]

NOTE.—(1) The case was decided both by the President and the Privy Council on the footing that the Free City of Danzig must be considered to be a new sovereign State. (See [1921] P. 162 and [1921] A.C. 338.)

(2) Observations were made by their Lordships (L.R. [1922] 1 A.C. at pp. 330, 331; 3 B. and C.P.C. at pp. 1044, 1045) on the question how far the rules of municipal law as to the formation, interpretation and discharge of contracts were relevant to international treaties. "It is not the function of a Court of Prize as such to be a censor of the general conduct of a belligerent, apart from his dealings in the particular matters which come before the Court, or to sanction disregard of solemn obligations by one belligerent, because it reprehends the whole behaviour of the other. Reprisals afford a legitimate mode of challenging and restraining misconduct, to which, when confined within recognised limits and embodied in due form, a Court of Prize is bound to give effect. In a matter, however, which turns on the obligation of a single and severable compact, the Court must inquire whether that very compact has been discharged and ought not to be guided by considerations arising only out of the general conduct of the war."

(3) In 1925 Great Britain exercised her right under the Sixth Hague Convention of denouncing it by addressing a notice to the Dutch Government; for her reasons, see *Miscellaneous Papers,* No. 19 (1925), Cmd. 2564.

vi.—On Neutral Persons and Property. Embargo. The Right of Angary

Case No. 289

Angary—Requisition of Property of Neutral Subjects—Duty of Compensation—Requisition of Shipbuilding Contracts of Norwegian Subjects in the United States.

NORWAY AND UNITED STATES (REQUISITION OF SHIPBUILDING CONTRACTS CASE).

Permanent Court of Arbitration. 13 *October,* 1922.

(VALLOTON, ANDERSON,[1] VOGT.)

THE FACTS.—This was a claim for compensation on behalf

[1] See Case No. 267 as to the participation of Mr. Anderson in the rendering of the award.

of certain Norwegian shipowners whose ships were requisitioned by the authorities of the United States during the World War. In September, 1916, there was established by the United States Shipping Act the United States Shipping Board "for the purpose of en-" couraging, developing and creating a naval auxiliary " and naval reserve and a merchant marine, to meet the " requirements of the commerce of the United States " with its territories and possessions and with all " foreign countries." On 6 April, 1917, the day of the declaration of war by the United States against Germany, the Shipping Board exercised its authority under Section 11 of the above Act and formed the United States Shipping Board Emergency Fleet Corporation. That Section authorised the Shipping Board to " form " under the laws of the District of Columbia one or " more corporations for the purchase, construction, " equipment, lease, charter, maintenance and opera-" tion of merchant vessels in the commerce of the " United States." After the declaration of war the powers of the Shipping Board were substantially enlarged. On 3 and 4 August the Fleet Corporation sent a general order of requisition to almost all the shipyards of the United States. The order requisitioned not only the ships and the material, but also the contracts, the plans, detailed specifications and payments made. After the examination of the plans, specifications and contracts, interests and names of owners, the Fleet Corporation required the shipbuilders to proceed with the completion of the ships. It appeared from the evidence produced before the Tribunal that the original contracts were not cancelled as the result of the requisition orders, and that the Fleet Corporation took over the legal rights and duties of the shipowners towards the shipbuilders. The shipbuilders were thus relieved of any obligation to the former owners. However, the Fleet Corporation took no steps, until 1919, to refund to the latter the progress payments made by them to the shipbuilders.

Among the property thus requisitioned were fifteen shipbuilding contracts of a number of Norwegian subjects. This property had not been restored to the owners by June, 1919, when the Treaty of Versailles was signed. The report of the United States experts

Case No. 289 ***contd.***

on the amount of just compensation was not available until 1919. Difficulties having arisen between the Norwegian owners and the Fleet Corporation as to the compensation to be granted to the former, the Government of Norway took up the matter and the claim was submitted, by a special agreement, to arbitration in conformity with the arbitration treaty between the two States signed on 4 April, 1908.

Held : (*a*) As to the law applicable by the Tribunal—see Case No. 261.

(*b*) Although the contracts in question were the property of Norwegian subjects, the United States were entitled, provided that just compensation was duly assessed and paid without undue delay, to requisition yards and factories within American jurisdiction and to expedite the construction of the ships for public use. However, although the emergency legislation of the United States in regard to requisition of the property of neutral subjects was not contrary to international law, the manner of its exercise by the authorities of the United States entailed the responsibility of the latter and entitled the Government of Norway to claim compensation on behalf of the shipowners. The Tribunal said : " It must be admitted, " in favor of the present claimants, that the American war " legislation gave a large discretionary power to the Shipping " Board and to the Emergency Fleet Corporation, and that " some officials do not seem, as regards the claimants, to have " always used their power in the true spirit of the American " Constitution, or of the Congressional Acts, or for instance of " Presidential orders of 1917 and 1918. As has already been " stated, the national peril was not such as to free them from " the obligation of making the necessary inventory and valua- " tion of all the property taken for the purpose of determining " and paying 'just compensation.' This was not a case of " 'requisition of neutral property' in the special meaning of " that term in the laws and customs of war. While the taking " or destroying of neutral property on the field of battle, or " in invaded territory, without preliminary compensation or at " least due process of law, is often excused on account of " extreme emergency, an essential difference must be made " here in favor of the claimants. The just compensation to " which they are entitled includes not only the items which " have been duly proved, but also those which could have been " proved and estimated if the officials of the belligerent state "had, in the interest of both parties, paid or offered payment, "or at least required expert valuation and inventory of the "neutral property taken with a proper representation of both "sides. The American authorities seem to have waited till "1919 to get the reports of their experts produced as evidence "of just compensation, . . .

"In the present instance the liability of the Emergency "Fleet Corporation is due to its disregard, not only of the "public law, but also of the municipal private law, as it should "have settled accounts and delivered the ships to their original "owners at least after the end of June 1919.

"The United States are responsible for having thus made "a discriminating use of the power of eminent domain towards "citizens of a friendly nation, and they are liable for the "damaging action of their officials and agents towards these "citizens of the Kingdom of Norway."

The United States had not proved that the Shipping Board or the Fleet Corporation acted in conformity with the liberal spirit of their municipal law, on which they have relied in the present arbitration, in applying the provisions of the Fifth Amendment to the Constitution in regard to protection of property—a constitutional provision which was "in complete "accord with the international public law of all civilized "countries." [1]

(*c*) The United States took over, in fact and in law, the contracts under which the ships built for the Norwegian owners were being or were to be constructed. As the result the claimants were fully and for ever deprived of their property. These acts amounted to a requisition by the exercise of the power of eminent domain within the meaning of the law of the United States.

The retention of the money of the claimants in the form of the progress payments made by them to the shipbuilders was unlawful. "Such action was not only contrary to international "law, but also to the municipal law of the United States. The "amounts of the progress payments should have been refunded "at the time of the requisition of the ships. There can be no "excuse for waiting until 1919 to make an assessment of these "amounts." Neither was there sufficient reason for keeping the property of the claimants after the signature of the Treaty of Versailles, in particular in view of the fact that

[1] The Tribunal here interpreted the word "property" used in the Fifth Amendment in order to show that it included all *jura in personam* and "choses "in action."

Case No. 289 ***contd.***

the property of other owners similarly requisitioned had been restored.

(*d*) The contention of the United States that in addition to the original value of the contracts no compensation is due when the contracts have been destroyed, or rendered void, or delayed in consequence of *force majeure* or " restraint of princes and " rulers," cannot be accepted. "Although 'restraint of princes' " may well be invoked in disputes between private citizens, it " cannot be invoked by the United States against the Kingdom " of Norway in defense of the claim of Norway. International " law and justice are based upon the principle of equality " between states. No state can exercise towards the citizens of " another civilized state the 'power of eminent domain' " without respecting the property of such foreign citizens or " without paying just compensation as determined by an im-" partial tribunal, if necessary."

(*e*) As to the amount of compensation and measure of damages, see Case No. 130.

(*f*) As to interest, see Case No. 131.

(*g*) As to the signature and the execution of the award, see Case No. 267. [Reports: *A.J.*, XVII (1923), pp. 362-399; Scott, *The Hague Court Reports* (2nd series, 1932), p. 40.]

NOTE.—The Tribunal distinguished the case of the Norwegian shipbuilding contracts from the requisition of a number of Dutch ships by the United States on the ground that the latter were completed and registered under the Dutch flag, while the claimants' ships were still under construction.

Effects of Outbreak of War—On Neutral Persons and Property —The Right of Angary—Requisition by British Government of Timber belonging to Egyptian Company.

COMMERCIAL AND ESTATES COMPANY OF EGYPT *v.* BALL.

England, High Court of Justice, King's Bench Division.
19 *April*, 1920.

[It will be more convenient to deal with this case (36 T.L.R. 526) in digesting *Commercial and Estates Company of Egypt* v. *Board of Trade*, L.R. [1925] 1 K.B. 271, in the next volume of this *Digest*.]

vii.—Trading with the Enemy

Trading with the Enemy—Enemy Nationals Resident or Carrying on Business in Countries subject to Capitulations—British Trading with the Enemy Proclamations—China. **Case No. 290**

SALTI ET FILS *v.* (BRITISH) PROCURATOR-GENERAL.

Great Britain, Privy Council, on Appeal from the Admiralty Division of the High Court of Justice sitting in Prize.
15 *July*, 1919.

THE FACTS.—The British Trading with the Enemy Proclamation (No. 2) of 9 September, 1914, prohibited all persons resident in British territory, *inter alia*, to supply "goods, wares or merchandise" to "any person or "body of persons of whatever nationality resident or "carrying on business in the enemy country."

The British Trading with the Enemy (China, Siam, Persia, and Morocco) Proclamation, 1915, applied the first-named Proclamation to "any person or body of "persons of enemy nationality resident or carrying on "business in China, Siam, Persia or Morocco in the "same manner as they apply to persons or bodies of "persons resident or carrying on business in an enemy "country."

A firm of diamond merchants of enemy nationality, duly authorised by licence of the Crown to carry on business in England, sent by post in September and November, 1915, certain registered packets of diamonds from London to a person of enemy nationality carrying on business in Shanghai. The diamonds were dispatched to him as their agent on sale for commission in pursuance of a pre-war agency agreement. The diamonds, having been returned from the British Post Office in Shanghai to the Chief Postal Censor in London, were seized by him and condemned by the Admiralty Court in Prize.

Held by the Privy Council on appeal: That the diamonds were rightly condemned as lawful prize. (Present: Lords Parmoor, Wrenbury and Sterndale and Sir Arthur Channell.) [Reports: L.R. [1919] A.C. 968; 3 B. and C.P.C. 374.]

NOTE.—The arguments turned almost entirely upon the construction of the two Proclamations. The case is digested merely as an illustration of the scope of the Trading with the Enemy Proclamations.

Case No. 291 **Effect of Outbreak of War—Trading with the Enemy—Allied Company Continuing to Carry on Business in Allied Territory Occupied by Enemy—Belgium.**

CENTRAL INDIA MINING COMPANY LIMITED *v.* SOCIÉTÉ COLONIALE ANVERSOISE.

England, Court of Appeal, on Appeal from High Court of Justice, King's Bench Division. 21 *November,* 1919.

THE FACTS.—The plaintiff company was registered in India. The defendant company was incorporated under the laws of Belgium and its registered office was in Antwerp. By a contract between the two companies made in Paris in January, 1914 (that is, before the outbreak of war), the plaintiff company agreed to sell a quantity of manganese iron ore to the defendant company during the years 1914 to 1917 inclusive for shipment to European and/or American ports. On the outbreak of war two of the directors of the defendant company transferred to England all the company's goods and a large sum of cash; one of these two (the managing director) came to England and there carried on business in his own name, but for the benefit of the company. All transactions in Belgium were closed.

In October, 1914, German troops occupied Antwerp, the defendant company's premises were converted into a national kitchen and a Red Cross hospital, and in February, 1916, the German authorities placed the company under compulsory administration. During the German occupation meetings of the board of directors and of the shareholders were held in Brussels at which was transacted formal business, such as the re-election of directors, the passing of accounts, the paying of dividends on preference shares, etc. These meetings were held in order to comply with the law of Belgium and to maintain the existence of the company. There were no new trading transactions during the occupation, but the debts owing to the company were collected and its liabilities discharged.

The British Trading with the Enemy (Occupied Territory) Proclamation, 1915 (dated 16 February, 1915, and made in consequence of the decision in

Société Anonyme Belge des Mines d'Aljustrel (Portugal) v. *Anglo-Belgian Agency*, L.R. [1915] 2 Ch. 409), applied the previous Trading with the Enemy Proclamations to "territory in hostile occupation as they "apply to an enemy country," and by a further Proclamation dated 14 September, 1915, the expression "enemy," which already included persons resident and carrying on business in enemy territory and companies incorporated in enemy territory, was "declared to include, and to have included, "any incorporated company or body of persons "(wherever incorporated) carrying on business in any "enemy country or in any territory for the time being "in hostile occupation."

On 24 October, 1918, the plaintiff company issued a writ, under the Legal Proceedings against Enemies Act, 1915, applying for a declaration that the contract of January, 1914, was as from 16 February, 1915, abrogated and of no force and effect, and that they were absolved from every duty and obligation thereunder. They based their claim upon the ground that the defendant company was "carrying on business" in territory under hostile occupation and was an "enemy."

The defendant company counter-claimed for a declaration that the contract was valid and subsisting, and that all deliveries under it were suspended during the war and for a reasonable period thereafter.

Rowlatt, J., held, in favour of the plaintiff company, that upon the construction of the Proclamations referred to above the defendant company was "carrying "on business" in enemy-occupied territory and that the contract was made void by the Proclamations. On appeal,

Held by the Court of Appeal (Bankes, L.J., and Duke, P.; Scrutton, L.J., dissenting), affirming the decision of Rowlatt, J.: That although the defendant company had not during the occupation engaged in any new commercial transactions it had done certain acts (*viz.* the collection of debts and discharge of liabilities) which amounted to "carrying on business"; that the contract of January, 1914, was one the performance of which would involve certain dealings of a kind prohibited by the Trading with the Enemy Proclamations; that conse-

Case No. 291 *contd.*

quently the defendant company was an "enemy" within the meaning of the Trading with the Enemy Proclamations with whom it was forbidden for the plaintiff company to trade; and that therefore the plaintiff company was entitled to a declaration that it was abrogated and of no force and effect as from 16 February, 1915, and that they were absolved and released from all obligations under it.

Scrutton, L.J., dissented on the ground that in his opinion the defendant company was not "carrying on business" in Belgium; that the defendant company might be held to be "resident" in Belgium, but that only "carrying on business" or incorporation was relevant under the Proclamations in the case of companies, and that this contract could have been carried out without anything having been done in Belgium at all, so that, it being possible to perform it in a legal way, it ought not to be avoided unless an intention could be shown to perform it in an illegal way (citing *Waugh* v. *Morris* (1873), L.R. 8 Q.B. 202). [Report: L.R. [1920] 1 K.B. 753.]

VI.—Enemy Character

i.—Of Individuals

Case No. 292

Nationality—Enemy Character—Presumed Retention of Nationality of Origin.

WOLFF (appellant) *v.* THE TREASURY (respondent).

Union of South Africa, Supreme Court (Appellate Division).

27 *June*, 1919.

(SOLOMON, A.C.J., C. G. MAASDORP, J.A., DE VILLIERS, A.J.A.)

THE FACTS.—Appellant was by birth a Bavarian subject. Between 1880 and 1883 he acquired the qualifications of a burgher of the Orange Free State, which he subsequently lost by residing outside the Free State for more than two years. At the time of the annexation of the Free State and the Transvaal he was resident in the Transvaal. The Orange Free State Provincial Division having made an order vesting in the Custodian of Enemy Property the custody and control of all the property of appellant within the jurisdiction of the Court,

Held: Since appellant did not become a British subject at the date of annexation of the Republics either as a burgher of the Orange Free State (which he no longer was), or from the mere fact of residence in the Transvaal, he had failed to show that he had ceased to be a Bavarian subject, and the order of the Provincial Division was properly made.

" The case . . . stands thus. It is established that the " appellant was by birth a Bavarian subject: the inference to " be drawn from that fact is that he still is a Bavarian subject, " and there is no evidence before us to rebut or to cast the " least doubt upon that inference. The respondent accordingly " has discharged the *onus* which lay upon him to prove that " the appellant is an enemy subject " (*per* Solomon, A.C.J., at p. 341). [Report: *The South African Law Reports*, [1919] *Appellate Division*, p. 336 ([1919] A.D. 336).]

NOTE.—The proceedings in the Orange Free State Provincial Division are not reported. But an identical decision on the same facts of the Transvaal Provincial Division is reported in *The South African Law Reports, Transvaal Provincial Division*, 1919 (*The Treasury* v. *Wolff*, [1919] T.P.D. 25), where reference is made to *Ex parte Weber*, printed in a note to *Ex parte Liebmann*, [1916] 1 K.B. 268, as bearing on the question of the retention of German nationality.

Enemy Character of Individuals—Effect of Marriage of British Woman to Enemy Subject.

See Case No. 144 (*Fasbender* v. *Attorney-General*).

Enemy Character of Individuals—Meaning of " German National " in Treaty of Peace of Versailles and British Treaty of Peace Orders.

See Case No. 144 (*Fasbender* v. *Attorney-General*).

Enemy Character—Test of—Residence.

See Case No. 271 (*Hughes* v. *Techt*: *Techt* v. *Hughes*).

Enemy Character—Effect of Divesting of Enemy Nationality by Claimants in Prize Proceedings.

See Case No. 288 (*The Blonde and other Ships*).

ii.—Of Corporations

[See also Part VI B: XI, NATIONALITY OF CORPORATIONS.]

Case No. 293 **Enemy Character—Corporations—Company Registered in Neutral Country—Enemy Nationality of Shareholders—Test of Effective Control.**

THE VESTA AND OTHER SHIPS.

England, the Prize Court. 19 *May*, 1920.

THE FACTS.—In proceedings by the Procurator-General for the condemnation, as good and lawful prize, of a certain cargo on the ground that it was enemy property, it appeared that the owner of the cargo was the Internationale Magneziet Werken, a limited company formed under Dutch law (whether before or during the Great War does not appear), with a capital divided into 100 shares of 1000 florins each. Of these shares, 98 were held by one of the directors, a German national, one by his son, and the remaining one by a Dutch national, the brother-in-law of the German holder of 98 shares. On 21 March, 1916, the German holder of 98 shares purported to transfer them to another Dutch national.

(The case involved a number of other points which are, however, not digested.)

Held by the President (Sir Henry Duke): That in view of *Daimler Co.* v. *Continental Tyre and Rubber Co.*, L.R. [1916] 2 A.C. 307, and other cases, "it is indisputable . . . that the "goods . . . were enemy goods." [Reports: L.R. [1920] P. 385; 3 B. and C. P.C. 716.]

On appeal to the Privy Council the above finding of the learned President that the Internationale Magneziet Werken possessed enemy character though formally a Dutch corporation was not contested. The appeal was allowed on other grounds. [Reports: L.R. [1921] 1 A.C. 774; 3 B. and C.P.C. 897.]

See also Case No. 294 (*The Hamborn*).

Enemy Character of a Ship—Neutral Flag—Enemy Ownership —Corporations—Test of Effective Control. **Case No. 294**

THE HAMBORN.

England, the Prize Court, and, on Appeal, the Privy Council.
31 *July*, 1919.

THE FACTS.—In October, 1915, the *Hamborn*, a steamship flying the Dutch flag, was captured by a British ship of war while on a voyage from New York to Cuba. She was owned by the Hamborn Steamship Company, a single-ship company registered in Holland, and all the shares in this company were held by two other companies (B. and C.) registered in Holland, and one of them (B.) managed the ship. All the directors of the B. and C. companies were Germans and resident in Germany. The shares in the B. company were held by a company registered in Germany and a German firm. The shares in the C. company were held by the B. company, and two other companies registered in Germany.

The net result was " that no one other than enemy " subjects was a director, manager or shareholder in " any of the companies which are supposed to have " had an interest direct or indirect in the Hamborn " Steamship Company or the *Hamborn*; and no " person other than a German [with the exception of " one Hungarian shareholder also an enemy subject] " had any pecuniary or beneficial interest to the " extent of even a pfennig in the shipping company " or the ship."

Held by Sir Samuel Evans, P.: That in these circumstances " The centre and whole effective control of the business of the " Hamborn Steamship Company was in Germany. Having " regard to these facts, the vessel must be regarded in this " Court as belonging to German subjects." The ship was accordingly condemned. [Reports: L.R. [1918] P. 19; 3 B. and C.P.C. 80.]

On appeal, the Privy Council (Présent: Lords Sumner, Parmoor, Wrexbury and Sterndale and Sir Arthur Channell) upheld this judgment, citing and applying *Daimler Co.* v. *Continental Tyre and Rubber Co.* (L.R. [1916] 2 A.C. 307). In the judgment of the Privy Council it was stated (at p. 995) that " there seems to have been no disguise or concealment or

Case No. 294 *contd.* "attempt to delude either the captors or the Court." (A point also arose upon Article 57 of the Declaration of London which it is unnecessary to digest.) [Reports: L.R. [1919] A.C. 993; 3 B. and C.P.C. 379.]

See also Case No. 293 (*The Vesta*).

Enemy Character—Corporations—The "Daimler" Control Test.

See Case No. 276 (*In re Badische Co.*).

iv.—Of Goods

Case No. 295

Enemy Character—Of Goods—Partnership in Neutral Country with German Co-partner—Shipment from New York to Sweden—Insurance of Cargo against Molestation—Criterion of Nationality or Domicile ?

HANDELSVENNOOTSCHAP ONDER DE FIRMA R. KUPSCH AND ABTAS, OF AMSTERDAM (appellant) *v.* N. V. AMSTERDAM-DELI BRAND- EN ZEEASSURANTIE-MAATSCHAPPIJ, OF AMSTERDAM, *ET AL.* (respondents).

Holland, *Court of Appeal of Amsterdam, First Chamber.* 1 *April*, 1921.

(Dr. W. BOOT, President; Drs. G. KIRBERGER and JOH. M. JOLLES, Judges.)

THE FACTS.—During the Great War, 500 bales of cocoa were shipped by an American partnership to Gothenburg (Sweden). They were consigned to a Swedish partnership of Stockholm, ostensibly for consumption in Sweden only, but they in fact remained there at the disposal of a Dutch firm, of Amsterdam, consisting of two partners, one of whom was a German subject. The cargo was insured by the defendant companies against molestation, on condition of "guarantee for "consumption in neutral countries, with neutral "shippers and consignees." On 6 January, 1916, the s.s. *Urna*, on which the cocoa was conveyed, was arrested by a British man-of-war and brought into Bristol. The cocoa not having been released by the British authorities, the owners abandoned it to the insurance companies and sued the latter for the amount insured. The lower Court rejected the claim.

Held on appeal: That the lower Court was justified by

reason of the German nationality of one of the partners in the Dutch firm in rejecting the claim. According to British doctrine, domicile and not nationality is decisive for the determination of the neutral or enemy character of a person. However, it is well known that this principle has often been abandoned in practice during the Great War, so that the owners were not justified in relying upon a favourable view being taken by the British authorities. Moreover, there is no reason to interpret the guarantee clause according to British conceptions only, since the owners ought also to have reckoned with the possibility of seizure of the cargo by the French, and in a French court the nationality and not the domicile of the owner is decisive. [Reports : *Weekblad van het Recht*, 13 June, 1921, No. 10726 ; *Nederlandsche Jurisprudentie*, 1922, p. 570.]

VII.—The Binding Force of the Laws of War

War—Rules of Warfare—Binding Force of—Necessity and Self-Preservation—Article 52 of the Fourth Hague Convention —German Requisitions in Belgium. **Case No. 296**

GERMAN REQUISITIONS (NECESSITY AND SELF-PRESERVATION) CASE.

Germany, Reichsgericht in Civil Matters. 1 *November*, 1922.

THE FACTS.—During the World War the German occupation authorities in Belgium requisitioned a motor belonging to a Belgian manufacturer. They then sold the motor to the defendant, who sold it under a guarantee to another governmental authority, which, in turn, sold it to the plaintiff together with the guarantee attaching to it. Subsequently the plaintiff was deprived of the motor by way of expropriation through the so-called Restoration Commission (*Rücklieferungskommission*) established in pursuance of the Treaty of Versailles and charged, *inter alia*, with the restitution to the lawful owners in France and Belgium of property taken away by Germany. The plaintiff maintained that the defendant never acquired property in the motor on the ground that the requisition, being contrary to the Hague Convention, was illegal [1] and that the Belgian

[1] Apparently contrary to Article 52 of the Fourth Hague Convention, which permits requisitions in kind only for the purposes of the army of occupation.

Case No. 296 *contd.*

owner therefore never lost his right of property in the motor.

Held, on final appeal on a point of law: That the action must be dismissed. The Belgian owner was deprived of his property by requisition effected by the German authorities.

(*a*) There is no doubt that the German authorities in Belgium took away the motor in question with the object of transferring the property in it to the German *Reich*. Accordingly, unless the requisition was illegal, the Belgian owner lost his property in the motor. Requisitions, being an act of sovereignty, are subject to judicial review only in so far as the judge has to investigate whether they have not been effected as the result of obvious excess of authority. Only if the latter question were answered in the affirmative could it be held that the owner retained his right of property. However, the question must be answered in the negative. The requisition, although contrary to the Hague Conventions, was lawful. For

(*b*) "It is a principle recognized in international law and "which must be applied also to the Hague Conventions, that a "State's right to self-preservation is superior to all obligations "undertaken in treaties, and that in case of necessity a State "may depart and go beyond the provisions of the Hague "Convention concerning the Laws and Customs of War on "Land." As the result of the measures of blockade molestation by the enemy, Germany was put in a position in which she had as a matter of necessity to adopt measures of an unusual nature. The German occupation authorities were competent to judge whether there was such necessity in the present case. [Report: *E.R.Z.*, vol. 105, p. 326.]

Hague Conventions—Effect of General Participation Clause.

See Case No. 288 (*The Blonde and other Ships*)

Binding Force of the Laws of War—Hague Conventions—Application in view of Conflicting Retaliatory Measures.

See Case No. 297 (*The Noordam* (*No.* 2) *and other Ships*).

Rules of Warfare—Binding Force of—Hague Conventions.

See Case No. 299 (*Prisoners of War* (*Germany*) *Case*).

VIII.—Enforcement of the Laws of War

i.—Reprisals

Reprisals—Maritime Reprisals—Conditions of Legality—Binding Force of the Laws of War—Eleventh Hague Convention. **Case No. 297**

It is not proposed to digest the decisions given upon the British Reprisals Orders in Council, but they involved a few points of principle which it may be convenient to summarise here.

(1) In *The Zamora*, L.R. [1916] 2 A.C. 77 (on appeal from Sir Samuel Evans, P.), although the validity of a Reprisals Order in Council was not actually in question in this case, the Privy Council, after pointing out that Lord Stowell's decision in *The Fox* (1811), Edw. 311, " proceeded upon the principle " that where there is just cause for retaliation, neutrals may by " the law of nations be required to submit to inconvenience " from the acts of a belligerent Power greater in degree than " would be justified had no just cause for retaliation arisen, a " principle which had been already laid down in *The Lucy*, " (1809) Edw. 122," continued as follows (at p. 98) : " An order " authorising reprisals will be conclusive as to the facts which " are recited as showing that a case for reprisals exists, and will " have due weight as showing what, in the opinion of His " Majesty's advisers, are the best or only means of meeting the " emergency ; but this will not preclude the right of any party " aggrieved to contend, or the right of the Court to hold, that " these means are unlawful, as entailing on neutrals a degree " of inconvenience unreasonable, considering all the circum- " stances of the case."

(2) In *The Stigstad*, L.R. [1919] A.C. 279 (on appeal from Sir Samuel Evans, P.), the validity of the British Reprisals Order in Council of 11 March, 1915, was challenged by neutral shipowners, and was upheld by the Privy Council, adopting and elaborating the second passage quoted above from their decision in *The Zamora*. (Present : Lords Sumner, Parmoor, Wrenbury and Sterndale, and Sir Arthur Channell.)

(3) In *The Leonora*, [1919] A.C. 974 (on appeal from Sir Samuel Evans, P.), the validity of the British Reprisals Order in Council of 16 February, 1917, was challenged by neutral shipowners and cargo-owners, and after a fresh consideration

Case No. 297 *contd.* the principle laid down in *The Zamora* and *The Stigstad* was applied and the validity of the Order in Council upheld. (Present : the same members of the Council.)

(4) In *The Noordam (No. 2) and other Ships*, L.R. [1919] P. 255, a further point was involved. Certain bonds, coupons and other securities had been seized, and the Crown asked for an order for their detention as being " goods which are of " enemy origin or are enemy property " under the British Reprisals Order in Council of 11 March, 1915. Lord Sterndale, P., held that, assuming the securities to be " postal corre- " spondence " within the meaning of the Eleventh Hague Convention—and he was not satisfied that this assumption was correct—it followed from the decisions in *The Stigstad* and other cases that " a Convention of this kind cannot deprive one " belligerent of the right of reprisal against another, especially " if that other belligerent is breaking every canon of inter- " national law ; and that the belligerent may take measures " against his adversary which are not justified by the Conven- " tion, just as he may take measures against him which are not " justified by the ordinary canons of international law " (at p. 263). The learned President ordered the release of certain of the securities as not being " of enemy origin " or " enemy " property " and ordered the detention of the remaining items. On appeal by the Procurator-General as to the items ordered to be released, the Privy Council held that they were " goods " which are of enemy origin " and varied the order of the learned President by ordering their detention. They also held that they were not " postal correspondence " within the meaning of the Convention, and accordingly they did not pursue the question whether the Convention would override the Reprisals Order in Council, L.R. [1920] A.C. 904. (Present : Lords Sumner, Parmoor and Wrenbury, the Lord Justice-Clerk and Sir Arthur Channell).

(5) Reference should also be made to *The Blonde and other Ships*, L.R. [1922] 1 A.C. at pp. 329-331 ; 3 B. and C.P.C. 1044, 1045, and, in particular, the passage quoted at p. 414 of this volume, Case No. 288.

ii.—Spies

Enforcement of the Laws of War—Spies—Conditions for Trial by Court-Martial. **Case No. 298**

UNITED STATES EX REL. WESSELS *v.* MCDONALD, COMMANDANT OF BROOKLYN NAVY YARD.

United States District Court, E.D. New York. 2 March, 1920.

THE FACTS.—This was a petition for habeas corpus. Wessels entered the United States in 1916 as an agent of the German Government. He used a false name and a forged Swiss passport. In May, 1918, he was arrested as a spy. He was indicted for conspiracy to commit espionage but was not brought to trial. Meanwhile he was kept in prison under presidential warrant as an alien enemy. In January, 1920, he was arrested by naval authorities in New York on the charge of being a spy, and court-martial proceedings were instituted. He petitioned the United States District Court for habeas corpus, contending that there was no jurisdiction to try him by court-martial since he had never been a member of the United States naval or military forces, since New York was not under martial law nor in the theatre of warfare, and since the regular civil courts were functioning. The Federal statutes provided for trial by court-martial of persons found in the United States in the capacity of spies. (39 U.S. Stat. L. 663.)

Held: That the writ must be denied. Congress has constitutional power to provide for the trial of spies by court-martial. When a person is restrained of his liberty by court-martial, the only question for the civil courts on habeas corpus is whether the court-martial has jurisdiction to try the petitioner. "The proceedings therein, if confined within the limits of their "jurisdiction, cannot be revised, altered, or controlled by the "civil courts." (265 Fed. 754, 760.) The Court distinguished *Ex parte Milligan,* 4 Wall. (U.S.) 2, on the ground that in the present case there was no such crime charged as would entitle the prisoner to a trial by judge and jury under the Fifth and Sixth Amendments to the Constitution. "The guaranties of "the Constitution apply only where a crime is charged. "Crime means offense against the government, as understood "when the Constitution was adopted. There was no such "crime known to the law as that of a spy then." (265 Fed.

Case No. 298 ***contd.*** 754, 762.) The Court pointed out the conditions of the World War which brought the port of New York within the field of operations and followed the Hague Convention of 1899 (32 U.S. Stat. L. 1818, 1819) in defining a spy as " an individual acting " clandestinely or on false pretenses, who obtains, or seeks to " obtain, information in the zone of operations of a belligerent " with the intention of communicating it to the hostile party." " (265 Fed. 754, 763.) [Report: 265 Fed. 754.] " Military " authorities should have power to try spies wherever found; " otherwise they may not be subject to trial for that offense. " In this great World War through which we have just passed, " the field of operations which existed after the United States " entered the war, and, especially in regard to naval operations, " brought the port of New York within the field of active " operations. The implements of warfare and the plan of " carrying it on in the last gigantic struggle placed the United " States fully within the field of active operations. The term " ' theater of war,' as used in the Milligan Case, apparently " was intended to mean the territory of activity of conflict. " With the progress made in obtaining ways and means for " devastation and destruction, the territory of the United " States was certainly within the field of active operations. " Great numbers of troops were being sent abroad and, in " larger numbers, sailing from the port of New York. Vessels " loaded with ammunition and supplies for the army were " daily, and frequently in a day, leaving this port. German " submarines were landing unheralded in our ports, before the " United States entered the war. Ships were being destroyed " within easy distance of the Atlantic coast; there was the " constant threat of and fear for airships above the harbor and " the city of New York on missions of destruction. A spy of " the enemy might well have aided these hostile operations. " It is not necessary that it be said of the accused that he " entered forts or armed encampments in the purposes of his " mission. But such we had in large establishments. It is " sufficient if he was here on the mission of a spy and com- " municated his intelligence or information to the enemy."

IX.—Prisoners of War

Prisoners of War—Legal Position of—Subjection to the Law of the Captor—Continuance of the Status of Soldier—Germany and the Hague Conventions. **Case No. 299**

PRISONERS OF WAR (GERMANY) CASE.

Germany, Reichsgericht in Criminal Matters. 4 *April*, 1922.

THE FACTS.—The accused was a German non-commissioned officer. He was taken prisoner by the French army. The French authorities then appointed him a camp non-commissioned officer. In this capacity he beat some German prisoners of war. He was now prosecuted on the ground of § 122 of the German Military Criminal Code, which punishes corporal punishment of subordinates. He was convicted.

Held, on final appeal on a point of law: That the conviction must stand. According to the view adopted in international law, the fact of capture terminates the relation of subordination to the national military authorities, which remains suspended for the duration of the status of prisoner of war. As, according to Article 8 of Hague Convention No. IV, prisoners of war are "subject to the laws, regulations, and orders in force in the "army of the State in whose power they are," the captor State is entitled to place new authorities over them. Thus a prisoner of war may himself be placed in a position of authority over other prisoners of war. Within the frame of the new military organisation created as the result of captivity prisoners of war are to be regarded as soldiers, and persons placed in command over them are to be regarded as military commanders. Accordingly the maltreatment of other prisoners of war by the accused must be regarded as maltreatment by a military commander of his military subordinates. § 122, which corresponds to a similar provision of French military law, is therefore applicable.

As to the Fourth Hague Convention, the Court pointed out [1] that "it was merely an international treaty which has never "been incorporated into German law." However, it is "recog-"nised law" (*anerkannten Rechtes*) that the provisions of this Convention "were valid during the World War as custom of

[1] It is somewhat difficult to follow this statement. The Fourth Hague Convention was signed by Germany and ratified by her on 27 November, 1909. The Convention was published in the German *Reichsgesetzblatt*, 1910, pp. 107, 132 and 375.

Case No. 299 *contd.* "war (*Kriegsgebrauch*) as between the belligerents, in particular between Germany and France." [Report: *E.R.S.*, vol. 57, p. 46.]

Case No. 300 **Prisoners of War—Detention of—After Conclusion of Peace Treaty—Whether Preserving the Character of Prisoners of War.**

PRISONERS OF WAR (BREST LITOWSK) CASE.

Germany, Reichsgericht in Criminal Matters.
1 *February*, 1921.

THE FACTS.—The accused was, it seems,[1] charged with having permitted the escape of some Russian prisoners of war entrusted to his custody. He was charged under § 121 of the German Criminal Code relating to the escape of prisoners generally. He pleaded, *inter alia*, that prisoners of war were not prisoners within the meaning of the Code, and alternatively, that he permitted them to escape after the Peace Treaty of Brest Litowsk was concluded (on 3 March, 1918).

Held, on final appeal on a point of law: That the conviction must stand.

(*a*) As prisoners are to be regarded all persons who in the public interest have been deprived of their personal freedom in accordance with the law and who are, as a result, in the power of the competent authority. This definition applies also to prisoners of war.

(*b*) The fact that the prisoners escaped after the conclusion of the Peace Treaty is irrelevant. According to Article 20 of the Fourth Hague Convention, prisoners of war ought to be sent home within the shortest possible period after the conclusion of the Treaty of Peace. The details of the release and of the sending home of the prisoners of war were regulated by special agreements concluded between Germany and Soviet Russia subsequent to the Treaty of Brest Litowsk. However, up to the time when they are handed over to their home State or its plenipotentiaries prisoners of war preserve their character as such. [Report: *E.R.S.*, vol. 55, p. 227.]

[1] The facts do not appear very clearly from the report.

X.—Non-Hostile Relations between Belligerents, Especially Armistices

Armistice—Carriage by Neutral Ship of Contraband to Enemy Base of Supply during Armistice—Seizure and Condemnation of Ship and Cargo—Effects of Armistice—Interpretation of Treaty Permitting Trade between Neutral Country and Enemy Country—Restriction to Trade Consistent with Neutrality. **Case No. 301**

THE RANNVEIG.

England, the Prize Court. 16 *March,* 1920.

THE FACTS.—On 11 November, 1918, an Armistice was concluded between the Allied Powers and Germany. On 6 March, 1919, the Armistice being still in operation, a British ship of war captured in the Baltic the Norwegian merchant ship *Rannveig* carrying a cargo of salted herrings, which had been declared to be conditional contraband by Great Britain, to Stettin, which had already been found by the British Prize Court to be a German base of supply.

The owners of the *Rannveig* based their claim for her release upon an agreement made between Norway and the United States of America on 30 April, 1918, with the assent of Great Britain and other Allied Powers, which permitted certain trade between Norway and Germany; the owners of the cargo based their claim for its release both on the agreement above mentioned and upon the fact of the conclusion of the Armistice, and contended that in view of the Armistice the dispatch of foodstuffs to an enemy base of supply raised no presumption of military use.

The Armistice contained the following provision:

"Article 26: The existing blockade conditions "set up by the Allied and Associated Powers are "to remain unchanged, and all German merchant "ships found at sea are to remain liable to capture. "The Allies and the United States contemplate the "provisioning of Germany during the armistice as "shall be found necessary."

The agreement between the United States of America and Norway contained the following provision:

Case No. 301 ***contd.***

"Article III. Norway will not export to the "Central Powers or their Allies foodstuffs of any "kind except fish and fish products. Fish and fish "products may be exported in quantities not to "exceed 48,000 tons per annum. . . . The export "of each class of fish and fish products is to be made "in the form in ordinary commercial use in the "past. . . ."

The agreement was made for the duration of the war subject to provisions for determination which do not affect this case. The shipment of fish on board the *Rannveig* at the time of her capture was within the limit of 48,000 tons per annum.

Held by the President (Sir Henry Duke): (*a*) That upon the construction of this agreement "there is nothing [in it] "which shows an intention to authorize Norwegian traders to "do any act inconsistent with neutrality. The Norwegian "trade with Germany in fish which is provided for is, in my "opinion, that trade only which is consistent with neutrality, "and not trade which is contraband. Applying every-day "rules of construction I come to a like conclusion with that "which Sir James Marriott expressed in 1778 in his judgment in "*The Vryheid* (Hay and Marriott, 188)—namely, that a treaty "right to trade with the enemy in goods which conditionally "are contraband must in the absence of express stipulation "be limited to 'goods going in the ordinary course of merchan-"'dise and for mercantile purposes (*i.e.* not to a German base "'of supply).'"

(*b*) That the express terms of Article 26 of the Armistice made it clear that the Armistice did not suspend the operation of the British Proclamations as to contraband. "I take it," said Sir Henry Duke, P., "to be a sound proposition that an "armistice does not necessarily imply the right to re-provision "a beleaguered area or to remove the blockade of a coast: "see Hall, 7th ed., p. 585; Halleck, 4th ed., vol. II, p. 351, "but I think the question need not be examined in this case" in view of the terms of Article 26. Both the ship and the cargo must be condemned as good and lawful prize. [Reports: L.R. [1920] P. 177; 3 B. and C.P.C. 740.]

NOTE.—This decision was affirmed by the Privy Council, L.R. [1922] 1 A.C. 97; 3 B and C.P.C. 1013, and the following comment upon the passage from the judgment of the learned President quoted at (*a*) above should be noted: "This passage, doubtless by inadvertence, appears to "assume that the carriage of the cargo in question would, apart from "the Norwegian-American Agreement, have been an unneutral act in "the carrier, and that to have permitted it to be shipped would have "been a breach of neutrality on the part of the Norwegian Government. "It is not, however, the crucial point of his decision. The carriage of "contraband, though hazardous, is not an unlawful or an unneutral "trade. . . ." (L.R. [1922] 1A.C. at p. 99; 3 B. and C.P.C. at p. 1017.)

Armistice—Legal Obligations Created by—No Effect on Internal Legislation. **Case No. 302**

MARTIN *v.* KEYAERTS AND LEYSEN.

Belgium, Commercial Tribunal of Brussels. 1 *February*, 1919.

THE FACTS.—Under the terms of the Armistice concluded on 11 November, 1918, the German Government bound itself to deliver to the Allied and Associated Powers all military supplies, victuals, etc., which had not been taken away during the time allowed for evacuation. On 15 November the defendants bought from a German officer, who was apparently acting in an official capacity, certain quantities of oils and fats; on the same day they re-sold them to the plaintiff, who knew their origin and took possession of them. On 17 November the Belgian army authorities seized the goods, claiming that they belonged to them by virtue of the Armistice of 11 November. The present action was brought by the purchaser to have the sale set aside, on the ground that the seller (defendant) had never been the owner of the goods sold (Article 1599 of the *Code Civil*).

Held: That the action was misconceived: the effect of the provisions of the Armistice was that the property in the articles and goods mentioned in that instrument "is not thereby *ipso* "*facto* transferred to the Allied Governments, since the goods "remain the property of the Germans if they take them away, "and only cease to be their property if they cannot take them "away within the time fixed; that it certainly appeared that "the German authority impliedly deprived itself of the right "to sell these things, but that is merely an obligation not to "do something, and this can have no effect on the transfer of "the actual right of property to a third party; on this point "it should be remarked that the armistice of 11 November "was a military agreement between enemy generals; that no

Case No. 302 *contd.*

"law or decree-law gave it form and force of law in Belgium; "that it has not been published in the *Moniteur*; in these cir-"cumstances the armistice could in no way modify the rules "of Belgian private law, nor the manner in which property is "transferred according to that law. It was therefore not "established that either the German authorities from whom "the defendant got his title to the goods, or the defendant "himself, was not the owner at the time when they sold." [Report: *Pasicrisie belge*, 1919, vol. III, p. 8.]

NOTE.—See in a contrary sense Case No. 303 (*State of Belgium* v. *Malfeit and Fischer*).

Case No. 303

Armistice—Legal Obligations Created by—Invalidity of Contracts in Contravention of.

STATE OF BELGIUM *v.* MALFEIT AND FISCHER.

Belgium, Civil Tribunal of Antwerp. 10 *May*, 1919.

THE FACTS.—See the relevant provision of the Armistice of 11 November, 1918, stated in the facts of the last preceding case (No. 302). On 11 November, C. Fischer, a German subject, bought from the German authorities a large quantity of tropical woods warehoused in Antwerp. It was intended to transport the wood to Holland, so it was arranged that payment should be made on delivery and on condition that the goods were not seized by the Dutch Government or by any other authority. As it proved impossible to transport the goods, Fischer sold them again the next day (12 November) to the defendant Malfeit. The Belgian State seized the wood, and brought an action to establish its ownership by virtue of the Armistice.

Held: That the claim was well founded. The circumstances revealed clearly the illegal motive and the bad faith which had characterised the transactions. The conditions inserted in the Armistice Agreement of 11 November, 1918, were specially intended to safeguard the higher interests of the Allied forces and, in consequence, the security of the Belgian State; it was the duty of all citizens to observe these conditions just as they observed the laws and regulations, and they can no more allege ignorance of the former than of the latter. Malfeit was thus prohibited from concluding the sale in question as it was established that the wood belonged to the German military authorities and proved that, without his intervention, these goods would necessarily have become the property of the Belgian State as war booty. [Report: *Pasicrisie belge*, 1919, vol. III, p. 152.]

NOTE.—The Tribunal does not say that the Belgian State had become the owner of the goods in virtue of and from the date of the Armistice. It confines itself to setting the sale aside and so leaves the State free to exercise the rights which the Armistice gave it. See in the same sense the decision of the Civil Tribunal of Antwerp of 3 April, 1919 (*Pasicrisie belge*, 1919, vol. III, p. 125), and see the contrary judgment of the Commercial Tribunal of Brussels, Case No. 302 (*Martin* v. *Keyaerts and Leysen*).

Armistice—Convention of 11 November, 1918—Germany's Undertaking to Surrender her Military Equipment to the Allies—Transaction effected by the German Authorities after the Signature of the Armistice but before the Cessation of Hostilities. **Case No. 304**

W. AND M. *v.* THE (FRENCH) STATE.

France, Tribunal Supérieur of Colmar. 4 *February*, 1920.

THE FACTS.—At 10 a.m. on 11 November, 1918, the claimants contracted with the German authorities at the General Headquarters of the 64th Division for the purchase of a certain quantity of unsawn wood. The Armistice Convention had been signed at 5 a.m. on the same day and hostilities were to cease six hours after, at 11 a.m. The Armistice Convention stipulated (Article 6) that military equipment should be handed over to the Allies. The claimants contended, however, that since the Armistice Convention was only due to enter into force six hours after its signature, the contract had been made at a time when the vendor still retained full capacity to sell.

Held: For the State. The clause providing for the cessation of hostilities six hours after the signature of the Armistice refers solely to hostile operations in the firing-line. It could not have had the effect of postponing for six hours Germany's obligation under the Convention, as from the time of signature, to carry out her engagements thereunder. [Report: Sirey, 1922, Part II, p. 57, with a note by Professor J. P. Niboyet.]

Case No. 305 **Armistice—Convention of 11 November, 1918, Article VI, § 3—International Obligation—Whether Part of German Law—Effect on Private Contracts—American Occupation of Coblenz—Article 43 of the Fourth Hague Convention.**

ARMISTICE AGREEMENT (COBLENZ) CASE.

Germany, Reichsgericht in Civil Matters. 19 *April,* 1921.

THE FACTS.—The defendant company bought on 25 November, 1918, from the German military authorities in Coblenz a large quantity of nails, horse-shoes, etc., the larger part of which it then sold to the plaintiff on 4 January, 1919. In February, 1919, the authorities of the United States army of occupation, basing themselves on Article VI, § 3, of the Armistice Agreement of 11 November, 1918, declared both transactions to be null and void and the property purchased by the plaintiff to be the property of the United States. The United States authorities then released this property and handed it over to the plaintiff on payment of the difference between the price paid by the defendant and that paid to him by the plaintiff. The United States authorities also ceded to the plaintiff their claims against the defendant. The present action was brought, *inter alia,* on the ground of unjustified enrichment, and also in reliance on the rights ceded to the plaintiff by the American authorities. The Court of First Instance dismissed the action. So also did the Court of Appeal, before which the plaintiff also pleaded *negotiorum gestio.*

Held, on final appeal on a point of law: That the claim must be dismissed.

(*a*) The obligation of Germany and the corresponding right of the United States as laid down in Article VI, § 3, of the Armistice Agreement constitute an international right and duty only. Article 212 of the Treaty of Versailles (which was not ratified by the United States) providing that Article VI of the Armistice Agreement shall be maintained and thus acquire the character of an internal law would have no retroactive effect. The Armistice Agreement was never assented to by the German legislative authorities and was not published in the Journal of Laws of the *Reich.* It did not acquire the force of a municipal law so as to render void contracts concluded in disregard of its provisions.

(*b*) It was true that the American military authorities declared, by a proclamation, on 14 January, 1919, as null and void purchases made after 11 November, 1918, from the German military authorities inasmuch as such purchases were contrary to the Armistice Agreement. However, this proclamation could not affect contracts validly concluded under private law. According to Article 43 of the Fourth Hague Convention the United States authorities were bound to respect the German laws so far as possible. It would have been sufficient for their purpose if they had declared the purchases in question as null and void so far as the United States were concerned. There was no reason to interfere with the relations of private law between the German military authorities and private purchasers, or between the latter and further purchasers. [Report: *E.R.Z.*, vol. 102, p. 106.]

Armistice—Whether Identical with the Cessation of the State of War—Armistice and War Clause in Contracts. **Case No. 306**

DÜSSELDORFER ALLGEMEINE VERSICHERUNGS-A.G. *v.* L.

Germany, Reichsgericht in Civil Matters. 15 *December,* 1922.

THE FACTS.—This was an action against an Insurance Company. The plaintiff forwarded on 2 November, 1918, a wagon-load of glass jars from Brussels to Cologne. The consignment, which was insured under an insurance policy containing the so-called war clause, never arrived at its destination. It appeared that it was captured by the Allied troops as war booty. The defendant company maintained that the Court was bound to enquire whether the consignment was seized before or after 11 November, 1918 (the day on which the Armistice Agreement was concluded), as in the latter case the war clause would no longer be applicable.

Held, on final appeal on a point of law: That the question of the date of the seizure was irrelevant. The Armistice does not put an end to the state of war. It merely aims at a temporary cessation of the hostilities. As the state of war continued, the possibility of warlike acts was not altogether excluded. [Report: *E.R.Z.*, vol. 106, p. 59.]

Armistice—Whether Amounting to Termination of War.

See Case No. 308 (*United States* v. *Hicks*).

Armistice—Armistice Agreement of November, 1918—As Part of German Law.

See Case No. 169 (*Immovables* (*Aliens in Germany*) *Case*).

XI.—Termination of War

Case No. 307 **Termination of War—Continuance of State of War until Exchange of Ratifications of Treaty of Peace—British Termination of the Present War (Definition) Act, 1918.**

KOTZIAS *v.* TYSER.

England, High Court of Justice, King's Bench Division.
13 *January*, 1920.

THE FACTS.—The plaintiff, being desirous of protecting himself against the consequences of the continuance of the Great War which prevented him from carrying on his business as a merchant, effected a policy of insurance with the defendant on 2 November, 1918, whereby the latter agreed to pay to the plaintiff a certain sum of money "in the event of peace between Great "Britain and Germany not being concluded on or "before the thirtieth day of June one thousand nine "hundred and nineteen."

A general Armistice between those two Powers, amongst others, took effect on 11 November, 1918. The Treaty of Peace of Versailles between Great Britain and other Allied and Associated Powers on the one hand, and Germany on the other hand, was signed on 28 June, 1919.

By the Termination of the Present War (Definition) Act, 1918, which became law on 21 November, 1918, it was enacted that the Crown should have power to declare by Order in Council "what date is to be "treated as the date of the termination of the present "war, and the present war shall be treated as having "continued to, and as having ended on, that date for "the purposes of any provision in any Act of Parlia-"ment, Order in Council, or Proclamation, and, except "where the context otherwise requires, of any pro-"vision in any contract, deed, or other instrument "referring, expressly or impliedly, and in whatever "form of words, to the present war or the present "hostilities. . . ."

On 21 August, 1919, the plaintiff commenced his action. No Order in Council or Proclamation had been issued under the Act above mentioned at that date or indeed up to the date of the judgment, 13 January,

1920; nor had the ratifications necessary to bring the Treaty into force been deposited at the latter date.

Held by Roche, J.: That peace had not been concluded on or before 30 June, 1919, and the plaintiff was therefore entitled to recover the sum insured by the policy: (1) upon grounds of the general principles of international law: "The authorities "show that, in the absence of any specific statutory or con-"tractual provision to the contrary, the general rule of inter-"national law is that as between civilized Powers who have "been at war, peace is not concluded until a treaty of peace "is finally binding upon the belligerents, and that that stage "is not reached until ratifications of the treaty of peace have "been exchanged between them" (at p. 77). (2) Nor could the defendant rely upon any date which might be fixed for the termination of the war under the Act above mentioned, for no Order in Council or Proclamation had been issued. (3) Moreover, the parties to the Treaty of Peace had themselves expressly agreed that the state of war should terminate upon the coming into force of the Treaty, which event had not yet occurred. [Report: L.R. [1920] 2 K.B. 69.]

See also Case No. 301 (*The Rannveig*), and Beckett in *L.Q.R.*, XXXIX (1923), pp. 89-97.

War—Termination of War—Armistice. **Case No. 308**

UNITED STATES *v.* HICKS.

United States District Court, W.D. Kentucky. 3 *April*, 1919.

THE FACTS.—Hicks was convicted of violating regulations made pursuant to a Federal statute concerning houses of ill fame near military camps during the war. (40 U.S. Stat. L. 76, 83.) It was conceded that such a regulation normally lay within the police power exclusively reserved to the States, and outside the sphere of the Federal Government, were it not for the unusual situation due to the war. The United States had declared on 6 April, 1917, that a state of war existed with Germany. On 11 November, 1918, the President read to both houses of Congress a proclamation that the Armistice had been signed, including a statement that "The war thus comes to an end." Great publicity was given to this event. The acts here charged were committed on 7 December, 1918. The question was whether that date was "during the

Case No. 308 *contd.*

"present war." Upon a motion by Hicks for arrest of judgment and a new trial,

Held : That a new trial must be granted. The Court took judicial notice of the proclamation and of the ending of the war. The statute here violated did not provide for the period of demobilisation ; and since it was a criminal statute it could not be extended by construction to cover that period. The Court said : "In advance of a treaty it is, of course, possible "for the war to break out again ; but, if it does not do so, "then certainly it was *in fact ended.*" (256 Fed. 707, 711.[1]) [Report : 256 Fed. 707.]

Case No. 309

War—Termination of War—Article 440 of the Treaty of Versailles.

SECCO MAIA & COMPANY *v.* UNIÃO FEDERAL.

Brazil, Supreme Federal Tribunal. 16 *December,* 1919.

THE FACTS.—This case involved the date of termination of the World War. The legislative Decree 3533 of 3 September, 1918, authorised the Executive, while the state of war lasted, to suspend importation and exportation of goods. The Executive took action under this authorisation, issued certain orders, and approved the appropriation of certain merchandise for the public good. After the Peace Treaty had been signed, and after it had been ratified by the Brazilian Congress, the plaintiffs sought from the Federal Judge of the First Chamber a prohibitory order against the Federal Government so as to permit the plaintiffs to exercise their export business without being subject to the power of the Government to appropriate goods. This application was refused, on the ground that the war had not yet ended. On appeal,

Held : That the judgment must be affirmed. The Government had full power to regulate commerce, or to restrict or suppress it entirely, during the war. The question was whether the cessation of hostilities and the signing and ratification of the Treaty of Peace by Brazil ended the war. "The approval "by Congress and the consequent ratification by the President "was not enough for a treaty of peace to enter into effect "when that same treaty had an express clause regulating the

[1] See Hudson, *The Duration of the War between the United States and Germany,* in *H.L.R.,* XXXIX, p. 1020.

" matter." Article 440 of the Treaty of Versailles provided that deposit of ratifications should be made at Paris as soon as possible, and that when the Treaty had been ratified by Germany and by three of the Principal Allied and Associated Powers it would enter into effect between the ratifying parties. At the time of the present action Germany had not yet ratified the Treaty. [Reports: *Revista do Supremo Tribunal*, vol. 24, p. 25; *Revista do Direito*, vol. 58, p. 551.]

NOTE.—There was a vigorous dissent, which referred to a " purely " fictitious state of war," saying that " peace is a fact which is re- " cognised throughout the whole world," and pointing out that the approval given to the Treaty by Congress included a statement that the acceptance of this Treaty put an end to the state of war with Germany.

There is a series of Cuban cases involving the question of the end of the war in which attempts were made to judge criminals by the military courts in a way allowed only during war. See the case of *Secondino García* (30 January, 1922), *Gaceta Official* for 25 March, 1922, p. 6340, in which it was held that the military courts were still competent because no treaty had been ratified with Hungary; and a similar report in *Gaceta Official* for 29 June, 1922, p. 1209.

B. WARFARE ON LAND

II.—Appropriation, Utilisation and Destruction of Enemy Property

Appropriation of Enemy Maritime Property on Land—Whether Maritime Prize or Not—Hot Pursuit.

See Case No. 344 (*The Anichab*).

III.—Occupation of Enemy Territory

i.—Nature and Effects of the Occupation

Nature and Effects of the Occupation—Maintenance of National Sovereignty—Legislative Measures of National Authorities—Effect in Occupied Territory—Suspension during Occupation. **Case No. 310**

AUDITEUR MILITAIRE v. G. VAN DIEREN.

Belgium, Council of War (Court-Martial) of Brabant.
31 *January*, 1919.

THE FACTS.—The Decree-Law of 8 April, 1916, issued by the Belgian Government during the period of occupa-

Case No. 310 *contd.*

tion, made the giving aid to the enemy, malicious denunciation to the enemy, etc., criminal offences. The accused, being charged under these heads, alleged in defence, *inter alia*, that he was in occupied territory at the dates of the acts with which he was charged.

Held by the Court-Martial: That the Decree-Law was applicable to the accused. On the basis of Article 43 of the Hague Convention, as interpreted by the Court of Cassation (judgment of 5 July, 1917; *Pasicrisie belge*, 1917, vol. I, p. 280), the Court held that in law national sovereignty subsisted in the occupied territory during the occupation, even when the occupying Power exercised *de facto* authority. It was true that a notice by the German Government in Belgium (4 January, 1915) proclaimed that "the Orders issued from this "day onwards by the King of the Belgians and the Belgian "ministers have not the force of law within the domain of the "German Government of Belgium." But this provision contravened the rights of sovereignty. By a Decree-Law of 8 April, 1917, the King declared: "subject to any express provision "to the contrary, the decree-laws, orders and regulations of "the legal authority are obligatory through the Kingdom. "The administrative and judicial authorities will apply them "concurrently with the liberation of the country, and without "further proclamation." Moreover, it has to be observed that the Code of Penal Procedure (Articles 8-14) allowed prosecution in Belgium for certain breaches of the law committed abroad. If a lawful sovereignty did not prevent these laws from having binding force but merely suspended their application while the offender was abroad, "it would be inconceivable that a simple "authority in fact resulting from a most flagrant usurpation "could render inoperative" penal provisions as to offences committed on the national territory. [Report: *Pasicrisie belge*, 1919, vol. III, pp. 1 *et seq.*]

NOTE.—This judgment was confirmed by the Military Court on 15 February, 1919. The Court of Cassation finally dismissed an application by the accused on 4 June, 1919 (*Pasicrisie belge*, 1919, vol. I, pp. 97 *et seq.*).

See to the same effect, in regard to the Decree-Law of 8 April, 1917, the decision of the Court of Cassation of 4 June, 1919 (*Pasicrisie belge*, 1919, vol. I, p. 153). An uninterrupted series of decisions recognises the obligatory force in the occupied territory of the orders of the Belgian Government. See decision of the Court of Cassation of 11 February, 1919, concerning the Decree-Law of 11 October, 1916 (*Pasicrisie belge*, 1919, vol. I, p. 9); judgment and decisions concerning the Decree-Law of 26 October, 1914, of the Civil Tribunal of Brussels of 10 March, 1919 (*ibid.*, vol. III, p. 112), of the Court of Appeal of Liège of 4 June, 1919 (*ibid.*, vol. II, p. 100), of the Court of Appeal of Ghent of 19 June, 1919 (*ibid.*, vol. II, p. 145), and of the Court of Cassation of 9 December, 1920 (*ibid.*, 1921, vol. I, p. 177); and decision of the Court of Cassation of 8 July, 1919, concerning the Decree-Law of 31 July, 1917 (*ibid.*, 1919, vol. I, p. 178).

Territory under Enemy Occupation—Nature and Effects of Occupation—Legislative Measure of the Lawful Authority —Obligatory Effect in Occupied Territory—Application in Occupied Territory. **Case No. 311**

DE NIMAL *v.* DE NIMAL.

Belgium, Court of Appeal of Brussels. 23 *April*, 1919.

THE FACTS.—The appellants having lodged an appeal on 15 February, 1915, against a judgment of the Court of First Instance of Mons, given on 30 October, 1914, the respondents asked that the application should be dismissed as being out of time, the period of three months fixed by the Code of Civil Procedure (Article 443) having expired. The appellants relied on the Royal Decree of 28 October, 1914, suspending periods of prescription and limitation in civil matters for the duration of the war.

Held: That the appeal lay. The legislative authority of the legal government no doubt loses strength as the enemy forces advance on the territory. In other words, new laws enacted by the legal authority in the endeavour to combat the occupant and to injure his power, are not capable of application in districts where a military occupation has been established. However, the present case has nothing to do with the struggle between the belligerents. It arises out of a measure intended to protect the interests of persons subject to the law. [Reports: *Pasicrisie belge*, 1919, vol. II, p. 83.]

NOTE.—This decision, based on the principle of the preservation of the sovereign power of the lawful authority in occupied territory, is of interest for two reasons: (1) it recognises not only the obligatory character of measures of the lawful authority, but also the application of these measures in occupied territory in certain circumstances; (2) it fixes, however, a reasonable limit to the efficacy of these measures by declaring them to be inapplicable in any cases in which they are aimed at injuring the occupying Power.

Case No. 312 **Legal Status of Occupied Enemy Territory—Prohibition upon the Export of French Silver Currency—Occupied Territory —Non-Assimilation to the National Territory.**

NAOUM AND OTHERS *v.* THE GOVERNMENT OF THE COLONY OF FRENCH WEST AFRICA.

France, Court of Cassation (Criminal Chamber).
20 *December*, 1919.

THE FACTS.—The export to foreign countries of French silver currency was prohibited by a law, dated 17 August, 1915, and applicable to French West Africa. The appellants attempted to export French currency to the German colony of Togoland, then under French military occupation. For this offence the Court of Appeal of Dakar had condemned each of them to imprisonment for six months and to the payment of a fine of 5000 francs.

Held : That the appeal against the decision of the Court of Dakar must be dismissed. " Territory under military occupa-" tion cannot be held to be part of the national territory." [Report : *Gazette du Palais*, 1920, I, p. 62.]

Case No. 313 **Occupation of Enemy Territory—Occupation Subsequent to the Armistice—Alsace-Lorraine—Provisional Administration—Power of the French Authorities.**

IN RE WEBER.

France, Court of Cassation (Criminal Chamber).
13 *November*, 1919.

THE FACTS.—Weber was found guilty of contravening the Order of the Prime Minister (*Président du Conseil des Ministres*), dated 26 November, 1918, concerning the exchange of German money. His appeal was founded on the plea that the Order was illegal.

Held : That the appeal must be dismissed. The territory of Alsace and Lorraine, reunited to France by the Armistice of 11 November, 1918, and the Peace Treaty of 28 June, 1919, had, from the commencement of their occupation, been placed under the authority of the Prime Minister (*Président du Conseil des Ministres*), who thus "was invested in virtue both of this "authority and of the right of occupation with power to issue "such regulations as were necessary for the security of the "army and the maintenance of public order and to attach "penalties for non-observance." [Reports: *Dalloz*, 1920, Part I, p. 77, with a note by Professor Marcel Nast; Sirey, 1920, Part I, p. 285.]

Alsace-Lorraine—Period between 11 November, 1918, and the Entry into Force of the Peace Treaty—Sequestration—Military Occupation—Legal Position of Sequestrator. **Case No. 314**

BOURGOIN (OFFICIAL SEQUESTRATOR) *v.* SOCIÉTÉ BELGE ÉLOI ET CIE.

France, Court of Appeal of Paris. 21 *June*, 1922.

THE FACTS.—The dispute arose out of dealings between Bourgoin, in his capacity as Sequestrator of the *Forges de Lorraine*, with the Belgian Company, *Éloi et Cie*, the dates of these transactions being the 28th and 31st October, 1919, *i.e.* in the period between the Armistice of 11th November, 1918, and the Peace Treaty. Bourgoin objected to the jurisdiction of the Commercial Court on the ground that the measures had occurred on territory subject to the law of war; they were, therefore, acts of State, and therefore not open to discussion by a court. The Court of First Instance rejected this contention.

Held on appeal: That the objection to the jurisdiction could not be sustained. The Sequestrator was a mandatory of Justice, not a State agent; his acts were cognisable by the ordinary judges. "The Court cannot accept the novel theory "advanced by the Liquidator-General to the effect that the "Sequestrators entrusted with the management of the *Forges* "*de Lorraine* when they entered into commercial contracts in "the execution of their duties were acting as agents (of the "State) on occupied territory, subject to the Law of War, and "under no control except that of the Hague Conventions." [Reports: *Dalloz*, 1924, Part II, p. 64; *Gazette du Palais*, 1922, II, p. 490.]

Case No. 315 **Enemy Occupation—Occupation by Virtue of the Armistice Agreement—Contractual as distinguished from Enemy Occupation—Continuation of Legislation of Lawful Sovereign—Hague Convention concerning Laws and Customs of Land Warfare—Occupation of the Rhine Bank.**

RHINELAND (GERMAN DECREES) CASE.

Germany, Reichsgericht for Criminal Matters.
29 *September,* 1921.

THE FACTS.—This was a prosecution in connection with a Decree for fighting venereal diseases issued on 11 December, 1918, by the Federal authorities. The offence was committed in February, 1920, in Saarbrücken (on the left bank of the Rhine), at that time occupied by the Allied troops. The accused denied that the German Decree was applicable.

Held, on final appeal on a point of law: That the conviction must stand. The occupation of the left bank of the Rhine took place in pursuance of the Armistice Agreement. It was a contractual, not a war occupation. German laws and decrees operated in the occupied territory unless the occupation authorities, for considerations grounded in the Armistice Agreement, objected to their entry into force or to their continued validity in the occupied territory. Even in regard to enemy occupation, Article 43 of the Fourth Hague Convention provides that the occupant shall take measures to restore and ensure public order and safety while respecting, unless absolutely prevented, the laws in force in the country. [Report: *E.R.S.*, vol. 56, p. 194.]

Case No. 316 **Occupation of Foreign Territory—Legal Position of Occupied Territory—Operation in Occupied Territory of Legislation of Lawful Sovereign—Occupation of Hungarian Territory by Serbian Troops—Insulting the Person of the Head of the Hungarian State.**

COMMUNE OF BÁCSBOROD CASE.

Hungary, Supreme Court. 12 *September,* 1922.
(*No. B.I.* 3223/1922.)

THE FACTS.—On 1 May, 1920, the accused, resident in the Commune of Bácsborod in the Bácsbodrog Department (*Comitat*), insulted the person of the head of the Hungarian State. This happened at a time when the Bácsborod Commune was occupied by Serbian troops in pursuance of the Armistice Agreement. The Treaty of Trianon subsequently restored the Commune to Hungary. According to a law passed in Hungary at the time of the Serbian occupation, insulting the person of the head of the State was made a crime.

Held: That the conviction of the accused on account of insulting the head of the Hungarian State must stand. "At "the time when the offence was committed as well as at the "time of the commencement of the prosecution proceedings "the accused was a Hungarian subject. He would have been "criminally liable even if the place in which the offence was "committed were to be regarded as being provisionally foreign "territory. This of course is not so in the present case seeing "that the place in question was not ceded even temporarily. "The fact of enemy occupation does not mean that either in "constitutional law or in international law the territory had "ceased to be Hungarian territory." [Report: *Büntetöjogi Döntvénytár*, vol. XV, Case No. 19.]

Occupation of Enemy Territory—Decrees of Occupying Authorities—Effect on Persons Not Resident in Occupied Territory. **Case No. 317**

CZECHOSLOVAK OCCUPATION (HUNGARY) CASE.

Hungary, Supreme Court. 25 *October*, 1922.
(*No. P. IV* 917/1922.)

THE FACTS.—The place where the plaintiff was resident was after the termination of the war occupied by Czechoslovak troops. During the Czechoslovak occupation the defendant repaid to the plaintiff a loan in Hungarian currency, as provided in the loan agreement. The plaintiff maintained that the loan ought to have been paid in Czechoslovak currency, as laid down in a Czechoslovak Governmental Decree issued during the occupation. The defendant was not resident in the occupied territory.

Held: That the claim must be dismissed. Up to the entry into force of the Peace Treaty the territories detached from Hungary and eventually ceded to the Czechoslovak State were merely under Czechoslovak occupation. Accordingly they must

Case No. 317 *contd.* be regarded during that period as being Hungarian territory. Hungarian law must be applied to transactions between Hungarian subjects resident in the territory in question. The plaintiff was not entitled to ask that, having regard to the Decree issued by the Czechoslovak authorities, the loan should be repaid in Czechoslovak currency. The Decree of the Czechoslovak Government could have no effect in regard to the modes of payment as between Hungarian subjects not resident in occupied territory. [Report : *Hiteljogi Döntvénytár*, vol. XVI, Case No. 1.]

Case No. 318 **Occupation of Enemy Territory—Status of Occupied Territory—Capitulatory Régime—Italian Occupation of Turkish Territory.**

BOLIOTTI *v.* MASSE.

Italy, Court of Rhodes. 31 *December*, 1920.

THE FACTS.—An Italian subject, one Boliotti, began before the Court of Rhodes civil proceedings against the brothers Masse, who were French subjects. The latter and the French vice-consul at Rhodes brought up as a preliminary point the question of the competence of the courts established there by Italy. It was maintained that, in view of the capitulary régime actually in force in Rhodes, proceedings between foreign citizens of different nationalities should be judged by the consular court of the defendant, hence the present case should be tried by the French consular court applying French law.

Held : That the Court had no jurisdiction. The courts of the first and second instance, established by Italy at Rhodes, although presided over by Italian judges, must be considered to be the successors to the former Ottoman judicial authority. If it is admitted that the title of Italy to its present possessions is that of warlike occupation, it necessarily follows that, in accordance with the usual principles of international law, the power which Italy exercises at Rhodes cannot be considered otherwise than as exercised as agent for the sovereign of the occupied territory, and within the limits of the rights appertaining to such sovereign. These courts cannot then be considered as tribunals derived from the legal order in Italy. The fact that Italian judges have been called to preside over them is not important ; one has to take into account the nature of the judicial organs themselves and not the persons of whom they are composed. As regards the application of Italian laws by these courts, these are applied not as forming part of Italian legislation but because they have become part of the local legislation, similarly with any other provision coming from the occupying authority adding to or modifying the *corpus* of the earlier Ottoman legislation either in order to meet new needs or to carry out particular ends imposed out of necessity by the Government or the Administration of the occupied territories. Consequently, as the capitulatory régime has remained in force at Rhodes, the courts established by Italy are not competent to judge a cause begun by an Italian subject against French subjects. [Report: *Foro Italiano*, vol. I (1921), pp. 518-528, with a critical note by Professor Cavaglieri.]

NOTE.—There are other judgments of the Court of Rhodes on this question, but to a different effect. See the judgments of 18 September, 1913, in *Foro Italiano*, vol. I (1914), p. 66; of 27 September, 1914, in *Rivista di diritto internazionale*, 1915, pp. 246 *et seq.*, with a critical note by Professor Anzilotti. See also on this series of cases Catellani, in *Rivista di diritto internazionale*, 1914, pp. 22-32; and Marinoni, in *Rivista di diritto e procedura penale*, 1914, fasc. 9, and 1916, fasc. 1.

Occupation of Enemy Territory—Status of Occupied Territory —Whether Foreign Territory—Dissolution of Austro-Hungarian Monarchy—Provinces Occupied by Italy. **Case No. 319**

GALATIOLO *v.* SENES.

Italy, Court of Cassation of Rome. 3 November, 1922.

THE FACTS.—By proceedings instituted on 19 June, 1920, the firm of Galatiolo, of Trieste, sued the firm of Senes, of Palermo, before the Civil and Commercial Court of that city to obtain payment of sixty thousand lire as damages due to the plaintiffs following upon failure to deliver certain merchandise. The plaintiffs maintained that the Court of Trieste was competent as being "the "reciprocal forum against foreigners," as laid down in Article 101 of the Austrian rules of procedure. The defendants contended that as Trieste had in the meantime become part of Italy it could not be regarded as foreign territory within the meaning of Article 101. The Court of First Instance decided in favour of the defendants. The Court of Appeal of Trieste reversed that judgment and held that in law, at the date of the institution of the proceedings by the plaintiff firm, the new provinces were still foreign territory as regards the

Case No. 319 *contd.*

Kingdom of Italy. Hence the Court of Trieste was competent, on the basis of the said Article 101. The firm of Senes appealed to the Court of Cassation.

Held: That the appeal must be allowed. Trieste could not for the purposes of the present action be regarded as foreign territory. After the constitution of the Kingdom of Italy, the recovery of the Italian Provinces, still under foreign domination, was considered to be in the nature of a *restitutio in integrum*. "Many of our laws have accorded to non-native "Italians a virtual Italian citizenship that had only to await "the reunion of those provinces with the mother country to "become effective. . . . With the complete dissolution of the "enemy army and the simultaneous dismemberment of the "Austro-Hungarian Empire, the national integration has been "accomplished almost automatically and *pari passu* with the "military occupation of the provinces. The Treaty of St. "Germain and the law of annexation [1] did not add anything "to the rights of sovereignty over these provinces, irrevocably "acquired by the Kingdom of Italy by reason of the victory "of our arms, which has given effect to the immanent right of "the nation to the lordship over the entire Italian territory. "Treaty and statutes will bring the present situation into "accord with the exigencies of international law. But it is "absurd to think that in the interval between the armistice "and the coming into force of the law of annexation, at a time "when not only the sovereignty of Austria-Hungary over these "provinces, but that very State, had disappeared, the two "provinces *disiecta membra* of a now destroyed organism have "been able to live a separate political life outside the sove-"reignty of the Italian State which had become responsible for "all its administration, justice, army and finance." [Report: *Foro delle nuove Provincie*, vol. II (1923), pp. 185-190.]

NOTE.—See for the thesis agreeing with the principles affirmed in this judgment, Salvioli, in *Archivio Giuridico*, April, 1922, pp. 149-160; and to the contrary, Cavaglieri, in the same, July, 1922, pp. 64-74.

Case No. 320

Occupation of Enemy Territory—Legal Nature of Occupation —Occupied Territory as Foreign Territory.

DEL VECCHIO *v.* CONNIO.

Italy, Court of Appeal of Milan. 24 November, 1920.

THE FACTS.—The marriage of two persons, originally

[1] The Italian law formally incorporating the ceded territories.

Italian citizens, was dissolved by a decree of divorce from the Court of Trieste during the period between the armistice and the annexation of Trieste by Italy. Trieste was occupied by Italian troops after the armistice. The question was whether or not the decree in order to be recognised in Italy should be treated like any other decree obtained in a foreign country, *i.e.* whether it should first be submitted to a judicial sentence and to the grant of an exequatur by a competent court.

Held: That an exequatur is necessary because the decree is a foreign one. While, at the end of the last century, the fact of war-time occupation alone put an end to the governmental power of the invaded State over its occupied territory, replacing it in full and perfect manner by that of the invading State, it had gradually come to be recognised that war-time occupation, instead of expressing itself in the mere exercise of power by the occupant, has given place to a legal relation regulated by international law. It is universally held nowadays that warlike occupation cannot attribute to the occupying State the sovereignty over the occupied territory. The destruction or modification of the rights of a vanquished State cannot be accomplished except by the treaty of peace or by annexation. If the territory taken from the enemy remains legally what it was beforehand, that is, foreign territory in relation to the occupying State, the authorities which such occupying State has found in the place and has deemed it convenient not to remove but to maintain in the exercise of their functions, must also be deemed to be foreign. Therefore the question of the territories of Venezia Giulia cannot yet be regarded as settled. The condition created by the armistice must be deemed as constituting war-time occupation in regard to the territory in question. [Report: *Foro Italiano*, vol. I (1921), pp. 208 *et seq.*, with a note by Professor Cavaglieri.]

NOTE.—See to the same effect *Calderoni* v. *Official of Civil Status of Genoa*, decided by the Court of Appeal of Genoa on 29 October, 1920. See in the contrary sense *Galatiolo* v. *Senes*, decided by the Court of Cassation of Rome on 3 November, 1922 (*Foro delle Nuove Provincie*, vol. I (1922), pp. 185-190).

Case No. 321 **Occupation of Enemy Territory—Nature and Effects of Occupation—Legislation of the Lawful Sovereign—Effect in Evacuated Territory.**

KULTURAS BALSS CO-OPERATIVE SOCIETY *v.* LATVIAN MINISTRY FOR HOME AFFAIRS.

Latvia, The Senate. 19 *November,* 1920.

THE FACTS.—The claimant, *Kulturas Balss* Co-operative Society, a publishing house, applied to the Senate to quash a regulation issued by the Ministry for Home Affairs on the ground of its being contrary to a Russian law on freedom of the press enacted on 27 April, 1917. The Ministry submitted, *inter alia,* that the Russian law on press freedom never acquired legal force in Latvia, as at the date of its publication one part of Latvian territory was evacuated by Russian civil authorities, while another part was occupied by the enemy.

Held by the Senate: That, while the application was to be rejected for other reasons, the Ministry was wrong in its interpretation of the influence of occupation and evacuation on the law. "The fact of occupation and evacuation does not in itself "preclude the coming into force, within the occupied or evacu-"ated parts of a State, of laws enacted by that State's central "authorities, so long as these parts are not separated from the "State by a public-law procedure." [Report: *Latvijas Senata administrativa departamenta spriedumi, in Iekslietu ministrijas vestnesis,* 1921, p. 52.]

NOTE.—The law existing at the date of the occupation is not invalidated by the new conditions, but the Senate seems to have adopted a novel view in holding that laws enacted after the date of evacuation in the non-occupied part of the State acquire *ipso jure* legal force within the territory subject to war conditions (*occupatio bellica*). This view may, perhaps, be open to criticism on the ground that, as to evacuated territory, the validity of new laws depends there upon the degree of effectiveness of the authority which the State still maintains, and that the substitution, in a military zone, of military authorities for civil authorities of the same State excludes explicitly or implicitly certain laws meant to be applied exclusively by civil authorities.

Occupation of Enemy Territory—Nature and Effects of the Occupation—Powers of the Occupant. **Case No. 322**

REPUBLIC *v.* RALSKI.

Poland, Supreme Court, Second Division. 16 *May*, 1922.

THE FACTS.—The defendant was convicted, in 1921, by the District Court of Grodno, of having, during the Bolshevik occupation of the district in question in 1920, charged a woman before the Bolshevik authorities with espionage in favour of Poland, whereupon she was shot by them. The judgment of the District Court established that the woman had not committed espionage but that the defendant, having quarrelled with her, took the opportunity of avenging himself. The offence of which the defendant was convicted was that of having falsely accused a person before the authorities. In his appeal he claimed, *inter alia,* that the conviction amounted to recognising the Bolsheviks as having exercised legitimate authority over the district in question.

Held: That the conviction must be affirmed. *De facto* power in territory which is occupied by enemy forces is temporarily in the hands of the occupant, who, under the rules of international law laid down in Articles 42 and 43 of the Hague Rules of Land Warfare, may exercise public power in that territory. [Report: Zb. O.S.N., 1922, No. 116.]

Armistice—Occupation of Enemy Territory—Occupation by Virtue of Armistice Agreement—Nature of Occupation.

See Case No. 315 (*Rhineland* (*German Decrees*) *Case*).

ii.—Legislative, Judicial and Administrative Functions of the Occupant

Territory under Enemy Occupation—Nature and Effects of Occupation—Legislative Measure of Lawful Power—Law Punishing Malicious Denunciation—Obligatory Effect in Occupied Territory—Position of Members of the Occupying Forces. **Case No. 323**

KAUHLEN CASE.

Belgium, Court of Cassation. 19 *October*, 1920.

THE FACTS.—The Decree-Law of 8 April, 1917, issued by

Case No. 323 *contd.*

the Belgian Government during the occupation, provided for the punishment of "any person who maliciously, by denunciation of any fact, real or imaginary, "exposes any person to enquiry, prosecution or "severities by the enemy." The applicant, having been found guilty under this Decree-Law by the Court of Appeal of Liège (20 July, 1920), moved to have the judgment quashed on the ground that this measure had no application to him as he belonged to the army of occupation.

Held: That the appeal must be dismissed. "The Decree-"Law of 8 April, 1917, applies to the person who gives the "information whatever his nationality, even if he belongs to "the army of occupation. The language of the law is per-"fectly general on this question. There is no principle of inter-"national law establishing an immunity which would be con-"trary to the spirit of the particular enactment as well as to "universal morality." [Report: *Pasicrisie belge*, 1921, vol. I, p. 100.]

Case No. 324

Enemy Occupation—Acts Contrary to the Laws and Customs of War—Treaty of Versailles, Articles 228 and 229—Whether the Jurisdiction instituted by those Articles was exclusive of Civil Jurisdiction.

BOCKSTEGEN'S CASE.

Belgium, Court of Cassation. 23 *March*, 1920.

THE FACTS.—Articles 228 and 229 of the Treaty of Versailles require the German Government to deliver up to the Allied and Associated Powers persons accused of having committed acts contrary to the laws and customs of war. The perpetrators of these acts were to be brought before the military tribunals of the Powers to which their victims belonged. In the present case the applicant was accused of a murder and an attempted murder. He was arrested by the Belgian authorities in Germany after the armistice and sent for trial to the Assize Court of Brabant on indictment by order of the prosecuting division (*Chambre des mises en accusation*) of the Court of Brussels (23 January, 1920). He then applied to the Court of Cassation on the ground that the Belgian military court alone had jurisdiction.

Held: That even if it be assumed that the acts with which the applicant was charged constitute "acts contrary to the "laws and customs of war" within the meaning of the above provisions of the Treaty of Versailles, still those provisions were not intended to, and did not, affect the rules as to jurisdiction which in Belgium apply to the prosecution of crimes committed within the kingdom by aliens not surrendered to the Belgian State by virtue of the treaties; that the decision attacked stated that the applicant was not a prisoner of war; that he was arrested at Krefeld on a warrant issued on 23 January, 1919, by the *Auditeur Militaire* of the 4th Division. From this it followed that the plea to the jurisdiction was without foundation. [Reports: *Pasicrisie belge*, 1920, vol. I, p. 104; 47 *Clunet* (1920), pp. 718 *et seq.*]

NOTE.—See to the same effect the decision of the Court of Cassation of 10 August, 1920 (*Pasicrisie belge*, 1921, vol. I, p. 84).

Courts Established by Occupying Power—Arbitral Tribunals as to Rent—Legality of. **Case No. 325**

CAMBIER *v.* LEBRUN *ET AL.*

Belgium, Court of Cassation. 4 *December*, 1919.

THE FACTS.—By an Order of the German Governor-General in Belgium of 10 February, 1915, arbitral tribunals for rent were set up and the ordinary courts of first instance were given jurisdiction on appeal from decisions of these tribunals. This was an application to the Court of Cassation to quash a judgment given in exercise of this jurisdiction by the Court of First Instance of Namur (3 April, 1917).

Held: That the application must be dismissed. It must be admitted that decisions given by courts established under the Order of the German Governor-General in Belgium of 10 February, 1915, bind the parties. However, these tribunals are not a creation of Belgian law. The decrees of the occupying Power, whatever they may be, do not emanate from the exercise of national sovereignty. They have not the validity of Belgian laws, but are merely commands of the enemy military authority, and are not incorporated in the legislation or the institutions of the country. Accordingly, the judgment attacked is not to be regarded as an act emanating from a court established by the Belgian legislature. The duty of the Court of Cassation is limited to the maintenance and protec-

Case No. 325 *contd.* tion, in the litigation brought before it, of the unity of the legal system which issues from the national sovereignty. It follows, therefore, that the decision attacked is not of the class which falls within the jurisdiction of the Court of Cassation. [Reports: *Pasicrisie belge*, 1920, vol. I, p. 1; *Belgique Judiciaire*, 1920, col. 10.]

NOTE.—See also the case of *Postula* v. *City of Liège*, decided by the Belgian Court of Cassation on 29 April, 1919. This was an appeal against a decision given by the President of the German Civil Administration for the Province of Liège acting in lieu of the Permanent Deputation of the Province, which alone legally has jurisdiction. It was held that as the decision appealed against did not come from a national court, the Court of Cassation, in virtue of the principles on which it was established, was not competent to deal with the appeal. [Report: *Pasicrisie belge*, 1919, vol. I, p. 132.] See in the same sense the decisions of the Court of 21 January, 1918 (*Pasicrisie belge*, 1918, vol. I, p. 177; *Belgique Judiciaire*, 1919, col. 384), and of 29 April, 1919 (second case, *Pasicrisie belge*, 1919, vol. I, p. 132).

See similar decisions of the Court of Cassation of 16 October, 1919 (3 cases, *Belgique Judiciaire*, 1919, cols. 1302 *et seq.*; *Pasicrisie belge*, 1919, vol. I, p. 225 *et seq.*; 47 *Clunet* (1920), p. 726 [decision incorrectly dated 26 October]), and of 4 December, 1919 (second case, *Pasicrisie belge*, 1920, vol. I, p. 1). For the same reasons the Civil Tribunal of Liège (*Godin* v. *Godin*, 26 January, 1920, *Pasicrisie belge*, 1920, vol. III, p. 168; *Belgique Judiciaire*, 1920, col. 133 and Note) was declared "without jurisdiction to take cognisance on appeal of "cases brought before it in application of German legislation."

These decisions illustrate an important development in the case-law of the Court of Cassation. While maintaining the legality of these arbitral tribunals and the obligatory character of their decisions, they refuse to assimilate the measures taken by the occupying Power to those emanating from the exercise of the national sovereignty. The Court of Appeal of Liège had already at an earlier date declared that "orders of the occupying Power do not constitute part of the national "system of law, which alone can be taken into consideration and whose "sanctions alone can be examined by Belgian courts—courts the status "of which has not been affected by the occupation" (7 May, 1919, *Belgique Judiciaire*, 1919, col. 1099). See also a decision of the same Court (19 February, 1919, *Pasicrisie belge*, 1919, vol. II, p. 45) declaring "that it was not for the administrative officials nor for the judicial "authorities to secure the execution of ordinances of the occupying "Power, which are essentially different from the national legislation "and can in no way be assimilated to it."

A decision of the Court of Cassation of 20 May, 1916, had admitted, on the contrary, that by reason of the ratification of the Hague Convention by the Belgian Law of 25 May, 1910, orders of the occupying Power made in virtue of Article 43 of the annexed Regulations derived from that law the same obligatory force as Belgian laws (*Pasicrisie belge*, 1915-1916, vol. I, p. 375; *Belgique Judiciaire*, 1919, cols. 148 *et seq.*). See on this award the observations and notes in *Belgique Judiciaire*, 1919, cols. 116 *et seq.* It is to be noted that in accordance with this decision of 4 December, 1919, the officials of the Court were forbidden to issue, with a view to execution, copies of decisions given by the courts set up by the occupying Power, on the ground that such a step would tend to attribute a legal character to " acts of force alien " to the national sovereignty " (*Official circular of* 6 *December*, 1919, *Belgique Judiciaire*, 1920, col. 12).

Legislation by Occupying Power—Effect on National Public Law—Conflict with Article 43 of Regulations annexed to Hague Convention No. IV of 1907. **Case No. 326**

COMMUNE OF GRACE-BERLEUR *v.* COLLIERY OF GOSSON LAGASSE AND ASSOCIATES.

COLLIERY OF GOSSON LAGASSE AND ASSOCIATES *v.* COMMUNE OF JEMEPPE.

Belgium, Court of Cassation. 29 *July*, 1919.

THE FACTS.—An Order of the German Governor-General, dated 3 December, 1914, had made resolutions of Communal Councils levying communal taxes subject to the approval of the Occupying Power, thus modifying the Belgian Law of 4 August, 1914. The Colliery Gosson Lagasse, having been ordered by the Court of Liège (25 July, 1917) to pay certain taxes imposed by the Commune of Jemeppe for the financial year 1913, appealed against the order on the ground, *inter alia*, that the approval of the German Governor was not given until 10 June, 1915, and contested the validity of the decision of the Court of Liège as violating the principle of the yearly character of the tax.

Held: That the appeal must be dismissed, seeing that on the question of the legality of the taxes the approval (of the German Governor-General) was immaterial. The Belgian Law of 4 August, 1914, on the subject of the delegation of powers, had provided that resolutions of Communal Councils levying communal taxes should be subject to the approval of Provincial Governors or, in their absence, the approval of the " permanent deputations." The German Order of 3 December, 1914, above referred to, which repealed this law and substituted the approval of the Occupying Power for that of the national authorities, cannot be regarded as a measure for restoring and assuring public order and safety in the occupied territory within the meaning of Article 43 of the Regulations annexed to the Hague Convention No. IV of 1907. [Report: *Pasicrisie belge*, 1919, vol. I, p. 199.]

Case No. 326 *contd.*

NOTE.—Although Belgian courts have, as a general rule, declared that they have no jurisdiction to interpret treaty provisions when the interests of the Belgian Government or relations between States are in question (Belgian Court of Cassation, 9 January, 1911, *Pasicrisie belge*, 1911, vol. I, p. 78 ; Ch. de Visscher, in *R.I.*, 1922, pp. 331 *et seq.*), they have always assumed the right to interpret the Hague Convention No. IV of 1907 (see Cases Nos. 325, 326). In fact, a judicial interpretation of this Convention is almost inevitable, as this Convention, as the Court of Appeal of Liège remarks (13 February, 1917, 44 *Clunet* (1917), p. 1809), only " produces its full effects at the time when diplo- " matic relations between the interested parties are broken off and a " common and amicable interpretation has become impossible."

Case No. 327

Legislative Measures of Occupying Power—German Order of 8 August, 1918—Validity—Article 43 of the Regulations annexed to Hague Convention No. IV of 1907.

BOCHART *v.* COMMITTEE OF SUPPLIES OF CORNEUX.

Belgium, Court of Appeal of Liège. 28 *February*, 1920.

THE FACTS.—The Order of 8 August, 1918, of the German Governor-General in Belgium declared void all purchases of vegetables not yet gathered. In the present case the appellant sued for the execution of a contract of this kind, basing his claim on the illegality of the German Order.

Held : That the contract is void, in accordance with the German Order " the legality and obligatory force of which it " would be idle to dispute . . . having regard to the tenor of " the Order and to the circumstances in which it was made." In fact, the occupying Power, even if it may have contemplated the possibility of a personal profit for its own nationals, nevertheless took its action with a view to regulating and diminishing the exorbitant price of vegetables. It acted in the place of the legitimate authority which for the time being had been ousted, and in conformity with the provisions of Article 43 of the Hague Convention. [Report: *Pasicrisie belge*, 1920, vol. II, p. 209.]

NOTE.—See in regard to this German Order similar decisions of the Court of Liège of 4 June, 1919 (*Pasicrisie belge*, 1919, vol. II, p. 137), of 25 June, 1919 (*ibid.*, 1920, vol. II, p. 208), and of 21 February, 1920 (*ibid.*, 1920, vol. II, p. 112). In a contrary sense, see Case No. 328.

Legislative Measure of Occupying Power—German Order of 8 August, 1918—Invalidity—Article 43 of Regulations annexed to Hague Convention No. IV. **Case No. 328**

DE BRABANT AND GOSSELIN *v.* T. AND A. FLORENT.

Belgium, Court of Appeal of Brussels. 22 July, 1920.

THE FACTS.—See Case No. 327 (*Bochart* v. *Committee of Supplies of Corneux*).

Held: That the German Order of 8 August, 1918, was not made with a view to assuring public order and security, but to starving the population. It went beyond the powers given to the occupant by Article 43 of the Hague Convention; it never had the force of law and cannot therefore avoid an agreement properly concluded by the parties. [Report: *Pasicrisie belge*, 1921, vol. II, p. 182, which gives only a summary of the decision.]

NOTE.—See in regard to this Order the decisions of the Civil Tribunal of Huy of 19 April, 1919 (*Pasicrisie belge*, 1919, vol. III, pp. 179 and 192), and of 20 January, 1920 (*ibid.*, 1920, vol. III, p. 59). In the contrary sense, see Case No. 327 (*Bochart* v. *Committee of Supplies of Corneux*).

Legislative Measure of Occupying Power—German Order of 8 August, 1918—No Part of National Legislation—Incompetence of National Tribunals to Interpret the Order and to Secure its Application. **Case No. 329**

MATHOT *v.* LONGUÉ.

Belgium, Court of Appeal of Liège. 19 February, 1921.

THE FACTS.—The German Order of 8 August, 1918, prohibited the sale of vegetables before they had been gathered. A bargain of this kind had been made by the parties in this case. Mathot not having performed the contract, Longué brought an action for rescission and damages, and was successful in the Court of First Instance. Mathot appealed. He based his case chiefly on the invalidity of the contract under the German Order of 8 August, 1918. Longué disputed the applicability of this Order in the present case, alleging that the contract did not relate to vegetables.

Held: That the appeal must be dismissed.

The Court declared that two issues were raised: (1) whether a Belgian court is competent to interpret an order of this kind

Case No. 329 ***contd.***

and to secure its application and execution; (2) whether the order in itself has any legal force whatsoever against a Belgian national.

As to the first point, it could not be admitted that a Belgian court or tribunal has any competence to interpret an act of a foreign authority and still less to secure its execution.

As to the second point, the Court proceeded on the principle recognised by the Court of Cassation that the orders of the occupying Power are not laws, but simply commands of the military authority of the occupant (see Case No. 325 and Note). The Court rejected the contention of the appellant that as the Belgian Law of 25 May, 1910, ratifying the conventions and declarations annexed to the final act of the Peace Conference (1907), provided that these conventions and declarations have full effect in Belgium, the orders of the occupying Power, which are not laws but merely commands of the military authority, nevertheless become Belgian laws which the Belgians must respect: "This inference, logically and legally inadmissible, "is based on a false premise—that is to say, the admission "... that Article 43 of the Hague Convention conferred upon "the occupying Power a positive right to legislate; but ... "it is inaccurate to say that by virtue of the Convention the "occupant has been given any portion whatever of the legis- "lative power; ... it appears from the text of the Convention "itself and from the preliminary work that all that was "intended ... was to restrict the abuse of force by the occupant "and not to give him or recognise him as possessing any "authority in the sphere of law." The law remains the apanage of the national authority exclusively, the occupant possessing *de facto* power and nothing more. It follows from this that the Belgian Law of 1910 could not and did not recognise the *de facto* power of the occupant as having the right to legislate.

Moreover, to admit that the occupying Power has any right to legislate ... would be to create very possibly and frequently an insoluble conflict between the decrees of the legal authority and those issued by the *de facto* power; this is inadmissible as being contrary to the absolute character of sovereignty. It followed from these considerations that the Order of 8 August, 1918, emanating from a *de facto* power, had no legal value and could not acquire such value by virtue of the Belgian Law of 1910, and that the Belgian courts could not base their decisions on such a decree. On these grounds the Court, rejecting all arguments based on the German order, recognised the validity of the contract and confirmed the original judgment given against the appellant. [Report: *Belgique Judiciaire*, 1921, cols. 438 *et seq.*]

NOTE.—This case marks the reversal of the current of decisions followed up till then by the Court of Liège in regard to the German order of 8 August, 1918: see Case No. 327, and the award of 23 June, 1920 (*Pasicrisie belge*, 1920, vol. II, p. 220, concerning the German order of 10 June, 1917). But it is of more general interest also. It contains the complete and logical development of the fundamental principle laid down by the Court of Cassation in its judgment of 20 May, 1916 (*Belgique Judiciaire*, 1919, cols. 167 *et seq.*; see also Case No. 325 and Note), all the consequences of which it seemed to admit, namely, that "the orders of "the occupying Power are not laws, that they could not be more than "commands of the military authority of the occupant." In spite of this principle, the Court of Cassation had recognised the obligatory effect of the orders of the occupant on the basis of the Belgian law ratifying the Hague Conventions; and had even declared itself incompetent to pronounce on the legality of these orders under Article 43 of the Regulations annexed to Convention No. IV. This decision of the Court of Liège rejects the argument based on the law ratifying the Convention, observing that this Convention does not imply that the occupant has any power over law, even within the limits fixed by Article 43. In so doing it puts aside as irrelevant for determining the legal value of these measures all considerations based on their conformity or otherwise with the Hague Conventions. From this latter point of view it dissociates itself entirely from most of the decisions given on this question. See the Note of M. Ch. Mons on this award, *Belgique Judiciaire*, 1921, cols. 441 *et seq.*

Courts Established by Occupying Power—Arbitral Tribunals as to Rent—Unfair Procedure—Invalidity of Judgments Rendered. **Case No. 330**

VERDYCK *v.* VONCKEN.

Belgium, Civil Tribunal of Antwerp. 7 *May*, 1920.

THE FACTS.—In execution of a decision (12 October, 1915) of the special arbitral tribunal on questions of rent established by the occupying Power (see Case No. 325), the defendant had seized and sold the furniture of the plaintiff, who was a refugee abroad at the time. After the war the plaintiff brought an action for damages against the defendant.

Held: The Tribunal ordered the defendant to pay damages. The judgment in virtue of which he had proceeded to sell the plaintiff's furniture was of no effect. It was true that the Court of Cassation, while maintaining that decisions given by such special arbitral tribunals have not the character of an act

Case No. 330 *contd.* emanating from a court established by the national legislation, affirms that these decisions are enforceable against the parties to the action (see Case No. 325). But a tenant who was abroad when the action was brought, and who was, and necessarily must have remained, a stranger to the proceedings taken against him, could not be regarded as a litigant party. Article 13 of the German order establishing these tribunals provides "that the "parties must appear in person before the arbitral tribunal." "This provision ignores the fundamental rules and principles "upon which modern civil procedure is based and which are "intended to secure the rights of the defence. . . ." The judgment therefore established no valid legal relation between the parties, and the decision of 12 October was merely a sham which cannot have any legal effect. [Report : *Pasicrisie belge*, 1920, vol. III, p. 156.]

Case No. 331

Courts Created by Occupying Power—German Tribunals in Belgium—Illegality of Judgments of.

SOCIÉTÉ SIEBERT *v.* BURM DE BELIE.

Belgium, Commercial Tribunal of Antwerp. 2 *May*, 1919.

THE FACTS.—The "Imperial District Court" (*Kaiserliches Bezirksgericht*) established at Antwerp by the German Governor-General gave judgment, on 31 July, 1918, against the defendant for payment of a certain sum by way of demurrage. The Commercial Tribunal of Antwerp ordered the plaintiffs in the original action, in default of appearance, to repay the amount. The plaintiffs in the original action before the Antwerp Court, through their sequestrators, moved to have this judgment set aside.

Held : That the motion fails. The Imperial District Court was a "court established by the enemy in opposition to the "courts of the country and in violation of international law." The decision "being illegal," the defendant was justified in claiming the restitution with interest of the amount paid. [Report : *Pasicrisie belge*, 1919, vol. III, p. 183.]

NOTE.—See in the same sense the judgment of the Correctional Tribunal of Ghent of 2 April, 1919 (*Public Prosecutor* v. *B. J. and R.* ; *Pasicrisie belge*, 1920, vol. III, p. 50), declaring that the Court had been set up illegally, "since the ordinary courts were competent," and denying legal authority to its decisions. See also the decision of the Court of Appeal of Liège of 7 February, 1919 (*Pasicrisie belge*, 1919, vol. II, p. 44).

Administrative Act of Occupying Power—Appointment of Judge—Lack of Authority—National Courts without Jurisdiction on Appeal. **Case No. 332**

ADRIAENSSENS *v.* *MINISTÈRE PUBLIC.*

Belgium, Police Court of Antwerp. 14 *May*, 1919.

THE FACTS.—This was an appeal against a decision dated 15 March, 1918, given by one H. Q., appointed by the occupying Power to sit as a magistrate at the Antwerp Police Court.

Held : That the Court had no jurisdiction. It was incompetent to decide an appeal from a judgment which was not given by a Belgian judge regularly appointed. The occupying Power had no right to interfere in the judicial business of the country. Having only a temporary power over the country, it could not confer upon a judge appointed by itself the security of tenure required by the constitution. Accordingly, H. Q. could not be regarded as a regularly appointed Belgian magistrate seeing that the occupying Power had excused the citizens whom it appointed to public offices from taking the political oath required by the Belgian Law of 18 June, 1869 (Articles 186 and 188) (Award of the Court of Cassation of 21 January, 1918 ; *Pasicrisie belge*, 1918, vol. I, p. 177). [Report : *Pasicrisie belge*, 1919, vol. III, p. 177.]

NOTE.—Similarly, the appointment of a notary by the occupying Power was declared void on the ground that it was contrary to the Hague Convention, and the execution of deeds before him was held to be a nullity (award of the Commercial Tribunal of Ghent of 22 January, 1921 ; *Clunet*, 49 (1922), p. 1038).

Military Occupation—Article 43 of the Hague Convention concerning the Laws and Customs of War on Land—Administrative Measures Taken by the Occupant—Removal of a Judge—Yugoslav Occupation of Carinthia. **Case No 333**

CARINTHIA (REMOVAL OF JUDGES) CASE.

Austria, Supreme Court in Civil Matters. 23 *April*, 1919. (*R. I* 56/19.)

THE FACTS.—At the end of November, 1918, one part of a district in Carinthia (Kärnten) was occupied by Yugoslav troops who removed the President of the District Court from his office and replaced him by a retired, formerly Austrian, judge. The latter gave

Case No. 333 *contd.*

judgment on 23 December, 1918, in a civil case without the parties raising objections to the jurisdiction of the Court. Several days later the Yugoslav troops were forced to withdraw and the former position in the organisation of the courts was restored. The defendant then appealed against the sentence rendered by the judge appointed by the Yugoslav authorities on the ground that the composition of the Court was not in accordance with the law. The Court of Appeal allowed the appeal on the ground that the judge appointed by the Yugoslav authorities did not subscribe to the oath of allegiance to the Republic of German Austria, and that therefore the composition of the Court was not in accordance with the law.

Held by the Supreme Court: That the decision of the Court of Appeal cannot stand. According to Article 43 of the Hague Convention concerning the laws and customs of war on land the occupant is entitled to take steps for the maintenance of public order and security. The judgment of the Court of First Instance was in accordance with this provision of the Hague Convention. [Report: *Entscheidungen des Obersten Gerichtshofes in Zivilrechtssachen,* vol. I (1919), No. 29, p. 103.]

Case No. 334

Occupation of Enemy Territory—Court Substituted for the Regular National Court by the Enemy—Article 43 of Hague Convention—Nullity in France of Judgments Rendered by a Court Irregularly Established by the Enemy.

In re X.

France, Court of Appeal of Nancy. 8 *January,* 1920.

The Facts.—The judges of the Court of First Instance of Briey and Longwy remained at their posts at the beginning of the German occupation. The German authorities subsequently relieved them of their functions and replaced them by a court established in the name of the German Empire. On 14 June, 1917, the woman X, charged with infanticide, was acquitted by a decision of this Court. When she was prosecuted anew for the same facts after the war, she contended that the German judgment ought to rank as a final decision and that she could not be tried a second time for the same offence.

Held: That the decision of 14 June, 1917, of the Court

created by the German authority could not produce any effect, direct or indirect, in France. The Court could not be recognised as having a legally constituted authority when the very object of its establishment was the suppression of the legally constituted court. Article 43 of the Hague Convention in no way authorised the occupying authorities to suppress in the occupied regions French courts which, so far from disturbing public order, safeguarded it. Moreover, the crime of infanticide is not among those reserved in principle by the law of war to the cognisance of the enemy as being likely to jeopardise the security of his army. [Reports: 47 *Clunet* (1920), p. 213; *Dalloz*, 1920, Part II, p. 415, with an unsigned note; *Gazette du Palais*, 1920, I, p. 1326.]

NOTE.—See also decision of the Court of Appeal of Douai of 15 May, 1919 (*Dalloz, ibid.*; 46 *Clunet* (1919), p. 770), holding for the same reasons that it was not for a French court to decide an appeal against a decision given by an enemy court in French occupied territory.

Occupation of Enemy Territory—Jurisdiction of Local Courts and of Military Tribunals—Article 43 of the Fourth Hague Convention—Occupation of the Left Bank of the Rhine—Question whether Conviction by Military Tribunal Prevents Further Prosecutions in the Local Courts. **Case No. 335**

RHINELAND OCCUPATION (JURISDICTION) CASE.

Germany, Reichsgericht in Criminal Matters. 23 *February*, 1920.

THE FACTS.—The accused was sentenced, on 3 March, 1919, by a British Court-Martial in the Rhineland to two years' imprisonment for being in possession of a loaded revolver and for threatening persons in order to induce them to part with money and provisions. The accused was then prosecuted in the same year by a German court for armed robbery and sentenced to five years' imprisonment. (It is not clear from the judgment in what way the accused came into the hands of the German civil authorities. Possibly he was handed over to them for the purpose of serving the sentence passed upon him by the Court-Martial.) The German Court admitted that the prosecution covered the same facts for which the accused had been previously sentenced by the Court-Martial, but was of the opinion that this did not prevent it from inflicting upon the accused a sentence for armed robbery. It was contended on behalf of the accused that in view of the consummated

Case No. 335 ***contd.***

proceedings before the British Court-Martial the German Court had no jurisdiction.

Held, on final appeal on a point of law: That German courts had jurisdiction and that the conviction must stand.

(*a*) The Armistice Agreement of 11 November, 1918, provided that the territory on the left bank of the Rhine should be administered by the local authorities under the supervision of the Allied Powers and of the United States. It did not say that the German courts shall be replaced by those of the occupying Powers. This was in accordance with Article 43 of the Regulations attached to the Fourth Hague Convention. Although the occupant is bound, except for compelling reasons, to leave intact the local courts, it may set up its own courts. According to international law the occupant may exercise through its own courts jurisdiction over the inhabitants in so far as this is necessary for the prosecution of criminal acts against the occupying Power, against the persons and property of the occupation authorities and of the army of occupation, or, generally, against the regulations issued for the security of the occupation. This was also recognised in Article 3 (*a*) of the Special Agreement relating to Article 428 of the Treaty of Versailles. Apart from these exceptions, the jurisdiction of local courts remains intact subject to the principle *ne bis in idem*.

(*b*) As to possible limitations arising from the application of the principle *ne bis in idem*, it must be remembered that the law applied by the courts set up by the army of occupation differs from local criminal law not only in regard to the source of its validity but in respect of its object—which is the security of the army and authorities of occupation. It is possible that the latter may create offences which are not recognised as such by municipal law. It may also happen that the criminal act is punishable by both systems of law, in which case the sentence of the court-martial precludes a further prosecution by the local court. However, there are possible cases of a mixed nature, *i.e.* arising out of offences which threaten in part the occupation (in the present case by carrying a loaded revolver) as such, and in part the normal life of the territory (in the present case by an act of armed robbery). In such cases the sentence of the court-martial punishes only part of the offence; the other part must be dealt with by the ordinary courts of the country. [Report: *E.R.S.*, vol. 54, p. 139.]

Power of Occupant to Alter Laws and Regulations—Repeal of Legal Moratorium by Occupant—Article 43 of Regulations Annexed to Hague Convention No. IV Respecting Laws of War on Land (1907)—German Occupation of Belgium—Jurisdiction of a Foreign Court in regard to Acts of Occupying Power. **Case No. 336**

CILLEKENS *v.* DE HAAS.

Holland, District Court of Rotterdam. 14 *May*, 1919.

(Dr. W. LUNSINGH TONCKENS, Single Chamber.)

THE FACTS.—By Decree of the King of the Belgians of 2 August, 1914, approved by the Law of 4 August, 1914, a moratorium was enacted up to 31 August, 1914, which was subsequently prolonged, for the last time by Decree of 21 January, 1915, for the whole duration of the war. On 5 January, 1916, the German Governor-General in Belgium issued an Order providing for the gradual abrogation of the moratorium, which was to cease on 8 November, 1916. This was an action of debt; the defendant recognised the plaintiff's claim, but invoked the moratorium. He maintained that the Governor-General's Order was illegal as being contrary to Article 43 of the Hague Regulations.

Held: For the plaintiff. The validity of the Order of the Governor-General results from Article 43 of the Regulations annexed to the Convention No. IV of 1907 concerning the Laws of War on Land, according to which the occupant is bound to take all steps in his power in order to re-establish and insure public order and safety in the occupied country, while respecting, unless absolutely prevented, the laws in force in the country. By the latter words the Article has clearly in view the laws which were in force before the war and not legal measures of a special character (such as a moratorium) taken during the war and in connection with it. Even if that were otherwise, it would in any case be in the interest of public order and safety to restrict the moratorium to the shortest possible term. At the moment of the repeal of the moratorium it was impossible to foresee the end of the occupation of the larger part of Belgium, so that it might have been desirable not to wait till the end of the war to terminate the moratorium. Consequently, this measure may be considered to have served the re-establishment and insurance of public order and safety in Belgium, and be considered as lawful. [Report: *Weekblad van het Recht*, 3 November, 1919, No. 10474.]

Case No. 337 **Occupation of Enemy Territory—Legislative Functions of the Occupant—Continuance of the Existing Laws—Articles 44 and 45 of the Hague Convention.**

REPUBLIC *v.* WEISHOLC.

Poland, Supreme Court, Second Division (*Full Meeting*).
17 *October*, 1919.

THE FACTS.—The defendant was convicted in 1919 by the District Court of Plock of having co-operated, during the German occupation of the (Congress) Kingdom of Poland in the World War, as a secret agent with the German Field Police in persecuting Polish social and political organisations and individual citizens, and further with having denounced certain individuals to the German police as Russian spies, thus causing their arrest. It was established, *inter alia*, that the defendant had been a confidential agent of the German police in the matter of local political conditions.

The Court of Appeal of Warsaw, on appeal, while reducing the sentence, confirmed the conviction, which it described as one for "having, as a Polish citizen, "co-operated with the German occupation authorities "in actions inimical to the Polish State and nation, to "wit, by being a paid agent of the German secret field "police, the purpose of which was to spy upon and "persecute all expressions of political life in Poland, "and of having in that capacity furnished the occupa-"tion authorities with information as to local political "conditions." The Court of Appeal held that the relevant Articles of the Russian Criminal Code were in force in Poland during the German occupation, since they were in force at the time when the occupation began; that "under the principles of the law of "nations, the territories which are occupied by the "enemy during the war do not cease to belong to the "State of which they had formed part before such "occupation, until special international treaties, or the "course of history, for instance the coming into exist-"ence of a new State even though not yet formally "recognised by other States, either make such terri-"tories part of the occupying State or make of them "an independent State. . . ." For the purpose of the present case it was enough to establish that throughout the World War the territory in which Weisholc had committed his acts did not form part of Germany. Under Part III of the Hague Convention, the occupant must respect the laws in force in the occupied territory unless this be absolutely impossible (Article 43), and must not compel the inhabitants either to give information about the army of the enemy (Article 44) or to take an oath of allegiance to the occupant (Article 45). The German occupation was throughout inimical and not allied, since allied occupation may take place only by the consent of the State to which the occupied territory belongs; but such consent had been granted neither by the supreme power of the Russian State nor subsequently by the supreme power of the Polish State. The German authorities could not repeal the relevant Articles of the Penal Code, although they could and did suspend their application by declaring that these Articles, among others, would not be applied. The Court held, moreover, that while the Articles in question spoke of Russian citizens, it was precisely as Russian citizens that Polish citizens were, in the period in question, protected by international law. On appeal to the Supreme Court,

Held, dismissing the appeal and repeating the arguments of the Court of Appeal, set out above: That the German occupying authorities neither could, under Article 43 of the Hague Rules, nor did repeal the Articles in question of the Russian Penal Code, and that "criminal acts, threatened with penalties in "laws . . . which are suspended by the enemy who occupies "the country but which are not legally repealed, and which "later are restored to practical application, may and should "be . . . punished. . . . This general principle is all the more "right and obvious in cases of high treason, since if any other "interpretation were adopted citizens might during every "invasion by an enemy betray with impunity, for his benefit, "their own country, as soon as that enemy had ordered and "proclaimed the repeal of the binding force of old laws, or the "suspension of their application." [Report: Zb. O.S.N., 1919, No. 65.]

NOTE.—See, for a discussion of the case, Roth, *Die Entstehung des polnischen Staates*, 63, 64; and Berezowski, in *Gazeta Administracji i Policji Państwowej*, 1924.

Case No. 338 **Occupation of Enemy Territory—Functioning of Courts in the Occupied Territory—Crimes Committed in Occupied Territory—Sentence by Courts of Occupying Power—Validity of Rule of *ne bis in idem*.**

REPUBLIC *v.* OFICYŃSKI.

Poland, Supreme Court, Third Division. 28 *October*, 1921.

THE FACTS.—The province of Galicia, which until 1918 formed part of Austria, was in part occupied in 1914 by Russian forces. The Austrian courts continued to function during the occupation. The defendant, after having been kept in gaol for a year pending investigation, was convicted by a court in Russia of murder committed in Galicia, and was sentenced to prison, where he served (in Russia) three years. After returning to his native place, where Polish authority was now established, he was convicted in 1921 on the same facts, by the District Court of Zloczów, of murder, and sentenced to death, the penalty being commuted to one of ten years' penal servitude. The Court directed that the four years spent in the Russian prison should be counted as service of part of the ten years' sentence. The defendant appealed to the Supreme Court, pleading that under international treaties the occupant is bound to maintain order in the occupied territory and that, since the occupant had given judgment in the case, the case could not be judged again by other courts without violating the principle *ne bis in idem.*

Held : That the appeal must be dismissed. Under Article 43 of the Hague Rules of Land Warfare, the occupant has the right to take steps aiming at the restoration and maintenance of public order and safety and respecting the laws in force unless prevented by insurmountable difficulties. He has no right to try, by his own courts and within his own territory, crimes committed within the occupied territory. It is, therefore, not necessary for the purposes of the present case to decide whether criminal judgments given by courts organised by the occupant on occupied territory must be unconditionally and always recognised, even after the occupation has come to an end, by the State whose territory has been occupied, and whether such judgments must be considered as definitely settling the cases in question. The judgment in this case having been given in Moscow, although Austrian courts had continued to function with the consent and under the supervision of the occupant in the territory in question, it must be considered as a foreign judgment, both as regards Austria and as regards Poland. Consequently, Polish courts were now competent to decide the present case. [Report : O.S.P., I, No. 473.]

Occupation of Enemy Territory—Article 43 of the Fourth Hague Convention—American Occupation of Coblenz.

See Case No. 305 (*Armistice Agreement* (*Coblenz*) *Case*).

Occupation of Enemy Territory—Judicial Authority—Existing Courts Presided over by Judges Nationals of the Occupying Power—Capitulatory Régime in Occupied Territory.

See Case No. 318 (*Boliotti* v. *Masse*).

iii.—Respect of Private Property. The Public Property of the Enemy State. Requisitions and Contributions

Requisitions—Validity of—Articles 52 and 53 of the Hague Regulations—Article 297 (*e*) of Treaty of Versailles—Place where " Exceptional War Measures " taken—Requisitions for Purposes other than the Needs of the Army of Occupation—Invalidity of Requisitions or Duty of Compensation ? **Case No. 339**

TESDORPF *v.* GERMAN STATE.

Anglo-German Mixed Arbitral Tribunal. 8 *November*, 1922, *and* 25 *April*, 1923.

(BOREL, VAUGHAN WILLIAMS, ZACHARIAS.)

THE FACTS.—This was a claim under Article 297 (*e*) of the Treaty of Versailles, which provided for compensation to be paid by Germany for damage caused by exceptional war measures taken by her with regard to property rights and interests in German territory as it existed on 1 August, 1914. At the outbreak of war the claimants had 1595 bags of coffee stored at Antwerp, where they were, in February, 1916, requisitioned by the German Fortress Governor of Antwerp. No receipt was given and no payments were made either to the owners of the coffee or of the warehouse. The coffee was then conveyed to Altona in Germany, where it was valued and distributed to various units of the

Case No. 339 *contd.*

German army. On behalf of the German State it was contended that the Tribunal had no jurisdiction on the ground that the coffee was requisitioned by the military authorities in Belgium; that the plaintiffs were thus deprived of their property in Belgium (and not in German) territory; and that the claim did not therefore fall under the provisions of Article 297 (*e*) of the Treaty. The plaintiffs contended that as no correct receipt was given for the coffee and as no price was paid for the goods taken away, the action of the German authorities could not be considered a lawful requisition under Articles 52 and 53 of the Regulations attached to the Fourth Hague Convention; that that action did not therefore cause the immediate expropriation of the goods in question; and that the goods were carried to and distributed in Germany while they were still the property of the plaintiffs.

Held: That the Tribunal had no jurisdiction.

(*a*) The military character of the requisitions which took place at Antwerp was sufficiently shown by the facts and circumstances of the case.

(*b*) While the seizures covered by Article 53 of the Regulations had no effect with regard to the passing of property in the articles seized (that Article providing expressly for the restoration at the end of the war of the articles seized), Article 52, relating to requisitions *in specie,* contemplated their immediate appropriation.[1] Such immediate appropriation is not excluded by the fact that the goods were not immediately valued and paid for.

(*c*) The Tribunal was not of the opinion that the seizure of goods at Antwerp was contrary to international law. There had undoubtedly been a certain misuse of the right of requisition by making the coffee available for parts of the German army other than those in the occupied territory. The fact that the limits laid down in Article 52 were disregarded cannot have the automatic effect of depriving the requisitions of their legal effect. There was no such sanction to be found in the Fourth Hague Convention, which merely provided that the State whose armies transgress the limits laid down in the Regulations is liable to indemnify. "The Tribunal are not of the opinion that "in the absence of an express provision avoiding wrongful acts,

[1] The Tribunal referred here to the clear provisions of Articles 415, 416 and 470 of the *Manual of Military Law* published by the British War Office (1914 edition).

" such a sanction is to be excluded altogether. This is a point " which must be decided according to the general rules and the " spirit of international law having regard to the actual cir- " cumstances of each case " (at p. 27). In the present case, having regard to the fact that the requisition took place for the needs of the army and with regard to stores of food warehoused in an important commercial seaport, the Tribunal did not consider that the circumstances of the requisition were such as to render it void in international law. [Report : *Recueil*, III (1924), p. 22.]

Occupation of Enemy Territory—Requisitions—Legal Nature of Requisition—Whether Conferring Title for the Transfer of Property—Articles 46, 52 and 53 of Hague Convention No. IV. **Case No. 340**

SALE OF REQUISITIONED OBJECT (CZECHOSLOVAKIA) CASE.

Czechoslovakia, Supreme Court of Justice.
12 *September*, 1922. (*No. R. II* 70.)

THE FACTS.—The Austro-Hungarian occupation military forces in Roumania requisitioned in November, 1917, an electric dynamo belonging to the plaintiff (a Roumanian firm). In July, 1918, the machine in question was sold by the Austro-Hungarian military administration to the defendant (a Czechoslovak firm). The plaintiff, the owner of the machine, claimed its restitution.

Held by the Court of First Instance : For the defendant. It may be agreed that no one can transfer to another more rights than he himself possesses. The main point at issue is whether or not the Austro-Hungarian military administration acquired, by the requisition, the property in the machine in question. This question must be answered in the affirmative, as it was proved that the requisition of the machine was effected in full conformity with the provisions of Article 52 of the Rules of the Hague Convention concerning laws and customs of war on land. Accordingly, the Austro-Hungarian military administration acquired the property in the machine and was entitled to sell it to the defendant.

Held by the Court of Appeal : For the plaintiff. The Opinion of the Court of First Instance, according to which the Austro-Hungarian military administration had acquired, by the requisition, the property in the machine, was erroneous.

Case No. 340 *contd.*

Article 46 in No. IV of the Conventions concluded at The Hague in 1899 and 1907, which, through the ratification by the Austro-Hungarian Monarchy and through the promulgation in the official collection of laws, became a source of law for its subjects, declares that private property in the occupied territory cannot be confiscated. Article 52 of the same Convention provides that requisitions in kind shall not be demanded from municipalities or individuals except for the needs of the occupying army. It appears from these provisions that where objects which cannot be consumed are concerned it is not possible to requisition the property in them, but only the use of them, as in that case the occupying army needs only their use and not their substance. In the same way as a house which has been requisitioned by the occupying army does not become its property by an adaptation or a partial reconstruction for the purposes of the occupying military forces, so also a machine cannot pass, by the requisition, into the property of the occupying forces. This Opinion is also confirmed by the provisions of Article 53 of the same Convention. Accordingly, a requisition calculated to effect a transfer of property is not permissible. It is unable in law to effect the transfer of the right of property.

Held by the Supreme Court of Justice: For the defendant. The comparison between a house and a machine, from which the Court of Appeal started, is not conclusive, as a house is an immovable object and a machine a movable one. Accordingly, the conclusions drawn from this comparison are not correct. The question whether the object can be consumed or not is not relevant for the decision whether a requisition gives rights of property or merely a right of use. Also, it is impossible to agree with the conclusions of the Court of Appeal drawn from Articles 46, 52 and 53 of the Hague Convention. Article 46 prohibits confiscation of private property, but requisition is not a confiscation (this appears from the fact that requisitions are dealt with separately in Article 52). Article 53 concerns seizure of public and of certain private property, which seizure is also different from requisition. Requisition in its literal meaning is identical with "demand," and this demand has, according to the law, the effect that the owner of the object demanded is obliged to comply with the demand and to deliver the object to the demanding authority, which, in turn, is obliged to pay in cash for the requisitioned object or to deliver a receipt (see Article 52, last paragraph, of the Hague Convention). From this latter requirement (payment in cash) it appears that the Opinion of the Court of Appeal that requisition gives only the use of the requisitioned object was not correct. Requisition is to be considered as a bilateral contract, *i.e.* a contract of sale, in which the absence of consent of the one contracting party (the owner who refused voluntarily to give his consent) is supplemented by a positive provision of the law. Requisition is, therefore, in legal analysis, a forced sale. The Court of Appeal, in order to substantiate its Opinion that the property cannot be requisitioned but only the use of the object, has referred to Article 52 of the Hague Convention, according to which requisitions can be demanded only for the purposes of the occupying army. However, this conclusion is not correct, as an object serves the purposes of the occupying army in the same way whether the property therein or only the use of it has been requisitioned. [Report: Váž. 1833 civ.]

NOTE.—Also discussed: (*a*) Binding force of the Treaty of Peace of St. Germain with regard to the Czechoslovak municipal sphere; (*b*) Binding force of the same Treaty as between Czechoslovakia and Roumania; (*c*) Article 249 of the same Treaty.

Law of War—Enemy Occupation—Act of Occupying Authority —Confiscation *quoad usum*. **Case No. 341**

PERKONS *v.* MEZDREJS.

Latvia, Senate. 22 September, 1922.

THE FACTS.—A farm belonging to the plaintiff was confiscated *quoad usum* during the war by the German occupation authorities as a punitive measure, the body of a murdered German soldier having been found on the premises. The occupation authorities subsequently leased the farm to a third person, during whose lease a foal was born out of a mare belonging to the farm live-stock. The foal, being in accordance with local law the property of the lessee, was sold by him to the defendant. The plaintiff claimed restitution of the foal on the ground that the confiscation of the farm was illegal. On the rejection of his claim by the Court of First Instance, the plaintiff appealed to the Senate.

Held by the Senate: That the decision must be affirmed. The measure taken was provoked by the hostile attitude of the local population towards the German occupation authorities. Such measures were to be considered as "*nécessité de guerre*,"

Case No. 341 *contd.*

which may be contrary to "*Kriegsmanier*." The general rules as to the competence of administrative bodies in time of peace, or the principle of criminal law that an individual is responsible only for himself, have no application in these cases. "All these "principles, true though they are, are inapplicable in time "of war and especially in relations between an occupying "authority and the inhabitants of an occupied province." In time of war not only a foreign Power but even the national Government may impose responsibility for the acts of other people, by inflicting, for instance, a money fine on a whole parish for destruction of telegraph or telephone wires without identifying the guilty person. "An occupying Power is forced "to an even greater degree to take determined and strong "action against the hostile population of an occupied province, "in order to maintain its authority and to secure its military "and civil rule and its army. The idea of war is in itself based "on the responsibility of the whole nation for the acts of a "part of it." [Report: *Senata civila kasacijas departamenta spriedumi*, 1922, p. 123.]

Case No. 342

Warfare on Land—Occupation of Enemy Territory—Respect for Private Property—Requisitions and Contributions.

SIUTA *v.* GUŻKOWSKI.

Poland, Supreme Court, Third Division. 15 *February*, 1921.

THE FACTS.—In February, 1919, while the Ukrainian forces were holding the district of Mościska, some of their representatives took certain horses out of the defendant's stable and sold them at once by public auction. The plaintiff purchased two of the horses. After the cessation of hostilities, the police took the two horses from the plaintiff and restored them to the defendant as the latter's stolen property. The plaintiff brought an action against the defendant, who pleaded that the plaintiff was a purchaser in bad faith since he knew that the action of the Ukrainians was illegal. The local court at Mościska gave judgment for the plaintiff, stating that the Ukrainian action was in law an act of requisitioning of private property by enemy forces (Article 52 of the Hague Rules), and thus deprived the defendant of his title to the requisitioned goods and made it possible for the plaintiff to acquire the property at a public auction.

The District Court of Przemyśl allowed the appeal of the defendant and dismissed the action, since under the Hague Rules requisitions in kind and of services are permissible only in order to satisfy the needs of the occupying army. It appears by contrast with this "cardinal principle of international custom" that nothing may be requisitioned except for the needs of the occupying forces, and that any act divesting inhabitants of their property as in the present case is illegal, since taking horses out of a stable and selling them to the local inhabitants has nothing to do with the needs of the army and any one purchasing horses in such circumstances must be considered as acting in bad faith. On appeal to the Supreme Court,

Held: That the judgment of the Court of Przemyśl was good in law and must be confirmed. [Report: O.S.P., I, No. 230.]

(For a discussion of the case see Rundstein, *ibid.*, 212-214, n. 1.)

NOTE.—The judgments of all three courts interpret both the Hague Rules of Land Warfare and the (Austrian) Civil Code, without discussing the question of the applicability of the Hague Rules to the Ukrainians, who were never recognised as belligerents or as insurgents.

Requisition—Article 52 or 53 of the Regulations annexed to Hague Convention No. IV of 1907—Requisition without a Requisition Receipt—Validity of—Passing of Property in Goods Requisitioned contrary to Article 52 or 53. **Case No. 343**

LAURENT *v.* LE JEUNE.

Belgium, Court of Cassation. 3 *March*, 1921.

THE FACTS.—The German troops had, on 22 August, 1914, taken a horse belonging to the plaintiff without giving him the receipt for a requisition required by Article 52 of the Hague Regulations. Finding the horse in the possession of the defendant, the plaintiff claimed restitution of his property before the Civil Tribunal of Arlon. That Court dismissed the action. The plaintiff then applied to the Court of Cassation, relying, *inter alia*, on the violation of Article 52 and on Article 2279 of the *Code Civil* so far as it authorises claims for the return of stolen goods. The representative of the Government, while supporting the claim to have the decision quashed, argued from the preparatory work of the Hague Con-

Case No. 343 ***contd.***

vention of 1907 (see Report of the Second Commission on amendments to the Regulations of 1899 concerning the laws and customs of war on land, *The Reports to the Hague Conferences of* 1899 *and* 1907, Oxford, 1917, p. 527) that the Article of this Convention which really applied was rather Article 53 concerning " all appli-" ances . . . adapted . . . for the transport of persons " or things. . . ."

Held : That the judgment of the Court below dismissing the claim must be quashed. It was immaterial whether there was a requisition not in accordance with the provisions of Article 52 or a seizure under Article 53 of the Regulations annexed to the Hague Convention. According to the findings, implied at any rate, of the judgment of the Court below, the plaintiff Laurent had received neither a requisition receipt nor payment nor restitution of his horse. The plaintiff had lost his property by an act of force against which he could not protect himself. The grounds on which the law admitted a claim for the return of stolen property applied exactly to the facts of the case. [Report : *Pasicrisie belge,* 1921, vol. I, p. 277.]

War on Land—Occupation of Enemy Territory—Respect of Private Property—Requisitions—Article 52 of the Fourth Hague Convention—Effect of Requisitions in the Field of Private Law.

In consequence of conflicting decisions as to the legal effect of requisitions effected by the Roumanian authorities during the occupation of Hungarian territory in 1919 (see the cases in the Supreme Court of Hungary—all reported *Polgarijogi Hatarozatok Tara,* III, p. 425—of *Vince* v. *Tompai,* 14 December, 1920; *Joo* v. *Kovacs,* 24 May, 1921; and *Fogelzinger* v. *Pinter,* 22 June, 1921), the Hungarian Supreme Court on 27 March, 1922, adopted a resolution to the effect that requisitions effected in time of occupation are to be regarded as unlawful if it appears from the circumstances that the purpose of the requisition was not to satisfy the needs of the occupying army but merely to compensate third persons affected by previous requisitions. The Court referred to Article 46 of the Hague Regulations laying down the principle of respect of private property, and to Article 47 prohibiting pillage. The Court stated that as a requisition constitutes an infringement of private property it must be interpreted restrictively, that is to say, that a requisition cannot be regarded as lawful if it is not made for the purpose expressly specified in Article 52 of the Hague Regulations.

Requisitions—Article 52 of the Fourth Hague Convention—Disregard of—Necessity and Self-Preservation—German Requisitions in Belgium.

See Case No. 296 (*German Requisitions (Necessity and Self-Preservation) Case*).

Requisitions—Alien Enemies—Articles 44, 49 and 52 of the Fourth Hague Convention.

See Case No. 171 (*Rymenans & Co.* v. *Germany*).

Requisitions—Capture of Maritime Property on Land—Article 53 of the Fourth Hague Convention.

See Case No. 344 (*The Anichab*).

iv.—Inhabitants. Services. Deportations. Hostages

Occupation of Enemy Territory—Position of Aliens Resident in the Occupied Territory before its Occupation by the Enemy—Subjection to French Law Concerning the Security of the French State.

See Case No. 162 (*In re Kirgis (Husband and Wife), Kaltenbach (Widow) and Others*).

C. WARFARE AT SEA

II.—Visit, Search, Capture and Destruction

(*a*) Of Enemy Merchantmen

Warfare at Sea—Capture of Maritime Property on Land—Article 53 of the Fourth Hague Convention—Whether Maritime Prize or Not—Hot Pursuit. **Case No. 344**

The Anichab.

England, the Prize Court, and the Privy Council on Appeal therefrom. 21 *July*, 1919; 13 *December*, 1921.

The Facts.—In the course of military operations by

Case No. 344 ***contd.***

British South African forces against German forces in German South-West Africa in 1914 and 1915 a launch, sixteen lighters and certain rope fenders used for the purposes of the trade of German liners were put on rail at German ports and moved up country to certain places distant 148 and 310 miles respectively from the coast. From six to nine months after the British occupation of these ports the places in the interior were captured by British military forces and the property above mentioned was seized, being found not afloat but ashore, the adjacent river not being passable.

The Procurator-General now asked for the condemnation of this (amongst other) property as good and lawful maritime prize, and the German owners of the property (the Woermann Line) claimed its release on the ground that, having been seized above high-water mark and up country, it could not be the subject of maritime seizure ; further, even assuming it to be war material, they as the owners claimed to be entitled to an indemnity under Article 53 of the Regulations annexed to the Fourth Hague Convention.

It was contended on behalf of the Crown that prize jurisdiction extends to goods brought on shore to avoid seizure (*Lindo* v. *Rodney* (1782), 2 Doug. 612 n., and *The Roumanian*, L.R. [1916] 1 A.C. 124), and that the British forces maintained a continuous and hot pursuit of the property until it was captured.

Held by the President (Lord Sterndale) : (*a*) That, while recognising, as was stated by Lord Parker in *The Roumanian* (*supra*), " that if property is liable to seizure at sea, and the " enemy succeeds in getting ashore and escaping with his " property, the belligerent who is trying to capture it has a " right to pursue him and to take the property from him," there was no evidence in this case upon which it could be held that the property had been taken in the course and as the result of hot pursuit.

(*b*) The craft in question, though capable of being put into the water again, were at the time of their capture " property " on land. They are taken by the land forces in land operations, and therefore I do not think they are the subject of " maritime prize." Accordingly " they must be released from " the Prize Court."

(*c*) That, it being impossible to say that there was no

reasonable ground for the seizure of the property, this was not a case in which a Prize Court should award damages against the captor.

(*d*) That Article 53 of the Regulations annexed to the Fourth Hague Convention provided that "indemnities" for certain property seized on land should be "regulated at the "peace," that is to say, by diplomatic action. It was not for a Prize Court to settle these indemnities. [Reports: L.R. [1919] P. 329; 3 B. and C.P.C. 611.]

[The learned President condemned other German property seized at ports in German South-West Africa as good and lawful maritime prize.]

On appeal to the Privy Council the judgment was affirmed upon the same grounds as those stated above. [Reports: L.R. [1922] 1 A.C. 235; 3 B. and C.P.C. 993.]

(*b*) OF NEUTRAL MERCHANTMEN

Warfare at Sea—Destruction of Neutral Merchantmen—Rescue and Recapture of Neutral Ships—Attempted Destruction of Norwegian Vessels by German Submarines—Rescue by British Submarine—Civil Salvage—General Rule that no Salvage is Payable—Exceptions. **Case No. 345**

THE SVANFOS; THE BORGILA.

England, Admiralty Court.[1] 13 *May*, 1919.

THE FACTS.—In April, 1917, an enemy (German) submarine stopped and completely reduced into her power two neutral (Norwegian) merchant ships, the *Svanfos* and the *Borgila*. Being unable to take them into port, the enemy submarine was about to destroy them as prize of war in accordance with the practice then being followed by German submarines. At that moment a British submarine arrived on the spot and drove away the German submarine by fire, whereupon the *Svanfos* proceeded on her way and the *Borgila*, being in a disabled condition, was taken into the temporary possession of the British submarine and later handed over to the care of a Norwegian ship of war.

The plaintiffs, who were the commander, officers and crew of H.M. Submarine G 7, claimed awards of salvage in respect of the services rendered by them to

[1] See p. 43, footnote.

Case No. 345 *contd.*

the *Svanfos* and the *Borgila*. The defendants were the owners of the *Svanfos*, her cargo and freight, and the owners of the *Borgila*.

Held by Hill, J.: That the plaintiffs were entitled to awards of salvage in respect of the services rendered to each of the ships. "The general rule that no salvage is given on the "recapture of an innocent neutral ship is based on the pre- "sumption that no peril is incurred by the capture, because "the neutral ship will be carried into the courts of the captor "and there justice will be done according to international law, "and the innocent owner will recover his ship, or its value "and expenses. But the general rule has no application where "the State of the captor and its courts are notoriously out- "raging international law, and have made it apparent that "justice will not be done, and that in defiance of international "law the neutral ship will be condemned or its destruction "justified by the courts of the captor" (at p. 196). The learned judge referred to Sir Samuel Evans, P., in *The Pontoporos* (L.R. [1916] P. 100), to Lord Stowell in *The Sansom* (1807) (6 C. Rob, at p. 413) and to cases decided by English courts both before and after the Peace of Amiens.)

The *Borgila* was a case of capture followed by recapture, the *Svanfos* a case of capture followed by rescue; nevertheless, in both cases salvage services were rendered (see *The Edward and Mary* (1801) (3 C. Rob. 305)). [Reports: L.R. [1919] P. 189; 3 B. and C.P.C. 470.]

NOTE.—The ascertained total value of the *Svanfos* and her cargo and freight was £94,072 and of the *Borgila* was £78,000. The awards made were in the case of the *Svanfos* and her cargo and freight £1000, and in the case of the *Borgila* £1200. In the case of the *Borgila*, which was disabled, part of the salvage service (included in the above award) was of a purely maritime character.

Case No. 346

Visit, Capture and Search of Neutral Merchantmen—Lawfulness of Search in Port.

THE BERNISSE; THE ELVE.

England, Privy Council, on Appeal from the Prize Court. 16 *December*, 1920.

In an action brought by neutral shipowners against the British Procurator-General for damages for the loss of one neutral vessel and damage to another while proceeding into a British port under orders given by a British cruiser, the following observation was made *obiter* by Sir Arthur Channell in delivering the Opinion of the Privy Council (Present: Lords Sumner, Parmoor, Wrexbury and Sir Arthur Channell):

"In this war it has been agreed that search at sea has "been practically impossible, and sending into port for "search has been almost universal."

[Reports: L.R. [1921] 1 A.C. at p. 463; 3 B. and C.P.C. at p. 777.]

NOTE.—See also *Netherlands American Steam Navigation Co.* v. *H.M. Procurator-General*, L.R. [1926] 1 K.B. 84; *Annual Digest*, 1925-1926, Case No. 370.

IV.—Prize Law

i.—Nature and Extent of Jurisdiction in Prize Courts

Prize Law—Nature and Extent of Jurisdiction in Prize Courts —Border-Line between Maritime Prize and Property Seized on Land and subject to Fourth Hague Convention.

See Case No. 344 (*The Anichab*).

iii.—Indemnities and Damages

Case No. 347

Capture by German Navy and Confiscation in Prize of Neutral (Dutch) Vessel for Carriage of Contraband—Return of Vessel after the War into Dutch Territorial Waters—Civil Embargo by Former Owner—Effect of Decision of Prize Court—Respect of Foreign Judgment—Refusal to Enter into Examination of Merits of Judgment—Reparation by way of Diplomatic Intervention only—Articles 21 and 22 of the Hague Convention No. XII of 1907 Irrelevant.

N. V. ZEETJALK "DE HOOP," OF AMSTERDAM (plaintiff) *v.* (1) N. V. WIJNNE EN BARENDS' CARGADOORS- EN AGENTURKANTOREN, OF DELFZIJL (HOLLAND) (defendant); (2) N. V. HERMES' SCHEEPVAART-, HANDELSMAATSCHAPPIJ EN BANK, OF THE HAGUE (intervener).

Holland, District Court of Groningen. 10 *June*, 1921.

(Jhr. Dr. D. R. DE MAREES VAN SWINDEREN, President; Dr. F. J. LISMAN and Prof. H. VAN GOUDOEVER, Judges.)

THE FACTS.—On or about 31 December, 1917, the Dutch "tjalk" (barge) *De Hoop* was captured in the North

Case No. 347 *contd.*

Sea by a German man-of-war, brought into a German port and confiscated in prize by a German court for carrying contraband. Subsequently, when the vessel again entered into a Dutch port, the former Dutch owner laid an embargo on the vessel there and filed a suit against the new owner (the defendant), laying claim to the vessel, alleging, *inter alia,* that the decision of the German Prize Court had lost its effect after the vessel's return to Dutch jurisdiction; that this was the more so as the confiscation had clearly been pronounced illegally and on insufficient grounds, since the German prize law in the matter of carriage of contraband was contrary to the Law of Nations and since the cargo had not really been destined to the person designated in the ship's papers as the consignee; that Article 431 of the Dutch Code of Civil Procedure forbids the execution of foreign judgments, and that Articles 21 and 22 of the Hague Convention No. XII of 1907 concerning the rights and duties of neutral Powers in case of maritime war imply the right of those Powers to restore to its owners a vessel captured by one of the belligerents while flying the national flag of a neutral Power, which enters later on into neutral territorial waters.

Held: That Article 431 of the Code of Civil Procedure has no other scope than to forbid the execution of foreign judgments in the proper sense of this term, *viz.* by means of seizure of the debtor's goods, or his imprisonment, but that it does not impede the recognition, in Holland, of a legal situation, or of a legal effect, which might have been created by a foreign judgment, *in casu* the loss of property; that Articles 21 and 22 of the Hague Convention No. XII of 1907 only determine the rights and obligations of neutral and belligerent States during the war, but that they do not contain any provisions about private rights in time of peace; further, that the plaintiff's contention as to the illegal character of the decision of the German Prize Court could not help him, since the rules of positive international law imply that reparation for a wrong suffered by an illegal confiscation in prize can only be obtained by way of diplomatic negotiation. [Report: *Weekblad van het Recht,* 9 August, 1922, No. 10907.]

E. NEUTRALITY IN GENERAL

I.—Nature of Duties of Neutrality

Neutrality—Duties of Neutrality—Goods Acquired by Acts of War in Occupied Territory—Transfer to Subsequent Buyers—Transport to Neutral Country—Detention by Neutral Government. **Case No. 348**

Bouman *v.* The State of the Netherlands.

Holland, District Court of The Hague, First Chamber. 1 *February*, 1921.

(Dr. A. H. du Mosch, President; Drs. J. van Gelein Vitringa and O. W. Sipkes, Judges.)

The Facts.—On 18 November, 1918, shortly after the armistice on the Western front, a vessel called *The Mina* (which had formerly belonged to a Belgian shipowner, and after having passed later on into the hands of the German military authorities during the occupation of Belgium, under the name of *The Wilhelm*, had finally been sold to a Dutch vendee, who re-christened it *W. P. Bouman I*) crossed the Belgian-Dutch frontier on the Scheldt, in order to escape recapture by the Belgians. The Dutch military authorities sequestrated the vessel upon its crossing the frontier, on the presumption that it had been acquired by the later owners in consequence of an act of war, the Dutch Government acting on the principle that their duty as a Government of a neutral State was to impede such property from entering into the free traffic of a neutral country. The Dutch purchaser of the vessel brought an action for reparation of the damage suffered by him in consequence of the vessel's detention from 18 November, 1918, till 1 July, 1919.

Held: For the defendant. The defendant Government was justified in invoking in favour of their attitude their obligation as a neutral Government under the Law of Nations not to admit into the free traffic within their territory ships and goods acquired in consequence of acts of war, such as capture, or requisition in an occupied belligerent country. The status of neutrality obliges a Government strictly to abstain from any act favouring either of the belligerents. Accordingly,

Case No. 348 *contd.* goods acquired by acts of war may not be freely admitted within neutral jurisdiction. Such admission to free traffic in a neutral country would imply recognition of possession obtained by acts of war, would allow such acts to produce a continuous effect in neutral territory and, consequently, would come to a passive assistance in assuring definitive effect to such acquisition. This was the more the case as the vessel's crossing of the Dutch frontier coincided with the evacuation of Belgium by the occupying Power and the presumption was obvious that the possessors would try still to bring their newly-acquired goods in safety on to neutral territory. [Report: *Nederlandsche Jurisprudentie*, 1921, p. 851.]

NOTE.—The above decision has been confirmed by the Appellate Court of The Hague (President, Dr. Polvliet; Judges, Drs. Polak and Van Slooten): judgment of 5 January, 1925 (Report: *Nederlandsche Jurisprudentie*, 1925, p. 402). The Court of Appeal based its decision on identical grounds, stating that the duty of the Dutch Government during the World War to maintain its neutrality precluded it from admitting into the free traffic in Holland ships or goods acquired by their present possessors in consequence of acts of war, and *holding*, moreover: That this point of view had been taken by the Dutch Government from the outset, that it had also been published by it and respected by the belligerents during the war, and that the Government was bound to adhere to this line of conduct, once adopted; that the Government feared that, after the conclusion of the armistice in November, 1918, the Germans would try to carry off to Germany captured or requisitioned goods from Belgium via Dutch territory; that Article 18 of the Armistice Convention prohibited the export of German vessels from Belgium, and that, therefore, the Dutch Government had enacted that no vessels would be allowed to enter into Dutch territory without being provided with a declaration from a Dutch consul in Belgium stating that they had not been captured or requisitioned in occupied territory during the war, nor belonged to the military stock; that the vessel had been retained only in view of an enquiry into its property and origin, which was the more justifiable on account of the successive changes of its name, and that the detention had not lasted longer than was strictly necessary in order to get certainty about the vessel's adventures; that the State of the Netherlands was not liable to damages for this detention, since "private municipal law, even without express reference, "must be deemed to be ruled by the generally recognised principles "of the Law of Nations."

Duty of Neutral State—Analogous Duty in Time of Peace to Prevent Hostile Expedition for Revolutionary Object—Forfeiture of Ship under British Foreign Enlistment Act, 1870.

See Case No. 122 (*The Harrier*).

Neutrality—In General—Treaties Relating to Neutral Commerce—Interpretation of.

See Case No. 301 (*The Rannveig*).

Duty of Neutral State—Analogous Duty in Times of Peace—Hostile Expeditions—The Law of the United States.

See Case No. 123 (*Gayon* v. *McCarthy*).

F. CONTRABAND

II.—Carriage of Contraband and Doctrine of Continuous Voyage

Declaration of Paris, 1856, Article 2—Enures for Benefit of Enemy Cargo-Owner as well as Neutral Shipowner. **Case No. 349**

THE DIRIGO, THE HALLINGDAL, AND OTHER SHIPS.

England, the Prize Court.[1] 14 *April,* 1919.

In this group of cases, which do not require a detailed digest, it was *Held* by the President (Lord Sterndale) that Article 2 of the Declaration of Paris (the neutral flag covers enemy's goods, with the exception of contraband of war) is not confined, in the benefits conferred by it, to the neutral shipowner but also protects the non-contraband goods of an enemy from seizure. Moreover, following Lord Parker in *The Hakan,* L.R. [1918] A.C. at p. 150, the enemy cargo-owner is permitted to appear and assert his rights under an international agreement. [Reports: L.R. [1919] P. 204 (at pp. 217 and 219), 3 B. and C.P.C. 439.]

Contraband—Treaty Permitting Trade between Neutral Country and Enemy Country—Interpretation.

See Case No. 301 (*The Rannveig*).

[1] In England in time of war jurisdiction in matters of Prize is exercised by the High Court of Justice (Probate, Divorce and Admiralty Division) as successor to the former High Court of Admiralty. Proceedings in the Prize Court thus constituted are entitled officially "In the High Court of Justice, "Probate, Divorce and Admiralty Division, Admiralty (In Prize)."—[Ed.]

INDEX

A

"Act of State," 21, 22
  plea of, in relation to aliens, 231-234
  State succession, 60
Actions, pending, effect of change of sovereignty, 89-91
Admission of liability, 373, 374
Agreements, inter-governmental, concluded without the consent of legislative organs, 313-315
Agriculture, regulation of conditions of. *See* International Labour Organisation
Aliens, 231-259
  access to courts, 243
  acquisition of immovable property, 239-242
  "act of State," plea of, 231-234
  admission of, 231
  allegiance of, 231-233
  companies formed by, 245, 246
  confiscation of property of, 238, 239
  criminal jurisdiction over, for acts committed abroad, 107-109
  damage done to property of, responsibility for, 173, 174
  discrimination against, 240, 241
  equality of treatment, limits of, 241
  exemption from security for costs, 243
  expulsion of, 251-259. *See also* Expulsion of Aliens
  guardians, acting as, 239
  non-discrimination, plea of, 247
Aliens—*continued*
  position of, 231-235
  protection by the national State, 235, 236
  "residence" of aliens, meaning of, 234
  treatment of, 237-247
Alsace, reunion with France, 448, 449
Alsace-Lorraine, Article 59 of the Treaty of Versailles, 92
Ambassadors. *See* Diplomatic Immunities
Amparo, 250
Anarchism, advocacy of, as reason for expulsion, 251-253
Anderson, Mr., refusal to sign award, 377, 378
Angary, 414-418
  compensation, allowance of interest, 191
  — measure of, 188, 189
  requisition of vessels, immunity from jurisdiction, 152, 153
Anglo-American doctrine, effect of war on contracts, 391
Annexation, effect on nationality, 201, 202
Antioquia, Government of, 285
Antwerp, occupation by Germany, 420
Arbitration—
  award, 375-381
  declaratory judgments, 375
  experts, 371
  function of, 367
  law applied, 369-371
  procedure, 371
  recommendations as an act of grace, 376
  refusal to sign award, 377, 378

Arbitration—*continued*
res judicata, 373, 374
stare decisis, 376
Archduke Charles Francis Joseph, 136
Argentina—
Bolivia, frontier with, 106
Constitution, Article 101..308
Germany, Treaty with (1857), 303
Great Britain, Treaty with (1825), 303
Italy, Consular Convention with, 303
nationality laws, 214, 215
naturalisation laws, 210, 211
Arkansas, admission to American Union, 96
Armed forces, foreign, jurisdiction over, 121, 122
Armistice, 435-441, 443
cessation of hostilities and signature of Armistice Agreement, 439
contraband, carriage of, during, 435
effect on internal legislation, 437, 438, 440
termination of war, 441-443
Armistice of 11 November, 1918.. 242, 435-441, 443, 444, 448, 449
Auflassung, 242
Australia, naturalisation in, 203, 204
Austria—
Code of Civil Procedure, Article 101..453
nationality law, 213
Penal Code, provisions as to counterfeiting currency, 317
Republic—
— beginning of existence of, 12, 13, 20, 21
— liability for obligations of Austrian Empire, 66-68
— officials of Austrian Empire, liability to take over, 74
Austria-Hungary—
Commercial Treaty with Germany, 68, 69
dissolution of, 20, 28, 132, 457
Extradition Treaties, how far applicable to Czechoslovakia, 259, 260
Austria-Hungary—*continued*
protected subjects in Egypt, 202
State succession, international conventions, 39
succession to property of, 58, 130, 131
United States, Treaty with (1848), 387, 388
Avulsion, 84, 96
Awards, arbitral, 375-381. *See also* under Arbitration
declarative or constitutive effect of, 87
declaratory judgments, 375
effectiveness of, 88
partial execution of, 87-89
recommendations as an act of grace, 376, 377
revision of, 379-381

B

Bakhmetieff, Russian representative in United States, 1917.. 52, 53
Bavaria, nationality in, 38, 39
Beaufort Convention (1787), 97
Behring Sea Arbitration Award, 177, 178
Belgium—
Code of Penal Procedure, crimes committed abroad, 446
compulsory administration, German measures, in, 321, 322
maintenance of sovereignty during German occupation, 445-447
Nationality Law (1909), 404
occupation by Germany, 445-447, 457-467, 481, 489
— trading with the enemy, 420-422
recognition of Finland, 153
requisitions, law of 1887 concerning, 121
sequestration of enemy property, 405
Belligerent forces, 386
Belligerents, acts of, 124-129
Berne Convention (1890), 71
Bilingual treaties, 339-341
Black Sea Company, Italian, 26, 27

Bohemia—
establishment of Czechoslovak sovereignty, 17-20
territory of, 11-14
Bolivia, frontier with Argentina, 106
Boundaries—
land boundaries, 95
water boundaries, 96-98
Boundary commissions, legal nature of, 84-89
Bratislava, part of Czechoslovakia, 15-17
Brazil—
aliens, expulsion of, 254-256
Constitution, Article 69 (nationality), 215
— Article 72 (aliens), 246
Penal Code, Article 4..158, 308
termination of war with Germany, 444
Brest Litowsk, Peace Treaty of, 242, 434
British Commonwealth of Nations, 39
Self-governing Dominion, naturalisation in, 203, 204
South Africa, Union of, status, 22
British Nationality and Status of Aliens Act (1914), Section 10.. 212
Brünn, Treaty of (1920), 214, 223
Buenos Aires, district of, 97, 98
Bulgaria, ex-Tsar of, property in England, 406
Burden of proof, in cases of option, 221

C

California, law of 1913 as to holding of land by aliens, 239
" State Waters," sea surrounding islands, 101
Calvo clause, 236
Canada, adhesion to Treaty concluded by Great Britain, 348
Extradition Treaty with Denmark, 275
Capitulations, régime of, 161
— in case of enemy occupation, 452
Cardozo, Judge, 388
Carinthia, occupation by Yugoslavia, 467
Causa proxima non remota inspicitur, 188
Cession, 84-89
effect on nationality, 243
requirement of formal delivery of possession, 84-89
Chaco. *See* Gran Chaco
Change of government, effect on extradition, 276
Charles Francis Joseph, Emperor of Austria, claim to exemption from jurisdiction, 136
" Chile order," 410
China—
Commercial Treaty with United States, 321
Treaties with France (1844 and 1858), 335
Civil law, application to international relations, 64
Claims—
effect of double nationality, 216
nationality of, 185
of individuals against foreign Governments, 184-188
presentation by Government, evidence of *bona fides* of claims, 187
Clarke, Mr. Justice, 182, 198
Clearing offices (under Peace Treaties), 392
Code Civil, action against debtor's debtor, 117
claims for breach of warranty of title, 120
Collisions, rules applicable to, 100
Colombia, Arbitration Agreement with Venezuela (1916), 371, 372
Comity, international, 25
Commercial missions, position of, 294-298
Companies, formed by aliens, 245, 246. *See also* Corporations
Compensation for confiscation of property, 56, 57
Compound interest, 191
Conclusiveness of acts of political departments, 22, 31, 57, 58. *See also* States, Recognition of, 43-47, *and* Governments, Recognition of, 47-58
Connecticut, Compensation Act, 351

Conservatoir derden-arrest, 22, 130
Constantinople, Inter-Allied Police at, 277
Constitutional limitations, treaty-making power, 316
Consular jurisdiction, 161
Consuls—
administration of estates by, 302, 303
archives, immunity of, 305
competence of, to claim jurisdictional immunities of vessels, 146
crimes not connected with the consular office, 307, 308
fiction of extraterritoriality, 304, 305
functions of, 300-304
immunities of, and of consular premises, 304-310
representatives of their States, how far, 301, 302
sequestration of property of enemy consul, 307
termination of mission of, 298, 299
waiver of privilege, 306
Continental doctrine, effect of war on private contracts, 391
Continuity of States, 30-35
Contraband, 491
carriage of, during armistice, 435, 436
Contracts (Private)—
Anglo-American doctrine, compared with Continental doctrine, 391
clause suspending deliveries during war, 393, 396, 397
concluded by means of a letter, 392
effect of war on, 390-400
executory contracts, 396-399
frustration, doctrine of, 395
partnership, 399, 400
performance involving intercourse with the enemy, 393
Conventions, international. *See* Treaties
Corporations, controlled by foreign State, jurisdiction over, 133, 134
enemy character of, 422-426
nationality of, test of control, 227, 230, 245, 394, 424-426
Costs, security for, exemption of aliens from, 243, 244
Counter-claims, against foreign governments, 23, 129, 132-135
Court-martial, foreign, recognition of judgment of, 29
trial of spies, 431
Courts, foreign, recognition of judgments of, 25
Cuba—
as party to the Universal Postal Convention, 314, 315
Constitution of, 28
nationality in, 93
workmen's compensation in, 93
"Curzon Line," 36
Custodian of Enemy Property (England), 397, 399, 400, 406-409
(Scotland), 398
(South Africa), 225
Customs territory, 42, 83
Cyprus, annexation by Great Britain, 199, 201, 202
nationality in, 199
Czechoslovakia—
establishment of, 11-20, 45
successor to Austria-Hungary—
— former officials, 73
— pecuniary obligations, 62
— treaties, 68, 71

D

Damages—
angary, in case of, 189
bona fides of claims to, 187
exaggerated claims to, 187
illegal detention, case of, 188
measure of, 187-190
Danzig, Free City of, jurisdiction of courts in actions begun before German courts, 89-91
— status of, 411, 412, 414
Declaration of Paris, Article 2.. 491
Declaratory judgments, 376
De facto belligerents, 386
De facto Governments, responsibility for acts of, 182-184
De facto subjects, 202

Delivery, formal, of territory, 84-89
Denial of justice, 331
Denmark, Extradition Treaty with Canada, 275
Derden-verzet, 126
Dies a quo, 192, 193
Diplomatic immunities—
  envoys, 285-287
  extraterritoriality, fiction of, 290-292, 304
  family of envoys, 287
  legation buildings, 289-292
  object of, 118
  obligations incurred before commencement of mission, 286
  retinue, 288
Disloyalty, as reason for cancellation of naturalisation, 209
Disputed territory, *de facto* jurisdiction over, 105, 106
Domicile, as test of enemy character of goods, 426, 427
Double nationality, 215-218
  burden of proof, 217, 218
  claims, effect on, 216

E

Economic Conference of Allied Governments (1916), 401
Egypt, date of independence, 204, 205
  Protectorate by Great Britain, 40-42
  — recognition of, 162
  Sanitary and Quarantine Council, 364
  Treaty with Greece (1913), 41
Ejusdem generis, doctrine of, 358
Eminent domain, 418
Enemy character—
  corporations, 424-426
  goods, 426, 427
  individuals, 422, 423
Enemy merchant ships in port, 410-414
Enemy subjects—
  effects of war on, 401-410
  in extraterritorial courts, 402, 403
  personal status, 401-406
  property of, 406-410
Enforcement of treaties, 319-324
Enlistment for service against foreign States, 180-182
Envoys. *See also* Diplomatic Immunities
  members of commercial mission, 294-298
  termination of mission of, 292, 293
Equality of States, 24, 332
"Equity," meaning of, 370, 371, 376, 377
Establishment of new States, 11-21
Esthonia, Government of, recognition by Great Britain, 43-46
Executive departments, construction of treaties by, 332, 333, 348, 349
Exequatur, of consuls, revocation of, 298, 299
Experts, functions of, in international arbitration, 371, 372
Expulsion of aliens, 251-259
  Brazilian law in the matter of, 254-256
  Mexican law in the matter of, 253, 254
  political activities, 252, 253
  procedure of, 257-259
  — in case of non-recognition of alien's Government, 258, 259
  — United States regulations on, 257, 258
  right of expulsion, 251-257
  — when inconsistent with treaties, 251, 252
  self-defence, as a measure of, 255, 256
Extradition, 259-281
  absence of extradition proceedings, 262
  amendment of request for extradition, 263, 264
  British Extradition Act (1870), 270, 271
  change of Government in State demanding extradition, 276
  conditions of, 270-277
  demand for, meaning of, 277
  extraditable crimes, 263-267, 272, 273
  nationals, of, 265, 269

Extradition—*continued*
objects connected with extraditable offence, 279, 280
political crimes, trading with the enemy, 265, 266
procedure of, 277-281
refusal of extradition, right of, 268
requests for, simultaneous, 278, 279
treaties, abrogation by municipal legislation, 7
trial for the same offence for which extradition is granted, 259, 260, 272-275, 277
waiver of extradition by offender, 280, 281
Extraterritorial courts, during war, *persona standi in judicio*, 401
Extraterritoriality, fiction of, 118, 119, 290-292, 304, 305

F

Federal States, 38, 39
conduct of foreign relations in, 39, 116
Ferdinand, ex-Tsar of Bulgaria, property in England, 406, 407
Finland, recognition by Belgium, 153
Fisheries, in territorial waters, jurisdiction over, 176, 177
Force majeure, 418
plea of, Treaty of Versailles, Article 131..169
Foreign armed forces, jurisdiction over, 121, 122
Foreign Enlistment Act (1870), British, 180
Foreign State—
armed forces abroad, 121
contracts in private law matters, 118, 122-124
exemption from jurisdiction, 114-135
governmental agencies abroad, 120-124
indirect impleading of, 116-118
submission to jurisdiction, implied, 114-116
Foreigners, criminal jurisdiction over, for acts committed abroad, 107-109
France—
China, Treaties with (1844, 1858), 335
Code d'Instruction Criminelle, Article 7..108
Code de Justice Militaire, 235
Code Pénal, Article 78..108
nationality in, 38, 39
Poland, attitude to restoration of, 37
Spain, Convention with (1862), 333, 334
Switzerland, Convention with (1869), as to jurisdiction, 122
United States, Agreement with (1918), 333
Frankfort, Treaty of (1871), 390
Friendly relations with foreign States, disturbance of, 127, 128
Frustration of contracts, 395
"Fundamental rights of man," 198

G

General participation clause in treaties, 411-413, 428
German East Africa, State succession, 61, 62
"German national," meaning of, 212, 224, 225, 423
German South-West Africa, occupation by British forces, 484, 485
Germano-Polish Paris Agreement (1920), 313, 314
Germany—
cessions to France under Article 357 of the Treaty of Versailles, 337, 349, 350, 367-369
Civil Code, Introductory Law, Article 88..242
Civil Procedure, Code of, 351
Constitution, Article 2..99, 290
— Article 4..151
— Article 45..314
— Article 78 (2)..116
— Article 82 (2)..99
— Article 83..99

Germany—*continued*
foreign relations, conduct of, 39
nationality in, 38, 39
nationality laws, 225, 226
Polish subjects, treatment of, 91-93
responsibility under Article 231 of the Treaty of Versailles, 169
territory of, 83, 99
treaties, effect of publication of, 322, 323
Treaty with Argentina (1857), 303
— with Austria-Hungary (of Commerce), 68, 69
— with France (1871), 39
— with Russia (1894), 242
— with Switzerland (Extradition), 268, 280
— with United States (1868) (Naturalisation), 208
Gomez, President, 180
Good morals, as requirement of naturalisation, 206, 207
Goods, enemy character of, 426, 427
Government, change of, effect on extradition, 276
Governments—
de facto, responsibility for acts of, 182-184
expulsion of aliens, 258, 259
foreign, recognition of acts of, 24-30
non-recognition, effect on immunities, 141, 142
recognition of, 44, 47-58
Gran Chaco, 106
Grants in perpetuity, 94, 95
Great Britain—
Arbitration Agreement (1910) with the United States, 193
law as to diplomatic immunities, 297, 298
Protectorate over Egypt, 40-42
— recognition of, 162
recognition of Esthonian Government, 43-46
— of Provisional Government of Northern Russia, 43, 44
termination of war with Germany, 442, 443
Great Britain—*continued*
Trade Agreement with Soviet Russia (1921), 49, 295, 296
Treaty with Argentina (1825), 303
— with Switzerland (1880) (Extradition), 270, 271
— with United States (1818) 236, 237, 331, 332, 335, 336
— — (1871), 327
— — (1899), 347
— — (1900) (Extradition), 272, 273
— — (1916), 4
Greece—
Consular Convention with United States (1903), 346, 347
landing of French troops at Piræus, 385
Treaty with Egypt (1913), 41
— with Turkey (1913), 389

H

Hague Convention No. I (for the Pacific Settlement of International Disputes), 85, 370, 378
applicability to States which have not ratified it, 3
Hague Convention No. IV (Laws and Customs of War on Land), Article 8..433
Article 20..434
Article 31..235
Article 42..457
Article 43..234, 440, 441, 446, 450, 457, 461-465, 467-475
Article 44..245, 472, 473
Article 46..477
Article 49..245
Article 52..245, 386, 427, 428, 475-483
Article 53..475-485
interpretation by municipal courts, 462, 464, 465
Hague Convention No. VI (Enemy Merchant Ships at the Outbreak of Hostilities), 410-414
Hague Convention No. XI (Restrictions on Capture in Maritime Warfare), 430

Hague Convention No. XII (Establishment of International Prize Court), Articles 21 and 22..488
Hague Convention of 1905 on Civil Procedure, 69-73, 122-124, 244, 300, 301, 352
Hague Conventions, in general, binding force of, 428
Haldane, Lord, on confiscation of enemy property, 409
Hamburg, free port of, 100
Heads of foreign States, exemption from jurisdiction, 136, 137
Heimatrecht, 15-18, 221
High seas, jurisdiction, 163
  marriage contracted on the high seas, 163, 164
Holland—
  Code of Civil Procedure, Article 26..325
  — Articles 376 ff., 126
  — Article 431..488
  designation of workers' delegates to International Labour Organisation, 361-363
  legislation of, relation to international law, 23
  municipal law, conformity with international law, 125-129
  neutrality, duties of, 489, 490
Holmes, Mr. Justice, 5, 328, 403, 404
Honduras, Extradition Treaty with Nicaragua, 269
Hostile expeditions, 180-182
Hovering laws, 111-114
Hungary—
  as party to the Hague Convention on Civil Procedure, 72, 73
  non-recognition of Soviet Government, 56, 57
  occupation by Czechoslovak troops, 451, 452
  — by Roumanian troops, 450, 451

I

Immigrants, Chinese, admission to United States, 198
Immunity from jurisdiction, diplomatic agents. *See* Diplomatic Immunities
  of public ships, 139, 140
Individuals. *See also* Aliens, Extradition, Nationality
  before international tribunals, 197
  de facto subjects, 202
  double nationality, 215-218
  enemy character of, 404, 405, 422, 423
"Industry," meaning of, 330, 331
Interest, 191-193
  compound, 191, 192
  dies a quo, 192, 193
  in case of exercise of right of angary, 191
International Health Convention (1892), 363, 364
International Labour Organisation—
  competence of, 328-330, 338, 342, 357-361
  designation of workers' delegates, 361-363
  objects of, 358-360
International law—
  binding force of, 3
  extent of, 3
  municipal law, relation to, 4-8, 124
  nature of, 3
  sources of, 3, 4
International Law Association, Hague Rules (1921), 151
International tribunals. *See* Tribunals, international
Interpretation of treaties. *See* Treaties, interpretation
Islands, measurement of territorial waters, 100-102
Italy—
  Argentina and consular convention with, 303
  Civil Code, Article 3..136
  — Article 9..304, 305
  Code of Civil Procedure, Article 105..136
  Code of Criminal Procedure, Article 5..305
  — Article 130..294
  — Article 635..260, 261
  — Article 641..260, 261
  — Article 642..277
  consular law of, 300
  recovery of provinces, 454
  Rhodes, occupation of, 452, 453

Italy—*continued*
Russia, Commercial Agreement with, 26, 27
— non-recognition of Soviet Government, 58, 294, 295
Switzerland, Extradition Treaty with, 261, 273, 274
United States, Treaty with (1871), 350, 351
— — (1913), 241
— — (concerning workmen's compensation), 319, 320

J

Japan, Treaty with United States (1911), 320
Judgments, continuance of, State succession, 77-79
Judicial authorities, pronouncements of, how far binding upon Governments, 22, 171, 172, 331, 332
Jurisdiction—
consular jurisdiction, 161-163
criminal jurisdiction over foreigners, 107-109
exemption from, foreign States, 22, 23, 91, 114-135. *See also* Recognition of States, 43-47, *and* of Governments, 47-58
— heads of foreign States, 136, 137
— public ships of foreign States, 137-158
extraterritorial jurisdiction, 161-163
high seas, 163, 164
hot pursuit, 164
hovering laws, 111-114
maritime frontiers, 111-114
national waters, 109-111
nationals abroad, 158-161
personal, 158-161
piracy, 164, 165
ports, 109-111
territorial, 105-109

K

Kansas, Workmen's Compensation Law, 319
Kerensky Government. *See* Russia, Provisional Government of 1917
"King's Resolution," Norway, 114
Krassin, M., head of Russian mission in Great Britain, 296, 297

L

Latvia, territory of, evacuation by Russian authorities, 456
"Law and equity," meaning of, 369-371
Law, natural, in the matter of State succession, 63
Laws of war, binding force of, 427, 428
Learned Hand, Judge, 139
Legal Proceedings against Enemies Act, 1915 (British), 421
Legation buildings—
extraterritoriality of, 118, 119
immunity of, 289-292
Liberec, district of, part of Czechoslovakia, 11-13, 17-19
Lien, maritime, foreign public ships, 148, 149
Liquor, importation into Norway, 113, 114
— into United States, 111, 112
Lombardy, cession to France, 88
Lorraine, reunion with France, 448, 449
Loss of nationality, 211-215, 225, 226
Loss of profits, damages for, 188, 189
Lübeck Bay, 98, 99

M

Main navigable channel doctrine, 97
Maritime belt—
breadth of, 100-102
law applicable in, 100
whether part of State territory, 98-100
Maritime frontier, 111-114
Maritime lien, foreign public ships, 148, 149
Maritime property, capture on land, 483-485
Maritime reprisals, conditions of legality of, 429

Marriage, contracted on the high seas, 163
— effect on nationality, 211
Marriott, Sir James, 436
Marshall, Chief Justice, on probable cause of seizure of ship, 172
Martial law, consideration by courts, 21
— Egypt, 42
Maryland, law on administration of estates, 346, 347
Measure of damages. *See* Damages, Measure of
Merchant ships (enemy) in port, 410-414
Mexico—
boundary with United States, 105, 106
Carranza Government, 53
Constitution, provisions as to ownership of land, 249
jurisdictional immunities in the United States, 25, 26
law in the matter of expulsion, 253, 254
nationalisation of petroleum in, 249, 250
nationality laws, 217, 218
Migratory Bird Treaty Act (United States), 4
Minorities Treaty, Czechoslovakia, 17
Mississippi, admission to American Union, 96
Missouri, State of, 4
Mixed arbitral tribunals, *stare decisis*, practice of, 376
Mixed boundary commissions, powers of, 89
Mixed Courts of Egypt, jurisdiction of, 40, 41, 161-163
Montenegro, as party to the Sixth Hague Convention, 410, 411
Moravia, territories of, 13, 14
Most-favoured-nation clause, 347, 350-352, 390
Municipal courts—
conclusiveness of evidence of, 176, 177
decisions of, whether binding upon Governments, 22, 171, 172, 331, 332
Municipal courts—*continued*
interpretation of treaties, conclusiveness of, 24
Municipal law—
effect on, of armistice agreements, 437-440
Holland, conformity with international law, 125-129
relation to international law, 4-6
— to arbitral decisions, 3, 7
Murmansk, Provisional Russian Government of, 50

N

Napoleon, restoration of Poland, 37
Nationality (*and see* Option of Nationality)—
admission to, 197, 198
cession, effect of, 243
change of sovereignty, effects of, 91-94, 199-202
claims, 185, 186
corporations, 227-230, 245, 246, 394
date of acquisition of, subsequent to option, 218, 219
de facto subjects, 202
double nationality, 215-218
Federal States, 38, 39
goods, test of enemy character of, 426, 427
individuals, as determining enemy character of, 422, 423
loss of, 211-215
naturalisation, 203-211
option of, 218-223
residence, as determining nationality on change of sovereignty, 94
statelessness, 224-226
Natural law, in the matter of State succession, 63
Naturalisation, 203-211
British self-governing dominions, in, 203, 204
cancellation of, 209, 210
invalidity of, in the event of return to country of origin, 204, 205
renunciation of, 208, 209

Naturalisation—*continued*
requirement of good moral character, 206, 207
Navigable channel, main, doctrine of, 97
Ne bis in idem, 470-472
Neutral merchantmen—
destruction of, 485-487
rescue and recapture of, 485-487
search in port, 486, 487
"Neutral property" clause in insurance policy, 230
Neutral property, requisition of, 414-418
Neutrality, duties of, transport of goods acquired by act of war, 489, 490
Neutrals, treaties permitting trade, interpretation of, 436
"New States," meaning of, 346
Nicaragua, Extradition Treaty with Honduras, 269
Nicholas II, 34
Non-discrimination, plea of, 244, 245, 247, 248. *See also* Aliens, discrimination against
North Dakota, taxation legislation, 6
North German Confederation, nationality laws, 217
Northern Russia, Provisional Government, 43, 44
Norway—
importation of liquor, 113, 114
territorial waters, limit of, 102, 114
Treaty with United States permitting trade with Germany, 435

O

Officials—
acts or errors of, responsibility of States for, 170, 171, 172
— ratification (implicit) of, 170
State succession, 73-75
— as to pensions, 66, 67
See also State Responsibility
Omsk Government, 32
Opium, 110, 111
Option of nationality, 218-223
burden of proof, 221, 222
conditions of validity of, 219

Option of nationality—*continued*
constitutive or declarative, 218, 219
date of acquisition, 218
expulsion subsequent to, 219, 220
persons over 18 years of age, 219
woman's right to, 220
"Ordinarily resident," 199
Ottoman Empire, nationality of subjects of, in Egypt, 40, 41
— in Cyprus, 202
Outbreak of war, effects of. *See* War

P

Panama Canal Zone—
Civil Code, 77
jurisdiction in, 94
Panama, Treaty with United States (1903), 94
Paris, Declaration of, Article 2..491
Parker of Waddington, Lord, on confiscation of enemy property, 409, 410
Partnership with enemy national, effect of outbreak of war, 399, 400
Permanent Court of International Justice, advisory opinions, 381
Perpetuity, grants in, 94, 95
Persona standi in judicio, 401-404
Philippine Islands—
Penal Code, piracy, 164
State succession, 59, 77
Piracy, 164, 165
Poland—
alien property in, 247, 248
Berne Convention (1890), as party to, 71, 72
Constitution, Article 81..7
— Article 95..247, 248
— Article 99..248
continuity of existence of, 33-38
establishment of, 47
Hague Convention on Civil Procedure, as party to, 70, 71
international law part of municipal law, 7
Land Reform Law of 1920..248

Poland—*continued*
partition of, 33, 34
recognition of, 33, 34
restoration of, 35-38
succession of, as to Austrian obligation, 63, 64
— as to Prussian obligation, 64, 65
Polish-German Paris Agreement (1920), 313, 314
Political crimes, trading with the enemy, 265, 266
Political departments. *See* Conclusiveness of Acts of Political Departments
Political rights, as distinguished from private rights, State succession, 76, 77
Political territory, as distinguished from customs territory, 83
Porto Rico, law of, 76
Portugal, confiscation of property of aliens, 238, 239
"Postal correspondence," meaning of, 432
"Pre-investigation" (in U.S.A., of national status of individual), 197
Preparatory work, consideration of, 342-344
Pre-war contracts. *See* Contracts (Private), effect of war on
Prisoners of war, 433, 434
detention of, after conclusion of peace treaty, 434
legal position of, 433
Private property (respect for). *See* War
Prize courts, British, jurisdiction of, 491
effect of decisions of, in neutral courts, 487, 488
Prize decree, effect of condemnation of ship, 107
Prize law, 487, 488
Proof, burden of—
in cases of option, 221, 222
in matters of double nationality, 217, 218
Protected persons, 202
Protectorates, 40-42
Protocols—
not submitted for ratification, 315
Protocols—*continued*
unratified, as distinguished from treaties, 186
Prussia—
conduct of foreign affairs, 116
responsibility for acts of Inter-Allied Plebiscite Commission in Upper Silesia, 179, 180
Prussian Tribunal for Conflicts of Jurisdiction, competence of, 115, 116
Public ships—
consuls, competence to claim immunity for, 146
immunity from jurisdiction, 137-158
maritime lien, 148, 149
non-recognition of Government ownership, effect of, 142
possession, as distinguished from ownership, determining exemption, 137-139
public purposes, when used for, 156
sale to private persons, position of, after, 148-150
salvage, claims for, 146, 147
trade, when engaged in, 137, 138, 140, 141, 146, 154, 157, 158
waiver of immunity, 145, 150-154
warrant of arrest, setting aside, 154-156

Q

Quarantine Council of Egypt, 364

R

"Race," meaning of, 222, 223
Rapallo, Treaty of, 28
Ratification, tacit, of acts of officials, 170
Real unions, 39
Rebus sic stantibus (private contracts). *See* Frustration of contracts
Recognition—
conditional, 58
de jure and *de facto*, distinction between, 50
foreign States, acts of, 24-30
Governments, of, 47-58, 141, 142

Recognition—*continued*
organs of, 47-51
retroactive effect of, 47-50
States, of, 43-47
— revocability of, 43, 45
Recommendations as an act of grace, 376, 377
Reprisals, how far a ground for termination of Convention, 414
maritime, British Orders in Council, conditions of legality, 429, 430
Requisitions, 427, 428, 475-483
contrary to Hague Conventions, whether invalid, 475, 476
military, how far subject to review by courts, 120, 121
neutral property, of, 414-418
receipts for, 481, 482
ships, in foreign waters, 161
transfer of property, whether conferring title for, 474-479, 482, 483
Res judicata, 373, 374
Residence, as determining nationality on change of sovereignty, 94 (Note)
" Resident," meaning of, 200, 201
Respondeat superior, 78
Restitution, French Commission of, in Belgium, 120
" Restraint of princes," 24, 418
Revision of arbitral awards, 379-381
Rhineland—
British courts-martial in, 469
occupation, nature of, 445
Rhodes, courts of, 452, 453
Rio Negro, territory of, 98
Riots, damage done to property of aliens, responsibility for, 173, 174
Rivers—
as boundaries, 84, 96-98
changes in course of, 97, 98
Roumania, occupation by Austria-Hungary, 477, 478
" Royal personage," meaning of, 341
Russia (*see also* Soviet Russia)—
administrative measures, how far enforceable in Poland, 75, 76
Russia—*continued*
Commercial Treaty with Germany (1894), 242
Confiscation Decrees, legality of, 49, 50
continuity of, 31-33
dismemberment of, 70, 71
Imperial Government, 30, 31
Provisional Government of 1917, 30-33, 43, 44

S

Saar territory, 83
whether part of Germany, 42
Salvage, claim for, jurisdictional immunities of foreign ships, 146-148
neutral merchantmen, in case of, 485-487
Sanitary Council of Egypt, 364
Schleswig, plebiscite in, 93
Scotland, Custodian of Enemy Property in, 398, 399
Scrutton, Lord Justice, on jurisdictional immunities of State-owned ships, 148
Seamen on foreign vessels, jurisdiction over, 109, 110
Search, of neutral merchantmen, 486, 487
Security for costs, exemption from, 243, 244
Self-preservation, as limiting the binding force of rules of war, 427, 428
Serbia, as party to the Sixth Hague Convention, 410, 411
Sèvres, Treaty of, 205
Shanghai, French Settlement at, 334, 335
Siege, state of, proclamation in Egypt, 42
Siège social, 344, 345
as test of nationality of corporations, 227, 228
Silesia, territories of, 13, 14
Slovakia, establishment of Czechoslovak sovereignty, 15-17
South Africa, Union of, Status of (in 1921), 22, 23
State succession in, 60
Sovereignty—
acts of, as distinguished from

Sovereignty—*continued*
transactions of private character, 22, 23
changes of, effects of, 89-94
— — on nationality, 91-94
— — on pending actions, 89-91
restrictive interpretation of treaties, reason for, 338
territorial, nature of, 83, 84
Soviet Russia—
Commercial Agreement with Italy, 26, 27
confiscation of private property, 26-28
Great Britain, recognition by, 49-51
non-recognition (Italy), 294, 295
— (Sweden), 54-56
— (United States), 51-53
Spain—
arbitrator between Colombia and Venezuela, 84-89
civil law, 76
France, Convention with (1862), 333, 334
Penal Code—
— Philippine Islands, in, continuing validity of, 77
— piracy, 164
State succession, 59
United States, Peace Treaty with, 93, 94
Special envoys, 294-298
Spies—
conditions of trial of, 431, 432
definition of, 235
St. Germain, Treaty of, 454
Article 62..231
Article 63..219, 220, 231
Article 70..213, 214
Articles 70-78..20, 21
Article 78..218, 220, 221
Article 80..218-223
Article 81..222
Article 177..316, 317
Article 179..316, 317
Article 206..317, 318
Article 208..318, 319
Article 248..345
Article 271..345
Article 318..64
establishment of Austrian Republic by, 20, 21
questions of State succession in, 75
Stare decisis, 376
State responsibility—
breaches of contractual obligations, 170
claims, 184
damages, 187-190
de facto Governments, acts of missions of, 182-184
decisions of municipal courts, 171, 172
executive action or inaction, 171-179
force majeure, plea of, 169
hostile expeditions, 180-192
interest, liability for, 191-193
State succession, 58-77
"act of State," 60
administrative measures, 75, 76
Austro-Hungarian Monarchy, in former, 130, 131
contractual and other obligations, 58-66
German East Africa, in, 61, 62
international conventions, 68-73
judgments of courts, 79
laws, continuance of, 76-78
officials, 73-75
pensions, 66-68
respect of private rights, 68
State territory. *See* Territory
Statelessness, 224-226
States (*see also* Foreign States)—
act of sovereignty, 21-23
acts in public capacity. *See* Jurisdiction, Exemption from Foreign States
beginning of existence of, 11-21
British Commonwealth of Nations, 39
composite, 38, 39
continuity of, 30-35
equality of, 24
establishment of, 11-21
extinction of, 35-38
federal, 38, 39
liquidation of, 130-132
practice of, as source of international law, 4
recognition of, 36, 43-47
— acts of, 24-30
— retroactive effect, 153, 154
transactions of a private character, 22, 23
unions of, 38, 39

Subjects abroad, jurisdiction over, 158-161
Succession of States. *See* State Succession
Sweden, recognition of Soviet Russia, 54-56
Swiss Federal Council, arbitrator between Colombia and Venezuela, 84-89
Switzerland—
  Convention with France (1869) (concerning jurisdiction), 122
  Extradition Treaties (Germany), 268, 280
  — (Great Britain), 270, 271
  — (Italy), 261, 273, 274

T

Tacit ratification of acts of officials, 170
Territorial waters (*see also* Maritime Belt)—
  as customs territory, 84
  breadth of, Norwegian claims, 114
  jurisdiction over, sea-fishing, 176, 177
  nature of boundary of, 112
  piracy, jurisdiction in the matter of, 164, 165
Territory—
  acquisition of, 84-89
  avulsion, 84
  boundaries, 95-98
  cession of, 84-89
  — effect on nationality, 243
  changes of territorial sovereignty, effects of, 89-94
  delivery of, formal, 84-89
  disputed, jurisdiction over, 105, 106
  foreign, occupation of, by virtue of Armistice Agreement, 450
  — — in time of peace, 94
  grants in perpetuity, 94, 95
  maritime belt, 98-102
  political, as distinguished from customs territory, 42
  territorial sovereignty, nature of, 83, 84
  territorial waters, 98-102
Texas, legislation concerning Chinese, 321
Thalweg, doctrine of, 96, 97
" Theatre of war," meaning of, 432
Theft, as defined in the Canadian Criminal Code, 275
Third parties, effect of treaties on, 324-326
Trading with the enemy, 419-422
  allied country under enemy occupation, 420-422
  as a political crime, 265, 266
  countries subject to capitulations, 419
Trading with the Enemy Acts (British), 394, 406-408
  — Proclamations (1914 and 1915), 419-421
Treaties (*see also* Agreements)—
  abrogation by subsequent municipal legislation, 7, 251, 252
  bilingual, interpretation of, 227, 228
  constitutional limitations, 316
  enforcement of, 319-324
  interpretation of, 328-353
  — bilingual treaties, 339-341
  — conduct of parties subsequent to conclusion of the treaty, 328, 329, 335, 336, 344, 345
  — effectiveness of treaty provisions, 336, 337
  — general purpose of the treaty, 329-331
  — most-favoured-nation clause, 347, 350-352, 390
  — municipal courts in, 24, 331, 332-335
  — preparatory work, 342-344
  — restrictive interpretation on account of infringement of sovereignty, 338
  — rules for, 344-350
  municipal law, relation to, 319-324
  performance of, 313-315
  publication of, effect of, 322, 323
  ratification of, 316-319
  — operation of, 319-324
  — reliance on unratified treaties, 316-318
  renewal of, tacit, 68, 69
  restrictive interpretation of, when constituting an exception to general principles of international law, 177, 178

Treaties—*continued*
State succession, as to, 68-73
termination of, 327, 328
— as the result of reprisals, 414
third parties, 324-326
war, effects of outbreak of, 387-390
Treaty of Peace Act (1919), Great Britain, 211
Treaty of Peace Orders (1919), 224
Treaty of Versailles. *See* Versailles, Treaty of
Treaty-making power, constitutional limitations, United States, 4-7
Trianon, Treaty of, 451
Article 231..345, 346
Article 254..345, 346
Tribunals, international, position of individuals, 197
Trieste, annexation by Italy, 455
Turkey—
abolition of suzerainty over Egypt, 40-42
diplomatic relations with United States, 142
Treaty with Greece (1913), 389
Turkish Purchases Commission in Germany, 114, 115

U

Ukraine, West Ukrainian Republic, 386
Union of South Africa. *See* South Africa, Union of
United States—
aliens, expulsion of, 251-253, 257-259
— internment of, during war, 208, 209
Arbitration agreement with Great Britain (1910), 193
army in France, jurisdiction over members of, 333
Chinese Exclusion Act, 112
Constitution, Amendments:
Fifth, 416, 417, 431
— — Sixth, 431
— — Tenth, 5
— — Fourteenth, 240, 241
— — Eighteenth, 327

United States—*continued*
Constitution—*continued*
— treaty-making power, conditions of, 4-7
Criminal Code, Sections 10 and 37..181, 182
France, Agreement with (1918), 333
Greece, Consular Convention with (1903), 346, 347
Hague Convention No. VI (1899 and 1907), 410, 411
Immigration Act (1917), 257, 258
Jurisdiction, over nationals abroad, 159-161
Liquor, importation of, 111, 112
— National Prohibition Act (1919), 327
Mexico, boundary with, 105, 106
Migratory Birds Treaty Act, 4
Philippine Islands, liability for Spanish obligations as to, 58, 59
Porto Rico, maintenance of Spanish law in, 76
Postal Convention, Universal, whether a " treaty," 314
Russian Government, Provisional (1917), recognition of, 31, 51-53
Seamen's Act, 109
Shipping Board, 414-416
— State commercial fleet, immunity of, 152
Termination of War (with Germany), 443, 444
Territory of, as theatre of war, 432
Treaties—
— with Austria (1848), 387, 388
— with China (Commercial), 321
— with Germany (1868) (Naturalisation), 208
— with Great Britain (1818), 236, 237, 331, 332, 335, 336
— — (1871), 327
— — (1899), 347
— — (1900) (Extradition), 372
— — (1916), 4
— with Italy (1871), 350, 351
— — (1913), 241
— — (Workmen's Compensation), 319, 320

United States—*continued*
Treaties—*continued*
— with Japan (1911), 320
— with Norway (permitting trade with Germany), 435
— with Panama (1903), 94, 95
— with Spain (Peace Treaty), 93, 94
Turkey, diplomatic relations with, 142
Upper Silesia, Inter-Allied Plebiscite Commission, 43, 179
Usury, German Decree, 83
Uti possidetis juris, principle of, 84-89

V

Venezuela, Arbitration Agreement with Colombia (1916), 371, 372
Venice, cession to France, 88
Versailles, Treaty of, Articles 45-50..83
Article 59..92
Article 87..118
Article 88, Paragraph 3 to Annex 2, 179
Article 91..92
Article 92..65
Article 119..61, 62
Article 212..440, 441
Articles 228 and 229..458, 459
Article 254..65
Article 255..65
Article 256..339
Article 276..351
Article 277..243
Article 278..92, 215
Article 287..70, 352
Article 291..242, 352
Article 292..242
Article 296..3, 216, 325, 344, 376, 392
Article 296 (2)..391
Article 297..321, 323, 325, 345
Article 297 (1)..405
Article 297 (*b*)..412
Article 297 (*e*)..227-229, 244
Article 298..321-323
Article 298 (*b*)..244
Article 299..342
Article 304..324, 344

Versailles, Treaty of—*continued*
Article 331..369
Article 339..337, 369
Article 357..337, 349, 367
Article 440..323, 350, 445
Part III, Section V, Annex, Paragraph 1..38
Part VIII, Annex 3..155
Part XIII, 328-331, 357-363
Vessels—
in foreign ports, jurisdiction over, 109-111
— of home State, 158, 159
public, exemption from jurisdiction, 137-158
wrongful seizure of, 171-179
Vienna, Congress of, 33-38
Violación de domicilio, 309

W

Wages, foreign seamen, question of jurisdiction, 109, 110
Waiver of exemption from jurisdiction, foreign States, 134, 135
public vessels, 145, 150-154
withdrawal of, 145
Waiver of extradition proceedings, 280, 281
War—
armistices, 435-441
belligerency, technical meaning of, 385
belligerent forces, 386
contraband of war, 491
enemy character—
— of corporations, 424-426
— of goods, 426
— of individuals, 422
indemnities, 487
laws of, binding force, 427
maintenance of national sovereignty, 445-448, 450, 451
neutral merchantmen, destruction of, 485
— search of, 486
neutrality, 489-491
occupation of enemy territory, 445-483
— legislative and judicial functions of occupant during, 457-475

War—*continued*
occupation of enemy territory—*continued*
— nature and effects of, 445-457
outbreak, effects of, 387, 418
— — on enemy merchant ships in port, 410-414
— — on enemy subjects, 400-410
— — on neutral property, 414-418
— — on private contracts (Anglo-American doctrine), 191, 390-400
— — on treaties, 387-390
prisoners of war, 433, 434
private property, respect for, 475-483
prize law, 487
reprisals, 429
requisitions, 475-483
spies, 431
termination of, 442-445
territory under capitulatory régime, 450-453
theatre of, 385
trading with the enemy, 419-422
warfare at sea, 483-488
— capture of maritime property on land, 483-485

Warfare at sea. *See* War
War profits, taxation of, 334
Warsaw, Duchy of, 34
Water boundaries, 96-98
changes in course of, 97
thalweg, doctrine of, 96
Weimar, German Constitution of (1919), 116
Withdrawal of privileges, necessity for notice of, 237, 238
Woman's right to option of nationality, 220, 221
Women, effect of marriage on nationality of, 212
World War, theatre of war, 432

Y

Yugoslavia—
occupation of Carinthia, 467
whether a new State, 346

Z

Zollausland, 83
Zollausschluss, 100
Zollinland, 83